Collectors Encyclopedia of

19th Century Hardware

Cutlery Tools, Kitchen, Small Farm Equipment, and miscellaneous items

with a 2004 Price Guide

(all original copy)

Originally copyrighted May 13, 1884
by Vajen & New, Indianapolis, IN

Reprinted in 2004

by
L-W Book Sales
PO Box 69
Gas City, IN 46933

VAJEN & NEW, INDIANAPOLIS, IND.

INDEX.

I

M

N

O

P

T

U

V

W

NARROW AND BROAD BUTTS.

WROUGHT AND CAST.

NARROW BUTTS.

Sizes	1	1¼	1½	1¾	2	2¼	2½	2¾	3	3½	4 in.
Cast, Fast Joint	....	....	...	....	....	....	....	....	....	....	....
Wro't, "	....	....	....	....	....	....	....	....	....	....	....
Light Wro't, Fast Joint		....	....	....	....	....	....	....	....	....	....
" Loose Pin		....	....	....	....	....	....	....	....	....	....

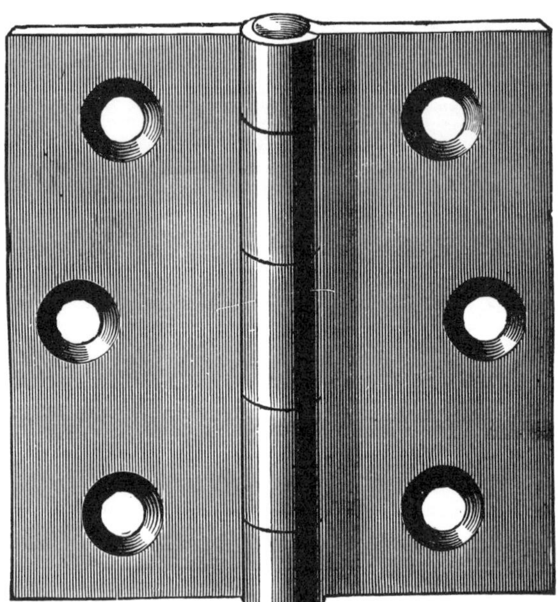

BROAD BUTTS.

Sizes	2x2	2x2½	2½x2½	3x3	3x3½	3½x3½	4x4	4½x4½	5x5
Cast, Fast Joint		......	......	......	......	......	......	......	......
Wro't, Loose Pin		......	......	......	......	......	......	......	......

Our wrought Butts are nicely finished with smooth, well-finished pins.

WROUGHT BUTTS.

WROUGHT IRON BACK FLAPS.

Sizes.. ¾in.... ⅞ in.... 1 in.... 1⅛ in.... 1¼ in.... 1⅜ in.... 1½ in.... 1¾ in.... 2 in....

WROUGHT TABLE HINGES.

Sizes. ⅞ in.... 1 in.... 1 ⅛ in.... 1¼ in.... 1⅜ in.... 1½ in.... 1⅝ in.... 1 ¾in.... 2 in....

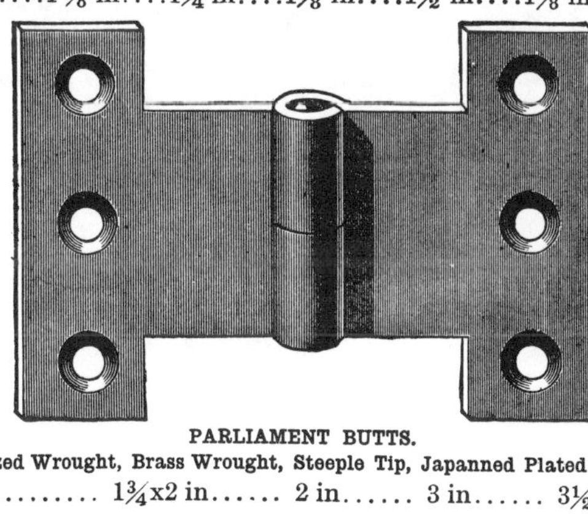

PARLIAMENT BUTTS.

Bronzed Wrought, Brass Wrought, Steeple Tip, Japanned Plated Acorn.

Sizes...................... 1¾x2 in...... 2 in...... 3 in...... 3½ in...... 4 in......

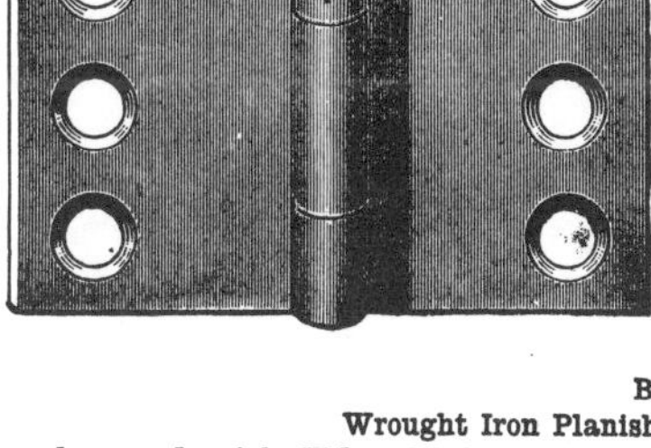

BLIND BUTTS.

Wrought Iron Planished, Wrought Iron Bronzed Brass.

Regular and with Edge Holes................. 1⅛ in...... 1¼ in...... 1⅜ in......

See Index for Brass Butts.

FIGURED CAST LOOSE PIN BUTTS.

STEEPLE TIPPED.

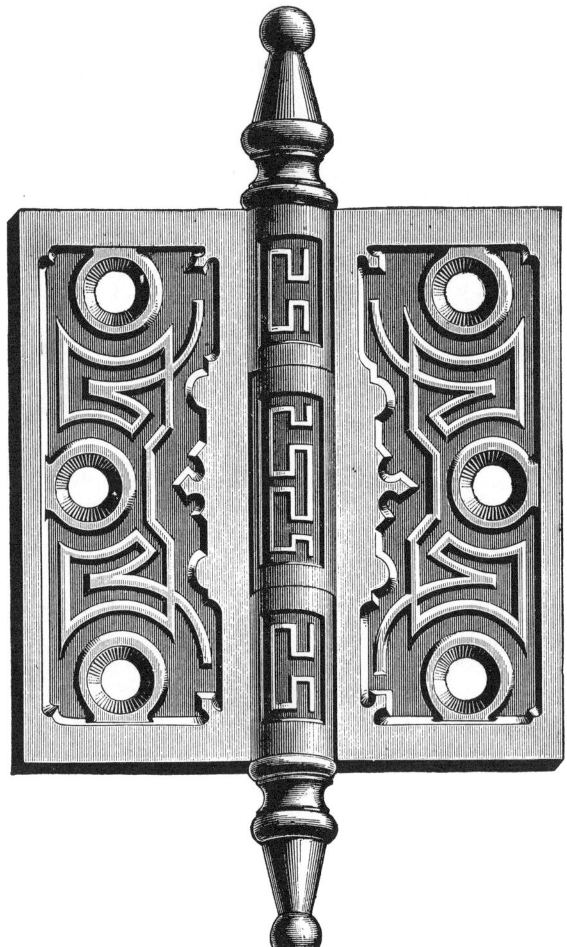

Sizes	2x2	2x2½	2½x2½	3x3	3x3½	3½x3½	3½x4
Plain	......	......	......	......	......	......	......
Japanned	......	......	......	......	......	......	......
" Silvered Acorn	......	......	......	......	......	......	......
Maroon Bronzed	......	......	......	......	......	......	......
Berlin "	......	......	......	......	......	......	......

Sizes	4x4	4x4½	4½x4½	4½x5	5x5	5½x5½	6x6
Plain	......	......	......	......	......	......	......
Japanned	......	......	......	......	......	......	......
" Silvered Acorn	......	......	......	......	......	......	......
Maroon Bronzed	......	......	......	......	......	......	......
Berlin "	......	......	......	......	......	......	......

PLAIN LOOSE PIN BUTTS.

STEEPLE TIPPED.

	2x2	2x2½	2½x2½	3x3	3½x3½	4x4	4½x4½	5x5
Boston Finish, Cast ..	......	......	......	......	......	......	......	......
Bronzed Wrought Iron	......	......	......	......	......	......	......	......
Nickel Plated " "	... ..	......	......	......	......	......	......	......

The above we can furnish in solid bronze metal, with steeple tips or with ball tips, as desired.

SPRING SCREEN DOOR HINGES.

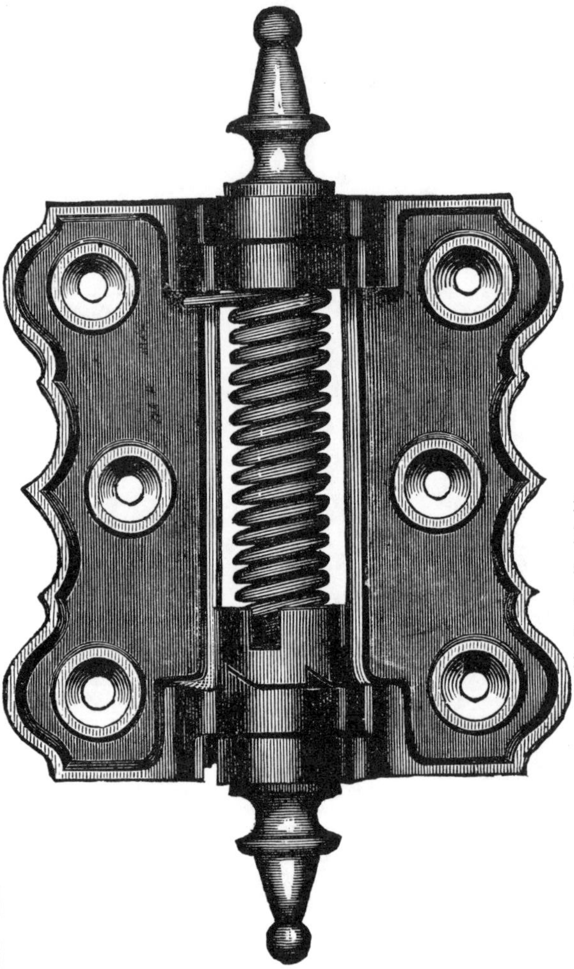

STANDARD SPRING HINGES.

No. 1, Surface......3x3 ......

No. 3, Mortise......3x3 ......

No. 5, Double Acting, ...

It will always be our aim to furnish the best hinge of this kind to be had for the money, and enable our customers to compete with other hinges on sale by other merchants which might be much inferior.

DEVORE'S SPRING HINGE.

The most practical low-priced Spring Hinge in the market. Simplest in construction, and **Most Durable.** Has uniform tension, holds the door firmly when closed, and when the door opens 130°, the action of the spring reverses, and holds the door open.

Size..................3x3 inch. ....

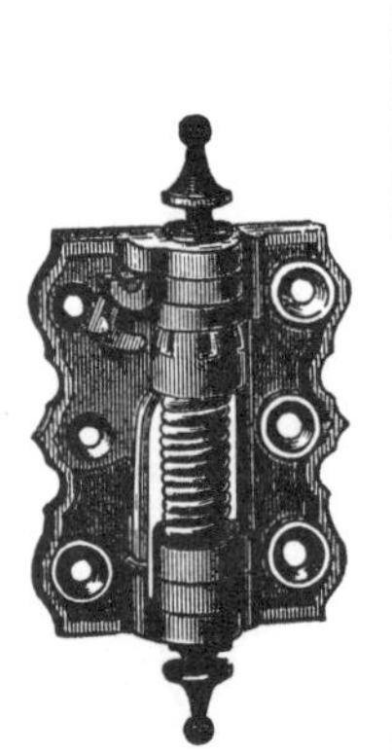

VAJEN & NEW, INDIANAPOLIS, IND.

SPRING HINGES.

GEM SPRING HINGES.

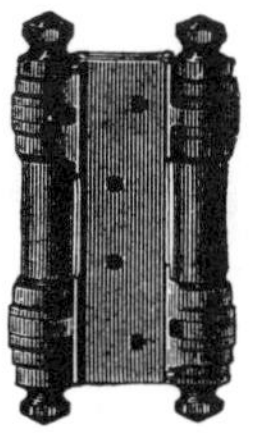

Double Acting.

Length.	For Doors.	Single Acting.	Double Acting.
3½ inch	¾ to 1⅛ inch	No. 63	No. 83
4 "	1 to 1⅜ "	" 64	" 84
5 "	1 to 1½ "	" 65	" 85
6 "	1 to 1¾ "	" 66	" 86
7 "	1¼ to 1⅞ "	" 67	" 87
8 "	1½ to 2¼ "	" 68	" 88
10 "	1¾ to 2½ "	" 69	" 89
12 "	2 to 3 "	" 70	" 90

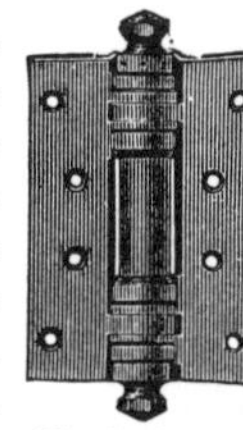

Single Acting.

The above numbers are for Japanned Hinges. They can also be furnished in Copper Bronzed, Real Bronze, or Polished Brass.

THE CHAMPION DOUBLE ACTING SPRING HINGE.

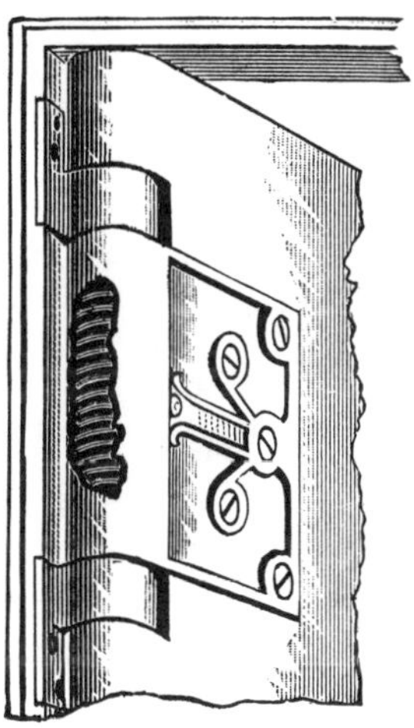

Nos.	35	40	50
For Doors	⅞ to 1⅛	1⅛ to 1⅜	1⅝ to 1⅞ in. thick.
Japanned	......	......	......

We claim for this Hinge the following merits, which make it superior to any other in the market:

1st. The spring is self-adjusting, and will hold its tension much longer than others.

2d. It is as strong as any butt, and will hold the heaviest door in its proper place without sagging.

3d. It is made of but three parts, thus being very simple and impossible to get out of order.

4th. It is both right and left hand, and single as well as double acting, the double acting being furnished at about the price of single acting of other manufacture.

5th. It is less cumbersome, and makes a more handsome finish when on a door.

MALLEABLE IRON, BRASS SPRINGS.

No. 240, Tuscan Bronzed.

2½ Inch, packed with screws ....

3 " " " " ....

Brass, Single Joint, to swing one way.

2⅜ Inch........................... ......

3 " ....

5 " ....

Brass, Double Joint, to swing both ways.

2⅜ Inch. For doors 1 in. thick or less, ...

3 " " " " " " ......

5 " " " " " " ......

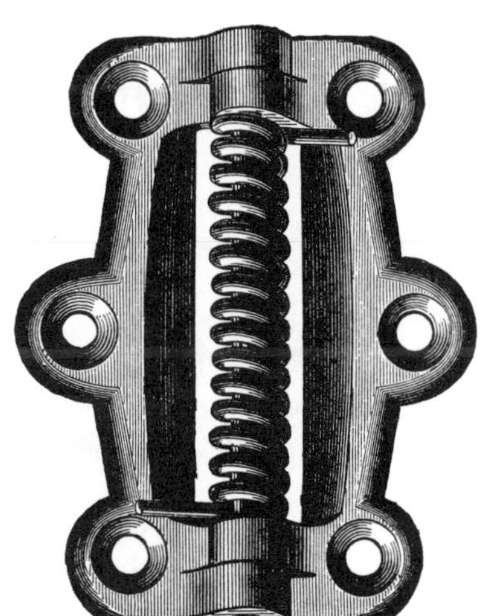

WROUGHT STRAP AND T HINGES, ETC.

Sizes	3	4	5	6	8	10	12	14	16 in.
Light Strap Hinges	....	....	....	....	....	....	....	....	....
Heavy " "	....	....	....	....	....	....	....	....	....

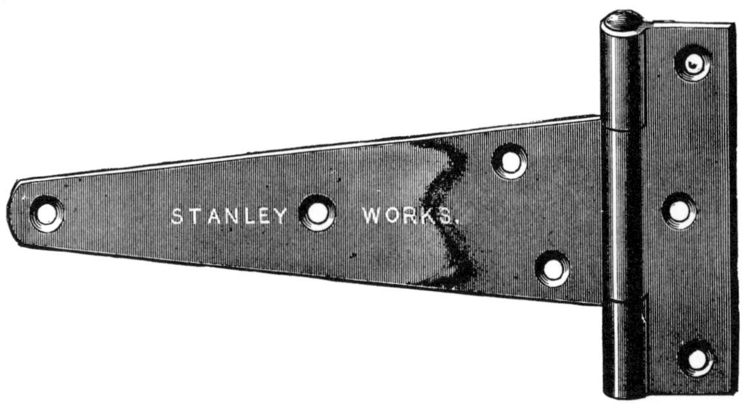

Sizes	3	4	5	6	8	10	12	14	16 in.
Light T Hinges	....	....	....	....	....	....	....	....	....
Ex. Heavy T Hinges	...	....	....	....	....	....	....	....	....

SCREW HOOK AND EYE HINGES.

Sizes	½	⅝	¾	⅞ in.
Per pound	......	......	......	......

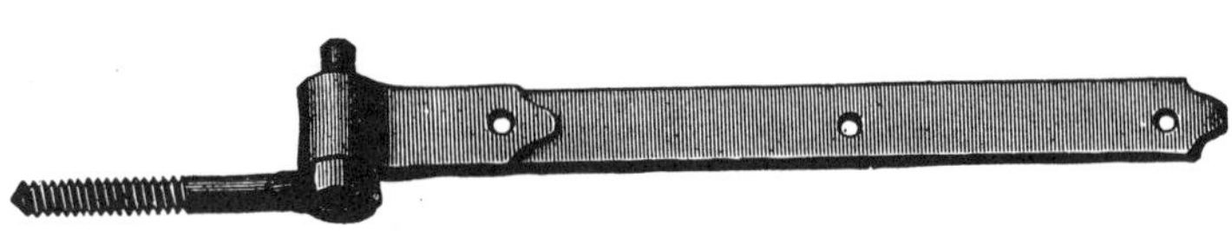

SCREW AND STRAP HINGES.

Sizes	6	8	10	12	14 to 36 in.
Per pound	......	......	......	......	......

VAJEN & NEW, INDIANAPOLIS, IND.

WROUGHT GOODS.

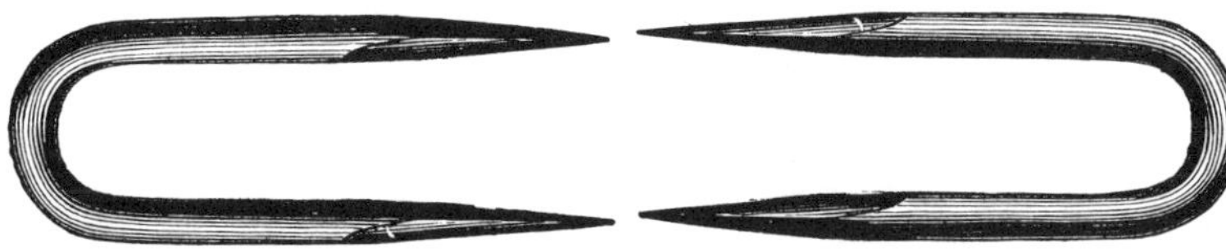

Wrought Staples	1	1¼	1½	1¾	2	2¼	2½	2¾	3	3½	4	4½	5	6 in.
	....	....	....	....	....	....	....	....	....	....	....	....	....	....

Wrought Hooks and Staples	2½	3	3½	4	4½	5	5½	6	7	8 in.
	....	....	....	....	....	....	....	....	....	....

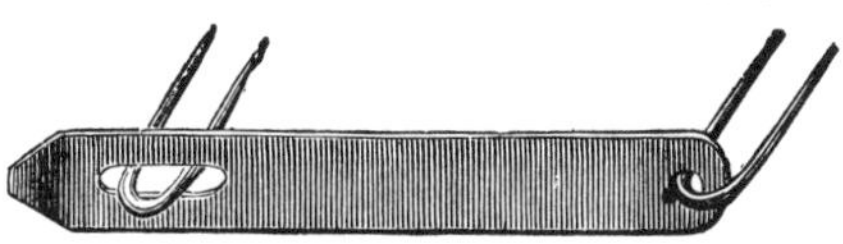

HASPS AND STAPLES.

Sizes..4 5 6 7 8 9 10 12 in.

... ...

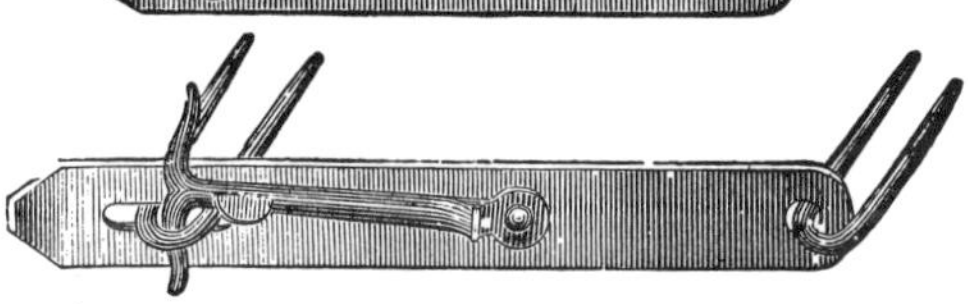

HASPS AND STAPLES, WITH HOOK.

Sizes...5 6 7 8 9 10 12 in.

... ...

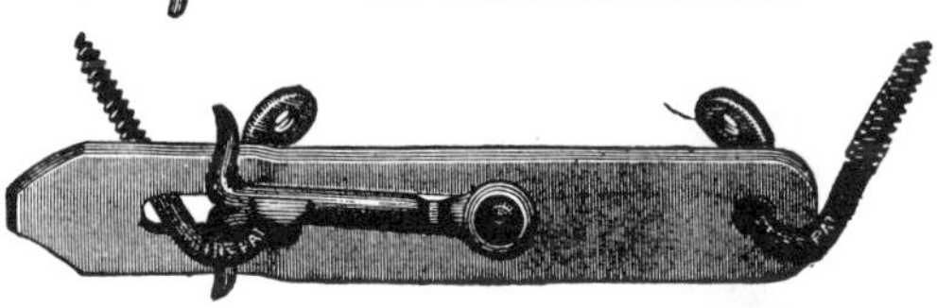

SMITH'S PAT. HASPS AND DOUBLE HOOKS, WITH SCREW STAPLES.

Sizes.6... 7... 8... 9... 10... 12... in

They screw into place without splitting the narrowest boards. The foot containing separate screw or nail, is securely covered by hasp, when in place.

BENT HASPS AND STAPLES.

Sizes...... 5.... 6.... 7.... 8.... in.

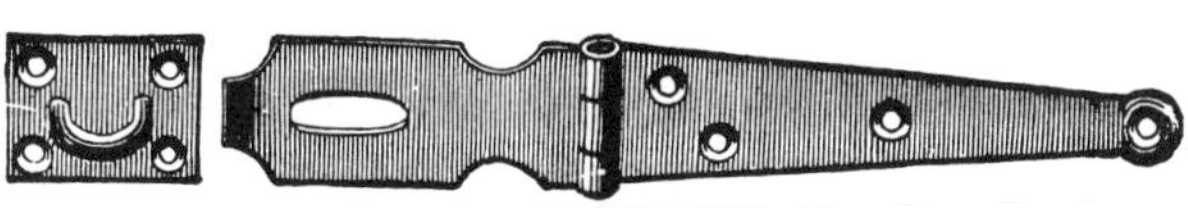

HINGE HASPS.

Size.... 3 4½ 6 8 10 in.

... ...

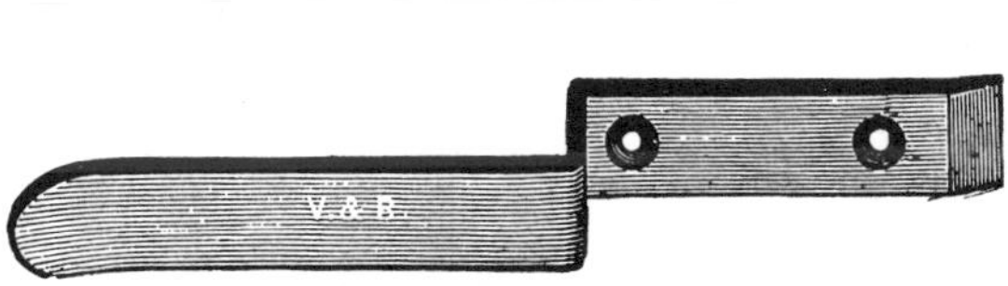

BAR STAPLES.

No. 1, Size of iron, 1¼x¼ in; wooden bar, 2x4 in.

No. 2, Size of iron, 1½x⅜ in; wooden bar, 2x4 in.

Per set, No. 1 .... No. 2 ....

SHUTTER HINGES.

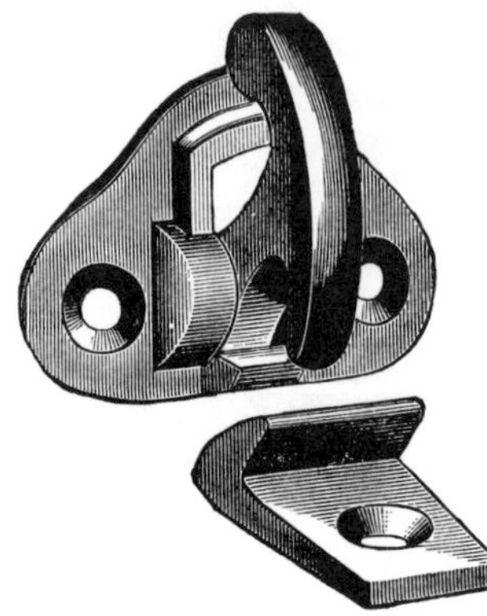

CLARK'S SURFACE GRAVITY-LOCKING BLIND HINGES.

CATCH FOR SAME.

No. 1, for wood, throws the blind 1¼ inches from the casing ......

No. 3, for brick, " " " 3¼ " " " " ......

SURFACE SHUTTER HINGES.

No. 4, for wood, 3⅛ in. when open ....

No. 5, for brick, 4½ " " " .....

This is the hinge mostly sold in this market for frame houses, and is self-locking.

REVERSIBLE SHUTTER HINGES.

Mortise.

No. 3, 3⅛ in. when open ......
No. 2, 4½ " " " ......
No. 1½, 5 " " " ......
No. 1, 5½ " " " ......
No. 0, 6¼ " " " ......
No. 00, 8⅛ " " " ......

Reversible, either right or left hand.

GATE HINGES AND LATCHES

MORTISE GATE LATCHES.

ST. LOUIS GATE LATCHES.

This is the selling latch of to-day.
Cheap and durable.

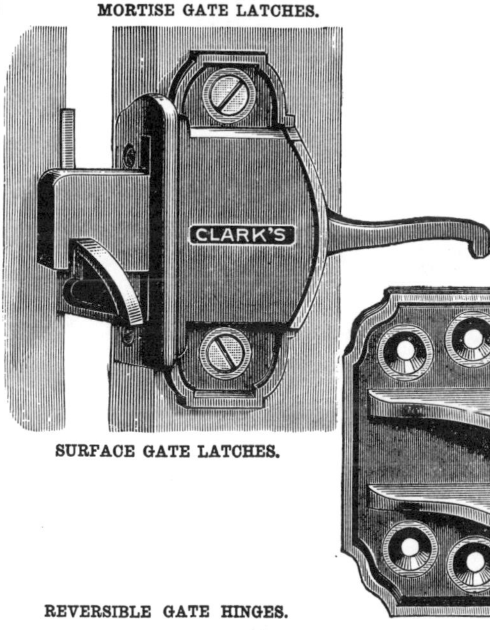

SURFACE GATE LATCHES.

REVERSIBLE GATE HINGES.

Self-Closing.

Will also hold the gate open when thrown back against the fence.

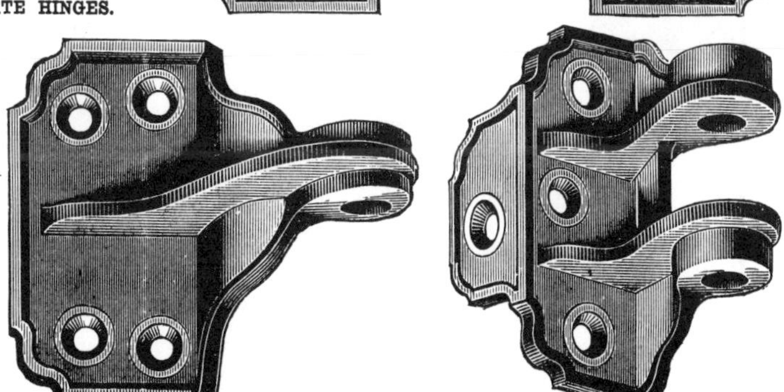

DOOR BOLTS.

SPRING BOLTS.

No. 315, Wrought Iron, Japanned .... 2...... 2½...... 3 .... 3½...... 4 in ....

No. 515, " Brass, Polished .... 2...... 2½...... 3...... 3½ .... 4 in .....

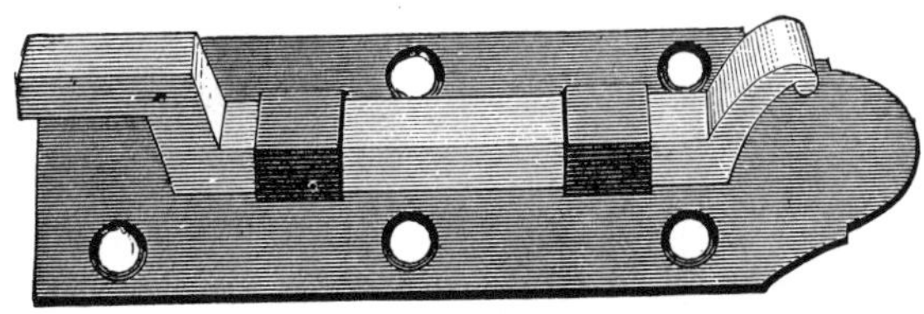

NECK BOLTS.

No. 325, Wrought Iron, Japanned .... 2½ ..... 3...... 3½...... 4 in......

No. 525, " Brass, Polished............. 2½ ..... 3 ..... 3½...... 4 in......

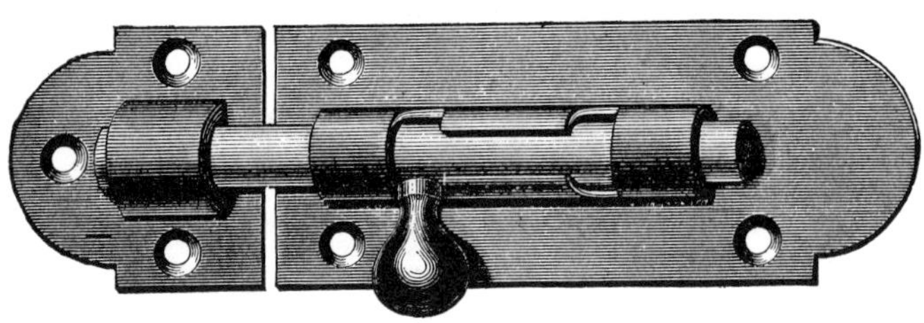

BARREL BOLTS.

No. 362, Cast, Japanned........................ 3...... 4...... 5...... 6 in......

No. 365, Wrought, Brass Knob, light.................... 2½...... 3...... 4 in .....

No. 367, " " " heavy .... 4...... 5...... 6...... 8 in......

No. 378, " " " .... 4...... 6 in......

No. 378 has a flat catch, and can be used to advantage in place of a neck bolt.

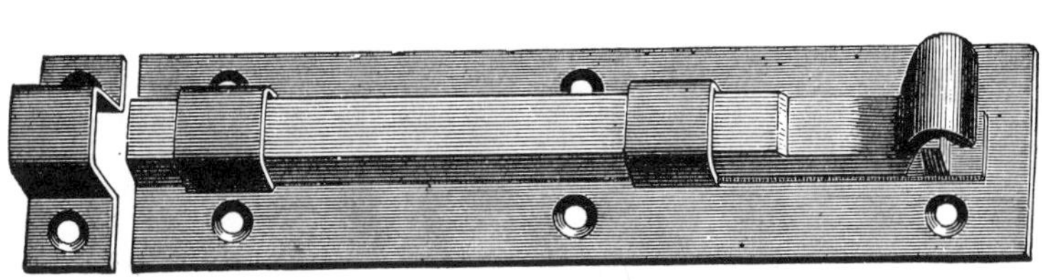

WROUGHT IRON SQUARE BOLTS.

No. 306, Japanned, Extra Heavy.......... 4...... 5...... 6...... 7...... 8 in......

No. 308, " " ", Floor Staples.......... 8...... 10...... 12 in......

DOOR BOLTS.

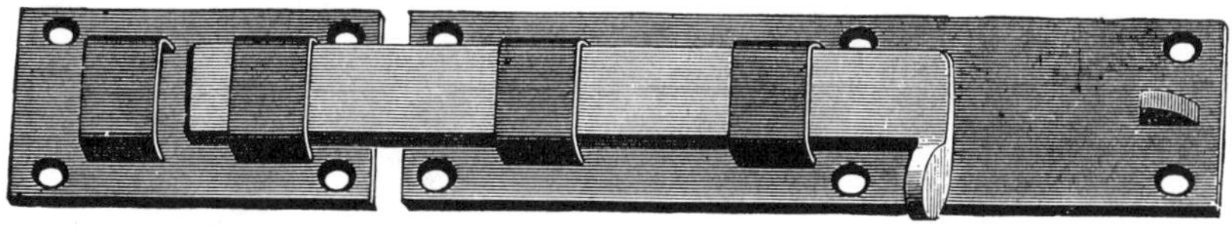

WROUGHT IRON SHUTTER BOLTS.

No. 335, Japanned Plate...................... 6...... 7...... 8...... 10 in......

WROUGHT IRON FLAT TAIL BOLTS.

No. 1048, Japanned Plates.......................... 12...... 15...... 18 in......

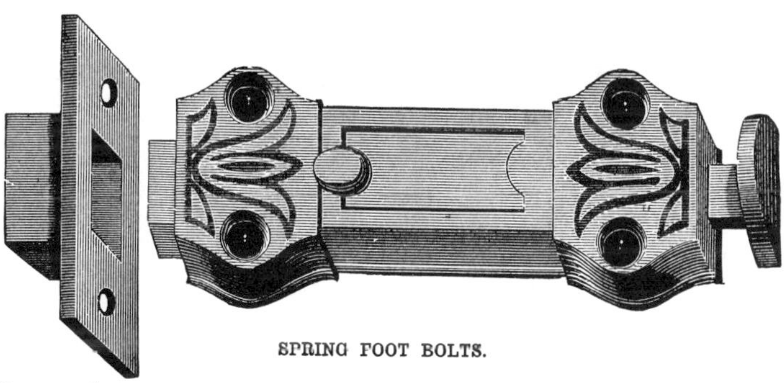

SPRING FOOT BOLTS.

No. 391, Japanned...... .... 6...... 8...... 10 in......

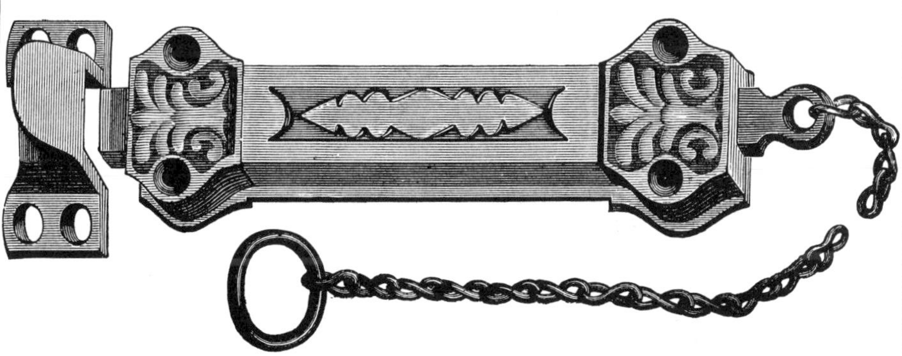

JAPANNED CHAIN BOLTS.

Sizes..................................	3	4	6	8
No. 383, Extra Heavy....................	......	......	......	....
No. 384, " " Reverse Bevel	......	......	......	......

DOOR BOLTS.

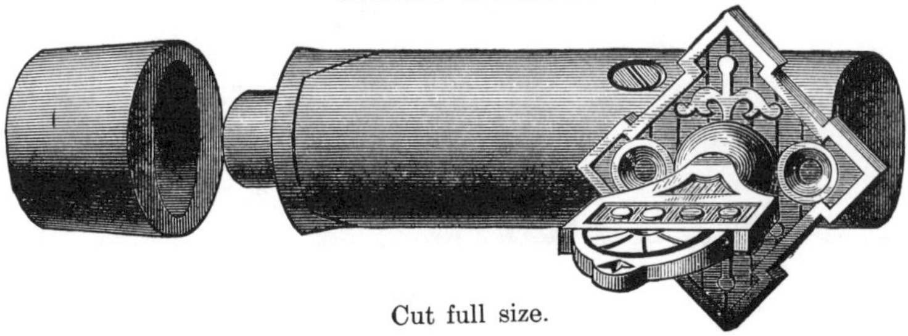

Cut full size.

MORTISE DOOR BOLTS.

No. 294, Berlin Bronzed Knob and Escutcheon ....
No. 297, Nickel Plated " " " ....
No. 298, Bronze Metal " " " ....

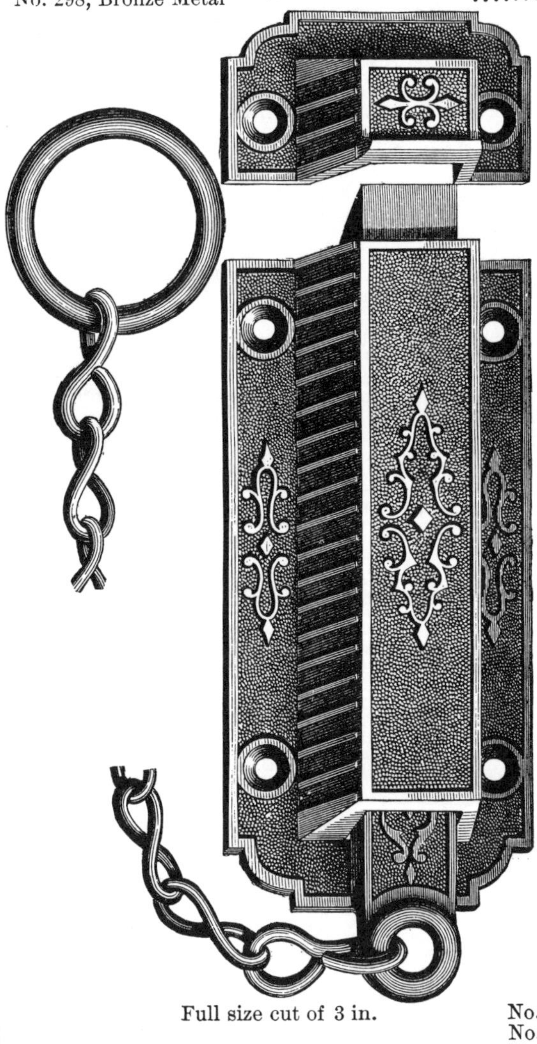

Full size cut of 3 in.

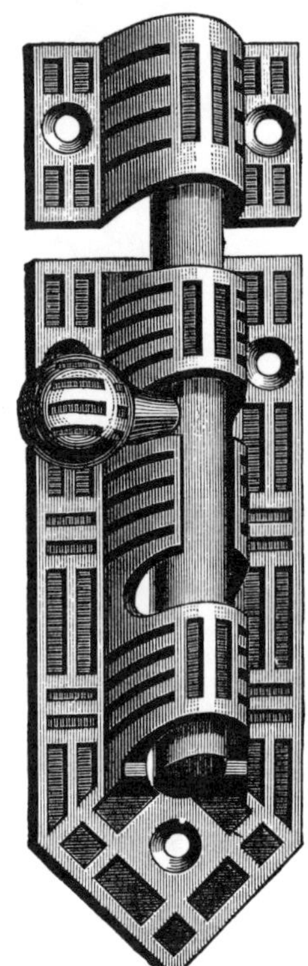

Cut full size.

BARREL BOLTS.

No. 460, Berlin Bronzed, 3 in ....

No. 860, Bronze Metal.. 3 in ....

No. 960, Imperial Bronze, 3 in ....

CHAIN BOLTS.

No. 481, Berlin Bronzed 3.... 4 in....
No. 881, Bronze Metal . 3.... 4 in....
No. 483, Berlin Bronzed 6.... 8 in....
No. 883, Bronze Metal . 6.... 8 in....

DOOR BOLTS.

Full size cut of 6 in.

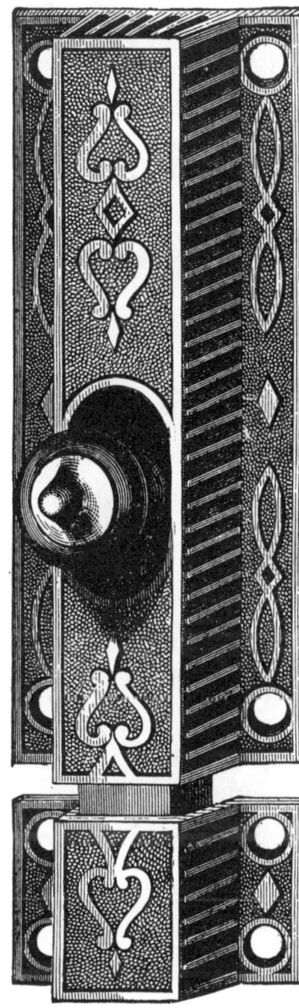

Full size cut of 4 in.

SQUARE CASED BOLTS.

Sizes	3	4 in.
No. 402, Berlin Bronzed, Bronze Knob	......	......
No. 404, Berlin Bronzed, Porcelain Knob	......	......

FOOT BOLTS.

No. 491, Berlin Bronzed	6	8 in	.....
No. 891, Bronze Metal	6	8 in	.....

VAJEN & NEW, INDIANAPOLIS, IND.

FLUSH BOLTS.

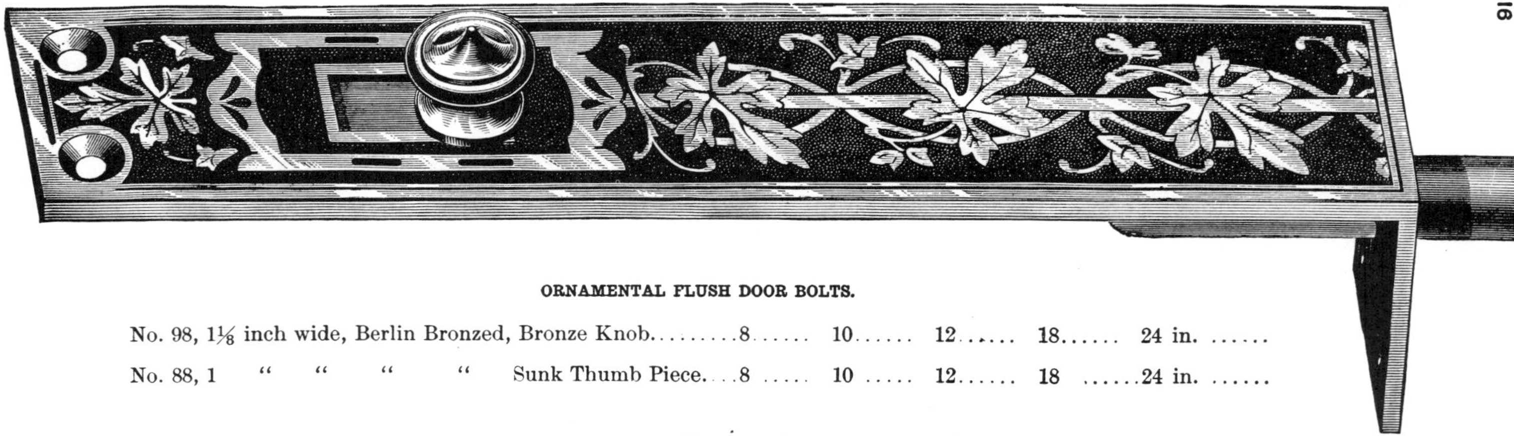

ORNAMENTAL FLUSH DOOR BOLTS.

No. 98, 1⅛ inch wide, Berlin Bronzed, Bronze Knob.........8...... 10...... 12...... 18...... 24 in. ......

No. 88, 1 " " " " Sunk Thumb Piece....8 ..... 10 ..... 12...... 18 ......24 in. ......

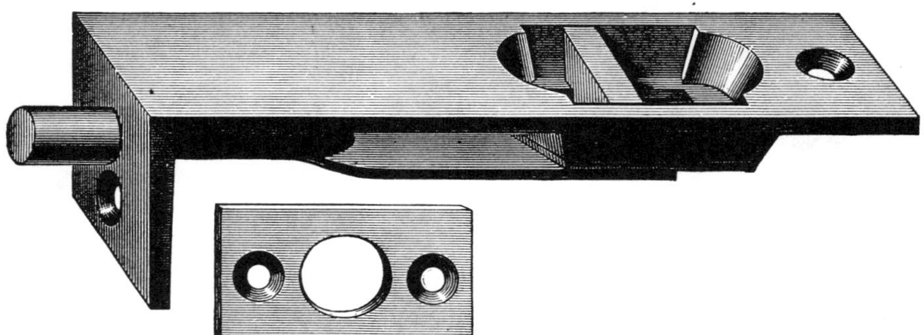

CAST BRASS FLUSH BOLTS.

Polished and Lacquered.

No. 60, ¾ inch wide .... 6...... 8...... 10 ..... 12 in. ......

No. 80, 1 " " ....10...... 12...... 18...... 24 in. ......

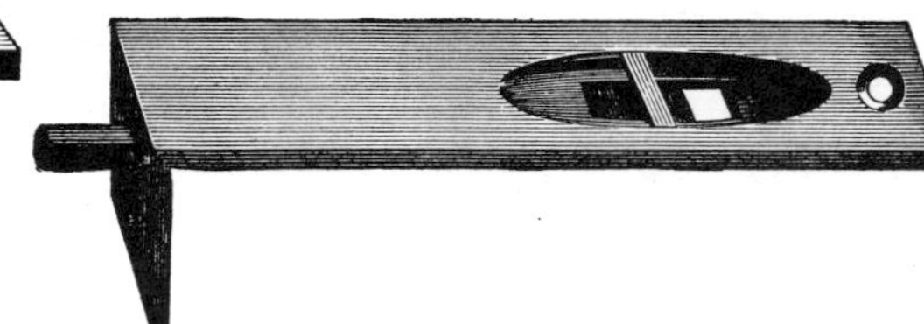

CAST BRASS FLUSH BOLTS.

Polished and Lacquered.

No. 30, ⅜ inch wide 2..... 2½.... 3.... 3½ in. ...

No. 40, ½ " " 2½.... 3...... 4.... 5 in....

FLUSH BOLTS.

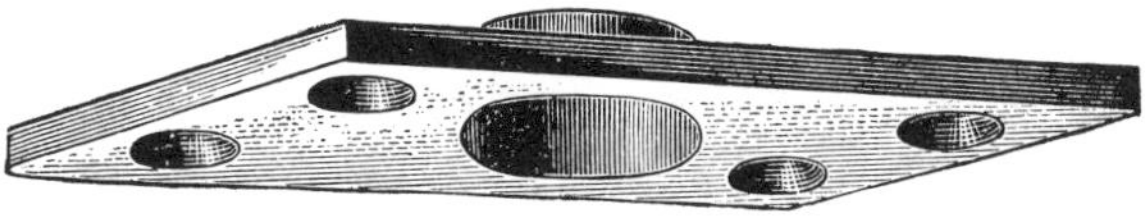

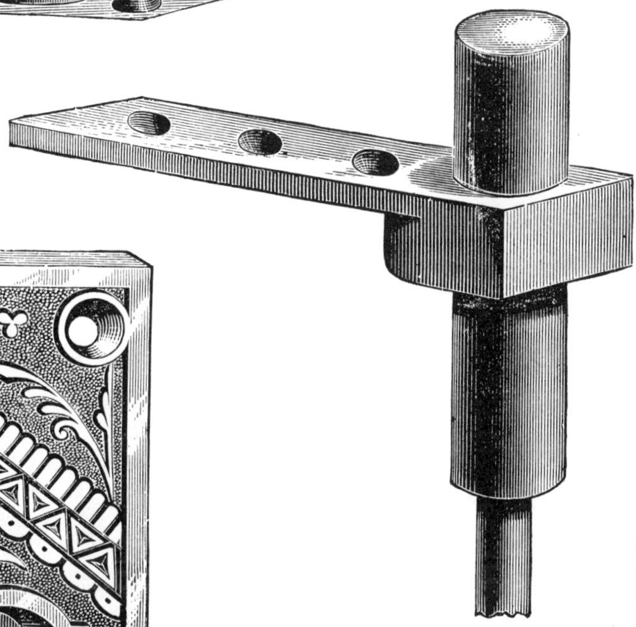

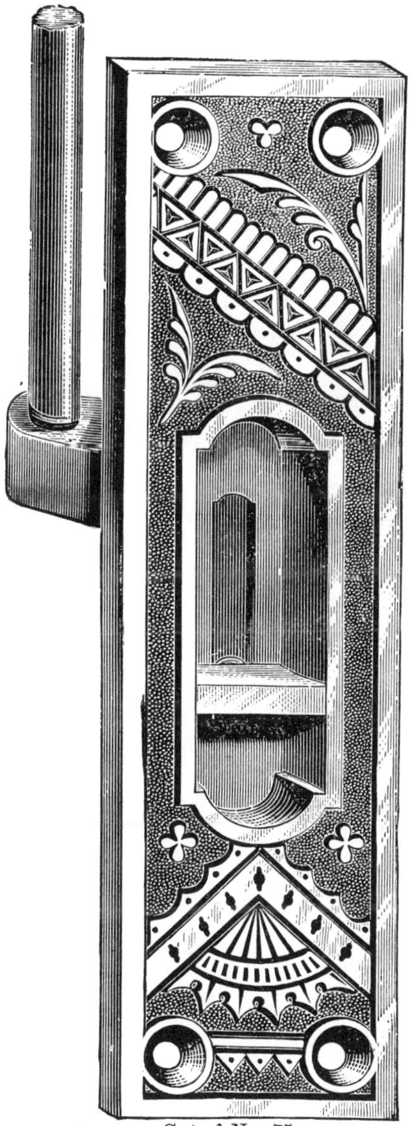

Cut of No. 75.

BRONZE METAL EXTENSION FLUSH BOLTS.

In three styles of finish, as follows:
No. 1, all Light Bronze.
No. 2, all Dark Bronze.
No. 3, Light Surface, Black Background.

No. 75, Sunk Thumb Piece.
No. 80, with Knob.

In the following sizes:

Nos.......	75	80	B 75	B 80
1½x8.....	......	......	......	......
1½x12....	......	......	......	......
1½x15 ...	......	......	......	......
1½x18 ...	......	......	......	......
1½x24....	......	......	......	......
1½x30....	......	......	......	......
1½x36....	......	......	......	......
1½x42....	......	......	......	......
1½x48....	......	......	......	......
1½x54....	......	......	......	......
1½x60 ...	......	......	......	......

"Branford" Bronze Flush Bolts are "Electro Bronzed Finish" on iron, in same patterns and sizes as above.
No. B 75, Sunk Thumb Piece.
No. B 80, with Knob.

No. 100, **Cast Brass Extension Flush Bolt can be made any desired length, increasing length of rod, by welding. The parts are similar to cuts on this page, excepting the plates are plain cast brass, polished and lacquered.** ....

CUPBOARD CATCHES, ETC.

JAPANNED CUPBOARD CATCHES.

No. 311, Fancy Brass Knob, Small size......... ......
No. 312, Fancy Brass Knob, Large size......... ......
No. 326, Porcelain Knob, Small size......... ......
No. 377, Porcelain Knob, Large size ....

Cut is full size of Nos. 311 and 326.

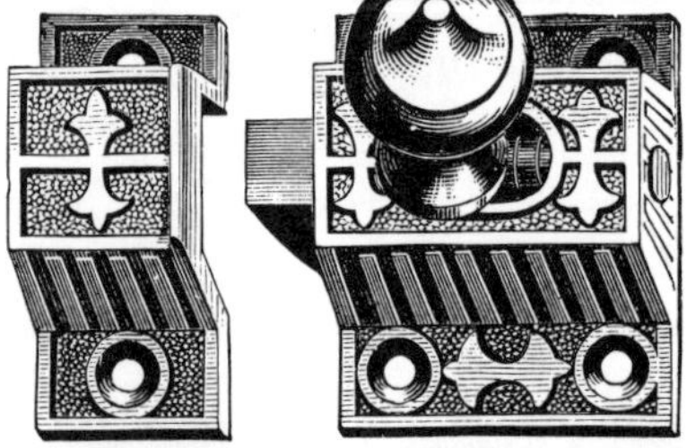

TUSCAN BRONZED FRENCH WINDOW CATCHES.

No. 3210, Bronze Metal Knob, packed with screws.......................... 1 in......
No. 3211, Bronze Metal Knob, packed with screws.......................... 1½ in.....
No. 3215, Porcelain Knob, packed wiih screws.......................... 1 in .....
No. 3216, Porcelain Knob, packed with screws.......................... 1½ in .....

Cut is full size of Nos. 3210 and 3215.

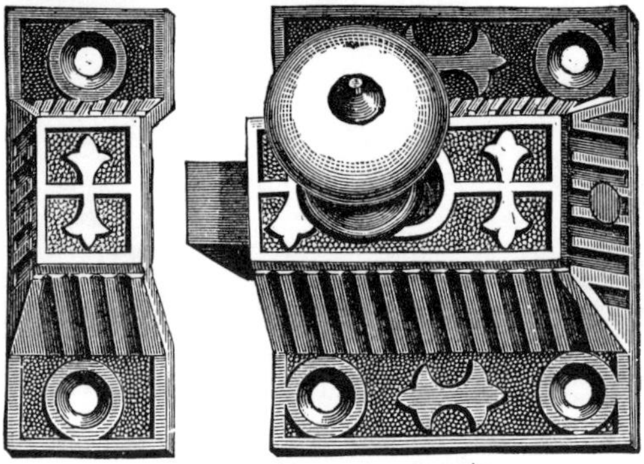

TUSCAN BRONZED FRENCH WINDOW CATCHES.

No. 3212, Bronze Metal Knob, packed with screws.... ......
No. 3217, Porcelain Knob, packed with screws ....

Cut is full size.

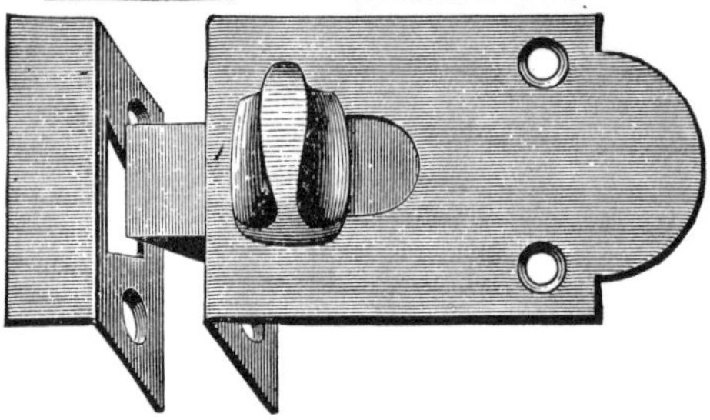

WROUGHT BRASS SHOW CASE CATCHES.

No. 1........................... ......

Cut is full size.

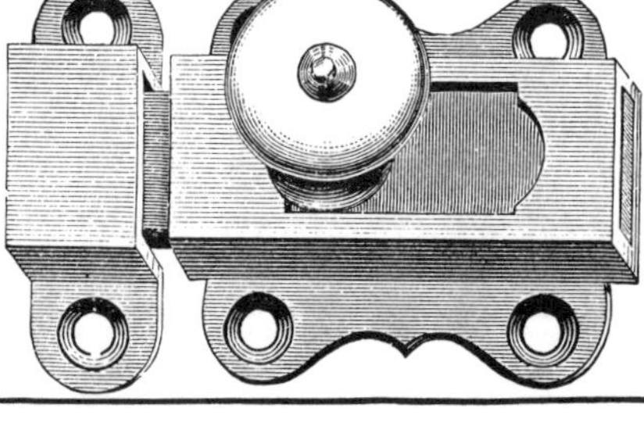

CUPBOARD BOLTS.

No. 205, Cast Brass, Porcelain Knob, 2¼ in......
No. 208, " " " " 3½ in......
No. 220, Tuscan Bronzed, Bronze Knob ....
No. 224, Tuscan Bronzed, Porcelain Knob............................ ......

Cut is full size of No. 205.

CUPBOARD TURNS.

No. 415.

CUPBOARD TURNS.

Kahala Bronzed,

No. 415, Packed with Screws ....

No. 420, Packed with Screws ....

With Lever Bolts.

No. 4430.

CUPBOARD TURNS.

No. 4230, Tuscan Bronzed.......... ......

No. 4430, Berlin " , Bronze Knob ....

Packed with Screws.

No. 4432.

CUPBOARD TURNS.

No. 4432, Berlin Bronzed, Bronze Metal T Handle ....

No. 4442, Berlin Bronzed, Bronze Metal T Handle ... .

No. 4852, Bronze Metal ....

No. 4952, Imperial Bronze ....

Packed with Screws.

BRASS FLUSH RINGS AND PULLEYS.

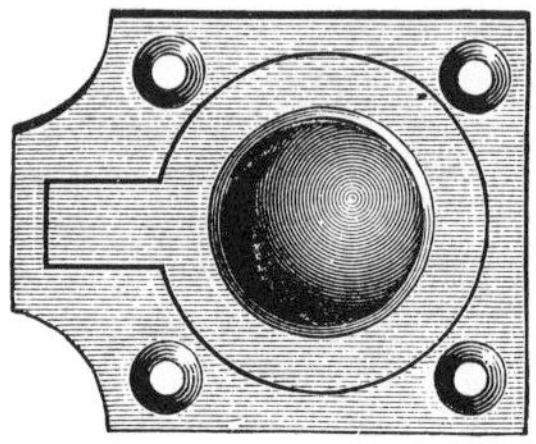

BRASS FLUSH RINGS.

Polished and Lacquered.......Inch, 1..... 1⅛..... 1¼..... 1⅜.....1½.....

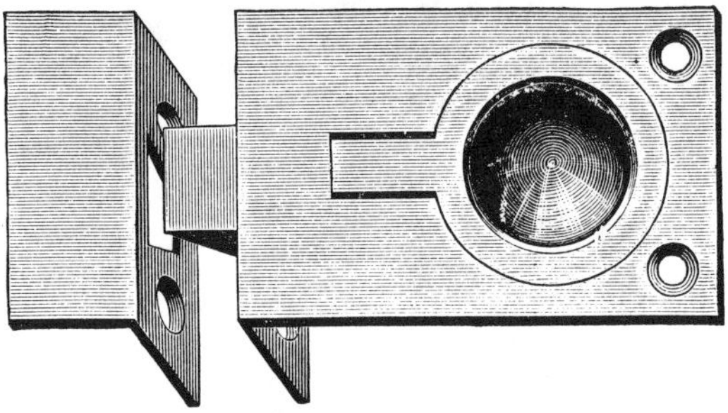

FLUSH RING SHOW-CASE CATCHES.

No. 25, Cast Brass, Polished and Lacquered ....

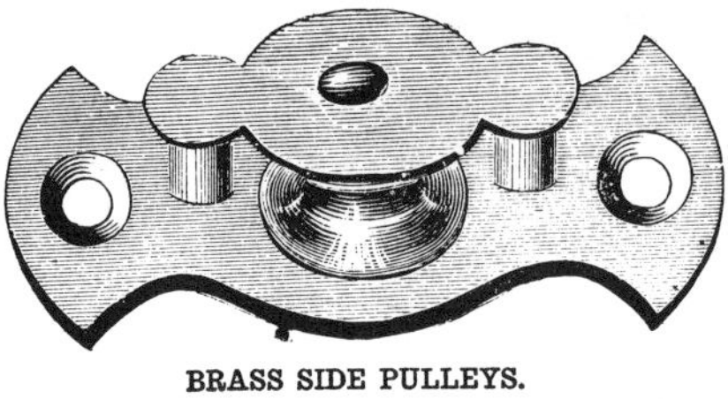

BRASS SIDE PULLEYS.

Inch	½	⅝
Single	......	......
Double	......	......

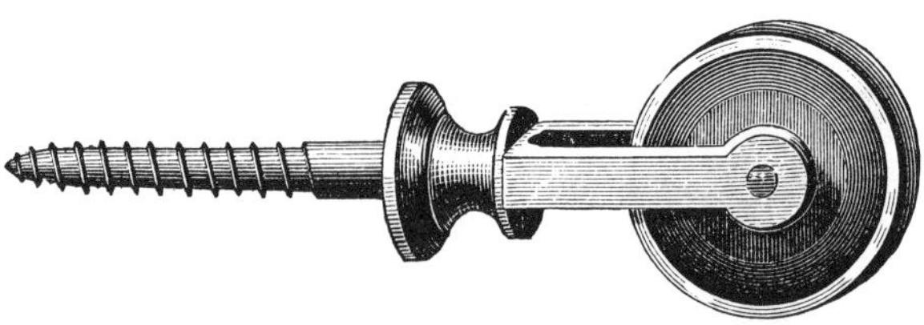

BRASS SCREW FULLEYS.

Inch	½	⅝	¾	⅞	1	1¼
Single	......	......	......	......	......	......
Double	......	......	......	......	......	......

WINDOW SPRING BOLTS.

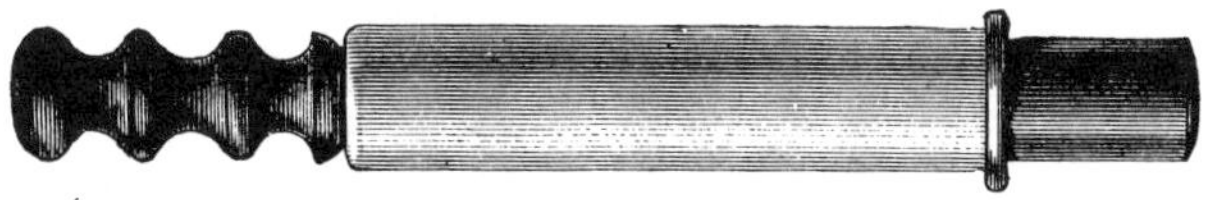

No. 15, Copper Bronzed. ....

No. 20, Silver Capped ....

No. 37, Wrought Iron, Tinned.. ......

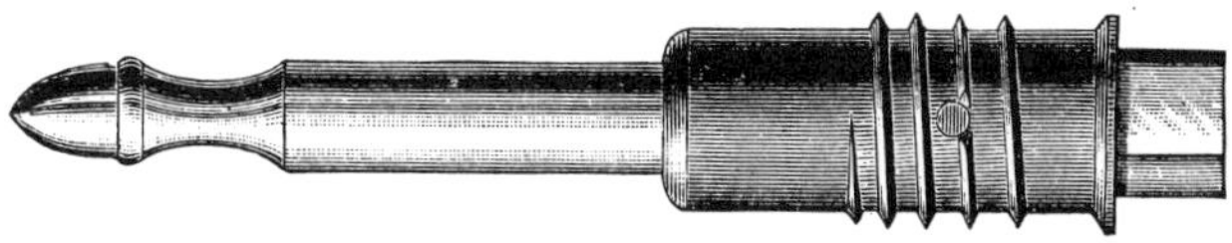

No. 101½, Copper Bronzed. ....

The case of this bolt is provided with a screw-thread, and when screwed into the sash, it is there to stay. The butt-end is flattened to fit a wrench, which will be found in every box containing half gross of bolts. By placing this wrench in a brace, it will be very easy to screw the bolt into the sash.

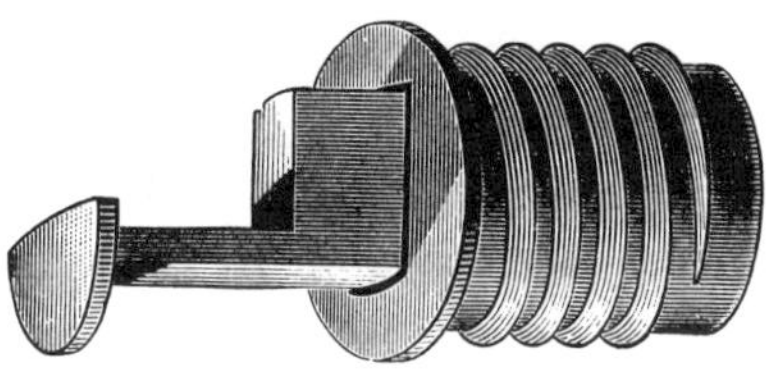

BABCOCK'S WINDOW SPRINGS.

No. 3, Brass Bolt................ ......

No. 4, Malleable Iron Bolt........ ......

WINDOW SPRINGS.

No. 5, Wrought Brass, Cast Brass Bolts, ...

No. 16, Wrought Iron, " " " ......

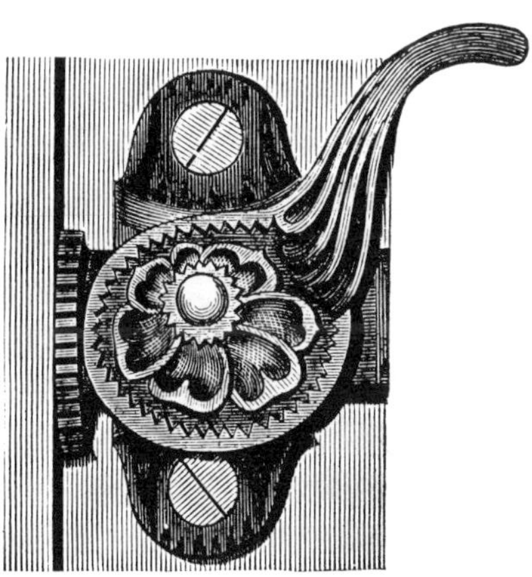

GARRETSON'S WINDOW LOCK.

Copper Bronzed..................... ......

Nickel Plated....................... ......

Holds the window firmly in any position. When locked, the sash can not be raised from outside, without breaking the window.

Is easily applied.

DRAWER PULLS.

Full size cut, No. 100.

Japanned.......................................No. 100, 2½ in....... No. 10, 4 in.......

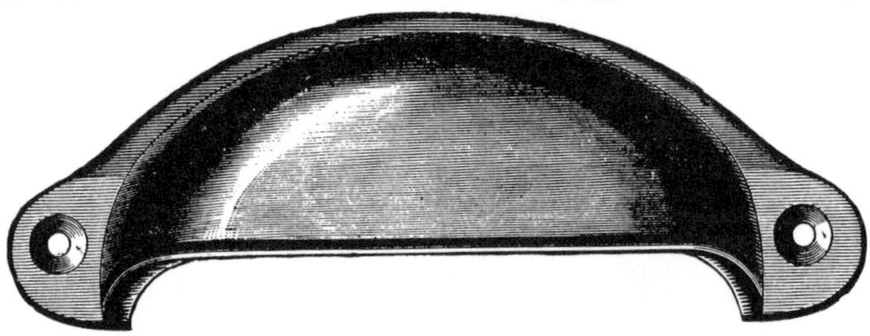

No. 30, Japanned.. ......

Full size cut of 456.

Berlin Bronzed....................................No. 556...... 456...... 356......

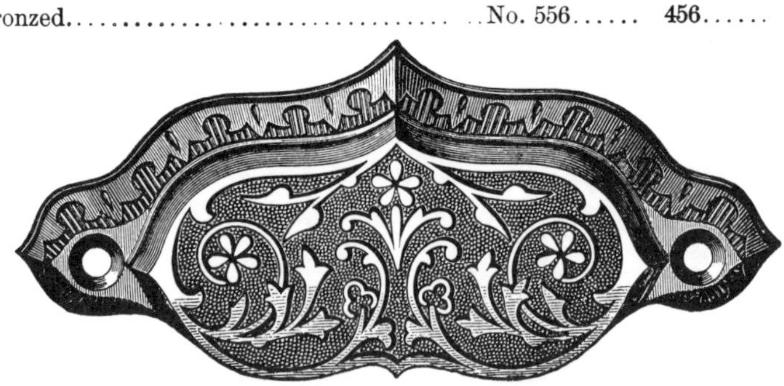

Full size cut of 476.

Berlin Bronzed....................................No. 576...... 476...... 376......

We have a number of other styles which we have not space to illustrate in this book.

DRAWER AND WINDOW PULLS, AND LIFTING HANDLES.

DRAWER PULLS.

No. 605, Tuscan Bronzed.. ......

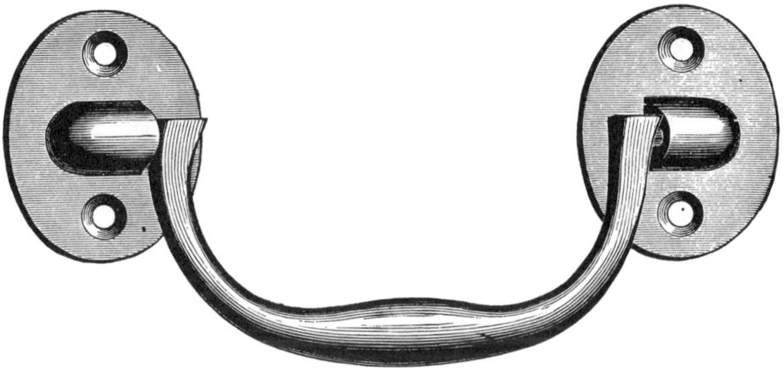

CAST BRASS LIFTING HANDLES.

No. 1, Polished and Lacquered........Sizes, 2½....... 3...... 3½...... 4 in.......

WINDOW PULLS.

No. 405, Berlin Bronzed........... ...... No. 805, Bronze Metal........... ......

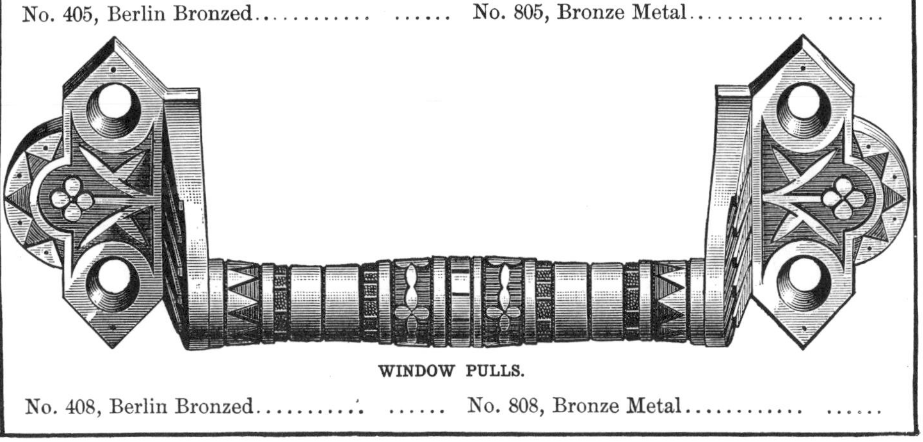

WINDOW PULLS.

No. 408, Berlin Bronzed.......... ...... No. 808, Bronze Metal........... ......

WARDROBE HOOKS.

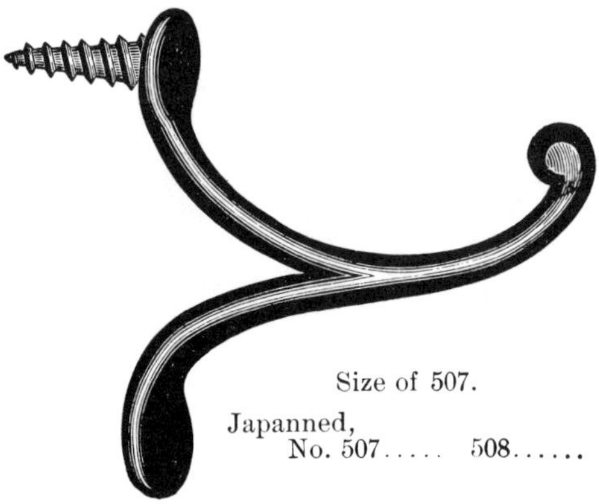

Size of 507.

Japanned,
No. 507..... 508......

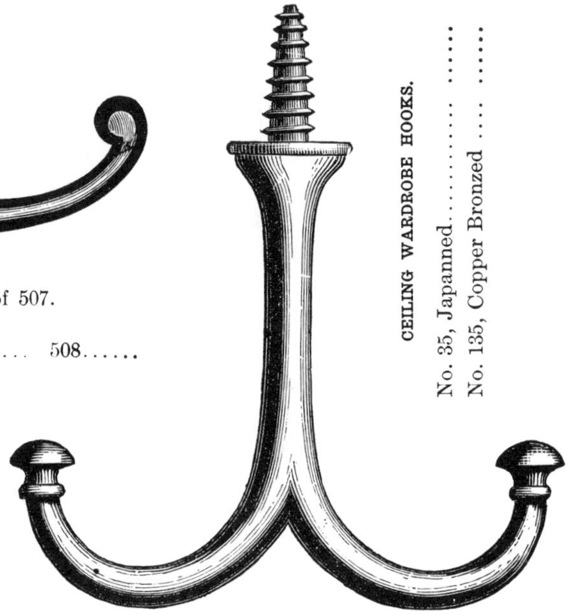

CEILING WARDROBE HOOKS.

No. 35, Japanned.......... ......
No. 135, Copper Bronzed ....

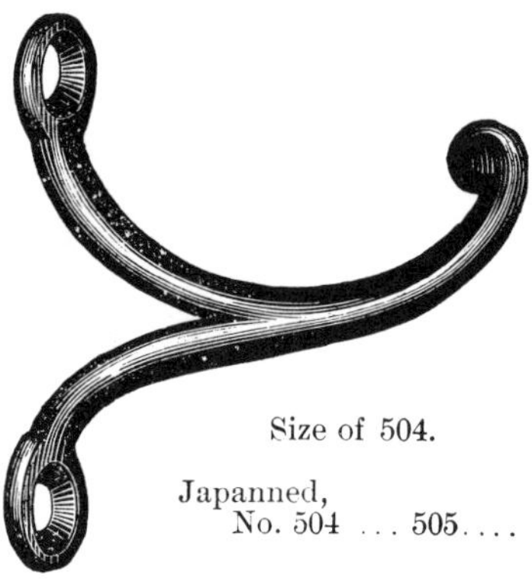

Size of 504.

Japanned,
No. 504 ... 505....

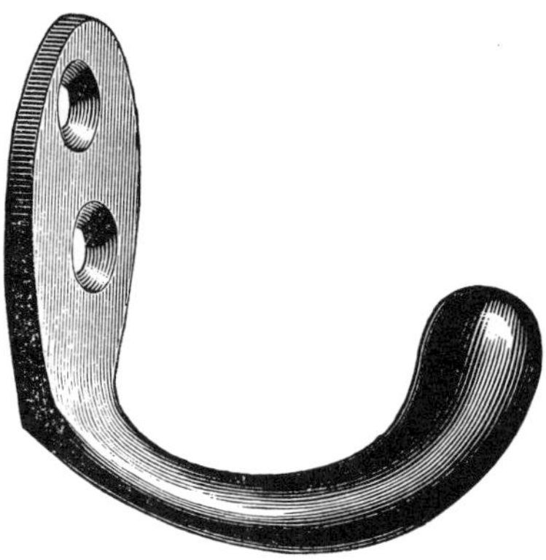

No. 515, Japanned.......... ......

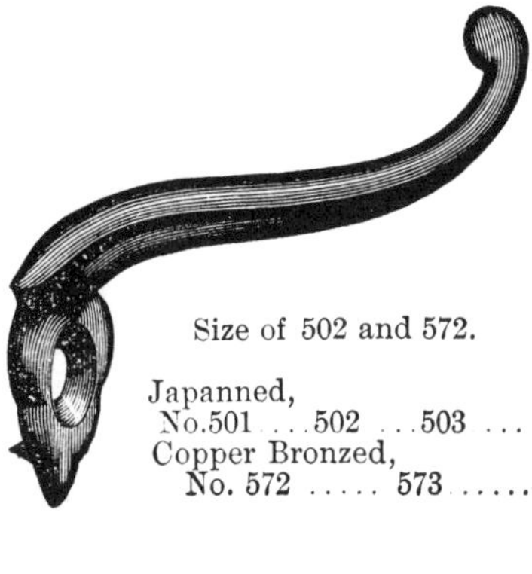

Size of 502 and 572.

Japanned,
No.501 ... 502 ... 503 ...
Copper Bronzed,
No. 572 ..... 573 .....

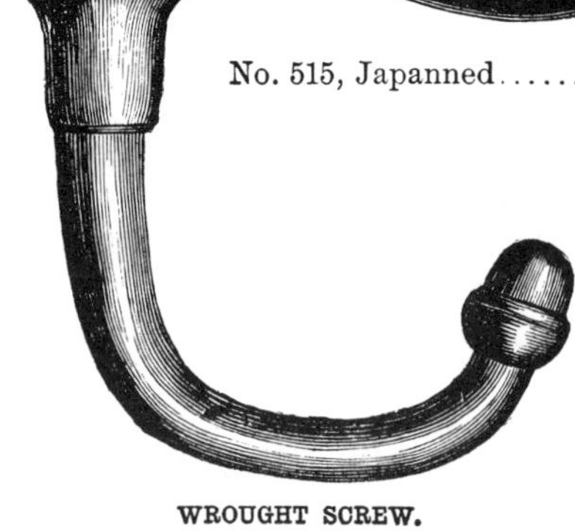

WROUGHT SCREW.

No. 30, Japanned........... ......

VAJEN & NEW, INDIANAPOLIS, IND.

COAT AND HAT HOOKS.

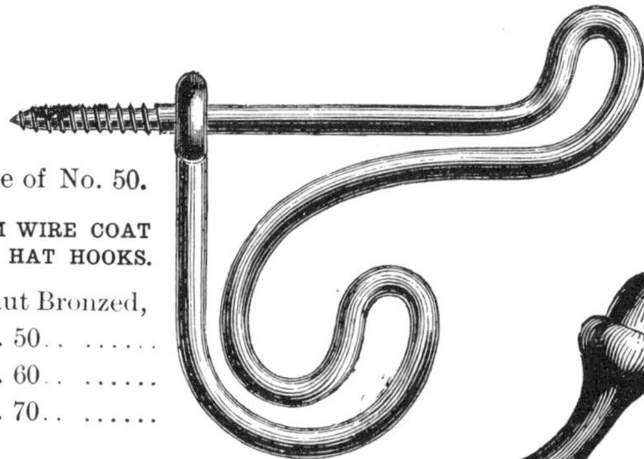

Size of No. 50.

GEM WIRE COAT AND HAT HOOKS.

Walnut Bronzed,
No. 50.. ......
No. 60.. ......
No. 70.. ......

Nos. 75 and 175.

Nos. 50 and 150

No. 75, Japanned ....
No. 175, Copper Bronzed ......
No. 50, Japanned ....
No. 150, Copper Bronzed ......

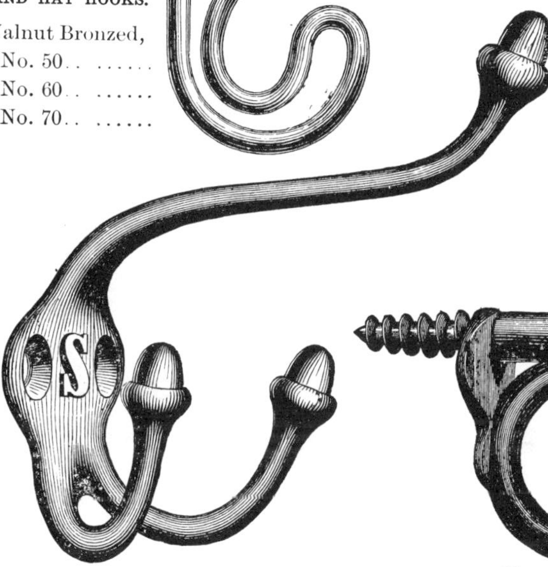

No. 20, Japanned ....
No. 120, Copper Bronzed..... ......

Size of 52 and 152.

Japanned,..... No. 52..... 53..... 54.....
Copper Bronzed, No. 152..... 153..... 154.....

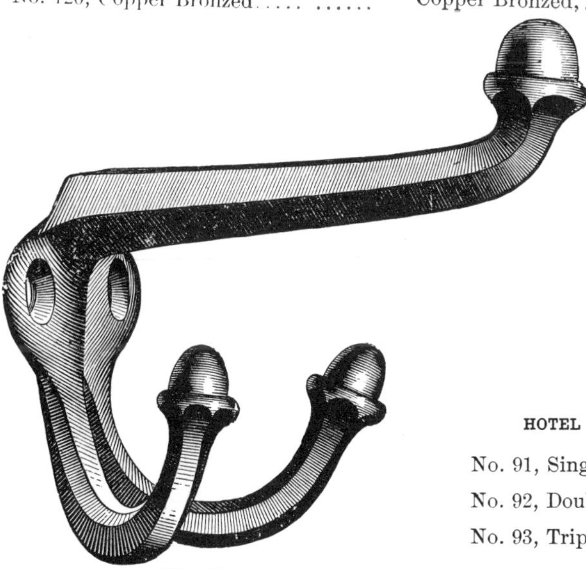

No. 93.

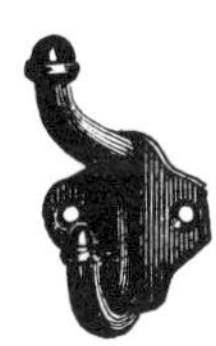

No. 92.

No. 91.

HOTEL OR SCHOOL HOUSE HOOKS.

No. 91, Single, Japanned ... .
No. 92, Double, " ....
No. 93, Triple, " ....

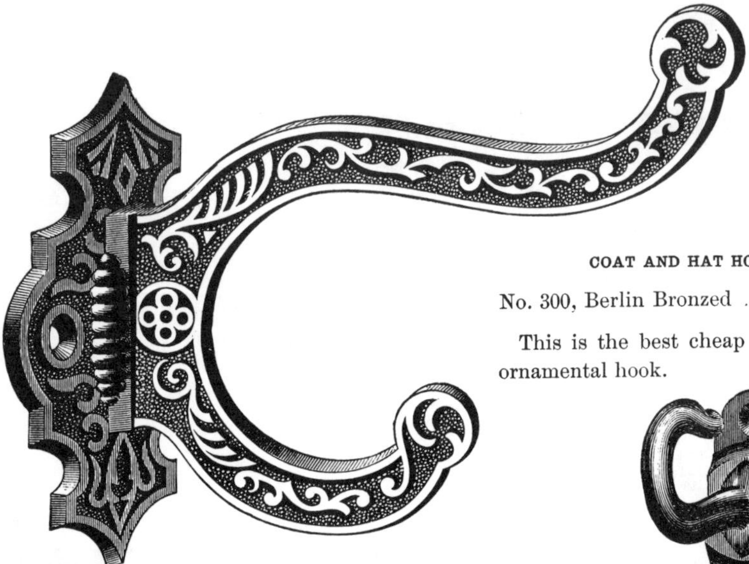

COAT AND HAT HOOKS.

No. 300, Berlin Bronzed ....

This is the best cheap hook for an ornamental hook.

No. 3.
CLOTHES LINE.

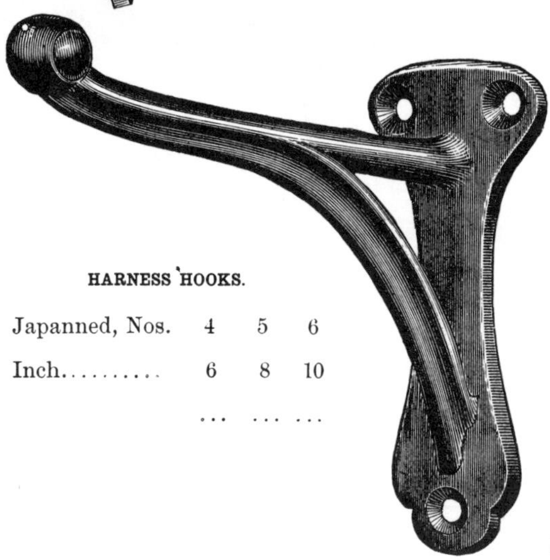

HARNESS HOOKS.

Japanned, Nos.	4	5	6
Inch..........	6	8	10
	...	...	...

Nos. 1 and 2.
CLOTHES LINE HOOKS .

Japanned Nos. 1 ... 2.... 3....

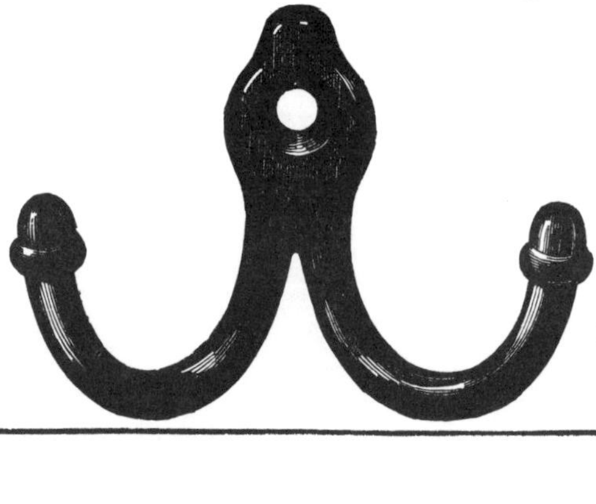

DOUBLE WARDROBE HOOKS.

Japanned....Nos. 541...... 542......

We have quite a variety of Fancy Coat and Hat Hooks, other than the ones illustrated on these pages.

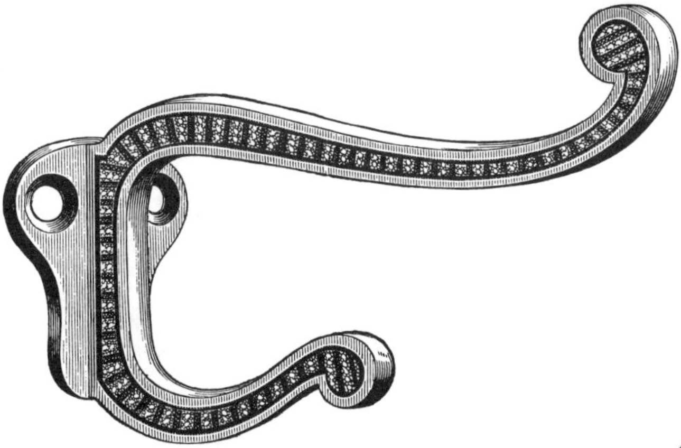

No. 791, Ornamental Bronze Metal, ...

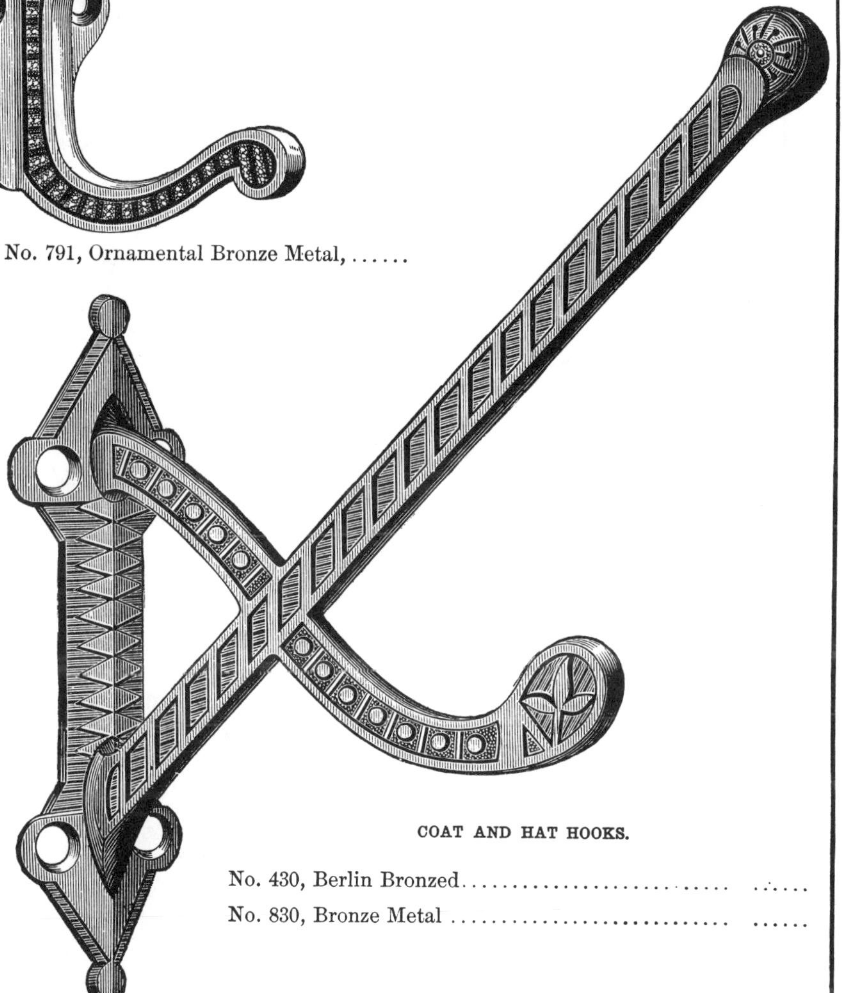

COAT AND HAT HOOKS.

No. 430, Berlin Bronzed.......................... ......

No. 830, Bronze Metal ....

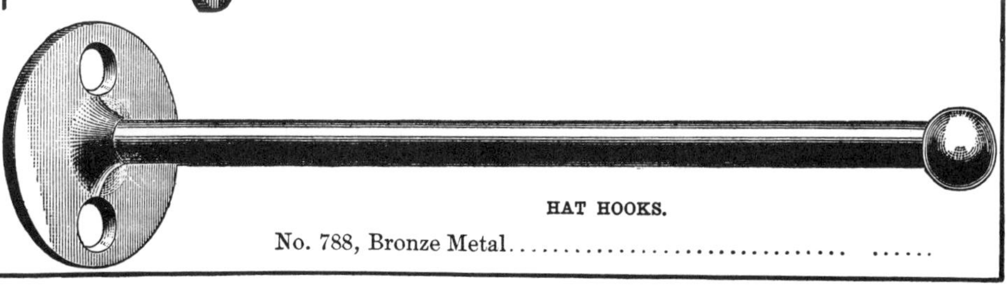

HAT HOOKS.

No. 788, Bronze Metal............................ ......

SASH FASTENERS.

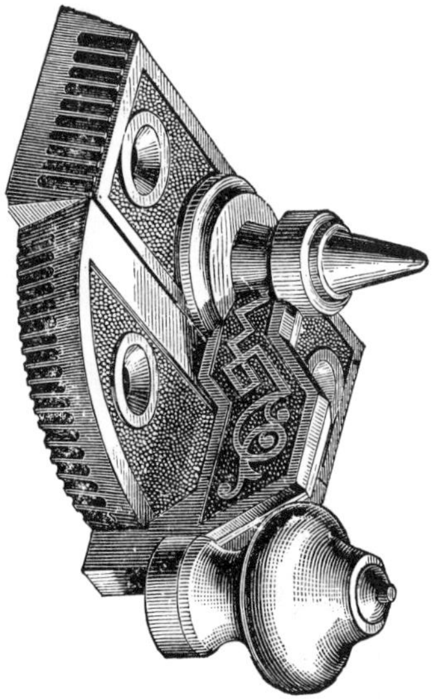

No. 38, Tuscan Bronzed........ ......
With Porcelain Knob.

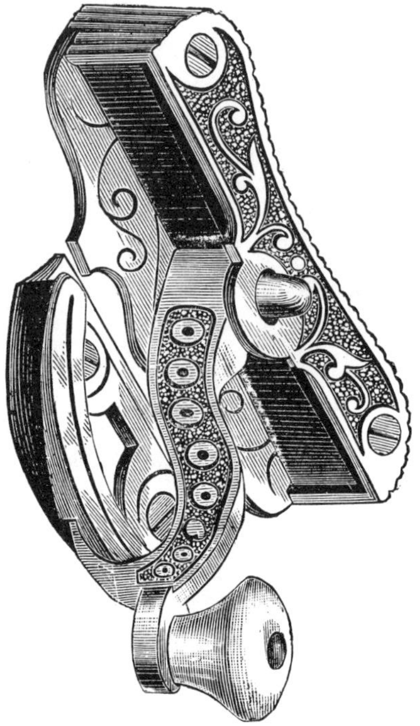

No. 15, Copper Bronzed, burglar proof .....
With Porcelain Knob.

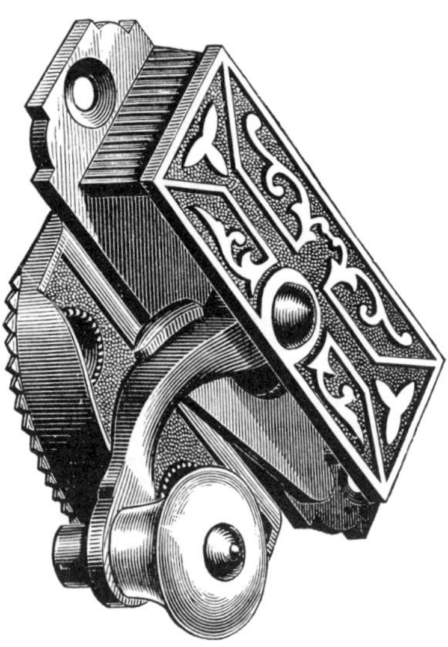

No. 521.

No. 520, Berlin Bronzed, Iron Knob, ...
No. 521, " " Porcelain " ......
Burglar proof.

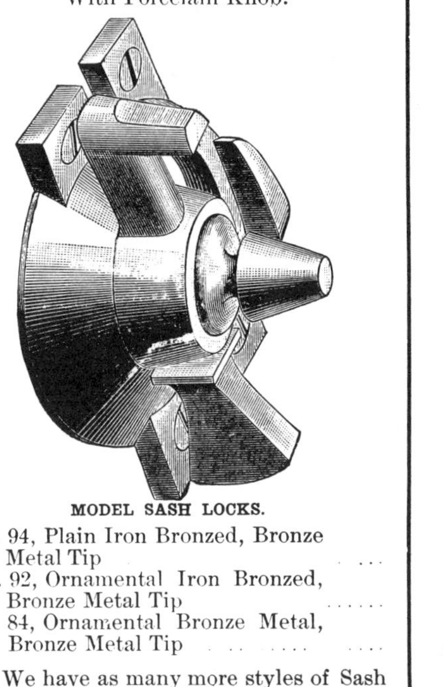

MODEL SASH LOCKS.

No. 94, Plain Iron Bronzed, Bronze Metal Tip ...
No. 92, Ornamental Iron Bronzed, Bronze Metal Tip ......
No. 84, Ornamental Bronze Metal, Bronze Metal Tip .. ..

All goods on this page packed with screws. We have as many more styles of Sash Locks, which we are unable to illustrate.

SASH LOCKS.

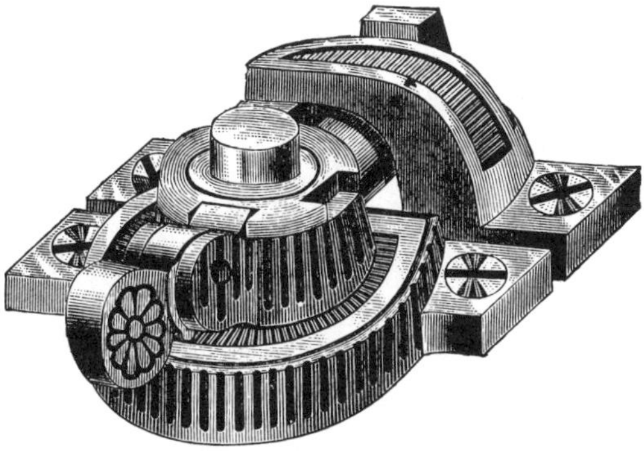

KEMPSHALL BURGLAR PROOF SASH LOCKS

No. 62, Polished Iron, Bronze Metal Tip and Drop ....
No. 66, Iron Bronzed, Brass Rivet and Iron Drop ....

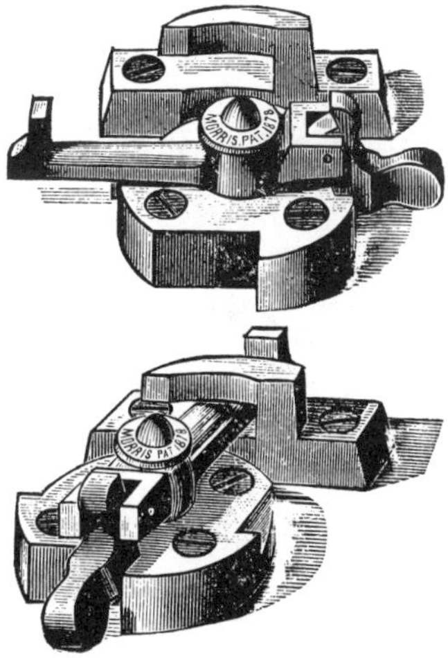

MORRIS BURGLAR PROOF SASH LOCKS.

No. 4½, Iron, Tucker Bronzed.... ......
No. 13, Plain Polished Iron, Boston Finish ....

MATHES BURGLAR PROOF SASH LOCKS.

No. 30, Ornamental Egyptian Bronzed, ...
No. 32, " Electro Bronze, Plated, ...
No. 33, " Bronze, Plated and Black Inlaid ....
No. 34, Ornamental Egyptian Bronzed, Genuine Bronze Lever... ....
No. 35, Ornamental Genuine Bronze, Bright or Statuary.............. ....

SECURE SELF-BOLTING SASH LOCKS.

No. 7, Lacquered Iron, Brass Cap and Knob ....
No. 27, Bronzed Iron, Bronze Cap and Knob ....
No. 55, Ornamental Bronze, extra heavy.................... ......

All goods on this page packed with screws. The above are the four best selling styles.

SASH PLATES, SASH PULL HOOKS AND SASH LIFTS.

Nos. 400 and 800.

Nos. 413 and 813.

Nos. 81 and 84.

SASH PULL PLATES.

No. 400, Round, Berlin Bronzed, packed with screws, ...
No. 800, " Bronze Metal, " " " ......
No. 413, Fancy, Berlin Bronzed, " " " ......
No. 813, " Bronze Metal, " " " ......

SOCKET WINDOW PULLS.

No. 81, Berlin Bronzed, packed with screws......... ......
No. 84, Bronze Metal, " " " ....

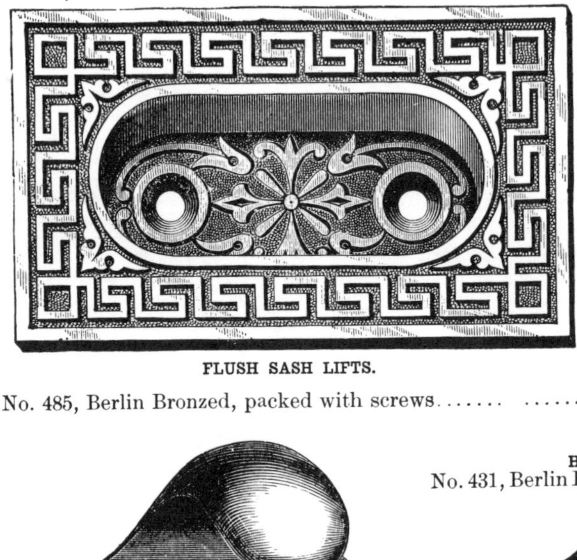

FLUSH SASH LIFTS.

No. 485, Berlin Bronzed, packed with screws....... ......

HOOK SASH LIFTS.

No. 431, Berlin Bronzed, packed with screws ...

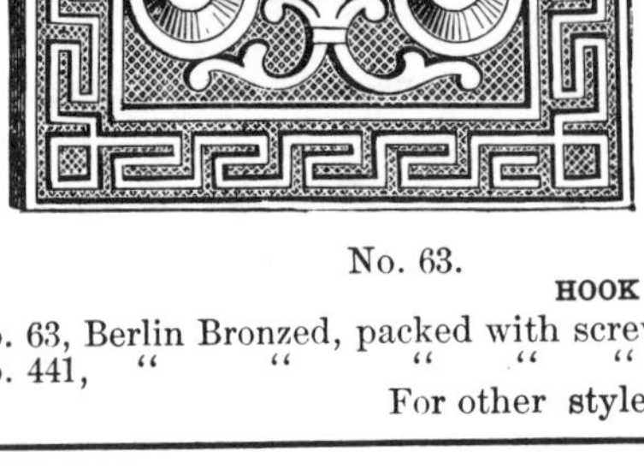

No. 63.

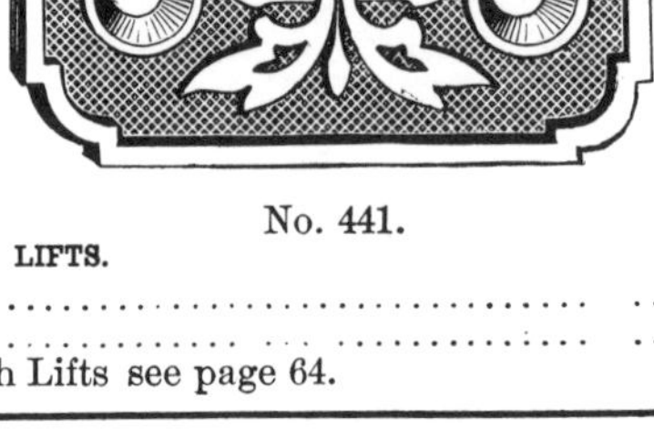

No. 441.

HOOK SASH LIFTS.

No. 63, Berlin Bronzed, packed with screws ....
No. 441, " " " " " ....

For other styles Sash Lifts see page 64.

VAJEN & NEW, INDIANAPOLIS, IND.

Full size cut of No. 21.

Berlin Bronzed Chest Handles........................ No. 20...... 21...... 22......

Half-size cut of No. 31.

FLUSH CHEST HANDLES.

Japanned, No. 31.... 32.... 33.... 34....

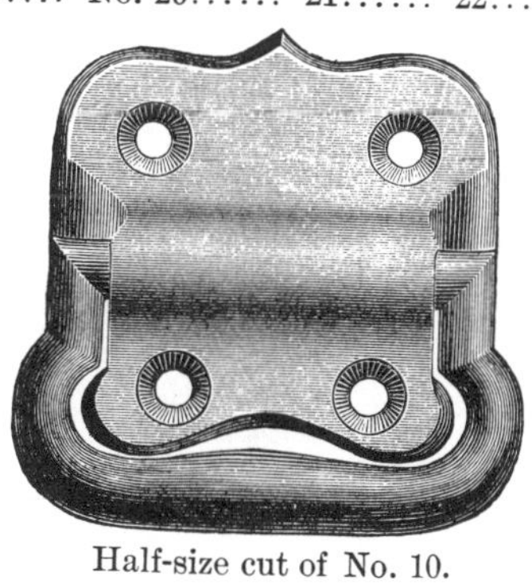

Half-size cut of No. 10.

CHEST HANDLES.

Japanned, No. 10.... 11.... 12.... 13....

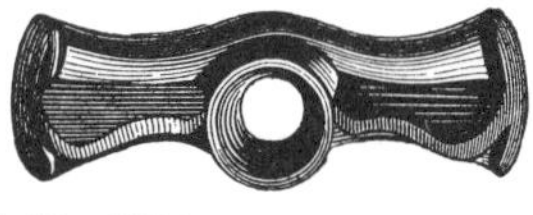

No. 10. JAPANNED DOOR BUTTONS.

In. 1½...1¾...2...2¼...2½...

No. 5. BRASS DOOR BUTTONS.

In. 1¼...1½...1¾...2....

DOOR BUTTONS ON PLATES.

No. 20, Japanned, 1½...1¾...2...2¼...2½ in...   No. 15, Brass, 1½....1¾....2 in....

SHUTTER BARS AND KNOBS.

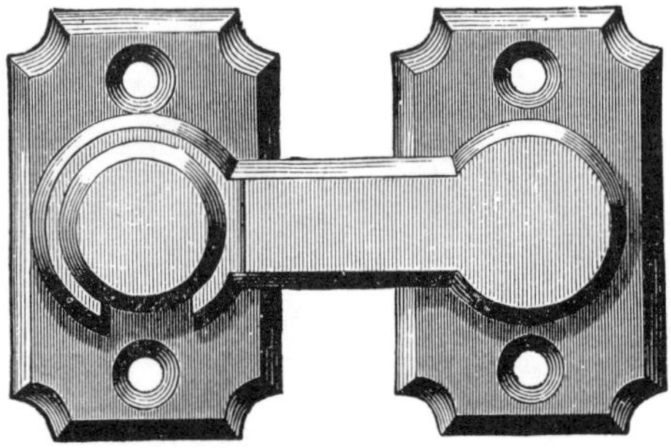

Full size cut of 2½ in.

Size	2	2½ in.
No. 71, Cast Brass	......	......
No. 72, Silver Plated	......	......

Full size cut of 2 in.

No. 105, Berlin Bronzed . 2...... 2½ in

Full size cut of 2½ in.

No. 55, Berlin Bronzed 2 .....2½ in......

Full size cut of 2½ in.

No. 165, Berlin Bronzed, 2..... 2½ in.....

Full size cut of 1⅛ in.

No. 52, Berlin Bronzed, ⅞..... 1⅛ in.....

All of the above packed with screws. For other styles of Shutter Bars see page 67. For other styles of Shutter Knobs see pages 67 and 97.

SHUTTER BARS AND HINGES.

Full size cut of 2½ in.

SHUTTER BARS.

No. 135, Berlin Bronzed, packed with screws.................... 2...... 2½ in......

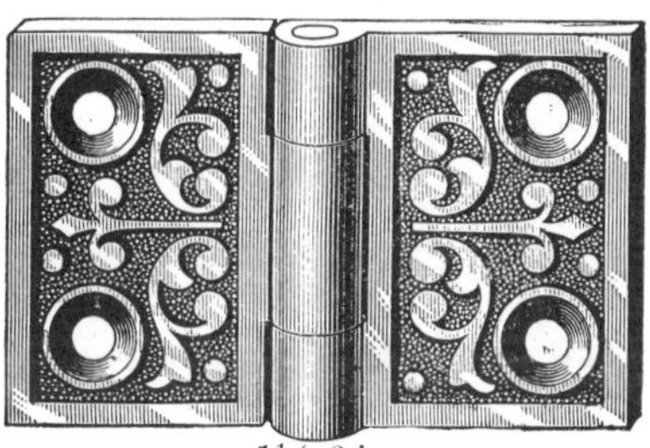

1¼x2 in.

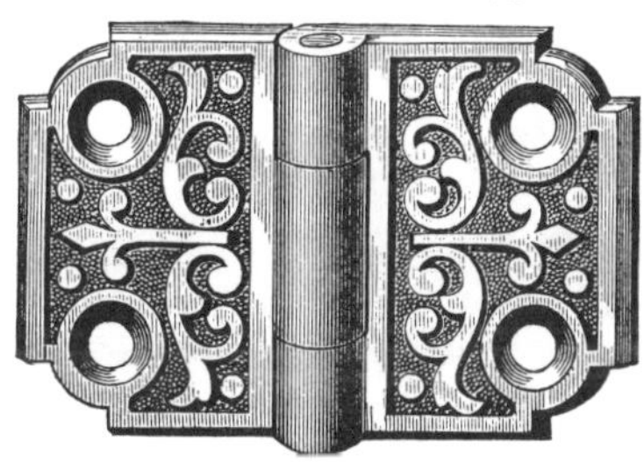

No. 411, Berlin Bronzed, with screws, 1¼x2 ..... 1½x2¼ in .....

No. 410, Berlin Bronzed, with screws, 1¼x2 in......

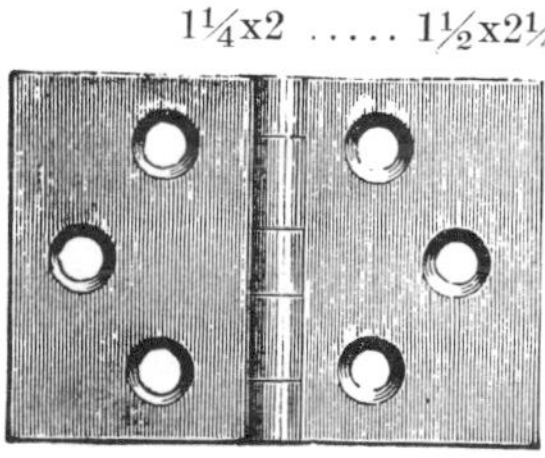

Desk.

Broad.

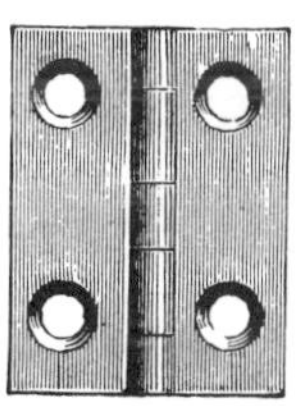

Middle.

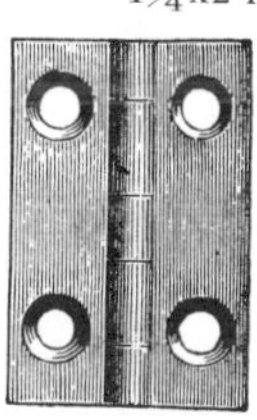

Narrow.

Full size cuts of 1 in.

WROUGHT BRASS BUTTS.

Narrow.

Inch.. ½.... ¾.... ⅞.... 1...... 1⅛.... 1¼.... 1⅜.... 1½.... 1⅝.... 1¾....
1⅞.... 2...... 2¼.... 2½.... 2¾.... 3...... 3¼.... 3½.... 3¾.... 4......

Middle.

Inch.. ½.... ¾.... ⅞.... 1...... 1⅛.... 1¼.... 1⅜.... 1½.... 1⅝.... 1¾....
1⅞.... 2...... 2¼.... 2½.... 2¾.... 3...... 3¼.... 3½.... 3¾.... 4......

Broad.

Inch.. ½.... ¾.... ⅞.... 1...... 1⅛.... 1¼.... 1⅜ ... 1½.... 1⅝.... 1¾....
1⅞.... 2...... 2¼... 2½.... 2¾.... 3...... 3¼.... 3½... 3¾.... 4......

Desk.

Inch..................... ½...... ¾...... ⅞...... 1........ 1⅛...... 1¼......
1⅜ .... 1½...... 1⅝...... 1¾...... 1⅞...... 2........

REGISTERS AND TRANSOM LIFTS.

ROUND REGISTERS.

Japanned.

Openings.	Registers.	Faces.	Floor Borders.
6 Inch,	......	......	....
8 "	......	......	....
9 "	......	......	....
10 "	......	......	....
12 "	......	......	....

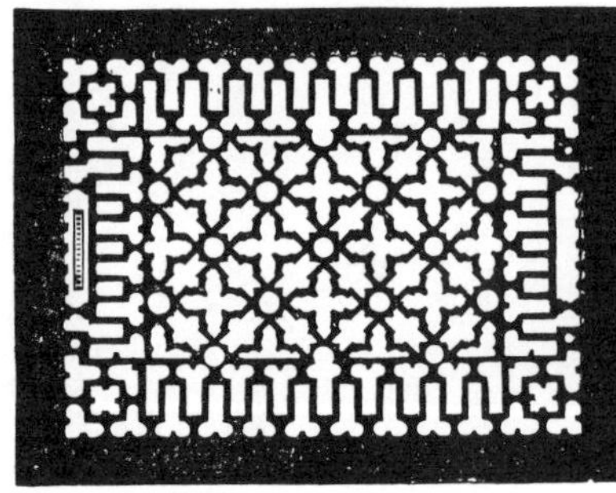

VERTICAL WHEEL REGISTERS.

Japanned.

Openings.	Registers.	Faces.	Floor Borders.
8x10 Inch,	......	......	....
8x12 "	......	......	....
10x12 "	......	......	....
10x14 "	......	......	....
10x16 "	......	......	....
12x12 "	......	......	....
12x15 "	......	......	....
14x18 "	......	......	....

Can also furnish Registers in White or Bronzed Faces.

For Hot or Cold Air, Floor or Wall. These Registers are the heaviest and best made in the market.

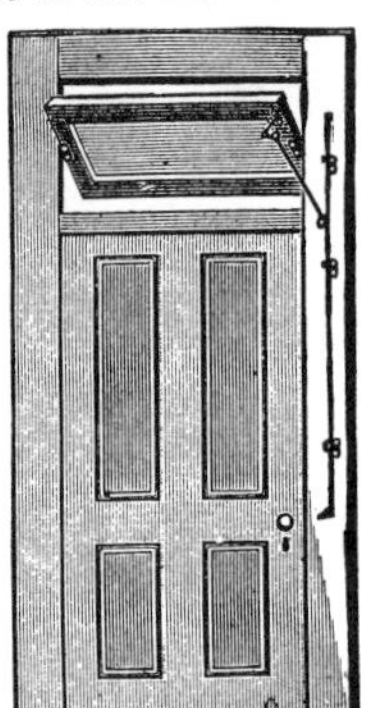

No. 1.

No. 3.

No. 4.

WOLLENSAK'S TRANSOM LIFTER AND LOCK.

Length	3	4	5	6	7	8	9	10 feet.
¼ Inch	......	......	......	......	......	......	......	......
5-16 "	......	......	......	......	......	......	......	......
⅜ "	......	......	......	......	......	......	......	......
½ "	......	......	......	......	......	......	......	......

Nos. 1 and 3 kept in stock; can furnish No. 4 when desired. Furnished in nickel plate or bronze to order.

With these Transom Lifters, ventilation is made easy. They are absolutely burglar proof. The transom can be locked in any position, and can not be tampered with from the outside.

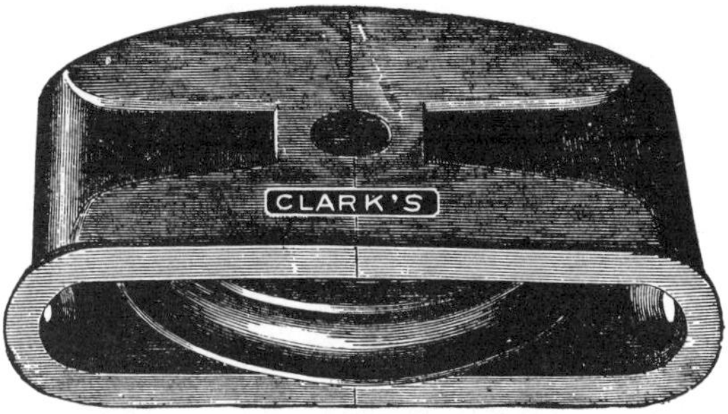

CLARK'S AXLE PULLEYS.

No. 20........................ 1¾...... 2 in......

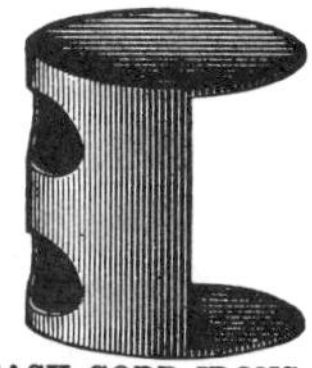

SASH CORD IRONS.

Smith's....... ......

EXCELSIOR AXLE PULLEYS.

No. 10, Plain, Polished Wheel	2	2¼	2½ in.	......
Polished and Bronzed, Plain Face	2	2¼	2½ in.	......
No. 200, Berlin Bronzed, Ornamental Face	2	2¼	2½ in.	......
Anti-Friction, Kahala Bronzed		2¼	2½ in.	......

Bronze Metal Front Pulley furnished to order.

IRON SASH WEIGHTS.

Round or Square, any weight desired.................................. Per lb ......

Also, Lead Sash Weights to order.

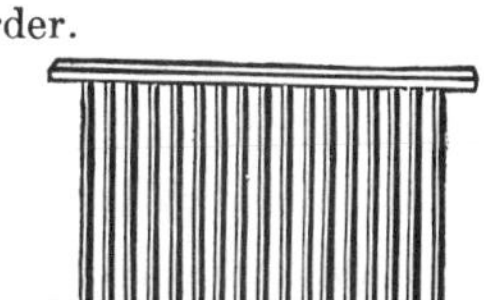

STAR ANCHORS.

FRAME ANCHORS.

JOIST SHOES.

FOUNDATION GRATES.

Fancy.

Size.	Weight.	Per lb
5x10 inches	4 lbs.	......
5x12 "	5¼ "	......
6x12 "	5½ "	......
8x12 "	7¼ "	......
8x16 "	11½ "	......
10x18 "	15 "	......
12x18 "	17½ "	......
12x21 "	20¼ "	......
12x24 "	22½ "	......

Plain.

Size.	Weight.	Per lb
5x10 inches	4 lbs.	......
5x12 "	4½ "	......
8x12 "	9 "	......
8x16 "	10½ "	......
10x16 "	12½ "	......
10x18 "	14 "	......
12x18 "	17¾ "	......
12x21 "	19½ "	......
12x24 "	22 "	......

SLIDING DOOR HANGERS.

WARNER'S SLIDING DOOR HANGERS.

No. 1, Berlin Bronzed, Flat or Astragal, including 28 feet of hardwood track, Per set....
No. 1, Bronze Metal, " " " " " " " " ....

These Hangers are entirely concealed from view, and run on a double track of hardwood, thus doing away with the ordinary floor track, and preventing any cutting of the carpet; they are adjustable in every particular in raising or lowering the door, thereby clearing the carpet of any unevenness of the floor. They are thoroughly made of malleable and wrought iron, the bearings being finished and lined with anti-friction metal. They run noiselessly, with perfect ease, and need no oiling. They can not get off the track. Nothing better for a sliding door.

THE DAVIS PARLOR DOOR HANGER.

No. 1, For Ordinary Doors, Per set .....
No. 2, For Ex.Heavy Doors, Per set......

No flanged wheels to cut, wear or get off the track; no cutting or defacing doors in hanging. Does not require an expert to put them up. Can be adjusted in a moment up or down, and are self-adjusting for any unevenness of the track. Strong and durable. Can not get off the track.

The best hangers will be found in our stock.

SLIDING DOOR SHEAVES.

Japanned Iron, Polished Wheel, Brass Pin Inch 3..... 4 ..... 5...... 6..... Wheels.
Anti-Friction, " 3..... 4..... 5...... 6...... "

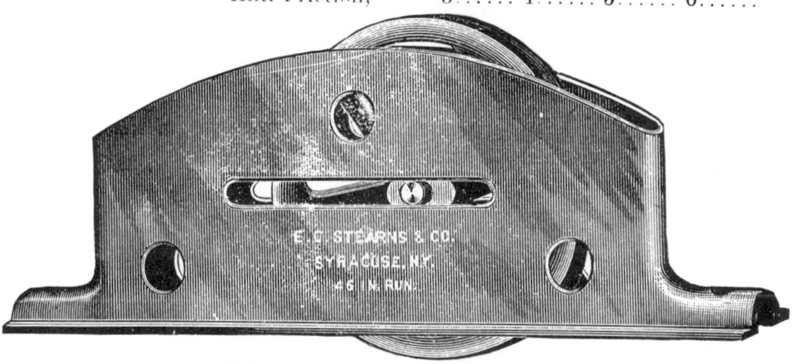

HATFIELD SLIDING DOOR SHEAVES.

Inch...............	2½.....	3.....	4 .....
Length of Run, Feet	33.......	42.....	46......

SLIDING DOOR RAIL.

Wrought Brass, Polished......1¼ in..... Bronzed Wrought Iron......1¼ in......
To be used with above Sheaves.

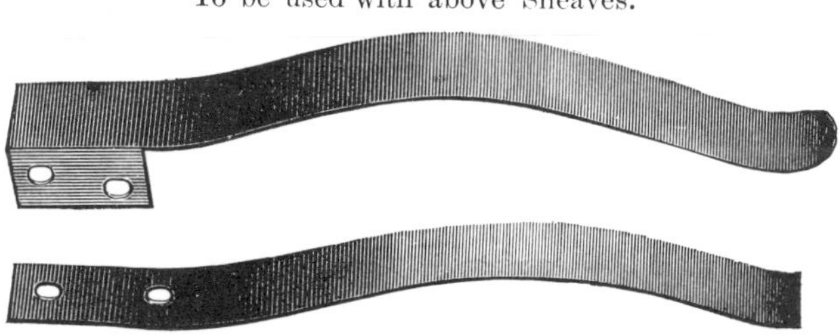

ANTI-RATTLING WINDOW SPRINGS.

Flanged.............. .... Plain......... ....
Totally prevent all rattling of windows. Can be easily applied where the sash works loose in the frame.

BARN DOOR HANGERS.

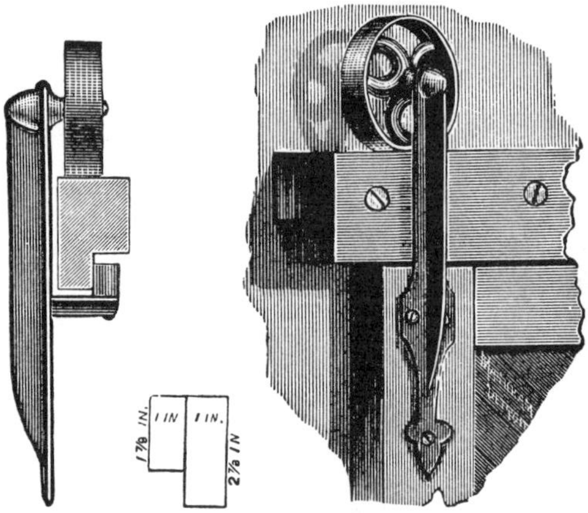

KIDDER HANGER.

4 Inch Wheel,...... 5 Inch Wheel,......

The above Hanger to run on a wood rail, the small anti-friction wheel keeping the door in place. Runs easy and with little noise.

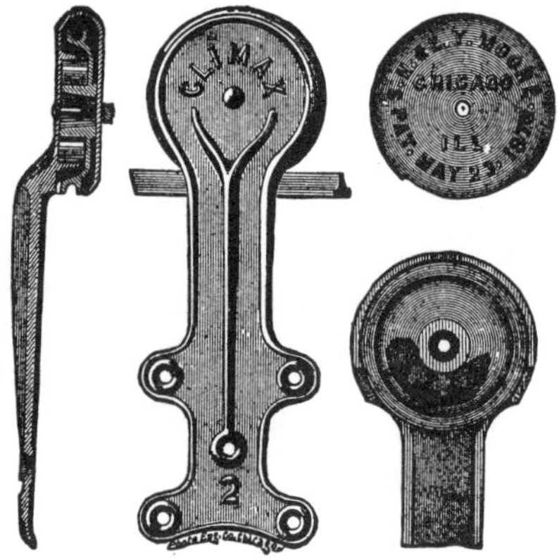

CLIMAX HANGERS.

No. 1, Large Size,.... No. 2, Medium, ...

No. 3, Small Size,....

The hub of the wheel in this Hanger revolves within a set of chilled rollers, giving ease of action and great durability, with no wear on the center pin.

CHECK BACK HANGER.

The old reliable Hanger to run on an iron rail.

3 Inch, Small.... ......
4 " Medium. ......
5 " Large.... ......

All Barn Door Hangers sold in pairs.

CRONK HANGER.

Wrought Iron. For Wood Rail.

This is a very simple constructed Hanger; strong, with steel axle pins. Nothing to break, and the door can not get off the track.

No. 4, Small Size, ...
No. 5, Medium " .....
No. 6, Large " ......

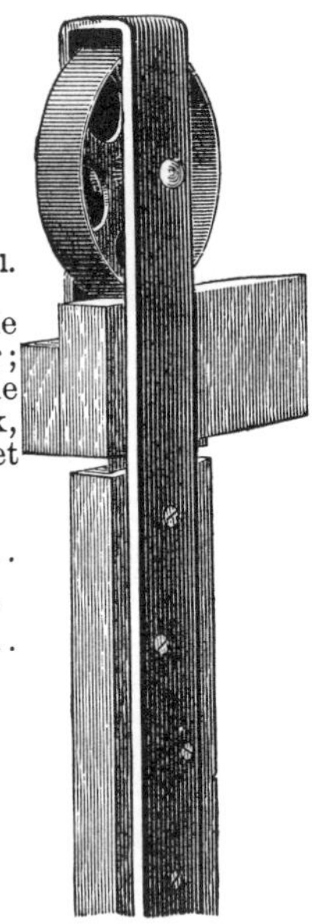

The latest improvements in Hangers will always be found in our stock.

ANGLE RAIL FOR CHECK BACK HANGER.

Single Flange........... Per foot...... Double Flange .... Per foot .....

SHUTTER TRIMMINGS.

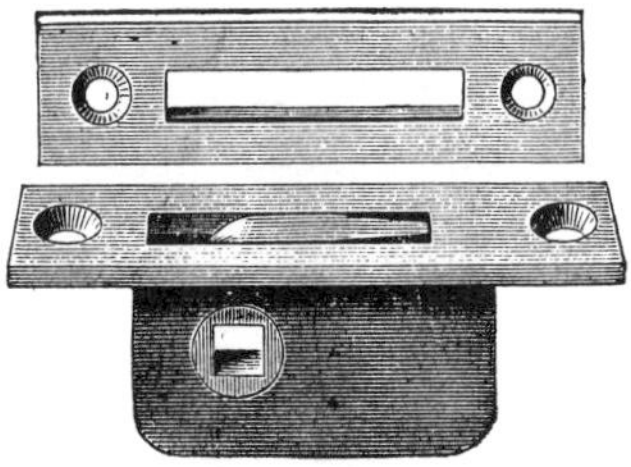

SHUTTER LOCKS.

No. 2, Polished Front and Strike, ...

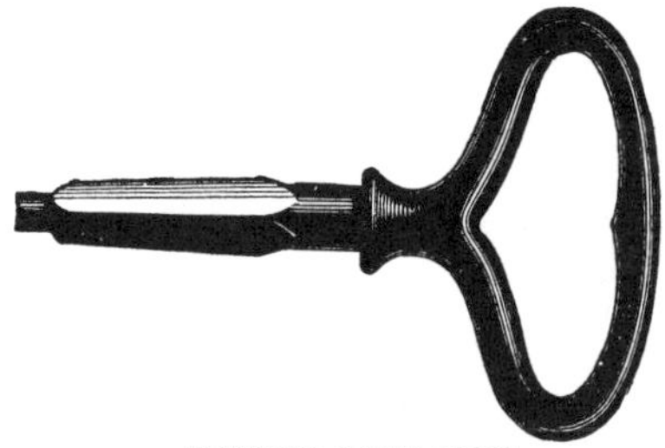

SHUTTER LOCK KEYS.

Japanned........................ ......

JAPANNED SHUTTER SCREWS.

Inch, $1\frac{3}{4}$ ..... 2...... $2\frac{1}{4}$...... $2\frac{1}{2}$ ..... 3......

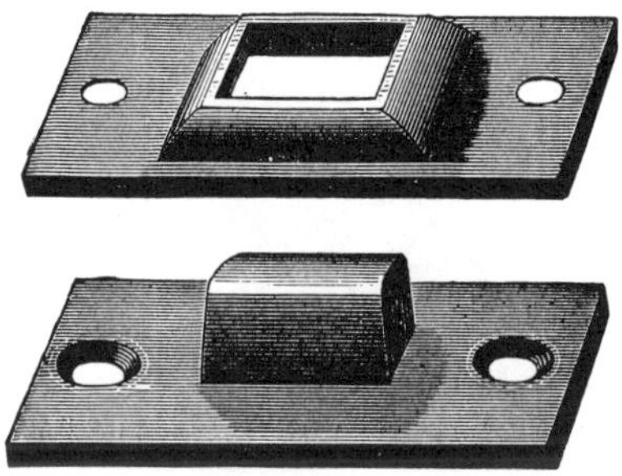

JAPANNED STUBS AND PLATES

No............. 1...... 2...... 3......

JAPANNED SASH CENTRES.

No 1..... 2 ..... 4...... 18...... 22......

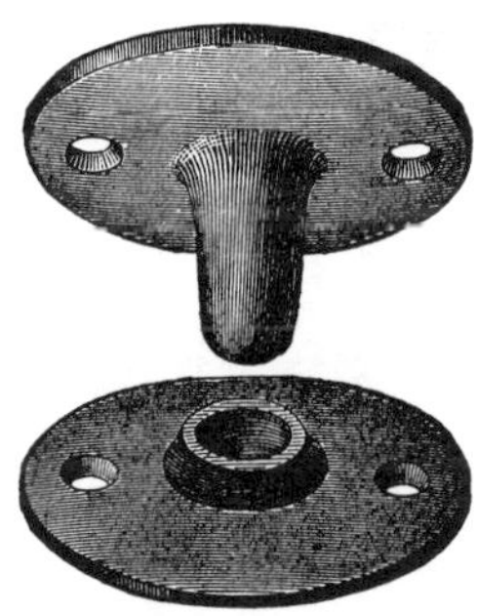

PORCH SUPPORTS.

Per pair..................... ......

GATE WEIGHTS.

Any size desired.

Per ℔...... ....

FOOT SCRAPERS.

No. 0, For Wood .. ....

No. 2, With Dish.. ....

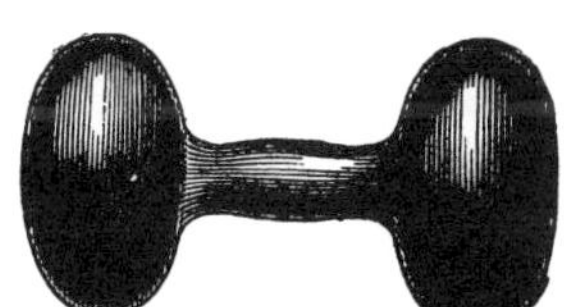

DUMB BELLS.

Common................. Per ℔....

Turned Handle, Wro't Centres, " ....

SASH ROLLERS AND REFRIGERATOR TRIMMINGS.

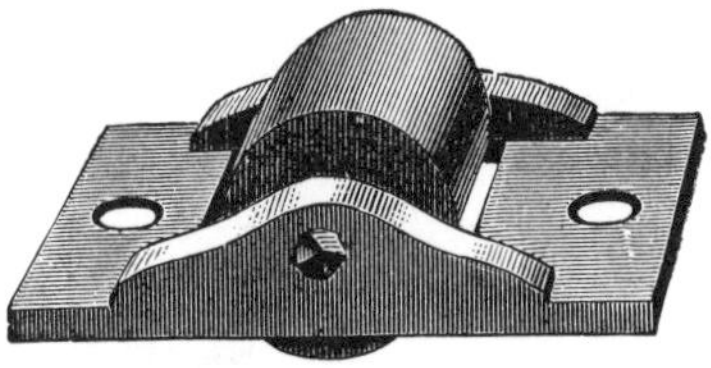

JAPANNED SASH ROLLERS.

No. 10,.... ⅝ ¾ ⅞ 1 1¼ in.

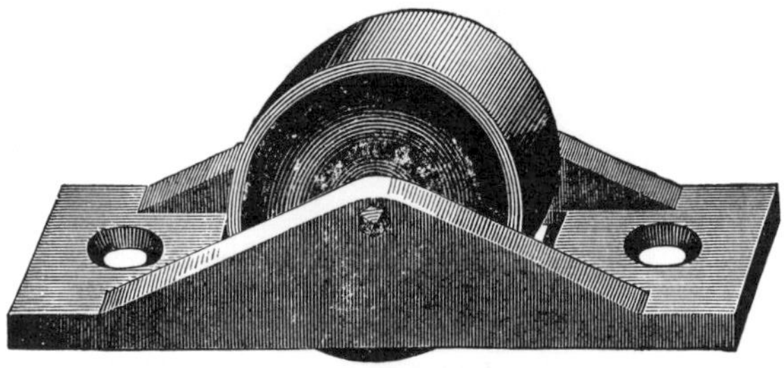

SASH ROLLERS.

.... Extra Heavy, Japanned.....Nos. 1...... 2...... 3......

REFRIGERATOR LATCHES.

	Bronzed Iron	Real Bronze	Nickel-Plated
Medium........	......	......	......
Large........	" "	" "	" " ......

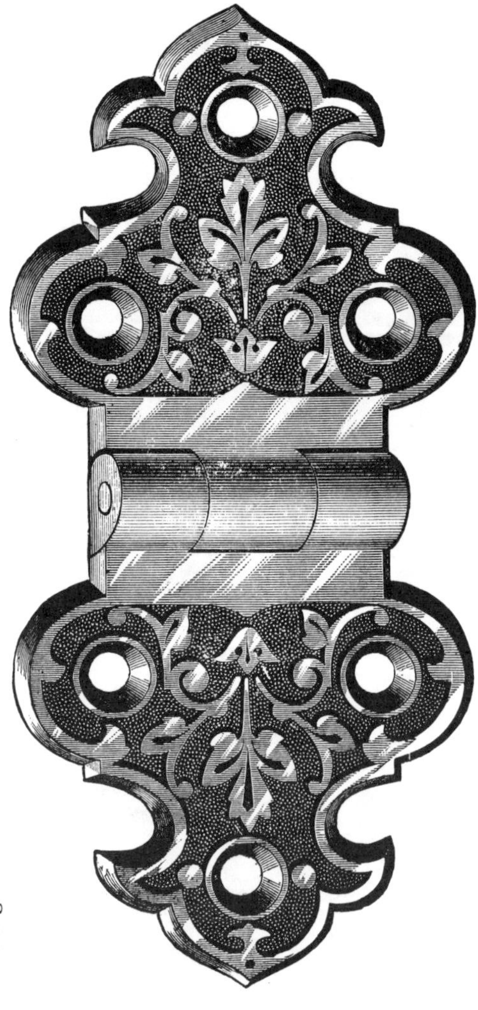

REFRIGERATOR HINGES.

No. 400, Berlin Bronzed, Brass Rivet................ 2½x5...... 4x6 in......

STAIR RAIL AND SHELF BRACKETS.

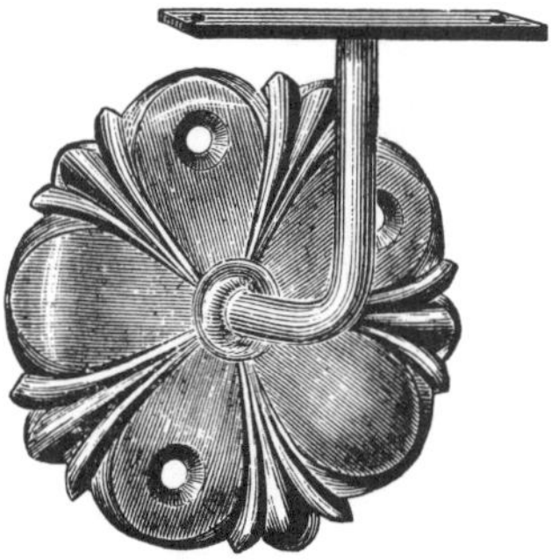

STAIR RAIL BRACKETS.

No. 1, Japanned.......... ......

STAIR RAIL BRACKETS.

No. 201, Tuscan Bronzed...... ......

No. 402, Berlin Bronzed....... ......

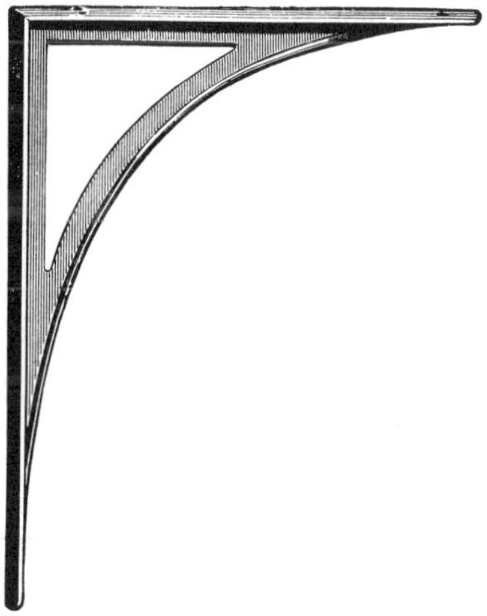

JAPANNED SHELF BRACKETS.

No. 44, Plain......3x4 4x5 5x6 6x8
....

8x10 8x12 10x12 12x14 12x20
....

No. 48, Heavy .... 16x20 .....

TUSCAN BRONZED SHELF BRACKETS.

No. 167 ..3x4.... 4x5 ... 5x7.... 6x8 ...

7x9.... 8x10... 9x12...

Other styles Fancy Brackets in stock.

DOOR SPRINGS.

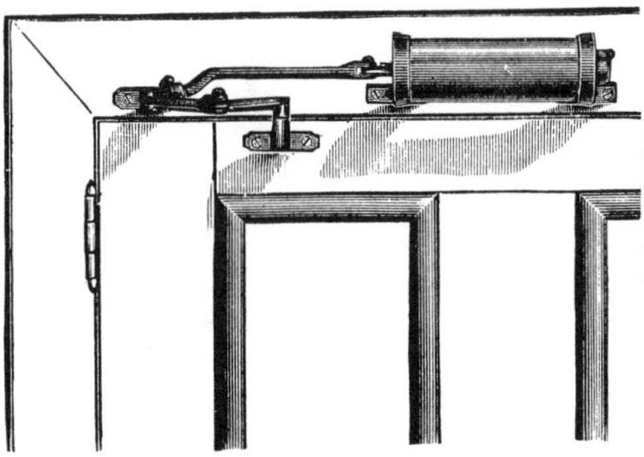

ELLIOTT PNEUMATIC DOOR CHECK.

Compact, Neat and Ornamental.

It is the most compact, symmetrical and efficient Door Check and Spring that has ever been put upon the market. Does not projcct perpendicularly and awkwardly ten or twelve inches into the room. Does not require the use of a spirit level or an experienced mechanic in attaching, but is so simple in construction, that any one can easily and properly adjust it. Does not require defacement of the casing or moulding in its application. Does not make a noise in closing the door, but is absolutely noiseless in its operation.

Try the Elliott Spring, if you would have the best.

No. 1, for doors uot exceeding 3½ feet wide by 3 inches thick ....
No. 2, " " " " 3 " " 2 " " ....
No. 3, " " " " 2½ " " 1½ " " ....
No. 4, " light doors in private residences...... ......

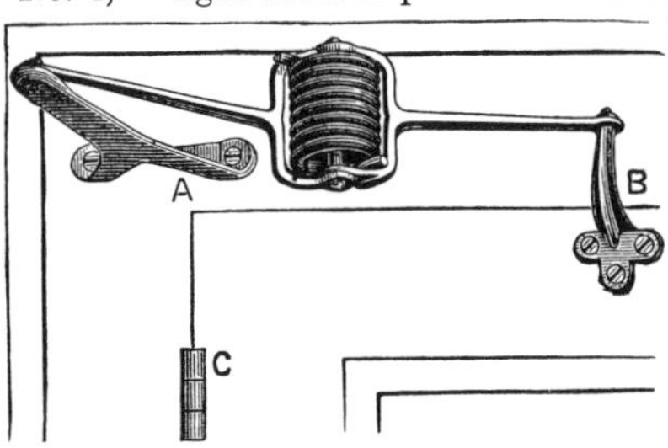

HERCULES REVERSE DOOR SPRING AND RETAINER.

Holds the door open as well as shut, and allows the door to stand at a right angle without the aid of any catch.

No. 1, for large doors...... ......
No. 2, " " " ......
No. 3, for medium doors ......
No. 4, " " " ......
No. 5, for screen doors ......

This Spring can be applied lower on the door where the door is not required to be thrown back, and Spring taken off and put on at pleasure.

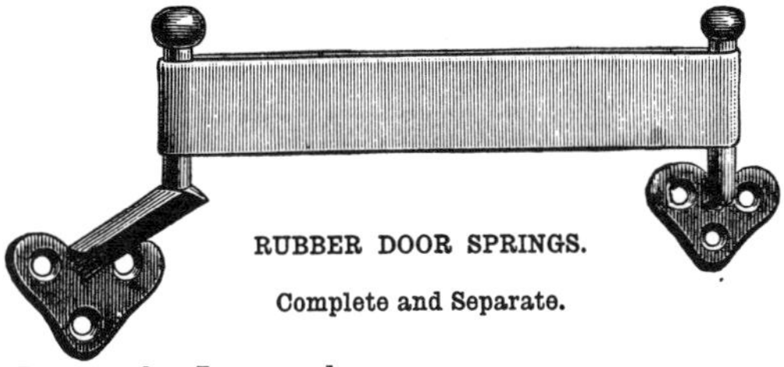

RUBBER DOOR SPRINGS.

Complete and Separate.

Irons only, Japanned...... ......
Rubber Bands only...... ......
Irons and Bands, complete...... ......

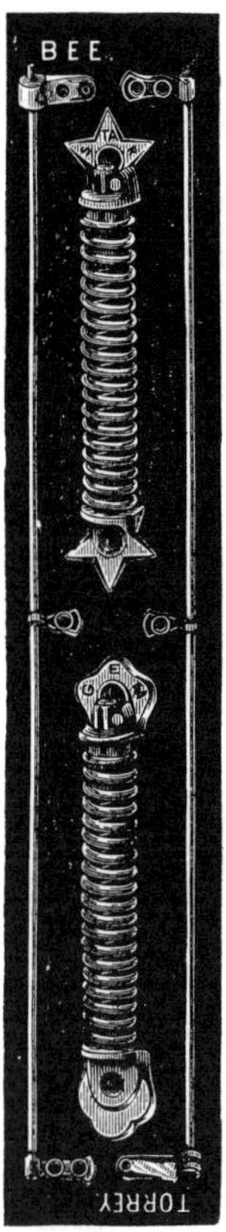

TORREY DOOR SPRINGS.

39 inch Rod, Japanned...... ......
44 " " " ....

WIRE COIL DOOR SPRINGS.

Nos.	10	9	8	6
Length	8......	9......	10......	12 in......

The size wire used is the same as the number of the spring.

PORCELAIN MOUTH PIECES.

No. 155, with Indicator.... ......

No. 159, without " ....

The metal in this whistle is japanned orange color.

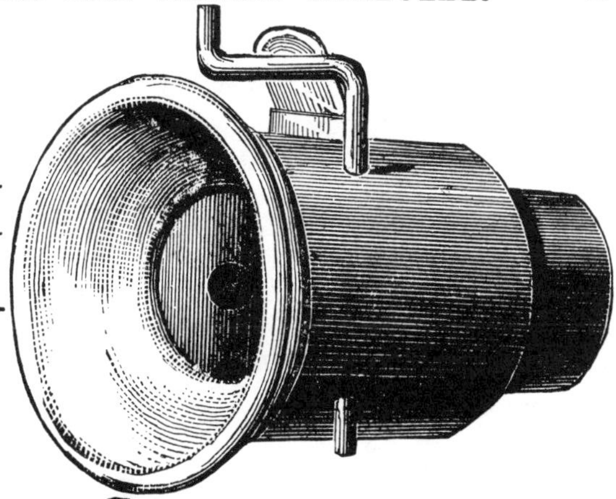

NICKEL-PLATED MOUTH PIECES.

No. 158½, with Indicator.. ......

No. 159½, without " .. ..

This whistle we can furnish in bronze to match other hardware.

Berlin Bronze.............. ......

Real " Ornamental.. ......

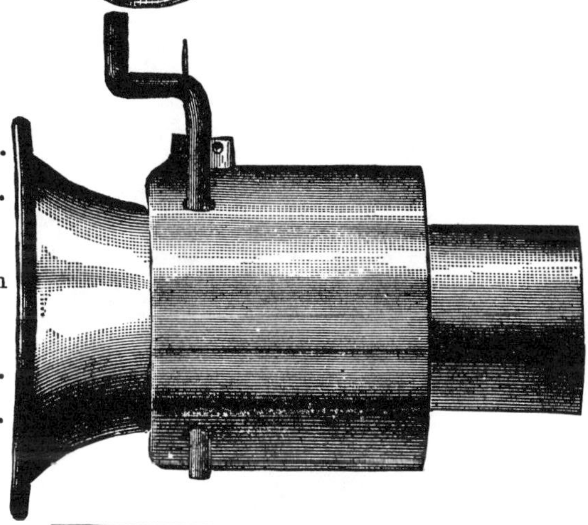

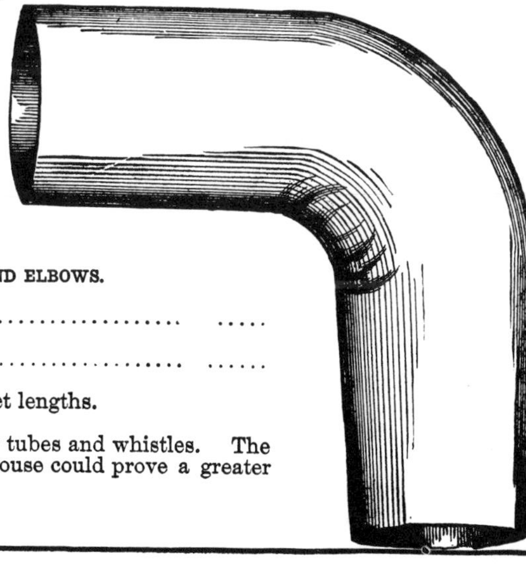

TIN SPEAKING TUBE AND ELBOWS.

Tube, 1 inch.. .....

Elbows, 1 inch ....

Tubing put up in five feet lengths.

Every house should have speaking tubes and whistles. The cost is trifling. No addition to the house could prove a greater convenience.

DOOR BELLS.

LEVER AND PULL DOOR BELLS.

Bell Metal.

No. 203½, 3½ In. Fancy Bells. . . . .

No. 205, 5 In. Fancy Bells. . . . .

Nickle Plated.

No. 213½, 3½ In. Fancy Bells. . . . .

No. 215, 5 In. Fancy Bells. . . . .

Berlin Bronzed.

No. 243½, 3½ In. Fancy Bells. . . . .

No. 245, 5 In. Fancy Bells. . . . .

The same bell can be used with a lever, a bell pull, or a slide pull. It can be put upon the door or upon the door jamb, or can be carried by the use of cranks to any place desired.

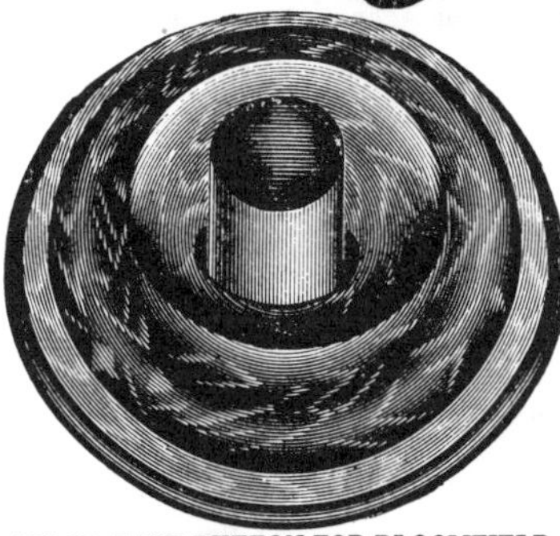

WOOD PUSH BUTTON FOR BLOOMFIELD GONG.

THE BLOOMFIELD DOOR GONG.

4 In. Bell . . . .

In this bell we present to the public a simple and reliable door bell. There are no springs or wires about it, consequently nothing to get out of order, and it is always ready when wanted. The outside fittings are similar to the electric bell, and can not be disarranged like the old-fashioned pull. They will fit any door from one to four inches thick, and can be put on by anyone, at little or no expense.

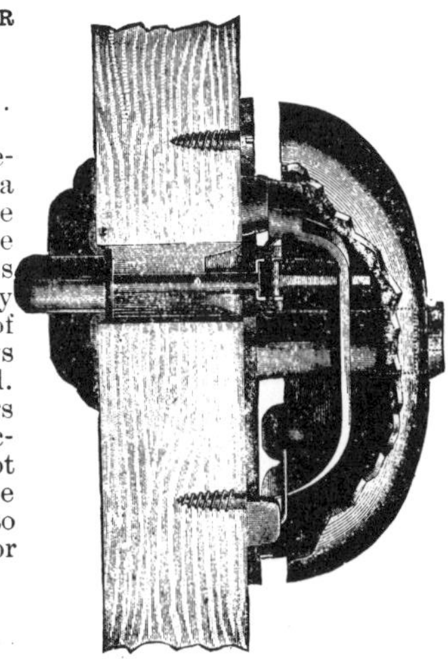

PNEUMATIC DOOR BELL.

Pneumatic Door Bell. . . . . 3. . . . . . 3½. . . . . . 4 in. . . . .
Flush and Surface Pushes, Wood. . . . Metal. . . Bronze. . . .
Foot Pushes, Brass . . . . Lead Tubing. . . . . per foot.

This bell can be placed in any part of the house, and is operated by compressed air. It is fast coming into use, and is highly appreciated by parties having them now in use. This bell is operated precisely same way as an electric bell.

DOOR BELL LEVERS.

No. 402, Berlin Bronzed... ......
No. 802, Bronze Metal ....
No. 902, Imperial Bronze.. ......
No. 708, Nickel Plated, Plain Pattern ....

No. 415, Berlin Bronzed, ...
No. 815, Bronze Metal, ...
No. 915, Imperial Bronze, ...

BELL PULLS AND BASE KNOBS.

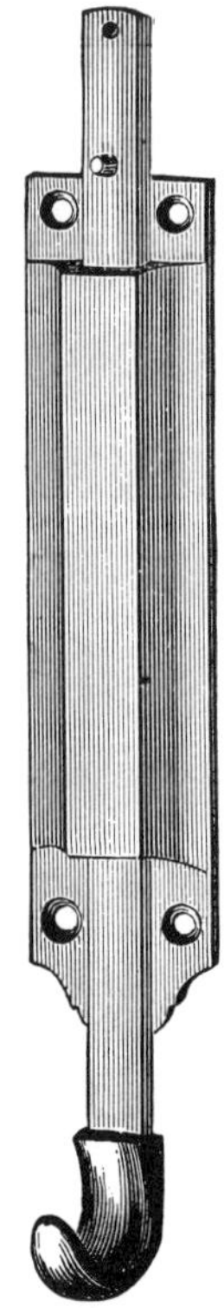

BELL PULLS.

No. 1401, Berlin Bronzed............ ....

No. 1801, Bronze Metal.............. ......

SLIDE BELL PULL.

No. 50, Brass......... ......

No. 705, Bronze Metal, ...

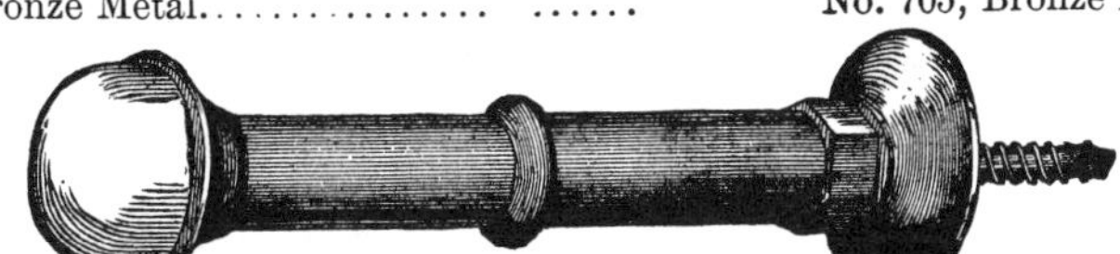

BRONZED IRON DOOR STOPS, RUBBER TIPPED.

The latest and the neatest ....

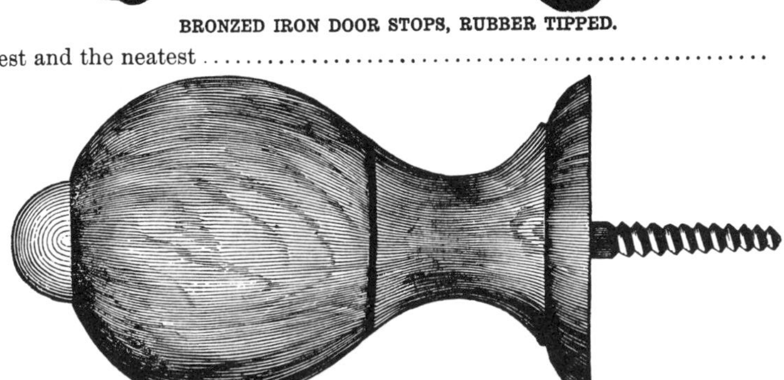

WOOD DOOR STOPS, RUBBER TIPPED.

Maple............ 2½ ..... 3 in...... Walnut............ 2½...... 3 in......

FLOOR DOOR FENDERS,

To screw on to the floor, with rubber on the side ....

YAJEN & NEW, INDIANAPOLIS, IND.

CHANDELIER HOOKS.

No. 55.

With 2½ Inch Screw.

No. 55, Berlin Bronzed................ ......

With 4 Inch Screw.

No. 27, Berlin Bronzed................ ......

No. 47, " " ....

No. 8027, Kahala..................... ......

For Gas Pipe.

No. 460, for ⅜ inch Gas Pipe.......... ......

LAMP HOOKS.

Japanned.....	1⅞	2	2¼	2½ in.
Nos...........	3......	4.....	5.....	6.....

Also many other styles.

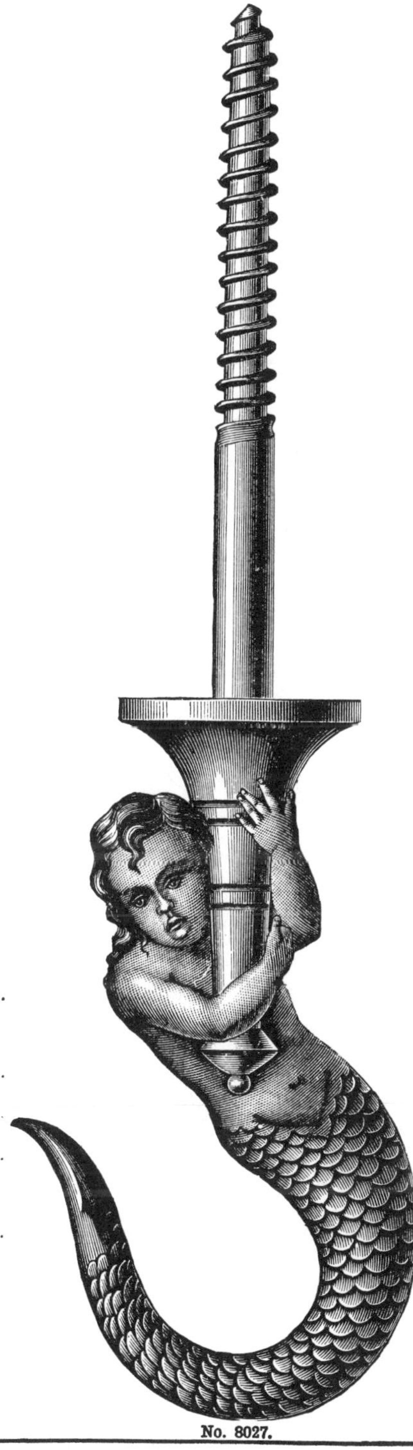

No. 8027.

THUMB LATCHES, STORE DOOR HANDLES, DOOR PULLS.

BARN DOOR LATCHES.

No.5,Japanned,wro't latch....

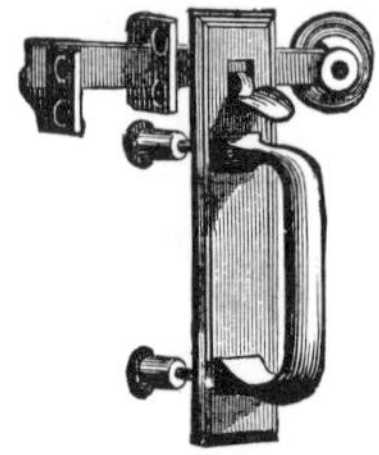

JAPANNED STORE DOOR HANDLES.

No. 6, Put on with Nuts .. ....
No. 16, With Plate........ ....
No. 25, Without Plate, Short Thumb Piece ... .
No. 26, Without Plate, Regular Thumb Piece ....

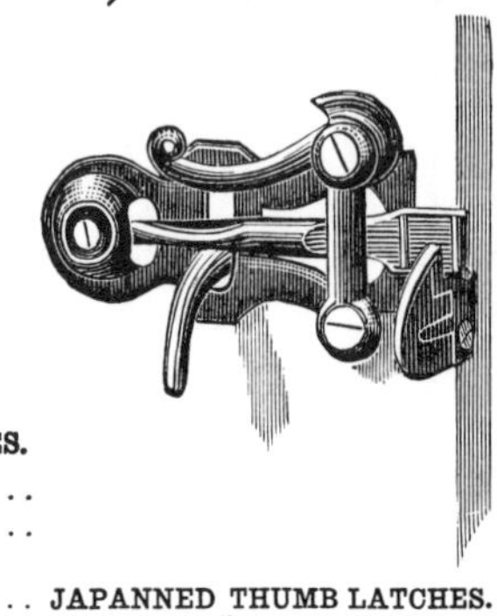

JAPANNED THUMB LATCHES.

	9 lb	6 lb to doz.
Nos....	2......	12......

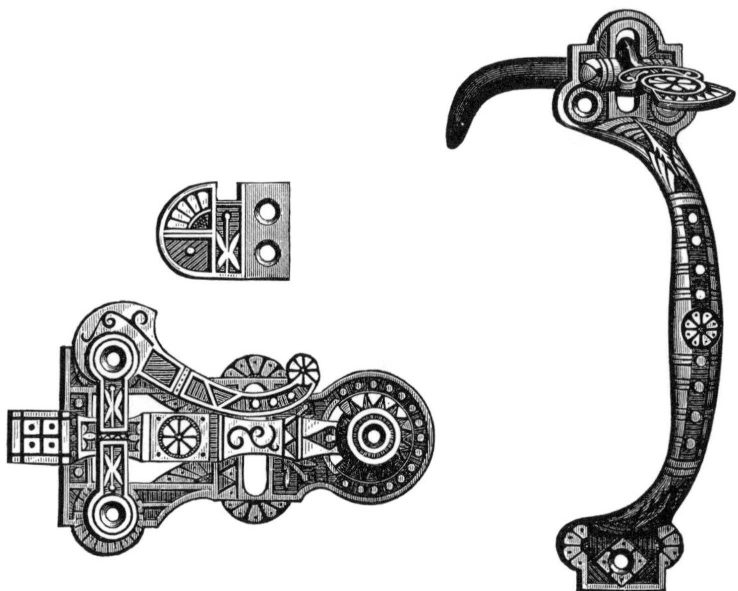

No. 62, Tuscan Bronzed Thumb Latches, packed with screws ....

JAPANNED DOOR PULLS.

No. 503, Oblique, Heavy ....
No. 504, Straight, " ....

TUSCAN BRONZED DOOR PULLS.

No. 508, Packed with screws......... ....

STORE DOOR HANDLES.

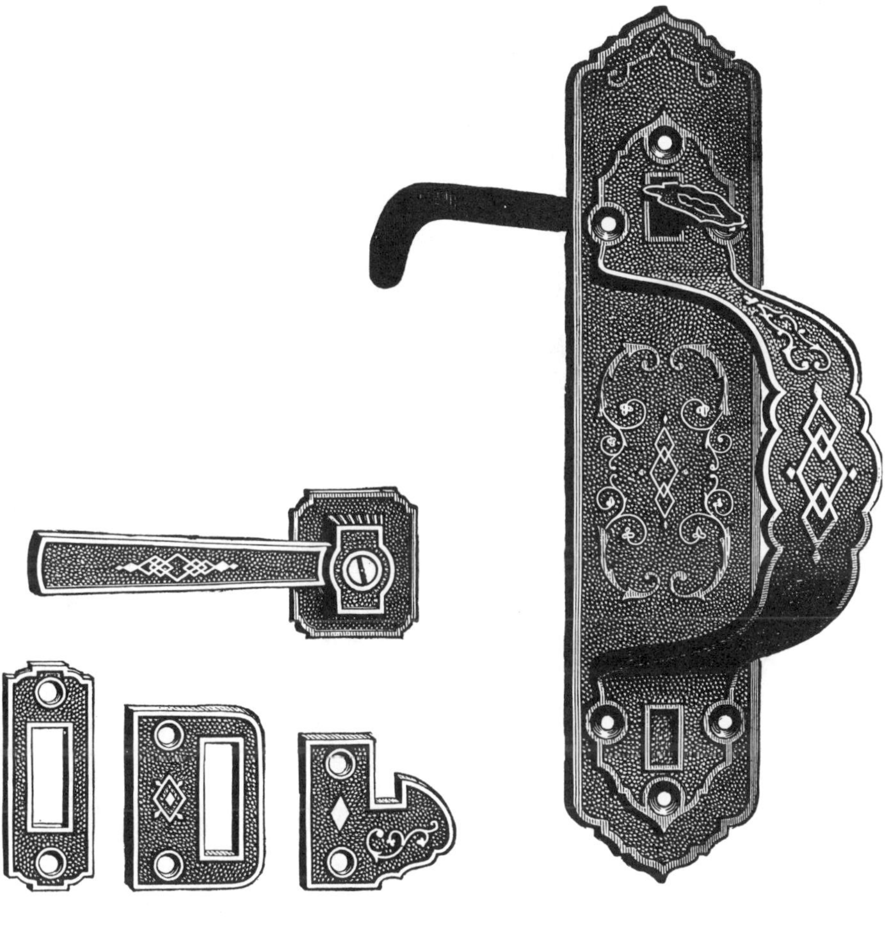

No. 18, Tuscan Bronzed, with Plate...

No. 20, " " " " ....

No. 29, Bronze Metal, " " ....

No. 81, Cast Brass, Silver Plated, with Plate...

Latches right or left hand. Suitable for doors single or double thickness.

STORE DOOR HANDLE AND LATCH.

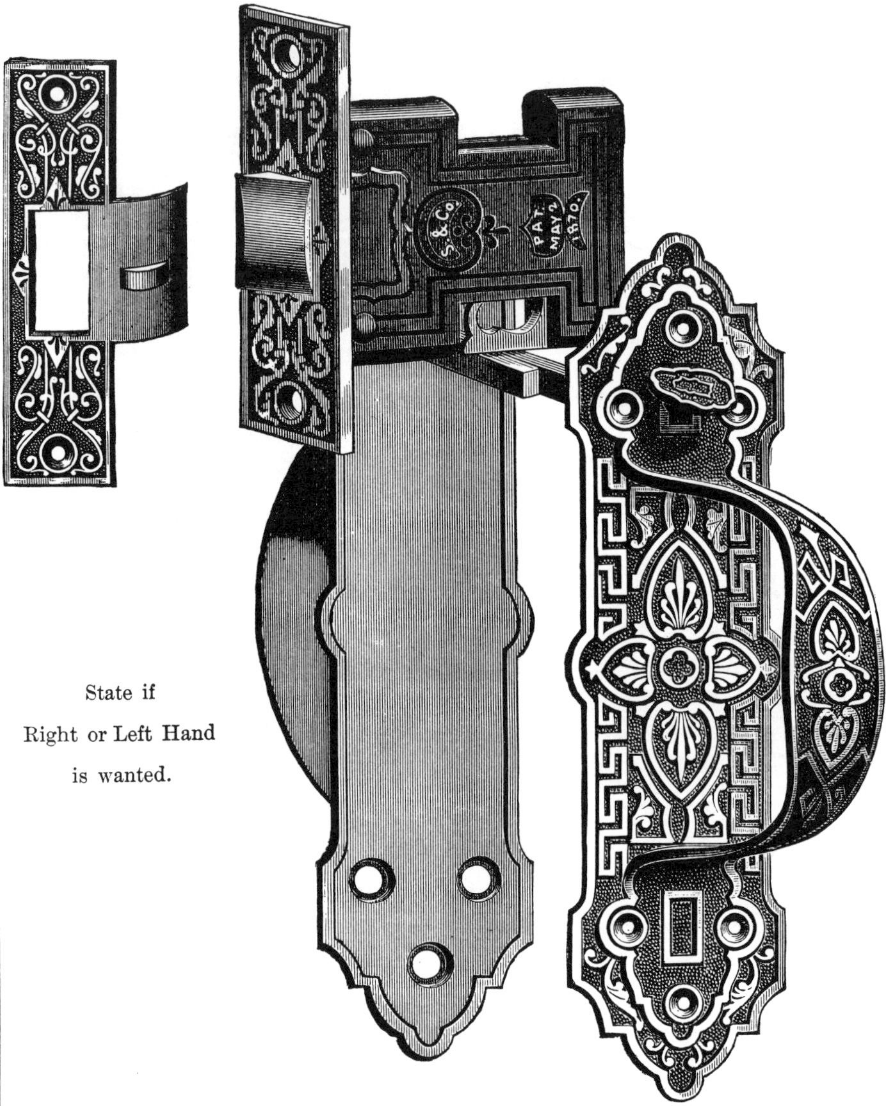

State if
Right or Left Hand
is wanted.

Half size cut of No. 445.

No. 445, Berlin Bronzed, Double Handle, round edge Mortise Latch, reversible, with Anti-Friction Roller Strike; Not Rabbeted.......................... ......

No. 449, Same description as No. 445, but Full Rabbeted...................... ......

No. 225, Bronze Metal, Double Handle, round edge Mortise Latch, $2\frac{3}{4}$x$3\frac{1}{4}$, reversible, with Anti-Friction Roller Strike; Not Rabbeted.................. ......

No. 229, Same description as No. 225, but Full Rabbeted..................... ......

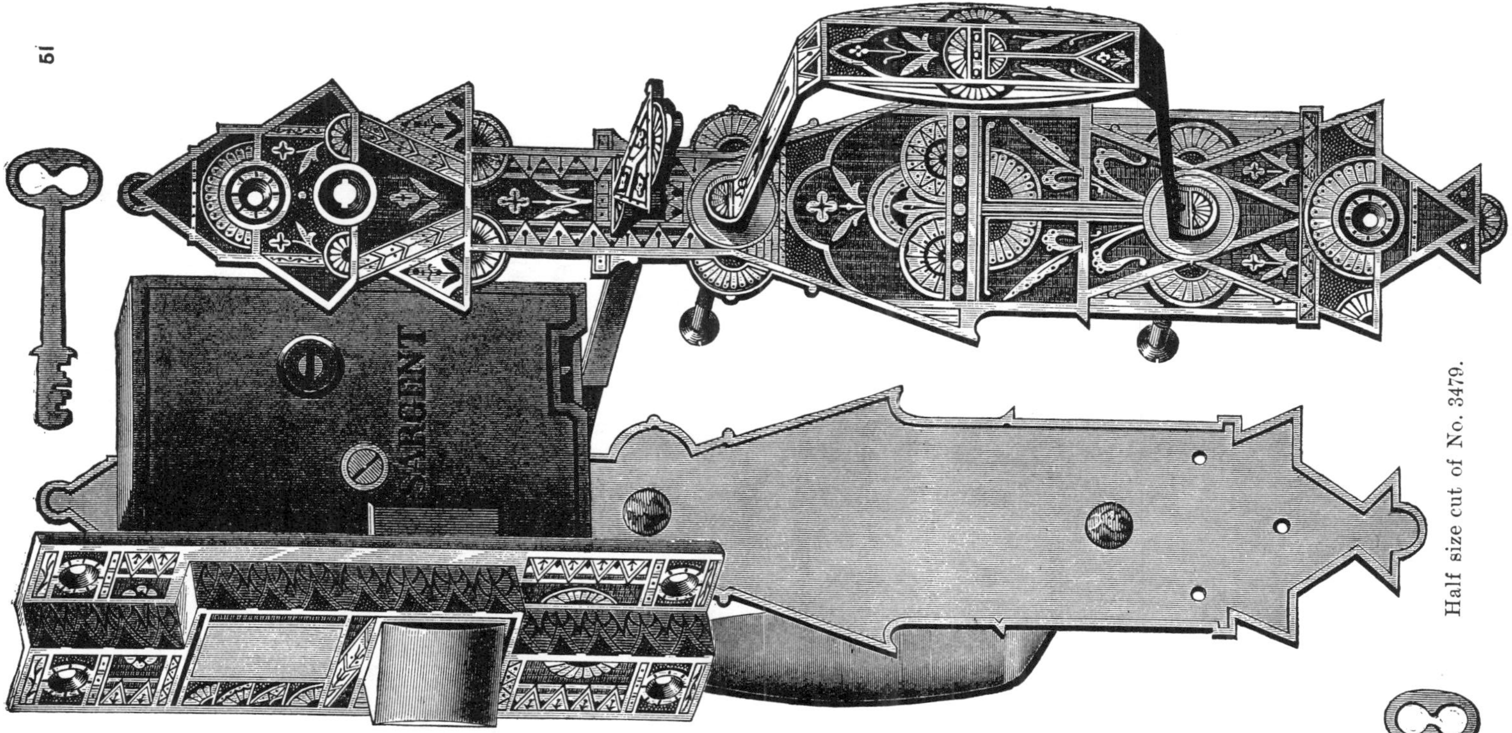

Half size cut of No. 3479.

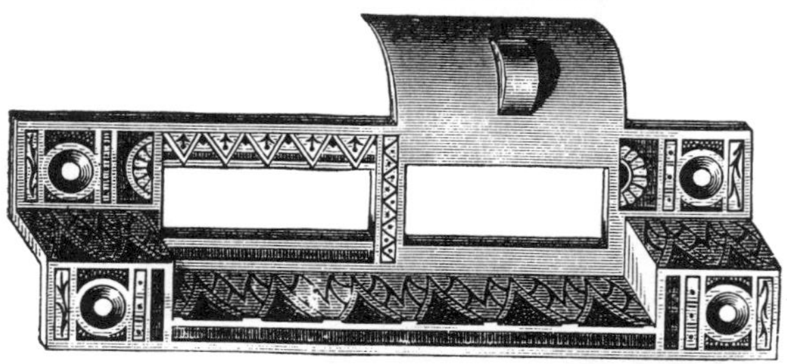

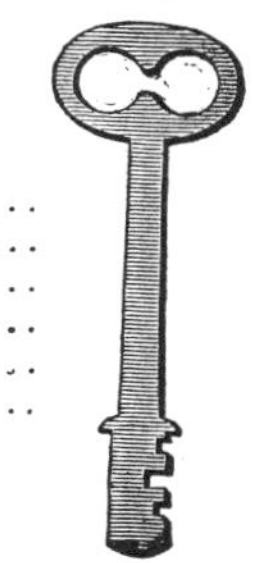

STORE DOOR HANDLES AND LOCK.

No. 3473,	Berlin Bronzed,	Not Rabbeted,	Handle,	Lock	and	Latch,	......
No. 3479,	" "	Rabbeted,	"	"	"	"	......
No. 3972,	Imperial Bronze,	Not Rabbeted,	"	"	"	"	......
No. 3978,	" "	Rabbeted,	"	"	"	"	......
No. 3973,	" "	Not Rabbeted,	"	"	"	"	......
No. 3979,	" "	Rabbeted,	"	"	"	"	......

Size of Lock and Latch for all above, 4¼x3 in; three tumblers.
Orders should state whether for right or left hand doors.
Nos. 3473, 3479, 3973 and 3979 have two flat steel keys.
Nos. 3972 and 3978 have two steel bit keys.

RIM DEAD LOCKS AND RIM LATCHES.

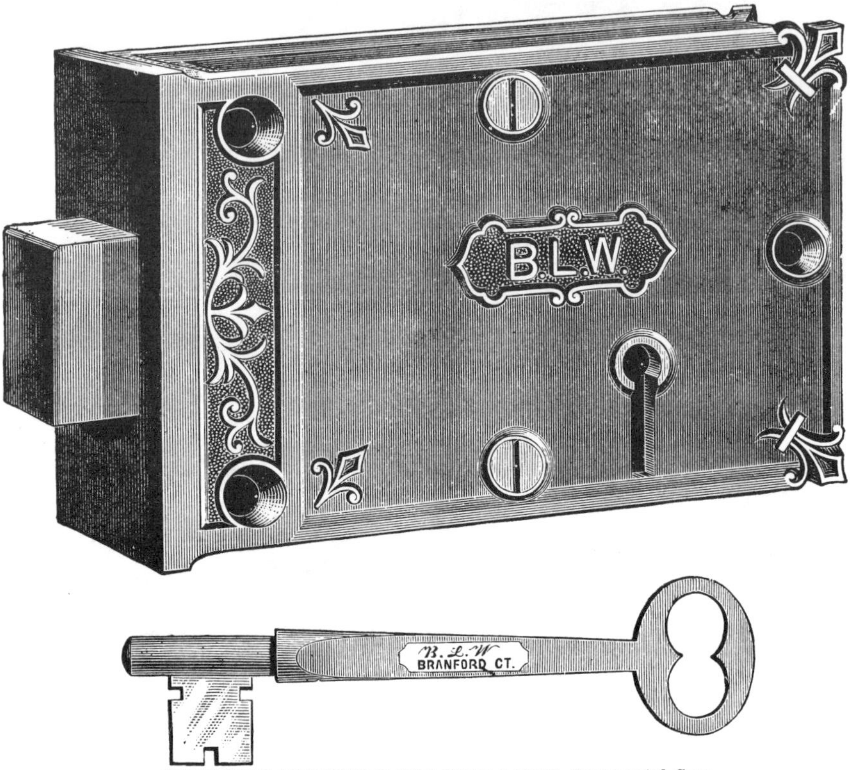

REVERSIBLE HORIZONTAL RIM DEAD LOCKS--Ornamental Case.

No. 0370, $2\frac{7}{8}$x$2\frac{1}{8}$, Iron Bolt, Nickel Plated Key, 1 Wrought Tumbler, 24 changes, ...
No. 0374, $3\frac{3}{8}$x$2\frac{1}{2}$, Same description as No. 0370 ......
No. 0378, 4x$2\frac{3}{4}$, " " " " ......
No. 0384, 5x$3\frac{1}{4}$, " " " " ......

HORIZONTAL RIM DEAD LOCKS--Plain Japanned Case.

With Cast Tumbler, in same sizes as above at less price.

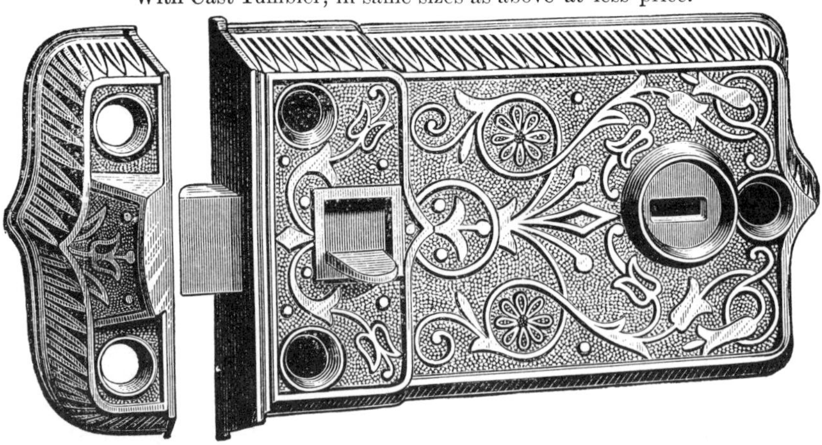

SUN KNOB LATCH.

Ornamental Iron, Bronzed Cases and Knobs, Size, $3\frac{1}{2}$x$2\frac{1}{4}$, Iron Bolt, Stop and Latch Bolt ......

RIM CUPBOARD LOCK AND KNOB LATCH.

UPRIGHT RIM CUPBOARD LOCK.

With Box, Mortise or Flat Strike. To reverse the Latch, take off the Cap.

No. 980, 3½x2. Iron Bolts, Malleable Iron Key, one Tumbler ....

HORIZONTAL RIM KNOB LATCHES, WITH SLIDE BOLT.

No. 203½, 3⅝x2½, Iron Bolt, Iron Hub, Iron Slide Bolt, Brass Sunk Thumb Piece ......

No. 204 B, 3⅝x2½, Brass Plated Iron Bolts, Solid Brass Slide Bolt Knob ....

No. 0203½, 3⅝x2½, same as No. 203½, but Ornamental Iron Bronzed Case...... ......

UPRIGHT RIM KNOB LOCKS.

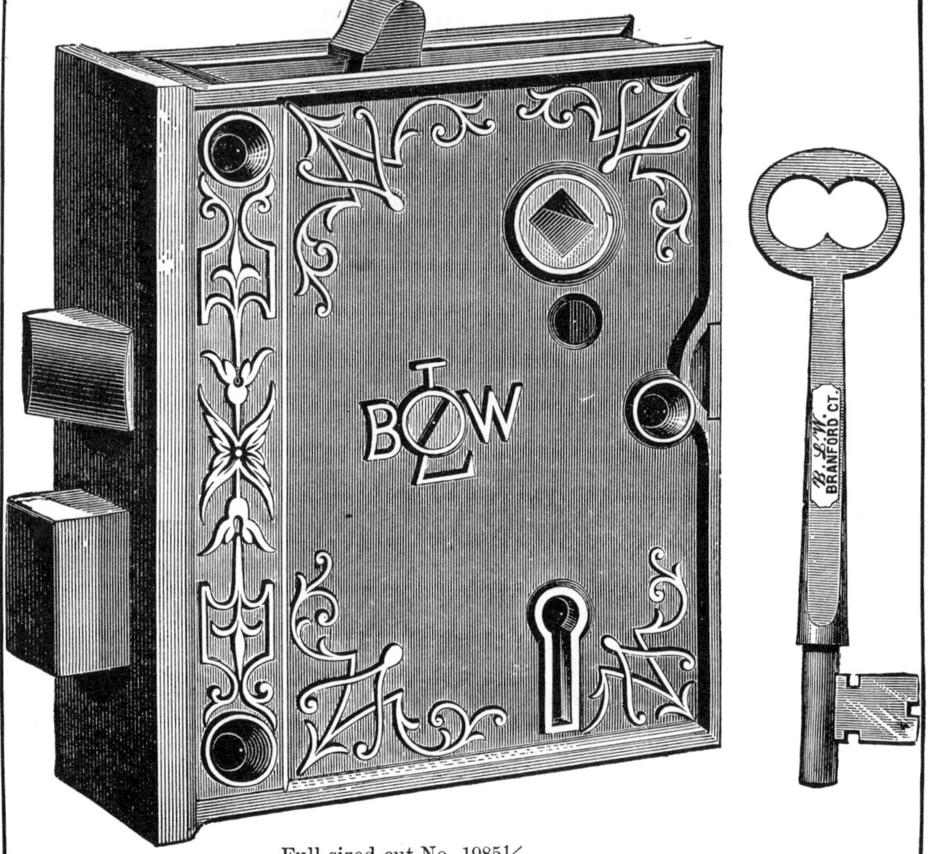

Full sized cut No. 1985¼.

REVERSIBLE UPRIGHT RIM LOCKS, ORNAMENTAL CASE.

No. 1990¼,	4⅛x3¼,	Iron bolts, malleable iron key,	1 tumbler, stop on latch… ……
No. 1985¼ N,	4⅛x3¼,	Iron bolts, nickel-steel key,	1 tumbler, stop on latch… ……
No. 1986¼ N,	4⅛x3¼,	Brass bolts, nickel-steel key,	1 tumbler, stop on latch… ……
No. 1990½,	4⅛x3¼,	Iron bolts, malleable iron key,	1 tumbler, iron slide bolt.. ……
No. 1985½ N,	4⅛x3¼,	Iron bolts, nickel-steel key,	1 tumbler, iron slide bolt.. ……
No. 1986½ N,	4⅛x3¼,	Brass bolts, nickel-steel key,	1 tumbler, brass slide bolt ……
No. 1941¼ N,	4½x3½,	Iron bolts, nickel-steel key,	1 tumbler, stop on latch… ……
No. 1942¼ N,	4½x3½,	Brass bolts, nickel-steel key,	1 tumbler, stop on latch… ……
No. 1941½ N,	4½x3½,	Iron bolts, nickel-steel key,	1 tumbler, iron slide bolt . ……
No. 1942½ N,	4½x3½,	Brass bolts, nickel-steel key,	1 tumbler, brass slide bolt. ……

UPRIGHT RIM LOCKS, PLAIN CASE.

To reverse the Latch, take off the Cap.

No. 962¼, 4¼x3½, iron Bolts, malleable iron Key, 1 Tumbler, stop on Latch…… ….

REVERSIBLE UPRIGHT RIM LOCKS, ORNAMENTAL CASE.

With Two Wrought Iron Rack Tumblers, 36 Changes.

No. 2738,	4⅛x3¼,	Heavy iron bolts, nickel-steel key, stop on latch………… ……
No. 2730,	4⅛x3¼,	Heavy brass bolts, nickel-steel key, stop on latch………… ……
No. 2738½,	4⅛x3¼,	Heavy iron bolts, nickel-steel key, iron slide bolt ………… ……
No. 2730½,	4⅛x3¼,	Heavy brass bolts, nickel-steel key, brass slide bolt……… ……
No. 2638½,	4½x3½,	Heavy iron bolts, nickel-steel key, iron slide bolt ………… ……
No. 2630½,	4½x3½,	Heavy brass bolts, nickel-steel key, brass slide bolt……… ……

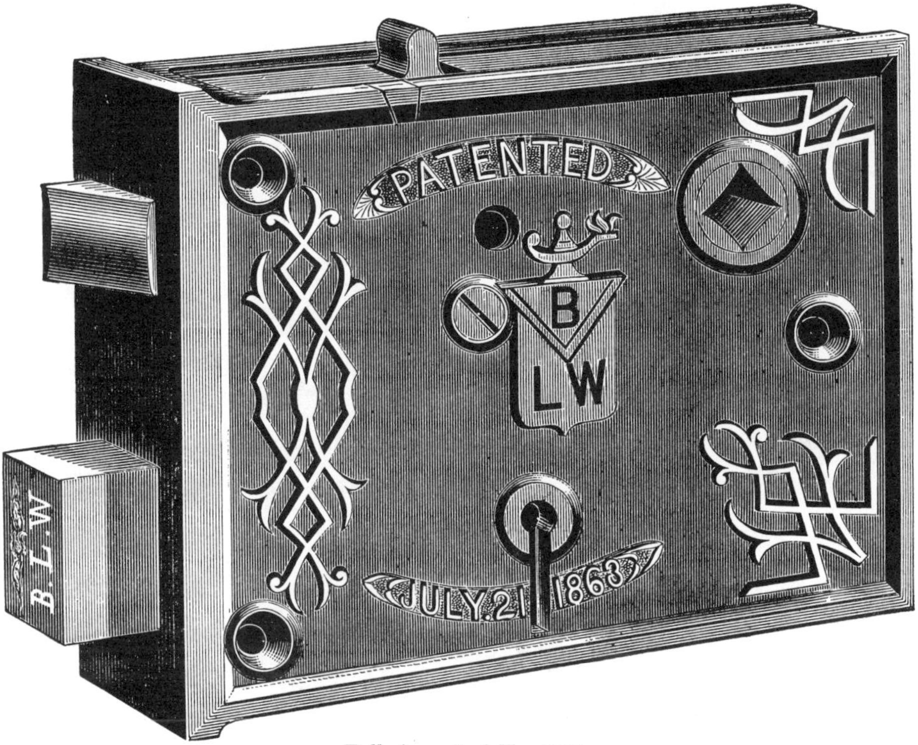

Full size cut of No. 0865.

REVERSIBLE HORIZONTAL RIM LOCKS.

Ornamental Case.

No. 0865, 4¼x3⅜, Iron bolts, malleable iron key, 1 tumbler, stop on latch.......... ......
No. 0966 N, 4¼x3⅜, Same as No. 0865, but with nickel-steel key.................... ......
No. 0967 N, 4¼x3⅜, Brass bolts, nickel-steel key, 1 tumbler, stop on latch........... ......
No. 0868, 5 x3½, Iron bolts, malleable iron key, 1 tumbler, stop on latch.......... ......
No. 0970 N, 5 x3½, Iron bolts, nickel-steel key, 1 tumbler, stop on latch............ ......

Ornamental Case, with Slide Bolt.

No. 0865½, 4¼x3⅜, Iron bolts, malleable iron key, 1 tumbler..................... ......
No. 0966½ N, 4¼x3⅜, Same as No. 0865½, but with nickel-steel key................ ......
No. 0967½ N, 4¼x3⅜, Brass bolts, nickel-steel key, 1 tumbler........................ ......
No. 0970½ N, 5 x3½, Iron bolts, nickel-steel key, 1 tumbler......................... ......
No. 0971½ N, 5 x3½, Brass bolts, nickel-steel key, 1 tumbler........................ ......

Any of the above locks, with nickel-steel keys, can be furnished with two tumblers.

Ornamental Case, with Wrought Inside Works.

No. 0666, 4¼x3⅜, iron bolts, nickel key, 2 wro't racktumblers, stop on latch, 36 changes.....
No. 0666½, 4¼x3⅜, Iron bolts, nickel key, 2 wro't rack tumblers, slide bolt, 36 changes......

Ornamental Case, Iron Bronzed, with Wrought Inside Works.

No. 00663, 4¼x3⅜, Iron bolts, nickel key, 1 wro't tumbler, stop on latch, 24 changes ......
No. 00663½, 4¼x3⅜, Iron bolts, nickel key, 1 wro't tumbler, slide bolt, 24 changes.... ......
No. 00670, 5 x3½, Iron bolts, nickel key, 1 wro't tumbler,,stop on latch, 24 changes ......
No. 00670½, 5 x3½, Iron bolts, nickel key, 1 wro't tumbler, iron slide bolt, 24 changes ......

Plain Case, Horizontal Rim Locks.

To reverse the latch, take off the cap.

No. 1465, 4¼x3⅜ Iron bolts, tinned malleable key, 1 tumbler, stop on latch........... ......

MORTISE AND RIM NIGHT LATCHES.

Full size cut of No. 165.

Yale, No. 43.

No. 154.

No. 156.

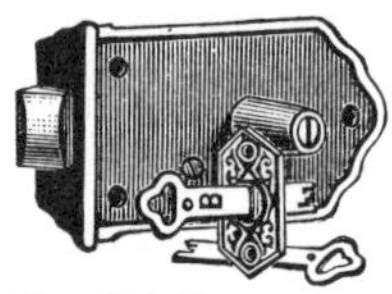

No. 165, Rear view.

No. 154, 4x3, Iron Bolt, Draw-back Knob, which stops the Latch by turning, 2 nickel keys. Ornamental Japanned Escutcheon..................

No. 156, 4x2¾, Same, except 2 flat steel Keys and Ornamental Bronzed Escutcheon........

No, 165, 4x2¾, Heavy brass Bolt, Draw-back Knob, which stops the Latch by turning, 3 brass Tumblers, 2 flat steel Keys, Ornamental Bronze Escutcheon, with revolving Key Guide..................

No. 227, 4½x3¼, Telescope self-adjusting Cylinder, extends from 1¼ to 2½ inches, with heavy brass bolts, 4 steel Tumblers, 2 nickel flat steel keys. Nickel-plated Escutcheon. Plated Draw-back Knob, 200 changes..................

No. 43, 3⅝x2⅜, "Yale," Japanned iron Case and Strike, Ornamental Bronzed Escutcheon, adjustable from ¾ to 3 inches. Bronze Knob..................

The above numbers kept in Reverse Bevel.

Yale, 73

MORTISE NIGHT LATCHES, FLAT FRONT.

Adjustable to Right or Left Hand Doors.

Yale Mortise Dead Lock.

For description see Index.

No. 72, 3½x3⅜, "Yale," Ornamental bronze knob, rose and short escutcheon, for doors 1¼ to 2½ in., thick. Finished brass front, 3 keys..................

No. 73, 3½x3⅜, "Yale," Same, excepting with long escutcheon, for doors 2½ to 3½ .....

No. 50, 3¼x2, Heavy brass front and bolt, plated thumb knob and plate, brass striking plate, 2 nickel keys, stop on latch..................

No. 1750, 3¼x2, Same description as No. 50, excepting with ornamental bronze front. ......

MORTISE NIGHT LATCHES, RABBETED FRONT.

No. 92, 3½x3⅜, "Yale," Ornamental bronze knob, rose and escutcheon, short, for doors 1¼ to 2½ in., thick, Finished brass front..................

No. 93, 3½x3⅜, "Yale," Same, excepting with long escutcheons for doors 2½ to 3½ ......

RIM STORE DOOR LOCKS.

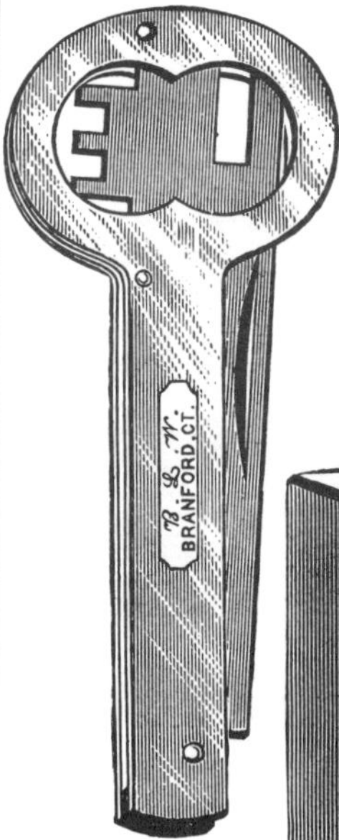

No. 11, Yale.

Full size cut Nos. 1145, 1150, 1155, 01145, 01150, 01155.

STORE DOOR RIM DEAD LOCKS, REVERSIBLE.

Ornamental Case, Japanned.

No. 1145, 5x3, Heavy iron bolt, 2 nickel folding steel keys, 1 tumbler, 12 changes.... ......
No. 1150, 5x3, " " " 2 " " " " 2 tumblers, 24 " ....
No. 1155, 5x3, " " " 2 " " " " 3 " 48 " ....

Ornamental Bronzed Case.

No. 01145, 5x3, Heavy iron bolt, 2 nickel folding steel keys, 1 tumbler, 12 changes... .....
No. 01150, 5x3, " " " 2 " " " " 2 tumblers, 24 " .. ..
No. 01155, 5x3, " " " 2 " " " " 3 " 48 " .. ..

UPRIGHT RIM STORE DEAD LOCKS, REVERSIBLE.

With Self-Adjusting Telescope Cylinder.

No. 1361, 5½x3, Heavy iron bolt, 3 nickel-plated flat steel keys, 5 steel tumblers, 100 changes, cylinder extends from 1¾ to 3¼ inches ....

No. 11, 2½x4, "Yale," Heavy brass bolt (2x½), japanned iron case and strike, ornamental bronze escutcheon, adjustable for doors ¾ to 3 inches thick........... ......

REVERSIBLE STORE DOOR KNOB LOCK.

No. 0435, 7x4½, Horizontal store door knob lock, heavy iron bolts, 2 nickel folding steel keys, 1 wrought tumbler ....

REVERSIBLE LEVER MORTISE KNOB LOCKS

VAJEN & NEW, INDIANAPOLIS, IND.

Above is full sized cut of Nos. 01800, 1503 N, 1518 N, 1518 N. Round edge.

No. 01800, 3½x3¼, Lacquered iron front, iron bolts, wro't iron strike, malleable iron key, 1 tumbler, 12 changes ....

No. 1503 N, 3½x3¼, Same as 01800, but with nickel-steel key ....

No. 1518 N, 3½x3¼, Same as 1503 N, but with brass front and bolts, and nickel-steel key ....

No. 1523 N, 4 x3¼, Same as 01800, but with nickel-steel key ....

No. 1538 N, 4 x3¼, Same as 1523 N, but with brass front and bolts ....

Same as Above, with Wrought Inside Work.

No. 1516, 3½x3¼, Heavy brass front and bolts, brass hub and striking plate, nickel-plated brass key, 1 wro't rack tumbler, 24 changes ....

No. 1541, 4 x3½, Same as 1516, but with 2 rack tumblers and 48 changes ....

No. 1561, 4½x3½, Same as 1516 ....

No. 1566, Same as 1561, 2 tumblers, 48 changes ....

No. 1571, " " 3 " 72 " ....

No. 1586, 5 x3¾, Same as 1516 ....

No. 1591, 5 x3¾, Same as 1586, but with 3 wro't tumblers, 72 changes ....

For further Descriptions and Prices, see Page 58 A.

VAJEN & NEW, INDIANAPOLIS, IND.

REVERSIBLE LEVER MORTISE KNOB LOCKS.

(For cut, see preceding page.)

MORTISE LOCKS, WITH THUMB-BOLT ATTACHMENT.

Wrought Inside Works.

No. 0586, 4½x3½, Heavy brass front and bolts, brass hub and striking plate, electro-plated thumb knob and plate, nickel thin bit key, 1 wrought rack tumbler, 24 changes . . . . . .

No. 0587, 4½x3½, Same as No. 0586, with 3 wrought tumblers, 72 changes . . . . . .

REVERSIBLE AND RABBETED FRONT DOOR MORTISE KNOB LOCKS, WITH NIGHT WORKS.

(For cut see following page.)

Plain Front.

No. 842, 4¾x3⅝, Brass front, bolt and striking plate, bronze thumb knob and plate, 1 wrought tumbler on large key, 2 nickle-plated flat steel night keys . . . . . .

No. 180½, 5½x4½, Same description as No. 842 . . . . . .

No. 1842, 4¾x3⅜, Ornamental bronze front and striking plate, bronze thumb knob and plate, 1 wrought tumbler on large key, 2 nickel-plated, flat steel night keys. . . . . . .

No. 1680½, 5x4½, Same description as No. 1842. . . . . . .

Rabbeted Front.

No. 852, 4¾x3⅝, Brass front and bolts, bronze knob and plate, 1 tumbler, 2 nickel-plated, steel night keys . . . . . .

No. 548, 5½x4¼, Heavy brass front, guarded brass bolts, brass strike, 1 wrought tumbler on large key, 3 wrought tumblers on night key, 2 nickel-plated night keys. . . . . . .

No. 1852, 4¾x3⅝, Ornamental bronze front and striking plate, bronze thumb knob and plate, 1 wrought tumbler, 2 nickel-plated, steel night keys. . . . . . .

No. 1649, 5½x3½, Same description as No. 1852 . . . . . .

Ornamental Iron Fronts, Electro-Branford Bronzed.

No. B 1842, 4¾x3⅜, Same description as No. 1842, but Branford bronzed. . . . . . .
No. B 1680½, 5 x4½, " " No. 1680½, " " . . . .
No. B 1852, 4¾x3⅝, " " No. 1852, " " . . . .
No. B 1649, 5½x3½, " " No. 1649, " " . . . .

Anti-friction Strikes furnished with Bronze Front Locks.

Be careful in ordering Rabbeted Locks, to state if Right or Left Hand is wanted. For Escutcheons, and Rose and Escutcheons Combined, see page 63.

FRONT DOOR MORTISE KNOB LOCKS.

REVERSIBLE AND RABBETED, WITH NIGHT WORKS.

VAJEN & NEW, INDIANAPOLIS, IND.

Full size cut of 842. For descriptions and prices see page 58 A.

VAJEN & NEW, INDIANAPOLIS, IND.

LOCKS AND LATCHES.

MORTISE KNOB LATCHES, FLAT FRONT.

No. 1, 3¼x1⅜, Lacquered iron front, iron bolt, wrought strike ....
No. 3, 3¼x1⅜, Heavy brass front, iron bolt, brass hub and strike ....
No. 4, 3¼x1⅜, " " " and bolt, brass hub and strike. ....
No. 20, 1¾x1⅜, Lacquered iron front, iron bolt and strike. ....
No. 21, 2¼x1¾, " " " " " " " ....
No. 22, 2¼x1¾, " " " brass bolt, iron " ....
No. 1704, 3¼x1⅜, Ornamental genuine bronze front, bolt and strike. ....

MORTISE KNOB LATCHES, RABBETED FRONT.

No. 26, 1⅝x1½, Lacquered iron front, iron bolt and brass strike. ....
No. 27, 2⅜x1¾, " " " brass bolt, hub and strike ....
No. 702, 3½x1¼, Heavy brass front, bolt, hub and strike. ....
No, 703, 3½x1¼, Lacquered iron front, brass hub and strike . ...

MORTISE DEAD LOCKS, FLAT FRONT.

No. 87, 2¾x1¾, Heavy brass front, bolt and strike, 2 flat steel keys, nickel-plated, 1 wro't tumbler, 24 changes ....
No. 75, 3½x2, Lacquered iron front, brass bolt, nickel-plated key, 1 wro't tumbler, 12 changes ....
No. 81, 3⅜x2½, Heavy brass front, bolt and strike, nickel-plated thin bit key, 1 wro't tumbler, 12 changes ....
No. 82, 5¼x2½, Heavy brass front, bolt and strike, 3 nickel-plated steel keys, 5 wro't detector tumblers, 500 changes, complete with escutcheons. ....
No. 1776, 3⅜x2½, Ornamental genuine bronze front, bronze bolt and strike, nickel-plated key, 1 wro't tumbler, 12 changes ....

"Yale," with One Escutcheon, to Unlock from One Side Only.

No. 352, 2⅜x3½, Heavy brass front, reversible for either right or left hand doors, ornamental bronze escutcheon, for doors 1¼ to 2¼ thick. ....

MORTISE DEAD LOCKS, RABBETED FRONT.

No. 84, 5¼x2½, Heavy rabbeted front, same description as No. 82. ....

"Yale," with One Escutcheon, to Unlock from One Side Only.

No. 372, 2⅜x3½, Heavy rabbeted brass front, (specify whether right or left hand lock is wanted); ornamental bronze escutcheons, for doors 1¼ to 2¼ thick.. ......

MORTISE KNOB LOCKS, RABBETED FRONT.

No. 168, 4½x3½, Lacquered iron front, brass bolts, hub and strike, nickel-plated steel keys, 1 wro't tumbler, 24 changes ....
No. 169, 4½x3½, Heavy brass front, bolts and strike, nickel-plated steel keys, 1 wro't tumbler, 24 changes ....
No. 170, 4½x3½, Lacquered iron front and bolts, brass hub and strike, nickel-plated steel key, 1 wro't tumbler, 24 changes ....
No. 1769, 4½x3½, Ornamental genuine bronze front, bolts and strike, nickel-plated steel key, 1 wro't tumbler, 24 changes ....
No. B1769, 4½x3½, Ornamental Branford bronzed, nickel-plated steel key, 1 wro't tumbler, 24 changes ....

MORTISE DOOR BOLTS.

No. 63½, 3⅜x1⅝, Lacquered iron front, iron bolt and strike, electro-plated thumb knob and plate ....
No. 66½, 3⅜x1⅝, Heavy brass front, bolt, hub and strike, electro-plated thumb knob and plate ....
No. 1766, 3⅜x1⅝, Ornamental genuine bronze front, bolt and strike, bronze thumb knob and plate. ....

REVERSIBLE UPRIGHT RIM FRONT DOOR LOCK.

No. 3640, 4¾x3¾, Heavy iron bolts, nickel-plated steel key, 1 tumbler on large key, 2 nickel-plated steel night keys, stop on latch, ornamental thumb knob ....

In ordering Rabbeted Front Locks, be particular to state which hand is wanted—Right or Left.

FLUSH SLIDING DOOR LOCKS.

ORIENTAL PATTERN.

For Double Doors. Ornamental Bronzed Front.
Astragal Front.

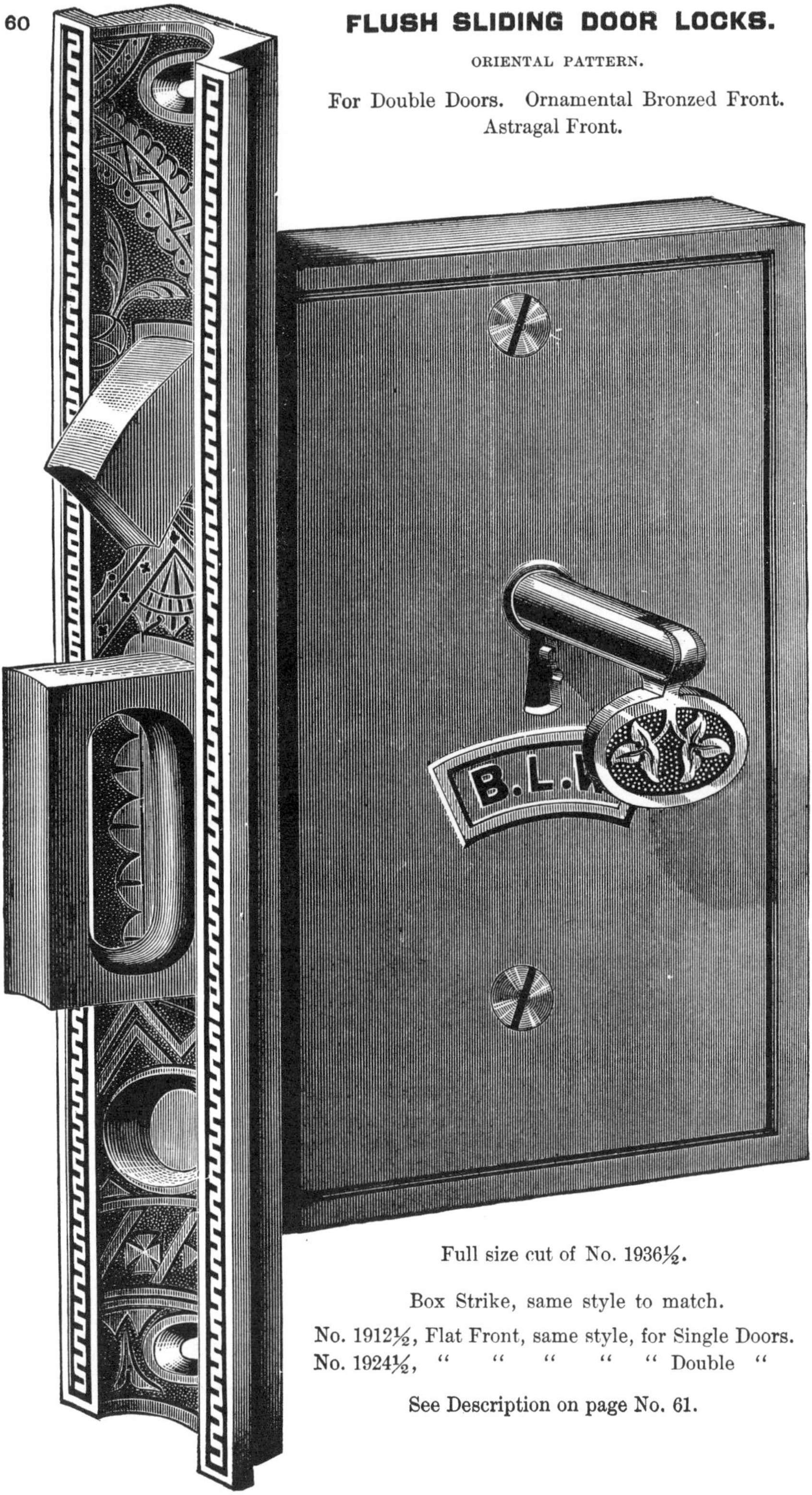

Full size cut of No. 1936½.

Box Strike, same style to match.

No. 1912½, Flat Front, same style, for Single Doors.
No. 1924½, " " " " " Double "

See Description on page No. 61.

VAJEN & NEW, INDIANAPOLIS, IND.

LOCKS AND LATCHES.

MORTISE SLIDING DOOR LOCKS, FOR KNOBS.

Plain or Flat Front.

No. 173, 4¼x3¼, Heavy brass front, bolt, hub and strike, nickel-plated key, 1 tumbler.......... ......

No. 1773, 4¼x3¼, Ornamental genuine bronze front, bolt and strike, nickel-plated key, 1 tumbler.......... ......

No. B 1773, 4¼x3¼, Ornamental "Branford Bronze," brass bolt and strike, nickel-plated key, 1 tumbler.......... ......

Astragal Front.

No. 175, 5x3½, Heavy astragal brass front, brass bolt and strike, nickel-plated key, 1 tumbler.......... ......

No. 1775, 5x3½, Ornamental genuine bronze front, bolt and strike, nickel-plated key, 1 tumbler.......... ......

No. B 1775, 5x3½, Ornamental "Branford Bronze," brass bolt and strike, nickel-plated key, 1 tumbler.......... ......

MORTISE SLIDING DOOR LATCHES, FOR KNOBS.

Flat Front.

No. 31, 3x2⅛, Heavy plain brass front, bolt and strike.......... ......

No. 1731, 3x2⅛, Ornamental genuine bronze front, bronze bolt and strike....... ......

Astragal Front.

No. 30, 3¼x2⅛, Heavy astragal brass front, brass bolt and strike.......... ......

No. 1730, 3¼x2⅛, Ornamental genuine bronze front, bronze bolt and strike. ... .

FLUSH SLIDING DOOR LOCKS.

Flat Front, for Single Doors.

No. 1912½, 5½x3½, Ornamental genuine bronze fronts, bolt and strike, nickel-plated key, 2 ornamental flush cup escutcheons.......... ......

No. B 1912½, 5½x3½, Same as above, in "Branford Bronze.".......... ......

Flat Front, for Double Doors.

No. 1924½, 5½x3½, Ornamental genuine bronze fronts and bolt, 4 ornamental flush cup escutcheons, nickel key.......... ......

No. B 1924½, 5½x3½, Same as above, in "Branford Bronze.".......... ......

Astragal Front, for Double Doors.

No. 1936½, 5½x3½, Ornamental genuine bronze fronts and bolt, 4 ornamental flush cup escutcheons, nickel key.......... ......

No. B 1936½, 5½x3½, Same as above, in "Branford Bronze.".......... ......

Orders for Flush Sliding Door Locks should give thickness of doors, otherwise they will be sent for doors 1¾ inches thick.

VAJEN & NEW, INDIANAPOLIS, IND.

MORTISE KNOB LOCKS.

REVERSIBLE LEVER. ORIENTAL PATTERN, BRONZE FRONT.

Electro-Plated Bronze Front Mortise Locks, or Bronze plated on iron, called "Branford Bronze." In same pattern and numbers as above, with the letter "B" prefixed, as B 1715, &c., &c.

Round Edge. Above is full sized cut of 1735.

No. 1715, 3½x3¼, Ornamental genuine bronze front, bronze bolts and striking plate, nickel flat steel key, 1 wro't rack tumbler, 24 changes............... ......
No. 1735, 4 x3¼, Same description as No. 1715............................. ......
No. 1740, 4 x3¼, Same as No. 1735, but with 2 wro't tumblers, 48 changes..... ......
No. 1760, 4½x3½, Same description as No. 1715............................. ......
No. 1765, 4½x3½, Same as No. 1760, but with 2 wro't tumblers, 48 changes..... ......
No. 1770, 4½x3½, Same as No. 1765, but with 3 wro't tumblers, 72 changes..... ......
No. 1785, 5 x3¾, Same description as No. 1715............................. ......
No. 1790, 5 x3¾, Same as No. 1785, but with 3 wro't tumblers, 72 changes..... ......

Bronze Front, with Thumb Bolt Attachment.

No. 1786, 4½x3½, Same as No. 1715, except with thumb knob and plate........ ......
No. 1787, 4½x3½, Same as No. 1786, but with 3 wro't tumblers, 72 changes..... ......
No. 1783, 4¾x4, Same description as No. 1786............................. ......
No. 1784, 4¾x4, Same description as No. 1787............................. ......

Cut of 2842.

Style of 2785.

ORIENTAL SQUARE PATTERN ESCUTCHEONS—GENUINE BRONZE METAL.

The following Escutcheons are the same in design as above:

No. 2860, Rose and Escutcheon combined for Locks No. 1715.
No. 2862, " " " " " " No. 1735, 1740.
No. 2864, " " " " " " No. 1760, 1765, 1770.
No. 2866, " " " " " " No. 1785, 1790.
No. 2868, " " " " " " No. 1786, 1787.
No. 2870, " " " " " " No. 1783, 1784.

No. 2854, Rose and Escutcheon combined for Locks No. 1842, 1852, 842, 852.
No. 2850, " " " " " " No. 1680½.
No. 2842, " " " " " " No. 1649.
No. 2780, Double Key-hole Escutcheon, " " No. 1842, 1852, 842, 852.
No. 2785, " " " " " No. 1649, 1680½.
Same numbers as above with "B" prefixed for Branford Finish Locks.

ORIENTAL PATTERNS.

BRONZE METAL DOOR KNOBS.
5-16 Plain Spindle.

No. 2336, Size, 2¼x2¼, Round Rose........ ....
No. 2366, Size, 2½x2¼, Round Rose........ ....

BRANFORD BRONZED DOOR KNOBS.

No. B 2336, Size, 2¼x2¼, Round Rose........ ....
No. B 2366, Size, 2½x2¼, Round Rose........ ....

BRONZE METAL DRAWER PULLS.

No. 175, Size, 3 in.... ....

BRANFORD BRONZED.

No. B 175, Size, 3 in.. ....

BRONZE METAL FLUSH SASH LIFTS.

No. 95, Size, 3½ in... ....

BRANFORD BRONZED

No. B 95, Size, 3½ in. ....

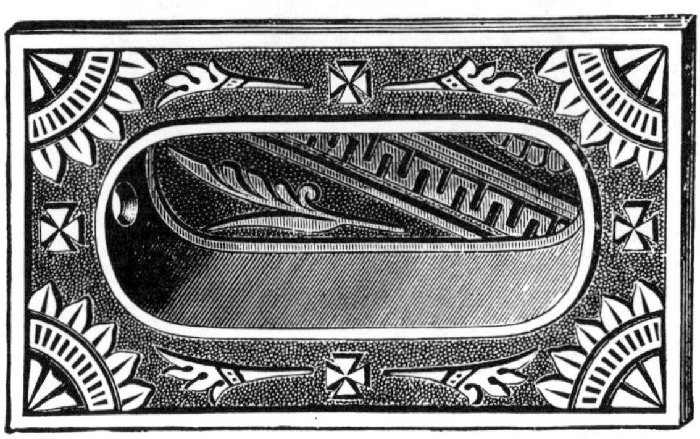

BRONZE METAL SASH LIFTS.

No. 90 ....

BRANFORD BRONZED SASH LIFTS.

No. B 90.................................. ......

We can furnish all the Oriental Patterns in OLD GOLD finish when desired.

BRONZE METAL DOOR BELL LEVERS.

No. 3358........................ ......

Various other patterns, with knob lever, with knob to pull, etc.

It is our intention to keep in stock a full assortment of Branford Bronzed Trimmings, and will get them in as fast as the factory make them. If Branford Bronzed is wanted give the Bronze number, prefixing a B.

BRONZE METAL PLATE ESCUTCHEON.

No. 2742........................ ......

BRONZZ METAL DOUBLE KEY-HOLE ESCUTCHEON.

No. 2580........................ ......

For Front Door Mortise Locks Nos. 842, 1842.

 ORNAMENTAL BRONZE AND BRANFORD BRONZE BUTTS.

This is the prettiest design in the market, and one of the latest. The solid bronze butts have steel washers, and the joints are perfectly finished .

BRANFORD BRONZED.

This bright electro-bronzed surface forms a pleasing contrast with the dark back ground and makes the Branford Bronzed a highly and attractive finish.

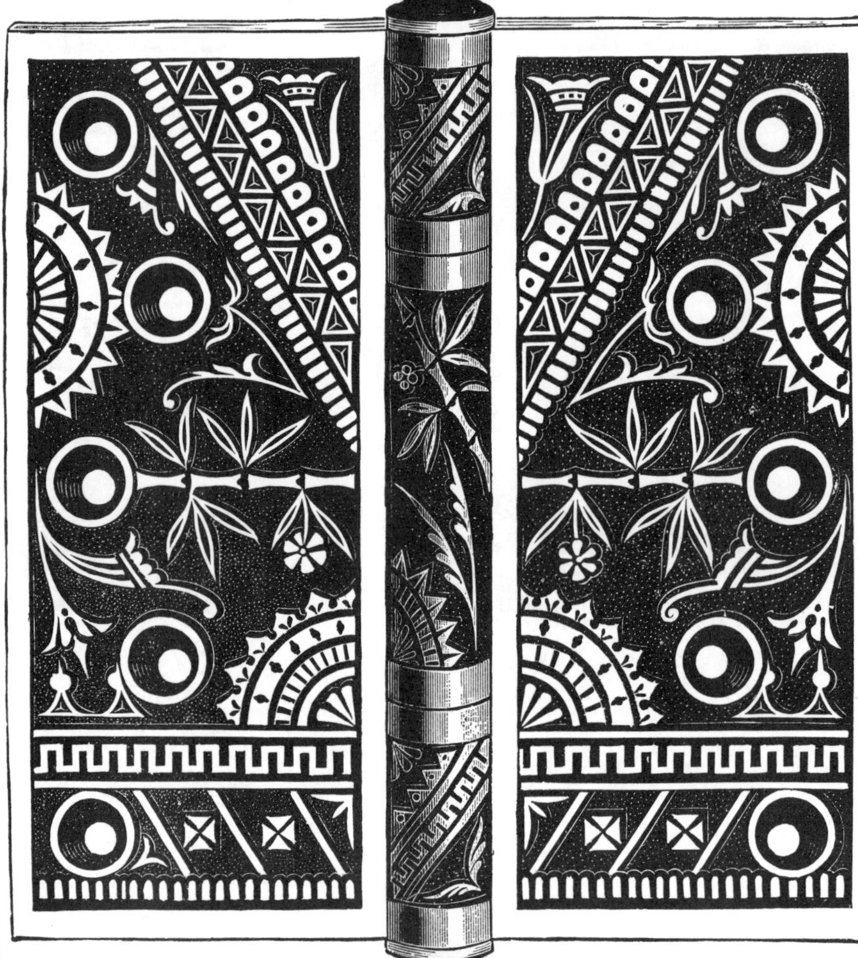

BRONZE METAL BUTTS.
Loose Pin.

	Size
No. 55, Size	2½x2½
" "	3 x3
" "	3½x3½
" "	4 x4
" "	4½x4½
" "	5 x5
" "	5 x6

BRANFORD BRONZED BUTTS.
Loose Pin.

	Size
No. B 55, Size	2½x2½
" "	3 x3
" "	3½x3½
" "	4 x4
" "	4½x4½
" "	5 x5
" "	5 x6

BRONZE METAL PARLIAMENT BUTTS.

No. 30, Ornamental Tip, Size, 1¾x2¾ . . .
No. 35, No Tip . . . . " 1¾x2¾ . . . .

BRANFORD BRONZED PARLIAMENT BUTTS.

No. B 30, Ornamental Tip, Size, 1¾x2¾ . . .
No. B 35, No Tip . . . . " 1¾x2¾ . . . .

BRONZE METAL SHUTTER HINGE.

No. 25, Size, 2x1½ . . . .

BRANFORD BRONZED SHUTTER HINGE.

No. B 25, Size, 2x1½ . . . .

BRONZE METAL SHUTTER HINGE.

No. 20, Size, 1¼x2 . . . .

BRANDFORD BRONZED SHUTTER HINGE.

No. B 20, Size, 1¼x2 . . . .

BRONZE METAL SHUTTER KNOB.

No. 150, Size, 1 in . . . .

BRANFORD BRONZED SHUTTER KNOBS.

No. B 150, Size, 1 in. . . . .

BRONZE METAL SHUTTER BARS.

No. 130, Size, 2 in. . . . .
No. 135, " 2½ in. . . . .

BRANFORD BRONZED SHUTTER BARS.

No. B 130, Size, 2 in. . . . .
No. B 135, " 2½ in. . . . .

DOOR KNOBS.

MINERAL DOOR KNOBS.

5-16, Plain Spindles.

No. 100, 2¼ Inch Rim, Japanned Neck and Rose.......................... ....

No. 102, 2¼ Inch, Mortise, Japanned Neck and Rose.................... ....

MINERAL CLOSET KNOBS.

No. 190, 2¼ Inch, Rim Japanned Neck and Rose. ....
No. 190½, 2¼ Inch, Mortise, Japanned Neck and Rose ....

Our knobs are undercut with bayonet fastenings, and not liable to come off.

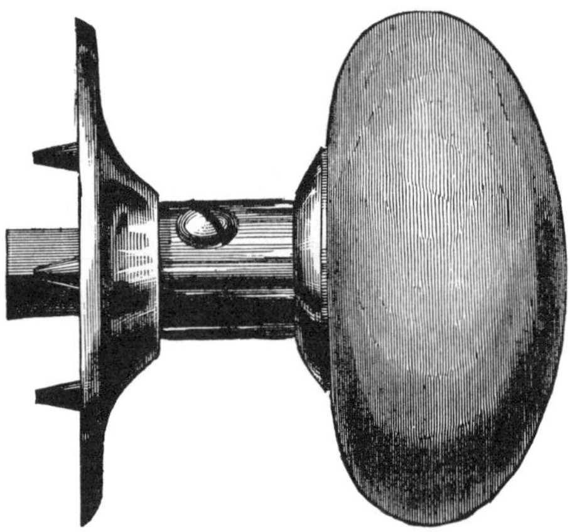

PORCELAIN DOOR KNOBS.

5-16 Plain Spindles.

No. 200, 2¼ Inch, Rim, Japanned Neck and Rose ....
No. 202, 2¼ Inch, Mortise, Japanned Neck and Rose. ....
No. 9100, 2¼ Inch, Rim with Band, Japanned Neck and Rose.... ....
No. 206, 1¾ Inch, Mortise, Japanned Neck and Rose. ....
No. 345, 2¼ Inch, Rim, Electro-plated Neck and Rose.. ....
No. 347, 2¼ Inch, Mortise, Electro-Plated Neck and Rose............ ....

Mortise and rim closet knobs furnished in all of the above.

JET DOOR KNOBS.

5-16 Plain Spindles.

No. 02410, 2¼ Inch, Rim, Bronzed Iron Rose....... ....

No. 02400, 2¼ Inch, Mortise, Bronzed Iron Rose....... ....

SIDE KNOB SCREWS.

Blued..... Tinned.....

Cut of No. 2320.

GENUINE BRONZE METAL DOOR KNOBS.
5-16 Plain Spindles.—Mortise.

No. 2320. Size, $2\frac{1}{4}$x$2\frac{1}{4}$, with round rose.................... ....

No. 2350. Size, $2\frac{1}{2}$x$2\frac{1}{4}$, same . ....

BRONZED IRON DOOR KNOBS.

5-16 Plain Spindles.—Mortise.

No. 02322. Size $2\frac{1}{4}$x$2\frac{1}{4}$, with round rose............ ....

Design similar to 2320.

This knob is electro-plated light color, to imitate genuine bronze metal.

Cut of No. 125.

BRONZED IRON DOOR KNOBS.

5-16 Plain Spindles.—Mortise.

No. 125, $2\frac{1}{4}$ in. with round rose ....

No. 126, $2\frac{1}{4}$ in. Rim, with round rose........... ....

This knob is Berlin bronze finish; can be used with other Berlin bronze trimmings, as well as separately.

Cut of No. 9993.

ROHIDA BRONZE DOOR KNOBS.

5-16 Plain Spindles.—Mortise.

No. 9993, $2\frac{1}{4}$ in. with round rose...... ....

Rohida Bronze is electro-plated, about same color as Branford bronze.

Escutcheon to match this knob, No. 9104.

We can also furnish Silvered Glass Front Door Knobs, Solid Brass and Nickel Plated Door Knobs

DOOR KNOBS.

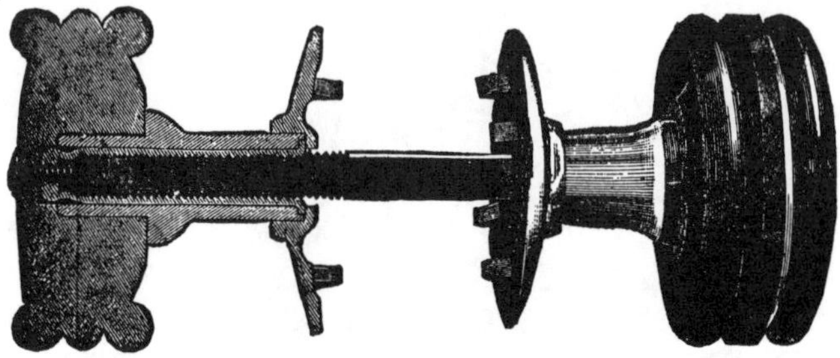

HIDDEN'S PATENT DOOR KNOBS.

Rim or Mortise.

No screws are used to secure knob or roses. Selected wood knobs for inside work only.

No. 8451, Walnut beaded, bronze necks and burnished bronze rose ....

No. 8445, Black ash beaded, nickel necks, nickel rose ....

HEMACITE DOOR KNOBS.

Color, Seal Brown.—Rim.

No. 405, Size, 2¼ in., with Round Hemacite Rose... ....

This is a very desirable inside knob.

Closet Knobs same number.

HEMACITE DOOR KNOBS.

Color, Seal Brown.

No. 339, Size, 2¼ in., Mortise, with Round Hemacite Rose ....

No. 431, Size, 2¼ in., Rim, with Round Hemacite Rose ... ...

This is called the Box Pattern, for inside work.

Closet Knobs same number.

No. 02501.

No. 010.

No. 9104.

ESCUTCHEONS.--Square Pattern.

No. 010, ¾ inch, Plated Plate for Narrow Bitt Keys. ......
No. 011, ⅞ " " " " " " ......
No. 10, ¾ " " " Wide " " ......
No. 11, ⅞ " " " " " " ......

BRONZED ESCUTCHEONS.—Ornamental Pattern.

No. 02501, ⅞ inch, Iron, Light Bronzed............. ......
No. 9104, ⅞ " Rohida Bronze.................. ......

All the new styles of Escutcheons will be found in stock.

No. 513.

HEMACITE ESCUTCHEONS.

Seal Brown Color.

No. 513, ⅞ inch, Hemacite..............
No. 506, ⅞ " " ....

See Index for Oriental Pattern Escutcheons.

No. 506.

COMMON NAILS.

12 16 20 30 40 50 60 d

COMMON NAILS.

10 8 7 6 5 4 3 d

FINE BLUED.

3 2 d

BARREL.

1⅛ 1 ⅞ in.

CLINCH NAILS.

2 2½ 3 in.

FENCING NAILS.

10 8 6 d

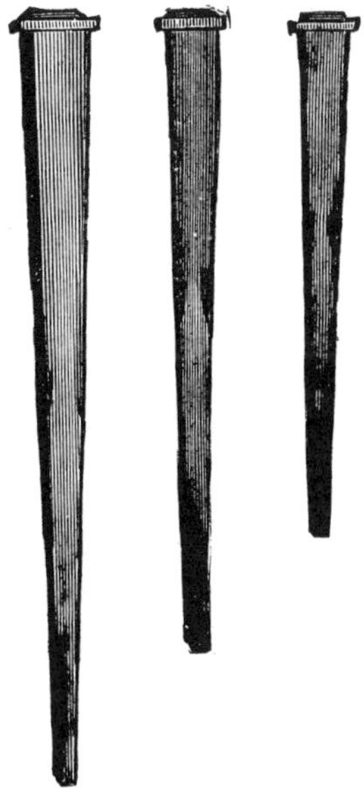

CASING NAILS.

6 8 10d

FINISHING NAILS.

⅜ ½ ⅝ ¾ 1 1¼ 1½ 1¾ 2 2¼ 2½ 3 in.

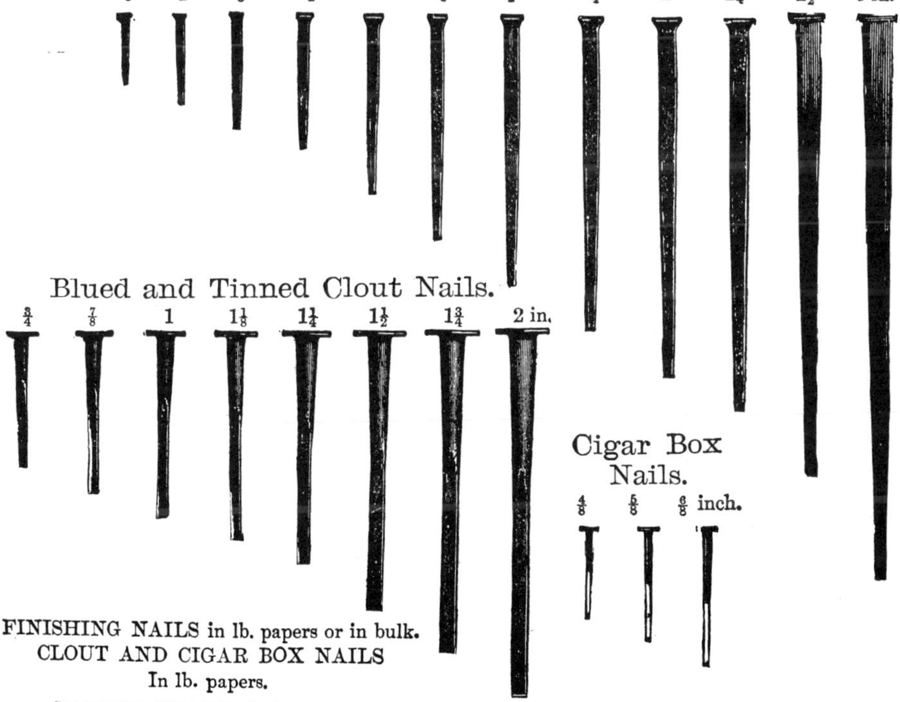

Blued and Tinned Clout Nails.

¾ ⅞ 1 1⅛ 1¼ 1½ 1¾ 2 in.

Cigar Box Nails.

4/8 5/8 6/8 inch.

FINISHING NAILS in lb. papers or in bulk.
CLOUT AND CIGAR BOX NAILS
In lb. papers.

PATENT BRADS, similar to above Finishing Nails, but lighter, and in smaller papers.

We buy none but the best in the above line. Wire and Tin Slating Nails.
See Nail Table on following page.

NAILS.

Extras in following list are to show the difference in cost of different sizes, and should be added to the rates quoted, or price of 10d to 60d.

10d to 60d Nails, Fence and Brads.			
8d & 9d,	" "	$ .25	above 10d Nails
6d & 7d,	" "	.50	" "
4d & 5d,	" "	.75	" "
3d	" "	1.50	" "
2d	" "	2.75	" "
3d Fine,	" "	3.00	" "
2d "	" "	3.75	" "
Clinch, all sizes		1.75	" "
Cut spikes, 3 to 8 in.		.25	" "
Barrel, 1½ inch		.75	" "
" 1⅜ inch		1.00	" "
" 1¼ inch		1.50	" "
" 1⅛ inch		1.75	" "
" 1 inch		2.50	" "
" ⅞ inch		3.00	" "
" ¾ inch		4.00	" "
Cut Boat Spikes		.75	
Casing & box, 4 to 20d		.75	Above common Nails of same size.
Finishing, 4d to 20d.		1.25	Above common Nails of same size.
Slating, 2d to 5d		.25	Above common Nails of same size.

Each Half Keg, 10 cents extra.

WROUGHT BOAT SPIKES. **Net.**

¼ inch square	per ℔	.....
5-16 "	"	.....
⅜ and 7-16 inch square	"	.....
½, 9-16 and ⅝ "	"	.....

LENGTHS AND NUMBER OF NAILS TO THE POUND.

DESCRIPTION.										
Sizes.	Common.	Clinch.	Fence.	Finishing	Fine.	Barrel.	Casing.	Brads.	Cut Spikes	Length.
¾ in.						800				¾ in.
⅞ in.						500				⅞ in.
2d.	800			1100	1000	376				1 in.
3d.	464			720	800	224				1¼ in.
4d.	296			523	368	180	398			1½ in.
5d.	224			410						1¾ in.
6d.	168	95	84	268			224	126		2 in.
7d.	120	74	64	188				98		2¼ in.
8d.	88	62	48	146			128	75		2½ in.
9d.	70	53	36	130			110	65		2¾ in.
10d.	60	46	30	102			91	55	28	3 in.
12d.	48	42	24	76			71	40		3¼ in.
16d.	36	38	20	62			54	27	22	3½ in.
20d.	24	33	16	54			40		14½	4 in.
30d.	17	20					33		12½	4½ in.
40d.	13						27		9½	5 in.
50d.	9½								8	5½ in.
60d.	8								6	6 in.
									5½	6½ in.
									4½	7 in.
									2½	8 in.

CUT BOAT SPIKES.

Size	No. to ℔	Size	No. to ℔	Size	No. to ℔
3½x¼	18	4 x5-16	9	8 x5-16.	3½
4 x¼	13½	4½x5-16	8	5 x⅜	5½
4½x¼	11¼	5 x5-16	7½	5½x⅜	5
5 x¼	10½	5½x5-16	6½	6 x⅜	4½
5½x¼	9½	6 x5-16	5¾	6½x⅜	4
6 x¼	8½	6½x5-16	4½	7 x⅜	3½
6½x¼	7½	7 x5-16	4	8 x⅜	3

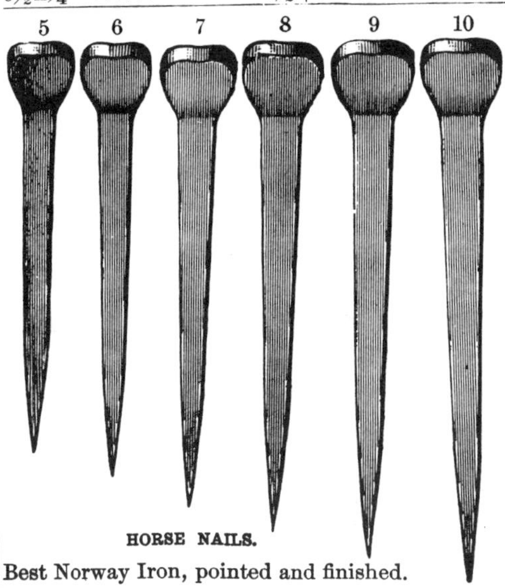

HORSE NAILS.

Best Norway Iron, pointed and finished.

25 lbs. in a Box.

HORSE AND MULE SHOES.

All sizes in Fore and Hind Shoes.

Full sized cut of No. 72.

No. 72, 2¼ in., Iron, ⅝ in. from selvedge edge to key pin, 4 keys to a doz. locks ....
No. 72, 2¼ in., " ⅝ " " " " 12 " " " ....
No. 423, 2½ in., " 13-16 " " " " 12 " " " ....
No. 161, 2½ in., " ⅞ " " " " 12 " " " ....
No. 185, 2½ in., " 1⅝ " " " " 12 " " " ....

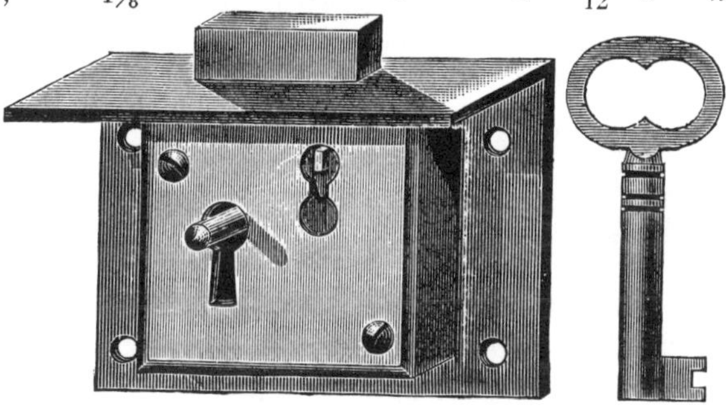

Full sized cut of No. 454.

No. 563, 1½ in., Iron, 2 secure levers, flat bow keys (all different) 12 to each doz. locks....
No. 454, 2 in., " " " " " " 12 " " " ....
No. 454, 2 in., " " " " " " 24 " " " ....
No. 455, 2 in., Brass, " " " " " 12 " " " ....
No. 455, 2 in., " " " " " " 24 " " " ....
No. 237, 2½ in., Iron, " " " " " 12 " " " ....

Full sized cut of No. 561.

No. 561, 2¼ in., Iron, 2 secure levers, solid steel bit, nickel keys (all different), 12 keys to each dozen locks.......... ....
No. 561, 2¼ in., Same, except 24 dozen keys to each lock.......... ....
No. 558, 2½ in., Same as No. 561.......... ....

Numbers given above are "Eagle" numbers.

CHEST AND TILL LOCKS.

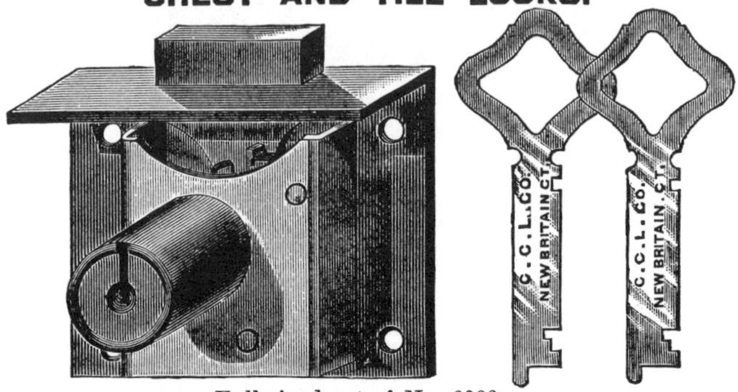

Full sized cut of No. 6080.

No. 6080, 1¾ in., Brass, 2 secure Levers, 2 Nickel-Plated, flat Steel Keys, (for ⅞ in. wood) ....
No. 6090, 1¾ in., Iron, 2 " " 2 " " " " " " " ....

Full sized cut of No. 6017.

No. 6018, 2¼ in., Brass, 2 secure Levers, 2 Nickel-Plated, flat Steel Keys, (for ⅞ in. wood) ...
No. 6017, 2¼ in., Iron, 2 " " 2 " " " " " " " ....

Full sized cut of No. 410.

No. 9, 4 in., Iron, Self-Locking, Double Link, Double Bit Key, 12 Keys to each dozen, all different ....

No. 250, 4 in., Brass, 4 secure Levers, Fine flat bowed Key, 24 Keys to each dozen, all different ....

255, 3½ in., Same description as No. 250, but Double Link ....

No. 410, 3 in., Iron, 3 secure Levers, Double Link, Fine flat bowed Keys, 12 Keys to each dozen, all different ....

Numbers given above are "Eagle" numbers.

CHEST AND TILL LOCKS.

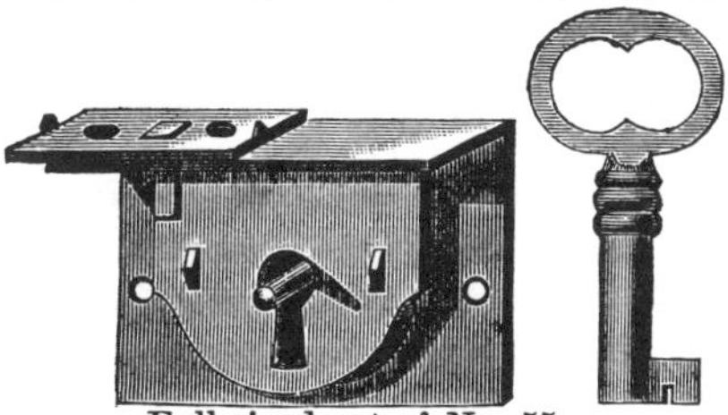

Full sized cut of No. 55.

No. 64, 2 inch, Iron, Double Link, 1 Ward, 12 Keys to each dozen........ ......
No. 55, $1\frac{1}{2}$ inch, " Single " 12 " " " ....
No. 189, $1\frac{1}{4}$ inch, Brass, Double " Tumbler, 12 " " " ....

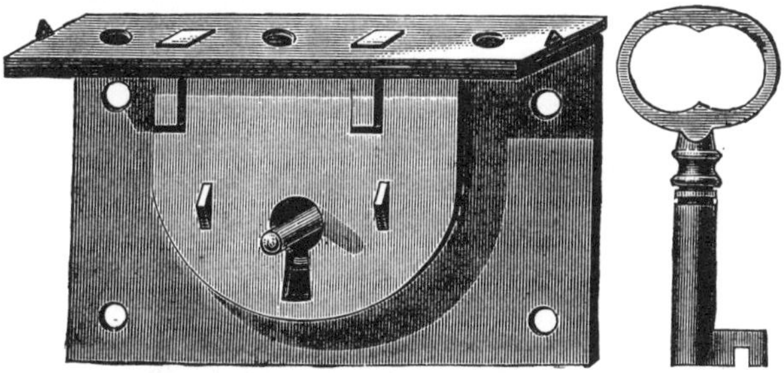

Full sized cut of No. 167.

No. 461, $2\frac{3}{4}$ in., Iron, Double Link, 2 Secure Levers, flat bowed keys, 12 to each doz.....
No. 166, $2\frac{1}{2}$ in., " " " 1 Ward, Assorted Fancy keys, 12 " ".....
No. 167, $2\frac{1}{4}$ in., " " " 1 " " " " 12 " ".....

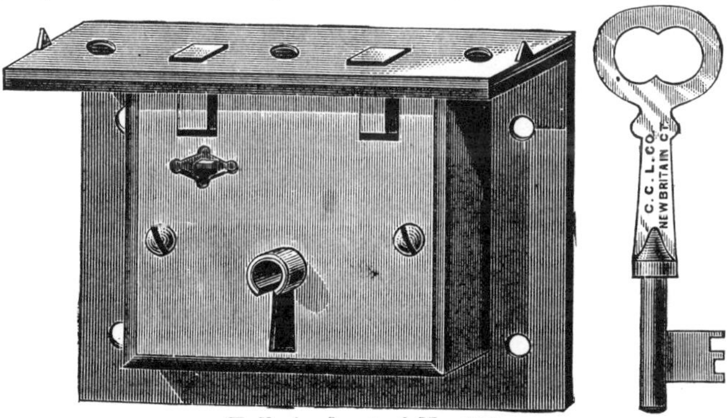

Full sized cut of No. 580.

No. 577, $3\frac{1}{2}$ inch. Iron, Double Link, 3 Secure Levers, Steel Nickel-Plated Keys, 12 to each dozen...
No. 580, $2\frac{1}{2}$ inch, Same as 577..

Cut of No. 161.

"YALE" DRAWER LOCK.

No. 161, Brass, for $\frac{7}{8}$ in. Wood ....
No. 163, " " 1 in. " ....
2 flat steel keys with each lock

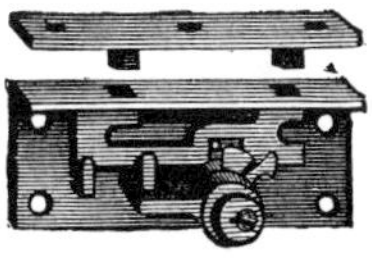

Cut of No. 121.

"YALE" CHEST LOCK.

No. 121, $4\frac{1}{4}$x$1\frac{3}{4}$, Brass, for $1\frac{1}{4}$ in. Wood, 2 flat steel keys with each lock. ... .

Numbers given (on first THREE illustrated) are "Eagle" numbers.

VAJEN & NEW, INDIANAPOLIS, IND.

VAJEN & NEW, INDIANAPOLIS, IND.

Full sized cut of No. 417.

No. 500, 3½x2 inch, Iron, Broad Bolt, Tumbler ....
No. 510, 3x1¾ inch, Iron, Broad Bolt, Tumbler ....
No. 417, 2¾x1¼ in., Iron, Broad Bolt, Tumbler ....
No. 415, 2½x1¼ in., Iron, Broad Bolt, Tumbler ....
No. 416, 2½x1¼ in., Brass, Broad Bolt, Tumbler ....
No. 508, 1⅞x¾ in., Brass, Broad Bolt, Tumbler ....

All of the above Locks shoot Bolt right and left.

Full sized cut of No. 571.

No. 567, 3½x2, Iron, Solid Square Box, Screwed, 2 Secure Levers, Broad Heavy Brass Bolt, Shoots Right and Left, Solid Steel Bit, Nickel-Plated Keys, all different, in each dozen ....

No. 567, 3 x1¼, Same as 567 ....

No. 1203, 2¾x1¼, " " 567 ....

No. 571, 2½x1¼, " " 567 ....

CORRESPONDING NUMBERS.

Eagle	500,	510,	417,	415,	416,	508,	567,	569,	1203,	571.
Corbin.....	709,	704,	703,	702,	0702,	0700,	743,	742		741.
Gaylord ..	87½,	369,	94,	96,	95,	98,	611,	633,		651.

Cut of lock No. 101.

"YALE" CUPBOARD LOCK.

No. 101, 2x1¾, Brass, for 1 inch Wood, 2 Keys with each Lock ....
Either Right or Left Hand.

Style of Yale lock key.

"YALE" SPRING CUPBOARD LOCK.

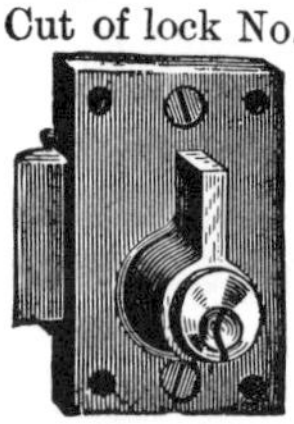

Lock No. 113.

No. 113, 2x1 5-16, Finished Brass for ⅞ in. Wood, 2 Keys to each Lock....... ......
Specify "Hand" wanted.

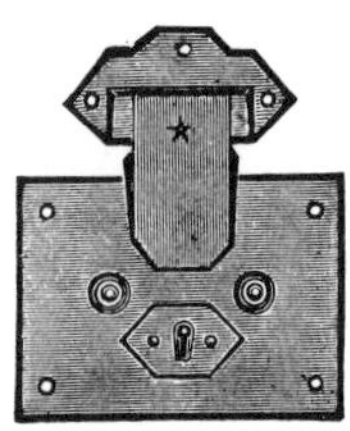

TRUNK LOCKS.

No. 0118½, 4¾ in., Brass spring hasp, flat steel keys..
No. 85½, 4 in., Iron, Japanned spring hasp, ... flat steel keys...... ....
No. 101½, 3½ in., Same description as 85½..... ....
No. 15, 3½ in., Iron, Japanned brass bush and drop, drilled pin'd key................. ....

VAJEN & NEW, INDIANAPOLIS, IND.

ESCUTCHEONS AND DROP HANDLES.

Brass Thread.
3/8, 1/2, 9-16, 5/8, 3/4. ....

No. 626.
Brass....

No. 122.
Nickel Plated......

No. 132.
Nickel Plated......

No. 742.
Nickel Plated .....

No. 740.
Nickel Plated......

No. 5.
Nickel Plated......
Gold Plated ......
Cut 2/3 size.

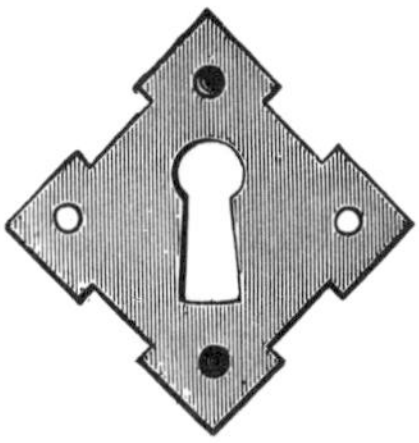

No. 3.
Nickel Plated......
Gold Plated ......
Cut 2/3 size.

No. 69.
Gold Plated......

No. 70.
Gold Plated .....

No. 182.
Nickel Plated......
Gold Plated ......
Cuts 2/3 Size.

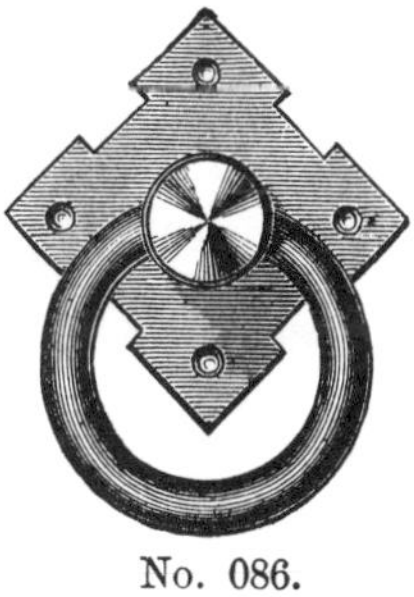

No. 086.
Nickel Plated......
Gold Plated ......

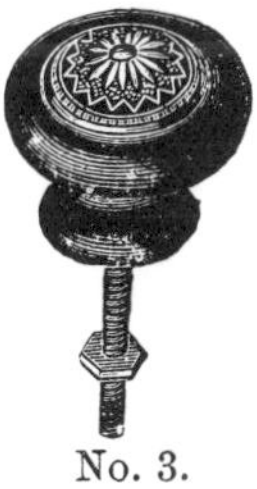

No. 3.

No. 3, Ebony Drawer Knobs, Gilt Center...................... ......

COMMODE BUTTONS.

No. 1, Ebony, Gilt Center ....
No. 2, Plain Ebony ....

Also a large assortment of other Drop Handles.

Fancy Escutcheons and Fancy Hinge Plates, Brass and Nickel Plated.

SHUTTER AND DRAWER KNOBS AND ESCUTCHEONS.

VAJEN & NEW, INDIANAPOLIS, IND.

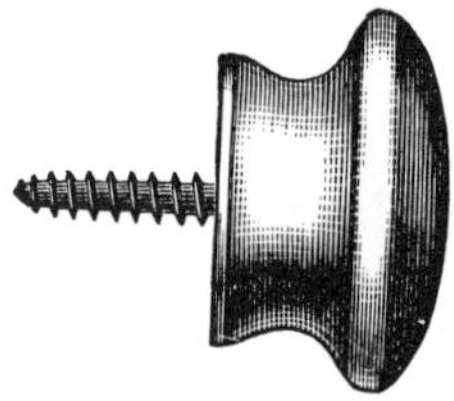

No. 1.

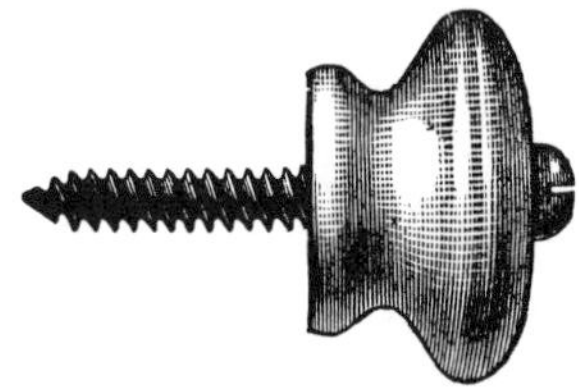

No. 15.

PORCELAIN SHUTTER KNOBS.

Inch	5/8	3/4	1	1 1/8	1 1/4	1 1/2	1 3/4	2.
No. 1, Fast Screw	....	....	....	....	....	....	....	...
No. 15, Round Tinned Screw,....	....	....	....	....	....	....	....	....

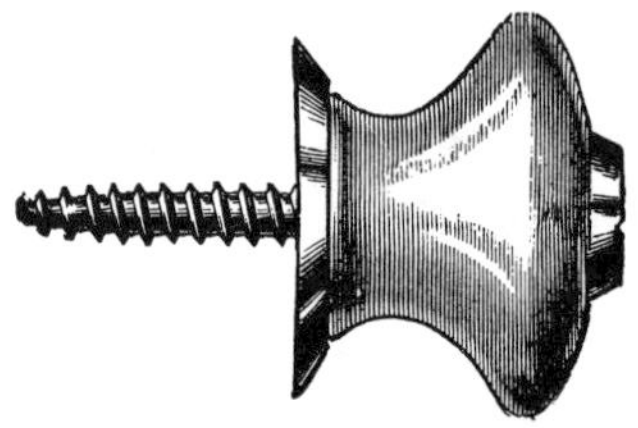

PORCELAIN SHUTTER KNOBS.

Silver Plated Base under Screw Head and Knob.

Inch	5/8	3/4	7/8	1	1 1/8
No. 40	......	......	......	......	......

No. 8.

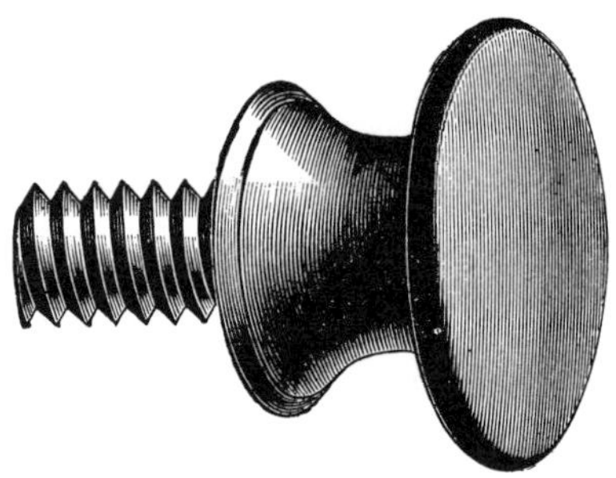

No. 9.

WALNUT OR OAK FURNITURE KNOBS.

Inch	1 1/2	2
No. 8	......	......

Inch	1 1/2	2
No. 9............	......	......

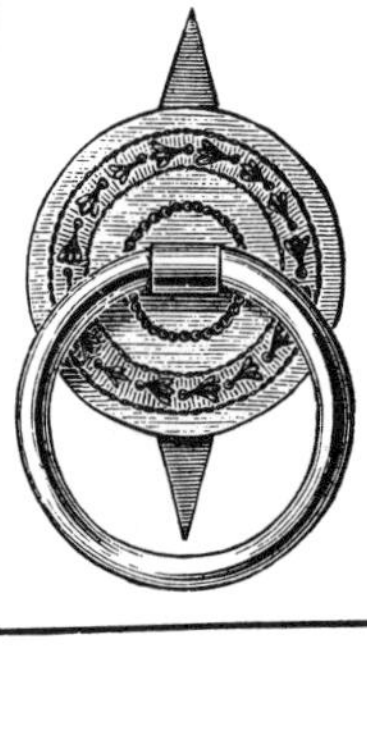

BRASS RING HANDLES.

Inch.... ... . 5/8 ..... 3/4...... 7/8......

WALNUT OR OAK ESCUTCHEONS.

Inch	5/8	3/4	7/8	1
Plain	......	......	......	......
Rabbet..........	......	......	......	......

CASTERS.

VAJEN & NEW, INDIANAPOLIS, IND.

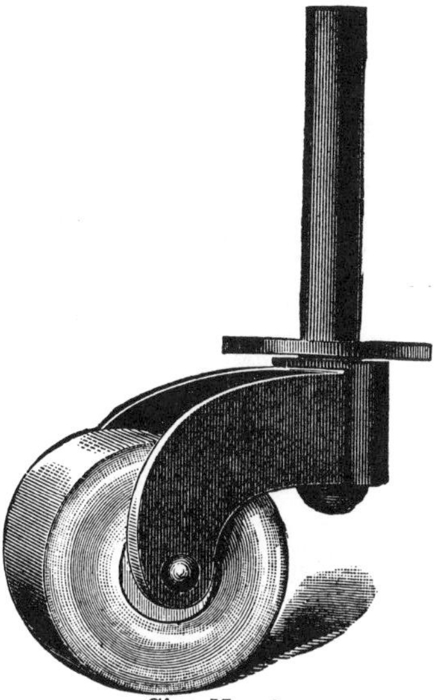

Size No. 3.

PHILADELPHIA PLATE.

LIST.

Nos.	2	3	4	5	6
Broz. Iron Wheel,	..	..	..	..	..
Porcelain "	..	..	..	..	..
Lignumvitæ "	..	..	..	..	..

Discount.......

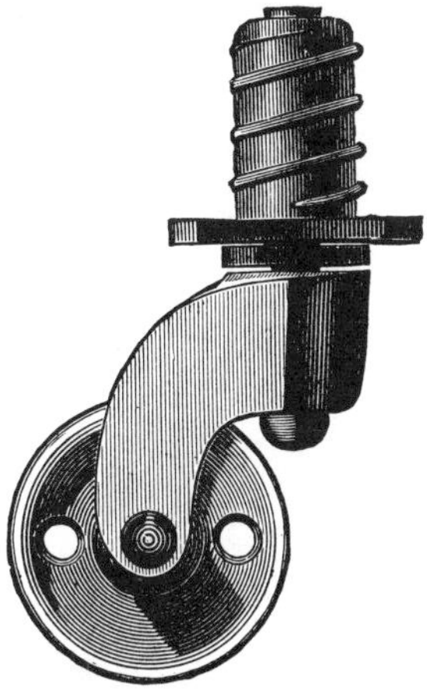

Size No. 2.

RICK BRO'S SCREW PLATE.

Wrought Pin and Washer. The Best Screw Plate Caster.

LIST.

Bronzed Iron Wheel,
Nos. 1..2..3..4..5..6..7 .
Porcelain Wheel,
Nos. 1..2..3..4..5..6..7..
Lignumvitæ Wheel,
Nos. 1..2..3..4..5..6..7..
Discount........

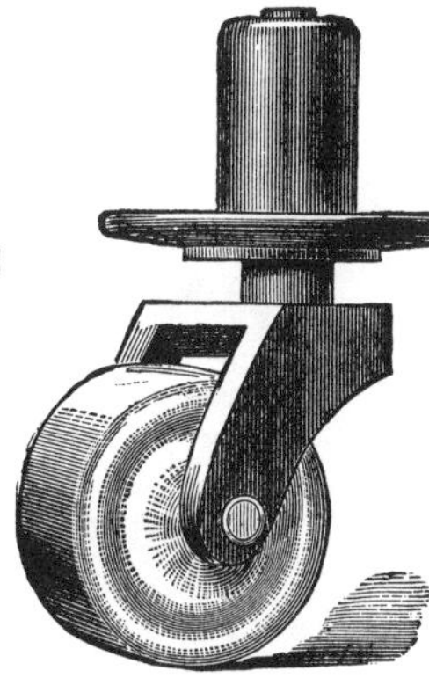

Size No. 2.

COMMON PLATE.

LIST.

Bronzed Iron Wheel,
Nos.1..2..3..4..5..6..7..
Porcelain Wheel,
Nos.1..2. 3..4..5..6..7..
Discount ....

MARTIN'S PATENT CASTERS.

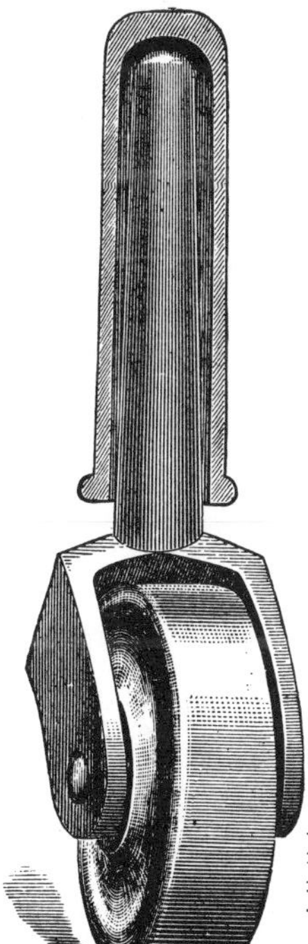

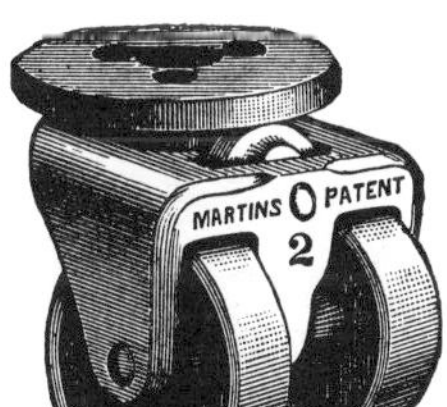

2/3 SIZE

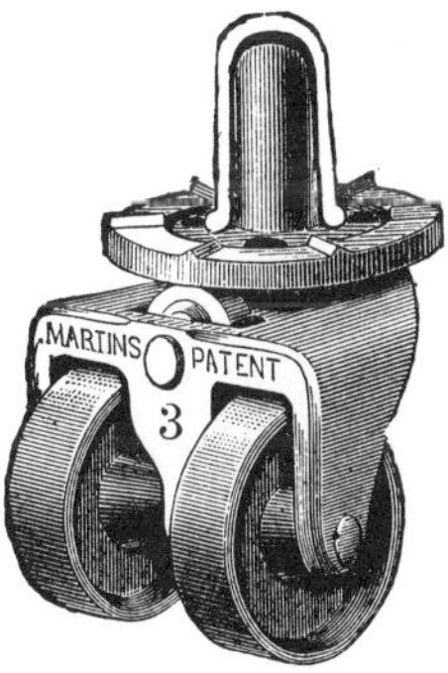

Martin's Casters, Round, Oblong and Stem Plate.

LIST.

No. of Caster	2	3	4	5	6	7	8	10	12	14
Size of Wheel	1 in.	1⅜	1⅝	1⅞	2	2¼	2¾	3⅛	4¼	4¾
Bronzed Iron Wheel,	...	...	...	...	...	...	...	...	...	...
Porcelain "	...	...	...	...	...	...	...	...	...	...
Lignumvitææ "	...	...	...	...	...	...	...	...	...	...

Discount ....

No. 6 is the Piano Caster—Larger Sizes for Refrigerators, Trucks, &c.

BED CASTERS.

LIST.

No.	1⅝, 1.	1⅝, 2.	1⅝, 3.	2, 1.	2, 2.	2, 3.
Bronzed Iron Wheel,	.....	.....	.....	.....	.....	.....
Porcelain "	.....	.....	.....	.....	.....	.....

Discount........

Heavy Store Truck Casters, Rubber Wheel Noiseless Casters.

SAND AND EMERY PAPER, ETC.

FLINT PAPER.

No. 00, 0, ½, 1, 1½, ...
No. 2, 2½, 3, ...

Flint Paper in Rolls of 50 Yards, 23½ in. Wide.

No. 00, 0, ½, 1, 1½, ... 2.. 2½.. 3.. 3½.. 4..

	Emery Paper.	Emery Cloth.
No. 00, 0, ½, 1, 1½	....	....
No. 2.	....	....
No. 2½	....	....
No. 3	....	....

GLUE.

No.......... A1...... A5...... B3...... B9 Ground......B10...... White......

Glue Pots on Page 179.

CHASE'S IMPROVED LIQUID GLUE

For Manufacturers', Office, and Household Use.

PRICE LIST.

1 oz., 1 doz. in box........ ......per doz.

2 oz., 1 doz. in box .... " "

Quarts .... " "

Can be furnished in large quantities for Manufacturers. Warranted not to deteriorate with age. It is a giant in strength, always ready for use and economical. Convenient for making all repairs about the house, for scrap books, &c.

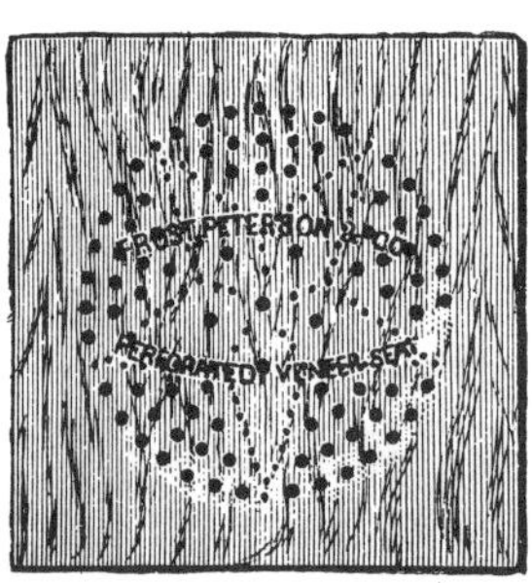

PATENT THREE-PLY VENEER CHAIR SEATS.

Only First-Quality kept in Stock.

Size..	12	13	14	15	16	17	18	20 in. sq.
Birch	....	....	....	....	....	....	....	....
Walnut....	....	....	....	....	....	....	....	....

CHAIR CANE.

Best Quality.

Fine Medium, or Heavy................... ......

Wide Binding.............................. ......

PICTURE AND FURNITURE NAILS.

VAJEN & NEW, INDIANAPOLIS, IND.

BRASS HEAD PICTURE NAILS.

No. 1, White Porcelain, Plain Rim.. ...... 1 1¼ 1½ 1¾ 2 2½ 3 3½ 4 in.

No. 9, White Center, Plain Rim ....

No. 9, Ruby " " " ....

No. 9, Blue " " " ....

No. 10, Solid Porcelain Head, ¾ inch ....

No. 11, " " " ⅞ inch ....

No. 100, Crystal Glass Center, Plain Rim ....

No. 105, Ruby Star " " " ....

No. 106, Green " " " " ....

No. 107, Blue " " " " ....

No. 34, Crystal Glass Center, Fancy Rim ....

No. 35, Ruby " " " " ....

No. 3, White Porcelain Center, Fancy Rim ....

FIRE GILT FURNITURE NAILS. CHINA NAILS AND DISCS.

No. 6 4 3 43 42 41 137½ 137½

Wire Nails on page 80.

CURTAIN AND PICTURE FIXTURES.

BRASS CURTAIN RINGS.

3/8 ½ 5/8 ¾ in.

No. 18............ 3/8 ...... ½...... 5/8...... ¾.....

DRAPERY HOOKS.

No. 327.

No. 327.. ......

PICTURE HOOKS.

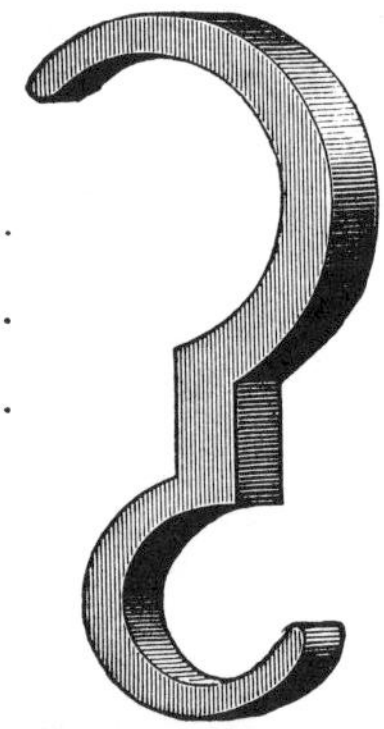

No. 030, Cast Brass, Unburnished, for 1½ in. Moulding, like cut......

No. 65, Stamped Brass, Fancy, for 1½ in. Moulding.......... ......

No. 72, " " Plain, " 1½ " ....

BRAIDED WIRE PICTURE CORD.

25 Yards in a Coil.

No. 0......

No. 1......

No. 2......

No. 3......

No. 4......

No. 5......

No. 0

No. 1

No. 2

No. 3

No. 4

No. 5

PALMER'S SELF-ADJUSTING SCREW PULLEY.

No. 1.................................... .....

PALMER'S SELF-ADJUSTING SHADE PULLEY.

No. 1.................................... .....

SCREW EYES.

No. 1 2 3 4

No. 5 6 7 8 9

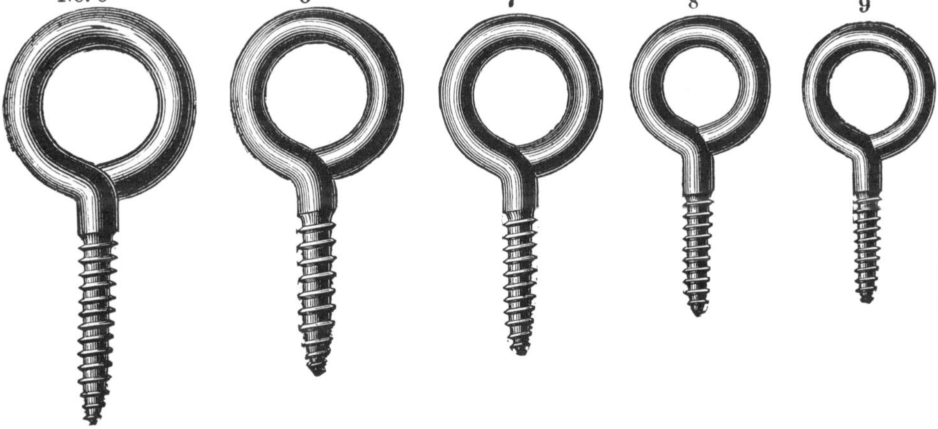

No. 10 11 12 13 14

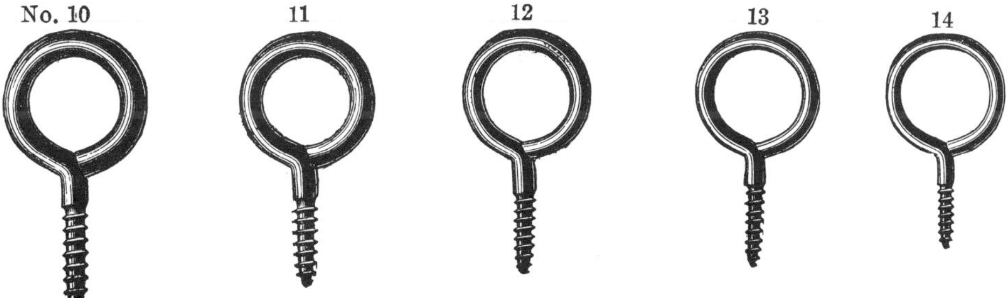

Bright Wire, well finished.

SCREW EYES AND SCREW HOOKS.

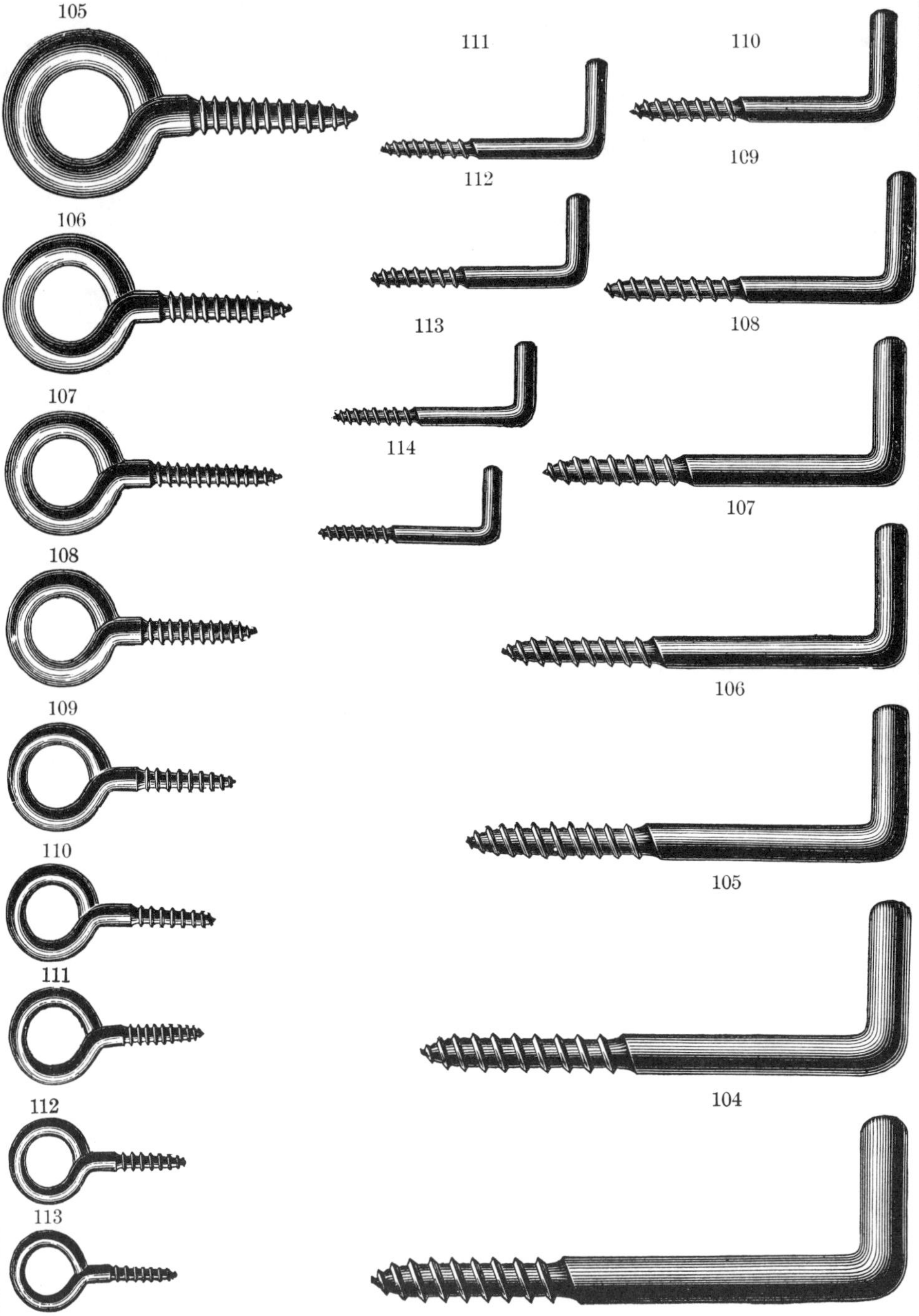

Bright Wire, well finished.

AWNING HOOKS, HOOKS AND EYES, &C.

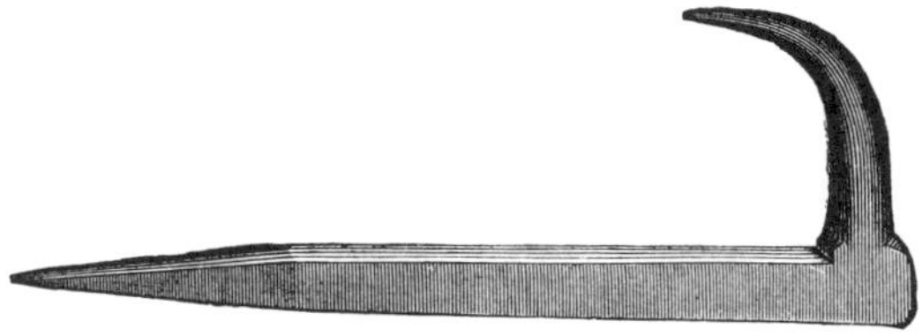

WROUGHT IRON AWNING HOOKS.

1¾ .... 2.... 2½.... 3.... 3½.... 4.... 4½.... 5.... 6 in. ...

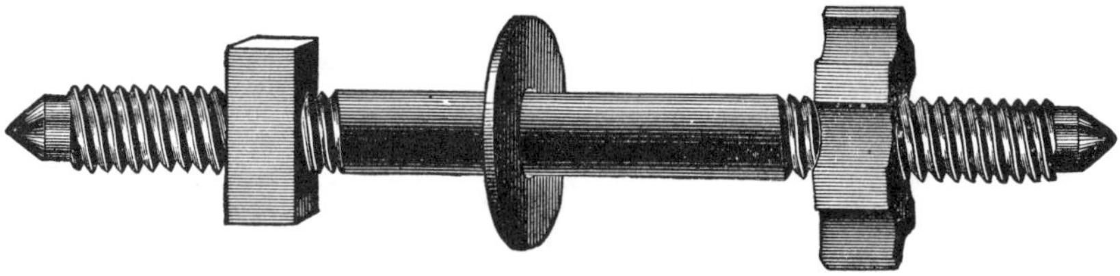

WROUGHT HAND RAIL SCREWS.

5-16 Iron, Two Nuts........................ 4...... 4½...... 5...... 5½ in......

POLISHED IRON HOOKS AND EYES

1½........ 2........ 2½........ 3 in.........

BRASS HOOKS AND EYES.

1...... 1¼...... 1½...... 1¾...... 2...... 2¼... 2½ in......

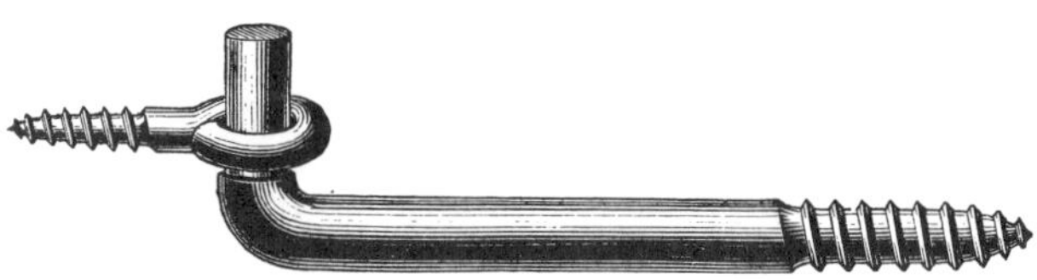

CORNICE HOOKS.

3.... 3½.... 4.... 4½.... 5.... 6.... 7.... 8.... 9.... 10.... 11.... 12 in....

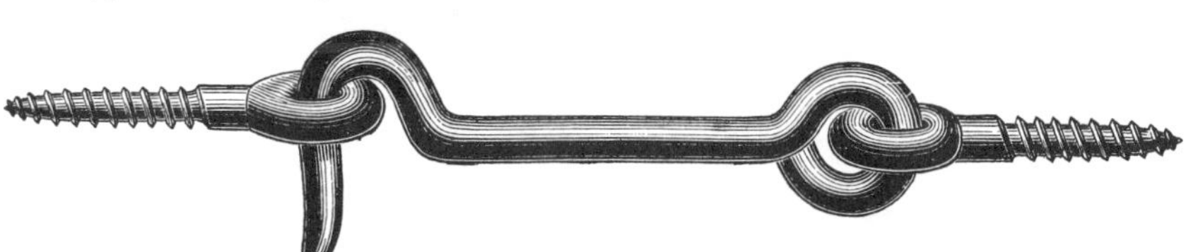

BRIGHT IRON GATE HOOKS AND EYES.

1½.... 2.... 2½.... 3.... 3½.... 4 in ...

SCREW AND DRIVE HOOKS.

TINNED TENTER HOOKS.

Per M,.... 3½ lb...... 4 lb..... 5 lb......

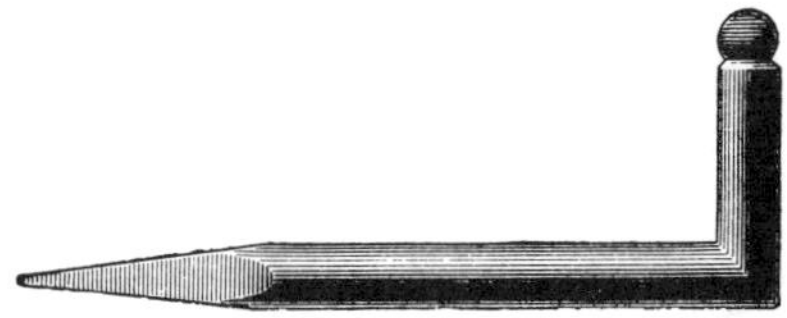

208

BRASS SCREW HOOKS.

No. 412.. ½.. ⅝.. ¾.. 1.. 1¼.. 1½in...

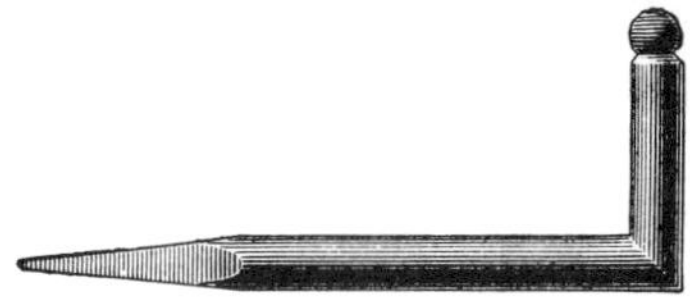

209

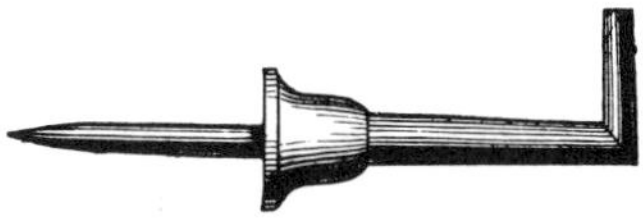

BRASS DRIVE HOOKS.

No. 405.... ½.. ⅝.. ¾.. 1.. 1¼.. 1½ in...

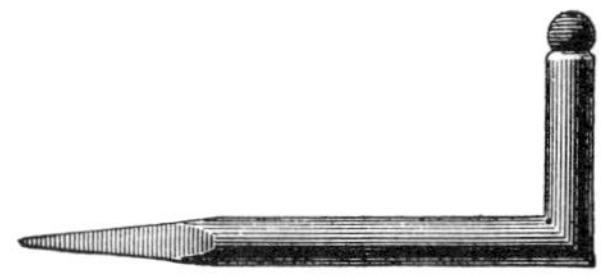

210

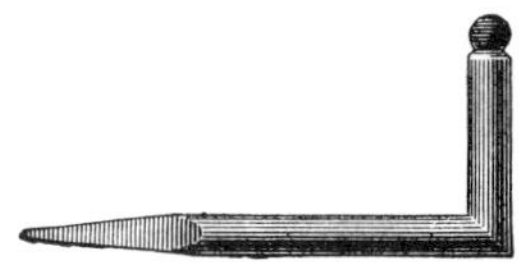

211

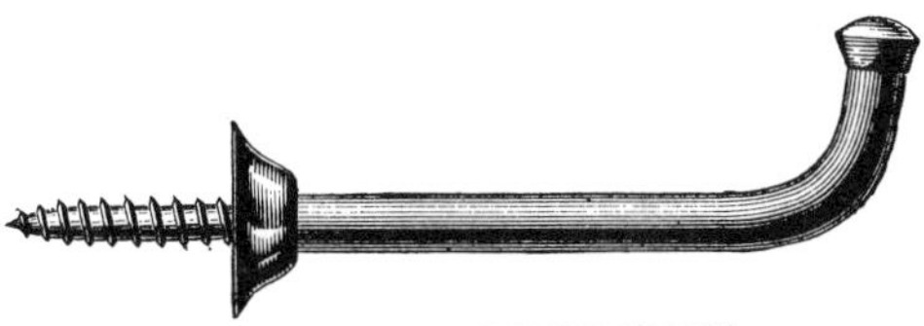

COPPERED WIRE SCREW HOOKS.

Brass Base........... No. 70 ..... 80......

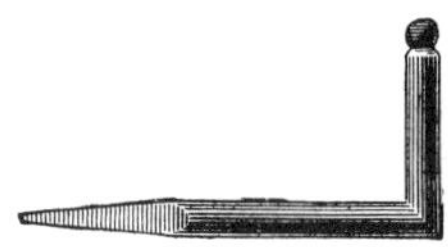

212

BRIGHT WIRE DRIVE HOOKS.

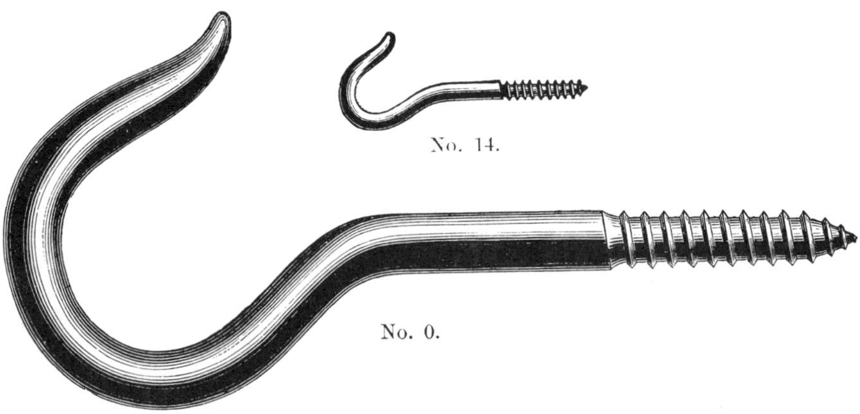

No. 14.

No. 0.

BRIGHT WIRE SCREW HOOKS.

No.......	0,	1,	2,	3,	4,	5,	6,	7,	8,	9,	10,	11,	12,	13,	14.
Per Gross,	....	....	....	....	....	....	....	....	....	....	....	....	....	....	....

KEYS.

VAJEN & NEW, INDIANAPOLIS, IND.

Yale Steel Blanks . . . .

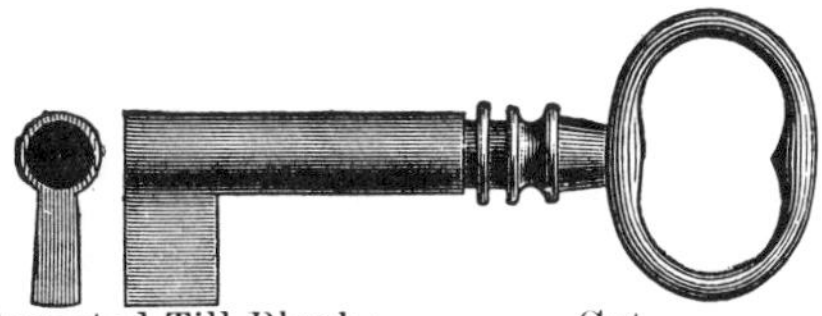

Assorted Till Blanks, ... Cut, ...

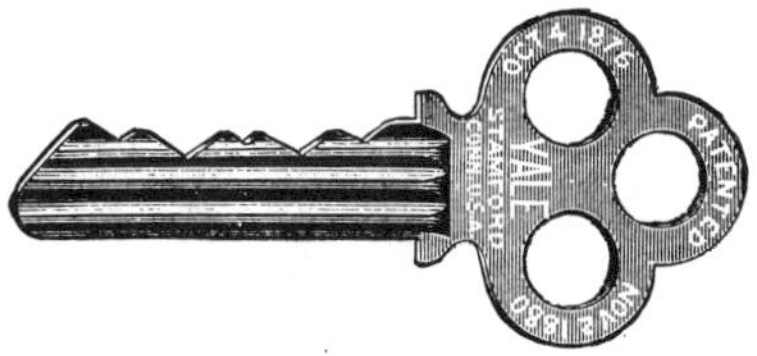

Yale Steel Blanks . . . .

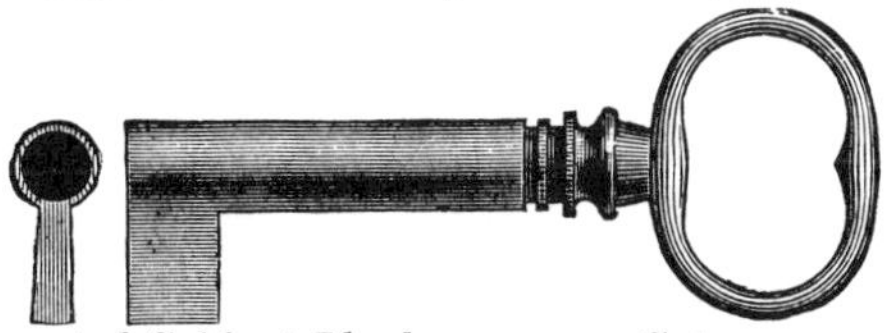

Assorted Cabinet Blanks, ... Cut, ...

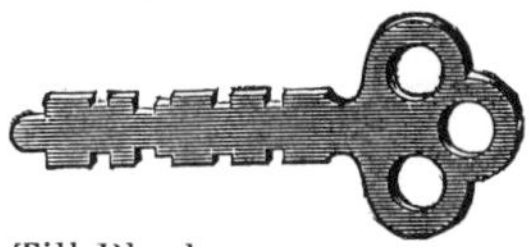

Steel Till Blanks . . . .

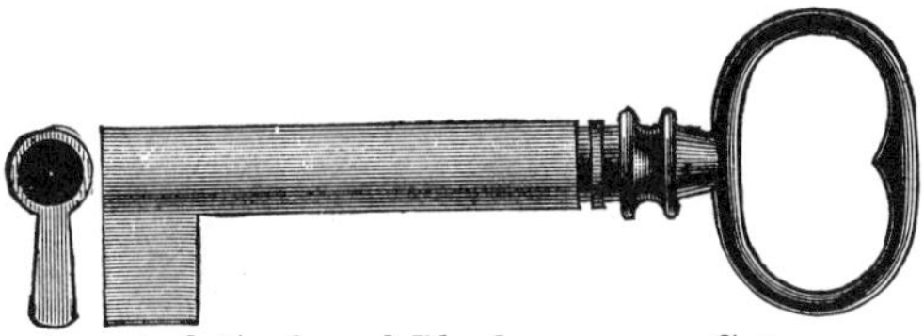

Assorted Cupboard Blanks, ... Cut, ...

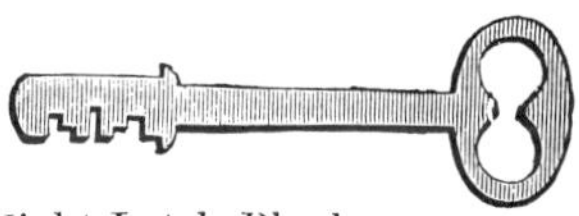

Night Latch Blanks. . . . .

PAD-LOCK KEYS.

Assorted Iron, Cut . . . .
" Brass Blanks . . . .

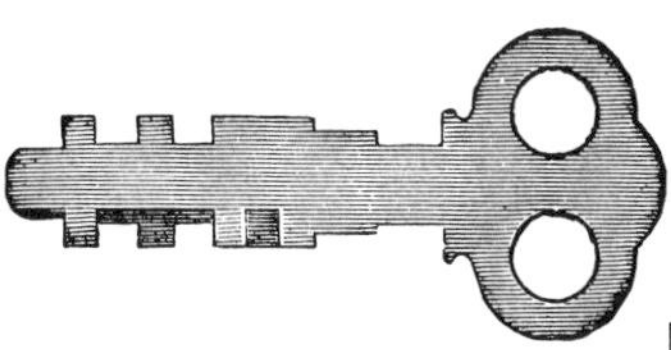

SCANDINAVIAN PAD-LOCK KEYS.

Iron, assorted . . . .
Steel, " . . . .

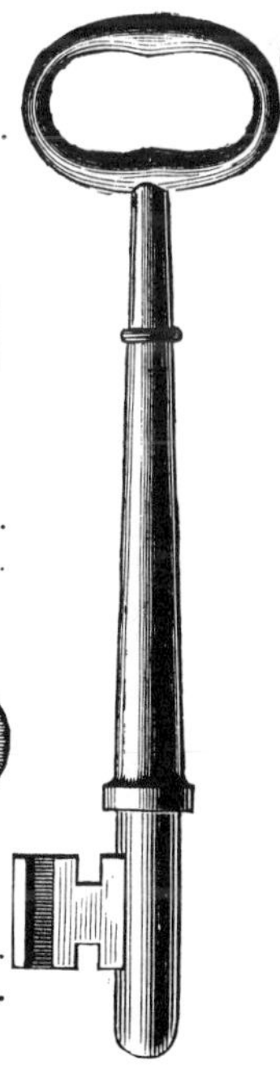

Short Bit.

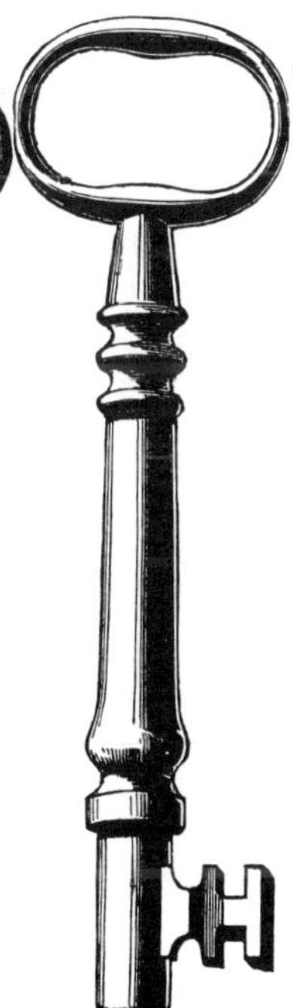

Heavy.

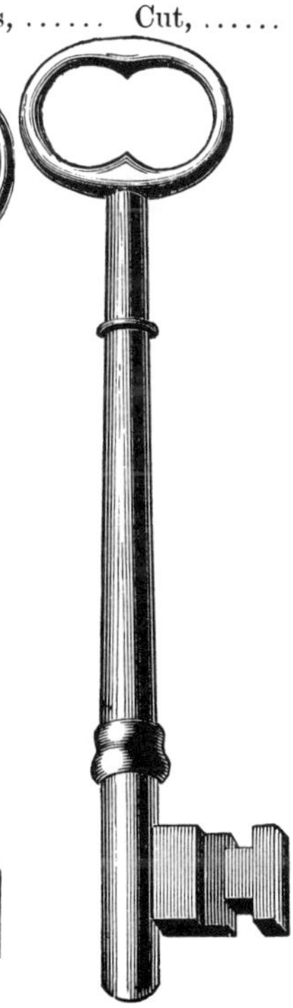

Long Bit.

Iron Door Keys, Cut, assorted, like above . . . .
" " " Blanks to File . . . .
Brass " " " " . . . .

Almost any Lock can be fit from our stock of Keys.
Bag, Trunk, Folding Store Door Keys and Skate Keys.

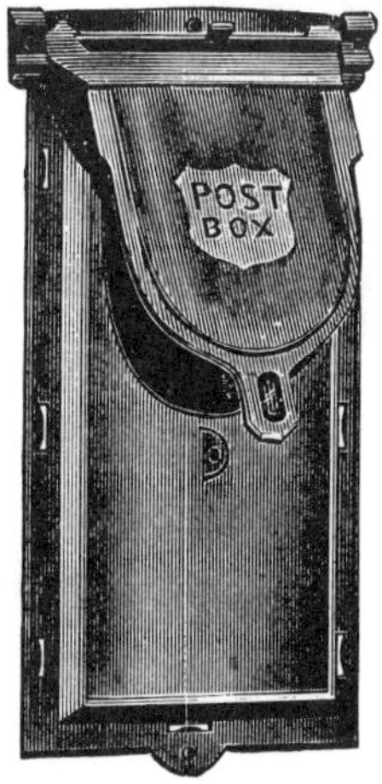

POST BOXES.

No. 1............ ......
No. 2............ ......

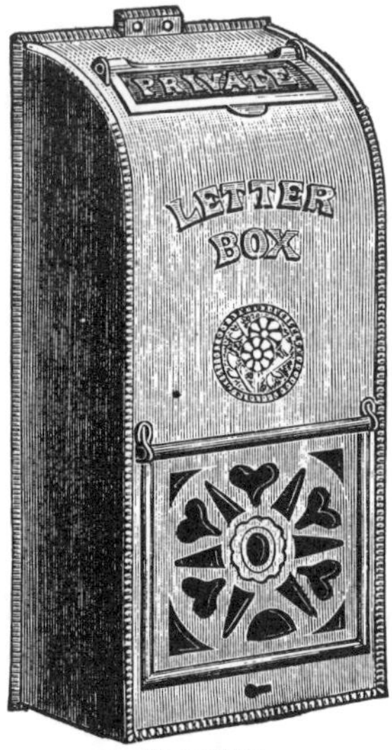

POST BOXES.

No. 4............. ......

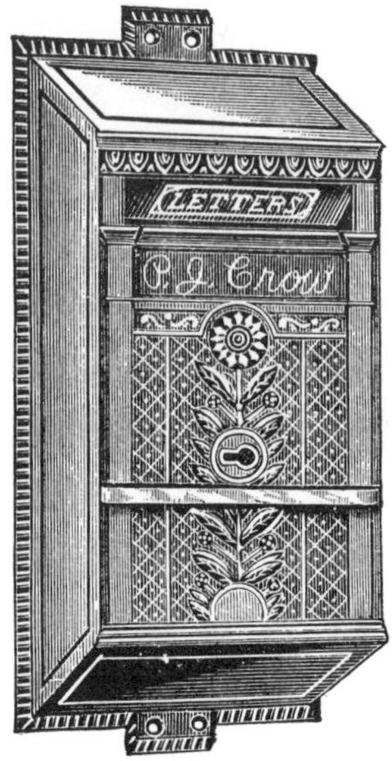

POST BOXES.

No.7.............. ......

LETTER BOX PLATES.

Berlin Bronzed.. No. 26...... 36......
Bronze Metal.. No. 29...... 39......

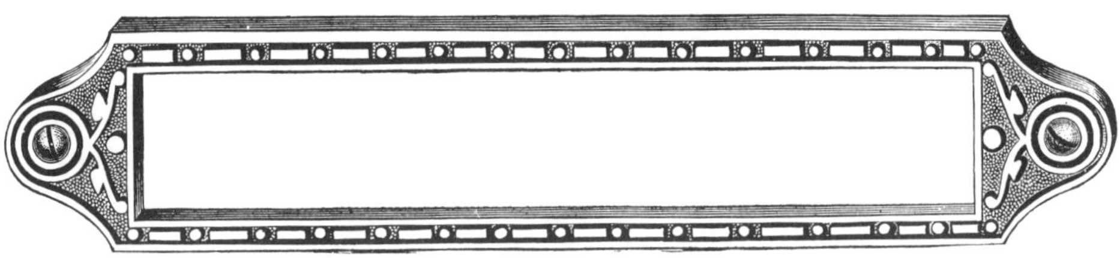

PEW NAME PLATES.

No. 3351, Berlin Bronzed, packed with screws...................................... ......
No. 2351, Bronze Metal, " " " ....

CORDAGE AND TWINES.

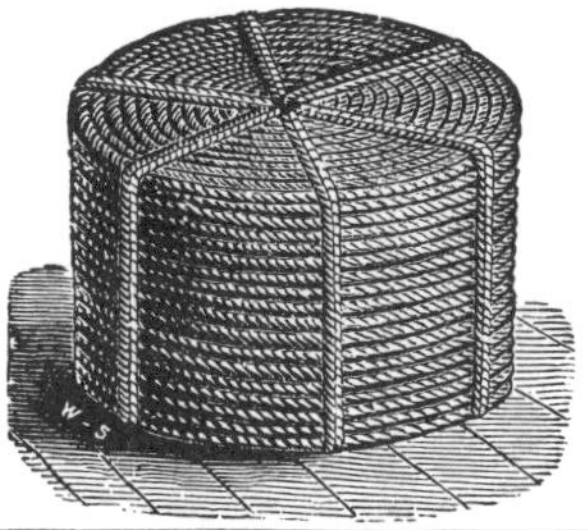

MANILLA ROPE,

½ in. diam. and upwards to 2 in.,.........per lb. ......
⅜ " " .... " ......
¼ " " and 5-16 diam .... " ......

SISAL ROPE.

½ in. diam. and upwards to 1 in.,........per lb. ......
⅜ " " .... " ......
¼ " " and 5-16 diam............... " ......

Hay Rope, 2, 3, 4 and 5 thread .... " ......
Hide Rope.......................... " ......
Lath Yarn.......................... " ......
Marline............................ " ......
Cotton Rope, 3-16.......... " ......
" " ¼ and larger.. " ......
American Hemp Sash Cord... " ......
Russia " " " .... " ......

Approximate Weight and Strength of Cordage, Manilla, Sisal, New Zealand, and Jute Ropes.
Weigh (about) alike.

Circumference in Inches.	Diam. in Inches.	No. of Feet in One Pound.	Str'g. New M'lla Rope
¾ in. 6 thr'd	1-4	43	450
1 in. 9 "	5-16	30	750
1⅛ in. 12 "	3-8	24	950
1 1-4	7-16	19	1,200
1 1-2	1-2	13 1-2	1,700
1 3-4	9-16	10	2,300
2	5-8	7 1-2	3,000
2 1-4	3-4	6	3,900
2 1-2	13-16	5	4,700
2 3-4	7-8	4	5,600
3	1	3 1-3	6,750
3 1-4	1 1-16	2 7-8	7,900
3 1-2	1 1-8	2 1-2	9,200
3 3-4	1 1-4	2 1-6	10,600
4	1 5-16	1 9-10	12,000
4 1-4	1 3-8	1 2-3	13,500
4 1-2	1 7-16	1 1-2	15,250
4 3-4	1 1-2	1 1-3	16,900
5	1 5-8	1 1-5	18,750
5 1-2	1 3-4	1	22,700
6	1 7-8	No. in. in lb.	27,000
6 1-4	2	9 3-10	29,300

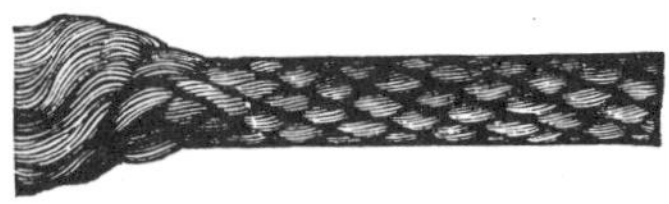

Silver Lake Braided Sash Cord.

No. 6, (3-16 in.) about 66 ft. to the lb. .....
" 7, " " 55 " " " " .....
" 8, (¼ in.) " 46 " " " " .....
" 9, " " 40 " " " " .....
" 10, (5-16 in.) " 30 " " " " .....
" 12, (⅜ in.) " 24 " " " " .....
Price of White Cotton...... ....
" " Drab " ....

TWINES.

Cotton Staging..................... ......
" Trot ....
" Bag..................... ......
" Wrapping ....
" Seine Twine, Soft.......... ......
" " " Hard......... ......
Hemp Twine, 2-ply, Fine, 2 oz.......balls
" " " " ¼ lb...... "
" " 2-ply, Med., ½ lb ..... "
" " 3-ply, " " ...... "
" " " Heavy 1 lb...... "
" Brick or Garden Lines in Hanks.....
Jute Wrapping Twine, 2 and 3-ply.. .....
" Wool Twine.................. .....
Sisal Bailing in Balls, 1 and 2-ply... .....
Flax Twine B, No. 12...... 18 ..... 24......
" Mattress, No.... 252...... 264......
" Broom Twine, in Hanks, Gray ....
" " " in Balls, " .. ...
" " " in Hanks, Red.. Blue..
" " " in Balls, " .. " ..
No. 10 H.B. Shoe Thread, 1 oz... 2 oz... balls

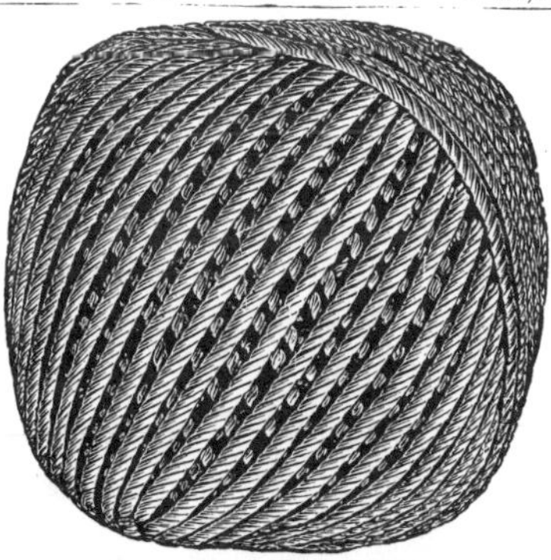

0
1
2
3

CHALK LINES.

Cotton Chalk Lines, No.12½... 13½... 14½...
In 20 Feet Hanks.

Silver Lake Braided, No. 0.. 1.... 2 .. 3....
In 20 Feet Hanks.—See Sizes in Cut.

Tarred Marline, Oakum Cotton Waste.

WIRE ROPE AND FIXTURES.

WIRE ROPE

BESSEMER STEEL—7 Wires to the Strand.

Inch	9-32	5-16	⅜	½
Breaking Strength	2.12	3.60	5.33	8.75 tons
Price Per Foot	......	......	......	......

These Ropes are best adapted for Guys, Standing Ropes, Ferries, Transmission of power, etc.

PLIABLE HOISTING ROPES—19 Wires to the Strand.

Inch	⅜	½	⅝	¾
Breaking Strength	2.15	4	5.87	9 tons
Price Per Foot	......	......	......	......

Other Sizes furnished in from two to four days after receipt of order.

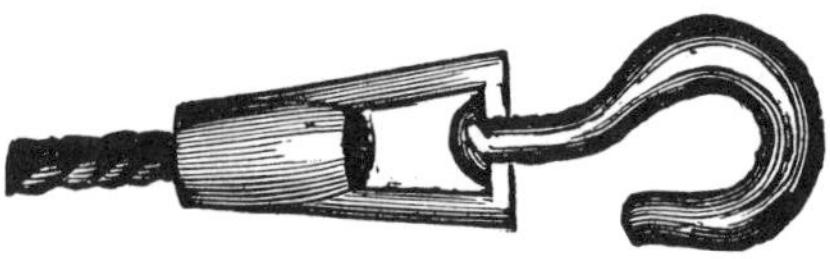

SOCKET AND SWIVEL HOOK.

For Rope, ⅜.... ½.... ⅝.... ¾ in....

CLOSED SOCKET.

For Rope, ⅜.... ½.... ⅝.... ¾ in....

WIRE ROPE CLAMPS.

For Rope, ⅜.... ½.... ⅝.... ¾ in....

OPEN SOCKET.

For Rope, ⅜.... ½ ... ⅝ ... ¾ in....

WIRE ROPE THIMBLES.

For Rope......⅜.... ½.... ⅝.... ¾ in....

WIRE ROPE SHEAVES.

Filled with Hard Rubber or Wood, Bored, Balanced and Painted.

Can furnish these Sheaves from 1½ to 12 feet in diameter.

WIRE.

SIZES AND CROSS SECTIONS OF WIRE.

These figures denote decimals of an inch.

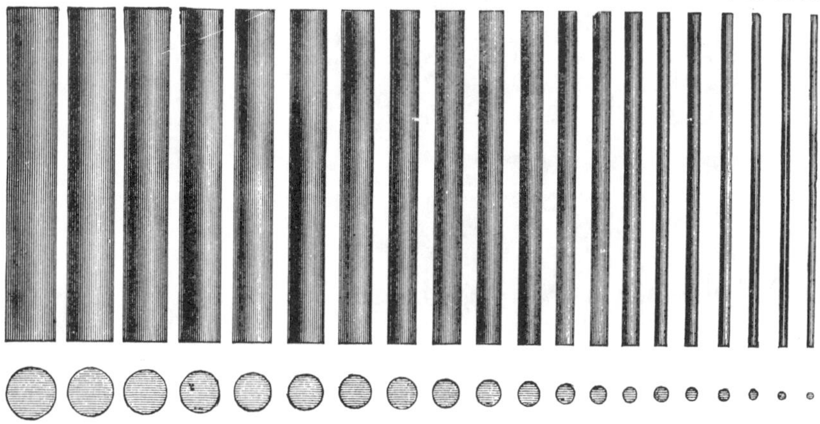

No.	Decimal of an inch	Number of feet of Iron Wire in a pound
1	.283	4.64
2	.263	5.37
3	.244	6.28
4	.225	7.45
5	.207	8.97
6	.192	10.45
7	.177	12.32
8	.162	14.73
9	.148	17.95
10	.135	22.33
11	.120	27.34
12	.105	34.21
13	.092	44 09
14	.080	58.91
15	.072	76.98
16	.063	101.48
17	.054	137.17
18	.047	186.33
19	.041	262 23
20	.035	344 82

Number of feet of Iron Wire in a pound.

BRIGHT, ANNEALED, COPPERED AND GALVANIZED WIRE.

Put up in 63 ℔. bundles.

Nos.......	0000 to 9,	10 and 11,	12, 13 and 14,	15 and 16, 17, 18.
Cts. per ℔	....	....	....	....

ANNEALED STONE OR WEAVING WIRE.

Nos........	19	20	21	22	23	24	25	26	27
Cts. per ℔....	....	....	....	....	....	....	....	....	.....
Nos........	28	29	30	31	32	33	34	35	36
Cts. per ℔....	....	....	....	....	....	....	....	....	.....

Nos. 19 to 36 put up in stones of 12 lbs. each.

TINNED WIRE.

Nos..................	0 to 10	10 to 11	12 to 14	15 to 16	17	18
Cts. per ℔...........	......	....	....	....	.....	....

TINNED BROOM WIRE.

Nos..	19 and 20	21 and 22	23 and 24
Cts per ℔................................	....	....	....

SPECIAL ANNEALED WIRES.

Steel Fence Wire, Nos. 8 and 9.... ...... Steel Baling Wire, Nos. 10 to 15..... ......

SPECIAL GALVANIZED WIRES.

Steel Fence Wire, Nos. 9.... 10.... 12.... Telephone and Telegraph, Nos. 10.... 12....

Other sizes in large quantities to special order.

We do not guarantee prices, as the iron market fluctuates. We can furnish all qualities of Wire, at best discounts ruling on day of shipment. Write for discounts when needing stock, and we will quote lowest prices.

ANNEALED STEEL WIRE.

In Quarter-pound Spools.

No.	18	20	22	24	26
Price	....	....	....	....	....

One dozen spools in a box.

Very convenient for retailing. In good shape for the customer, saves cutting small pieces from large coils—saves time.

HAIR WIRE—Small Spools.

Nos	24	26	28	30	32	34	36
Black	....	....	....	....	....	....	....
Plated	....	....	....	....	....	....	....
Brass	....	....	....	....	....	....	....

This Wire is indispensable to any miscellaneous stock of merchandise. Is used largely in making Wax and Paper Flowers.

MUSIC AND PIANO WIRE.

Smith's Patent Steel Music Wire, Nos. 8 .... 9.... 10.... 11.... 12.... French Gauge. In packages of 1 ℔ each. Used by Tile and Brick Makers.

STUB'S POLISHED ROUND STEEL WIRE.

In 1 foot lengths. Stub's Gauge.

Nos................	1 to 2	16 to 19	31 to 35.....	50 to 60 .....
Nos................	3 to 7......	20 to 25......	36 to 40......	61 to 70......
Nos................	8 to 15......	26 to 30	41 to 50......	A to Z......

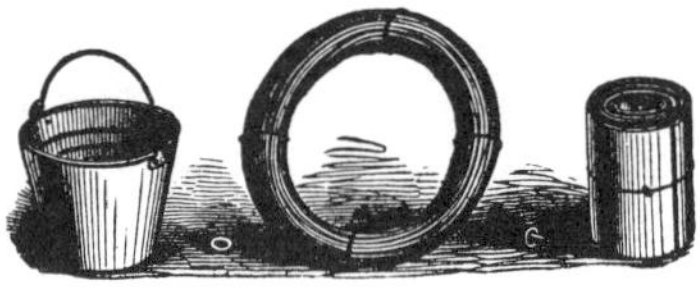

BRASS SPRING WIRE.

Nos	0 to 16	17 & 18	19 & 20	21	22	23	
Per ℔	....	....	....	....	....	....	
Nos	24	25	26	27	28	29	30
Per ℔	....	....	....	....	....	....	....

High and Low Brass Wire furnished in quantities.

COPPER WIRE.

Nos	0 to 20	21	22	23	24	25	27	28	30
Per ℔	......	......	......	......	......	......	......	......	......

ROLL AND SHEET BRASS.

Brown & Sharpe's Gauge the Standard. List January 17, 1884.

COMMON HIGH BRASS, Wider than and including.	In. 2 10	In. 10 12	In. 12 14	In. 14 16	In. 16 18	In. 18 20	In. 20 22	In. 22 24	In. 24 26	In. 26 28	In. 28 30	In. 30 32	In. 32 34	In. 34 36	In. 36 38	In. 38 40	In. 40
To No. 20 inclusive	.21	.22	.23	.25	.27	.29	.31	.33	.36	.39	.42	.46	.50	.55	.60	.65	Sp'l price not less than 80c.
Nos. 21, 22, 23 and 24 ...	.22	.23	.24	.26	.28	.30	.32	.34	.37	.40	.43	.47	.51	.56	.61	.68	
Nos. 25 and 26..........	.22½	.23½	.24½	.27	.29	.31	.33	.35	.38	.41	.44	.48	.52	.57	.63	.71	
Nos. 27 and 28..........	.23	.24	.25	.28	.30	.32	.34	.36	.39	.42	.45	.49	.53	.58	.65	.75	

Add ½c per ℔ additional on each No. thinner than Nos. 28 to 38, inclusive. Discount....
Brass thinner than No. 38 is Plater's Brass, at ....55 cents.

GERMAN SILVER.

In Sheets and Rolls. Brown & Sharpe's Gauge the Standard.

18 per cent., per ℔ .... 80 cents.

Discount...........

BRASS KETTLES.

13 in. and under, per ℔.......... ...... 14 in. and over, per ℔.......... ......

Size	7	8	9	10	11	12	13	14	15	16	17	18	19	20	21	22
Weight	1	1½	2¼	2¾	3½	4¼	5	5¾	6¾	7¾	9	10½	12	14	16½	19¾
Gallons	½	1	1½	2	2½	3	4	5	6	7½	9	10½	12	14½	17	20

COPPER KETTLES furnished in any size desired.

4 x 4 Mesh.

5 x 5 Mesh.

6 x 6 Mesh.

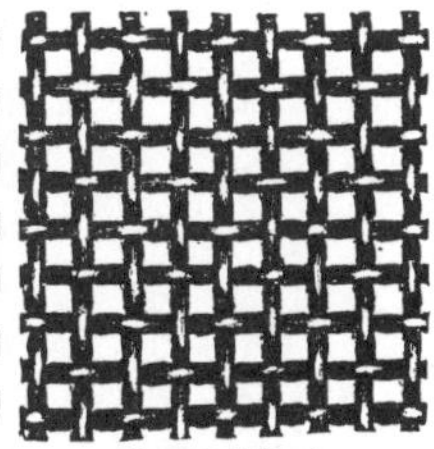
8 x 8 Mesh.

2 x 2 Mesh.

WOVE WIRE CLOTH.

Standard Hardware Grade.

Number of Mesh to the Inch.

2x2......	5x5......	10x10......	16x16......
3x3......	6x6......	12x12......	18x18......
4x4......	8x8......	14x14......	20x20......

Sold by the square foot. 36 in. wide.

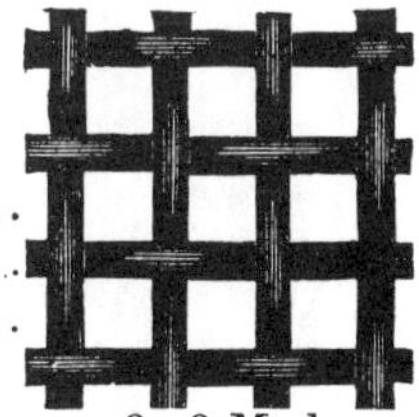
3 x 3 Mesh.

Heavy Grade.

No. of Mesh......................	2x2	3x3	4x4	5x5	6x6	
Plain Cloth......................	......	......	......	......	......	square foot.
Galvanized Cloth	......	......	......	......	......	" "

36 in. wide.

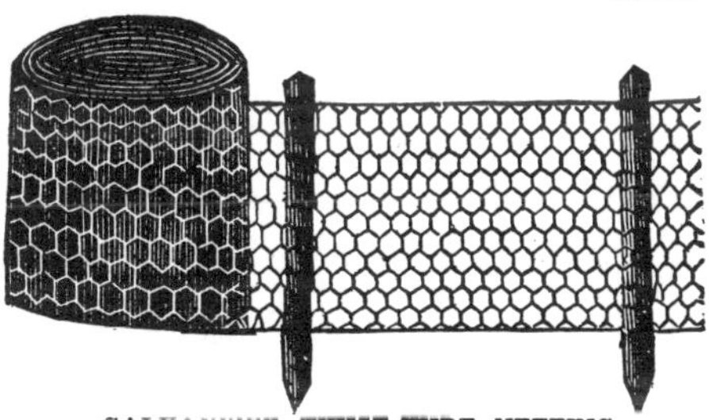

GALVANIZED TWIST WIRE NETTING.

Mesh..	½	⅝	¾	1	1¼	1½	2 in.
Square Ft.....	....	....	....	....	....	....	..

Galvanized Wire Netting is used for a great variety of purposes where an inexpensive protection is required, for Henneries, Pigeon Houses, for Drying Glue, Fruit, etc. 36 in. kept in stock.

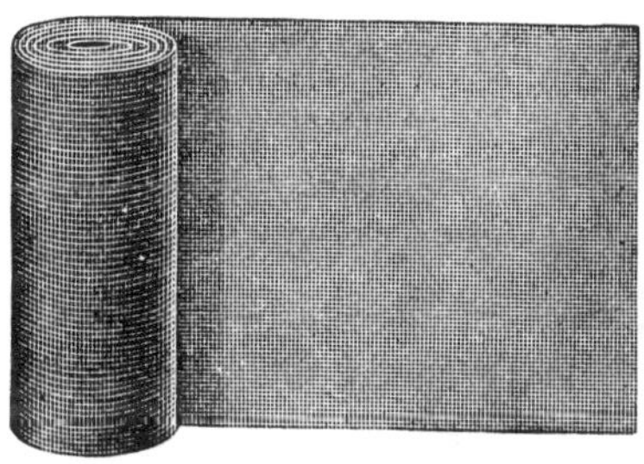

PAINTED WIRE CLOTH.

Green, Drab or Black. In 50 or 100 Feet Rolls.

24 to 48 in. Wide, per square foot.. ....

Our Wire Cloth is the Best in the market.

FIGURED WIRE CLOTH.

Per Square Foot................. ......
36 in. wide.

LANDSCAPE WIRE CLOTH.

Per Square Foot................. ......
Ordered to fit the opening.

BARB FENCE WIRE AND FENCING.

BARB FENCE WIRE.

The days of wood fencing will soon be with the past. Iron and steel are rapidly superceding. It is only within a few years that Barb Wire Fence has crept into general use. It is now well known that for economy, durability and strength, it can not be excelled. Is everlasting in its character, at less than half the cost of the less durable wood.

Strong winds do not affect them, nor snows break them down.

Prairie fires will not burn them.

They are easily and cheaply put up.

Painted ....

Galvanized ....

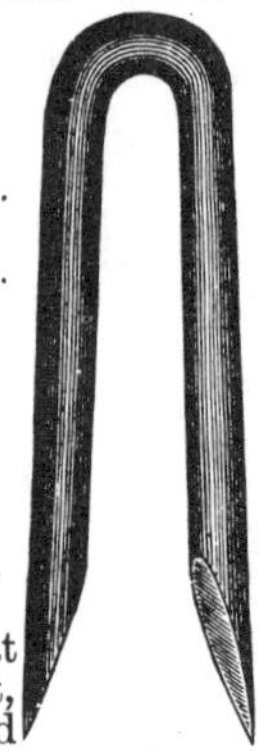

FENCE STAPLES.

Self-Color, 1¼ inch, Per ℔ ....

Galvanized, 1¼ inch, " " ....

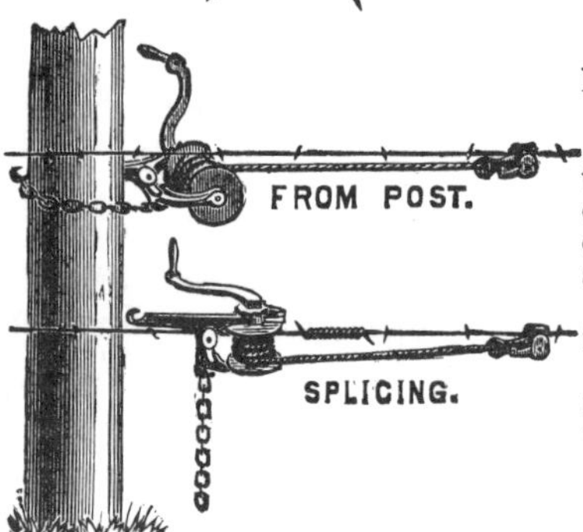

LITTLE GIANT BARB FENCE STRETCHER.

Price........................ ......

This is the only stretcher made that the latch will adjust itself to the ratchet, either side of the post or at either end of the wire, or either side up. Used for stretching and splicing.

For raising hogs, cattle or any other weight it is indispensable.

This stretcher being fastened to the post, it is not necessary to hold it up with one hand and undertake to turn the windlass with the other.

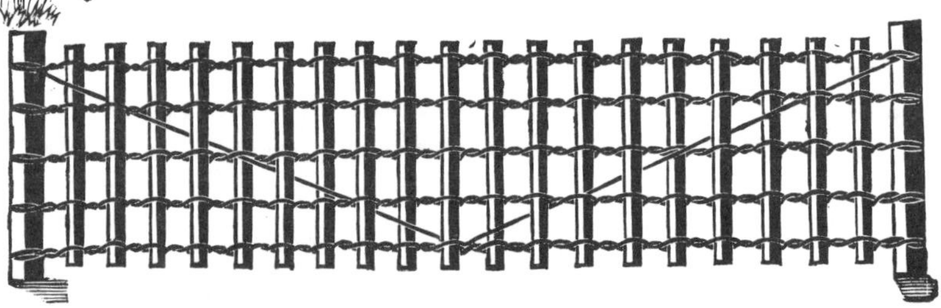

SHELLABERGER FENCE.

Light, Strong, Durable, Cheap. Perfectly Tight. Visible as Plank.

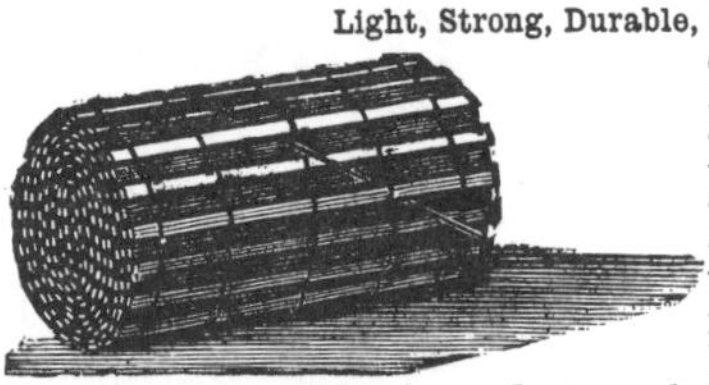

The above cut represents the combination fence, composed of five two-strand cables of the best annealed Bessemer steel wire, firmly interwoven with slats at a uniform distance of 2½ to 3 inches apart; the slats are of first quality; thus we have a fence that will turn all kinds of stock, from the smallest pig to the meanest mule, without endangering the life of any. It is five times as strong as barb wire, will last as long, visible as plank, and at much less expense.

Price, per rod.. ......

PAD-LOCKS.

R. R. SWITCH-LOCKS.
No. 85, Brass . . . .

No. 44, Brass . . . .
No. 55, Nickel Plated, ...

No. 42, Brass . . . .
No. 53, Nickel Plated, ...

CAST BRONZE METAL SPRING PAD-LOCKS.

Brass Keys . . . . No. A, 1 in . . . . . . 70, $1\frac{1}{8}$ in . . . . . 72, $1\frac{1}{2}$ in . . . . . .
Flat Steel Keys . . . . No. 072, $1\frac{1}{2}$ in . . . . . . 073, $1\frac{3}{4}$ in . . . . . .

CAST BRONZE METAL SPRING PAD-LOCKS—With Chain.

Brass Keys. . . . . No. 77, 2 in . . . . . . No. 81, $2\frac{1}{4}$ in . . . . . .

SCANDINAVIAN PAD-LOCKS.

Malleable Iron, painted Red, 2 keys, No. 860 . . . . . . 861 . . . . . 862 . . . . . .

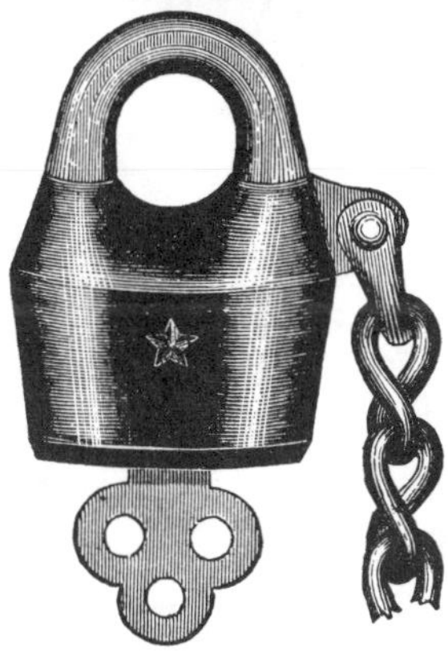

SCANDINAVIAN PAD-LOCKS.

Two flat steel Keys to each Lock. Shackle secured to the Lock-box.

Without Chain.

No. . .	224	225	226	227	228
Inch .	$1\frac{1}{2}$	2	$2\frac{1}{2}$	3	$3\frac{3}{4}$
	. . .	. . . .	. . . .	. . . .	. . . .

With Chain.

No.	224½	225½	226½	227½
Inch . . .	$1\frac{1}{2}$	2	$2\frac{1}{2}$	3
	. . . .	. . . .	. . . .	. . . .

See Dog Collar Locks, page 201.

VAJEN & NEW, INDIANAPOLIS, IND.

PAD-LOCKS.

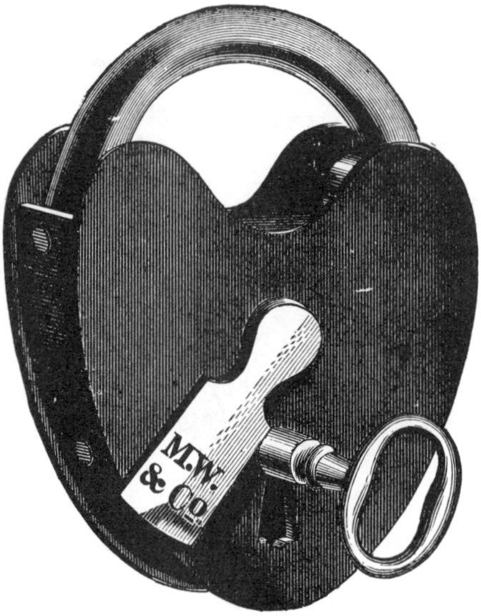

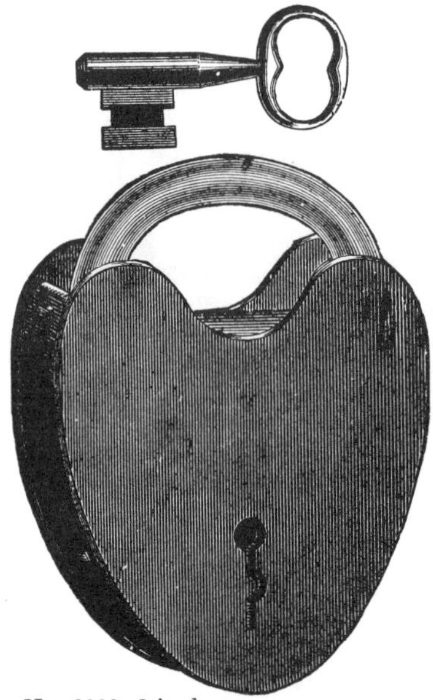

No. 00, 2¼ inch, Brass Drop............ .....
No. 1, 2½ inch. " " ... .
No. 16, 2¼ inch, Brass Drop, with Chain .....

No. 0000, 2 inch ....
No. 000, 2¼ inch........ ......

FLAT STEEL KEYED PAD-LOCKS.

No. 1029, 2¼ in., Brass Drop and Bushing, 1 key...... 2 keys......
No. 1030, 2½ in., Brass Drop and Bushing, 1 key .... 2 keys......
No. 1033, 2½ in., Brass Bushing, Double Bit Key....... ...1 key...... 2 keys......
No. 1058, 2½ in, Brass Bushing, Wide Bit Key..............1 key ..... 2 keys......

With Chain.

No. 1032, 2½ in., Engraved Drop, Brass Bushing..........1 key... .. 2 keys......
No. 1060, 2¼ in., Brass Drop and Bushing, ...1 key...... 2 keys......

SELF-LOCKING PAD-LOCKS.

No. 1047, 2½ in., Brass Drop and Bush, Double Bit Key ...1 key.... 2 keys ..
No. 1048, 2½ in., Brass Drop 1 key ... 2 keys....
No. 1050, 2½ in., Brass Drop and Bushing..1 key.... 2 keys....................

With Flat Steel Keys.

No. 1052, 2¼ in., Brass Drop and Bushing..1 key ... 2 keys....................

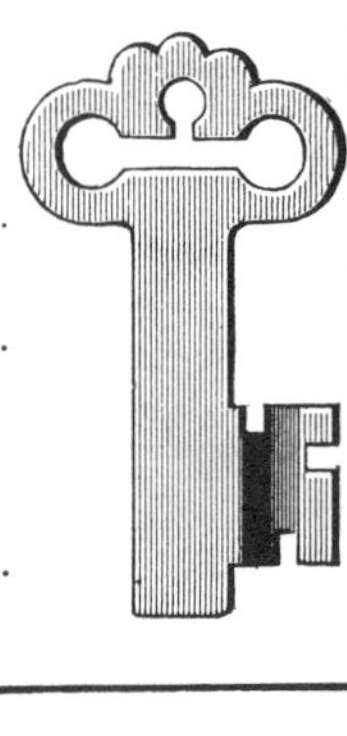

No. 1052.

CHAIN.

JACK CHAIN.

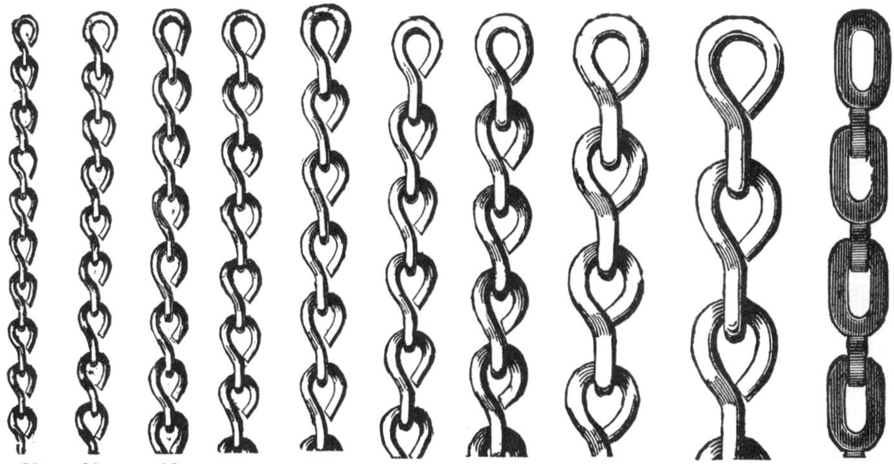

No. 22 20 18 17 16 15 14 12 10 No. 2 Safety.

No.	8	9	10	11	12	13	14	15	16	17	18	19	20	21	22	24
Iron	....	....	....	....	....	....	....	....	....	....	....	....	....	....	....	....
Brass	....	....	....	....	....	....	....	....	....	....	....	....	....	....	....	....

Brass Safety, No.....................3-0...... 2-0...... 0...... 1...... 2...... 3......

Sash Chain, Heavy.................. ...... Light........................... ....

HALTER CHAINS.

No. 4-0..... 3-0..... 2-0..... 0..... 1..... 2..... 3..... 4..... 5..... 6 ..... 7....

COW TIES—Ohio Pattern.

No. 4-0 ....
" 3-0.......... ......
" 2-0.......... ......
" 0............ ......

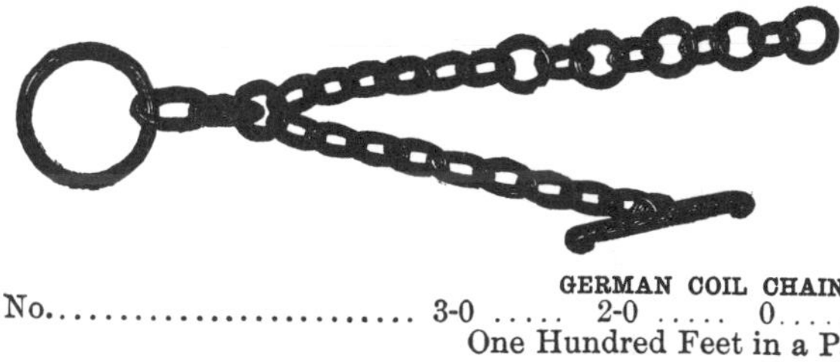

CLOSED RING.

No. 4-0........................ ......
" 3-0........................ ......
" 2-0........................ ......
" 0........................ ......

GERMAN COIL CHAIN.

No........................ 3-0 ..... 2-0 ..... 0..... 1...... 2...... 3...... 4......

One Hundred Feet in a Package.

CHAINS.

Until recently we have depended almost entirely upon the manufacturers in Europe for this class of goods. We are happy to state, that the large sums of money annually sent, from our shores in the payment for the same, is rapidly decreasing. Our own capital and labor having recently been largely invested in this branch of Manufacture, producing chains superior in every respect to those of foreign make.

CHAIN AND METALS.

COIL CHAIN—Black or Self Color.

	3-16	¼	5-16	⅜	7-16	½	⅝	¾ Inch
Weight of 1 foot.....	0.325	0.650	0.967	1.383	1.767	2.633	4.217	5.75
Breaking Weight....	2240	4256	6720	9634	13216	17248	26880	38752
Price per lb......	......	......	......	......	......	......	......	......

TOOL STEEL—Round, Square or Octagon.

¼ 5-16 ⅜ ½ ⅝ ¾ ⅞ 1 in ....Per lb. ......

BRASS KEY TAGS.

Round and Octagon.

Price ....

Large Size, Scolloped, for Hotels.

Price ....

Baggage Checks in Several Styles.

The above Lettered or Numbered to Order.

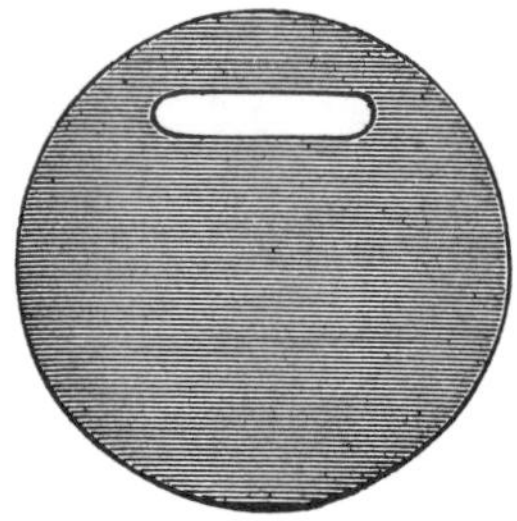

GALVANIZED WIRE CLOTHES LINES.

No. 19........... ...... 20............ ......

100 Feet in a Coil.

SOLDER.

No. 1 Refined.................. ...... Half and Half.................. ......

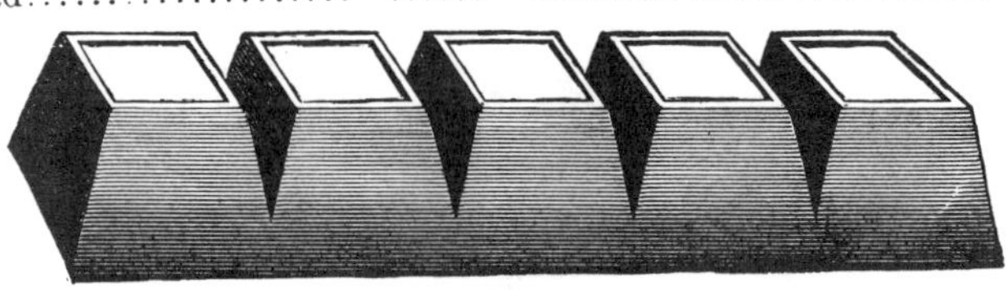

BABBIT METAL.

No. 4...... 3...... 2...... 1...... Crescent...... Extra...... Genuine......

BAR LEAD.

3 Bars to the Pound.. ......

PULLEYS.

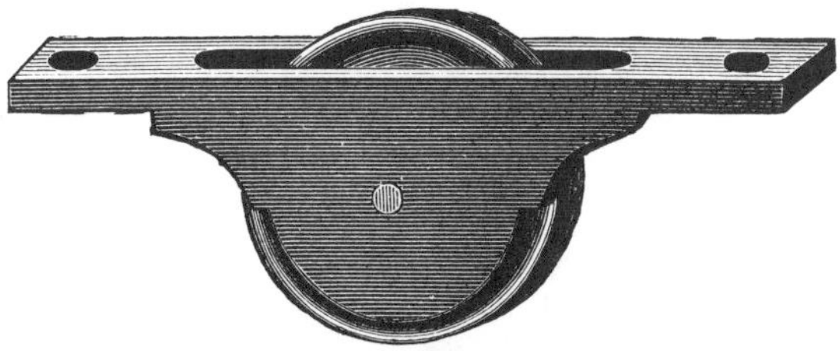

DUMB WAITER PULLEYS.

No. 40, 3 Inch, Heavy, Iron Wheel (4 in a set).......................... Per set.....

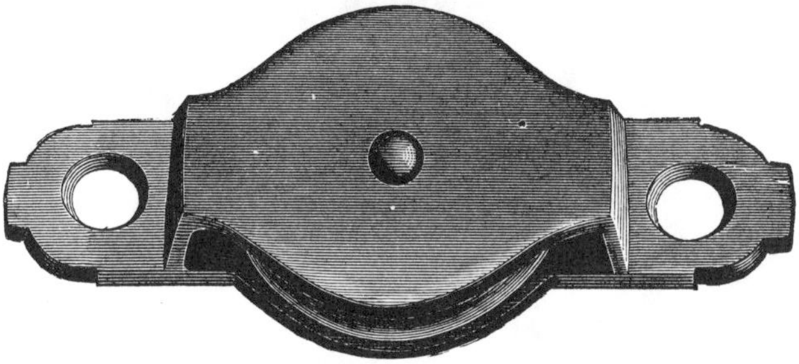

SIDE PULLEYS.

No. 25, Japanned........ 1½...... 1¾..... 2...... 2¼...... 2½...... 3 in......

SCREW PULLEYS.

Sizes	1½	1¾	2	2¼	2½	3 in.
No. 45, Single	......	......	......	......	......	......
No. 47, Double	......	......	......	......	......	......

No. 55, Upright .... 1¾..... 2 in......

No. 75, Awning Pulleys, Single .... 2..... 2½ ..... 3 in......

No. 77, " " Double........................ 2 ..... 2½...... 3 in......

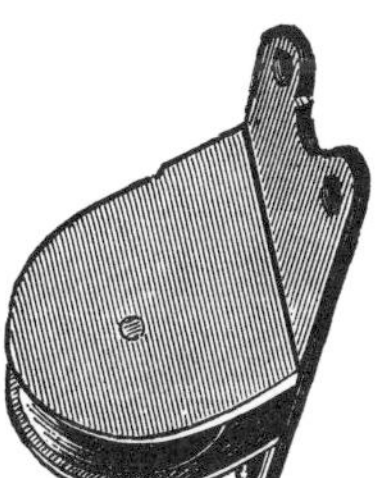

HOT HOUSE PULLEYS.

Inch	1¾	2	2¼
No. 85, Single	......	......	......
No. 87, Double	......	......	......

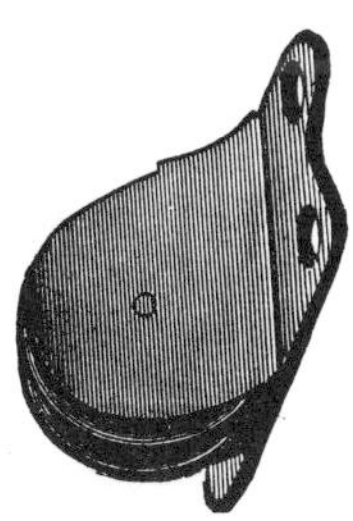

CLOTHES LINE PULLEYS,

No. 68, Jointed, with Cam. Fastening...... ......

PULLEYS AND TACKLE BLOCKS.

WELL WHEELS.

8........ 10........ 12 in........

Extra Heavy.

12 .... 16........ 20 in........

HAY FORK PULLEYS.

6 Inch, Swivel Eye, Japanned.

Iron Wheel, ... Wood Wheel, ...

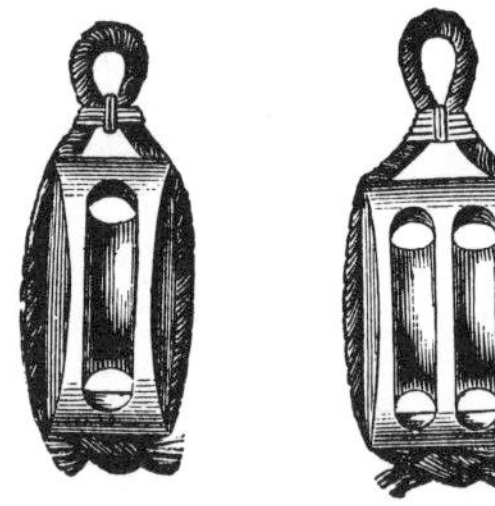

INSIDE IRON STRAPPED BLOCKS.

Size.	For Rope.	Single.	Double.	Snatch Blocks.
4 in.	½ in.	......	......	......
5 in.	⅝ in.	......	......	......
6 in.	¾ in.	......	......	......
7 in.	⅞ in.	......	......	......
8 in.	1 in.	......	......	......
9 in.	1 in.	......	......	......
10 in.	1⅛ in.	......	......	......

ROPE STRAPPED AWNING BLOCKS.

Single ...... Double ......

GALVANIZED IRON AWNING PULLEYS.

Single. ¾ .... 1 ..... 1¼ in .....

Double. ¾ ..... 1...... 1¼ in......

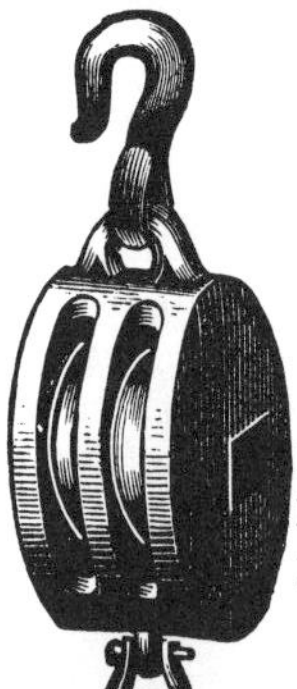

HEAVY, THICK MORTISE BLOCKS.

Size.	For Rope.	Single.	Double.
6 in	⅞ in.	......	......
7 in	1 in.	......	......
8 in	1⅛ in.	......	......
9 in	1¼ in.	......	......
10 in	1⅜ in.	......	......
11 in	1⅜ in.	......	......
12 in	1½ in.	......	......

WESTON'S "DIRECT" DIFFERENTIAL PULLEY BLOCKS.

Capacity.	Lift.		
⅛ ton	5 ft.	....	......
¼ ton	6 ft.	....	.....
½ ton	7 ft.	....	......
1 ton	8 ft.	....	......
1½ ton	8½ ft.	....	......
2 ton	9 ft.	....	......

Extra length chain furnished to order. One man can lift 1000 ℔. They hold the load at any point and can not run down.

SCYTHES, SNATHS AND CORN KNIVES.

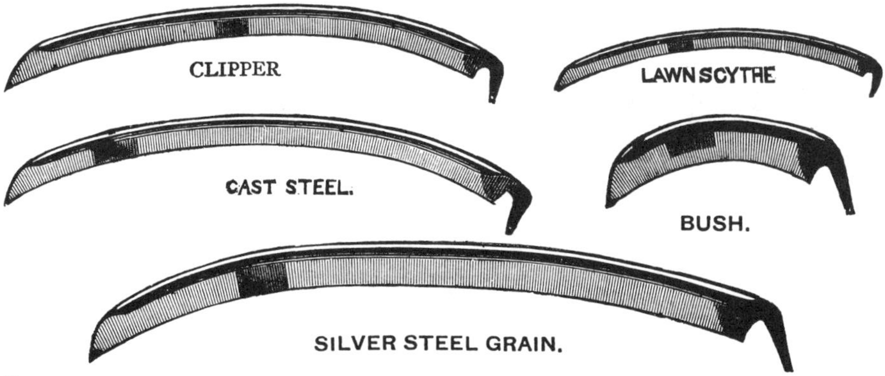

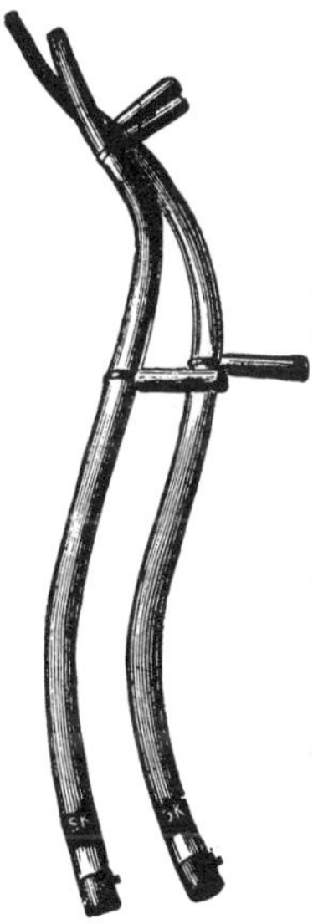

SCYTHES.—Assorted Lengths.

Clipper Grass, Full Polished, Bronzed Back, Sharp and Boxed. ......
Clipper Lawn, " " " " " " ......
Clipper Grain, " " " " " " ......
Cast Steel Grass, Edges, " Painted " In Straw......... ......
Cast Steel Lawn " " " " " ....
Rail Road, " " " " " ....
Weed, " " " " " ....
Bush, " " " " " ....

SCYTHE SNATHS.

No. 2, Screw Nib, Iron Ferrules on Nib.................... ......
No. 00, Adjustable Patent Loop, Iron Ferrules on Nib........ ......
Bush, Double Ring, " " " ....
Bush, Adjustable Patent Loop, " " " ....

GRAIN CRADLES.—In the White or Painted.

Turkey Wing, Complete, with Silver Steel Scythes............ ......

Other styles and shapes furnished to order.

GRAIN CRADLE FINGERS.

In the White Wood.. ......
Painted.. ......

CLIPPER CORN KNIVES.

Bronzed and Sharpened for Use.................................. ......

This Knife is heavy and well made.

VAJEN & NEW, INDIANAPOLIS, IND.

RAKES AND GRASS HOOKS.

HANDLED SOCKET MALLEABLE IRON RAKES.

Best quality Malleable Iron and finished Ash Handles.

No. of Teeth .... 10...... 12 ..... 14...... 16 .....

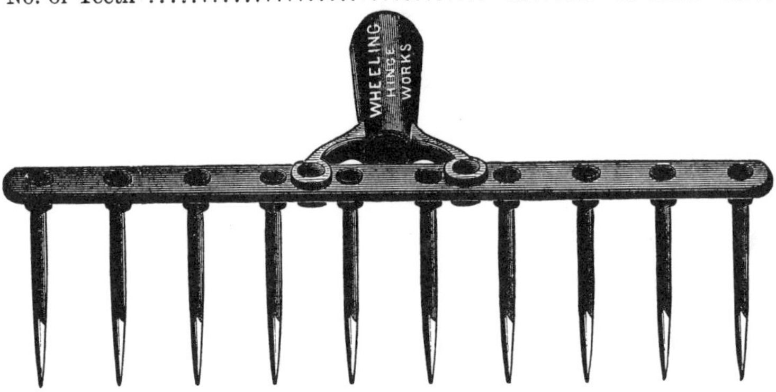

HANDLED WROUGHT STEEL RAKES.

Socket Handle, Steel Head and Teeth, Polished Points, with Polished Ash Handles. Lighter than wrought iron, and much stronger.

No. of Teeth.................. 10...... 12...... 14...... 16......

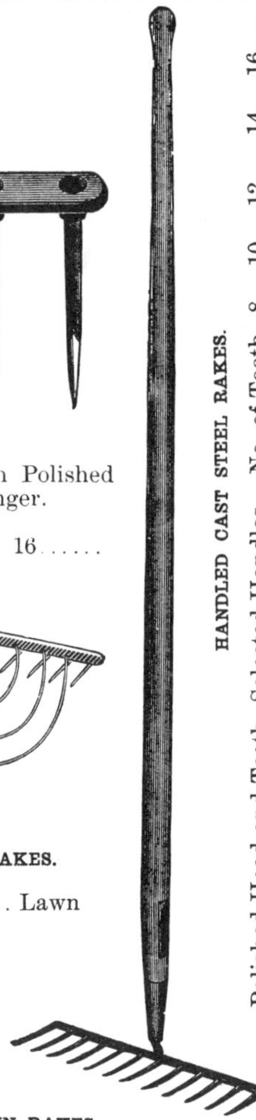

HANDLED CAST STEEL RAKES.

Polished Head and Teeth, Selected Handles. No. of Teeth, 8 . . 10 . . 12 . . 14 . . 16. . .

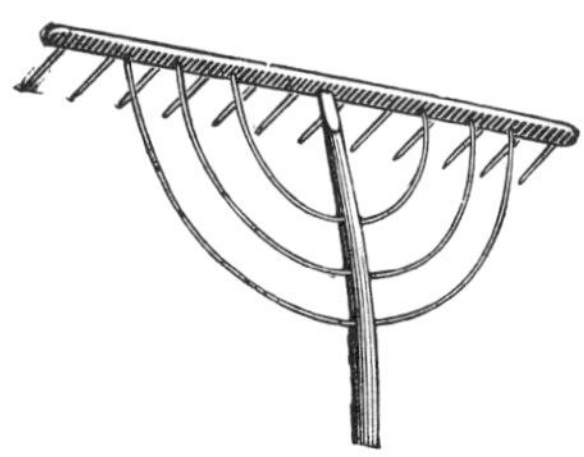

WOOD HAY RAKES.

Teeth, 8 ... 10... Lawn

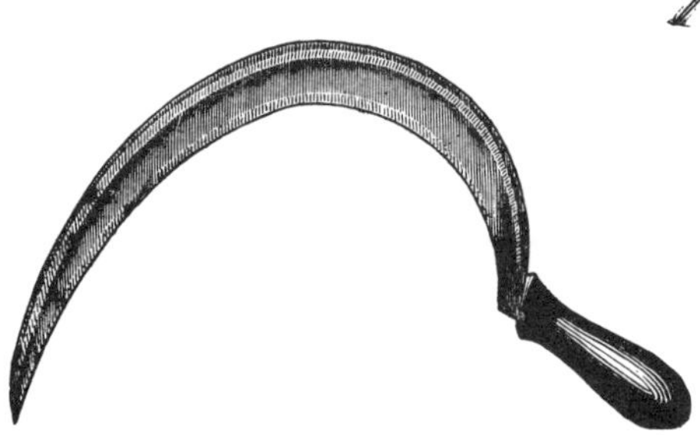

GRASS HOOKS.

Nos................1...... 2...... 3.....

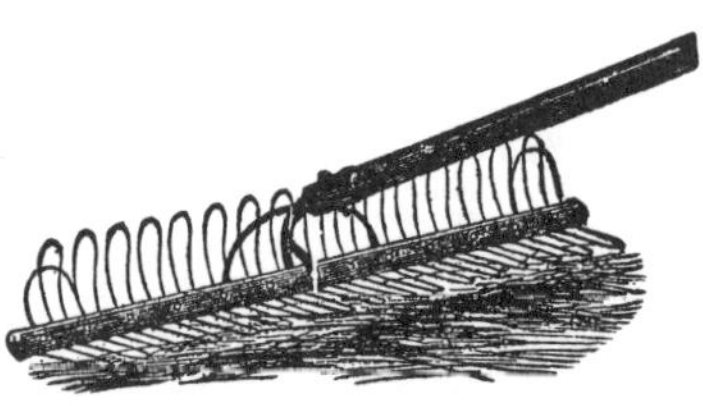

DAVIS LAWN RAKES.

Does not injure the grass. A backward push cleans the teeth from leaves or rubbish .....

HAY AND MANURE FORKS.

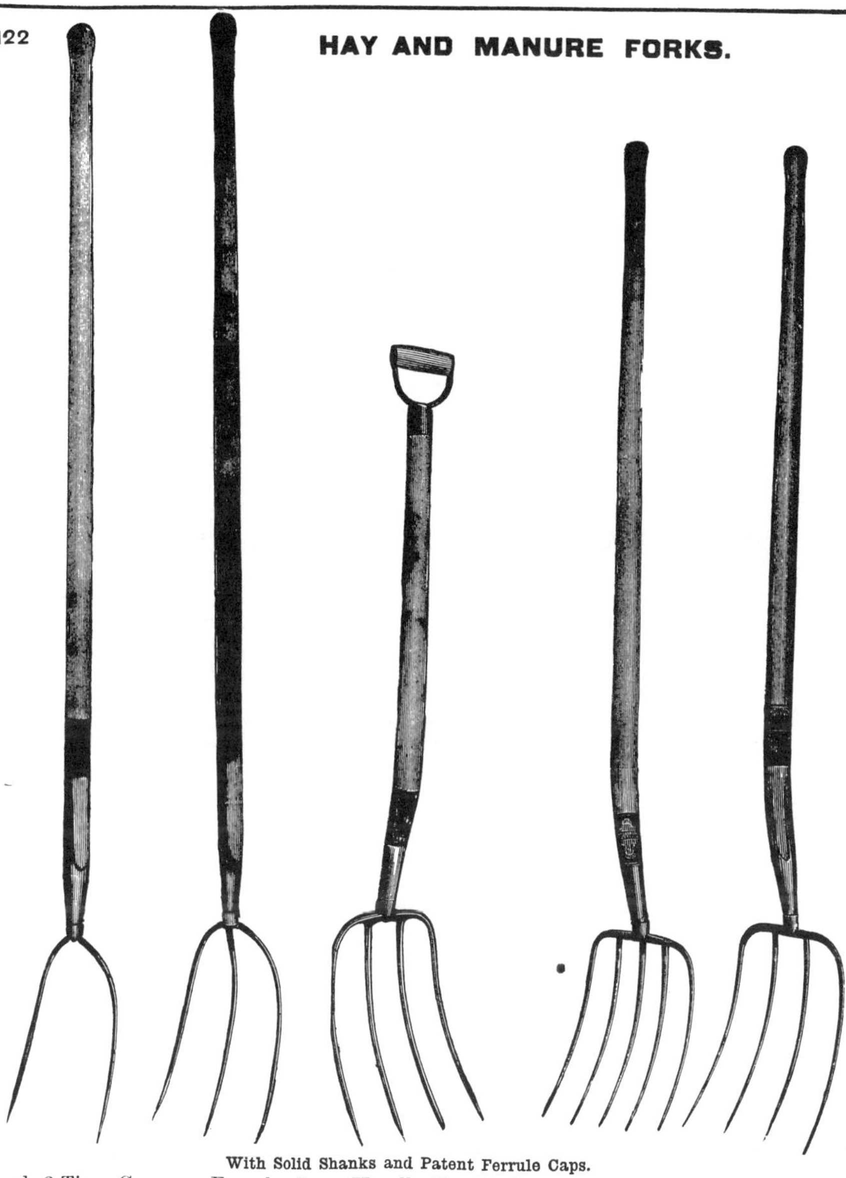

With Solid Shanks and Patent Ferrule Caps.

Oval,	2	Tine,	Common	Ferrule,	Long		Handle	Hay	Forks
"	2	"	Strap	"	"		"	"	
"	3	"	Common	"	"		"	"	
"	3	"	Strap	"	"		"	"	
"	4	"	Common	"	Long,	Bent	Handle	Manure	Forks
"	4	"	Strap	"	"	"	"	"	"
"	4	"	Common	"	"D"		"	"	"
"	4	"	Strap	"	"		"	"	"
"	5	"	Strap	"	Long		"	"	"
"	5	"	"	"	"D"		"	"	"
"	6	"	"	"	Long		"	"	"
"	6	"	"	"	"D"		"	"	"

Above Goods are first quality and bronzed finished, with first quality selected handles. Hay Forks, with handles, not exceeding 6 feet, one price. Longer handles, additional price.

FORKS, HOOKS AND HOES.

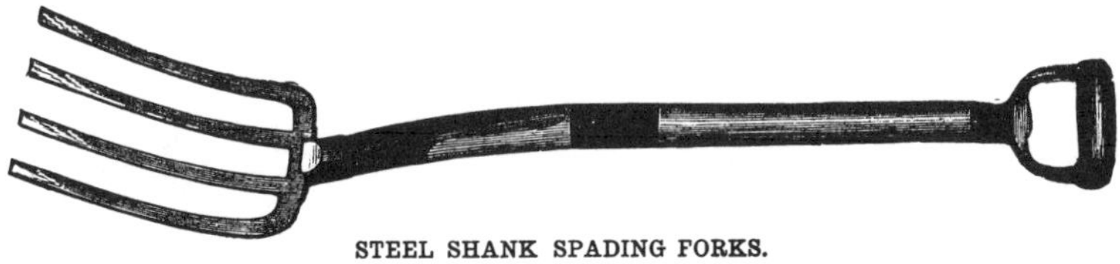

STEEL SHANK SPADING FORKS.

Heavy Angular, 4 Tine, "D" Handle, Common Ferule ....
" " " " " " Strap " ....

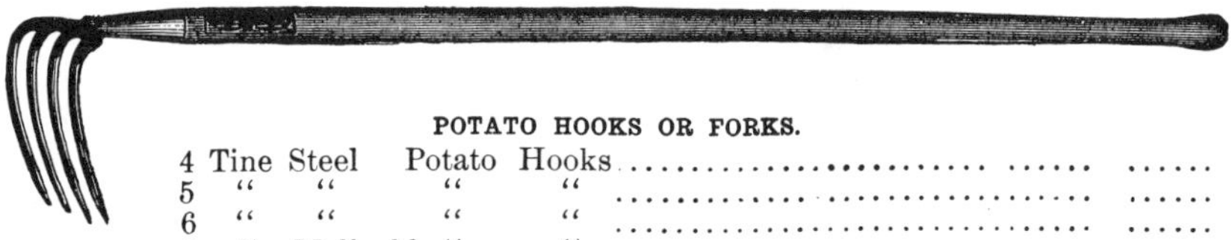

POTATO HOOKS OR FORKS.

4 Tine Steel Potato Hooks ....
5 " " " " ....
6 " " " " ....
4 " Malleable " " ....
5 " " " " ....

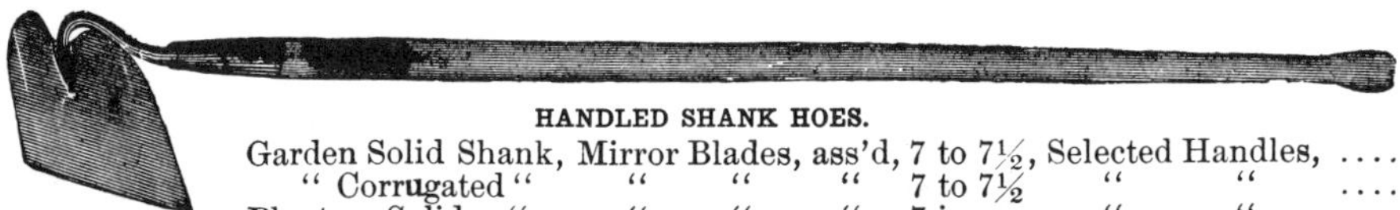

HANDLED SHANK HOES.

Garden Solid Shank, Mirror Blades, ass'd, 7 to 7½, Selected Handles, ...
" Corrugated " " " " 7 to 7½ " " ....
Planters Solid " " " " 7 in. " " ....
" " " " " " 7½ in. " " ....
Street Commissioners' Solid Shank " " " 12 in. " " ....

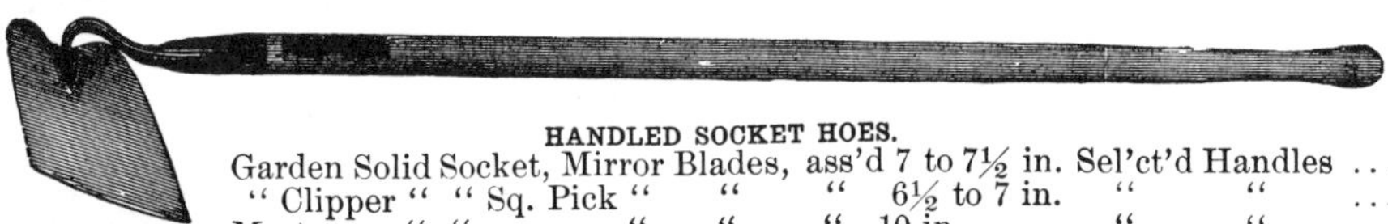

HANDLED SOCKET HOES.

Garden Solid Socket, Mirror Blades, ass'd 7 to 7½ in. Sel'ct'd Handles ....
" Clipper " " Sq. Pick " " " 6½ to 7 in. " " ....
Morter " " " " " 10 in. " " ....

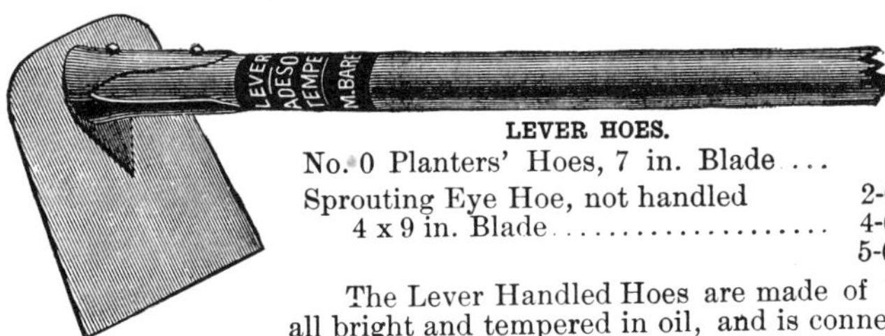

LEVER HOES.

No. 0 Planters' Hoes, 7 in. Blade ...
Sprouting Eye Hoe, not handled
4 x 9 in. Blade ....

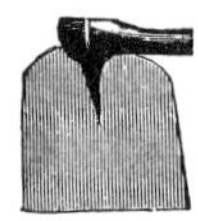

German Handled Hoes.

2-0—6½ in. Polish'd Blade . .
4-0—6 in. " " . .
5-0—5 in. " " . .

The Lever Handled Hoes are made of best crucible steel, blade all bright and tempered in oil, and is connected to the handle by two malleable iron ferules. When the bolt is withdrawn, as shown above, the ferules, working on the fulcrum surface, expand in the blade which is securely held by two hooking lugs, hooking through it.

LEVER GARDEN OR WEED HOES.

2 Prong ....
1 Broad Point ....

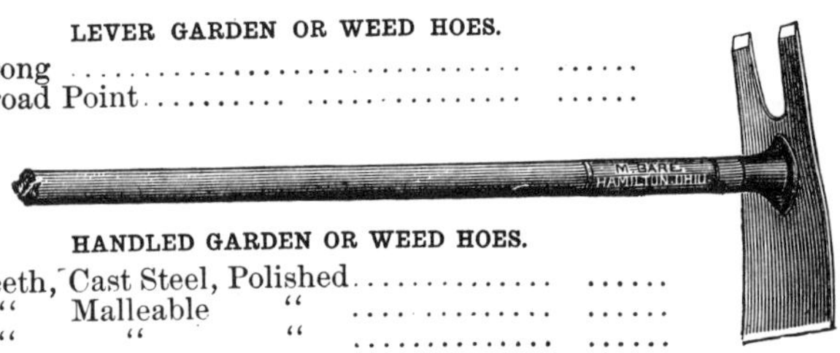

HANDLED GARDEN OR WEED HOES.

4 Teeth, Cast Steel, Polished ....
4 " Malleable " ....
6 " " " ....
6 " " " ....
Round Point, Malleable Shank, Polished Steel Blade, ...
Square " " " " " " ......
Two Prong " " " " " ......

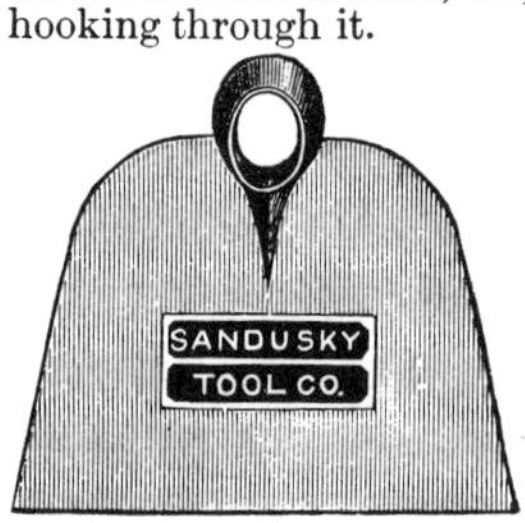

Planters Cast Steel Hoes Half Bright.

No.	00.	0.	1.	2.	3.
	...	...	...	...	...

VAJEN & NEW, INDIANAPOLIS, IND.

SHOVELS, SPADES AND SCOOPS.

VAJEN & NEW, INDIANAPOLIS, IND.

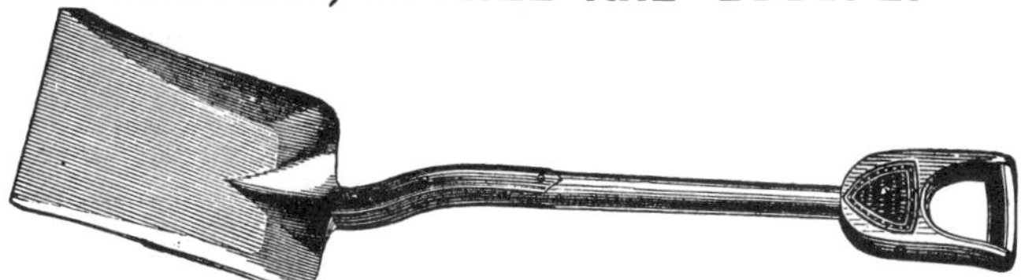

D Handle Shovels, Square Point, Solid Cast Steel, Polished, No. 2 3 4 5 6 7

D " " " " " " " Chisholm's No. 2..........
D " " Round " " " " Polished No. 2............
D " " Square " Steel Edge Black, No. 2 3 4 5 6 7 8 9 10 12

D " " " " Iron Back Strap, Polished No. 2............
D " " " " " " " " Boys'............
D " Coal " " " Solid Cast Steel, ½ " No. 2............
Long Handled Shovels" " " " " " " 2............
" " " Round Point " " " " " 2............
" " " " " Iron Back Strap, " " 2............

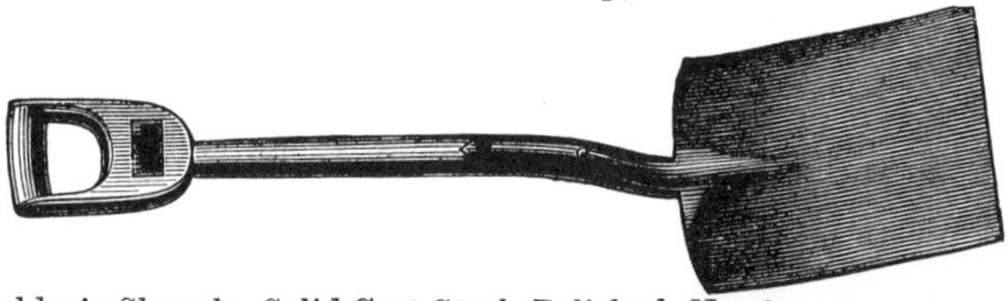

D Handle Molder's Shovels, Solid Cast Steel, Polished, No. 2..................

D Handle Spades, Solid Cast Steel, Polished, No. 2..........................
D " " Back Strap Iron, " " 2..........................
D " " " " " " Boys..........................
D " " Chisholm's " No. 2..........................
Long " " Solid Cast Steel, Square Point, Polished, No. 2 ....

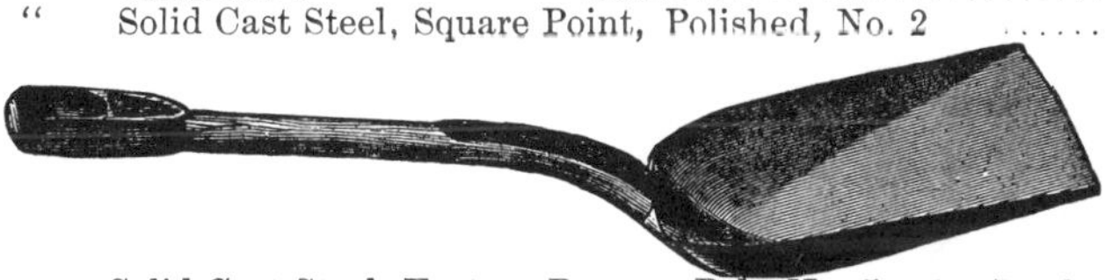

D Handle Scoops, Solid Cast Steel, Eastern Pattern, Pol., No. 5 6 7 8 9 10 12

D " " " " " Western " " No. 1.... 2.... 3.... 4 .. 5....
D " " " Iron " " " No. 1.... 2.... 3... 4 ... 5....
D " Furnace Scoops, Solid Cast Steel, " No. 2................
Half Polished Scoops—50 cts. per doz. less on List Price. Large Saw Dust Scoops.....

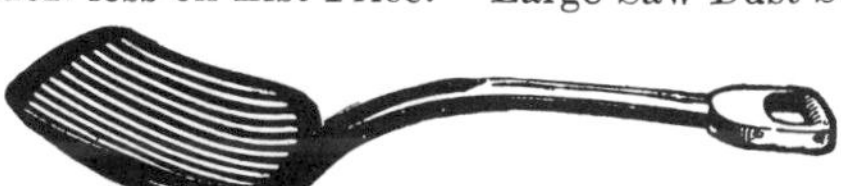

Mal. Iron Screening Scoop, one size.....

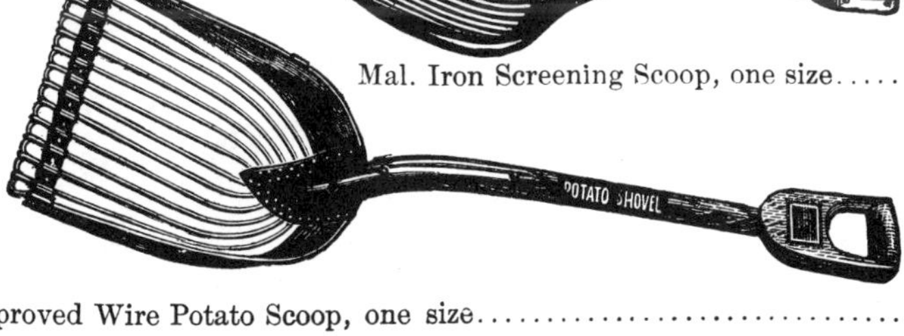

Patent Improved Wire Potato Scoop, one size..............................

TILE SPADES AND DITCHING TOOLS.

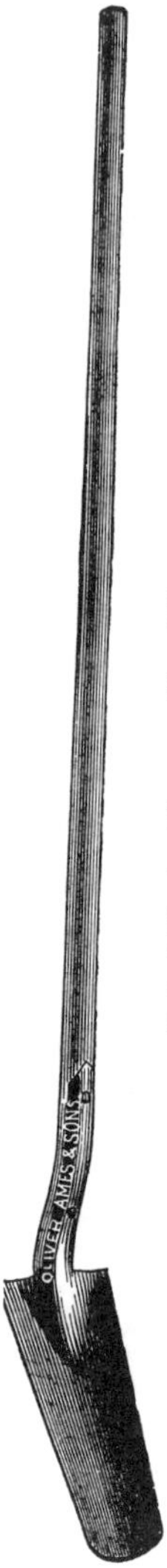

Cut of Drain Cleaner, No. 842.

Cut of Drain Spade, No. 93.

Cut of Drain Spade, No. 92.

Cut of Drain Spade, No. 91.

Cut of Ditching Spade, No. 181.

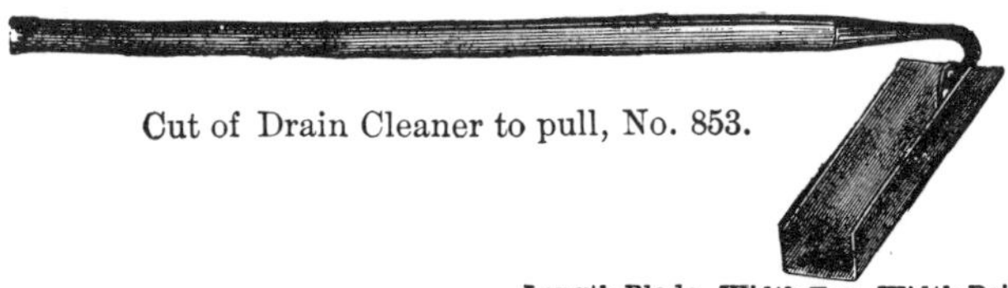

Cut of Drain Cleaner to pull, No. 853.

				Length Blade.	Width Top.	Width Point.	
Drain Spades,	No. 93,	Black	....	18 in.	4½ in.	3 in.	......
" "	No. 92,	"	....	17 in.	4½ in.	3 in.	......
" "	No. 91,	"	....	17 in.	5½ in.	4½ in.	......
Ditching "	No. 181,	"	....	14 in.	5¾ in.	6½ in.	......
" "	No. 181,	"	....	16 in.	5¾ in.	6½ in.	......
Post "	No. 173,	"	....	15 in.	5¾ in.	6½ in.	......
" "	No. 173,	"	....	16 in.	5¾ in.	6½ in.	......
" "	No. 173,	"	....	18 in.	5¾ in.	6½ in.	......

Drain Cleaners, No. 842, Flat, to push, 6½ in. at shoulder, 5 in. at point...
" " No. 853, Square, to pull, 4½ in. wide ....
" " No. 861, Round, to push and pull, 4½ in. wide.... ......

Post Spades are slightly more concave than the so-called Ditching Spades, and are in much greater demand for ditching purposes.

No. 121, Chisholm's 18-in. Ditching Spade. The Strap and Blade are made from one solid piece of sheet steel. Polished........ ....

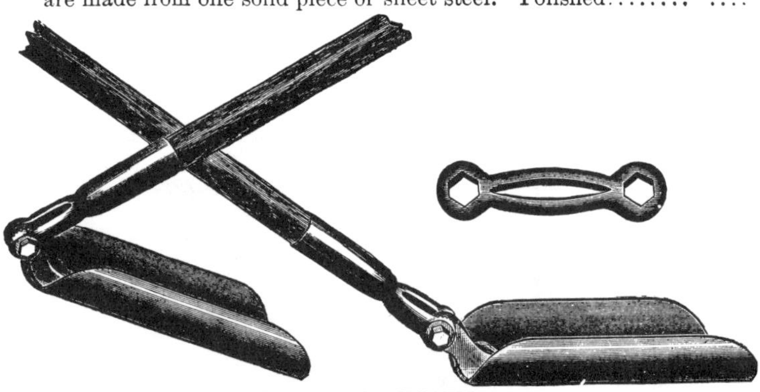

ADJUSTABLE HANDLE TILE CLEANER.

No. 2, 4 in. Wide............... ...... No. 3, 5 in. Wide............... ......

SHOVELS, SCOOPS AND HANDLES.

CHISHOLM'S STEEL SHOVELS AND SCOOPS.
The Srongest and Most Durable.

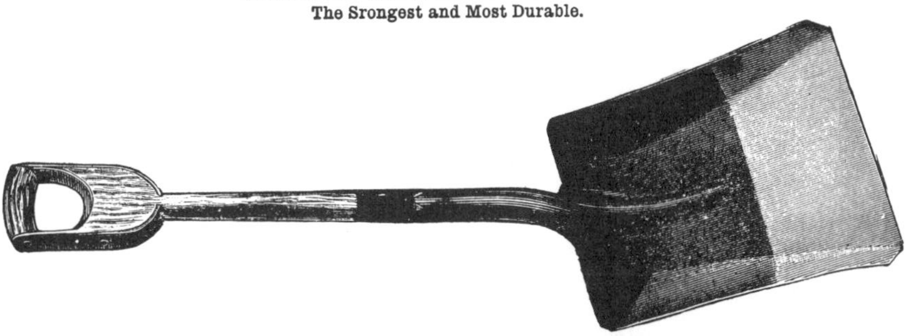

Coal Shovels, Solid Cast Steel.........................Nos. 1...... 2...... 3......

Scoop Shovels, Solid Cast Steel.......Nos. 4...... 5..... 6...... 7...... 8......

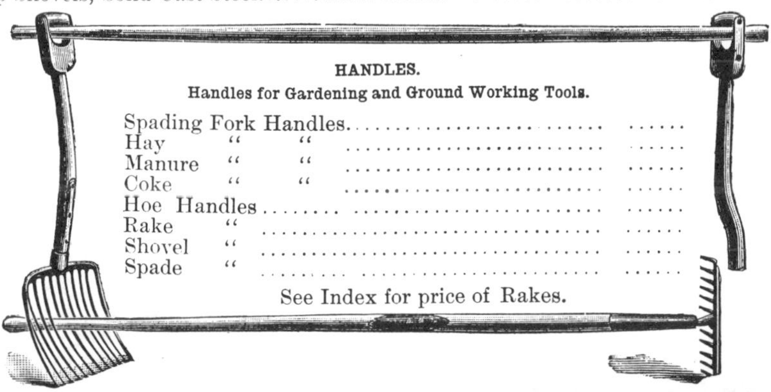

HANDLES.

Handles for Gardening and Ground Working Tools.

Spading Fork Handles	....	......
Hay " "	....	......
Manure " "	....	......
Coke " "	....	......
Hoe Handles	....	......
Rake "	....	......
Shovel "	....	......
Spade "	....	......

See Index for price of Rakes.

COKE FORKS.—Solid.

For Coke and Coal.

Diamond D Handle,

Tines 10 . . .. 12 ......

FIELD AND LAWN ROLLER.

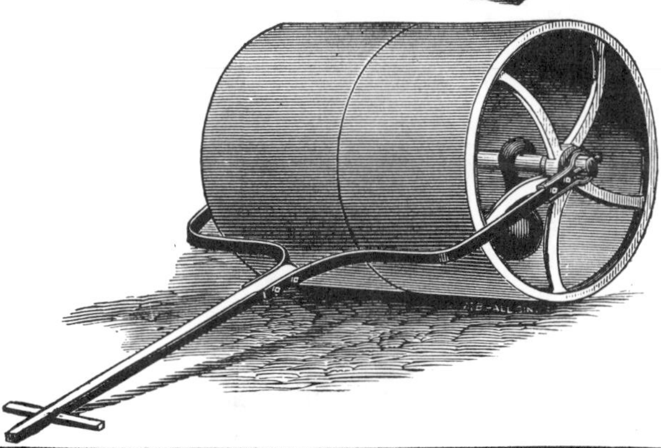

This Roller has two rolls, 20 inches in diameter, 12 in. face, each with weights which hang suspended in the Roller.

Every lawn should be rolled in the spring before cutting with a Lawn Mower.

VAJEN & NEW, INDIANAPOLIS, IND.

THE "BUCKEYE" JUNIOR LAWN MOWER

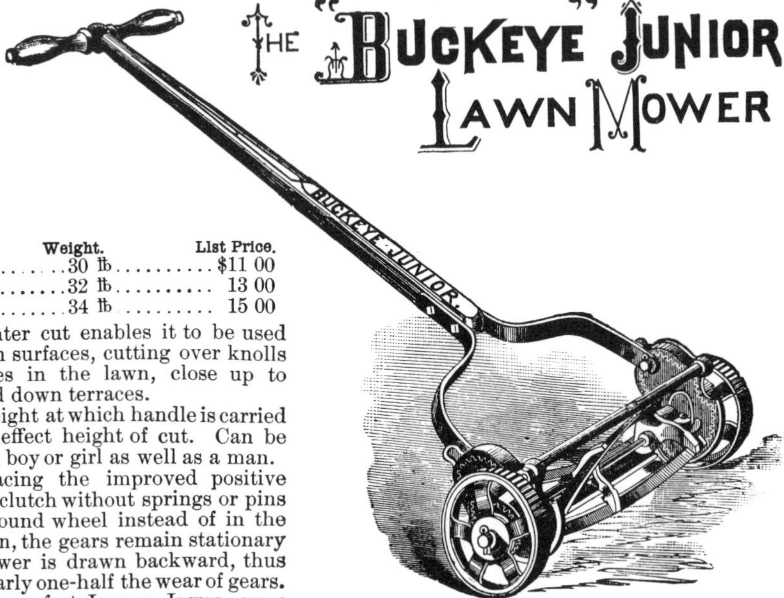

Size.	Weight.	List Price.
10 Inch	30 ℔	$11 00
12 Inch	32 ℔	13 00
14 Inch	34 ℔	15 00

Its center cut enables it to be used on uneven surfaces, cutting over knolls and ridges in the lawn, close up to walks and down terraces.

The height at which handle is carried does not effect height of cut. Can be used by a boy or girl as well as a man.

By placing the improved positive noiseless clutch without springs or pins in the ground wheel instead of in the reel pinion, the gears remain stationary when Mower is drawn backward, thus saving nearly one-half the wear of gears.

It is a perfect LITTLE JEWEL, very compact, thoroughly made of best material and beautifully finished.

"BUCKEYE" SENIOR.

Size.	Weight.	List Price.
10 Inch	30 ℔	$13 00
12 Inch	32 ℔	15 00
14 Inch	34 ℔	17 00
16 Inch	36 ℔	19 00
18 Inch	38 ℔	21 00

BUCKEYE JUNIOR and SENIOR Lawn Mower.

WITH GRASS-BOX ATTACHMENT.

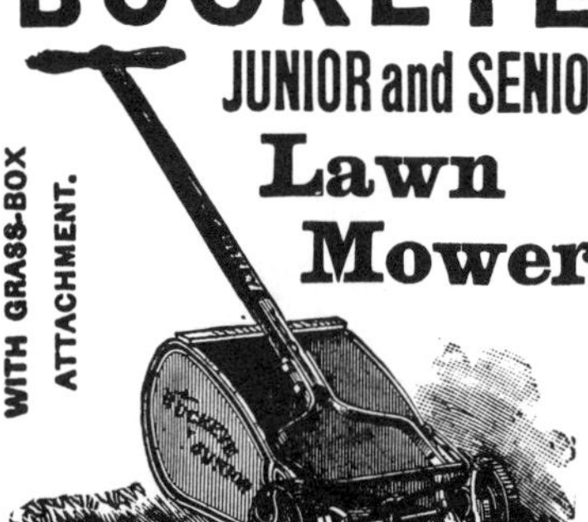

With independent internal gears separate from the ground wheels, perfectly encased to prevent gravel, dirt or grass from being carried into them by the ground wheels. Has an adjustable roller running the entire width of the machine, to regulate the height of cut. It has adjustable handles, and adapts itself to the irregularities of the surface. Ease of work and not liable to get out of or-order. It is a perfect LITTLE BEAUTY, being compact, thoroughly made of the best material and beautifully finished. It is the most perfect Lawn Mower in the market.

Grass Box Attachment for either Senior or Junior Mower ......

HOSE REELS AND NOZZLES.

HOSE REELS.

For Lawns and Pavement.

These Reels are latest improved; bent side pieces. They stand much firmer upon the ground than any other. No castings that are liable to break. The Reel is very large, enabling Hose to be used when partly wound up, protecting it from injury and allowing water to pass through freely.

No. 1, To carry from 50 to 100 ft. ¾ in. Hose, 8 in. wheels............ ......
No. 2, To carry from 100 to 150 ft. ¾ in. Hose, 13 in. wheels............ ......
No. 1, With Drum............ ......
No. 2, " " ....

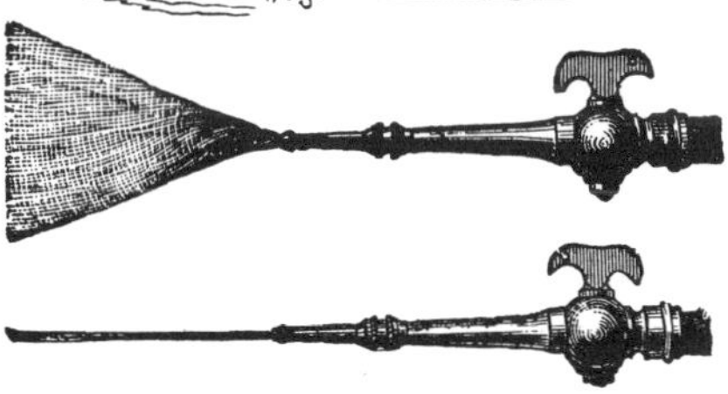

MAGIC NOZZLES.

¾ Inch .... 1 Inch..... ......

Will throw either single jet or spray.

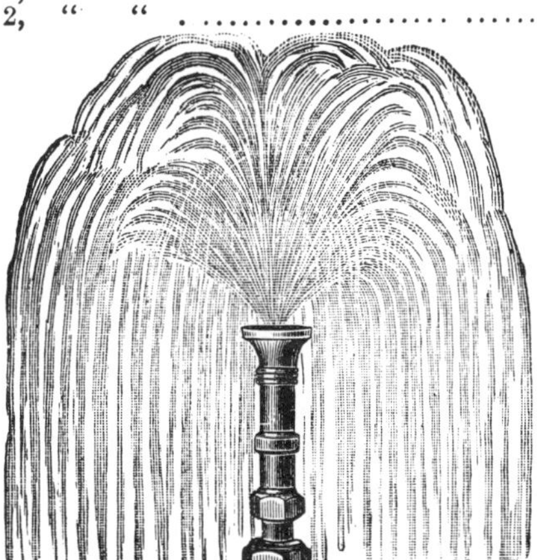

LOWELL SPRAY NOZZLES.

¾ Inch............ ......

Will throw either single jet or spray.

COTTON HOSE.

¾ Inch............ ......

This Hose is mil-dew proof. and guaranteed in every respect.

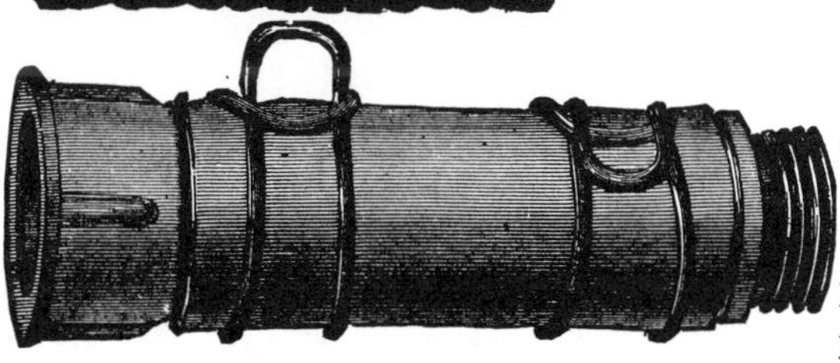

3-Ply Rubber Hose, ¾...... 1 in...... 1½ in......
In different grades. See page 129.

CALDWELL'S HOSE STRAPS.

¾	1	1¼	1½ in.
Nos. 6 & 8,	10 & 12,	14 & 16,	18 & 20.
....	....	....	....

HOSE STRAP FASTENERS.

No. 1, ½ to 1 in., inclusive.. ....

No. 2, 1¼ to 2½ in., " .. ....

HOSE, BELTING AND NOZZLES.

HOSE NOZZLES.

Inch .... ¾ ..... 1..... 1¼..... 1½.....

HOSE COUPLINGS.

Inch .... ¾ ..... 1..... 1¼..... 1½.....

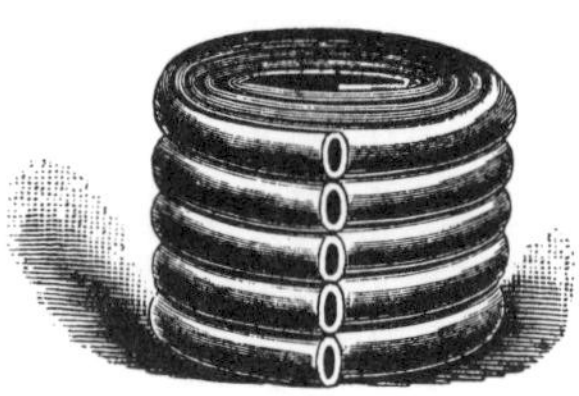

RUBBER HOSE—Three Ply.

	¾	1	1¼	1½ in.
Plumbers'.............	......	......	......	......
Standard,.............	......	......	......	......
Extra.................	......	......	......	......

LEATHER BELTING.

Size	1	1½	2	2½	3	3½	4	4½	5	5½	6 in.
Pr ft.,	.9	.15	.21	.27	.33	.39.	.45	.51	.57	.63	.69

Size	7	8	9	10	11	12	13	14	15	16 in.
Pr ft.,	.81	.93	1 05	1.17	1.29	1.41	1.53	1.65	1.80	1.94

Discount..................

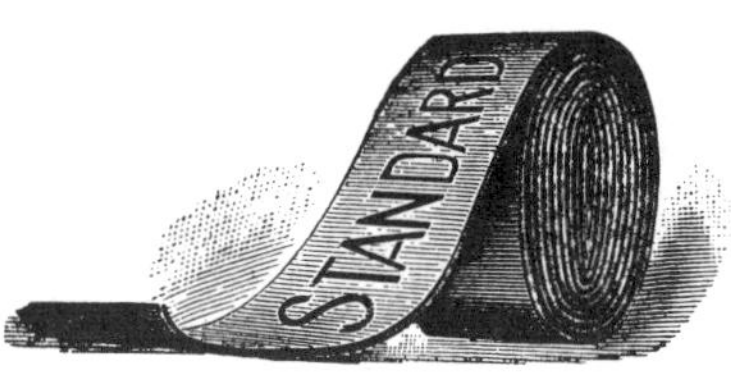

RUBBER BELTING.

Size..........	1	1¼	1½	2	2½	3	3½	4	5	6	7	8 in.
2-Ply..........	.7	.9	.11	.15	.18	.22	.26	.30	....	....	....	....
3 "	....	....	....	.17	.22	.26	.30	.34	.43	.52	.60	.70
4 "	....	....	....	.21	.26	.31	.37	.42	.52	.62	.73	.84

Size...........	9	10	11	12	13	14	15	16	18	20	22	24 in.
3-Ply...........	.80	.90	1.00	1.08	1.18	1.28	1.38	1.50	1.70	1.90	2.12	2.36
4 "	.95	1.07	·1.18	1.30	1.42	1.54	1.66	1.78	2.02	2.26	2.52	2 80

Discount..................

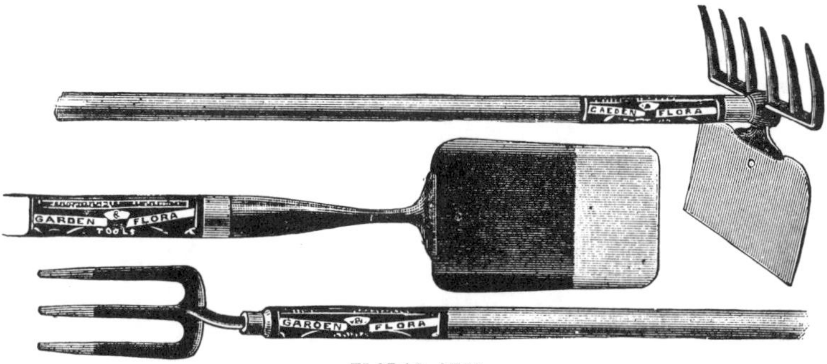

FLORAL SETS.

No. 2, Cast Iron Spade, Hoe and Rake, Painted in 3 Colors, 30 in. Handles ... .
No. 4, Cast Steel Spade, Malleable Iron Fork, and Hoe-Rake, with Steel Blade, Polished, and 30 in. Varnished Handles.............................. ......

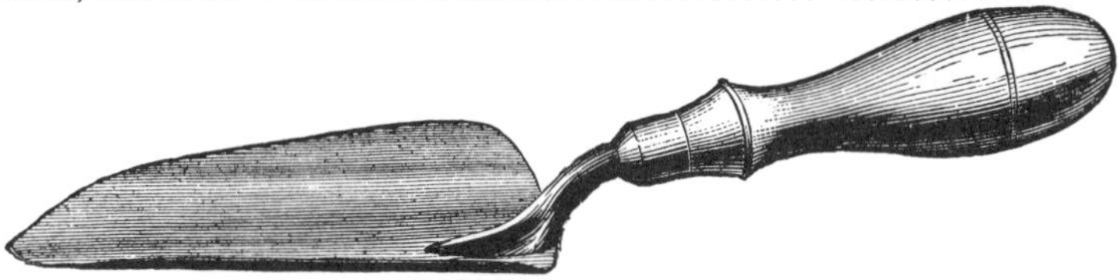

GARDEN TROWELS.

Cast Steel, Polished Blades ....6 ..... 7...... 8 in......

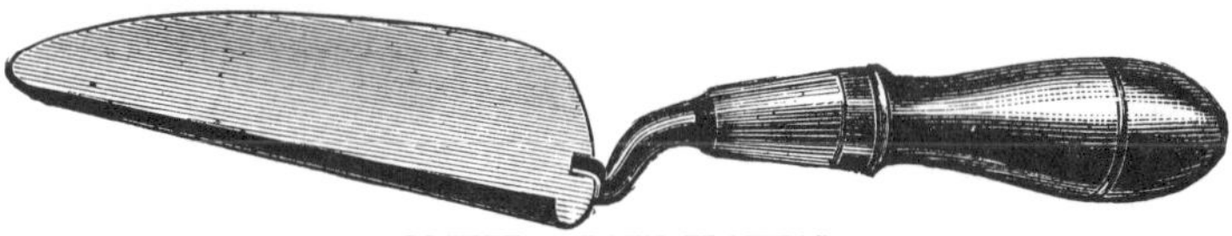

SOCKET GARDEN TROWELS.

Cast Steel, Polished Blades..............................6...... 7...... 8 in......

EXCELSIOR WEEDING HOOK.

Tinned Malleable Iron............ ......

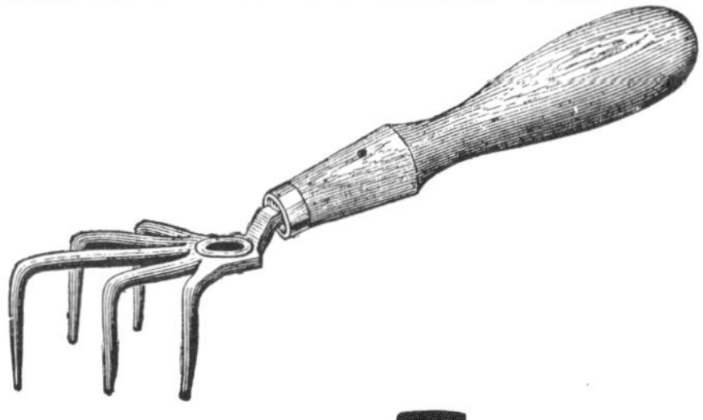

SCUFFLE HOES.

Cast Steel, Polished Blades, 8 in......

EDGING OR BORDER KNIVES.

Cast Steel, Polished Blades, 9 in......

All the latest and best Garden Tools kept in stock.

PRUNING SAWS AND SHEARS.

The Knife and Saw are both made of the best cast steel, and can be used with or without a pole. The saw can be detached when the hook alone is to be used, and attached again for use on limbs too large for the cutter. It combines two useful tools in one, without increase of cost to the consumer.

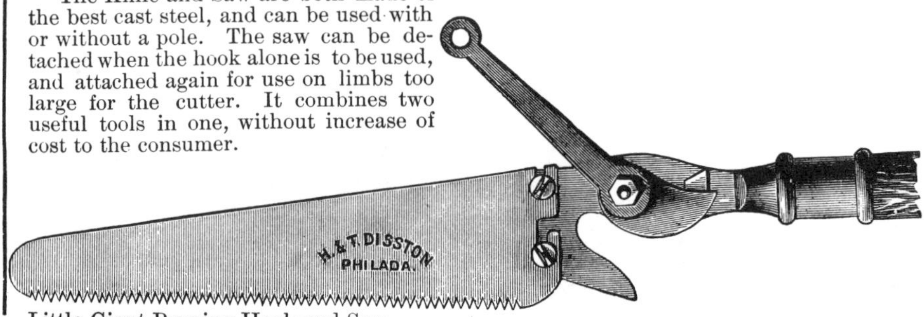

Little Giant Pruning Hook and Saw. ....

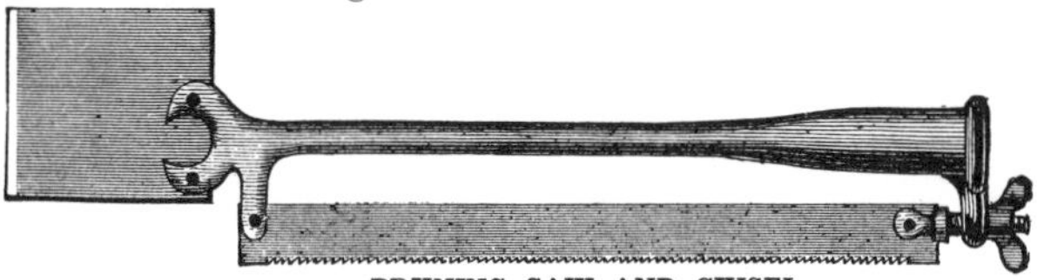

PRUNING SAW AND CHISEL.

Cast Steel Saw and Chisel, Malleable Iron Shank......... .....

Feet, 8..... 10.....

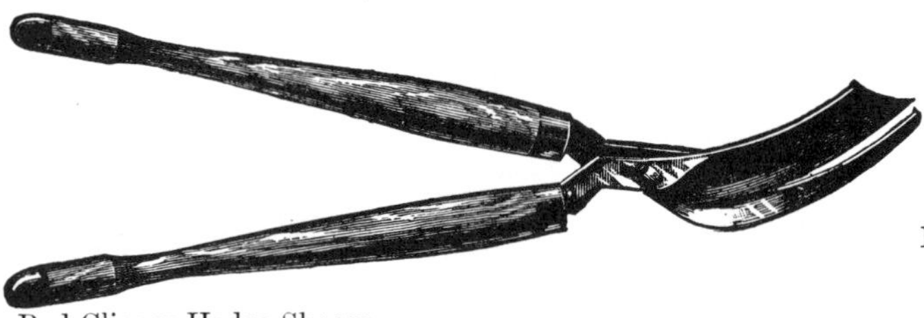

Red Clipper Hedge Shears.. ......

Buckeye Pruning Shears. ....

These justly celebrated Pruners are receiving praise wherever they are in use. They are to supercede all others; light, to take the place of the common hand shear, and strong enough to be used instead of the heavy, cumbersome large ones. A superior tool for tree and shrub trimming, It is needed by every one who has no more than a garden to keep in trim, while in an orchard it is an indispensable article, it being of such weight and size that it does not weary one to use it, and will do any work required of a pruner.

Price ....

These Shears have a hinge movement. The Shank is attached on the opposite side of the hook, operating as a lever to the blade, thereby preventing any springing of the blade, which has proved so objectionable in other shears. When the Shears need grinding, by simply removing one bolt, the knife can be turned around so as to be ground on an ordinary grindstone.

HAY KNIVES AND POST-HOLE DIGGERS.

THE "LIGHTNING" HAY KNIVES.

For cutting fine feed from bale; to cut down mow or stack; to cut corn stalks for feed; to cut peat, or for ditching in marshes, it is not excelled.
Price ....

HEATH'S UPRIGHT HAY KNIVES.

The spear-cutting edge, the comparative ease in working, and the direct pressure downwards, enables one to cut loose hay or straw easier than with any other knife.
Price ....

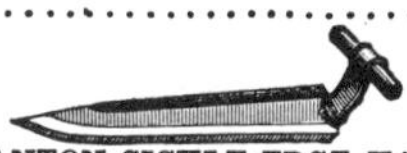

THE CANTON SICKLE-EDGE HAY KNIFE.

One of the best, fastest and easiest cutting Knives made.
Price..............................

FISHER'S PATENT HAY KNIFE.

Price..............................

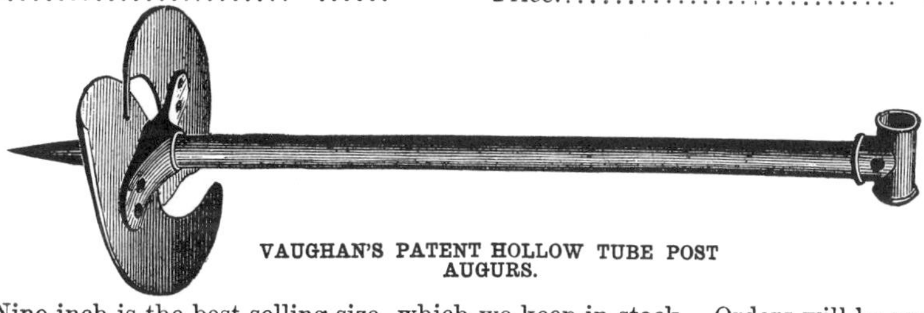

VAUGHAN'S PATENT HOLLOW TUBE POST AUGURS.

Nine inch is the best selling size, which we keep in stock. Orders will be accepted for 4, 5, 6, 7, 8 in. to ship from factory. 7 in., best size for posts to drive.......

"EUREKA" POST-HOLE DIGGER.

The blades are made of best cast steel. The head pieces of best malleable iron, and the handles of white ash. The blades are nine inches long. The length, complete, five feet. Weight about nine pounds.

Price..

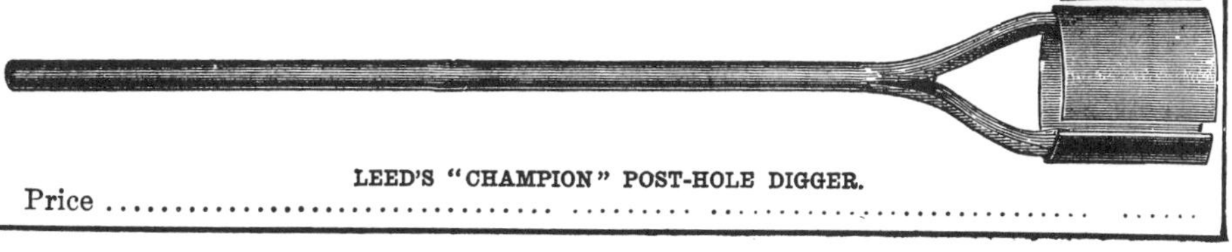

LEED'S "CHAMPION" POST-HOLE DIGGER.

Price ....

VAJEN & NEW, INDIANAPOLIS, IND.

ICE CREEPERS, PEG FLOATS, &C.

TINNED BUCKLES.

Inch	5/8	3/4	7/8	1
	....	....	....	....
Inch	**1¼**	**1½**	**1¾**	**2**
	....	....	....	....

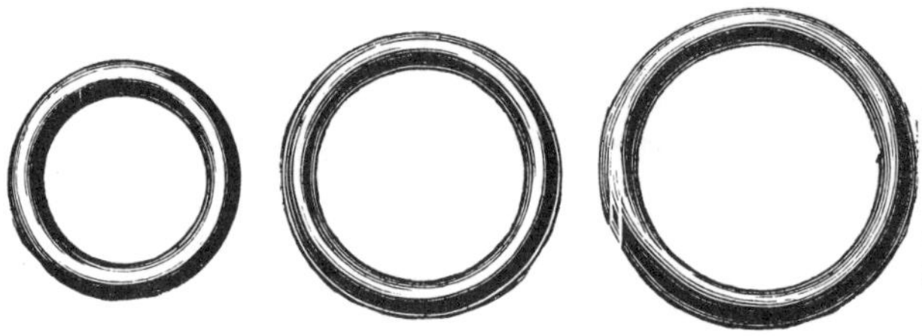

HARNESS RINGS.

Inch	½	5/8	¾	7/8	1
Japanned	...	...	...	...	...
Tinned	...	...	...	...	...

Inch	1¼	1½	1¾	2
Japanned	...	...	..	...
Tinned	...	...	...	...

PEG FLOATS.

Plain.............................. ...... Swivel.......................... ......

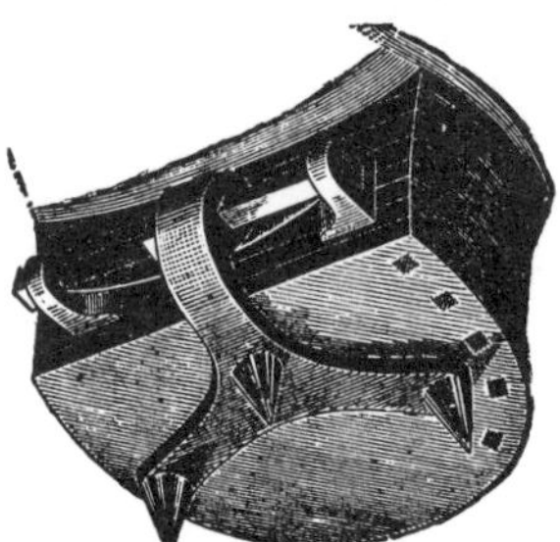

CHAMPION ICE CREEPERS.

Price.............. ......

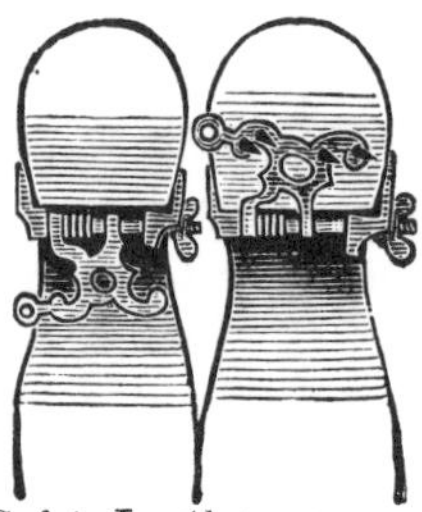

Safety Ice Creepers...
Acme " " ...

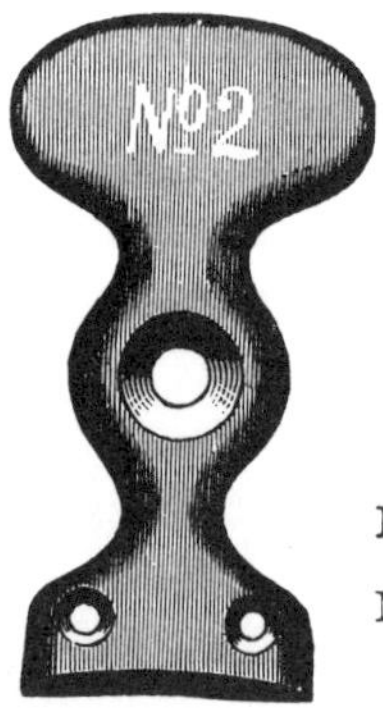

HEEL STIFFENERS.

Nos................. 3x...... 4x......

STANDARD PEG BREAK.

To Fasten on the Counter.

No. 20, Cast Steel, with Clincher..... ......

No. 50, Adjustable Cutter............ ......

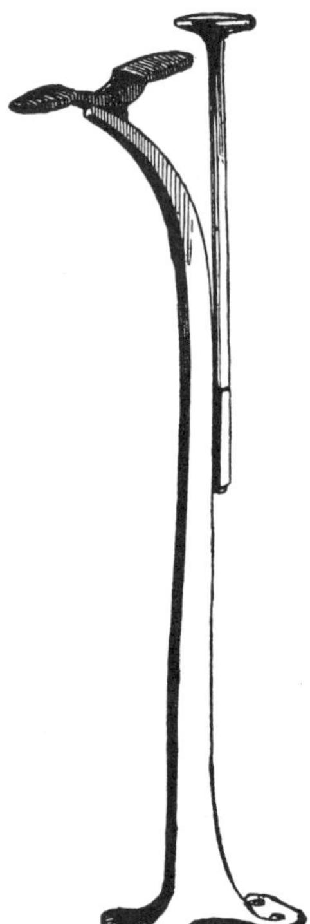

Cut of No. 20.

FINIAL.

ETHAN ALLEN VANE.

Ornamental Iron Finials,
Tower Ornaments,
Roof Crestings,
Stable Fixtures.

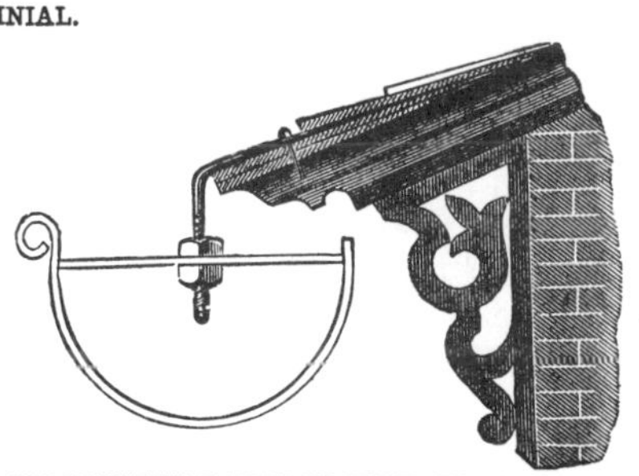

WOODRUFF'S EAVES-TROUGH HANGERS.

Price.............................. ......

WEATHER VANES.

Horse Vanes....	24 in	31 in. long	......
Bull "	....	33 in. "	......
Cow "	.... 28 in......	36 in. "	.....
Sheep "	....	32 in. "	.....
Hog "	.... 35 in......	42 in. "	.....
Rooster "	.... 24 in	32 in. high	......

Our Vanes are full-bodied and life-like, made of pure copper, which is gilded with genuine gold leaf. Warranted to remain bright in any climate.

THE WAYNE CHEAP CUTTING BOX.

Price........................... ......

STABLE SUPPLIES.

VAJEN & NEW, INDIANAPOLIS, IND.

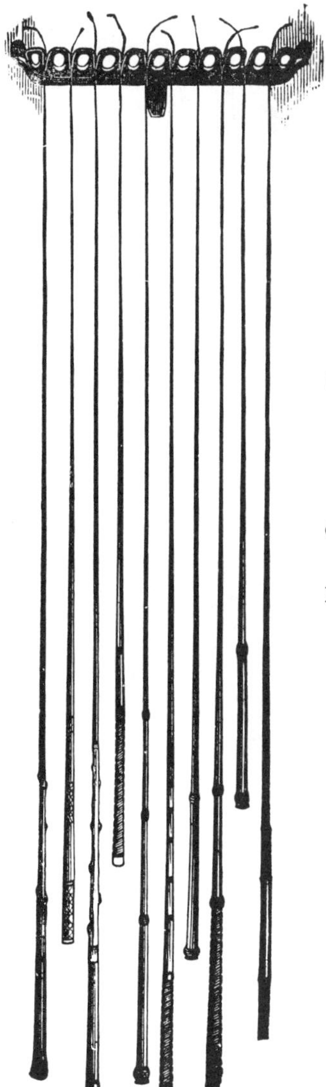

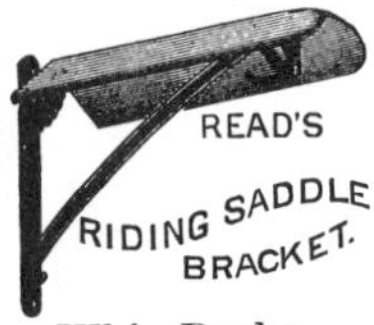

Whip Racks,
Harness Hooks,
Adjustable Buggy
Wrenches,
Chamois Skins,
Sponges,
&c.

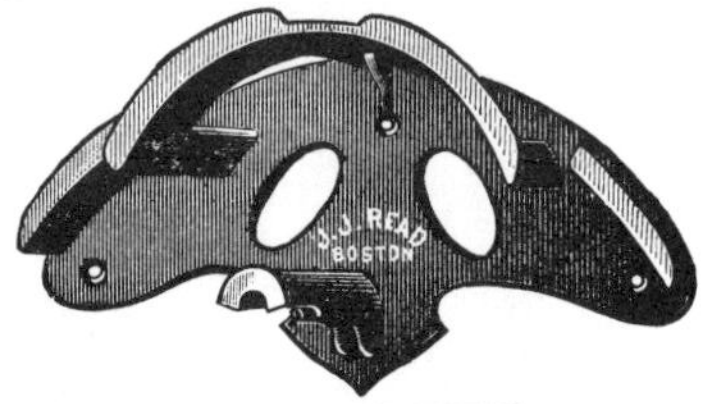

HARNESS BRACKET.

Holds the whole Harness, taking no more room than the ordinary hook, and can be used for both single or double harness. The harness can be placed upon or removed as easily as on the common hook.

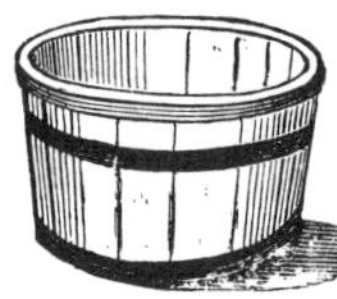

FOOT TUB.

HORSE PAIL.

Oak and Pine flush-bottom Pails.

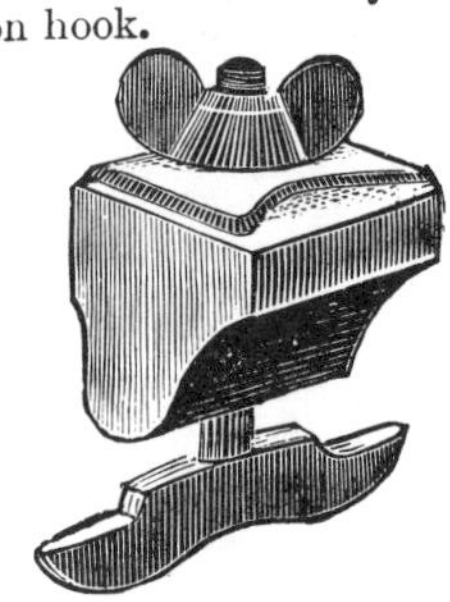

Adjustable Anti-Shaft Rattler.

WHIPS.

Buggy, Carriage and Coach Whips,
Drover and Teamster Whips.
A good assortment in all
the different grades.

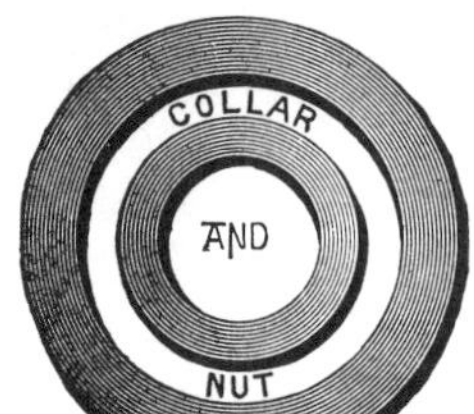

LEATHER CARRIAGE WASHER.

Size of axle,	¾	⅞	1	1⅛	1¼	1½
For Collar,	...	...	...	...	...	...
For Nut,	...	...	...	...	...	...

BROOMS.—Flat Hickory Splint.

For Stable and Warehouse use. Have no equal for durability and hard service.

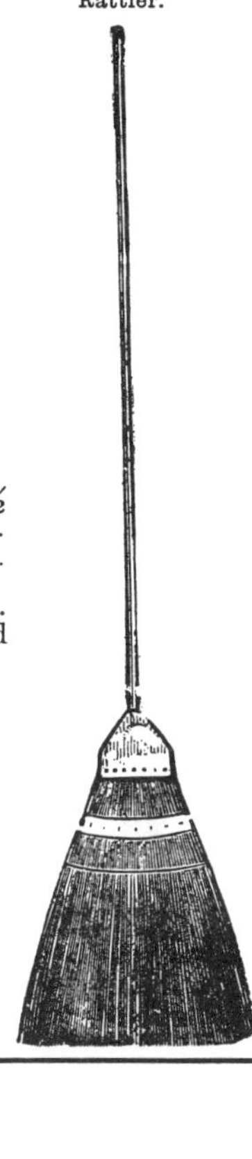

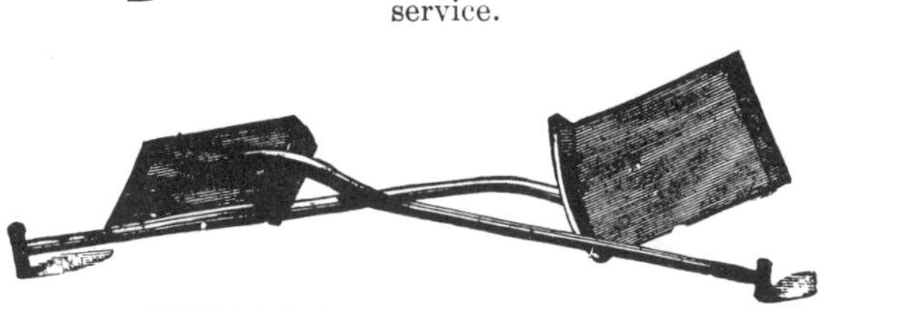

WOODEN SNOW AND STABLE SHOVELS.

Wagon Jacks, Wood Stable Forks, Rakes, Wood Measures, Curry Combs and Brushes.

EXPRESS WAGONS, SLEIGHS AND TRUCKS.

No. 4, Wheels, 10 and 14 in.; Body, 12½ x 26 in.; varnished. A strong, serviceable Wagon ....

No. X4, Same as No. 4, witn solid iron axles and iron boxes in hubs. ....

BENT KNEE SLEIGHS.

No. 2, Neatly Painted and Ornamented, ...
No. 3, " " " " with Swan Necks.............. ....

OAK SLEIGHS.

No. 1.................................... ......

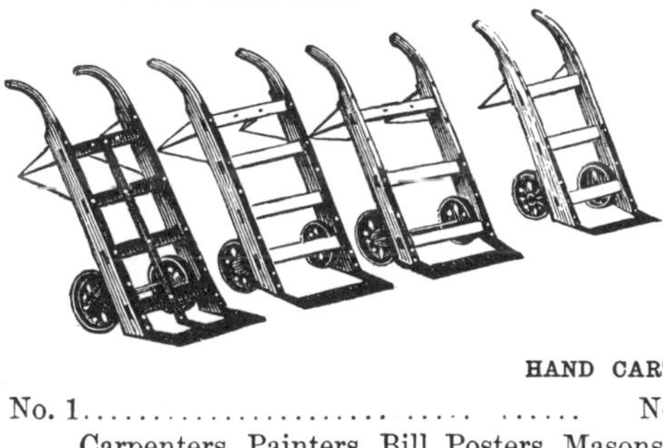

STORE TRUCKS.

Nos....	1	2	3	4
Half-Ironed..	....	....	....	....
Full " ..	....	....	....	....

Discount ....

Flour Barrel and Sack Trucks.

HAND CARTS.

No. 1.............................. ...... No. 2............................. ......

Carpenters, Painters, Bill Posters, Masons, etc., will find this Cart ahead of anything for carrying toools and light material. Farmers, too, use them to good advantage about the orchard or garden.

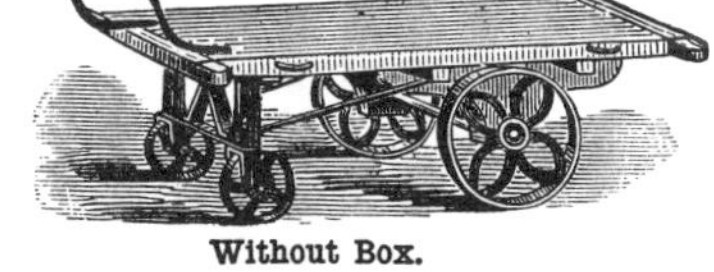

Without Box.

With Box.

REYNOLDS' IMPROVED MERCHANTS' AND WAREHOUSE TRUCKS.

With Box...................... ..... Without Box.................... .....

Size, 2 feet 6 inches wide by 5 feet long. Running gear so arranged that it can be run on elevator or scales from any angle, as it turns in exactly its own length. Capacity of box, 16 to 20 bushels.

WHEELBARROWS AND SCRAPERS.

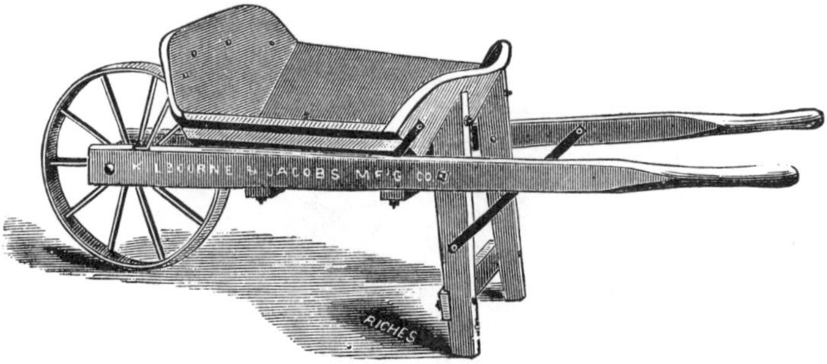

RAILROAD BARROWS.

Common ... . Bolted, Wood Wheel.. ...... Bolted, Iron Wheel.. ......

Large Size Sawdust or Salt Barrow ....

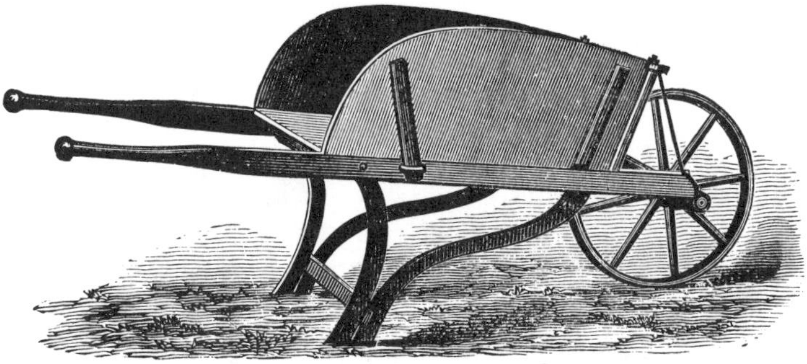

GARDEN BARROWS.

Small .... Medium......... ..... Large........... ......

Nicely painted, strong and durable.

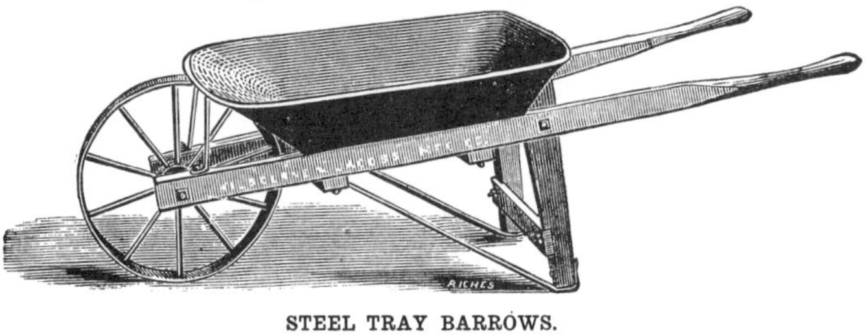

STEEL TRAY BARROWS.

No. 1, Capacity, 3½ cubic feet.... ...... No. 2, Capacity, 5 cubic feet ....

Trays stamped from a solid plate of steel, without seam or rivets, and have great strength without unnecessary weight.

SOLID STEEL SCRAPERS.

No. 1, Carries 7 feet of earth ....
No. 2, " 5 " " ....
No. 3, " 3 " " ....

Made of a single sheet of steel, pressed into the best and most practical shape for working.

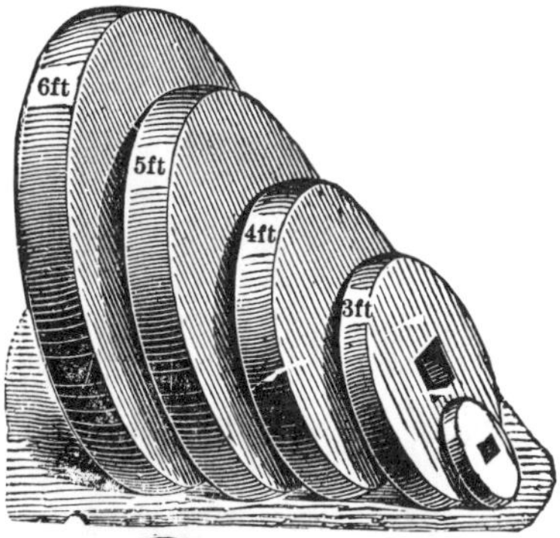

GRIND STONES.

From 20 to 500 pounds.

Price, per lb. . . . .

KITCHEN GRIND STONES.

8 in . . . . 10 in. . . . . . 12 in . . . . .

MOUNTED GRIND STONES.

Nos. . . . 1. . . . 2. . . . 3. . . .

GRIND STONE HANGERS.

Length of Shaft .15 . . . . 17. . . . . . 19 . . . . . 22. . . . . . 24 in . . . . .

SCYTHE STONES.

Indian Pond (Red End), ½ Gross in Box. . . . .

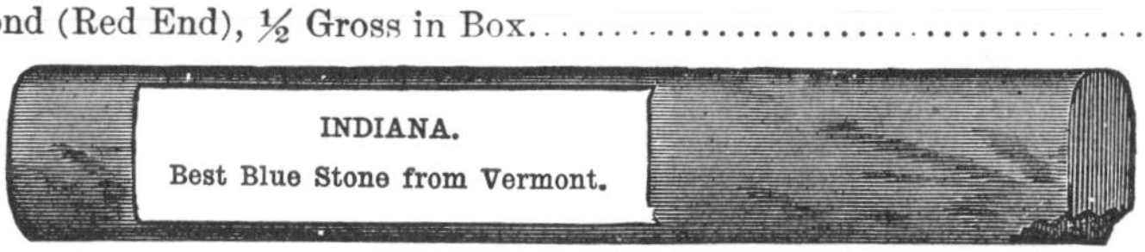

Indiana (Special), ¼ Gross in Box . . . .

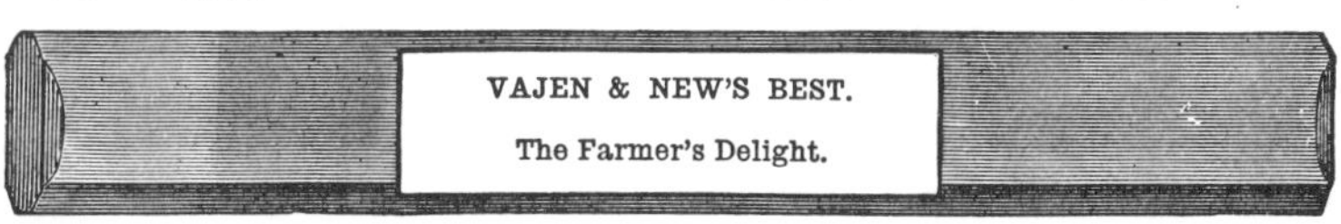

Farmer's Delight, ¼ Gross in Box . . . .

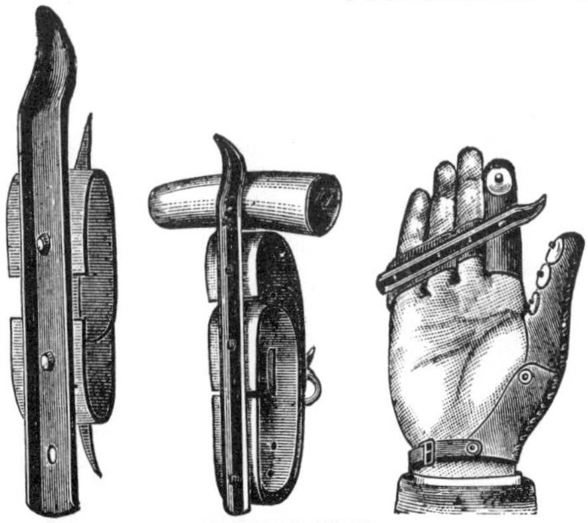

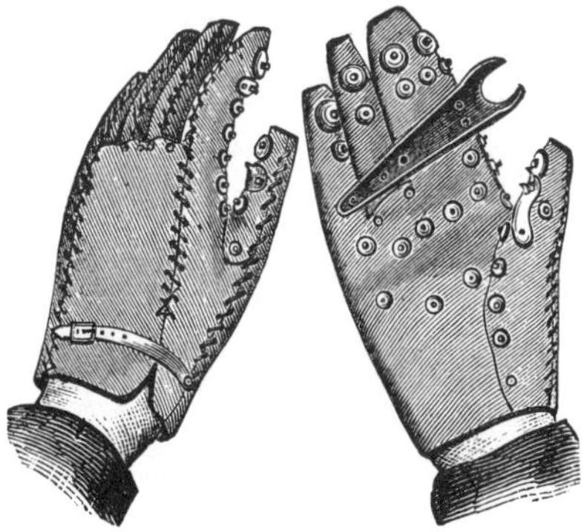

HUSKING PINS.

No. 60 ... No. 65.... No. 70....

HUSKING GLOVES.

No. 50, Laced.................. ......

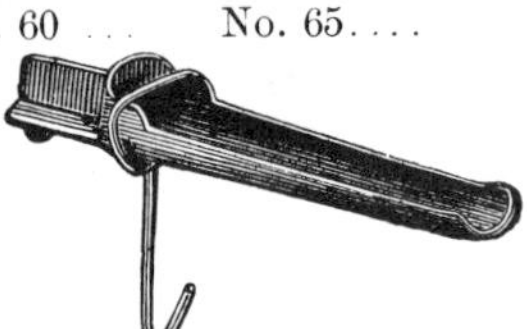

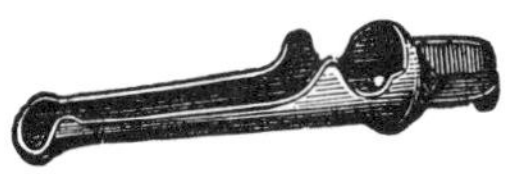

EUREKA SAP SPOUTS.

No. 1, With Heavy Wire Hanger, that does not break like Hangers cast on the spout..................... .....

No. 2, Without Hanger..... .....

Acknowledged by sugar-makers to be the best Spouts in the world, and that their yearly gain in sap more than pays their price.

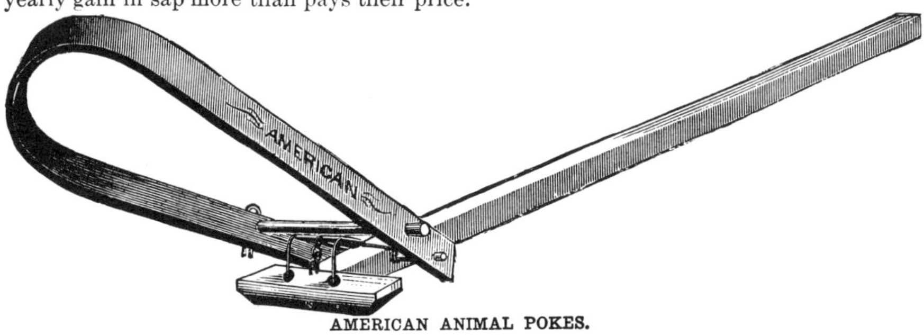

AMERICAN ANIMAL POKES.

These Pokes are made in a thorough workmanlike manner, from best selected stock of oak and hickory for the wood part, and the best of malleable iron and cast steel for the springs, cross head and spurs. Price..................... ......

HALTERS.

Rope, Common......................... ......

Rope, Braided ....

Web, Assorted Colors ....

WEANERS, HOG RINGS AND RINGERS.

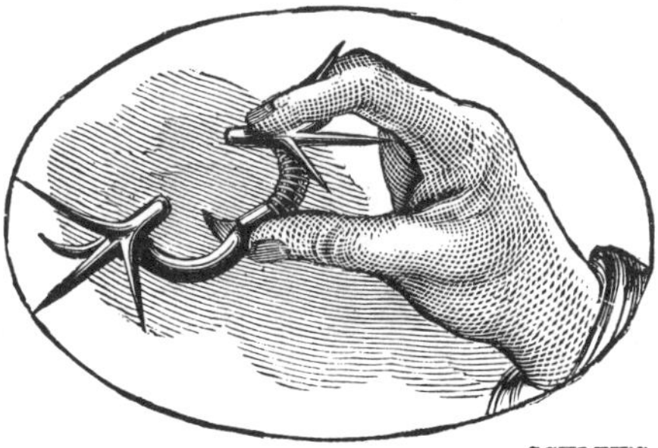

SCHLEY'S WEANERS.

No. 2, To Eight Months.......... ...... No. 3, Yearlings................. .....

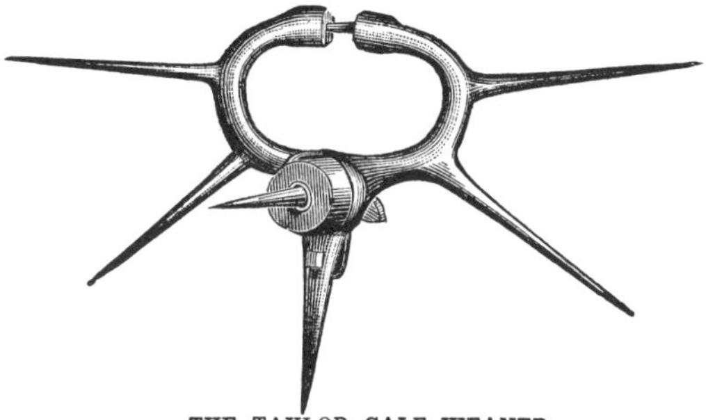

THE TAYLOR CALF WEANER.

It is self-fastening. The fastenings are made of brass, and can not stick fast while in use. It passes through the tissue of the nose, making it impossible for the animal to lose it. The nose heals over the same as an ear-ring in the ear, preventing chaffing, or irritating the nostril by sliding out. No. 2................................ ......

RICE'S WEANERS.

To 1 Year.	1 to 2 Years.	Grown Cows.
Nos. 1......	2	3 ....

BLAIR'S HOG RINGERS AND RINGS.

Blair's "Boss" Ringer will close any single wire ring made.

Blair's Hog Rings.... ...... Blair's Pig Rings.... ......

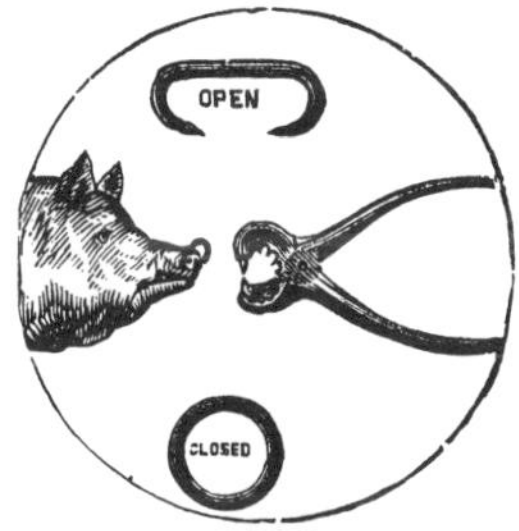

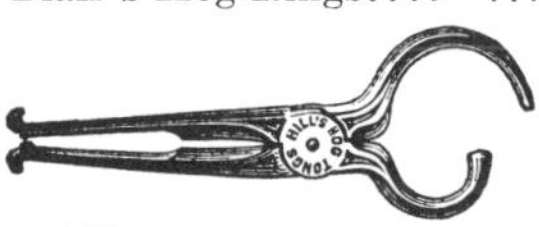

Hill's Hog Holder.. .....

Hill's Improved Hog Ringers.......... ....

Closes all sizes of Rings.

HILL'S RINGS.

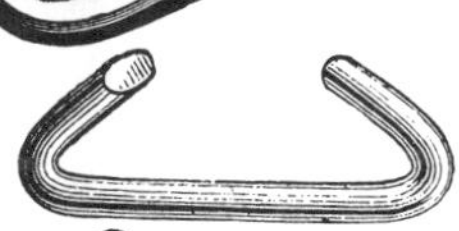

No. 1, Pig...........

No. 2, Shoat........

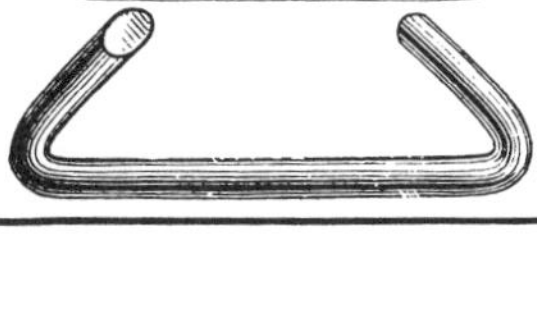

No. 3, Hog.........

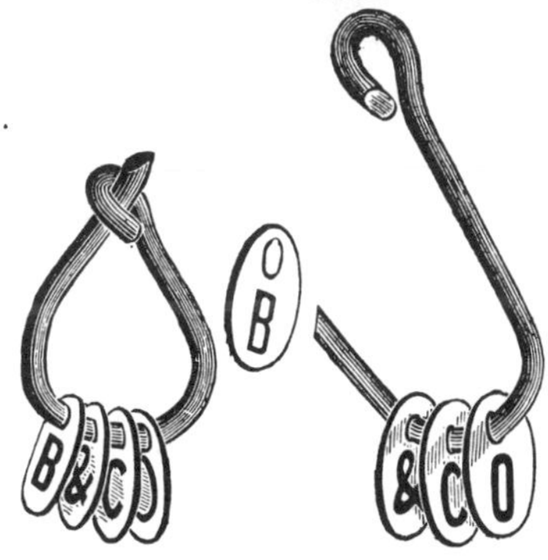

THE PERFECT STOCK MARK.

Is capable of any nuumber of combinations without complication....

CATTLE LEADERS, HORSE MUZZLES, &C.

CATTLE LEADERS.

No. 51, Malleable Iron, Brass Wire Spring......

No. 52, " " " " " ......

BULL RINGS.

Polished Steel, 2... 2½... 3 in...

" Copper, 2... 2½... 3 in...

CARRIAGE KNOBS.

No. 75, Japanned ... .

No. 11, " Small ....

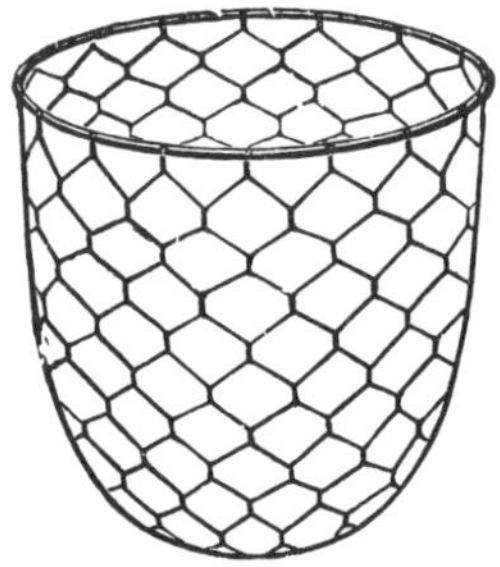

HORSE MUZZLES.

Japanned ....

Galvanized ....

OX BALLS.

Heavy, Octagon, Solid.

Nos. 12....13....14....

S HOOKS.

Wrought Iron.

1½	2	2½	3 in.
....	....	....	....

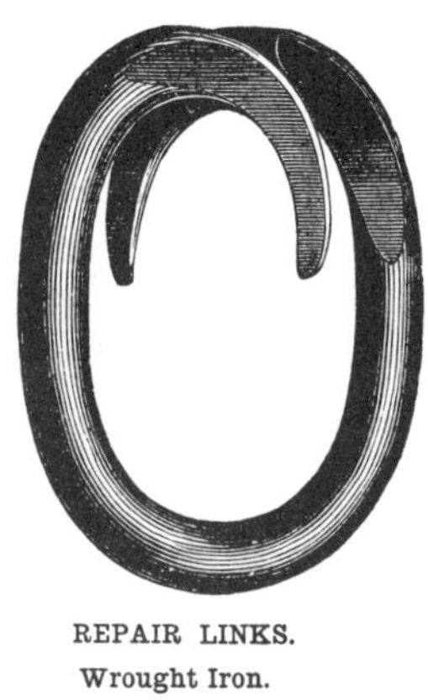

REPAIR LINKS.

Wrought Iron.

3-16	¼	5-16	⅜ in.
....	....	....	....

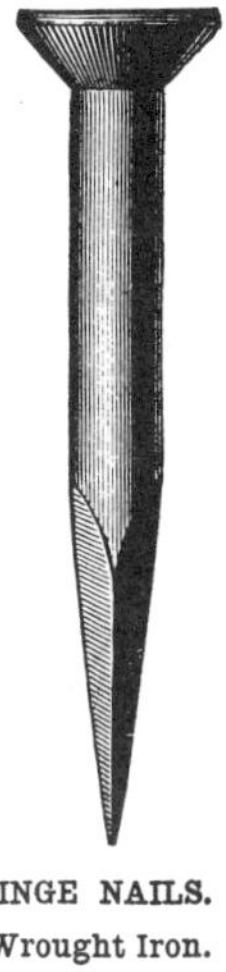

HINGE NAILS.

Wrought Iron.

¼x2	2½	3	3½ in.
....	....	....	....

HAND GONG AND CALL BELLS.

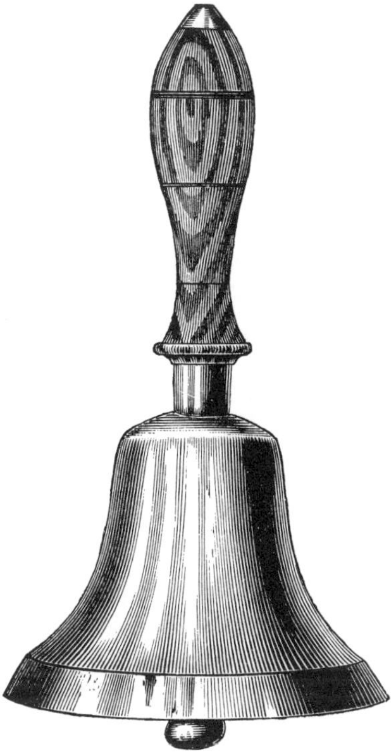

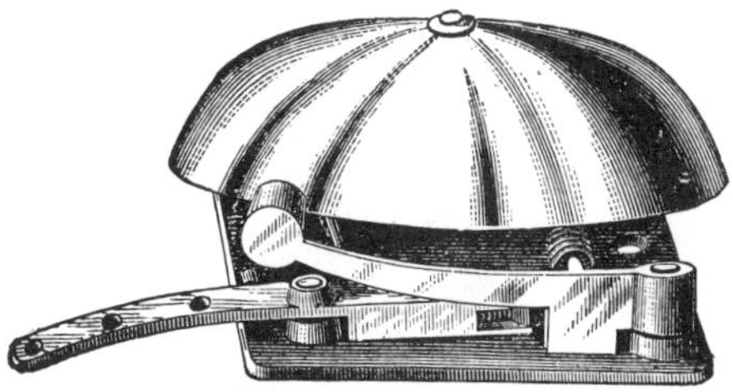

TRIP GONG BELLS.

Polished Bell Metal.

3... 4... 5... 6... 7... 8... 10 ... 12 Inch....

HAND BELLS.

Enameled Wood Handles.

No. 0.... 1.... 2 .. 3 ... 4.... 5 ... 6.... 7....

" 8.... 9... 10 .. 11.. 12 . 13... 14.. 15....

SWISS HAND BELLS.

Nickel Plated.

No. 2.... 4..... 6..... 8..... 10...... 12......

MILKMAN'S BELLS.

No. 20, 8⅝ in., Extra Heavy, Pure Metal, ...

No. 2600.
Bronze Base.
....

No. 2900.
Bronze Base.
....

No. 8050. ....

No. 3000.
Gilt Base.
....

No. 3200.
Gilt Base.
....

No. 4400.
"Hotel," Gilt Base.
....

CHURCH, FARM AND COW BELLS.

STEEL ALLOY CHURCH AND SCHOOL BELLS--Gold Bronzed.

These Bells are cast from an alloy of cast steel and crystal metal, and can be relied on under all circumstances and in all seasons. We have five sizes, as follows:

No.	Diam. Bell.	Weight Com.	Price.
4½	21 in	150 lb	......
5	24 in	225 lb	......
6	26 in	325 lb	......
7	32 in	600 lb	......
8	36 in	850 lb	......

The style of mounting these Bells is represented in the cut, and includes Wood Frame, Iron Wheel, and for Nos. 7 and 8, Tolling Hammers without extra charge.

These Bells are offered to the trade as the best of their class. They are uniform in shape, and finished in a first-class manner. The mountings are graceful in appearance and perfectly adapted to the duty they are to perform. The quality of material used is the best, and only experienced workmen employed in their production.

FARM BELLS--Richly Bronzed.

We have four sizes of Farm Bells, as follows:

No.	Diameter of Bell.	Weight Complete.	Price.
1	15 in	40 lb	......
2	17 in	50 lb	......
3	19 in	75 lb	......
4	21 in	100 lb	......

The style of mountings used for these Bells is represented in the cut. No. 4 Bell can be furnished with upright for platform or belfry if desired.

WILSON'S STOCK BELLS.

Nos.	0	1	2	3	4	5	6	7
	....	...	....	....	....	....	....	....

CAST SHEEP BELLS.

Strapped.

No. 2	......
No. 3	......
No. 4	......

SLEIGH BELLS.

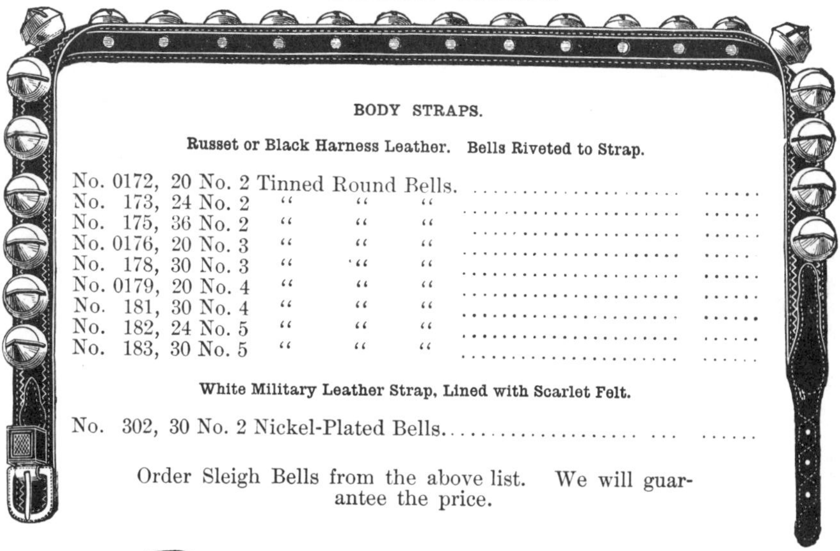

BODY STRAPS.

Russet or Black Harness Leather. Bells Riveted to Strap.

No. 0172,	20 No. 2 Tinned Round Bells	....	......
No. 173,	24 No. 2 " " "	....	......
No. 175,	36 No. 2 " " "	....	......
No. 0176,	20 No. 3 " " "	....	......
No. 178,	30 No. 3 " " "	....	......
No. 0179,	20 No. 4 " " "	....	......
No. 181,	30 No. 4 " " "	....	......
No. 182,	24 No. 5 " " "	....	......
No. 183,	30 No. 5 " " "	....	......

White Military Leather Strap, Lined with Scarlet Felt.

No. 302, 30 No. 2 Nickel-Plated Bells.................... ....

Order Sleigh Bells from the above list. We will guarantee the price.

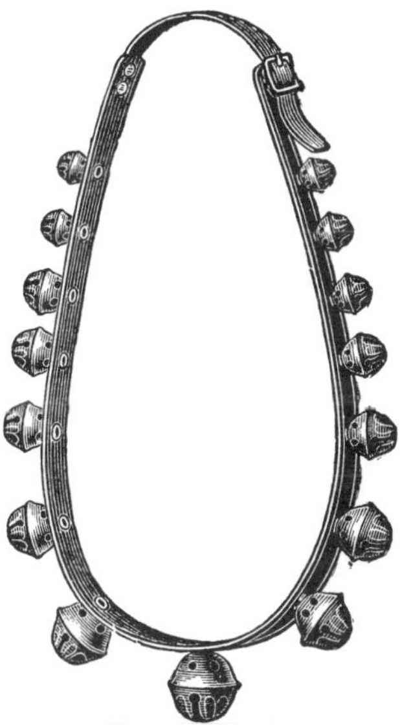

NECK STRAPS.

Polished Round Bells, Riveted.

No. 26,	9 Bells,	Nos. 1 to 5	....
No. 31,	11 "	Nos. 2 to 7	....
No. 37,	13 "	Nos. 2 to 8	....
No. 45,	15 "	Nos. 3 to 10	....

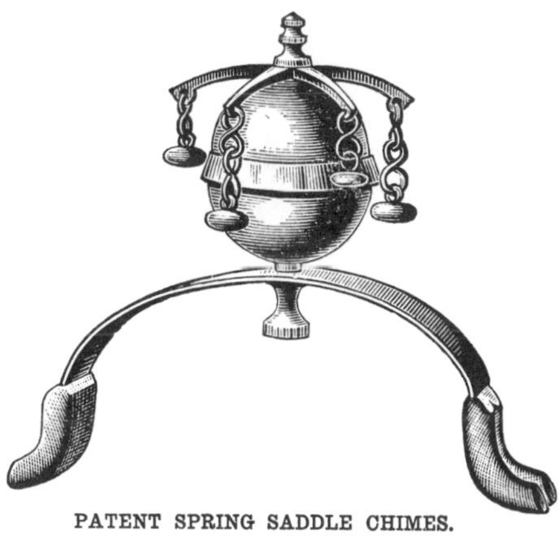

PATENT SPRING SADDLE CHIMES.

Nickel-Plated...................... ......

Gold " ....

This new style Chime spreads over the Saddle Hook and holds tightly on the rein loops; easily put on or taken off.

SHAFT BELLS.

White Metal.. ......

Nickel-Plated.. ......

SLEIGH BELLS AND HOUSE BELLS.

Polished.

ROUND BELLS.

Tinned. To Screw On.

No. 1 ....
No. 2....................... ......
No. 3....................... ......
No. 4 ....
No. 5 ....
No. 6 ....

Tinned.

Nos.	0	1	2	3	4	5	6	7	8	9	10	11	12	13	14	15
Polished	....	....	....	....	....	....	....	....	....	....	....	....	....	....	....	....

SHAFT CHIMES.

White Metal Bells ....

Nickel Plated Bells ....

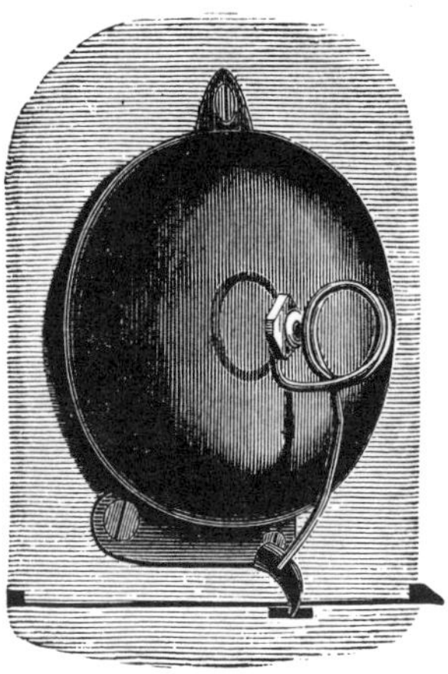

ALARM DOOR BELLS.

Bronzed Steel............ ....
Polished Bell Metal ....

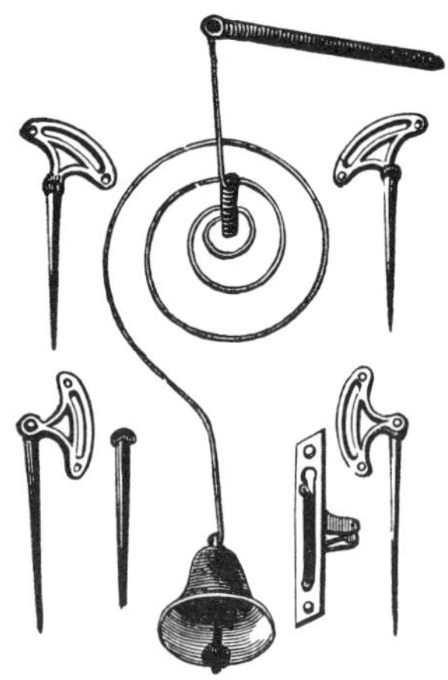

HOUSE BELLS ON CARRIAGES.

No. 113, With Spikes only ....
No. 123, Complete as per cut..... ......

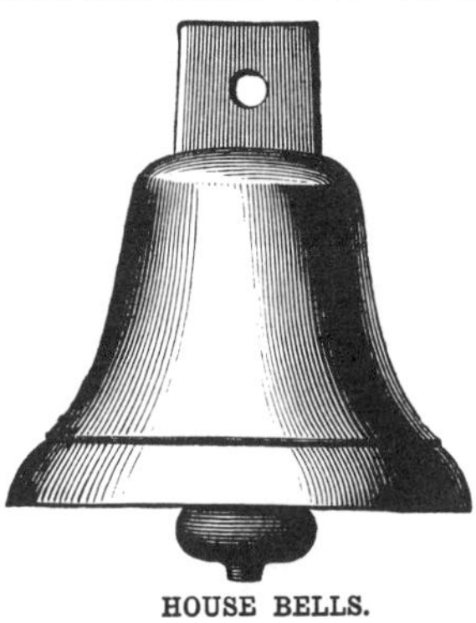

HOUSE BELLS.

Polished ....

CAR BELLS—With Snap.

Polished ....
Tinned ....

FIRE SETS, FIRE STANDS AND POKERS.

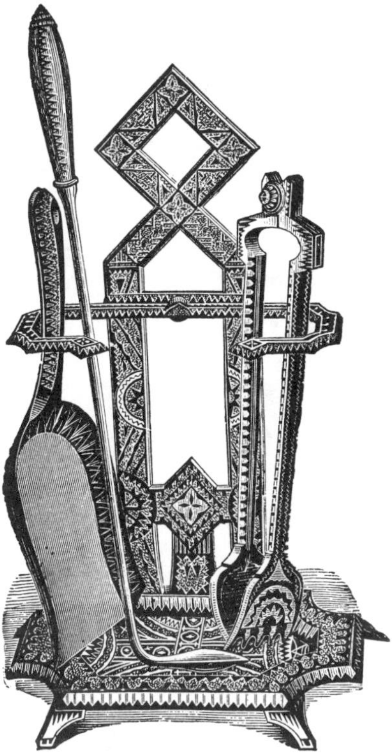

COTTAGE FIRE IRON SETS.

No. 1, Stand, Assorted Colors........ ......
No. 5, " " " ....
No. 9, " and Set, Assorted Colors. ......

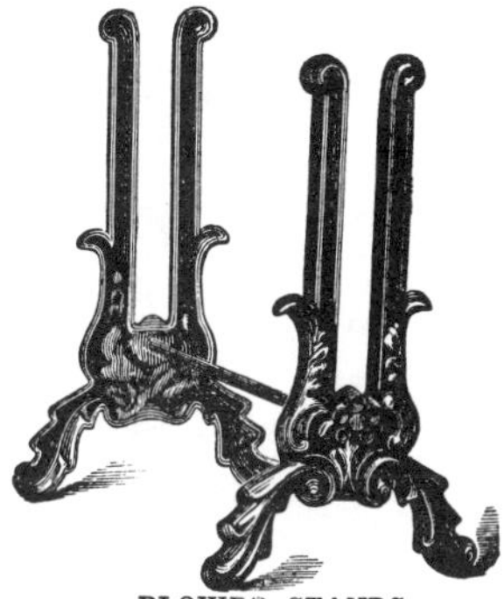

BLOWER STANDS.

No. 3.................. ......

FIRE IRON STANDS.

No. 28, Berlin Bronzed, 23 in. high...
No. 36, " " 24 " ...
No. 38, " " 26 " ...

WROUGHT IRON POKERS.

No. 1, Cast Handle.. ......

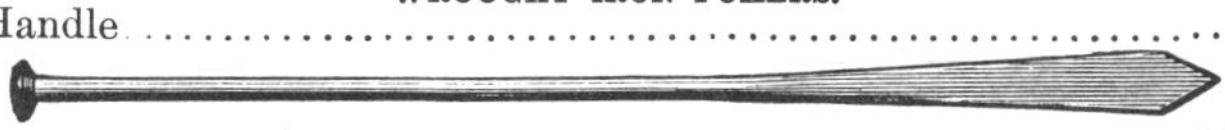

Size..	20	24	28 in.
Nos..	1.....	2	3......

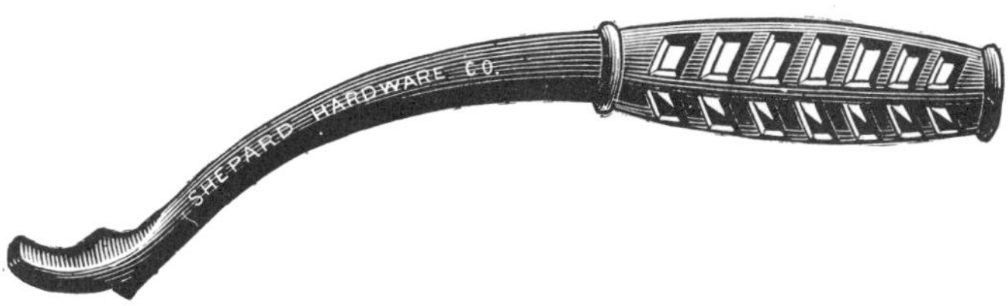

STOVE-LID LIFTERS.

Iron Handle ....

COAL SHOVELS AND TONGS.

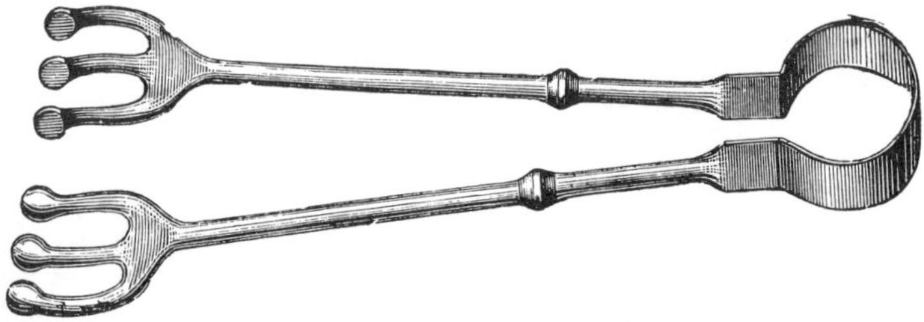

No. 1, Japanned................ ...... No. 2, Tinned ....

With Flat Steel Spring. Will pick up a pin or a cocoanut.

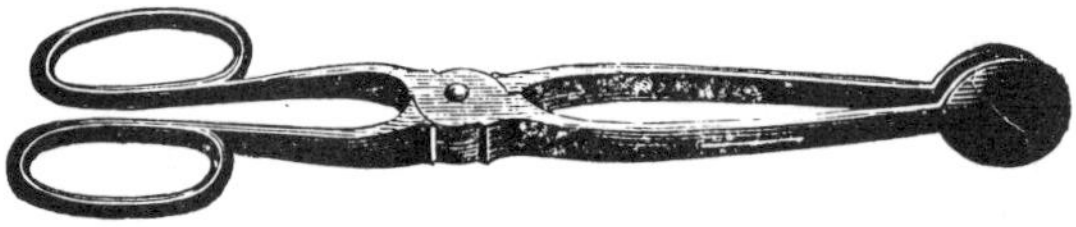

No. 1, 13 in. Long...... ......

Cast Japanned. Opens 6 inches.

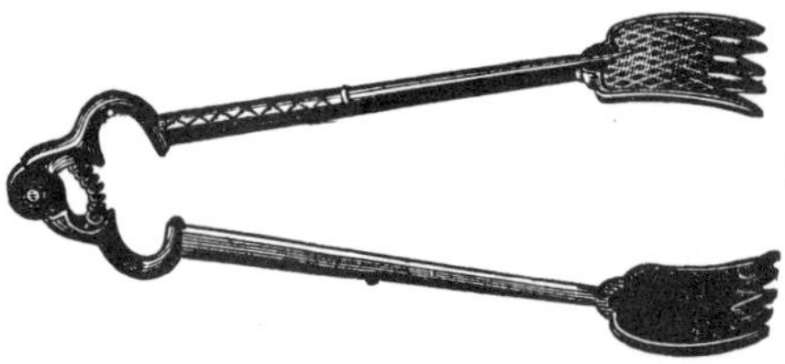

No. 40, With Spring, Bronze Finish.. ......

WROUGHT IRON FIRE SHOVEL.

Half Oval Handles.

No. 1.......................... ......

WROUGHT FIRE SHOVELS.

Nos.........	2....	3....	4 ...	5 ...
Length of Handles	15	17	18½	24 in.

ONE-PIECE CORRUGATED SHOVELS.

No. 15, Gem, Japanned, Length 16 in....................................... ......
No. 25, " " " 23 in....................................... ......

No. 57, Japanned, Round Handle, Length 23 in.............................. ......
No. 157, Tinned, " " " 23 in.............................. ......

COAL HODS, COAL VASES AND ANDIRONS.

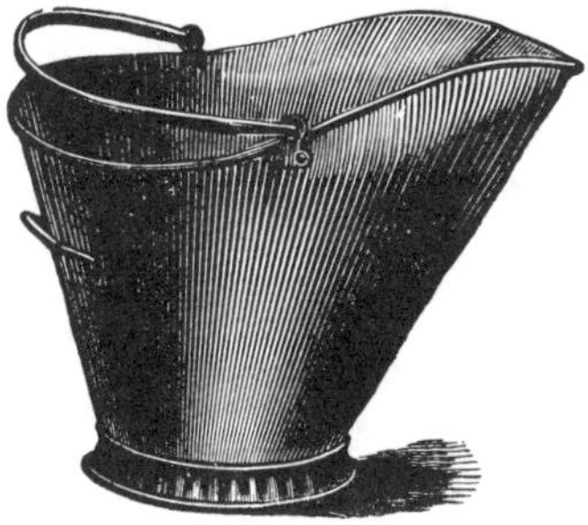

PRESSED COAL HODS.—Square Mouth.

Size...............	16	17	18	19 in.
Japanned	......	......	......	......
Galvanized	......	......	......	......
Japanned, Gold Band,	......	......	......	......

PRESSED COAL HODS.—Funnel Mouth.

Size..................	16	17	18	19 in.
Japanned	.....	......	......	......
Galvanized	......	......	......	......
Japanned, Gold Band.	......	......	......	......

COAL VASES.

No. 199, Square Front, Black Ground, Ornament on Cover and Front, Plain Gilt Lines ....
No. 202, Octagon Front, Same as above ....

PALACE COAL VASES.

No. 226, Round Front Corners, Black Ground, Ornamentation on Cover and Front, Fine Gilt Lines—hand work, ...
No. 228, Octagon Front, Same as above ....

Prices do not include Shovels, Tongs and Poker.

BRASS ANDIRONS.

No. 100, 12 in. High............ ......
No. 101, 16 in. " ....
No. 149, 20 in. " ....

COMMON DOG IRONS.

Nos..	1	2	3	4	5
Lbs..	15	18	20	24	28 per Pair.
	....	....	....	....	....

VAJEN & NEW, INDIANAPOLIS, IND.

FIRE IRONS AND FIRE SETS.

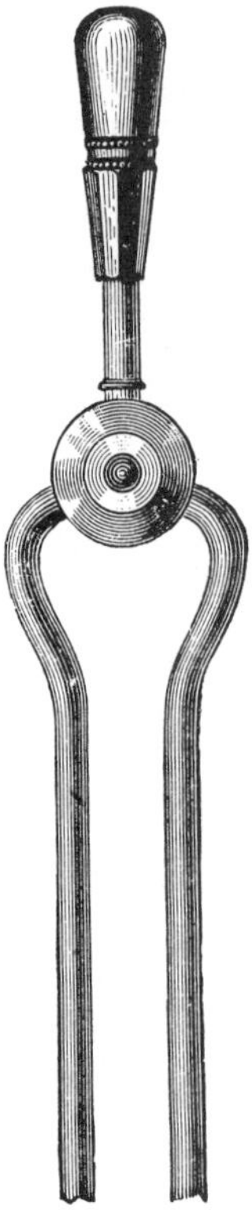

No. 42.

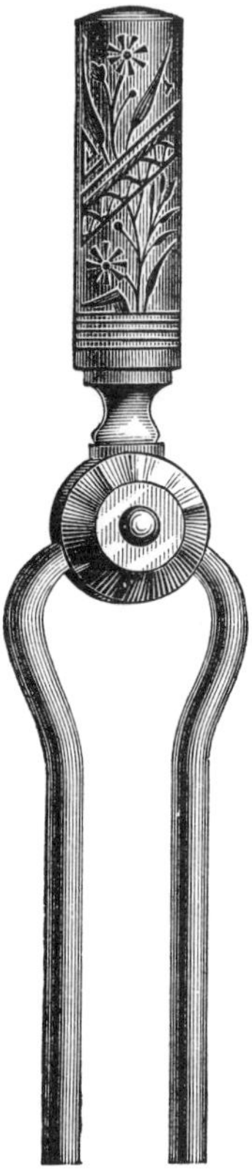

Nos. 50 and 51.

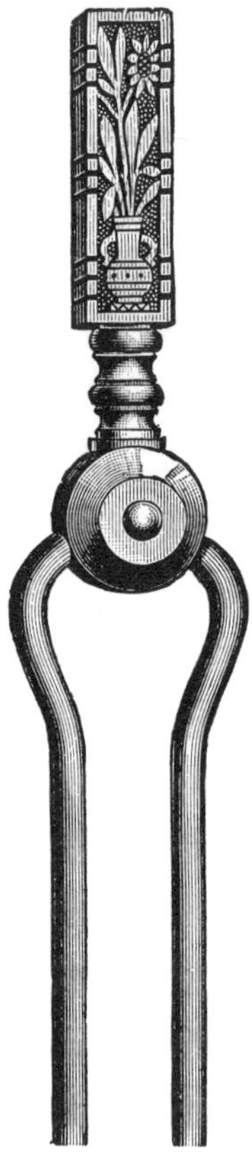

Nos. 55 and 56.

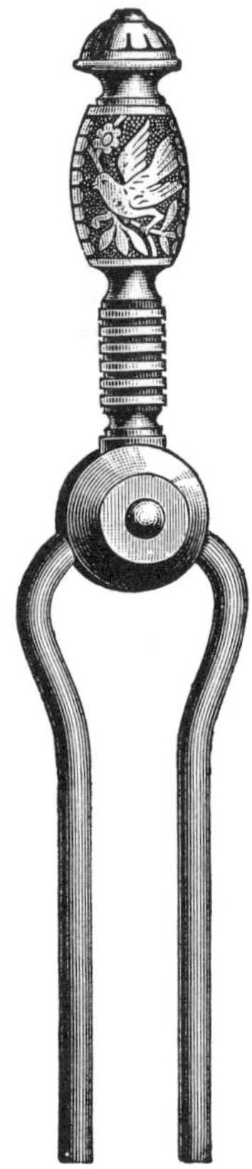

Nos. 65 and 66.

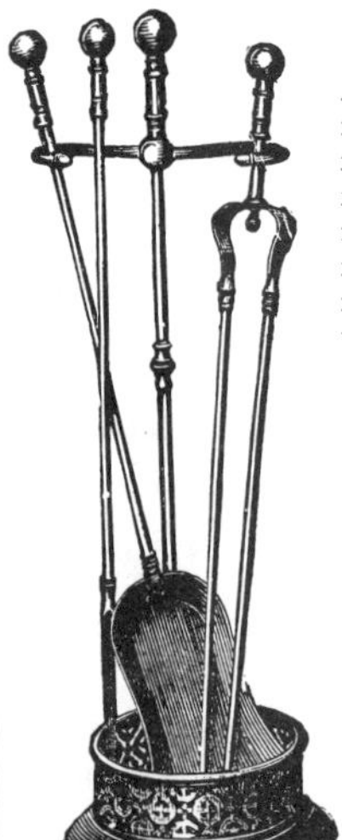

POLISHED STEEL FIRE IRONS.

No. 42, Beaded and Hexagon Ormolu Head ....
No. 50, Gold Lacquered Head.......................... ......
No. 51, Ormolu Bronze " ....
No. 55, Gold Lacquered " ....
No. 56, Ormolu Bronze " ....
No. 65, Gold Lacquered " ....
No. 66, Ormolu Bronze " ....

POLISHED BRASS FIRE SETS.

Andirons, Coal Hods, Coal Vases, Coal Grabs, Blower Stands, and Ornamented Brass Coal Hods.

Brass Fenders of any desired size, in a great variety of designs, furnished to order.

FANCY FIRE BELLOWS.

For Fire Places.................. ......

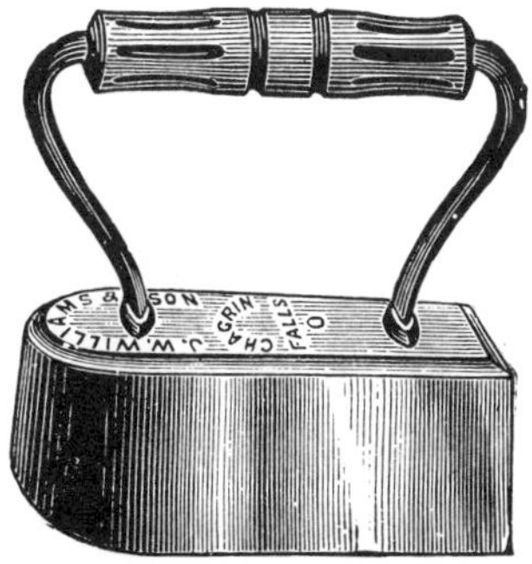

LAUNDRY POLISHING IRONS.

No. 1, For Shirt Fronts, Highly Finished........................ ....

STAR IRONS.

With Hollow, Perforated Iron Handles.

No. 70, Nickel-Plated...... ....
No. 75, Plain Polished. ... .
No. 100, Girl's Iron, Nickel-Plated. ....
No. 105, Girl's Iron, Plain Polished. ....

LAUNDRY POLISHING IRONS.

No. 2, Weight, 4...5...6...7...8 lbs...

TAILORS' IRONS.

Planed Face, Extra Polished.

Weight, 13 ...15...18 ...21....24 lbs....

See Gas Irons, page 202.

PLANED FACE, EXTRA POLISHED.

5 to 10 Pounds................. ......
100 lbs. in a Case.

MRS. POTTS' COLD HANDLE SAD IRONS.

Three Irons, One Handle and Stand constitute a set. These Irons have a detachable walnut handle, which never becomes hot.

No. 50, Nickel-Plated, in Sets............ ......
No. 55, Plain Polished.................... ......
No. 50, Nickel-Plated, Nos. 1, 2 or 3 with Handles............................... ....
No. 55, Plain Polished, Nos. 1, 2 or 3, with Handle.......................... ......

DOUBLE FLUE CHARCOAL IRONS.

Used in almost every city. The best thing out. Has flues at back to regulate the heat, and a ventilator on top, for protecting the hand.

Laundry, 8 lbs ....
Seamstress, 14½ lbs ....
Tailor, 20 lbs ....

FLUTING MACHINES.

GENEVA HAND FLUTER.

Price .. ..

The old reliable white metal Fluter.

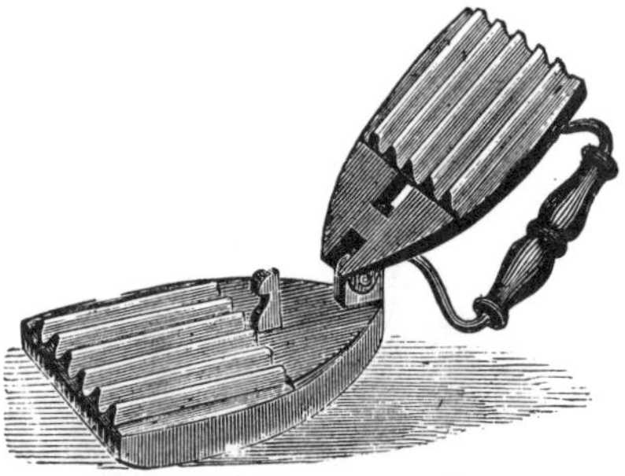

MONROE'S FLUTING SAD IRON.

Price ....

A Fluter and Sad Iron combined.

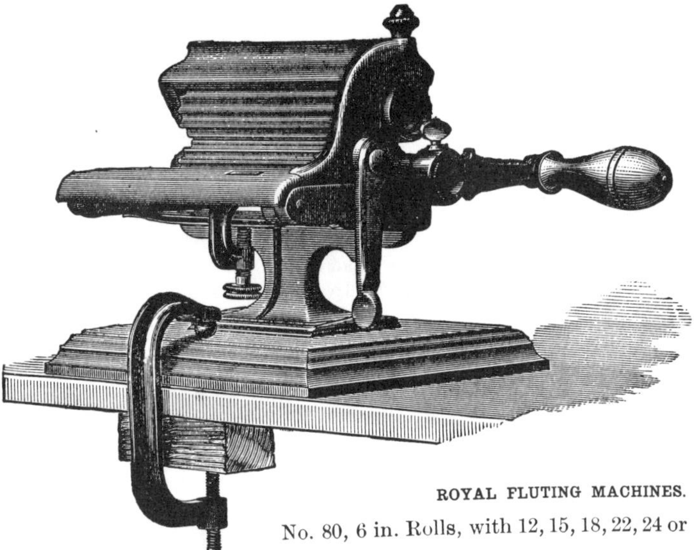

ROYAL FLUTING MACHINES.

No. 80, 6 in. Rolls, with 12, 15, 18, 22, 24 or 30 Flutes, ...

KNOX FLUTING MACHINES.

6 in., with 12, 15, 18, 22, 24 or 30 Flutes .....

See the Erie Fluter, Page 202.

SHEPHARD HAND FLUTERS.

No. 85, 3¼ in. Wide . ...

No. 98, 2⅞ in. Wide ....

No. 110, 3¼ in. Wide . ...

Both Roller and Plate Polished and Nickel Plated.

COFFEE MILLS.

ENTERPRISE COFFEE AND SPICE MILLS.

No. 2 ....

These Mills are desirable for Druggists and Family use. We can furnish our customers with any of the larger sizes when desired.

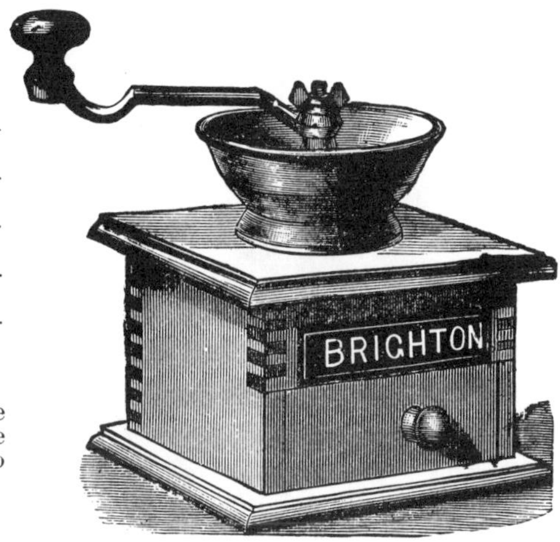

BRIGHTON BOX MILLS.

No. 1, Iron Hopper....................

No. 3, " " ....

No. 14, Plated ....

No. 16, " ....

No. 18, " ....

We do not hesitate to warrant these Mills to give satisfaction, as well as the numerous other patterns which we keep in stock.

WEBB'S STANDARD COFFEE MILLS.

No. 101, Medium size..

No. 102, Large " ..

The iron cover to this Mill is much desired by many, making it one of the best sellers.

COFFEE AND CRACKER MILLS.

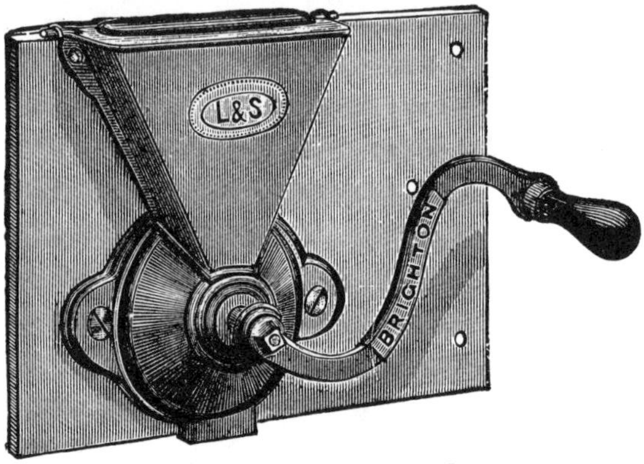

BRIGHTON SIDE COFFEE MILLS.

Nos. .... 101 ...... 202 .... 303 ..... 404 ......

BRIGHTON CRACKER AND BREAD MILL.

Price. ....

A Family Mill for grinding Bread, Crackers, Coffee, Spice, etc., and what every good housekeeper should have.

This Mill will fill a want long felt by every cook and housekeeper. It does away with that laborious and unsatisfactory method of crushing crackers with the rolling-pin; it enables the use of scraps and dry pieces of bread, which otherwise would be lost. It will grind fine or coarse, as desired.

As a Coffee Mill, it has no equal, and boarding-house keepers will find it admirably suited to their wants for this purpose.

PEERLESS.

No. $2\frac{1}{2}$, Rolls 10 x $1\frac{7}{8}$ in., Family Size . . . .

No. 3, Rolls 11 x $1\frac{7}{8}$ in. . . . .

No. 4, " 12 x 2 in . . . .

No. 5, " 14 x $2\frac{1}{4}$ in . . . .

The above Wringers will fit stationary or round tubs, thick or thin, and is the best known Wringer made.

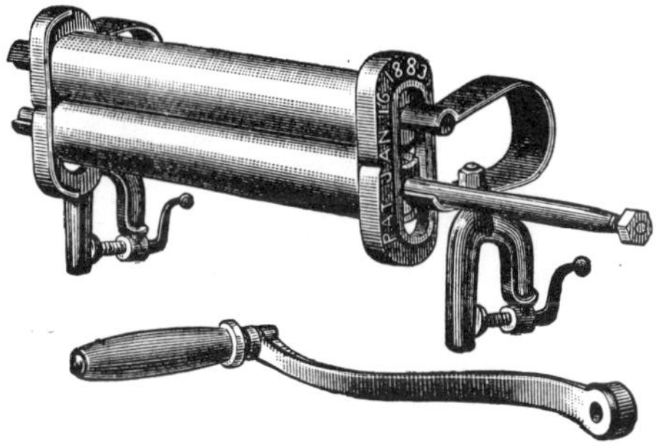

No. 99.

Iron Frame, Improvement on Eureka .

By turning handle backwards once around, the rolls can be separated, thereby relieving the pressure when not in use.

EXCELSIOR.—With Folding Bench.

No. A, Family Size, Rolls, 10 x $1\frac{3}{4}$ in. . . . . . .

The operator can stand erect while Wringing, with one hand free to spread and guide the clothes, instead of being required to steady the Wringer or tub. When not in use the Wringer can be readily detached from the bench, the latter folded, and both stored away in less space than is required for the usual "old chair."

Our Wringers all have the best rubber rolls, and guaranteed to give the best of satisfaction.

ENTERPRISE CHERRY STONER.

No. 1.................... ......

A new Cherry Stoner, which we particularly recommend to those desiring rapid work. It can be adjusted by thumb screws to adapt it to the different sizes of cherry stones. It will be found very rapid in its work, and a decided improvement over others of this class.

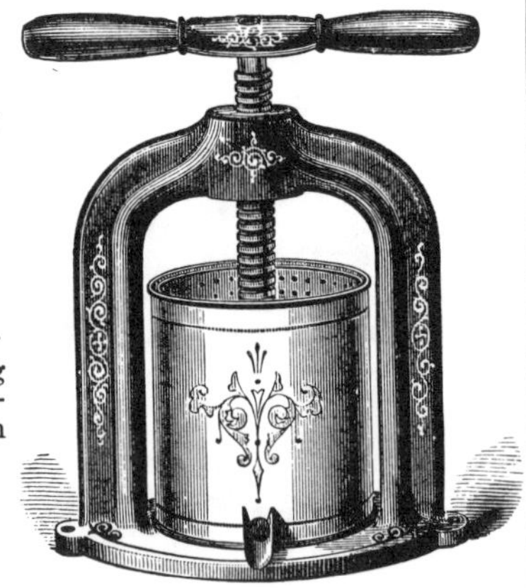

ENTERPRISE TINCTURE PRESS.

Quarts ....1.... 2.... 4.... 8....

A Druggist's Tincture Press, which is very strong and durable, as well as reasonable in price. Druggists will find this Press suitable for their wants, in making tinctures, decoctions, infusions, &c.

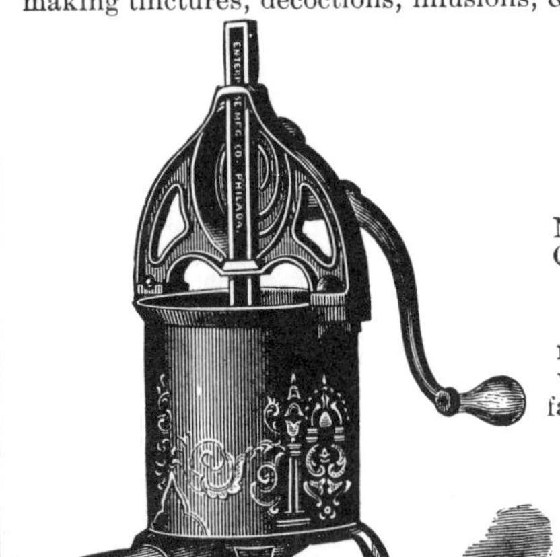

ENTERPRISE COMBINED SAUSAGE STUFFER,
Fruit, Lard and Jelly Press.

Nos............	5....	15....	25 ...	35....
Quarts.....	2	2	4	8
	Rack.	Screw.	Screw.	Screw.

These are decidedly the easiest working and most durable machines ever manufactured, and will be found useful for many purposes in every family.

VEGETABLE GRATERS.

Price ....

The best thing yet found for grating horse-radish, pumpkin, squash, carrot, cocoanut and other vegetables, or crackers, cheese, &c.

Apple Parers.... ....

Apple Parers, Corers and Slicers.. ....

Peach Parers.... ....

Potato Parers.... ....

WHITE MOUNTAIN FREEZER.--Triple Motion.

It has no equal.

Size.	List Price.	Size.	List Price.
2 Quarts	$3 75	10 Quarts	$10 00
3 "	4 50	15 "	15 00
4 "	5 50	20 "	20 00
6 "	7 00	25 "	25 00
8 "	8 00	50 "	60 00

Fly Wheels for 8, 10, 15, 20 and 25 qts., extra, $5
" " " 50 qts., extra..............$10
Discount...........

Power Freezers, 25 and 50 qts. furnished to order. Packing Cans and Tubs furnished to order.

The White Mountain Freezer has three motions. The center beater shaft has lifter arms, or floats, which mix the cream in the middle, turning opposite the outside beater. The outside beater scrapes the cream off the can, and has floats extending to inside beater, which throws cream to center, when it is thrown back by the inside beater to the outside, the can at the same time turning in an opposite direction, making three simultaneous motions, thus mixing the cream thoroughly and evenly. These beaters are of malleable iron and coated with pure block tin. The White Mountain Freezer has no large surfaces of zinc in contact with the cream, but tin instead. Families especially should look to this, as Freezers put away damp will, when dry, show oxide of zinc, which is a well-known poison.

NORTH POLE FREEZER.—Double Motion, Top Crank.

Size.	List Price.
2 Quarts	$3 00
3 "	3 50
4 "	4 50
6 "	5 50
8 "	6 50
10 "	8 00

Discount...........

This Freezer is a marvel of simplicity; will freeze cream in from five to ten minutes; is a good, reliable, cheap freezer.

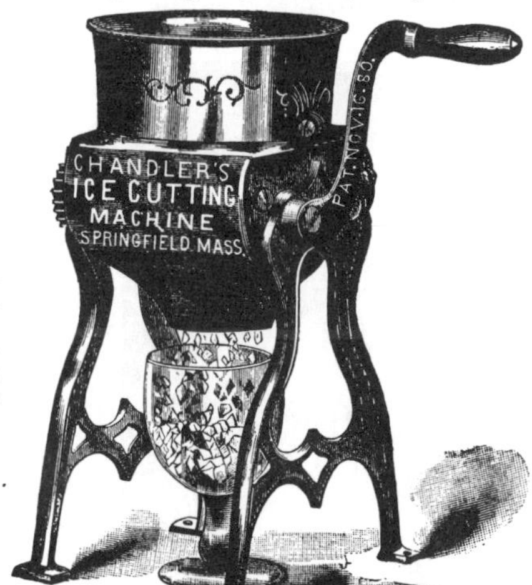

CHANDLER'S ICE CUTTING MACHINE.

Indispensable for family use. No chilled hands. A small, compact, simple, strong and cheap machine, which cuts ice into small, diamond-shaped pieces with the utmost ease and rapidity. Occupies a space only eight inches square. For Iced Tea or Coffee, or Ice Cream it has no equal.

No. 1........ ...... No. 2........ ......

COOLERS.

Galvanized Iron Ice Chambers. Fancy Colors. New Ornaments.

Bronzed Lever Faucets, 2...... 3 ...... 4 ..... 5 Gal .....

These Coolers are well packed, and constructed with the view of saving all the ice possible.

COOLERS.

Galvanized Iron Ice Chambers. Fancy Colors. New Ornaments.

Nickel-Plated Faucets, 2...... 3 ..... 4 .... 5 Gal .....
8 ... 10......12 " .....

Porcelain-Lined Ice Chambers.

Patent Self-Closing Faucets, 2 .. 3....4... 6....8 Gal....

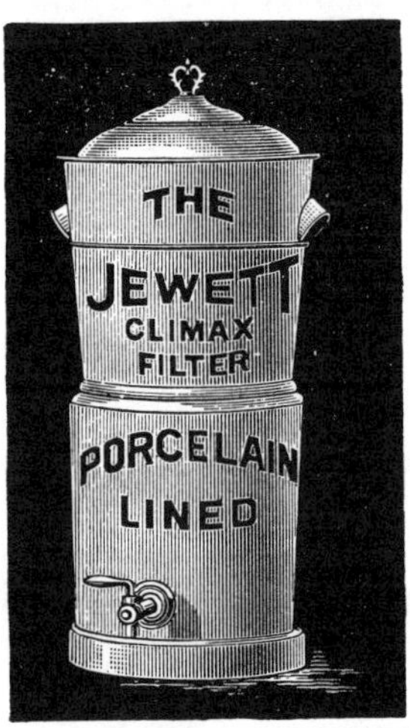

THE CLIMAX FILTER.

With Solid Iron Reservoir, Lined with White Porcelain.

No..................	52	53	54	55
Reservoir...........	2	3	4½	6½ Gals.
Price	......	......	......	......

A Filter for the million. The filtering medium is enclosed in a substantial shell of galvanized iron, fitted to the top of a porcelain-lined, cast-iron reservoir. This reservoir does not pretend to be a cooler, but still may be found a valuable substitute for such.

The No. 53 is the best family size, and always kept in stock.

CARPET SWEEPERS AND STRETCHERS.

STAR CARPET SWEEPER.

Price ....

This Sweeper sweeps close to the wall and base board, and also has rubber cushions around the box to keep the Sweeper from marking the furniture; the rubber is vulcanized on the wheels, merits which no other Sweeper possesses. The brush can be raised or lowered on either side. The only one which has the same mechanical movement as used in sweeping with a broom. We warrant it to take up what a broom will leave, even to wet sand.

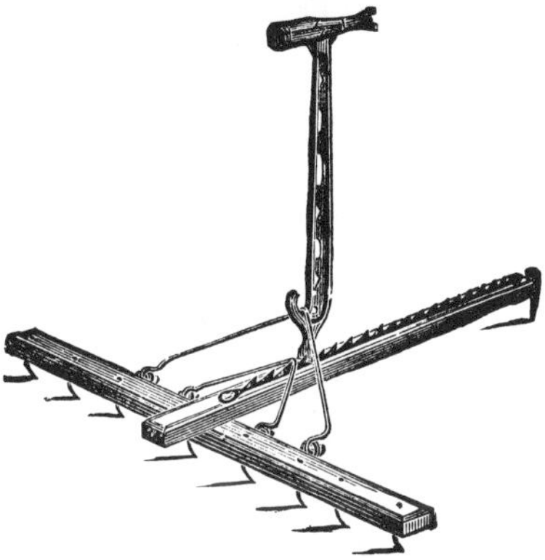

EXCELSIOR CARPET STRETCHER,

And Tack Hammer Combined.

Price ....

The most compact and complete machine ever offered to families for putting down carpet. Saves Labor, Time, Temper, Backache and Profanity.

Its merits are proved. It is needed. Every family should have one. It does its work effectually, handling the most obdurate carpet like a charm.

CARPET STRETCHER HANDLES.

30 Inches (will fit all stretchers) . ...

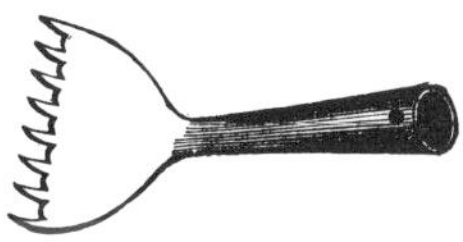

No. 2.

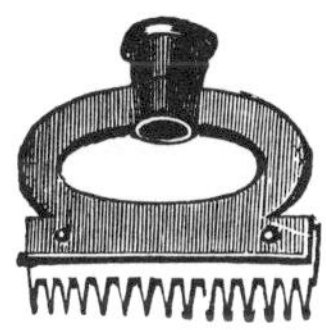

No. 1.

CARPET STRETCHERS.

No. 1, Cast Steel Teeth............ ....
No. 2, Socket, Cast Steel.......... ....

WHISK BROOMS.

Pocket...... Hand..... Barber's Whisk Brooms......

HOUSE BROOMS.

Nos. .... 1...... 2...... 3, Heavy......

STABLE OR STREET BROOMS.

Hickory Splint................................ ......
Rattan.. ......
Steel... ......

HAND BELLOWS, MOPS, &C.

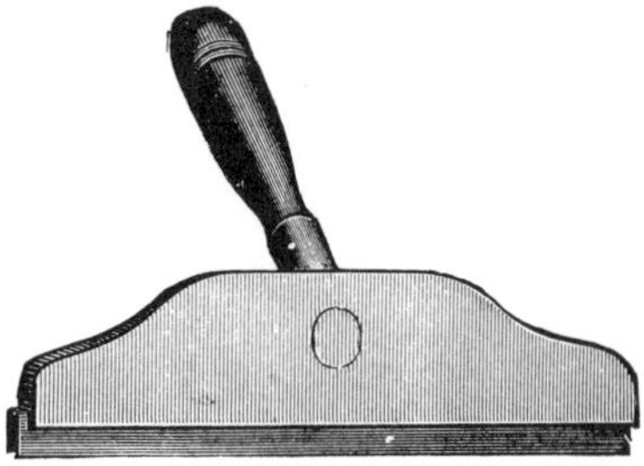

PERFECTION WINDOW CLEANERS.

Inch.. 8 ..... 10 .... 12...... 14......

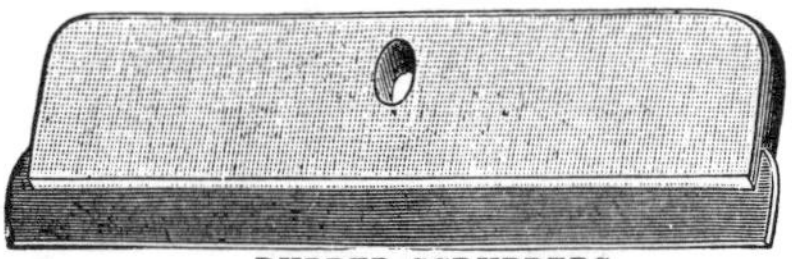

RUBBER SCRUBBERS.

Inch .... 12 ..... 14 ....

MOP AND BRUSH HOLDER.

Will hold a Mop or Brush equally well and is adjustable to any size brush.

COTTON MOPS.—Full Weight.

12 ... 14.... 16 ... 18 ... 20 ... 24 oz....

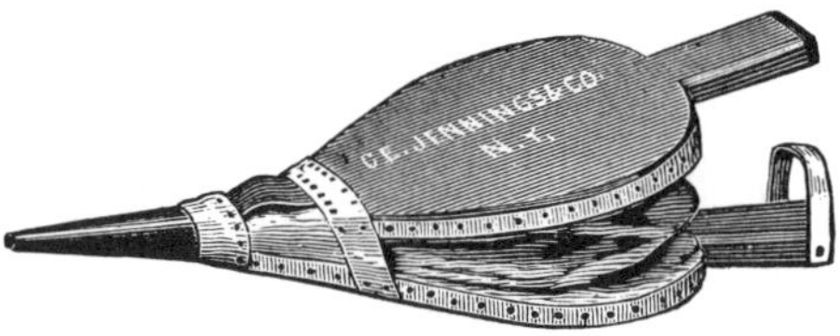

HAND BELLOWS.

Inch.. .. 8...... 9...... 10......

See Moulders' Tools for Moulders' Bellows.

GEM TOWEL RACKS.

Nickel Plated Tips..... ....

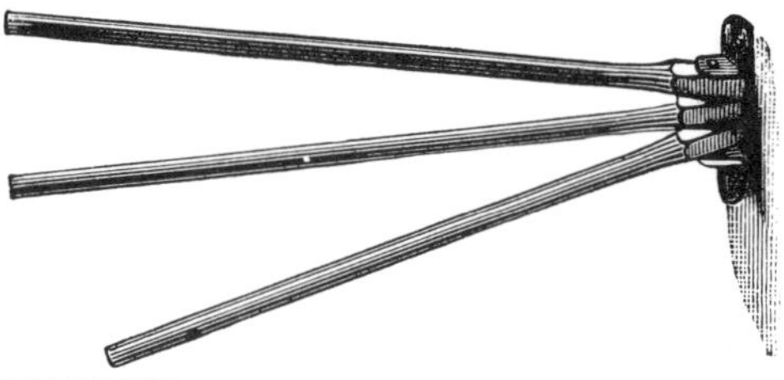

SHOE BLACKING.

The Genuine V AND N French Blacking.

No. .... 1...... 2...... 3......

This is the best Blacking in the market. **Try it.**

RISING SUN STOVE POLISH.

Price ....

DIXON'S STOVE POLISH.

Price.........

Sold in any quantity desired.

BASKETS, PUMPS, HODS, SAW BUCKS, ETC.

Willow Market Baskets,
Split Market Baskets,
Oak Feed Baskets, with Bail,
Split Baskets, 1 and 1½ Bushel.

Willow Clothes Baskets,
Split Clothes Baskets, Square.
Rattan Baskets, 1, 2, 3, 4, 5 Bushel.
Split Hampers, Rattan Hampers.

WRAPPING PAPERS.

White Tea ...... Manilla.... ...... Rag..... ...... Straw ... .

CHAIN PUMPS.

Price.................. ......

Complete with Chain, Fixtures, Tubing and Rubber Buckets, for 10 ft. well or cistern.

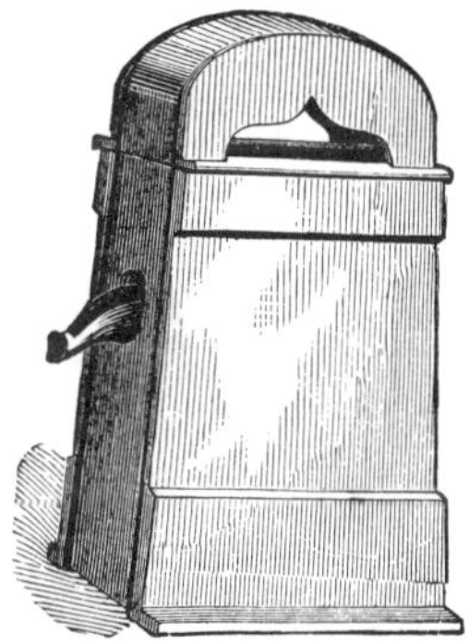

HODS.

Mortar Hods, Water Tight.. ......
Brick " ....

Mortar Hods made of soft wood, kiln dried, sides rabbeted, and all joints put together with white lead.

SAW BUCKS.

Plain.................................... ......
Folding ....

Made of hard wood, very strong.

VAJEN & NEW, INDIANAPOLIS, IND.

MISCELLANEOUS GOODS.

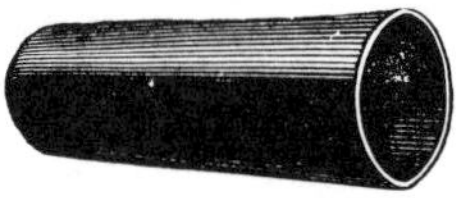

CANE AND UMBRELLA FERRULES.

Steel, Closed End, Assorted..... ......

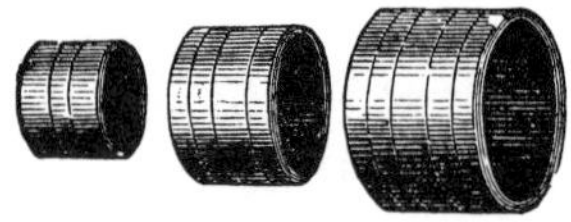

WROUGHT SEAMLESS BRASS FERRULES.

Assorted ....

MALLEABLE IRON FERRULES.

Assorted, $\frac{3}{4}$ to $1\frac{1}{8}$ in ....

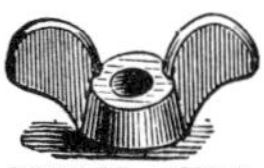

THUMB NUTS.

For 3-16 $\frac{1}{4}$ 5-16 $\frac{3}{8}$ $\frac{1}{2}$in.
....

HARROW TEETH.

Plain Iron	$\frac{3}{4}$.....	$\frac{7}{8}$... ..	1 in	.....
Headed "	$\frac{3}{4}$.....	$\frac{7}{8}$	1 in	.....
Plain Steel.....	$\frac{5}{8}$	$\frac{3}{4}$	$\frac{7}{8}$ in	.....
Headed "	$\frac{5}{8}$.....	$\frac{3}{4}$.....	$\frac{7}{8}$ in	.....

Malleable Corner Irons or Braces.

$4\frac{7}{8}$ inches long by $\frac{3}{4}$ inches wide................ ......

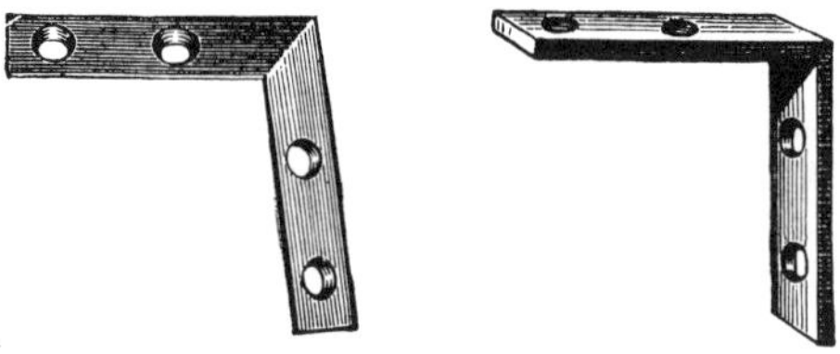

CORNER IRONS.

Malleable....$2\frac{1}{2}$x$\frac{1}{2}$...... $2\frac{3}{8}$x$\frac{1}{2}$ flat ....

Wrought, Inch $\frac{3}{4}$....$\frac{7}{8}$....1 $1\frac{1}{8}$ $1\frac{1}{4}$

QUOITS.

Japanned, per set of four ....

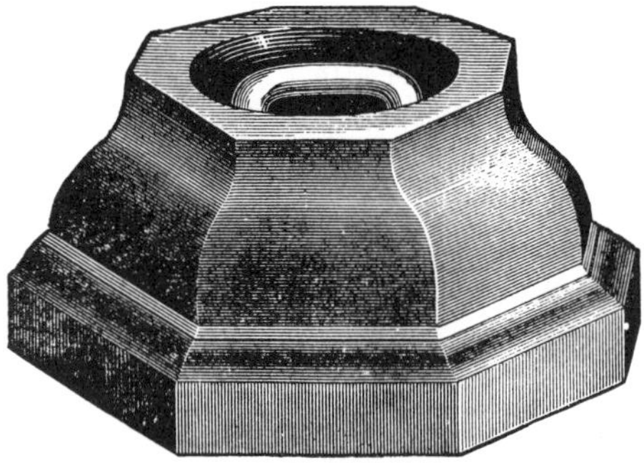

HITCHING WEIGHTS.

Pounds...	12	15	18	21	24	27	30
Per lb......							

We have Horse Weights in other styles than the one illustrated above.

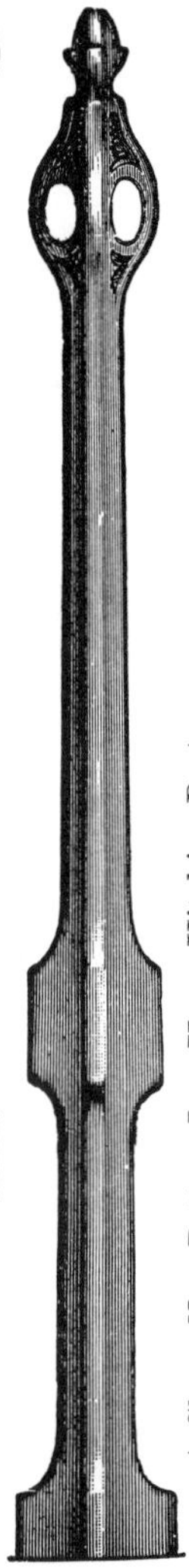

A Cheap New Pattern Iron Horse Hitching Post ....

SCALES AND STEELYARDS.

UNION COUNTER SCALES.

Single Beam, Tin Scoop, Japanned............ ......
Double " " " " ....
Single " Brass," " ....
Double " " " " ....

JAPANNED TEA SCALES.

No. 1, Capacity, .. 4 lb .... No. 6, Capacity, .. 6 lb......

HATCH'S COUNTER SCALES.

Capacity, 8 lb ....

STEEL PIVOT TRIP SCALES. — With Brass Scoop.

Handsomely Ornamented, Japanned Red.

Nos......	2	3	4	5
Capacity..................	8	4	2	2 lb
Without Side Beam	......	......	......	......
With " "	......	......	......	......

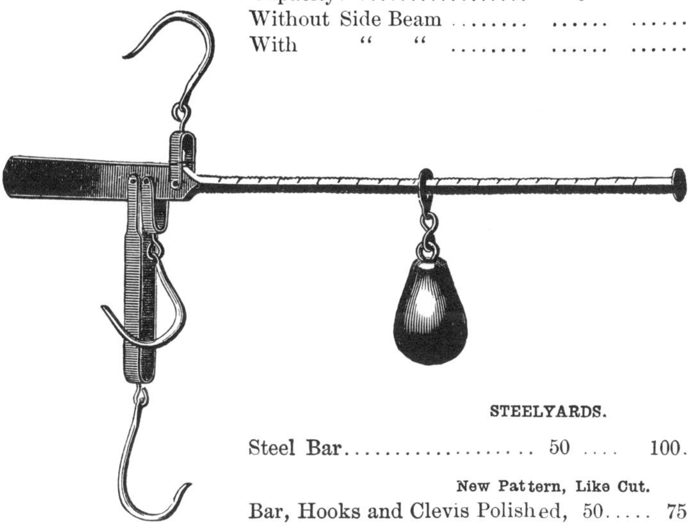

STEELYARDS.

Steel Bar.................. 50 .... 100...... 150......

New Pattern, Like Cut.

Bar, Hooks and Clevis Polished, 50..... 75..... 100 lb.....

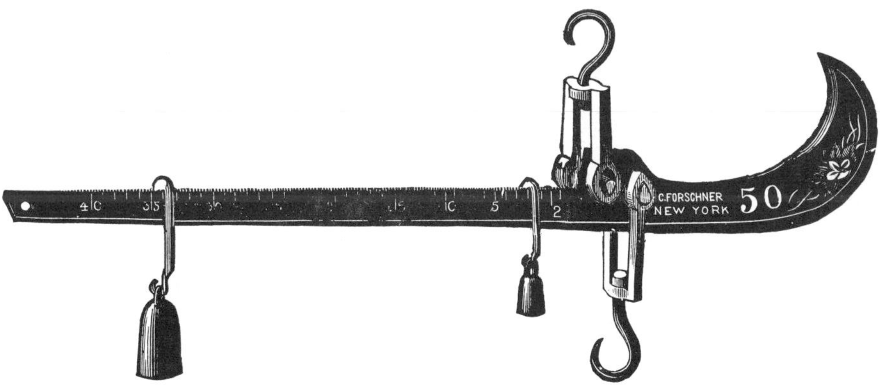

SCALE BEAMS.

To Weigh ....250...... 300...... 400...... 500...... 700 lb......

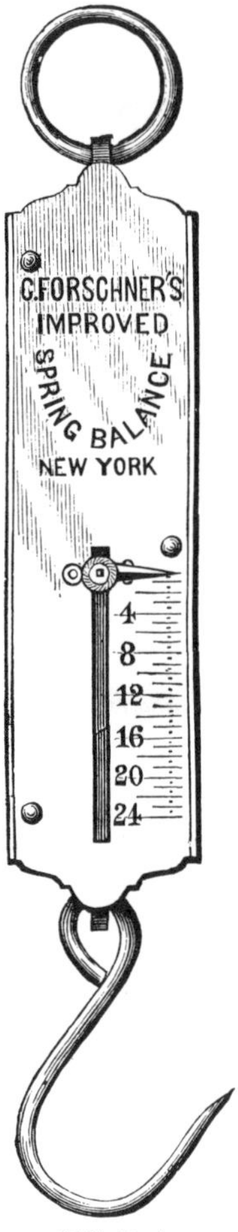

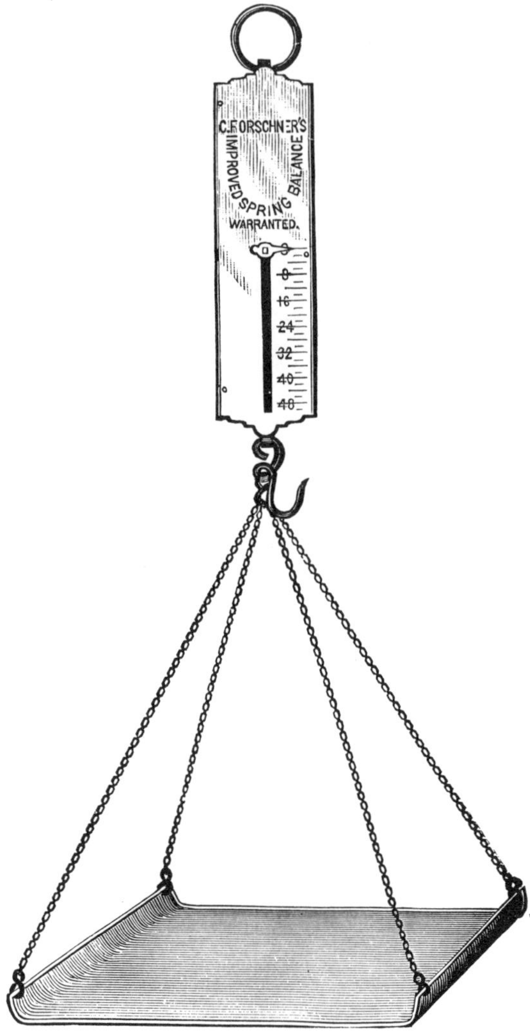

With Hook.

No. 11, 24 lb by ½ lb, Light, Straight ....
No. 12, 48 " 1 " " " ......
No. 16, 24 " ½ " Heavy, " ......
No. 19, 50 " 1 " " " ......
No. 25, 24 " ½ " Round ....
No. 26, 50 " ½ " " ....

With Round Pan.

No. 27, 24 lb by ½ lb, Round ....
No. 32, 24 " ½ " Straight ....
No. 35, 50 " 1 " " ....
No. 61, 10 " 1 oz, Circular ....

With Square Pan.

No. 40, 24 lb by ½ lb, Straight.... ......
No. 43, 50 " 1 " " ....
No. 77, 30 " 1 oz, Circular... ......

Circular Balances, with Glass Sash.

No. 114, 30 lb by 1 oz, Square Pan ......
No. 121, 30 " 1 " Tinned Iron Bows and Swivel ....
No. 126, 30 lb by 1 oz, Deep Tin Pan, Brass or Iron Bows .. ..

Boston Market Scales.

No. 140, 30 lb by 1 oz, Porcelain Pan, Nickel-Plated Bows.......... ......

United States Market Balances.

30 lb by 1 oz, Large Dial, Nickel-Plated Glass Sash, Porcelain Pan, Nickel-Plated Bows and Swivel ....

TRYERS AND TESTERS.

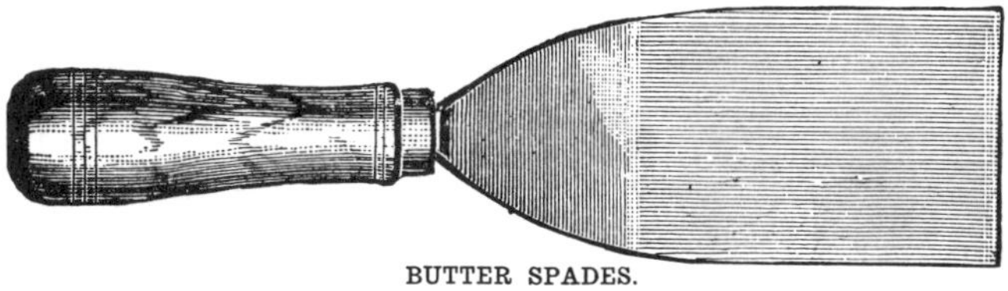

BUTTER SPADES.

Cast Steel, Tinned, for cutting and extracting Butter, Lard, Tallow, etc., from a tub or firkin ....

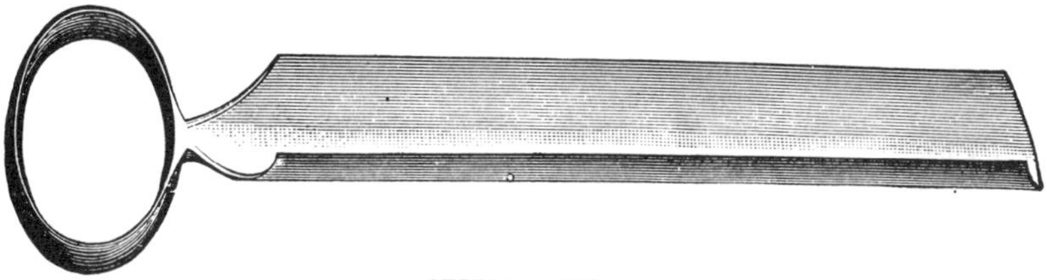

CHEESE TRYERS.

Forged Solid Cast Steel, Nickel-Plated.......................... 5...... 6 in ....

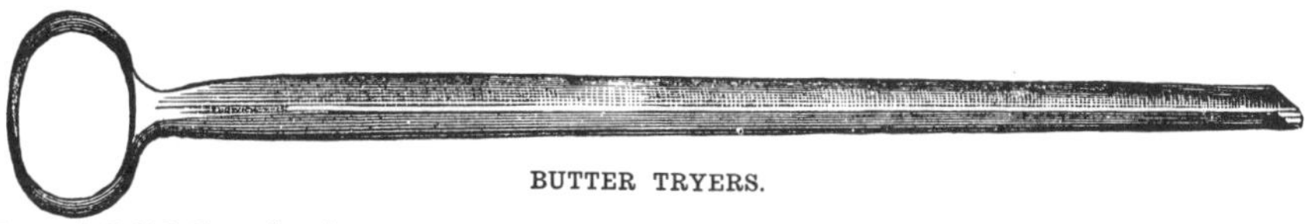

BUTTER TRYERS.

Forged Solid Cast Steel .... 18 in ...

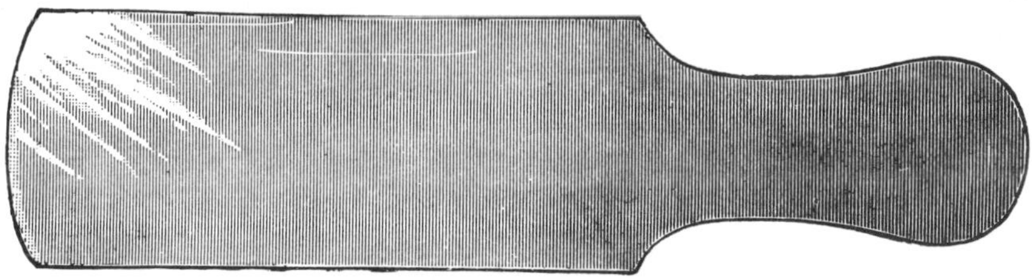

FLOUR TESTERS.

Cast Steel, Nickel-Plated ....

COFFEE TRYERS.

Cast Steel, Solid Points.. .....

HAM STRINGERS.

No. 1, Cast Steel.. ....

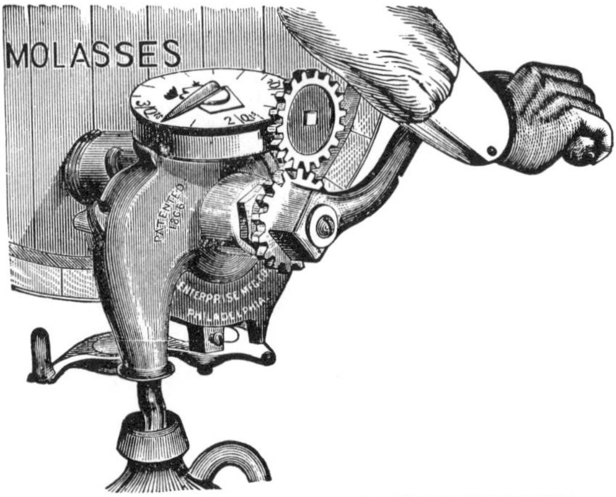

IMPROVED PATENT SUCTION AND FORCE MEASURING PUMPS.

Price ....

For molasses, thick oils, varnish, tar, &c.

ENTERPRISE "CHAMPION" SMOKED BEEF CUTTER.

Price ....

The best and cheapest in the market. A necessity for all grocers.

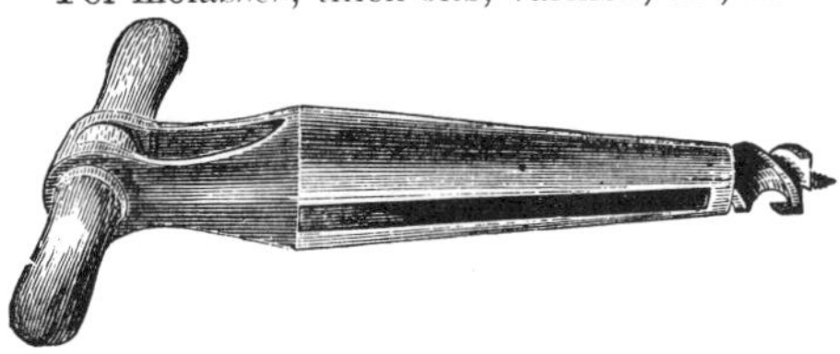

ENTERPRISE IMPROVED BUNGHOLE BORER, OR HOLLOW AUGUR.

No. 2, To 2 Inch Hole.............................

TUCKER'S ALARM MONEY DRAWER.

Price ....

It is made of hard wood; has six round cups for coin; is always set; is as easily opened as a common drawer; will sound the alarm promptly if tampered with by a thief. Combination changed in a SECOND. Need no key; no repairs.

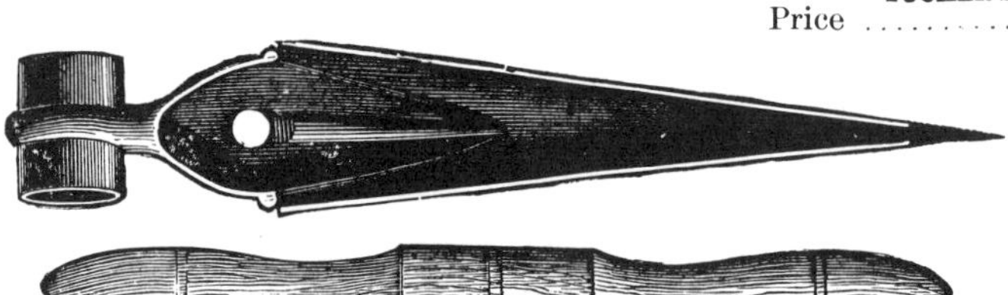

TAP BORERS.

1¾ Inch....................... 2 Inch..................

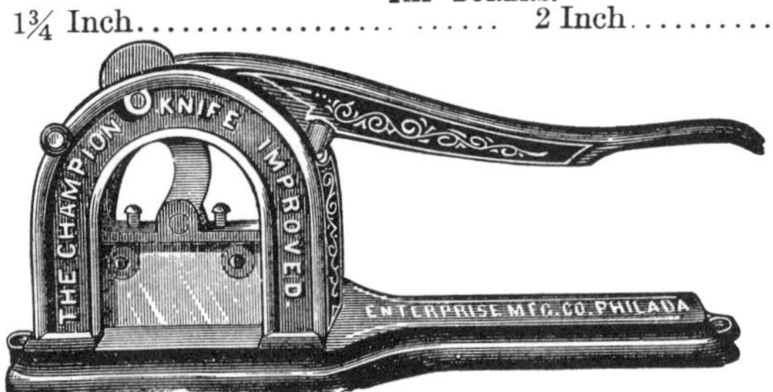

ENTERPRISE "CHAMPION" TOBACCO, ROOT AND HERB CUTTERS.

No. 1 .... No. 2..................

TOBACCO CUTTERS.

All Iron Bronzed.

No. 2 ....

Also "American" Tobacco Cutters.

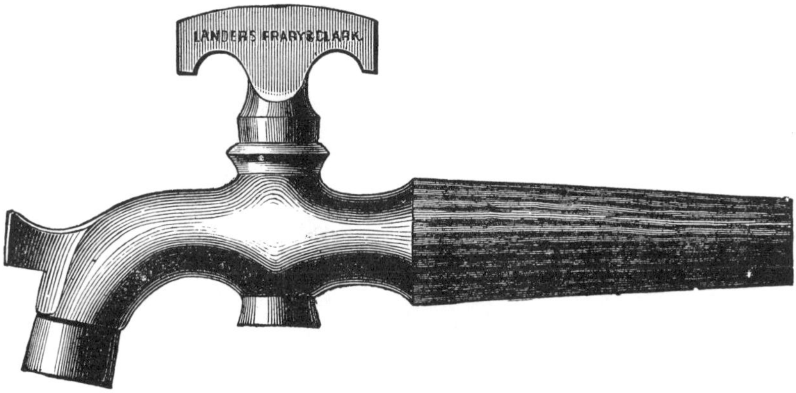

BRASS RACKING COCKS.

Size....	¼	5-16	⅜	½	⅝	¾	⅞	1 in.
Fast Key, to Drive	......	......	......	......	......	......	......	......
" " " Screw	......	......	......	......	......	......	......	......
Loose " " Drive	......	......	......	......	......	......	......	......
" " " Screw	......	......	......	......	......	......	......	......

BRASS GLOBE COCKS.

Size	¼	⅜	½	⅝	¾ in.
T Handle, Screw Shank	......	......	......	......	......
T " Tinned "	......	......	......	......	......

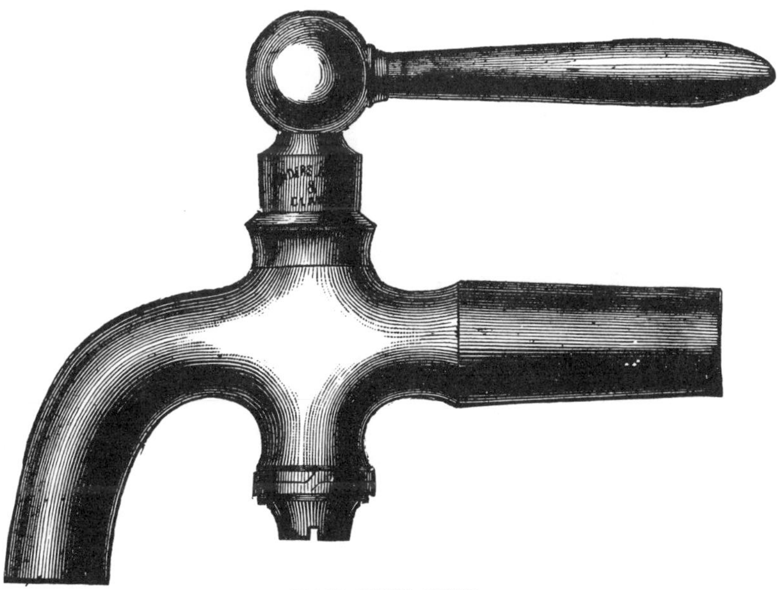

BRASS LEVER BIBBS.

Size	¼	⅜	½	⅝	¾	⅞	1 in.
Tinned Shank	......	......	......	......	......	......	......
Screw "	......	......	......	......	......	......	......

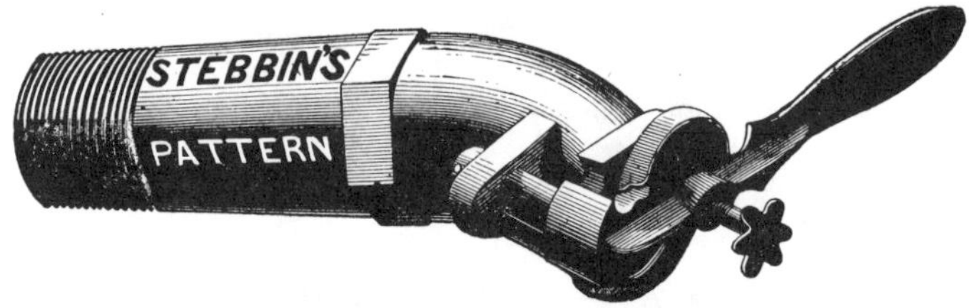

STEBBIN'S PATTERN MOLASSES GATES.

Nos. .... 1...... 2...... 3...... 4......

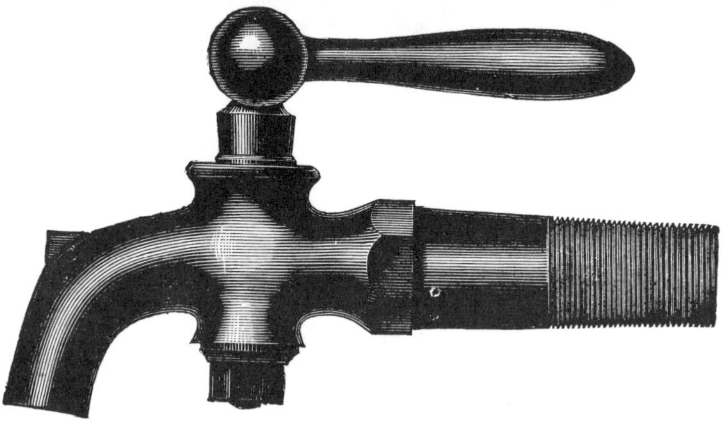

PETROLEUM FAUCETS.

Size	½	⅝	¾	1 in.
Screw Shank	......	......	......	......
Tinned "	......	......	......	......

IRON MEASURES.

Half-Bushels .... Pecks ..... Half-Pecks .... Quarter-Pecks...... Quarts......
In Nests (Half-Bushels, Pecks, Quarter and Half-Pecks, and Quarts)............ ......

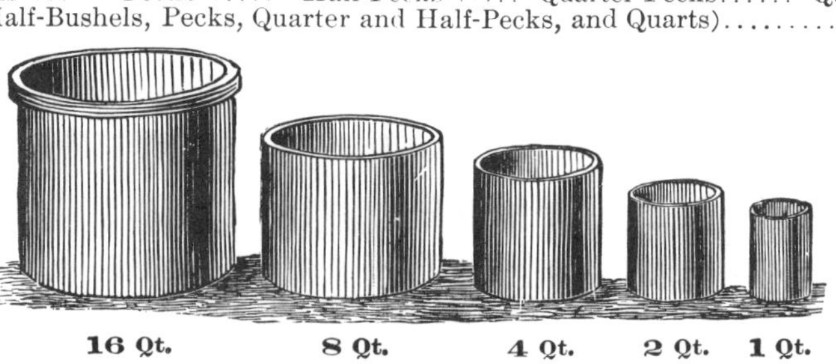

16 Qt. 8 Qt. 4 Qt. 2 Qt. 1 Qt.

WOOD MEASURES.

Half-Bushels ..... Pecks ... Half-Pecks...... Quarter-Pecks ..... Quarts......
In Nests (Half-Bushels, Pecks, Quarter and Half-Pecks, and Quarts)............ ......

CAN OPENERS, NUT CRACKS, &C.

SARDINE KNIFE OR CAN OPENER.

Iron Handle . . . .

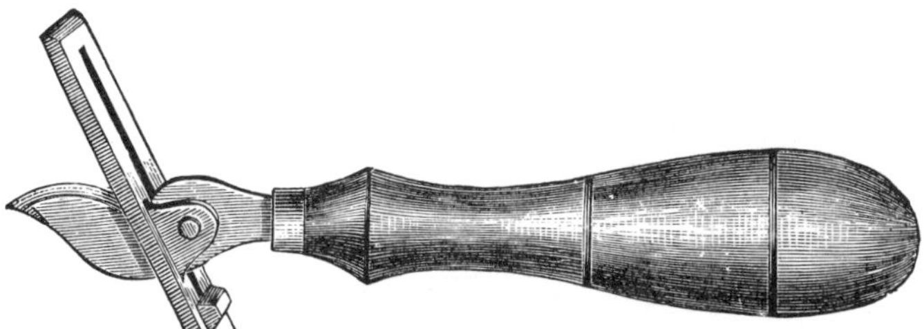

SPRAGUE'S CAN OPENER.

Wood Handle . . . . Iron Handle. . . . .

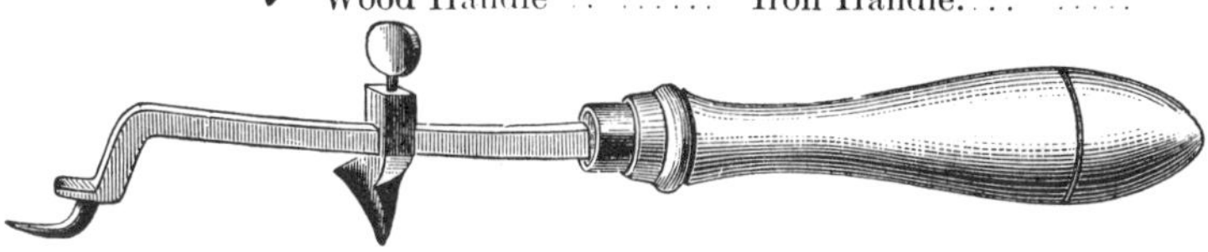

STAR CAN OPENER.

No better Can Opener in the market.

Solid Cast Steel, Rosewood Handle . . . .

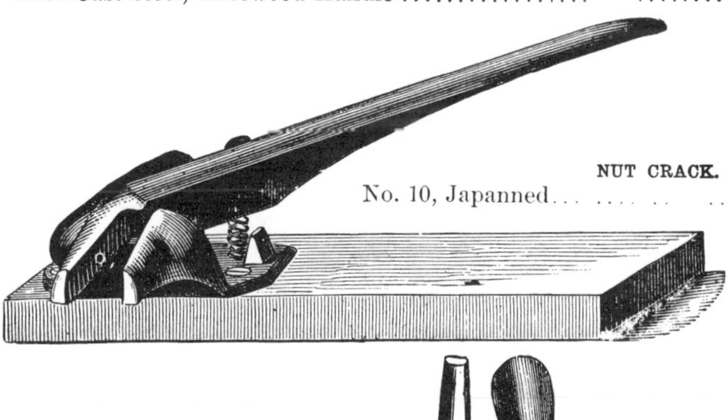

NUT CRACK.

No. 10, Japanned . . . .

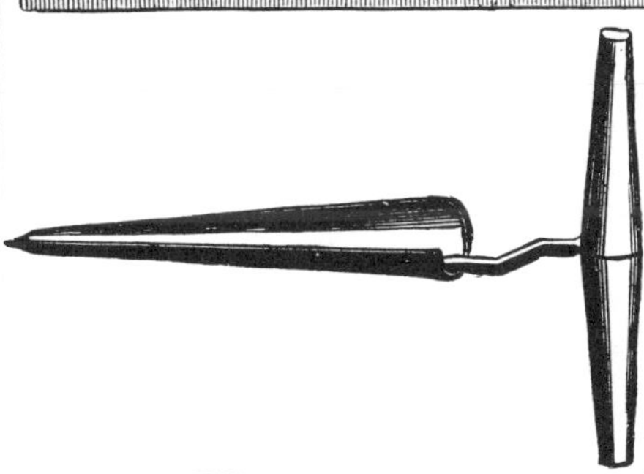

BUNG BORERS.

Bores to $1\frac{1}{2}$ Inches . . . .

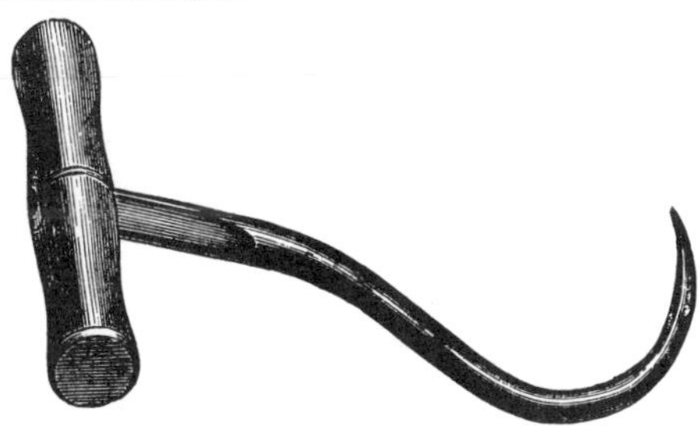

Hay Hooks . . . .

Cotton Hooks. . . . .

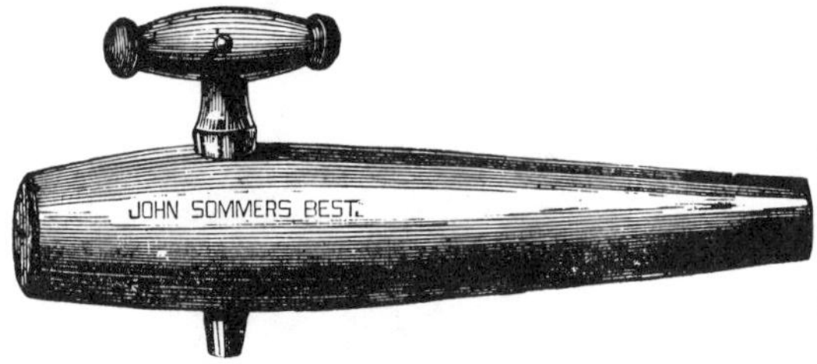

BLOCK TIN KEY FAUCETS.

Nos	0	1	2	3	4
Length	7	9	12	14	18 in.
Price	....	....	....	....	....

The Key or Stopper is pure block tin, warranted not to corrode.

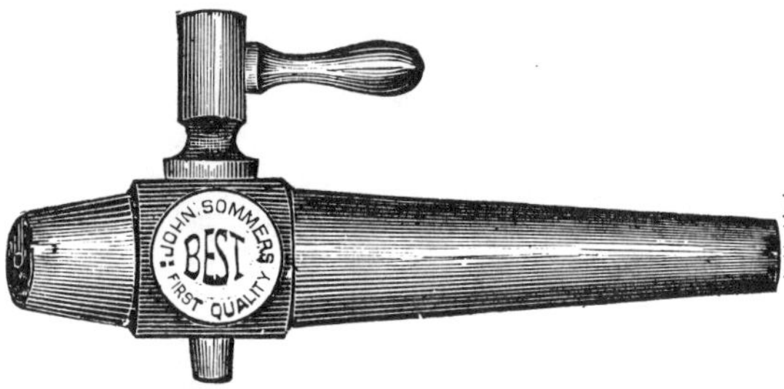

CORK LINED FAUCETS.

Nos.	0	2	4	6	8	8½	9
Length	6	7	8	9	10	12	18 in.
Price	...	...	...	...	...	...	...

RED CEDAR FAUCETS.

8 Inch.......................

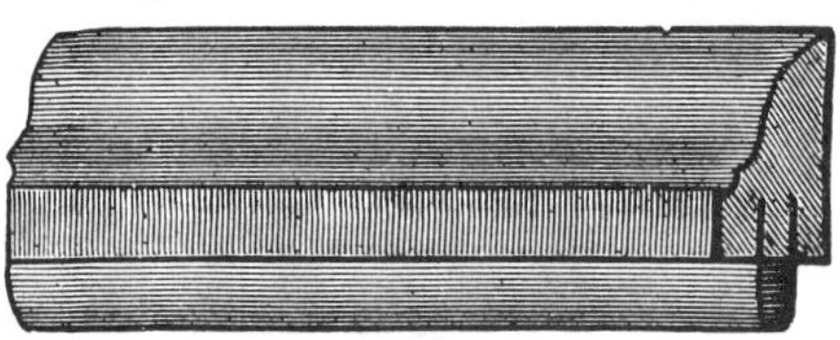

No. 1.

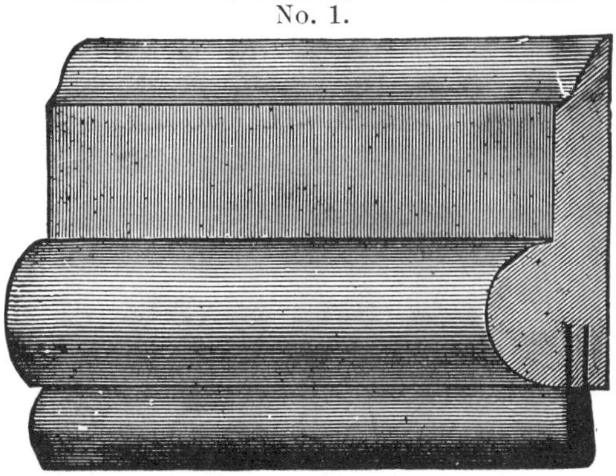

No. 4.

WEATHER STRIP.

No. 0, Applies to parting strip of windows.

No. 1, Applies to stop bead of windows and sides of doors.

No. 2, Applies to center rail of windows.

No. 3, Applies to center of double doors.

No. 4, Applies to bottom of doors.

Nos...	0	1	2	3	4
Price per ft.....	....	....	....	....	....

The cheapest and best Weather Strip in the market. Keeps out the cold, excludes rain, snow and dust. Will save its cost in fuel. Made of black walnut, with rubber inserted according to illustration.

ICE PICKS, LEMON SQUEEZERS, &C.

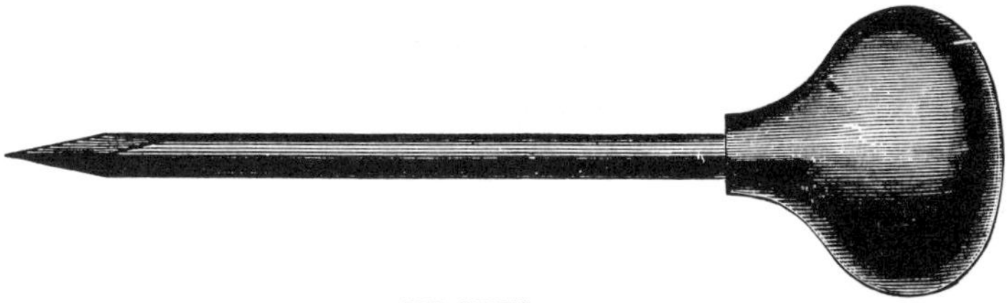

ICE PICKS.

Iron Handle.. ......
Wood Handle...Nos. 0...... 1......

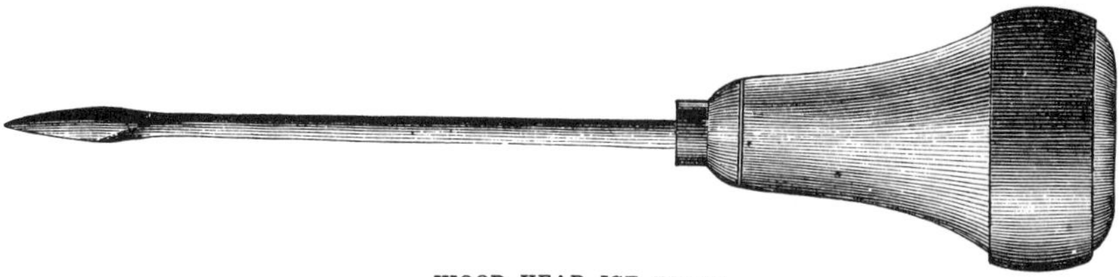

WOOD HEAD ICE PICKS

No. 3, For Breaking Ice into Small Pieces, Malleable Iron Band on Handle..... ......

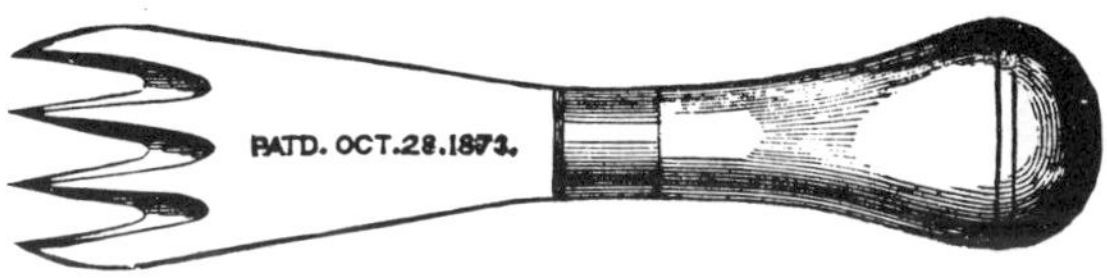

ICE CHISELS.

Cast Steel...................... ...... Converted Steel................. ......

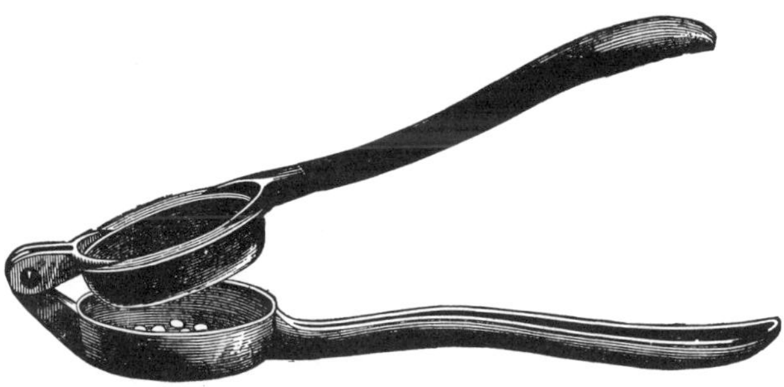

Tinned Malleable Iron Lemon Squeezers.. ......

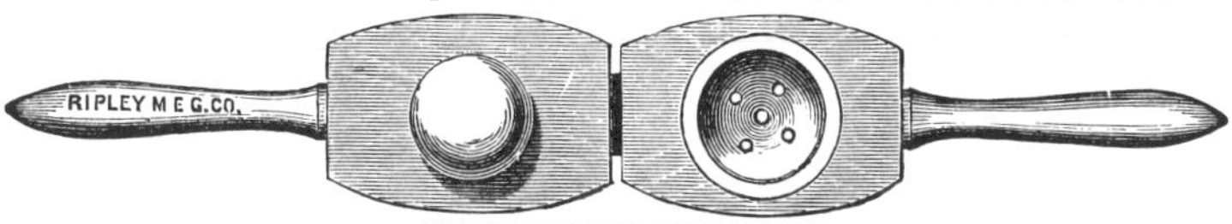

WOOD LEMON SQUEEZERS.

Common Wood................. ...... With Porcelain Bowl.............. ......

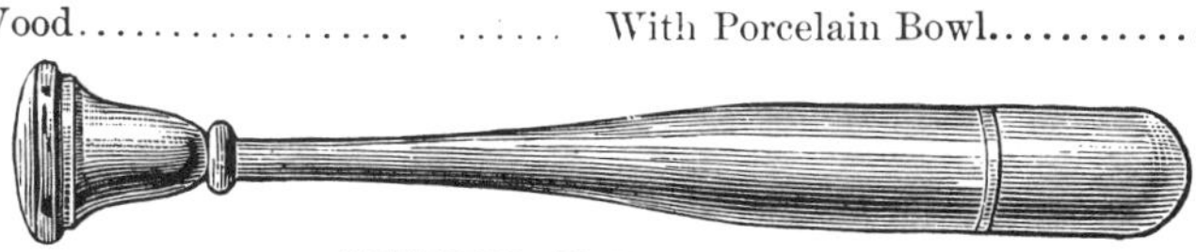

MUDDLERS, OR TODDY STICKS.

Assorted Styles and Sizes.................................... ....

MINCING KNIVES AND STEAK HAMMERS.

No. 1.
Polished Steel Blades,
Polished Handles.. ....

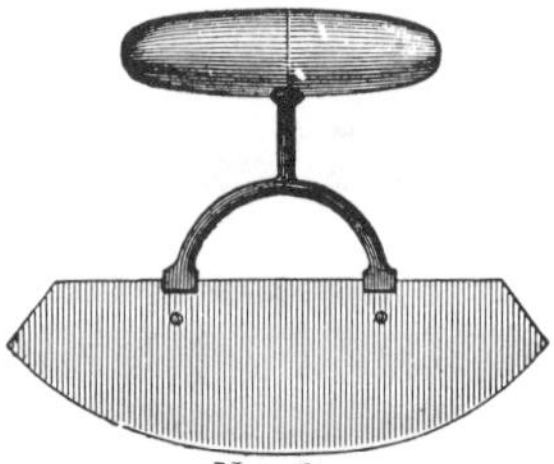

No. 2.
Polished Steel Blades,
Stained Handles. ......

No. 4.
Polished Steel Blades,
Stained Handles ....

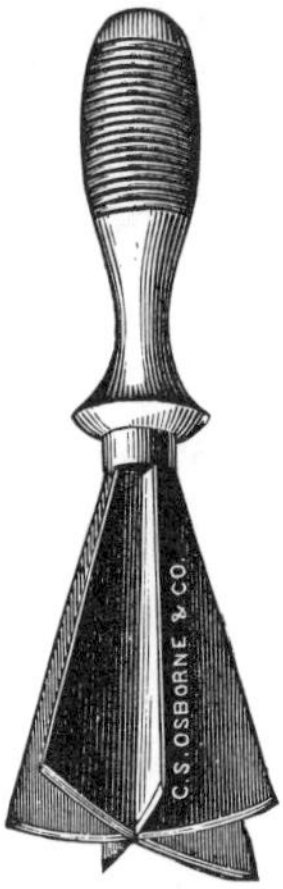

VICTOR MINCING CHOPPER.

6 Blades ....

No. 5.
Fine Polished Steel Blades,
tempered; iron handles. ....

No. 7.
Forged Cutlery Steel, tempered, Ebony polished handles ....

STEAK HAMMERS.

No. 8, Tinned....................................... ......

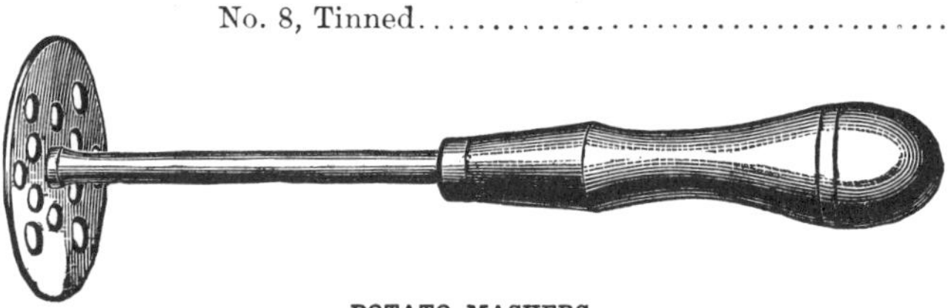

POTATO MASHERS.

Tinned... .....

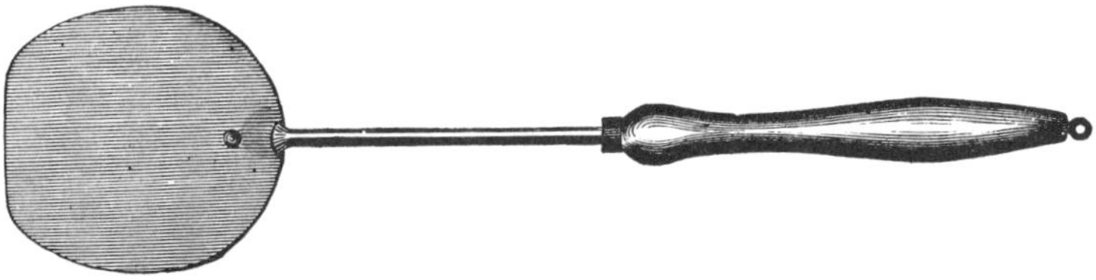

CAKE TURNERS.

No. 5, C. S. Polished Blades, Fancy Black Handles.......................... ......

MEAT CUTTERS.

Enterprise Meat Choppers.

No. 10, Clamps to Table, ...

No. 12, Screws to Table, ...

Chops 1 lb of Meat per Minute.

These Choppers do not grind or tear the meat, but as their name implies, chop it, precisely like the snipping process of a pair of scissors.

Nothing can excel them in cutting Sausage Meat, Hash, Mince Meat, Suet, Clams, Tripe, Codfish, Peppers, Chicken Salad, Chicken Croquettes, and Cabbage: also for mashing Potatoes, Pulverizing Crackers, Cutting Cocoanut for confectioner's use etc.

AMERICAN MEAT CHOPPERS.

No. 1,	8 in. Cylinder,	cuts	3 lbs. in 3 minutes....	.....
" 2,	10 "	"	" 5 to 6 " " 3 "	......
" 3,	12 "	"	" 8 to 10" " 3 "	......
" 4,	15 "	"	" 60 to 70 lbs. in an hour .	.....

With the American Chopper, a child six years of age can cut as much meat, in three or four minutes, as can be cut in an hour with the old chopping knife and tray.

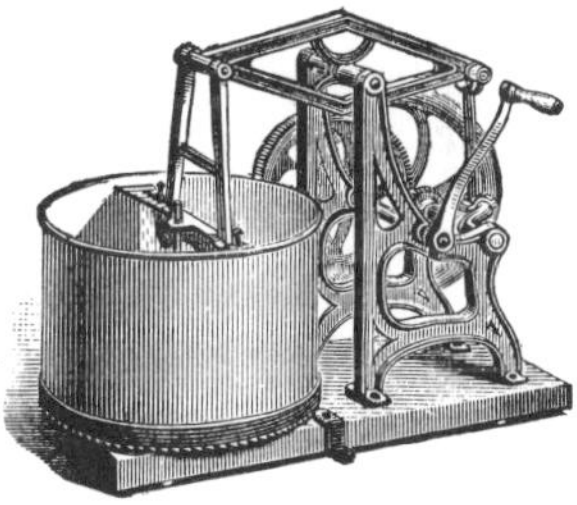

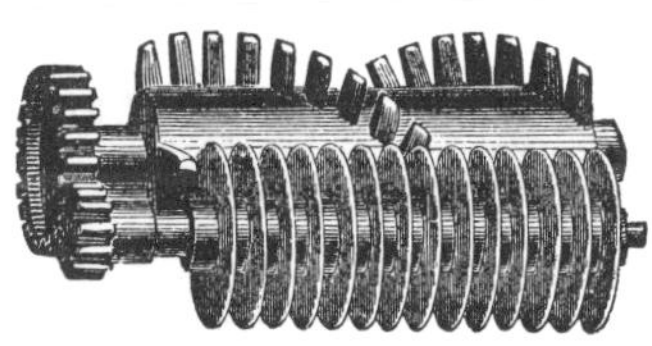

MEAT CUTTERS.

Perry's Patent.

No.... 200 . . . 300...... 400......

MEAT CUTTERS AND STUFFERS.

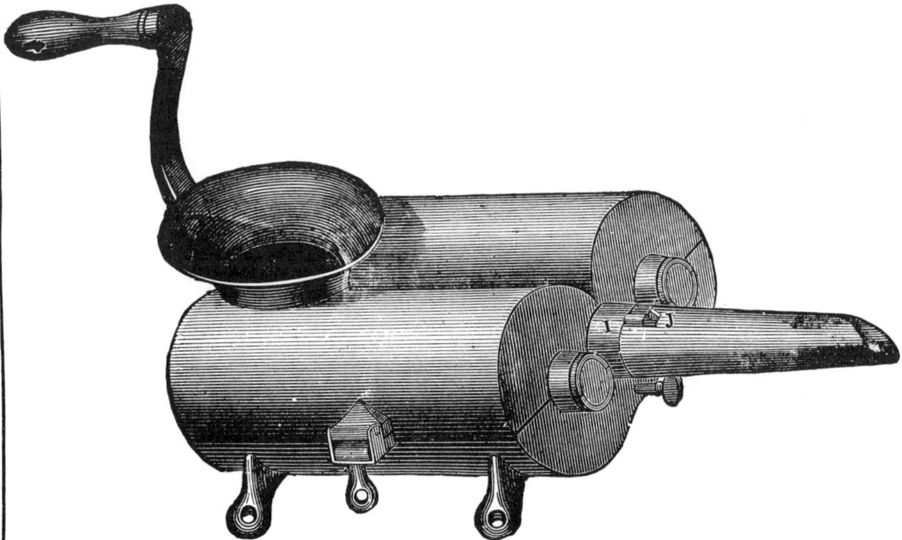

HALE'S PATENT MEAT CUTTER AND STUFFER.

Will Cut from 3 to 5 lbs. per minute.

No.. 10 ..... 11 ..... 12..... 13.....

SAUSAGE FILLER.

No. 1, For Family Use... ......
No. 0, For Butcher's Use.. ......

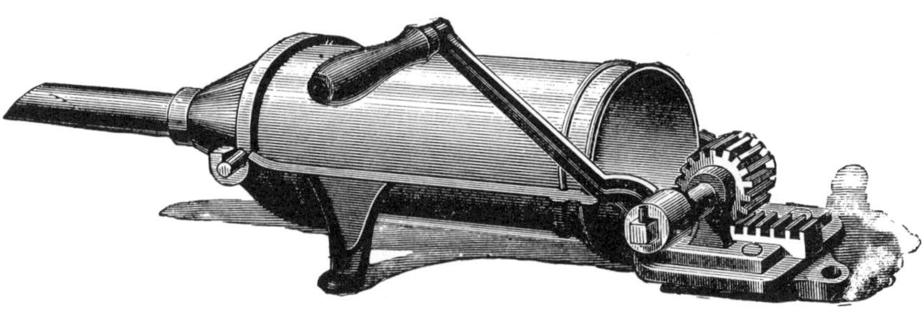

SAUSAGE FILLER.

Railroad.. ......

VAJEN & NEW, INDIANAPOLIS, IND.

LADDERS AND STAGES.

STEP LADDERS.

Feet	3	4	5	6	7	8	9	10	12	14	16
Plain	....	....	....	....	....	....	....	....	....	....	....
Patent, with Lock	....	....	....	....	....	....	....	....	....	....	....

Made of Clear Norway Pine, Strong and Light.

IMPROVED LONG LADDERS.

Feet.	10	12	14	16	18	20	22	24
	....	....	....	....	....	....	....	....

These Ladders are perfectly made. Very light, and capable of resisting a heavy load.

PATENT EXTENSION LADDERS.

Made in two sections. Especially adapted for the use of Painters, Lightning Rod Men and Tinners.

Feet	20	22	24	26	28	30	32
	....	....	....	....	....	....	....
Feet	34	36	38	40	42	44	46
	....	....	....	....	....	....	....
Feet	48	50	52	54	56	58	60
	....	....	....	....	....	....	....

Made of Clear Norway Pine, with Hickory Rungs; self-acting gravity hooks of the best malleable iron, by means of which the Ladder can be adjusted at any desired height.

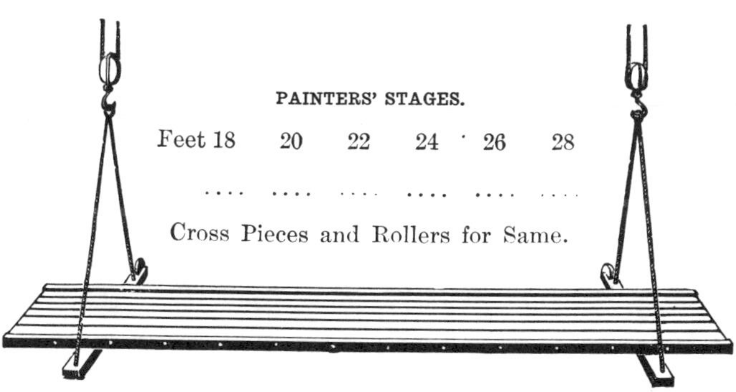

PAINTERS' STAGES.

Feet 18	20	22	24	26	28
....	....	....	....	....	....

Cross Pieces and Rollers for Same.

See Index for Stage Rope, and Block and Tackle.

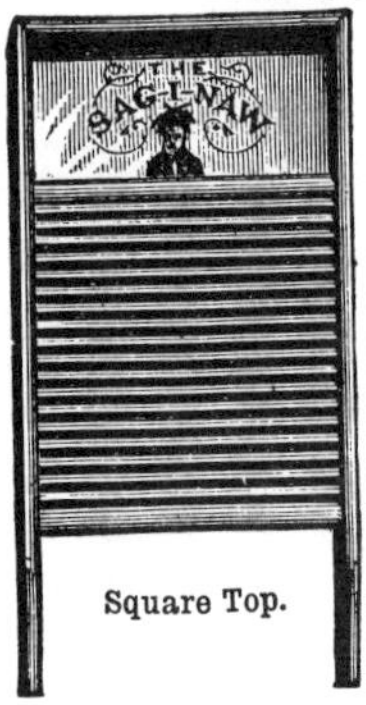

Square Top.

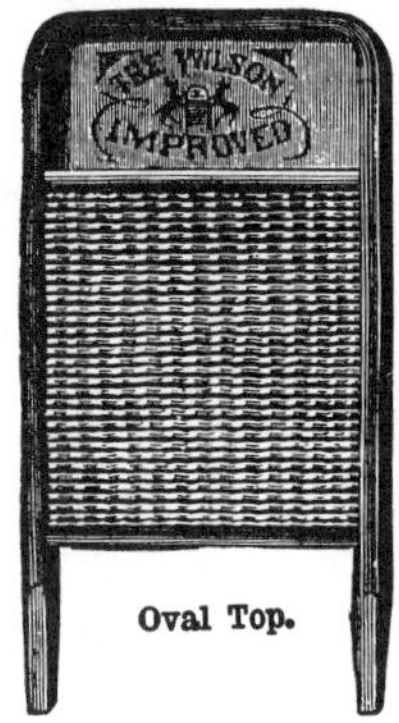

Oval Top.

SQUARE-TOP WASH BOARDS.

Single...... ...... Double...... ......

Oval Top.

Single...... ...... Double...... ......

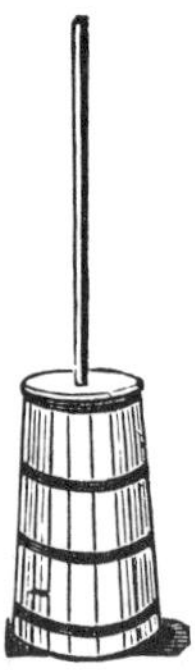

CHURNS.

Nos......	1	2	3	4
Pine.....	......	......	......	......
Ash.....	......	......	......	......
Mixed Cedar.	...	......	......	......

Our Churns are well finished, with straight, smooth-planed dashers.

UNIONS.

No. 1..	......
No. 2..	......
No. 3..	......

Union.

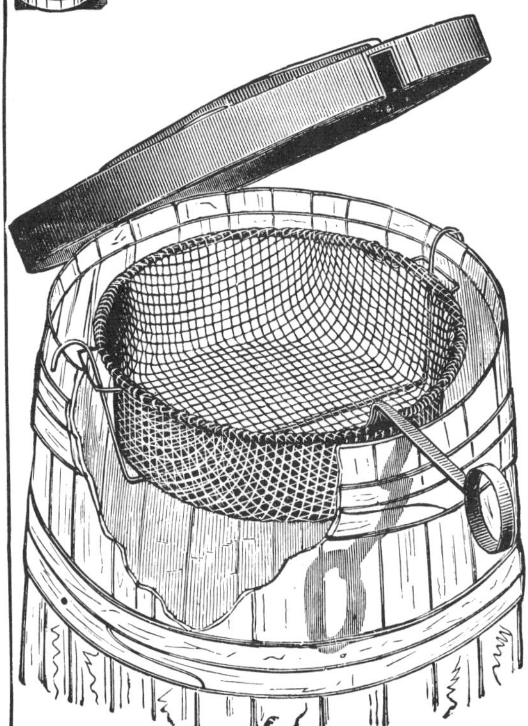

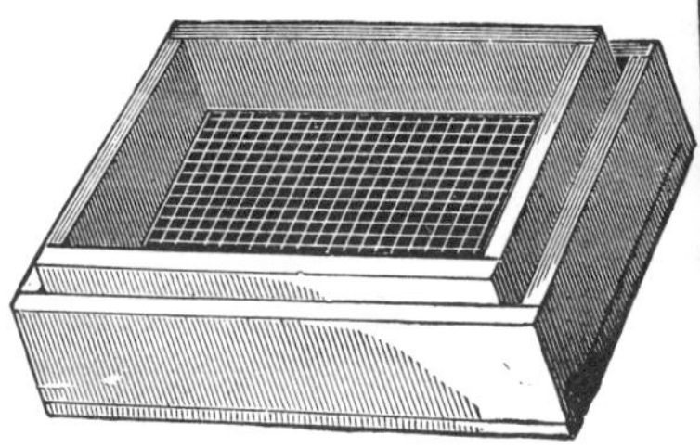

ASH SIFTERS AND COAL SIEVES.

Nos..........	1	2	3
Square, Nested	.....	......	......

A cheap Ash Sifter, within the reach of every one.

AMERICAN COAL SIEVES.

Galvanized, with Cover...... ......

This is the favorite Boston Ash Sifter. In using this, you need not consult your neighbor's weather vane, to decide which is the wind side of the barrel.

BIRD AND SQUIRREL CAGES.

ROUND AND SQUARE BIRD CAGES.

In Japanned Colors .... Brass ....

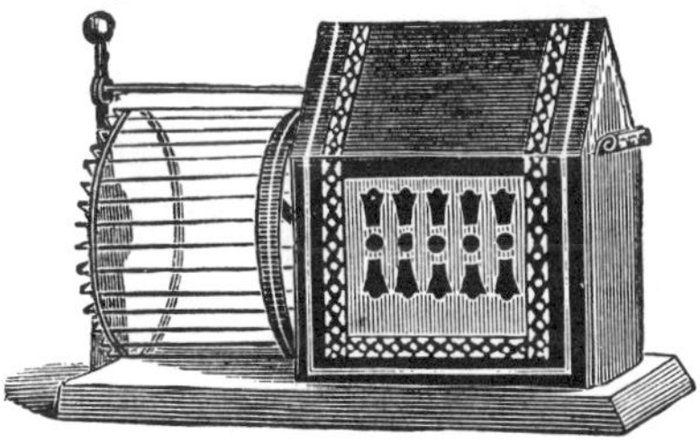

SQUIRREL CAGES.

Tin ....

WOOD BIRD CAGES.

All Styles and Sizes ....

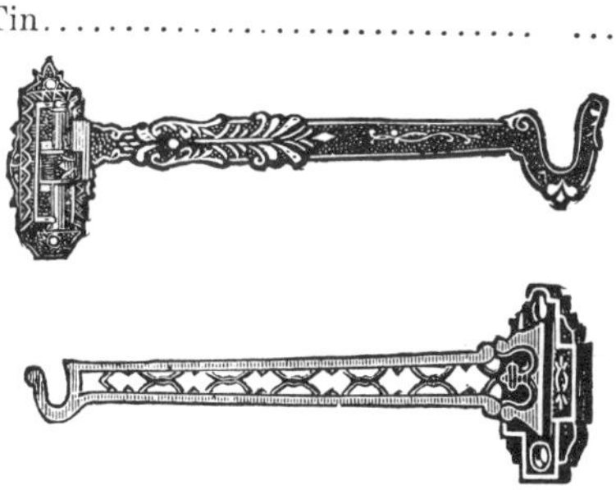

BIRD CAGE HOOKS.

See Index for styles and numbers.

PATENT BIRD CAGE SPRINGS AND HOOKS.

Brass Wire ....

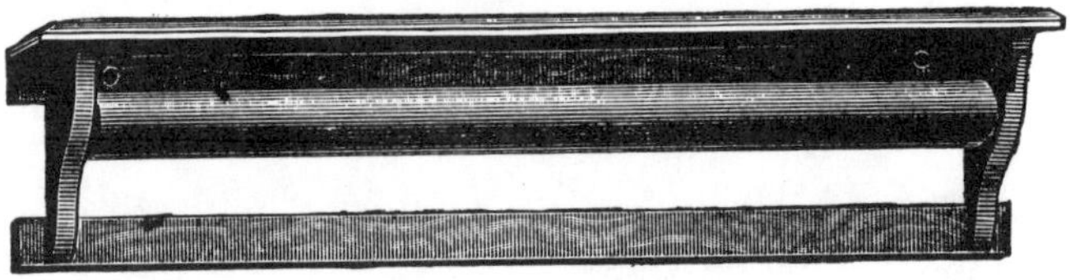

TOWEL ROLLERS.

No. 1, With Iron Brackets ... . No. 2, With Shelf.................... ......

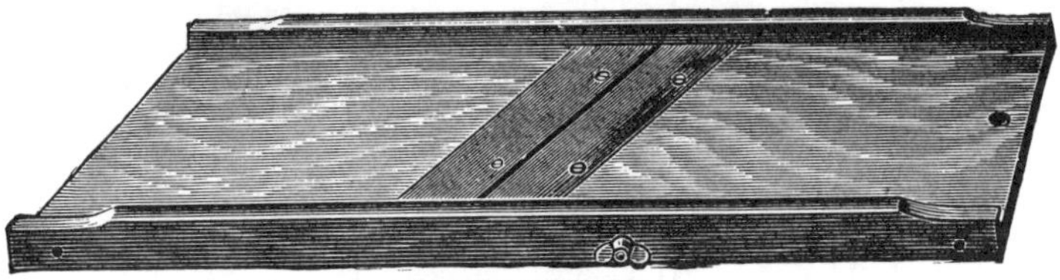

SLAW CUTTERS.

1 Knife......... ...... 2 Knives......... ...... Vegetable Slicers........ ......

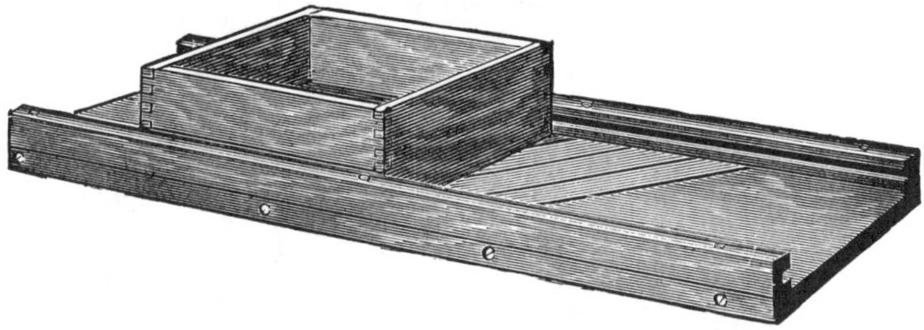

KRAUT CUTTERS.—With Box.

3 Knives. .... 8x24...... 9x28......

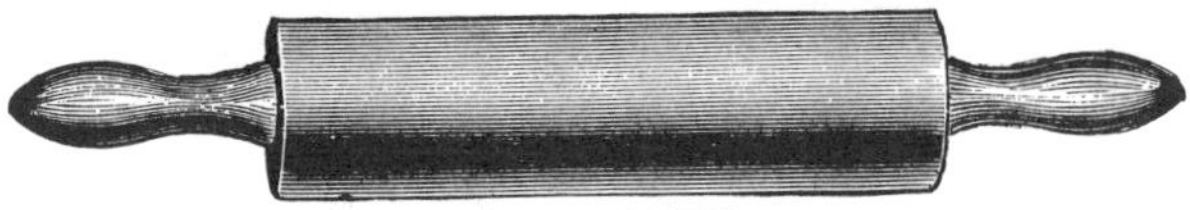

ROLLING PINS.

Tight Handle.................... ...... Loose Handle.................... ......

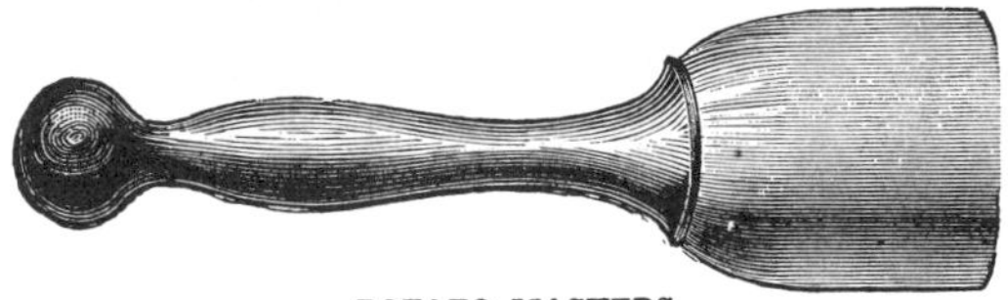

POTATO MASHERS.

Wood.. ......

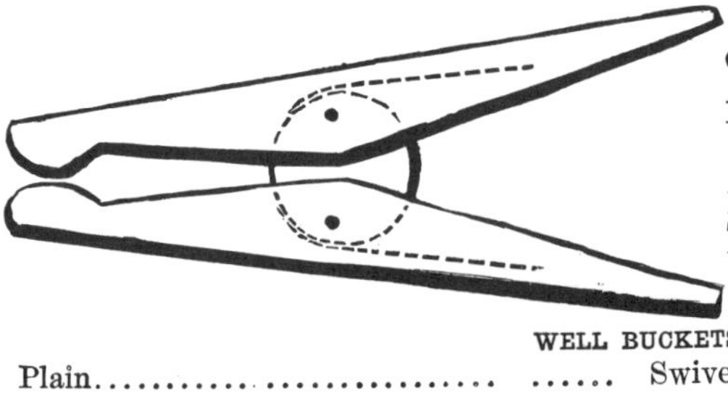

CLOTHES PINS.

Common .... Spring..... ....

Buckets.	2 Hoop	3 Hoop
Pine..............	......	......
Cedar..............	......	......

Horse Buckets, Pine......Oak........

Tubs ....Nos. 1.... 2.... 3....

Wood Bowls..Nos..	1	2	3	4	5
	...	...	...	...	...

WELL BUCKETS.

Plain......................... ...... Swivel........................ ......

SIEVES, RIDDLES AND SAND SCREENS.

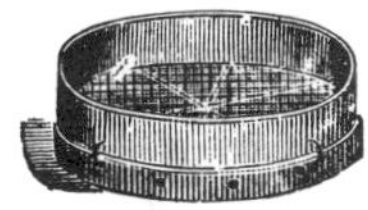

WOOD RIM SIEVES.

Nos..........	14 & 16	18	20	22	24
	......	......	......	......	......

These Sieves are well made, free from splinters. Wire well fastened to the frame, with cross wire to strengthen them.

METALIC SIEVES.

	Plain.	Plated.
14 and 16 Mesh	....	......
18 "	....	......
20 "	....	.....
24 "	....	.....

ELECTRIC SIFTERS.

Combined Sifter, Mixer, Scoop, Rice Washer and Strainer .....

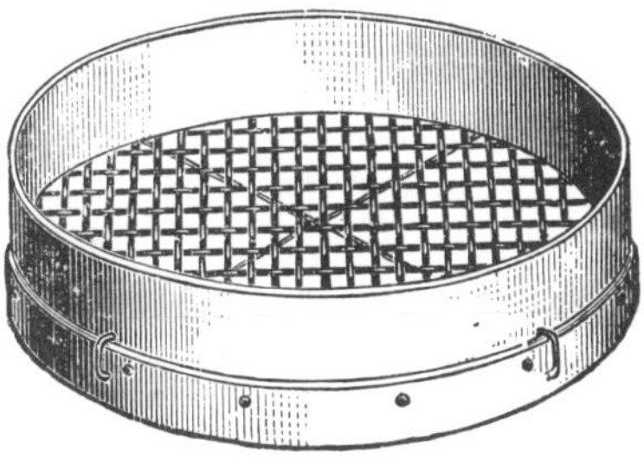

RIDDLES.

Steel Foundry, 2 to 16 Mesh..............		......
Brass " 2 to 16 "	....	......
Grain or Sand, 2 to 16 "	....	......

Riddles made smooth, with riveted rim.

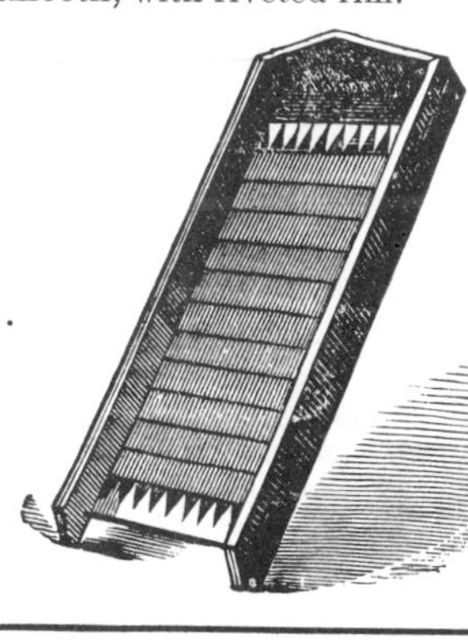

LIME AND SAND SCREENS.

2, 3, 4, 5, 6 Mesh.......................... ......

COAL SCREENS.

3/8, 1/2, 5/8, 3/4, 7/8, 1, 1 1/4, 1 1/2, 1 3/4, 2 in. Mesh.... ....

Screens are made of steel wire and well made frames.

VAJEN & NEW, INDIANAPOLIS, IND.

THE HANDY FAMILY GLUE POT.

Price ....

Will be found convenient in making repairs about the house, and will save its cost many times.

Each Glue Pot in a neat paper box.

GLUE POTS.

Nos	0000	000	00	0	1	2	3	4	5	6
Enameled..	....	....	....	....	....	....	....	....	....	....

Well made, and without sand cracks. Nothing better in the market.

MASLIN KETTLES.

Quarts	2	3	4	5	6	7	8
Enameled		....	....	....	....	....	....
Quarts		10	12	14	16	18	20
Enameled		....	....	....	....	....	....

The enamel lining in these kettles is first class.

IRON MORTARS.

Inch	4......	5......	6	7......	8......

Used by Druggists and in the Culinary Department.

Should grace the shelves in every kitchen pantry.

For crushing sugar, salt or for pounding hard bread and for many other uses.

IRON SUGAR KETTLES.

10 to 30 Gallons, With or Without Bale ....

Weight, about 3 lb to the gallon capacity, without bail.

JAPANNED WARE.

TEA TRAYS.
Japanned, Fancy Borders.

Inch	12	14	16	18	20	22	24	26	28
	...	...	...	...	....	...	...	..	...

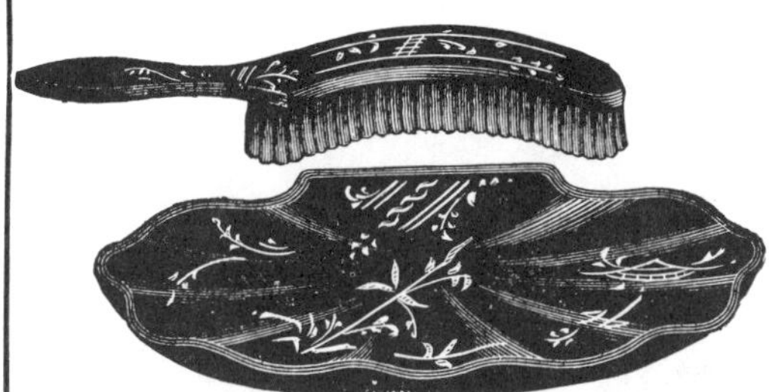

Crumb Brush and Tray............... .....

Children's Trays............ ......

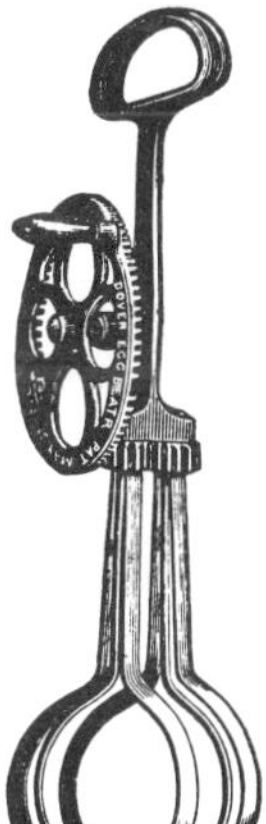

DOVER EGG BEATER.
No. 2, Family Size.. ....

Beats the whites of two eggs so perfectly in ten seconds that the cup may be inverted without any of the beaten mass falling.

SPICE BOXES.
In several styles.

SQUARE CAKE OR BREAD BOXES.
Small..... Medium.... Large....

CASH BOXES.

Nos.	1	2	3
Size	12	10½	9¼ in.
Plain Handle, For Padlock	....	....	....
Sunk Handle, with Lock	....	....	....

LETTER BOXES.
1 Part ....
2 Part.......................
3 Part.......................

TIN MATCH SAFES.
Price......... ....

TEA OR COFFEE CANS.
1 ℔....... 2 ℔.......

Bill and Stamp Boxes.

TOILET SETS.

A full assortment in all the latest designs, and all styles and colors.

Gold Banded ....

Ornamented........ ......

SPITTOONS AND CUSPIDORES.

Iron Spittoons, Large, for Public Buildings, &c........ ......

Japanned Tin Cuspidores, Assorted Colors........ ......

Brass Cuspidores........Small...... Large ......

Brass Cuspidores, Loaded Bottom, Large... ....

Nickel-Plated Cuspidores ....Small...... Large ......

Iron Cuspidores, Porcelain Lined, Assorted Colors........ ......

TINWARE.

Pieced and Stamped Ware, Covered Buckets, Dinner Buckets, Flaring Buckets, Dutch Buckets, Strainer Buckets, Coffee Pots, Measures, Sauce Pans, Tea Kettles, Steamers, Wash Boilers, Wash Bowls, Dippers, Milk Strainers, Milk Pans, Dish Pans, Rinsing Pans, Pudding Pans, Pie Pans, Tin Cups, Coal Oil Cans, Fruit Cans, Funnels, Sprinkling Pots, Tea Pots, Biscuit Cutters, Horseradish Graters, Ladles, Slop Jars, Chamber Pails, Dust Pans, Cake Pans, Sauce Pans, &c.

Discount on Pieced Ware........ ...... Discount on Stamped Ware........ ......

Stove Pipe, Elbows, Flue Stops, and Dripping Pans.

NEW STANDARD OCTAGON TEA POTS.

Made of finest prime charcoal tin, specially selected for this purpose, on account of its heavy coating and brightly polished surface. Handsome shape and finish, riveted handles of new design; large opening at top; stamped bottoms, fluted spouts, spun bell covers; every pot tested. Low price.

Pints........ 3...... 4...... 5......

BIRD CAGE HOOKS.

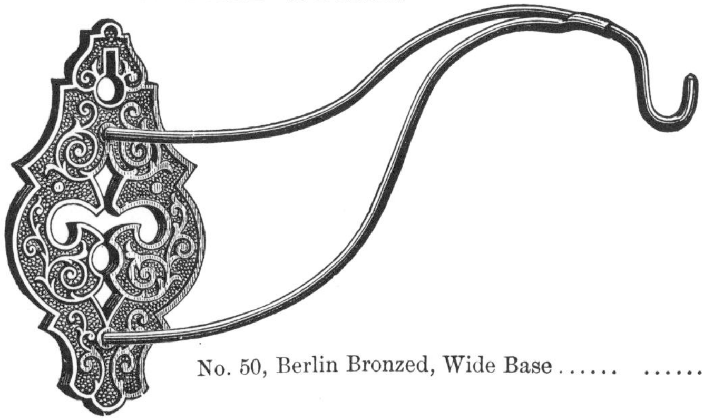

No. 50, Berlin Bronzed, Wide Base ....

No. 37, Berlin Bronzed....
No. 47, " " ....
With Swinging Hook. ....

PAPER CLIPS.

No. 40, Berlin Bronzed.............. .....
No. 43, Bronze Metal................ .....

PAPER FILE HOOKS.

No. 24, Tuscan Bronzed.

Match Safes, Style E, Berlin Bronzed...... ....

BOOT-JACKS, DOOR CHECKS, TWINE BOXES.

BOOT-JACKS.

No. 30, Bronzed...... ....

Folding Boot-Jacks................ ......

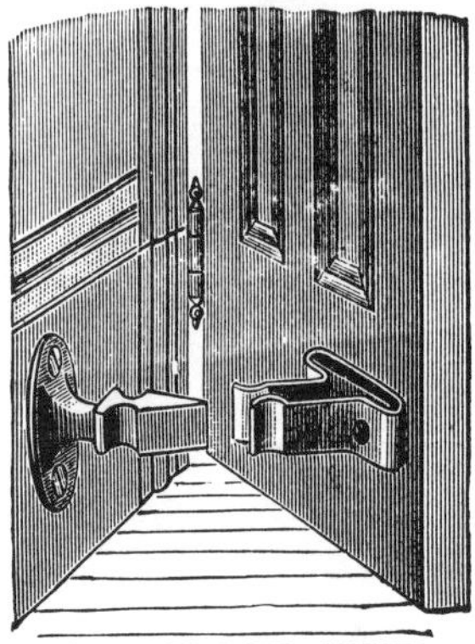

EXCELSIOR DOOR CHECKS.

Bronzed............... ... .

Brass...................... ......

DOUBLE BOOT-JACK.

Two Sizes in One.

No. 25, Berlin Bronzed.. ......

CHANDELIER HOOKS.

To Screw on to Gas Pipe.

No. 460, Berlin Bronzed . ...

TWINE BOXES.

For Large Balls of Twine.

No. 3, Adamantine Bronzed............. ......

VAJEN & NEW, INDIANAPOLIS, IND.

LANTERNS.

BRILLIANT.

The most convenient coal oil lantern for family use . . . .

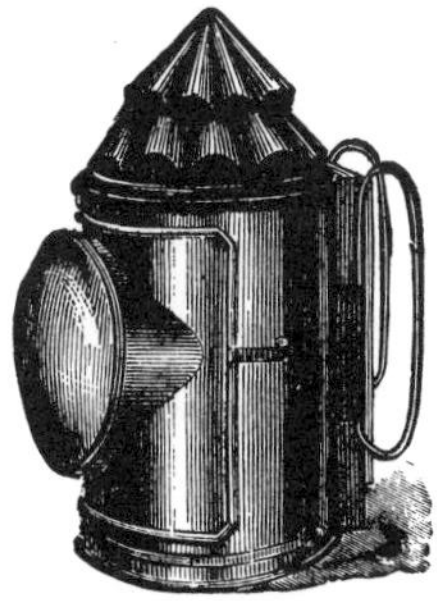

POLICE BULL'S EYE.

In Tin . . . .

In Brass . . . .

For lard and sperm oil.

RAIL ROAD.

Single Guard . . . .

Double " the Strongest and Best, ...

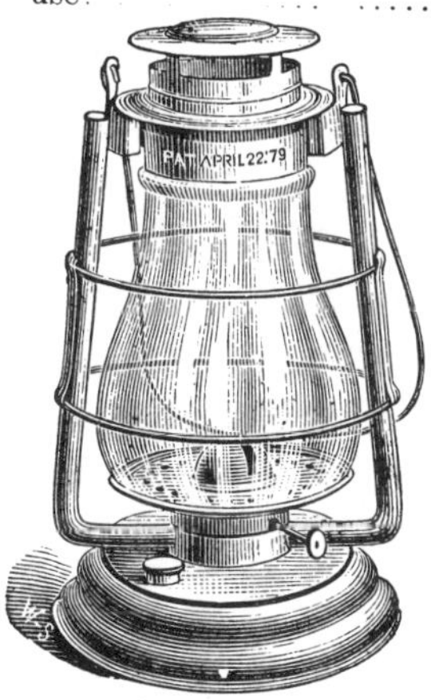

THE BOSS.

Tubular . . . .

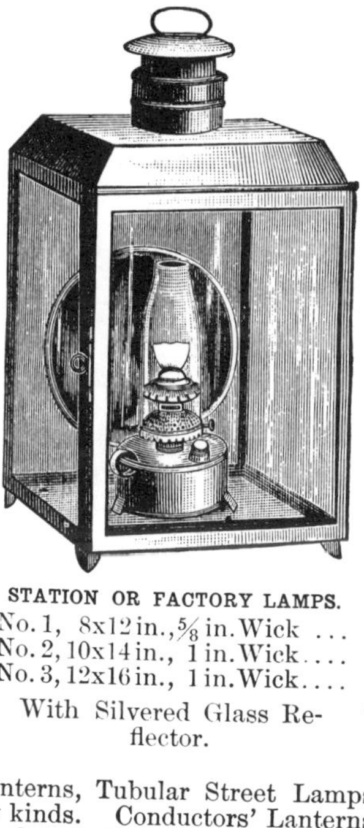

STATION OR FACTORY LAMPS.

No. 1, 8x12 in., 5/8 in. Wick . . .

No. 2, 10x14 in., 1 in. Wick . . . .

No. 3, 12x16 in., 1 in. Wick . . . .

With Silvered Glass Reflector.

LITTLE BOSS.

Tubular, Tin . . . .

" Brass . . . .

Coal Oil, Candle and Oil Lanterns, Tubular Street Lamps, Pocket and Small Brass Lanterns of many kinds. Conductors' Lanterns, Nickel Plated. Red and Blue Lantern Globes.

HEADQUARTERS FOR TORCHES AND CAMPAIGN GOODS.

Our stock is most complete in this line, when there is a demand for these goods. Write for Prices.

During the campaigns we will issue a list of the different styles kept by us in stock.

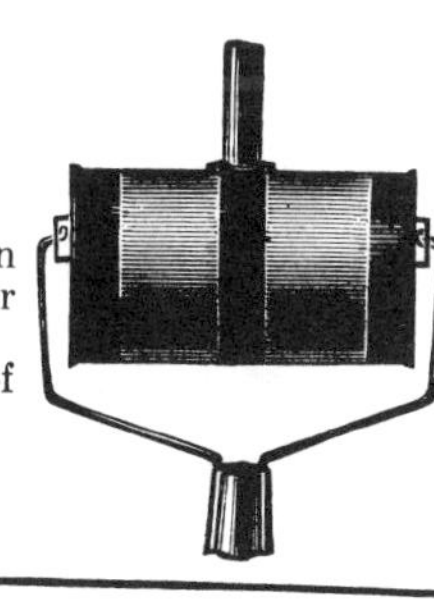

OARS.

Very Best Quality Selected White Ash.

Length, 6 to 8 ft., per ft.. ......

Spruce Spoon Oars, 7.... 8 ft....

TACKLE PULLEYS.

Size,	¾	1	1¼
Single	....	....	....
Double	....	....	....

HOOKS AND THIMBLES.

½	⅝	¾	1
....	....	....	....

SISTER HOOKS.

¼	⅜	½	⅝
....	....	....	....

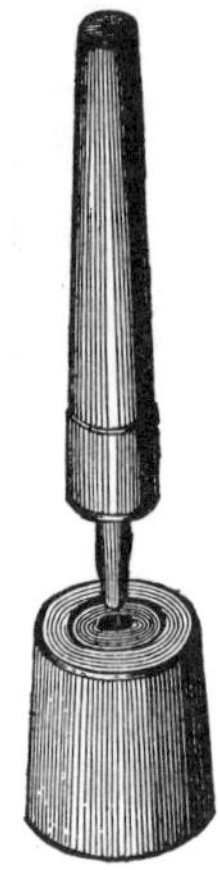

GROMMET SETS.

No. 2....... ......

LINE CLEATS.

No. 1, 4½ in. long.....
No. 2, 6 in. " ......

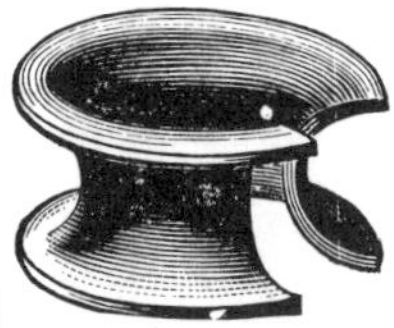

OPEN THIMBLES.

¼ to 1 in ....
1¼... 1½... 1¾... 2...

BRASS GROMMETS.

No. 2, With Washer,
Per Gro...... ......

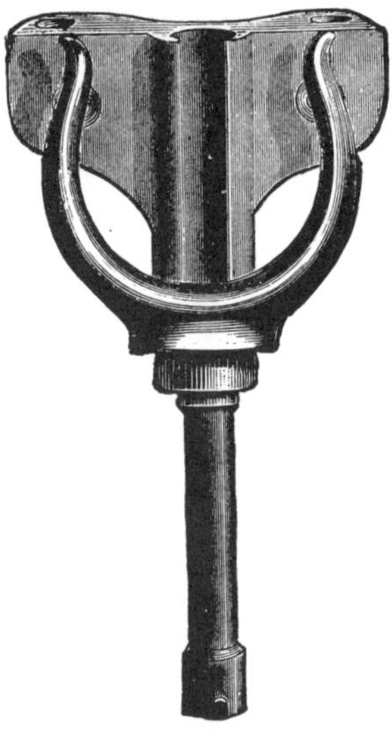

ACME ROW LOCKS.

Per Pair ....

These row locks can be dropped down below the top of the gunwale, when not in use.

ROW LOCKS.

No. 1, Per Pair......... ......
No. 2, " " ....
Canal " " ....

Canal Row Locks are hung to the oars, which allows them to be left in place on the boat; bolt going through the oar and made fast.

Lignumvitæ Cock Eyes......
Awning Makers' Palms......

ANCHORS.

6 to 9℔, Per ℔.... ......
10 to 18℔, " ....

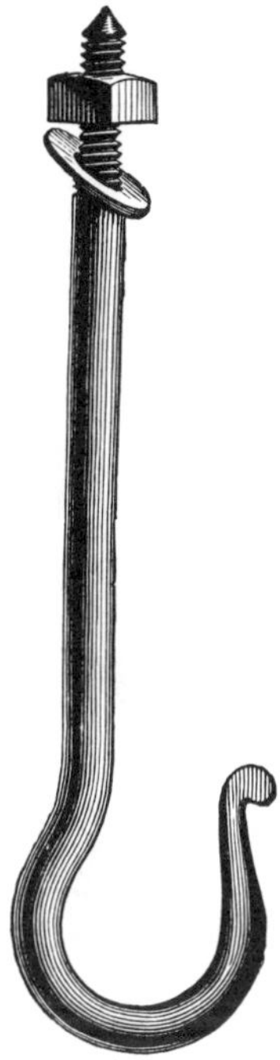

HAMMOCK HOOKS.

No. 58, Tinned, with Plate ....
No. 68, " " Screw.................. ......

WELL WHEEL HOOKS

No. 15, Wrought Iron..

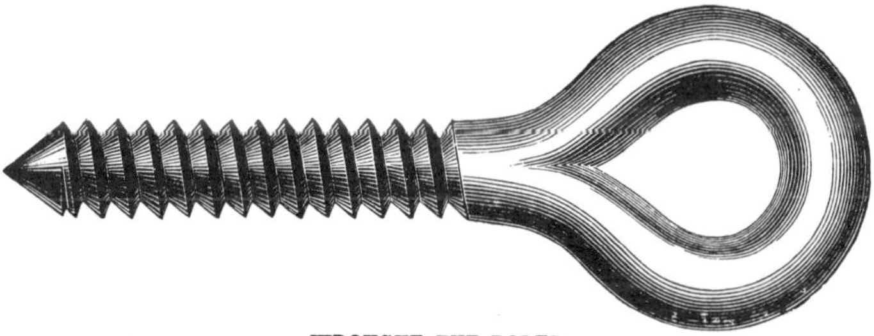

WROUGHT EYE BOLTS.

No. 102, Galvanized ....Inch, 3/8 .... 1/2 .... 5/8 .....

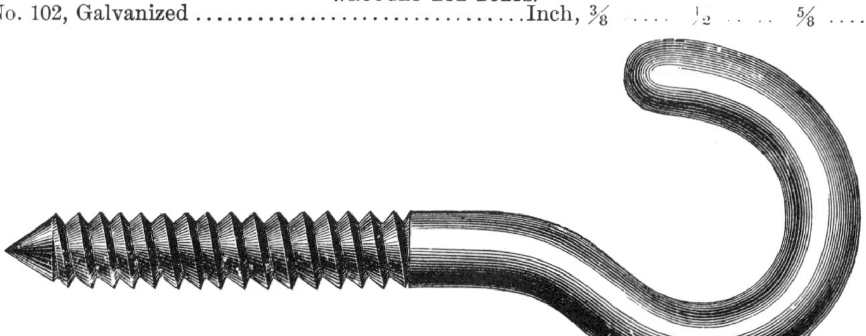

WROUGHT SCREW HOOKS.

No. 112, Galvanized ....Inch, 3/8 .... 1/2 .... 5/8 .....

SNAPS, CARDS, WEDGES, ETC.

VAJEN & NEW. INDIANAPOLIS, IND.

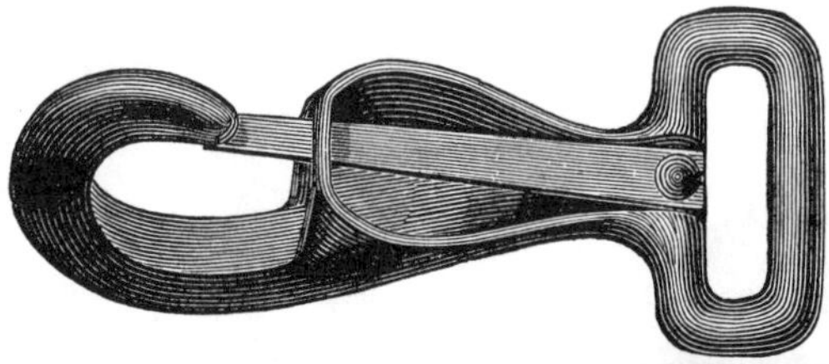

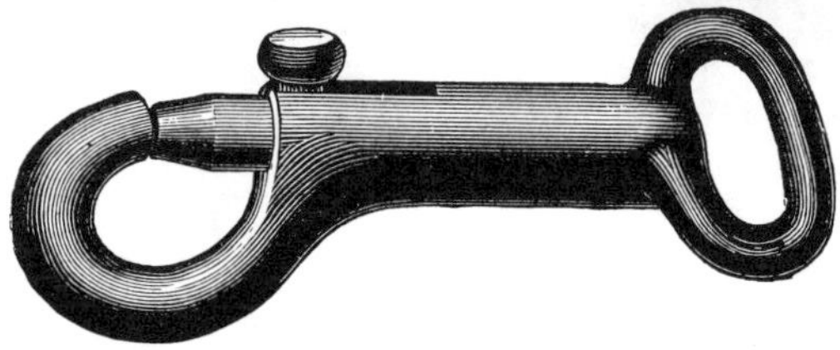

HARNESS SNAPS.

Size of Eye ... ¾ ⅞ 1 1¼
Nos........... 1 2 4 5
Japanned ....
Size of Eye . . 1½ ⅞ round, ⅜ round
Nos 6 20 30
Japanned ....
Size of Eye.... ¾ ⅞ 1 1¼
Nos..... .....1 1 12 14 15
Tinned........ ....
Size of Eye . . 1½ ⅞ round, ⅜ round.
Nos 16 120 130
Tinned.......... ....
Size of Eye .....¾ ⅞ 1 1¼ 1½
Nos. 101 102 104 105 106
Tuscan Bronzed ....
Size of Eye....... ⅜ round, ¾ round.
Nos 130½ 131
Tuscan Bronzed..... ....

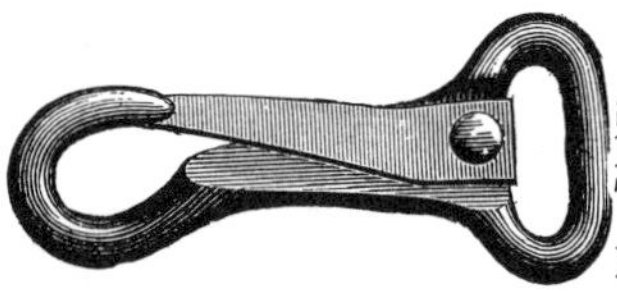

GERMAN HARNESS SNAPS.

Size of Eye .... ½ ⅝ ¾ ⅞ 1 1¼ 1½ ¾ round.
Nos...........20¼ 20½ 21 22 24 25 26 61
Tuscan Bronzed ... .

Baby Snaps, Very Small, Tinned ....

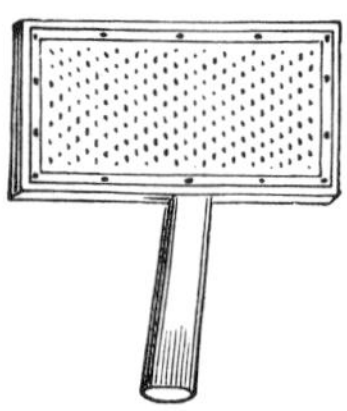

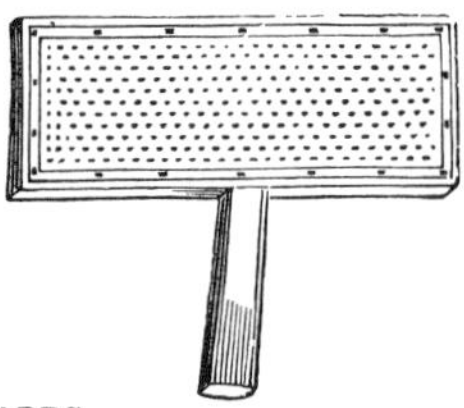

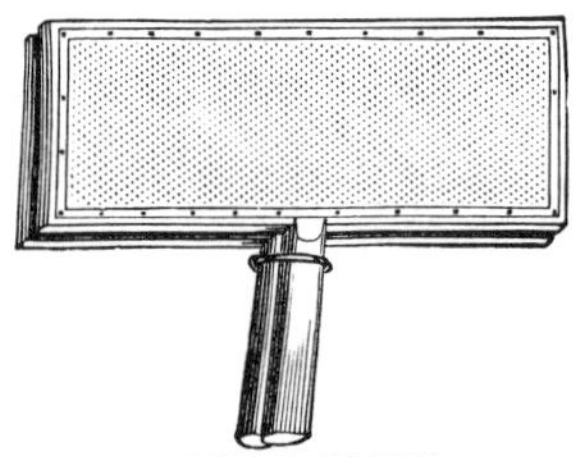

HORSE CARDS.

No. 3, Small.... ...... No. 1, Large.... ......

WOOL CARDS.

No. 8A, Best Quality.... ......

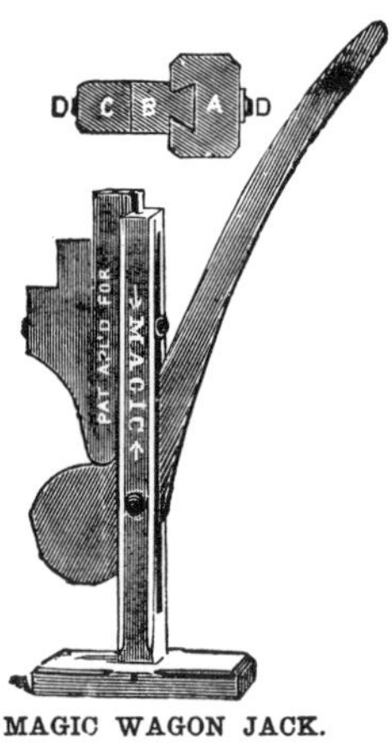

MAGIC WAGON JACK.

No. 17, Self-adjusting....

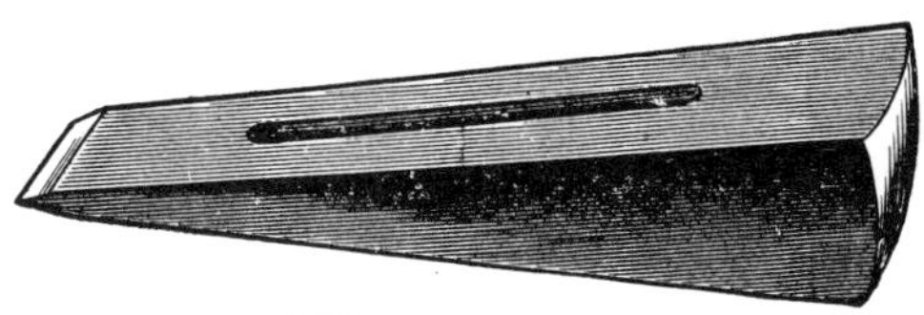

WEDGES.

Iron........ ...... Steel......... ......Per lb

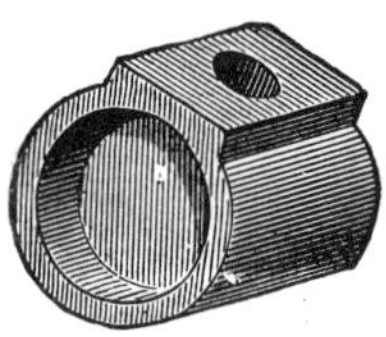

IRON MAULS.

Sunk Face.

8 to 16 lbs.......

Handled and Filled.

Lbs. 8.... 10.... 12....

PREPARED CHALK AND LEAD PENCILS

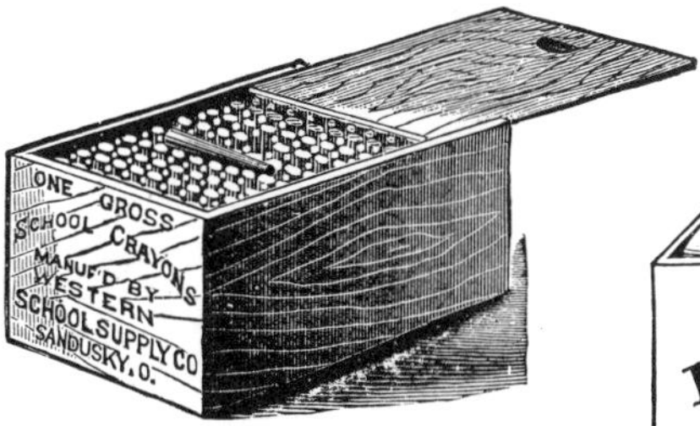

WHITE CRAYONS.

1 Gross in Box, Per Gross....

CARPENTER'S CHALK.

Half Gross in Box..White.... Blue.... Red... Per Gross.

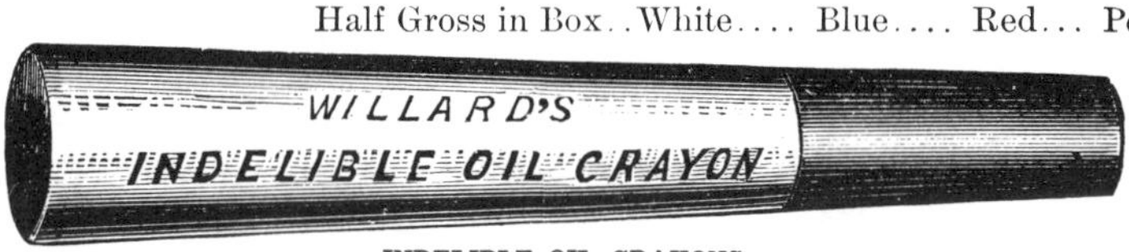

INDELIBLE OIL CRAYONS.

Will mark on Wood, Cloth, Paper, Tin, Iron, Crockery, Glass, &c. Are positively Indelible. Three Colors—Black, Blue and Red.. ......

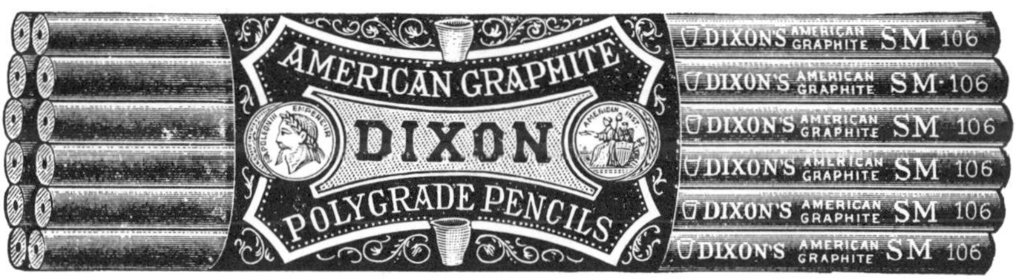

LEAD PENCILS.

No. 259, Plain Cedar ....
No. 373, Polished, Round Black... ......
No. 374, Century, Hexagon, Cedar Color.............................. ......
No. 152, Round, Satin Finish....S.M ......
No. 153, " " " ....M. ......
No. 154, " " " ....H. ......

CARPENTER'S PENCILS.

No. 236, 9 Inch, White Wood, Oval.. ......
No. 410, 7 " Polished Cedar, Oval.. ......
No. 411, 9 " " " " ....
No. 512, 9 " " " " Beveled Edges.................................. ......

METAL POLISH, CUTLERY ROLLS AND SHOW CASES.

STANDARD METAL POLISH AND RUST ERASER.

Price ....

The only preparation that will erase rust or varnish from any metai of an originally bright surface, and (if the face is not eaten off) polish as bright as ever.

Apply it on your machinery, edge tools, base-burner stoves, cutlery, gun or rifle barrels, silver, tin and table ware, nickel-plated show cases; in fact, anything that needs cleaning, polishing and preserving.

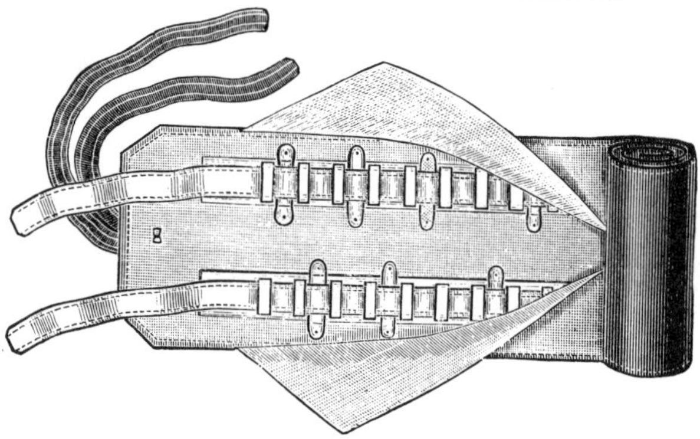

CUTLERY ROLLS.

For Table and Pocket Knives, Shears, Razors, &c.

Can furnish the above in Chamois Lined, Cashmere Lined, or Canton Flannel Lined, to order.. ......

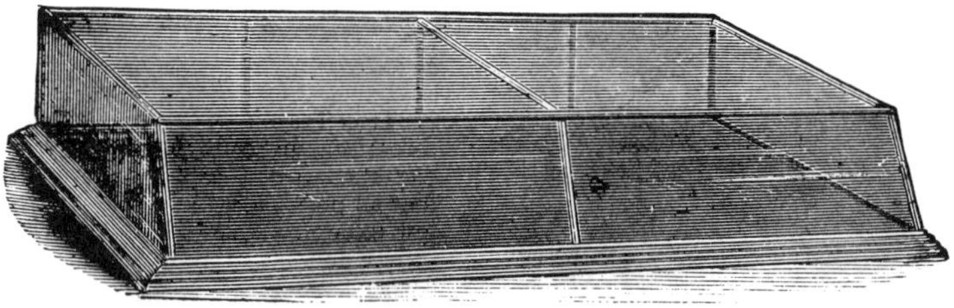

SHOW CASES.

No. 1, Mansard...... No. 2, Square..... No. 3, Round Front ..... Metal Frame.
No. 5, " ..... No. 6 " ...... No. 12, " " ...... Metal Joint.
No. 7, New Style Round Front .... Metal Frame.

Can furnish any of the above styles, from 2 to 12 feet.

RAT TRAPS.

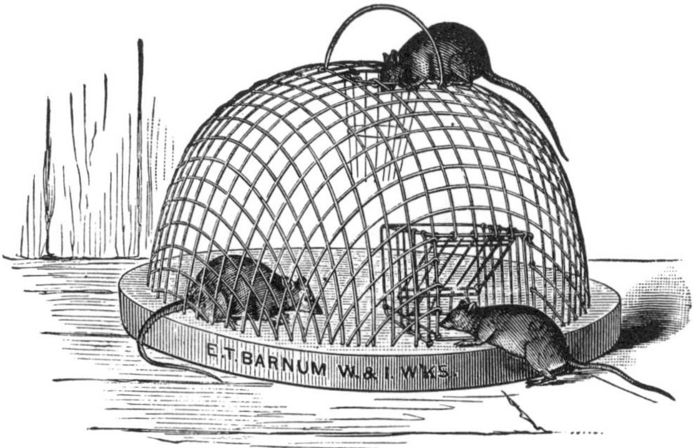

NEW CRIMPED RAT TRAP.

No. 18, Tinned Wire, Wood Bottom ....

This Trap has been received with great favor by the trade, and by its superior merit is rapidly taking the place of all the old styles of round Rat Traps.

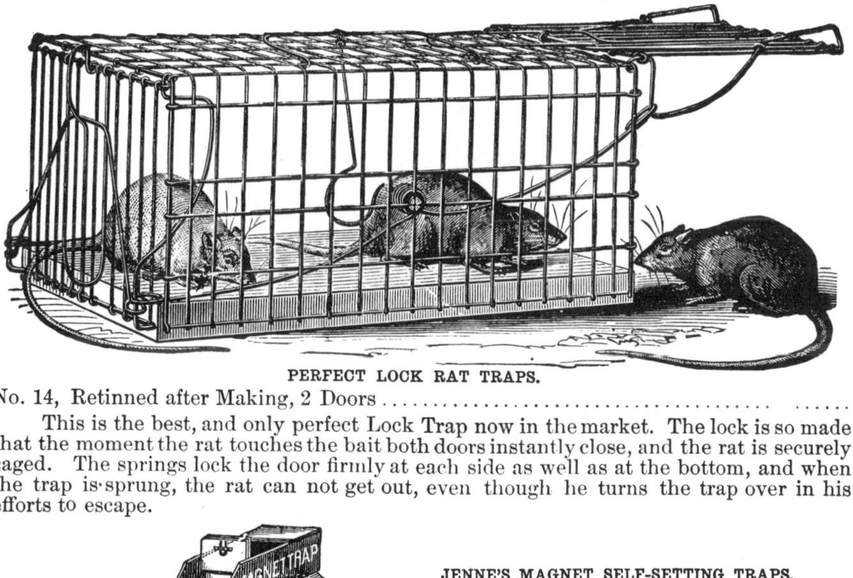

PERFECT LOCK RAT TRAPS.

No. 14, Retinned after Making, 2 Doors ....

This is the best, and only perfect Lock Trap now in the market. The lock is so made that the moment the rat touches the bait both doors instantly close, and the rat is securely caged. The springs lock the door firmly at each side as well as at the bottom, and when the trap is sprung, the rat can not get out, even though he turns the trap over in his efforts to escape.

JENNE'S MAGNET SELF-SETTING TRAPS.

Price... ....

This Trap is guaranteed to be a success, if the directions are followed. There are no pains nor expense spared to make every trap as near perfect as possible. All of the different traps, with few exceptions, hold the few victims they catch, either dead or alive, for the inspection of all the rest. The balance, of course, can't be caught, and get credit for being very smart The fact is, a drowned rat tells no tales. Any person with one of these traps and an abundance of good bait, managed discreetly, can catch every rat about any building or premises.

VAJEN & NEW, INDIANAPOLIS, IND.

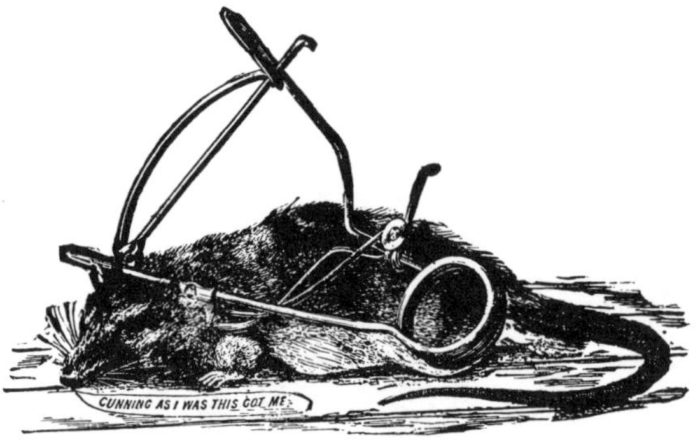

"LITTLE THROTTLER TRAP,"

CERTAIN DEATH.

Price.................... ......

Requires no bait.

This is a new trap, and meets with ready sale.

SURE DEATH RAT TRAP.

Price................. ......

The Best Cheap Rat Trap made.

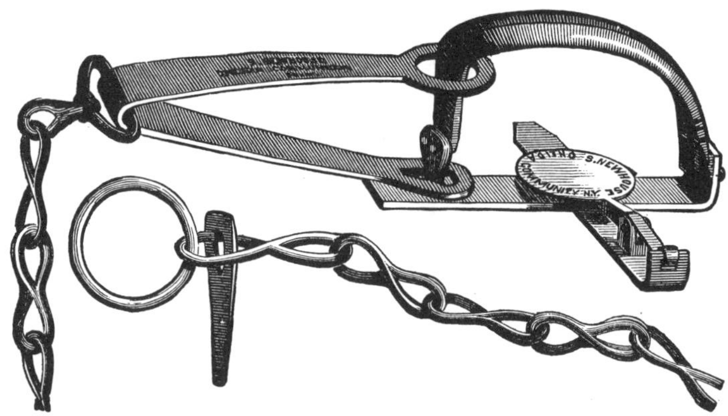

STEEL TRAPS.

With Chain.		Newhouse.	Hawley & Norton.
No. 0,	Rat	......	......
No. 1,	Muskrat....................................	......	......
No. 1½,	Mink..	......	......
No. 2,	Fox	......	......
No. 3,	Otter..	......	......

MOUSE AND MOLE TRAPS.

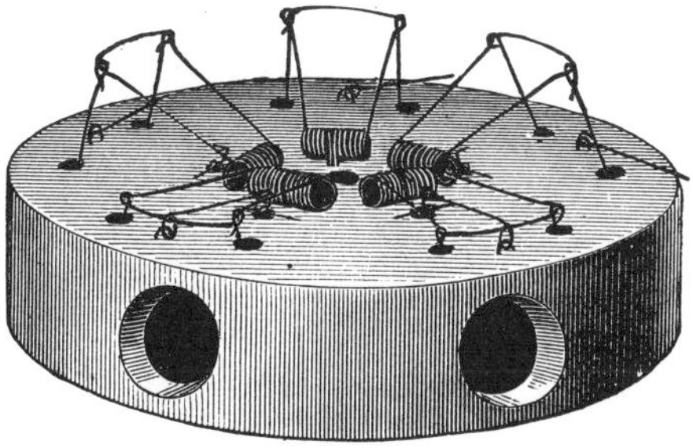

ROUND WIRE.

No. 1 ....

CHOKER.

Holes......1 2 3 4 5 6

Price, Per Dozen Holes ....

REVOLVING TRAP.

Bottom 3 x 6½ inches.

Price ....

This Trap will catch the mouse, as well as furnish good amusement for the children.

CYCLONE.

Price.................. ......

Can be approached from all sides. Simple and effective.

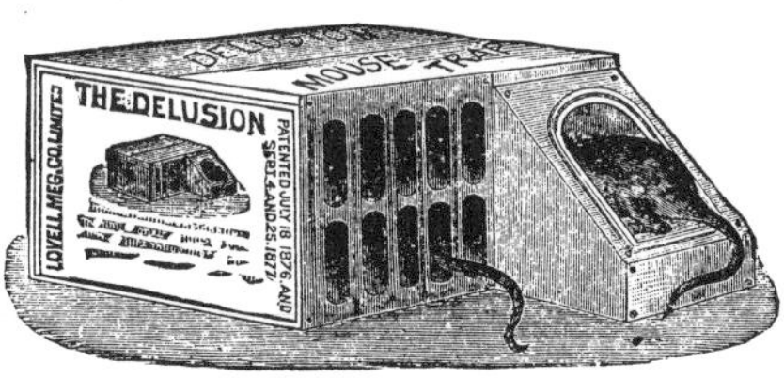

DELUSION.

Price ....

Self-setting. Each mouse caught resets the trap.

MABBETT'S MOLE TRAP.

Price...................................... ......

The engraving tells the story. Placed in the tracks of moles, this Trap is sure to catch them.

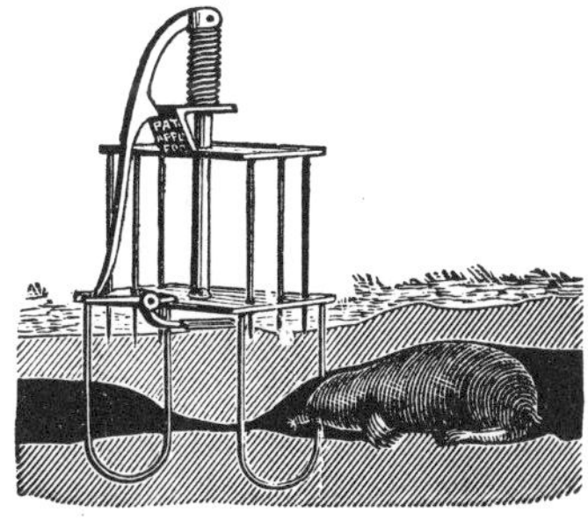

FLY TRAPS, CORN POPPERS, &C.

PARAGON.

Green ....

BALLOON.

Tinned Wire.................. ......

These are the leading Fly Traps in the market.

DISH COVERS.

	Blued.	Tinned.
6 Inch.........	......	......
7 Inch.........	......	......
8 Inch.........	......	......
9 Inch.........	......	......
10 Inch.........	......	......

HANGING BASKETS.

Painted Green.

Several Patterns.

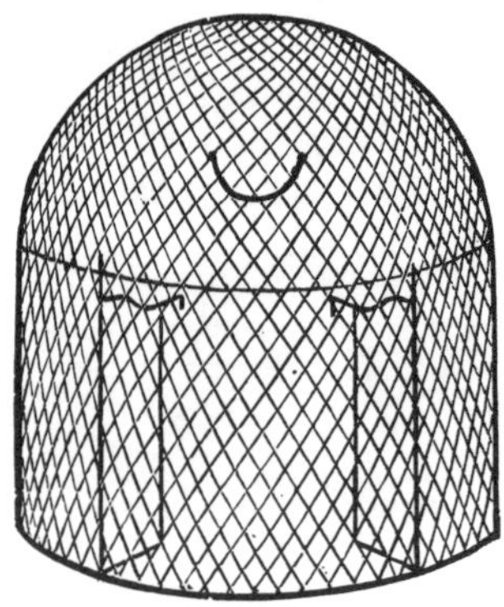

SPARK GUARDS.

Round Top..... ....

Square Top................. ......

Round and Square Top Brass Fire Guards furnished to order.

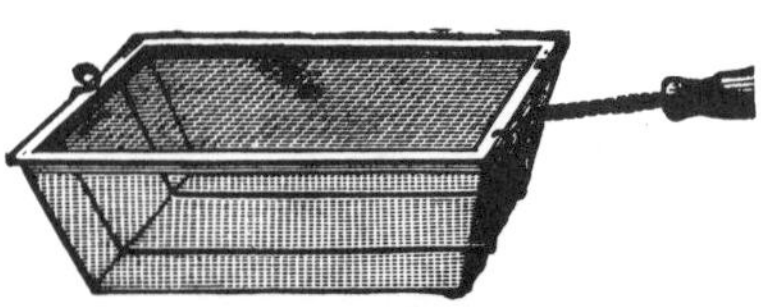

SQUARE CORN POPPERS.

Price................. ......

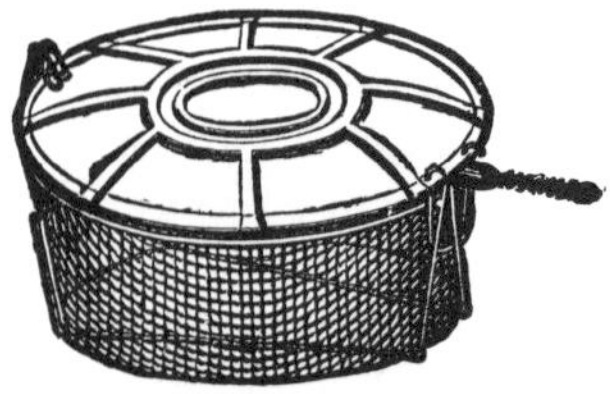

ROUND CORN POPPERS.

Price.................... ......

Our Corn Poppers are well made with good redwood handles.

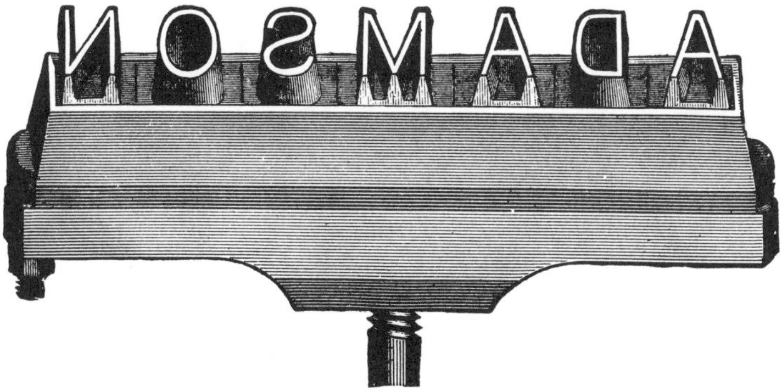

ADAMSON BRANDING IRON.

Names or Numbers in ¼, ⅜ and ½ in. can be furnished, and extra letters or figures when desired.

Four sizes for.	5	7	9	11 Type.
Size of Type, ¼ in.	......	......	......	......
" " ⅜ in.	......	......	......	......
" " ½ in.	......	......	......	......

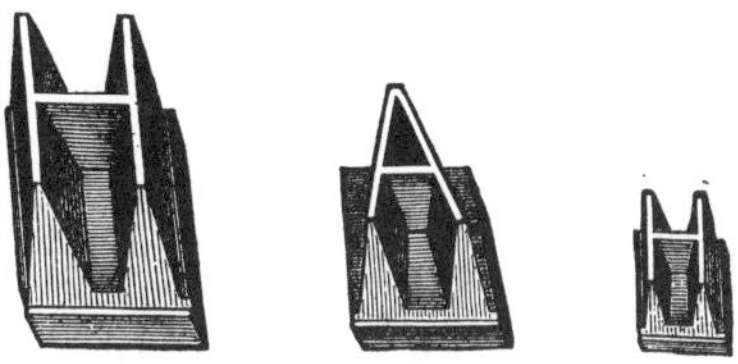

½ in. ⅜ in. ¼ in.

COPPER TYPE FOR BRANDING IRON.

SIZES ARE:

1½ inch. 1 inch. ¾ inch. ½ inch.

STENCILS.

Letters.

½ in....
¾ in....
1 in....
1½ in....

Figures.

½ in....
¾ in....
1 in....
1½ in....

Stencil Letters and Figures can be joined together, so as to form any word, name or address. STENCIL BRUSHES ND STENCIL INK.

STEEL LETTERS, FIGURES AND STAMPS.

Size	Show'g Height	Price per Alphabet	Price per set Figures	Single Letter.	Size	Show'g Height	Price per Alphabet.	Price per set Figures	Single Letter.
1-32	A	......	......	..	1-4	......	......	......	....
1-20	A	......	......	..					
1-16	A	......	......	....	5-16	A	......	......	....
3-32	A	......	......	....					
1-8	A	......	......	....	3-8	A	......	......	....
5-32	A	......	......	....					
3-16	A	......	......	....	7-16	......	......	......	....
7-32	A	......	......	....	1-2	......	......	......	....

Steel Name Stamps furnished to order.

VAJEN & NEW, INDIANAPOLIS, IND.

2 in.

PLATED NUMBERS.

¾ .... 1 .... 1¼ .... 1½ .... 2 in ....

PORCELAIN NUMBER PLATES.

Price ....

For Street Doors and Hotel Numbers.

1 in

¾ in.

PLATED NUMBERS.

Same as above.

PLATED NUMBER PLATES.

Price ....

For numbering Street Doors, Hotel Rooms, Church Pews, Armories, etc. They are easily cleaned with a chamois skin or dry woolen cloth.

1¼ in. Roman.

MOULDERS' PATTERN LETTERS AND FIGURES.

Roman Letters and Figures.

Sizes..	3-16	¼	5-16	⅜	½	⅝ in.
	....	....	....	....	....	....
Sizes..	¾	⅞	1	1¼	1½	2 in.
	....	....	....	....	....	....

See that you measure correctly.

We have a complete cabinet in stock.

1 in. Roman.

By the increase of bevel, which make the draft, they draw from the sand free, and the edges of the letters are more readily reached by the scratch brush.

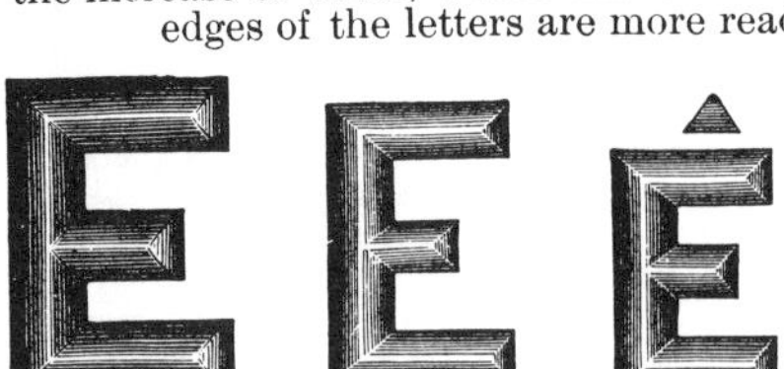

¾ in. ⅝ in. ½ in.

GOTHIC STYLE, SHARP FACE.

Sizes ...	¼	⅜	5-16	½	⅝	¾	1 in.
Let. or Figs. ...	...	...	...	...	...	...	...

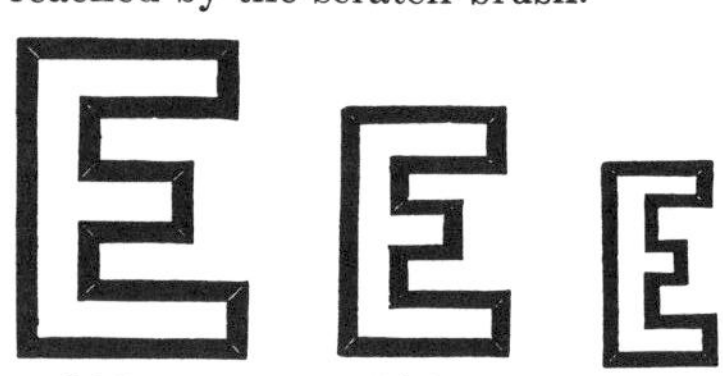

¾ in. ⅝ in. ½ in.

GOTHIC STYLE, FLAT FACE.

Sizes	¼	⅜	5-16	½	⅝	¾	1 in.
Let. or Figs. ...	...	...	...	...	...	...	...

The above styles are the ones most used; other styles in stock, and special styles to order.

PAINT BRUSHES.

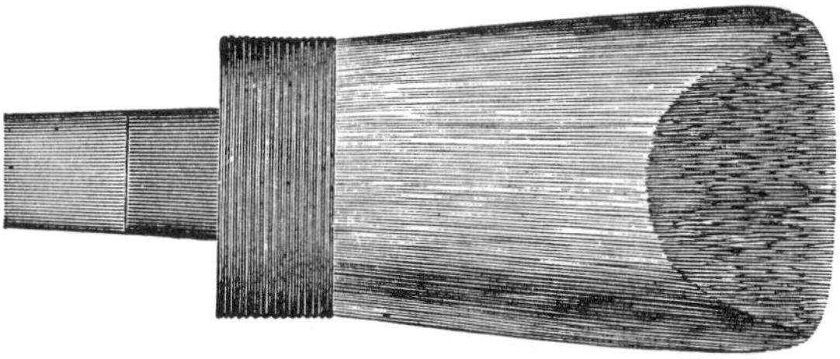

OVAL PAINT BRUSHES.—Wire Bound.

No. 6 . . . .
No. 5 . . . .
No. 4 . . . .
No. 3 . . . .
No. 2 . . . .
No. 1 . . . .
No. 1–0 . . . .
No. 2–0 . . . .
No. 3–0 . . . .
No. 4–0 . . . .

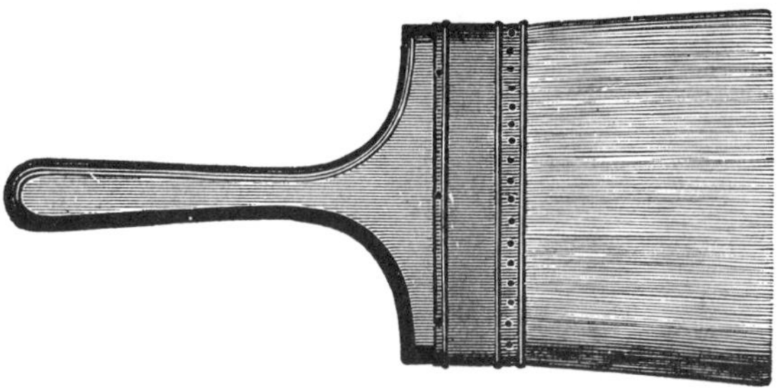

KALSOMINE BRUSHES.

All White Bristles.

Extra Length.

7 Inch . . . .
8 Inch . . . .

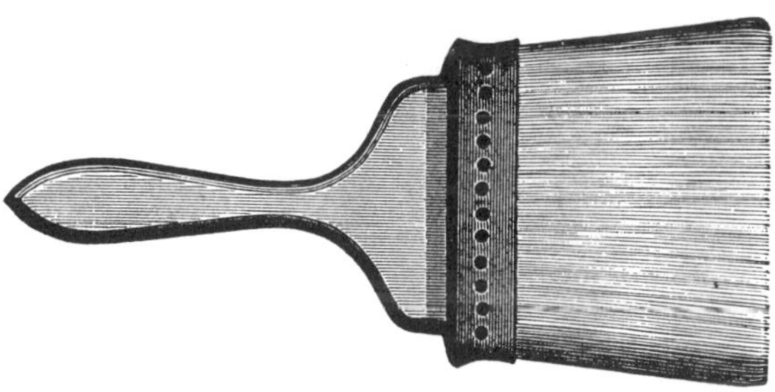

FLAT WALL BRUSHES.

All White Bristles.

3½ Inch . . . .
4 Inch . . . .
4½ Inch . . . .
5 Inch . . . .

SASH BRUSHES.

French . . . . Nos. 1 . . . . . . 2 . . . . 3 . . . . 4 . . . . .
Flat . . . . Nos. 1 . . . . . . 2 . . . . . . 3 . . . . 4 . . . . .

PAINTERS' DUST BRUSHES.

Round Block.

Price . . . .

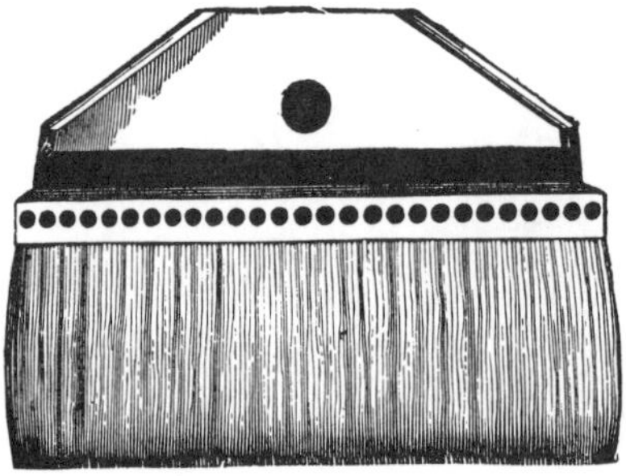

WHITEWASH BRUSHES.

Nos	1	2	3	3	5	6
All Bristle......	....	....	....	....	....	....

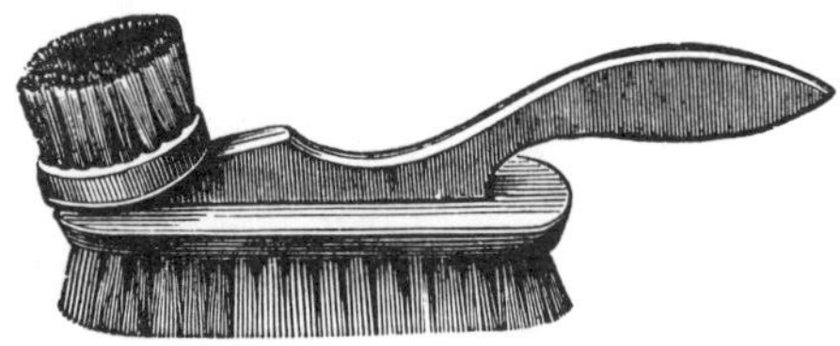

SHOE BRUSHES.

A Full Line in All Grades.

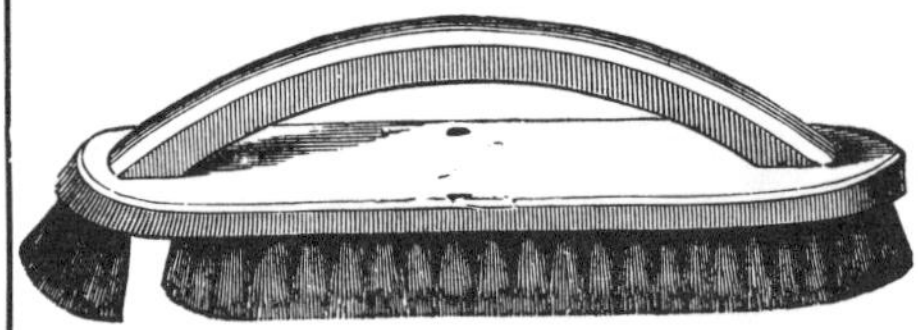

STOVE BRUSHES.

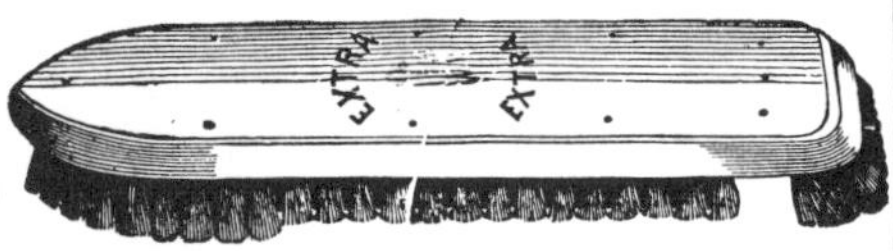

SCRUB BRUSHES.

In ordering Shoe, Scrub and Stove Brushes, state about the retail price of the brush wanted, and the order will be filled to your satisfaction.

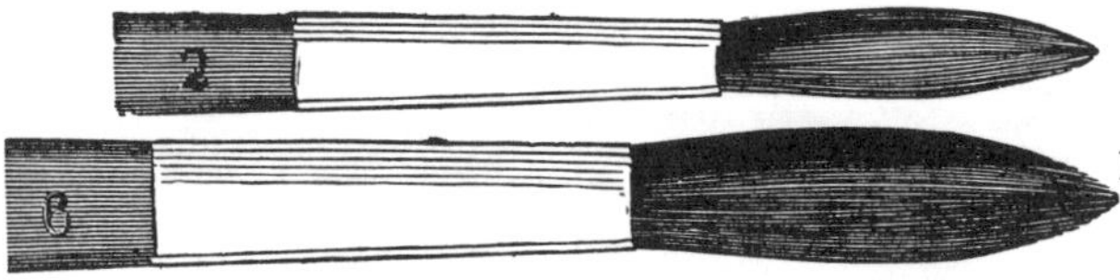

MARKING BRUSHES.

Round Cedar Handles.

Nos.	1	2	3	4	5
	....	....	....	....	....

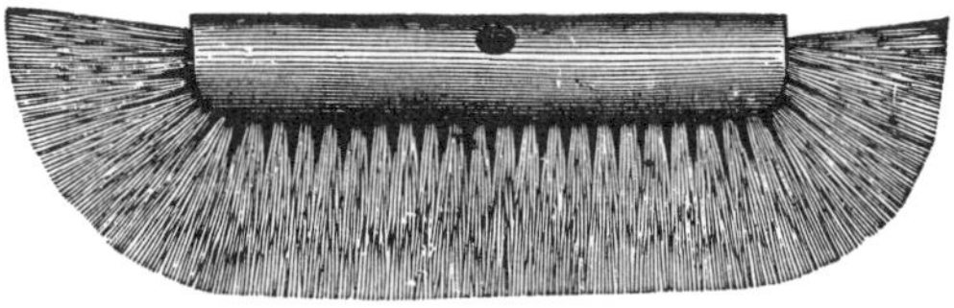

Window Brushes, all Bristle	....	......
Floor " "	....	......

COUNTER BRUSHES.

	Small.	Medium.	Large.
Plain	......	......	......
Fancy	......	......	......

TURKEY FEATHER DUSTERS

Inch.10....12....14....16....

BRUSHES.

LEATHER BACK.

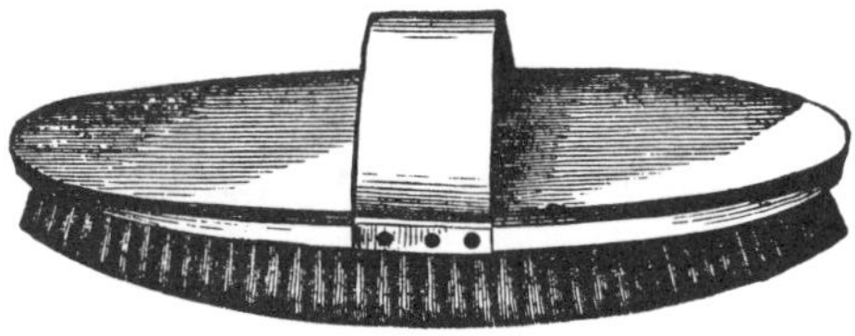

WOOD BACK.

Tampico, Paint Stub, American and Russia Bristle. A full line, from the cheapest to the best. State in your order the retail price of brush wanted.

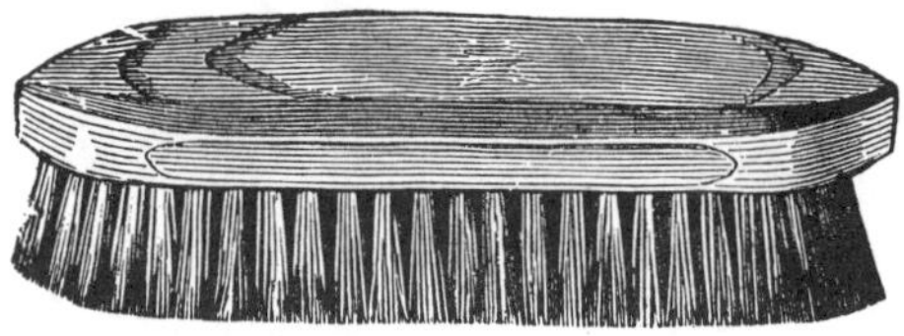

RICE ROOT DANDRUFF BRUSHES.

For Manes and Tails.. ......

STENCIL BRUSHES.

Nos............................1...... 2...... 4...... 6 ..... 8...... 10......

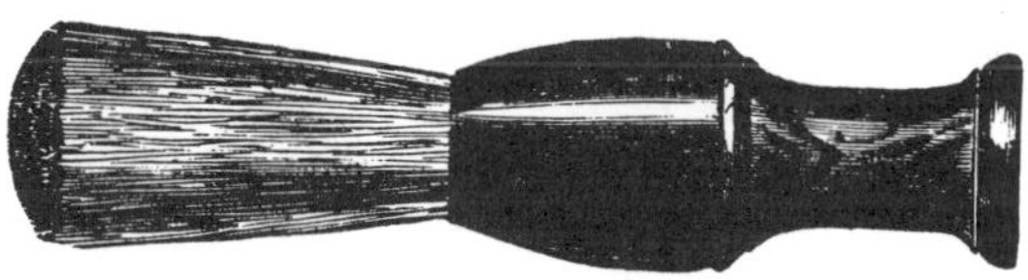

LATHER BRUSHES.

Nos............... 125...... 127...... 128 ..... 175...... 185 ..... 195......

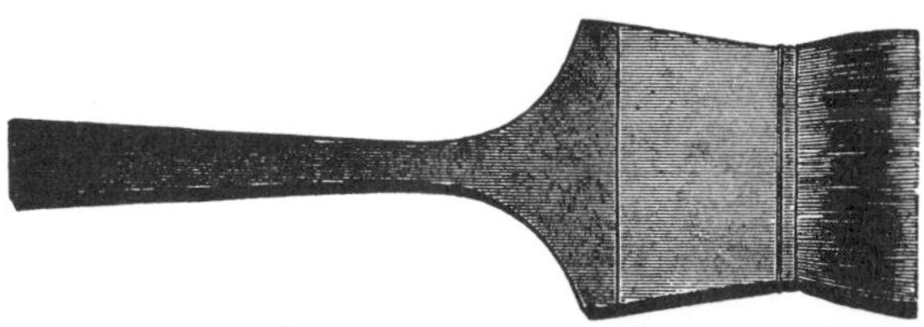

ENGLISH FLAT C. H. VARNISH BRUSHES, OR COPYING BRUSHES.

2½ Inch.. ......

CURRY COMBS.

No. 400, 6 Bars, Open Back, Japanned ....
No. 405, 8 " " " " ....
No. 417, 8 " **Closed** " " ....
No. 415, 6 " " " Brass...... ......

No. 60, 8 Bars, Open Back, Japaned...... ......
No. 62, 8 " Closed Back, Tinned Frame, Japanned...... ......

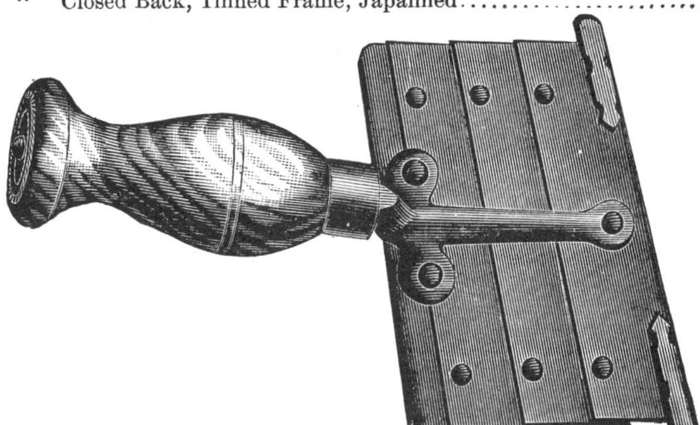

No. 228, 6 Bars, Japanned, Crank Shanks...... ......
No. 234, 8 " " " " ....
No. 234½, 8 " Tinned, " " ....
No. 240, 2 " Japanned, with Mane Comb...... ......

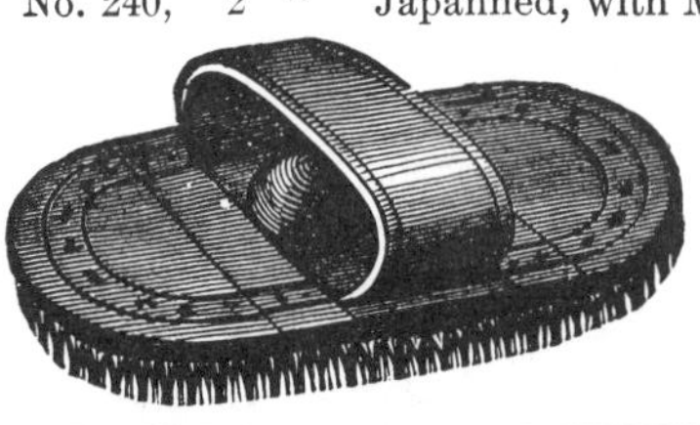

RUBBER CURRY COMBS.

Price ....

The above are only a few of the many styles in stock.

THERMOMETERS.

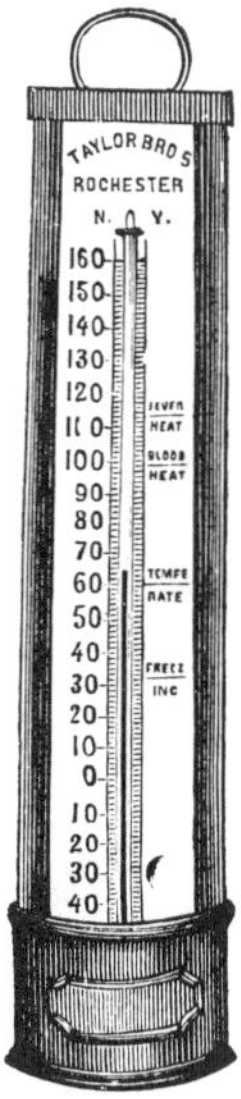

Tin Case.

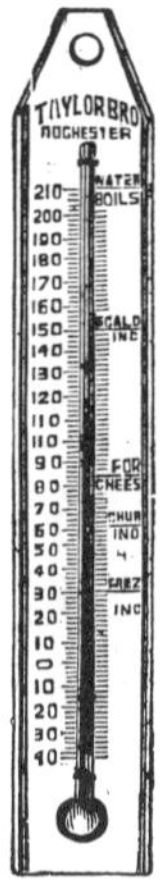

Flange Dairy.

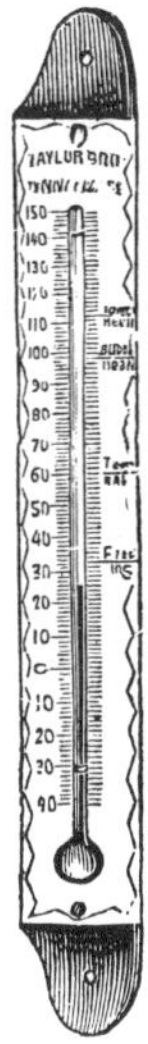

Window.

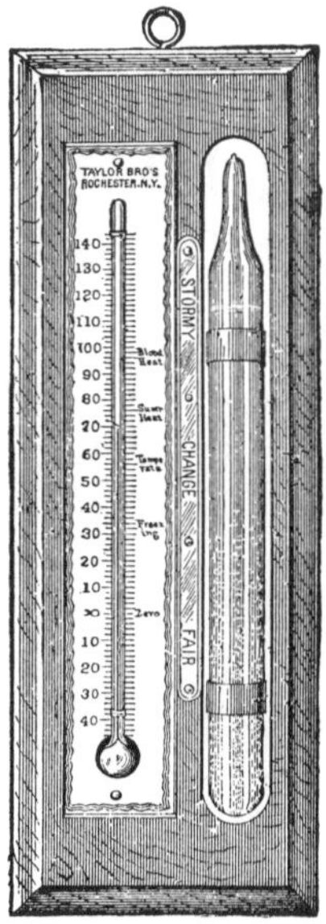

Storm Glass, or Barometer and Thermometer Combined.

Tin Case.	Flange Dairy.	Window.	Storm Glass.
7 In., Japanned...	7 In....	8 In....	Price.. ....
8 In., " ...	8 In	For fastening in corner of window outside.	
10 In., "	10 In....		

Cabinet Thermometers, Walnut Case .... 8 in...... 10 in......
Lactometer, for Testing Milk.. ......

SPECTACLES.

Assorted...... Blued...... Plated Rims......................... 1 Dozen in a Box.
Plain, Blue, London Smoke and Periscopic Glasses............................ ......
Goggles..Plain...... Green......

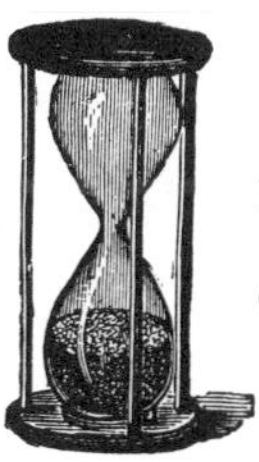

EGG GLASSES,

Or Three-Minute Glass.

Price....... ... .

To be used by the cook in timing the eggs when boiling.

LINEN PROVERS.

Price.................................... ......

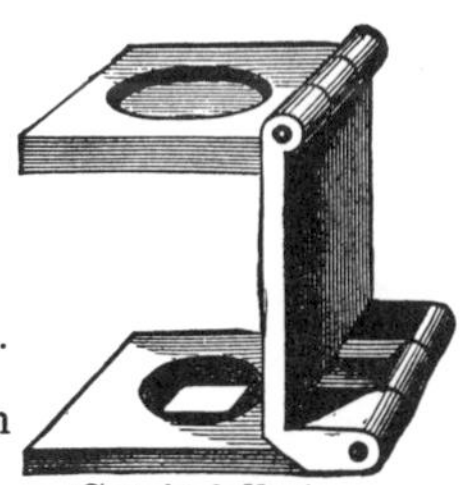

This Magnifying Glass can be folded up into a small space; can be carried in the vest pocket and used for many purposes.

Cut is full size.

DOG COLLARS AND MUZZLES.

DOG MUZZLES.
Assorted Sizes.

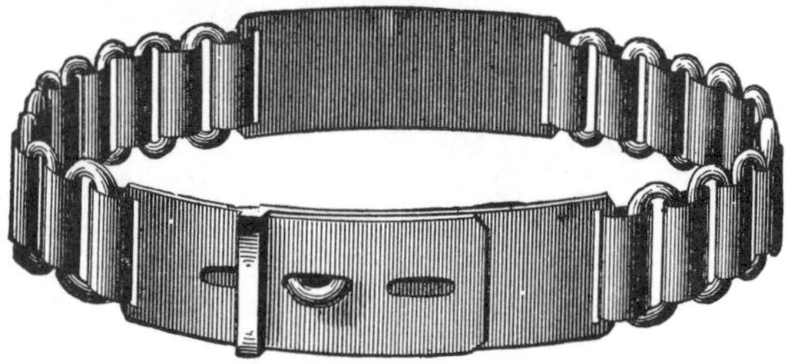

PLAIN NICKEL-PLATED CHAIN DOG COLLARS.

Nos	A	B	C	CX	D
Width.....	½	⅝	¾	1	1⅛ in.
Length ...	9 to 13,	11 to 15,	15 to 19,	17 to 21,	17 to 23 in.
Price	......	......	......	......	......

Leather and Nickel-Plated Collars in great variety.

Pointer and Setter Collars; Calf Collars.

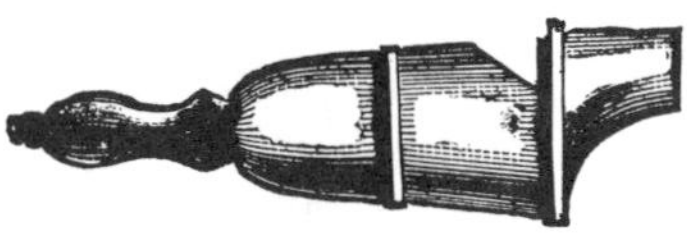

DOG CALLS.

Nos. 2 ..... 3 ..... 4..... 5.....

See Index for Police Whistles.

DOG COLLAR LOCKS.

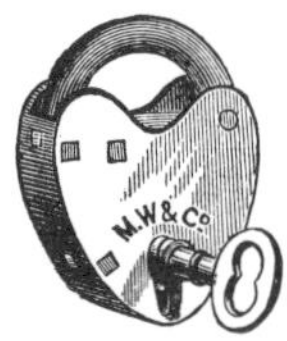

No. 40.	No. 301.	No. 302.
Brass.....	Nickel......	Nickel......
Nickel....	Gilt.........	Gilt.........

No. 110.

Charm.

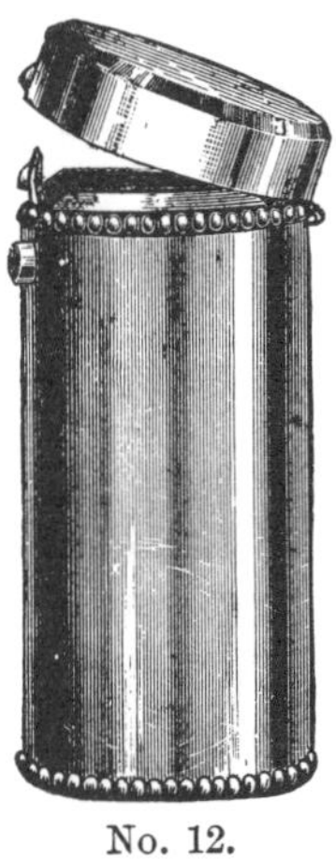

No. 12.

POCKET MATCH SAFES.—Nickel-Plated.

No. 110 ....
Charm.. ......
No. 12 ....

TOILET IRONS.

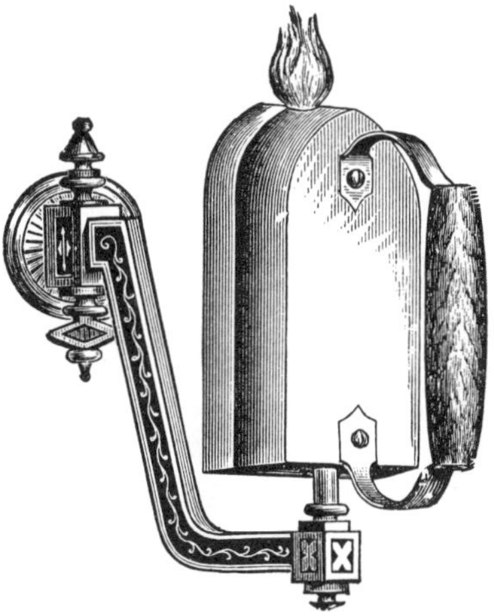

Cut of No. 1 Iron.

TOILET GAS SMOOTHING IRONS.

Can be heated in three minutes on any ordinary gas bracket. Nickel-Plated and highly finished.

No. 1, Designed for Gentlemen and used for Ironing Silk Hats. . . . .
No. 2, Designed for Ladies for Ironing Small Articles . . . .
No. 3, Designed for Milliners and Dressmakers' use . . . .

Parties boarding or traveling will readily appreciate the value of these Irons.

CURLING IRONS.—Highly Polished.

No. 1. . . . Small . . . . Medium. . . . . . Large. . . . . .

No. 3

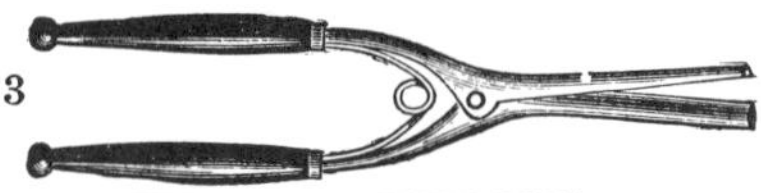

THE NEW FRIZZING IRON.
A Child Can Use It.

Polished Wood Handle-Plated. . . . .

No. 2

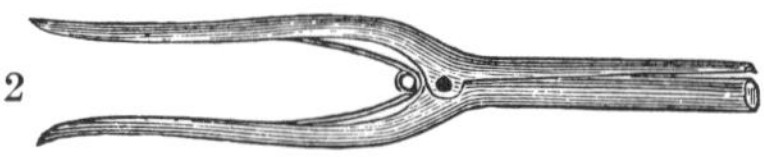

THE BANG FRIZZING IRON.
Nickel-Plated.

Particularly adapted and invented for the new prevailing style—the English or Langtry Bang. . . . .

No. 5

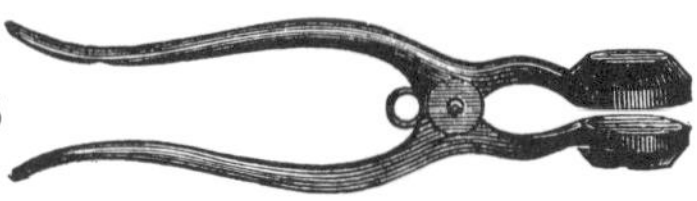

SELF-ACTING PINCHING IRON.
Nickel-Plated.

For Crimping, Waving and Frizzing the Hair; a tedious task made easy by the use of this Iron. . . . .

No. 4

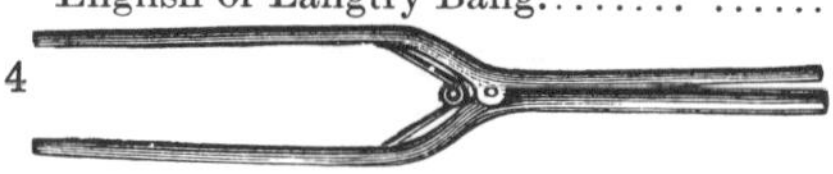

THE NEW FRIZZING IRON.
Polished and Nickel-Plated.

For the same purpose as No. 3, but larger. Used mostly by Hairdressers. . . . .

PINKING IRONS.
Cast Steel.

All sizes, from ¼ to 1 Inch.
Diamond. . . . .
Scollop . . . .

No. 6

SELF-ACTING CRIMPER AND WAVER.
Nickel-Plated.

Ladies, in whatever capacity, should avail themselves of an early opportunity of using this Crimper. . . . .

A LOW PRICE FLUTER.

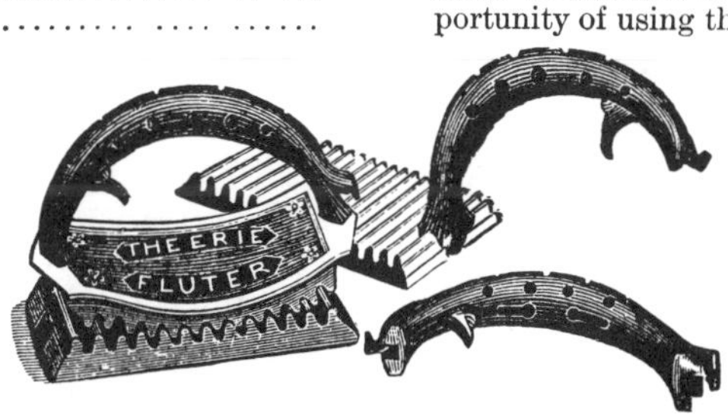

ANY CHILD CAN USE THEM.

THE ERIE FLUTER.

Polished and Bronzed, Having Adjustable Cold Handle. . . . .

See Irons and Fluters, pages 150 and 151.

HORSE AND HAIR CLIPPERS.

HORSE CLIPPERS.

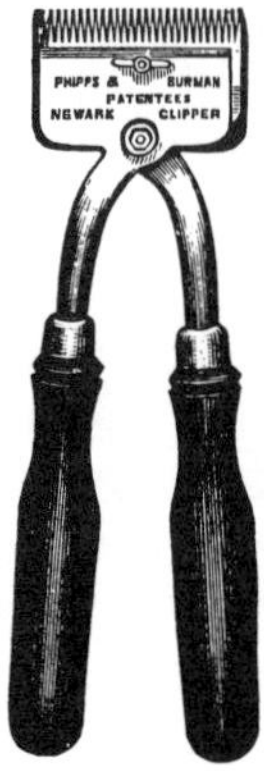

Newark.

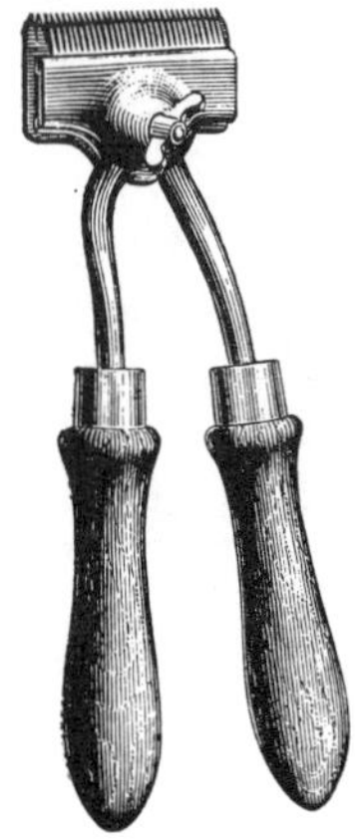

Brown & Sharpe.

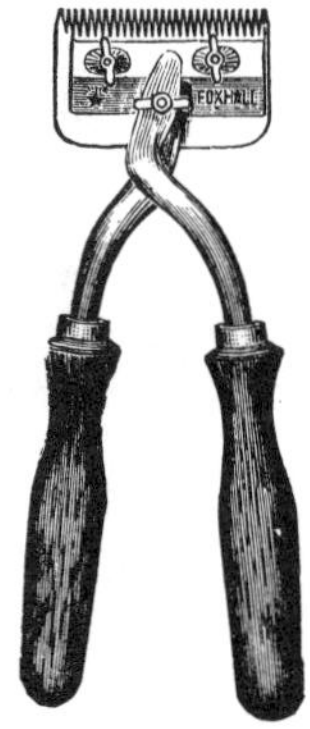

Foxhall.

Foxhall, Light Colored Handles, a Good, Cheap Clipper........................ ......
Newark, Ebonyed Handle, a Good, Medium Priced Clipper... ....
Brown & Sharpe, A Good Clipper—as Good as any in the Market.............. ......

Newark and Foxhall Clippers have leather cases for cutter.

REVERSIBLE HORSE CLIPPERS.

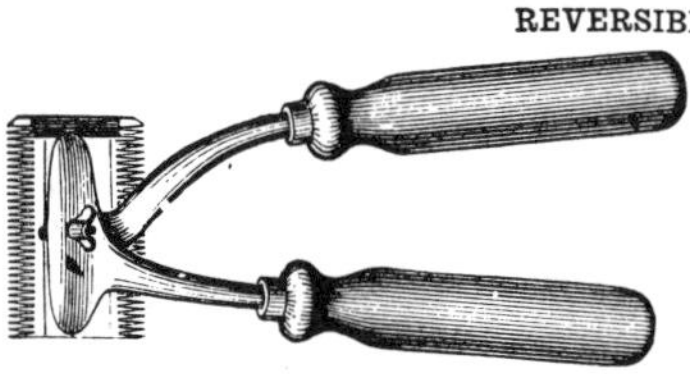

World's.

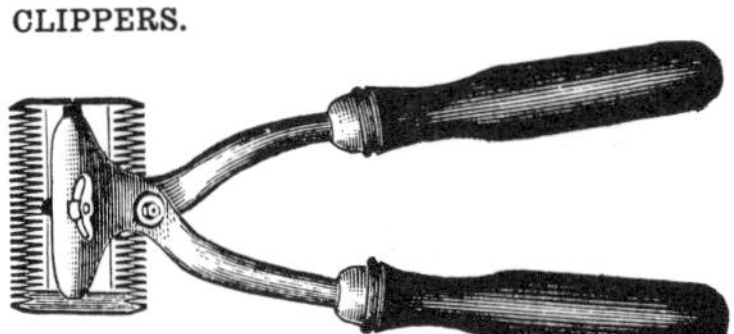

Apex.

World's Reversible, Ebonyed Handles, Self-Sharpening......................... ......
Apex Reversible, Self-Sharpening, the best Reversible Clipper in the Market... ......

Each one has a Leather Case for the Cutter.

Bent Trimming Shears also in stock.

BARBERS' HAIR CLIPPERS.

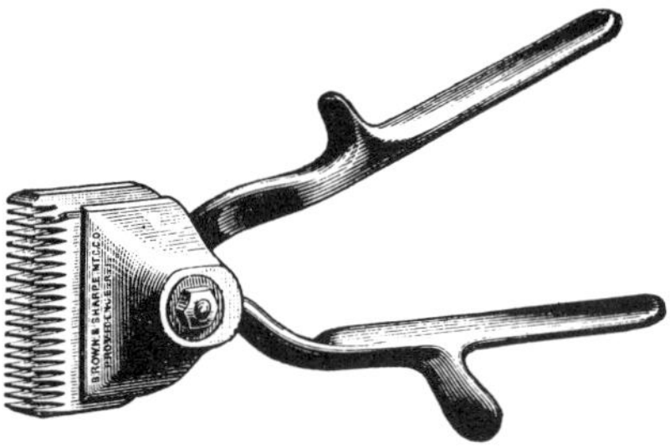

Brown & Sharpe.—Nickel-Plated.

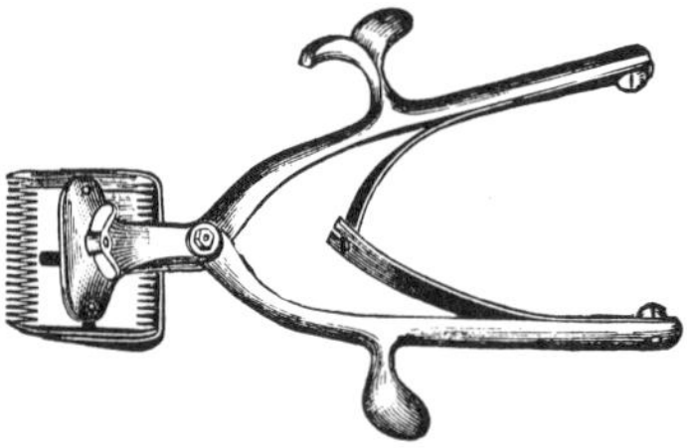

Duplex.

In Four Sizes—

No. 0, Toilet, Cuts Hair very short......
No. 1, Cuts Hair 1/8 inch long..........
No. 2, " " 1/4 " " ....
No. 3, " " 5-16" " ....

This is the popular Clipper

REVERSIBLE TOILET CLIPPER.

This is a new Clipper, both knives being the same size- We hope soon to have this Clipper with two sized knives, to cut Hair one-eighth and one-quarter.

The above is the best line of Clippers in the market to-day; the best will be found in stock at any time. Caution—Never apply files or grindstones to the Clippers.

Barbers' Cast Steel Shears and the best brands of Razors all warranted.

RAZORS.

We take great pride in keeping a large and well selected stock of these goods. We import all our Razors from Sheffield, and warrant them to give satisfaction. Our stock will be found at all times large and well assorted. For convenience in ordering we have divided these goods into five classes, as below.

Class A, Plain Ground, Heavy, Cheap Razors, Black Handles ....

Class B, Same as the above, but better finished, " " ....

Class C, Good, Medium Priced, Hollow Ground, White Bone and Black Handles ...... 3/8 ...... 1/2 ...... 5/8 ...... 3/4 ...... in.

Class D, Extra Hollow Ground, Ivory, White Bone and Black Handles ...... 3/8 ...... 1/2 ...... 5/8 ...... 3/4 ...... in.

Class E, Full Concaved, " " " " " ...... 3/8 ...... 1/2 ...... 5/8 ...... 3/4 ...... in.

Price given is on Black Handle. White Bone Extra. .... Ivory Extra ....

VAJEN & NEW, INDIANAPOLIS, IND.

RAZORS, STROPS AND HONES.

See Page 204 for Full and Complete Line of Razors.

No. 18, Magic, Large, with Hone ....

No. 96 C, 13½ in., One Side Oval ....

No. 8, 13½ in., Double Rod Frame ....

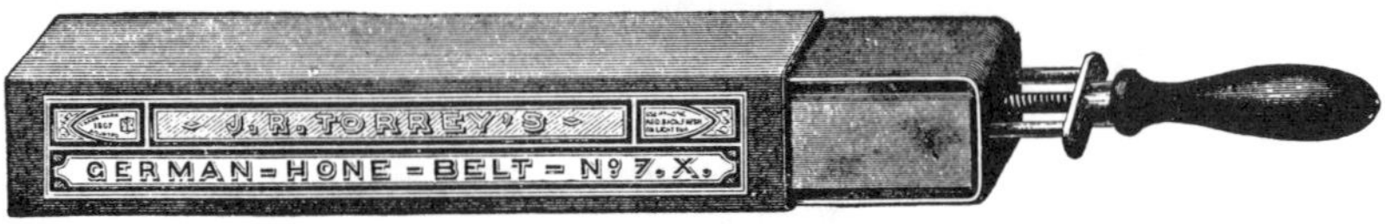

No. 7X, German Belt, with Hone, Double Rod and Screw ....
No. 022, " " " " " " " ....

No. 200, Cushion Belt, Imitation Morocco Case, Fine Leather Finish ....

RAZOR HONES.

7 in., Selected.. ...... 7 in., Extra Fine.. ...... 8 in., Extra Fine.. ......

BARBERS' SWING STROPS.

Russia Leather, No. 1A...2A... Canvas, No. 4A... Canvas and Russia Leather, No. 5A...

HEADQUARTERS FOR

AMERICAN AND ENGLISH

POCKET CUTLERY.

OUR STOCK COMPRISES THE CHOICE PATTERNS

IN THE BEST BRANDS.

An Endless Variety to Select From.

Stock Complete in Every Respect.

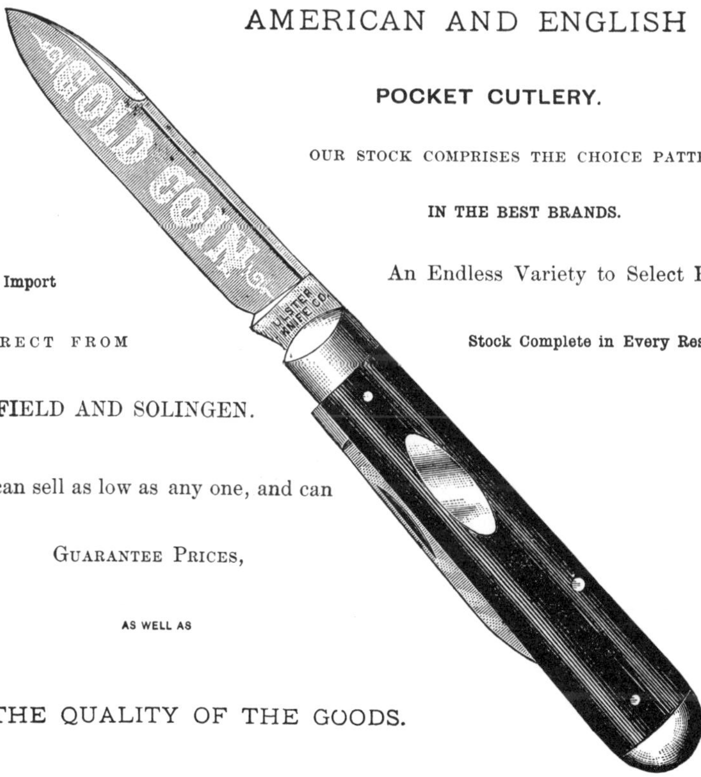

We Import

DIRECT FROM

SHEFFIELD AND SOLINGEN.

We can sell as low as any one, and can

GUARANTEE PRICES,

AS WELL AS

THE QUALITY OF THE GOODS.

Pen, Pocket and Jack Knives a Specialty.

Examine our Stock. It will interest you. About 1000 patterns.

VAJEN & NEW, INDIANAPOLIS, IND.

This cut kindly furnished by the Northfield Knife Co.

The largest assortment of Pocket Knives, from the best to the cheapest.

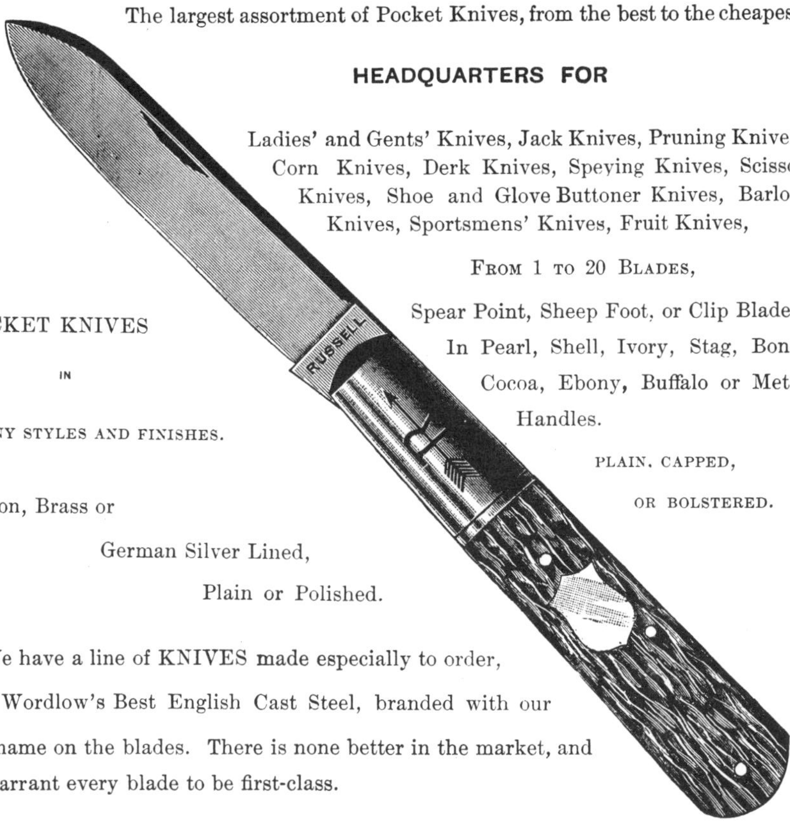

HEADQUARTERS FOR

Ladies' and Gents' Knives, Jack Knives, Pruning Knives, Corn Knives, Derk Knives, Speying Knives, Scissor Knives, Shoe and Glove Buttoner Knives, Barlow Knives, Sportsmens' Knives, Fruit Knives,

FROM 1 TO 20 BLADES,

Spear Point, Sheep Foot, or Clip Blades, In Pearl, Shell, Ivory, Stag, Bone, Cocoa, Ebony, Buffalo or Metal Handles.

PLAIN, CAPPED, OR BOLSTERED.

POCKET KNIVES IN MANY STYLES AND FINISHES.

Iron, Brass or German Silver Lined, Plain or Polished.

We have a line of KNIVES made especially to order, from Wordlow's Best English Cast Steel, branded with our own name on the blades. There is none better in the market, and we warrant every blade to be first-class.

This, the most important branch of our business, seems to be treated most mildly, and yet it has received the most consideration. To attempt to illustrate the many different patterns of Pocket Knives carried by us, would simply be impossible, and would require a book several times larger than our entire Catalogue.

COLUMBIA PATTERN.

No. 8, Tea Spoons.............. ...... No. 16, Table Spoons........... ......

No. 20, Table Forks.................................... ......

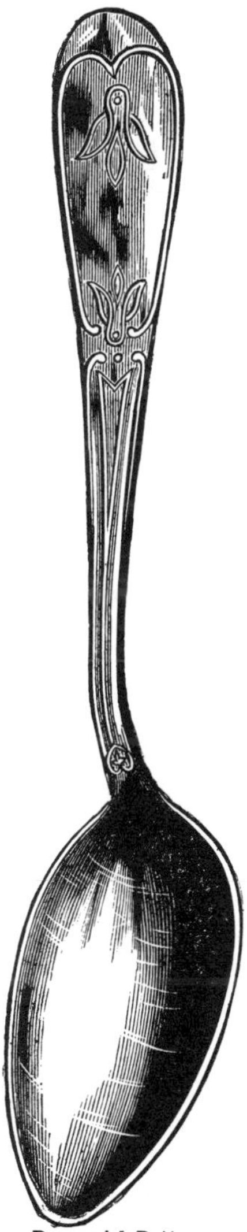

Brunswick Pattern.

BRITANNIA SPOONS.

No. 1000, Tea Spoons, Tipped Pattern.................. ......
No. 1000, Table " " " ....
No. 950, Tea " Brunswick Pattern................ ......
No. 1900, Table " " " ....

GERMAN SILVER SPOONS.

Tipped Pattern, Tea .... Table........... ......

SILVER PLATED SPOONS AND FORKS.

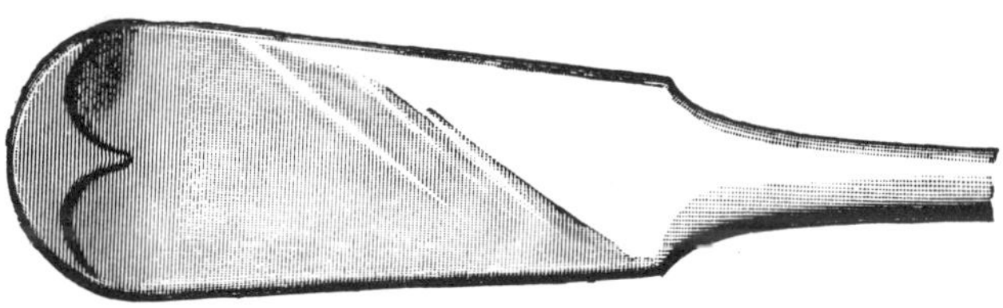

Tipped Pattern.

Tea Spoons ....
Table Spoons.. ......
Medium Forks.. ......

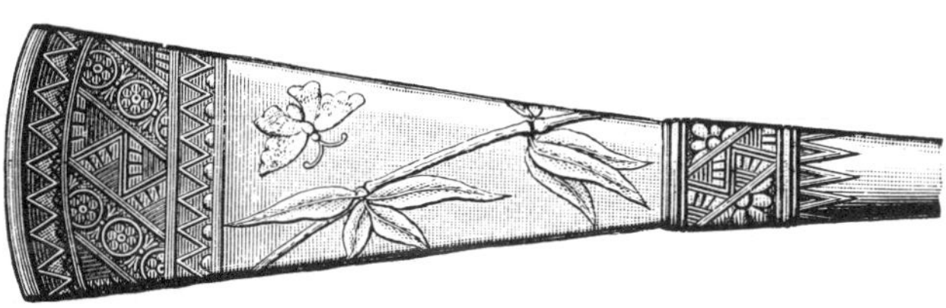

Japanese Pattern.

Tea Spoons.. ......
Table " ....
Medium Forks.. ......
Sugar Shells.. ......
Butter Knives ....

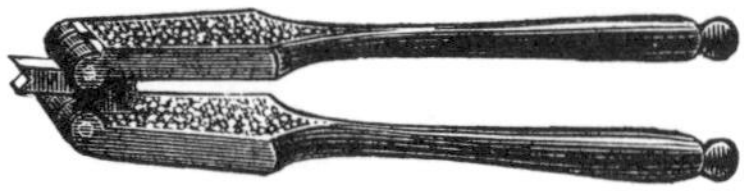

NUT CRACKS.

Iron, Bronzed.... ...... Nickeled ... .
Steel, Nickeled ....

PLATED STEEL NUT PICKS.

Sets of Half-Dozen ....
" " " and 1 Crack ....
" One " ....
" " " and 2 Cracks ....

In Paper and Wood Cases.

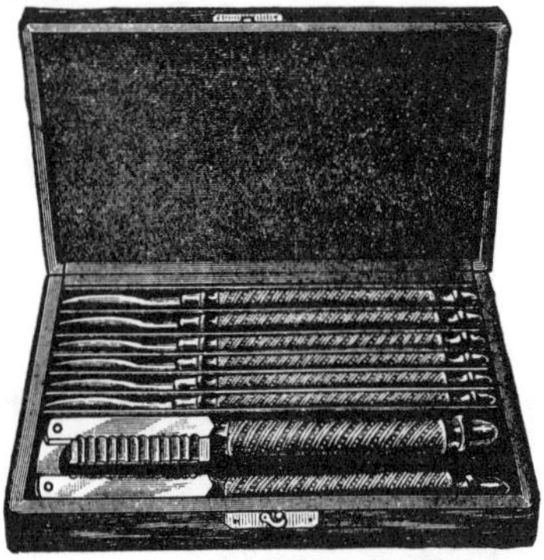

NUT PICKS AND CRACKS.

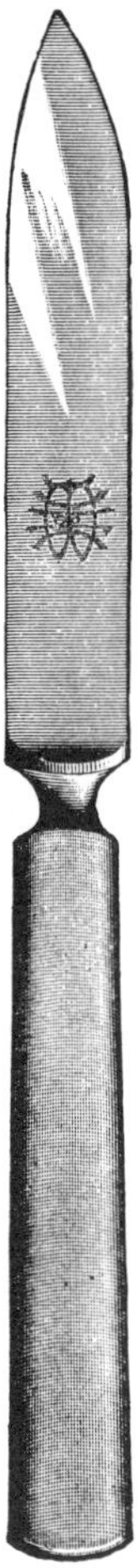

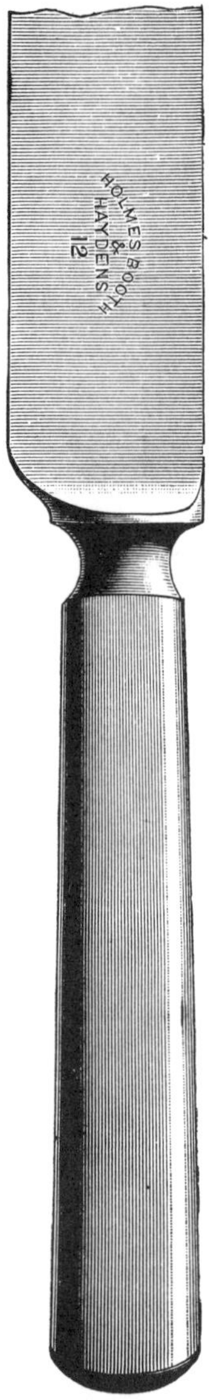

Single Plated, Solid Handle, Medium Knives.......... ...... Forks......... ......
Triple " " " " .... " ....
" " " Dessert " ....
Plated, Solid Handle, Fruit Knives ....
" Pocket " " ....
" " " with Nut Pick ....

CHILD'S SETS.

Wood Handles..... Bone Handles......
Silver Plated ....
" " with Napkin Ring..... ......

CARVERS.

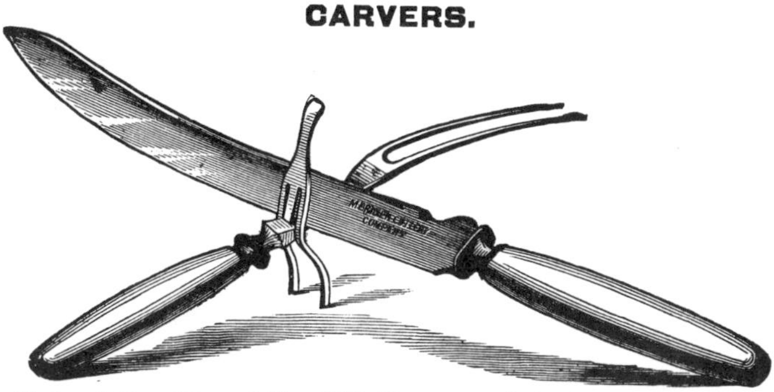

Style of No. 678 and No. 1078 Carvers and Patent Guard Fork.

PLAIN CARVERS.

No. 149, Rosewood.. . .... No. 249, Ebony .. .. No. 549, Bone .. ..

No. 161, Rosewood.. ...... No. 261, Ebony... ...... No. 561, Bone .. ..

RUBBER HANDLE CARVERS.

No. 675, Straight Handle........ ...... No. 678, Swelled Handle. ....
No. 675, " " Steels... ...... No. 678, " " Steels.. ......

CELLULOID HANDLE CARVERS.

No. 1075, Straight Handle........ ...... No. 1078, Swelled Handle ....
No. 1075, " " Steels.. ...... No. 1078, " " Steels.. ......

STAG HANDLE CARVERS.

No. 1217......................... ...... Steels ....

No. 1275 .... Steels ....

The above Carvers, priced by the pair, will be furnished in sets, and put up in handsome satin-lined cases if desired. We have the largest and best selected stock of Carvers in the State. Our assortment is always complete, embracing Ivory, Walrus and Pearl Handles, in Plain, Sabre and Scimeter Blades; also Game Carvers; in fact, all styles from the Plainest to the Finest.

FRENCH COOKS' KNIVES.

Inch	6	7	8	9	10	12
	......	......	......	......	.....	......

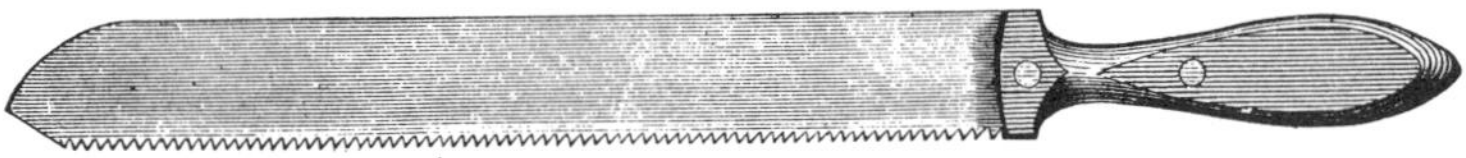

HAM SAW AND KNIFE COMBINED.

12 Inch, Cast Steel Blade ....

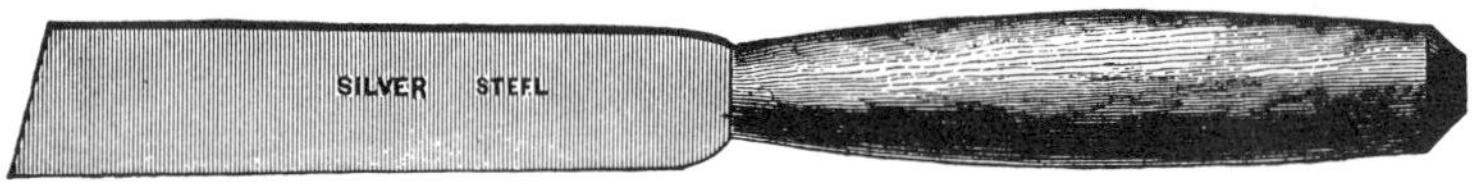

SHOE KNIVES.

Nos.	1	2	3
Square Point	......	......	......
Round "	......	......	......
Skivers	......	......	......

FLUTED POTATO KNIVES.

Price ....

VEGETABLE KNIVES.

Price ....

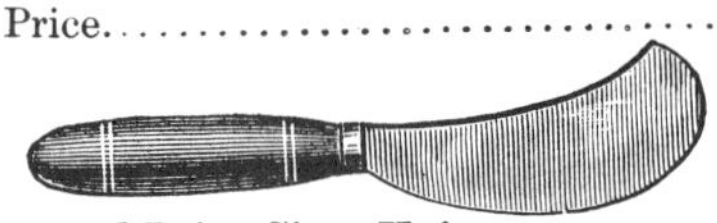

Round Point Cigar Knives.. ....

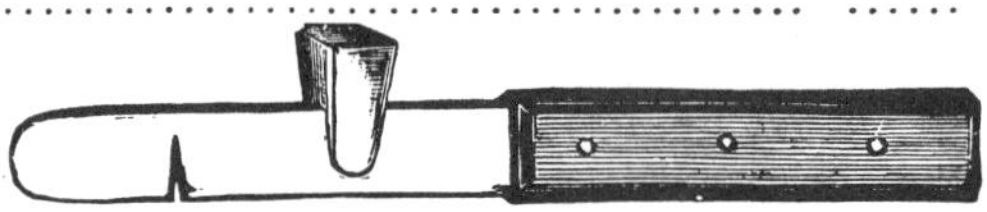

CIGAR BOX OPENERS.

Price ....

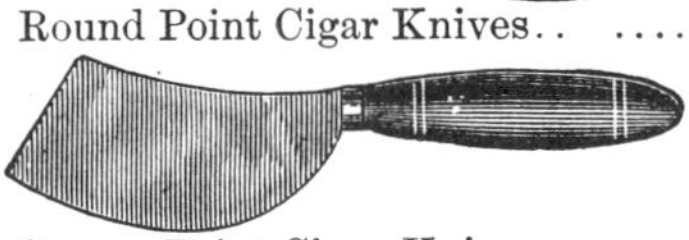

Square Point Cigar Knives.. ....

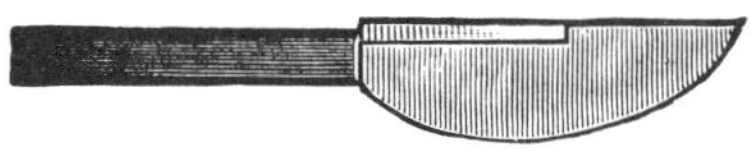

Cincinnati Pattern Cigar Knives ....

CIGAR BUTT CUTTER.

Price ....

TABLE CUTLERY.

The following priced with Three-Pronged Forks.

No. 12, Rosewood.... ...... No. 22, Ebony.... ...... No. 52, Bone.... ......

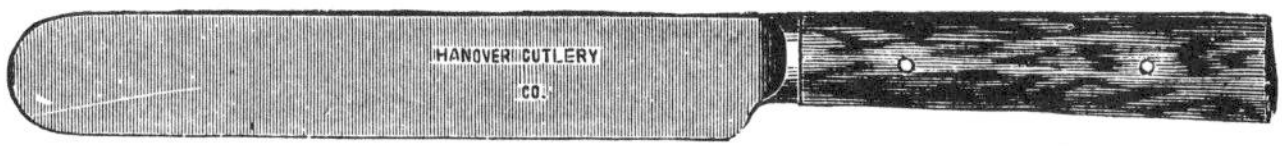

No. 12 B, Rosewood.. ...... No. 22 B, Ebony.. ...... No. 52 B, Bone.. ......

No. 12 C, Rosewood.. ...... No. 22 C, Ebony.. ...... No. 52 C, Bone.. ......

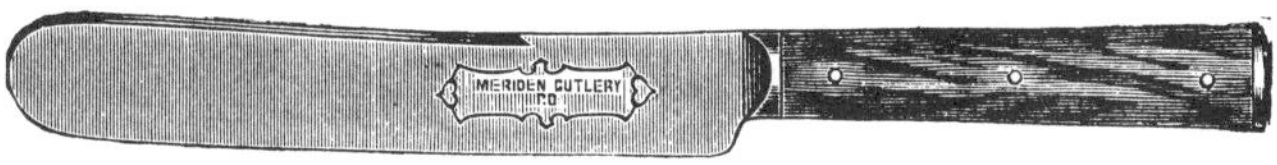

No. 11892, Rosewood.. ...... No. 22892, Ebony.. ...... No. 55892, Bone.. ......

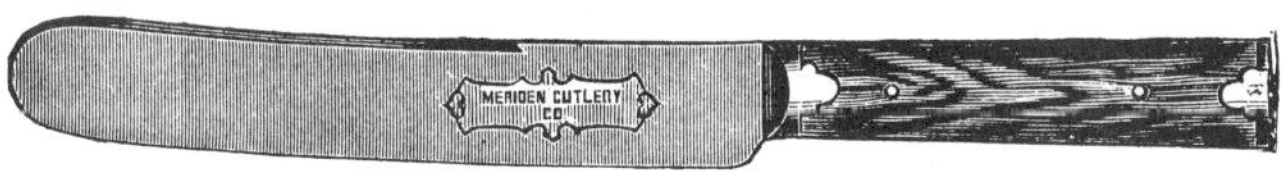

No. 11312, Rosewood............. ...... No. 22312, Ebony............. ......

No. 11352, Rosewood,............. ...... No. 22352, Ebony............. ......

No. 1171, Rosewood............. ..... No. 2271, Ebony............. ......

No, 1621, Rosewood.. ...... No. 2621, Ebony.. ...... No. 5621 Bone.. ......

No. 819, Iron Handled.. ......

The above illustrate a few of our most saleable patterns. We have also a fine line of Desserts and Moits.

Medium Knives and Forks, same price as Table Knives and Forks.

Dessert Knives and Forks, 50 cts. per gross less than Table Knives and Forks.

Knives only advance, No. Bolster, extra, $1.50, Bolster $2.00 per gross on Knives and Forks.

All the New Desirable Patterns kept in Stock and Furnished at Factory Prices.

TABLE CUTLERY.

TO BE USED WITH PLATED FORKS.

RUBBER HANDLE KNIVES.

No. 617, Medium .... Desserts ....

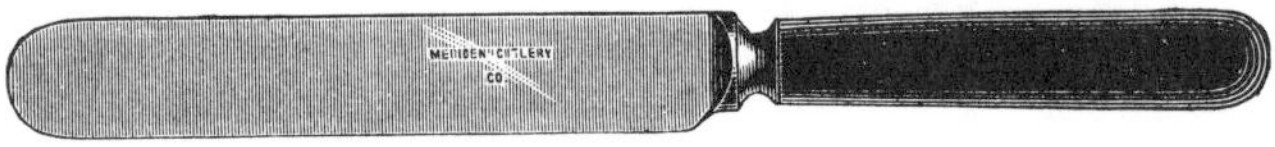

No. 675, Medium .... Desserts ....

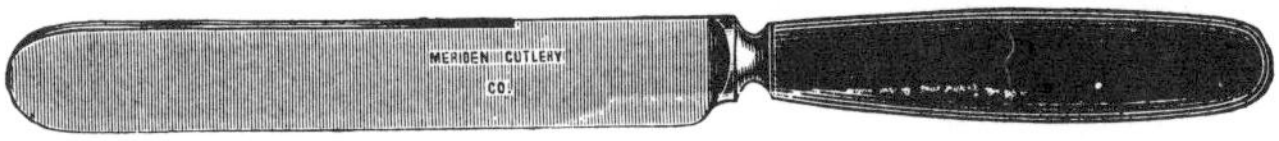

No. 678, Medium .... Desserts ....

CELLULOID HANDLE KNIVES.

No. 1017, Medium .... Desserts ....

No. 1075, Medium .... Desserts ....

No. 1078, Medium .... Desserts ....

IVORY HANDLE KNIVES.

No. 476, Medium .... Desserts ....

PEARL HANDLE KNIVES.—In Satin Lined Cases.

Medium .... Per Doz. Desserts .... Per Doz.

For Plated Handle Knives, see page 209.

Ivory, Pearl and Celluloid Handle Knives, with Plated Blades, in stock.

BUTCHER AND BREAD KNIVES.

BEECH HANDLE BUTCHER KNIVES.

Inch..... 6...... 6½...... 7...... 8...... 9...... 10..... 11...... 12......

BEECH HANDLE STICKING KNIVES.

Inch.. 6...... 6½...... 7......

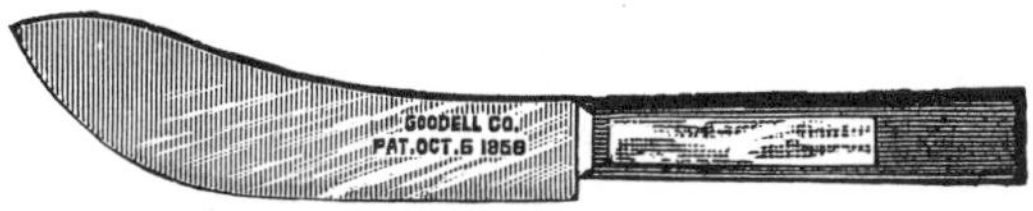

BEECH HANDLE SKINNING KNIVES.

Inch.. 6..... 6½...... 7......

ROSEWOOD HANDLE BUTCHER KNIVES.--Bolstered.

Inch.. 6...... 6½...... 7...... 8...... 9......

ROSEWOOD HANDLE STEAK KNIVES.—Bolstered.

Inch.. 10..... 11...... 12......

ROSEWOOD HANDLE STICKING KNIVES.—Bolstered.

Inch.. 6...... 6½......

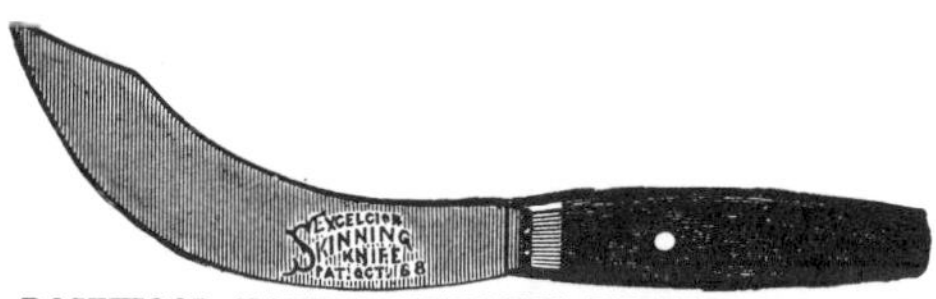

ROSEWOOD HANDLE SKINNING KNIVES.—Bolstered.

Inch.. 6...... 6½......

BREAD KNIVES.

No. 44, Cocoa Handle.............. ...... No. 144, Ebony Handle.......... ......

No. 244, Royal Slicer, Cocoa Handle.. ......

Ferruled Handle.. ......

WILSON'S BUTCHER KNIVES.

Inch. .5½. . . .6. . . . 6½. . . . 7 . . . 8. . . . 9. . . . 10. . . . 11. . . . 12. . . .

WILSON'S STICKING KNIVES.

Inch. . . . . .5½. . . . . 6. . . . . 6½. . . . . 7. . . . .

WILSON'S SKINNING KNIVES.

Inch. . . . . .5. . . . . 5½ . . . . 6 . . . . 6½. . . . . 7. . . . .

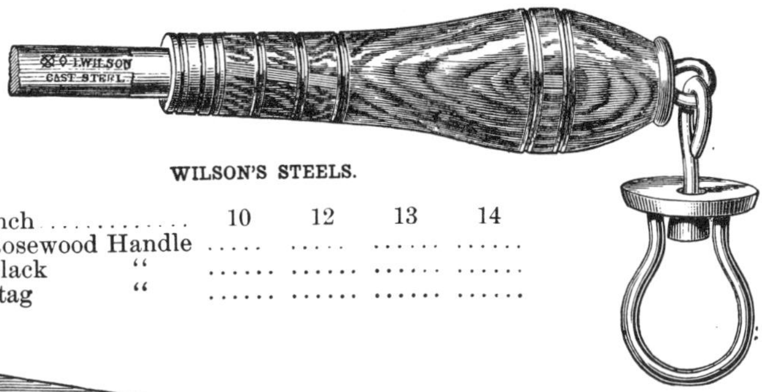

WILSON'S STEELS.

Inch	10	12	13	14
Rosewood Handle	. . . .	. . . .	. . . .	. . . .
Black "	. . . .	. . . .	. . . .	. . . .
Stag "	. . . .	. . . .	. . . .	. . . .

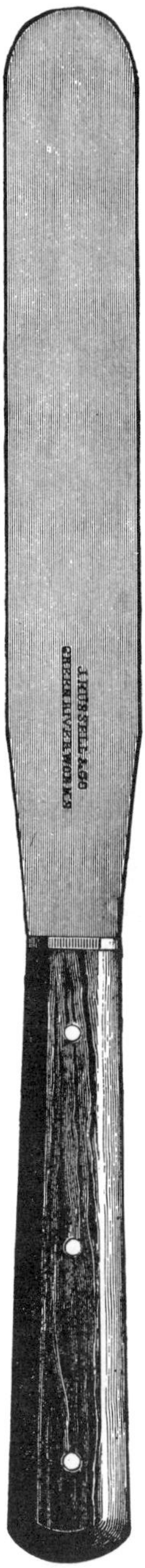

PATENT PALLET KNIVES, OR SPATULAS.

Inch. . . . . 3. . . . . 4. . . . . 5. . . . . 6. . . . . 8. . . . . 10. . . . . 12. . . . . 14. . . . .

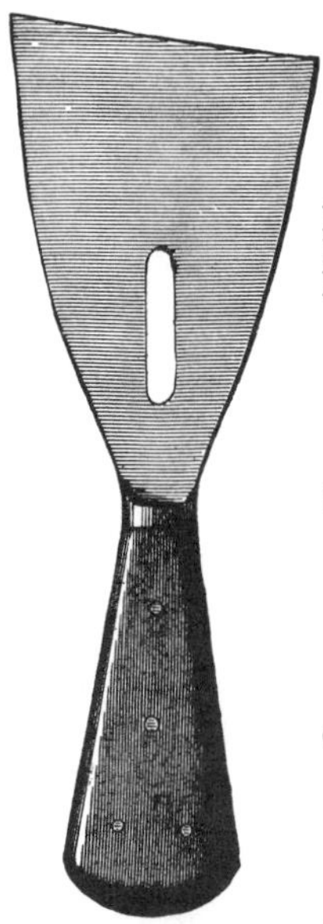

SCRAPING KNIVES.

In. . 3 . . . . 3½. . . .

KITCHEN KNIVES.

No. 15690, Rosewood Handle. . . . .
No. 13, Beech Handle. . . . .
Plain Round Handle. . . . .

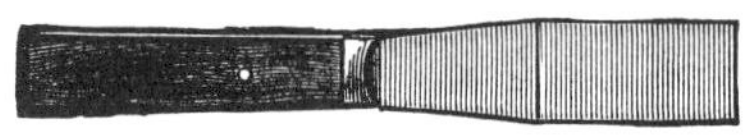

PUTTY KNIVES.

Square Point. . . Plain . . . . . Bolstered . . . . .
Stiff or Elastic.

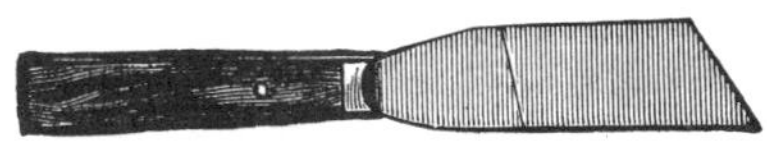

PUTTY KNIVES.

Clipped Point . . . .

BAND KNIVES.

Sickle Edge. . . . .

IRON SPOONS, FORKS, &C.

VAJEN & NEW, INDIANAPOLIS, IND.

TINNED IRON SPOONS.

No. 305, Tea, Brunswick Pattern ....
No. 40, Table. " " ....

No. 23, Tea, Rose Pattern.......... ......
No. 46, Table " " ....

SOLID IRON BASTING SPOONS.

Tinned .... 10..... 12 .... 14..... 16...... 18......

FLESH FORKS.

Iron Handle.......... Inch 2 ..... 3......Prong

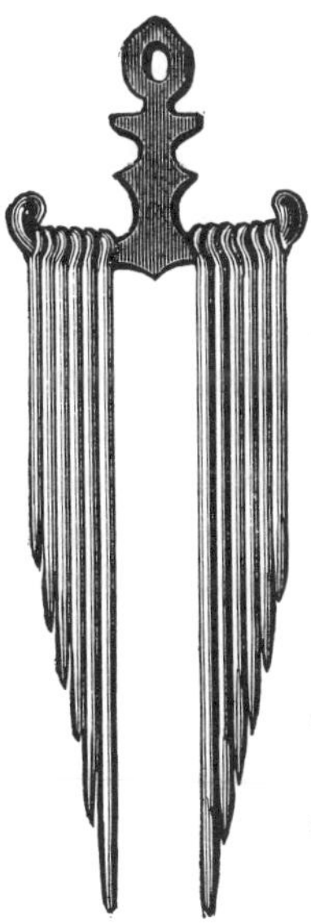

VEGETABLE FORKS.

Wood Handle ....

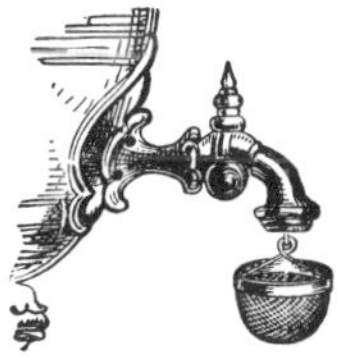

COFFEE STRAINERS.

No. 1, Wood Handle.......... ......

TEA STRAINER.

Tinned ....

INSECT POWDER GUNS.

This Insect Power Gun is so constructed that it can not choke..... ....

STEEL SKEWERS.

Set of 12..........

Paste Jaggers ....

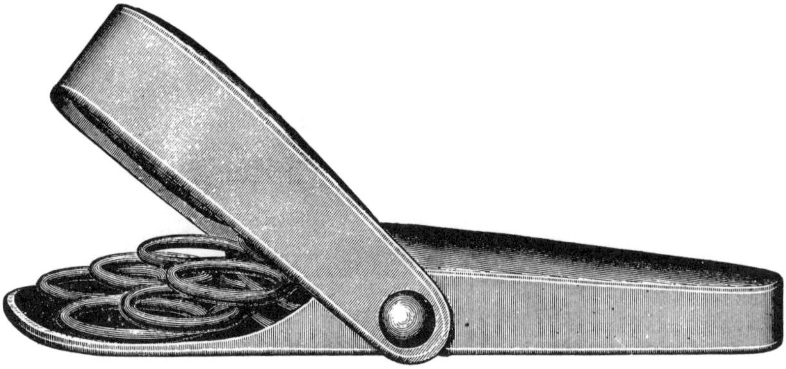

SCISSORS —In Leather Cases.

Nickel-Plated.	Gold-Plated.	Leather-Covered.
Sets of.....3 ..... 4......	Sets of ...3...... 4......	Sets of.....3...... 4......

Plush, or Velvet Cases, Silk Lined, also in stock.

READING GLASSES.

German Silver Rim, Ebony Handle, Best Quality....Inch....2...... 2½...... 3......

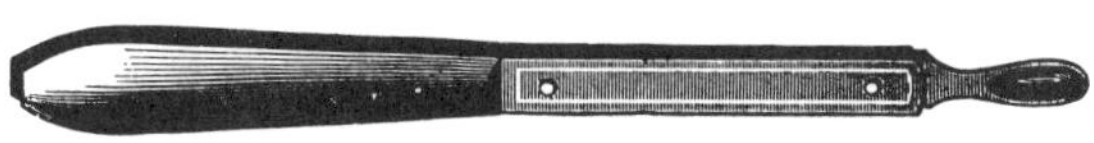

STEEL TWEEZERS AND EAR SPOONS

In several styles.

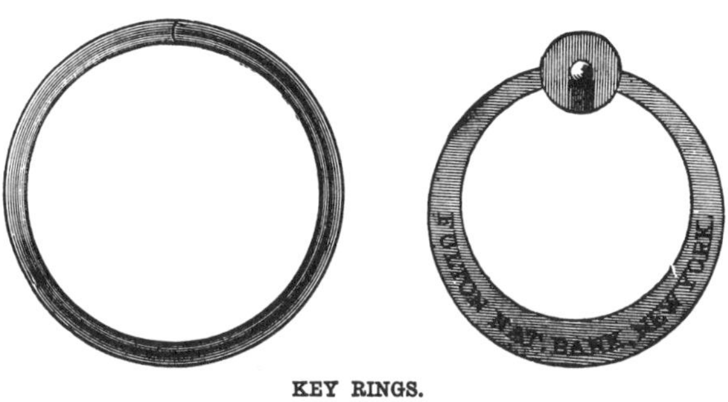

KEY RINGS.

An endless variety of Key Rings and Split Rings in the different sizes.

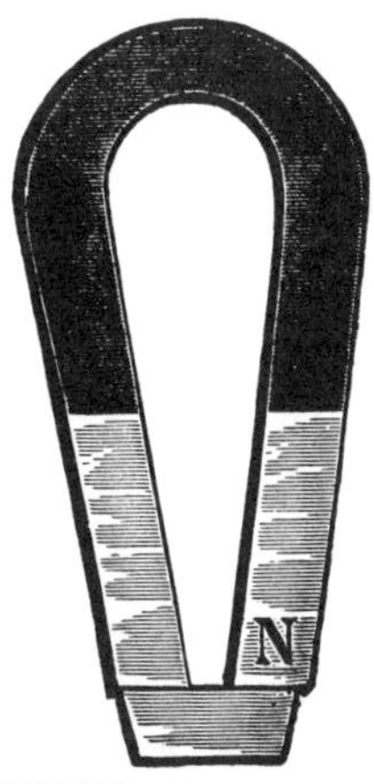

HORSESHOE MAGNETS.

In., 2½.... 3.... 4....

SHEARS AND SCISSORS.

STRAIGHT TRIMMERS.—With Steel Blades.

Inch....	6	6½	7	7½	8	8½	9	10
Japanned....	....	....	....	....	....	....	....	....
Nickeled	....	....	....	....	....	....	....	...

Second Grade, Nickeled .... 8.... 8½ in....

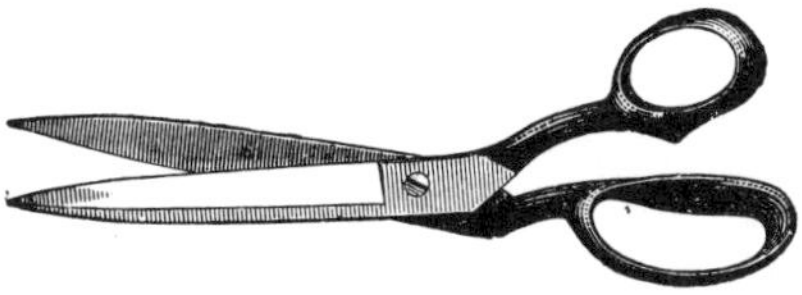

BENT TRIMMERS.—Solid Steel Blades.

Inch	9	10
Japanned	....	....
Nickeled	....	....

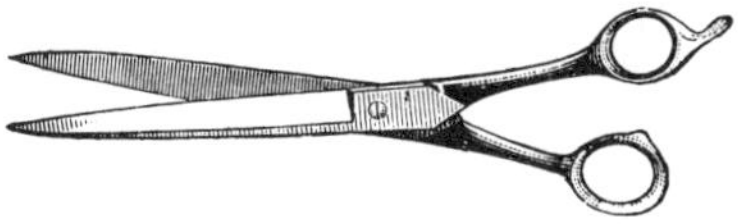

BARBERS' SHEARS.

Solid Cast Steel, Inch.. 7½.... 8 ... 8½....
Nickel-Plated.

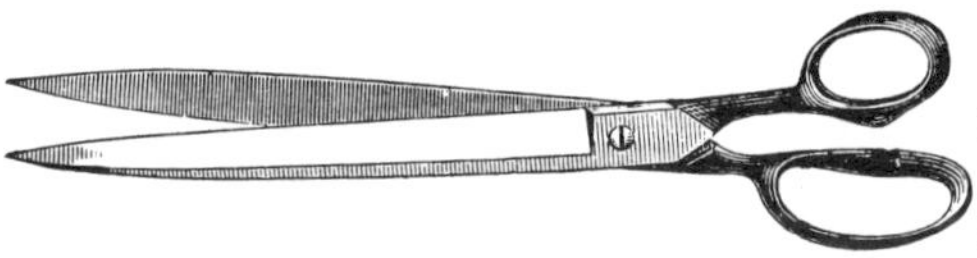

BANKERS' SHEARS.

Inch..............	12	14	16
Japanned.........	....	....	....
Nickeled..........	....	....	....

SCISSORS.

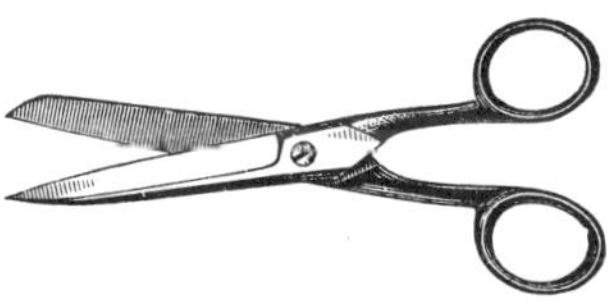

Inch..........	4	4½	5	5½	6	6½	7
Plain Bows ...	....	....	....	....	....	....	....
Beveled " ...	....	....	....	....	....	....	....
Nickeled	....	....	....	. ..	....	....	....

BUTTONHOLE SCISSORS.

Without Set Screws	....
With " "	....

POCKET SCISSORS.

Inch	3½	4	4½	5
Plain Bows.......................	....	....	....	....
Beveled "	....	....	....	....
Nickel Plated....................	....	....	....	....

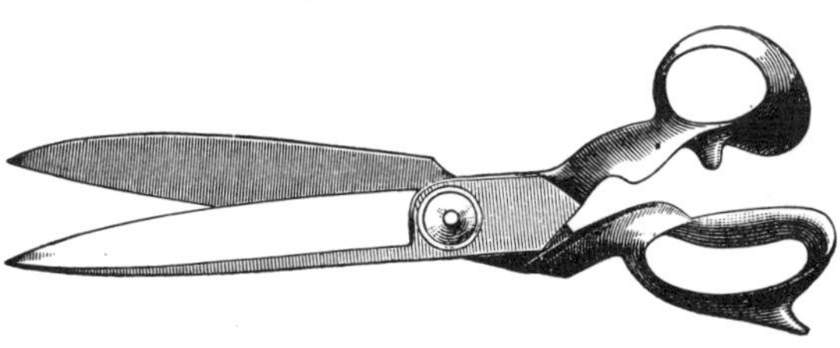

TAILORS' SHEARS.

Nos	5	6	7
Plain	....	....	....
Nickel Plated.	....	....	....

POCKET FOLDING SCISSORS.

Assorted, Blunt and Sharp Points .... Small ..... Large .....

Nickel-Plated, and furnished with a neat Morocco Case.

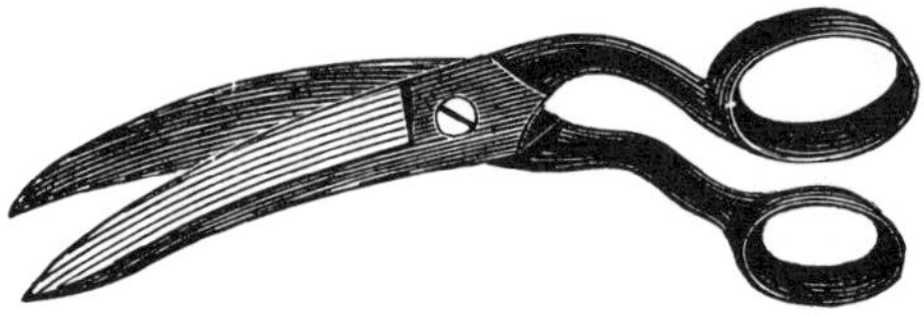

HORSE CLIPPING SHEARS.

9 Inch ....

Made of best cast steel.

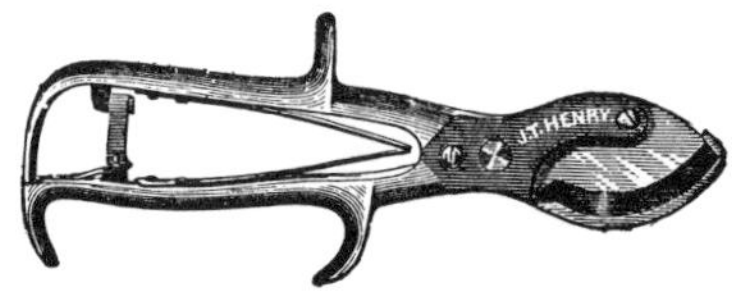

PRUNING SHEARS, OR SHEEP TOE TRIMMERS.

No. 1............ ....

No. 2 ....

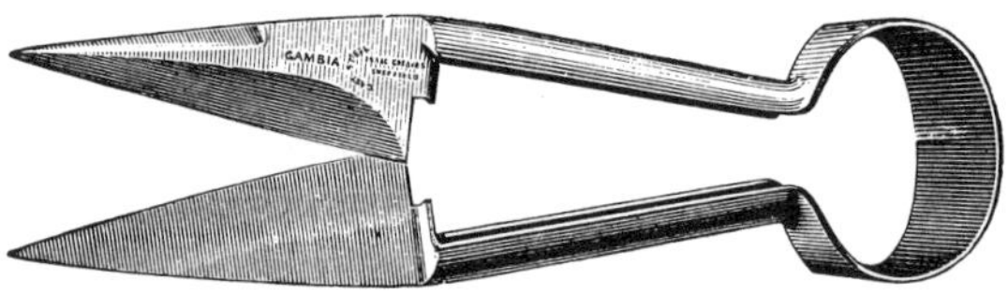

Half Ground Blades, Black Bow ....

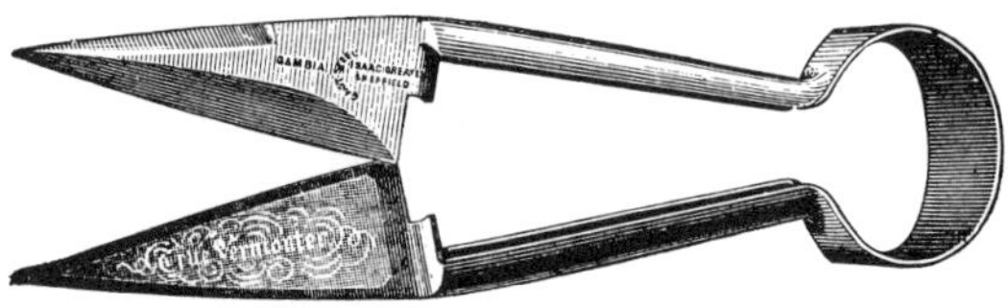

Polished Swaged Blades, Black Bow ....

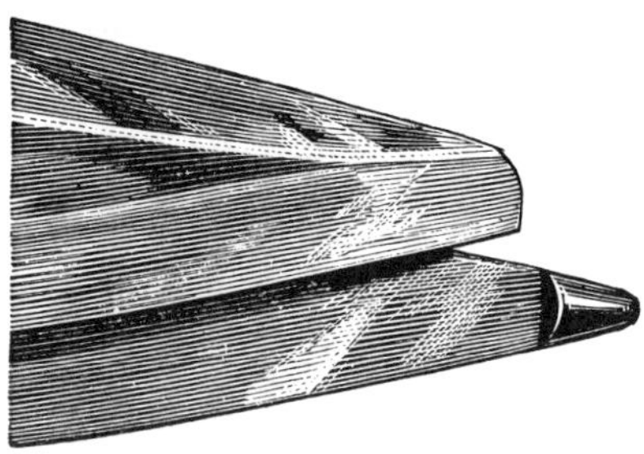

SHEEP SHEARS.—With Patent Guard Points.

Price.. ......

It effectually prevents cutting or wounding the animal while shearing, thereby enabling the shearer to work much faster.

HANDCUFFS, NIPPERS AND WHISTLES.

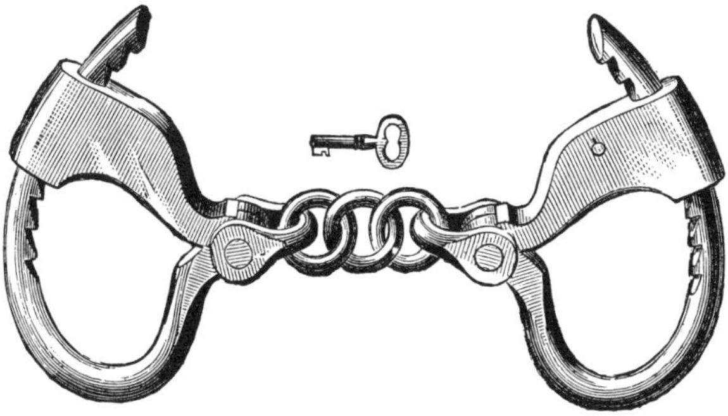

PATENT ADJUSTABLE DOUBLE LOCK HANDCUFFS AND LEG IRONS.

These Shackles are instantly adjustable to limbs of any size. They can be used in all cases with the certainty that they will fit exactly and securely.

Handcuffs, Polished.. ......
" Nickled... ......
Leg Irons, " ... .

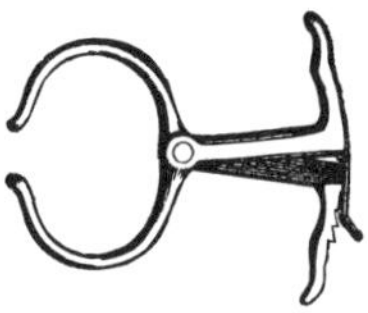

PHILLIPS' PATENT NIPPERS.

Nickel-Plated.................. ....

TOWER'S CHAIN NIPPERS.

Nickel-Plated ....

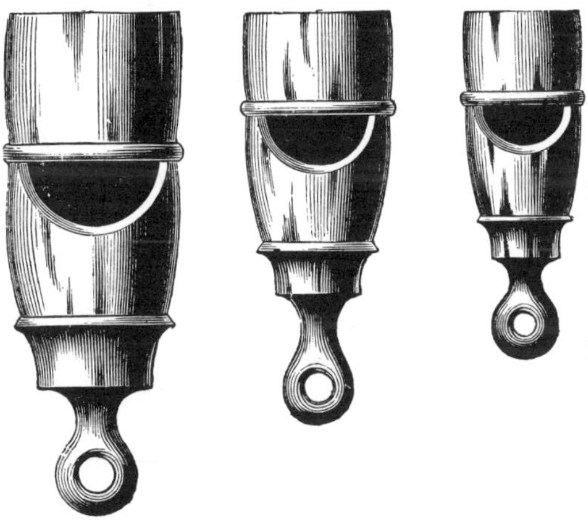

POLICE WHISTLES.

Britannia.

Nos....1.... 2 ... 3 .... 4 .... 5 ...

DUPLEX POLICE CALLS.

Nickel-Plated ....

GLASS CUTTERS.

No. 9, Combination Glass Cutter, Knife Sharpener and Can Opener......... ......
No. 10, Same, with Corkscrew......... ......

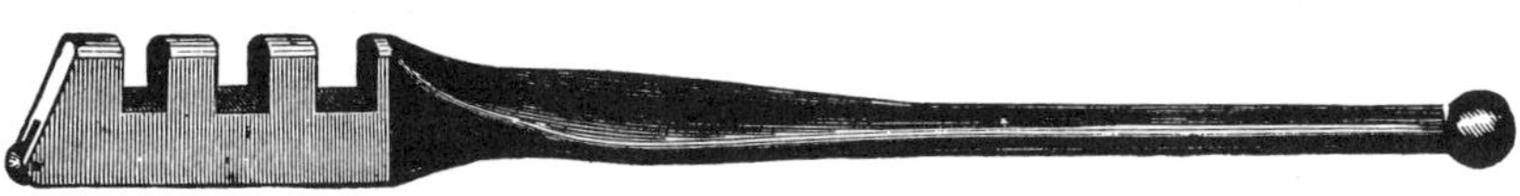

Cut of No. 1.

No. 1..... ...... No. 4, With Putty Knife..... ...... No. 5, Heavy..... ......

CORK-SCREWS.

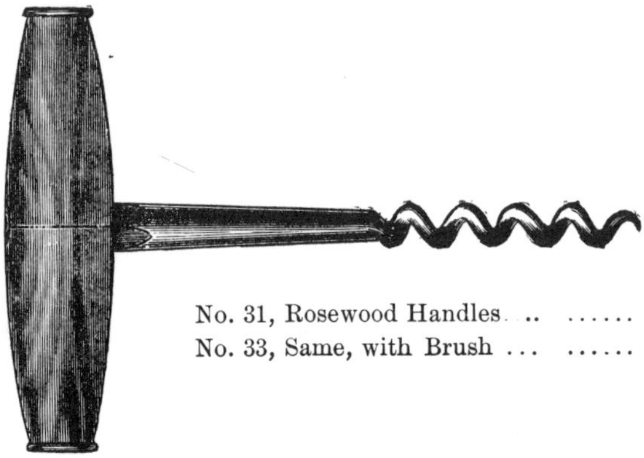

No. 31, Rosewood Handles.. .. ..
No. 33, Same, with Brush ... .

POCKET CORK-SCREWS.

No. 64.... ....

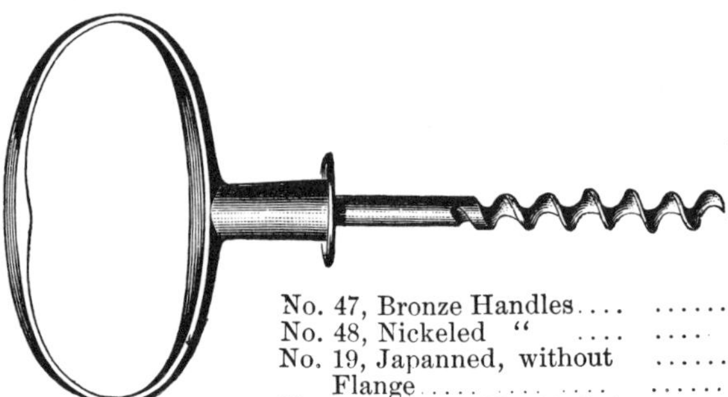

No. 47, Bronze Handles.... ......
No. 48, Nickeled " ....
No. 19, Japanned, without Flange.... ....
No. 18, Same as No. 19, but Spiral Coil ....

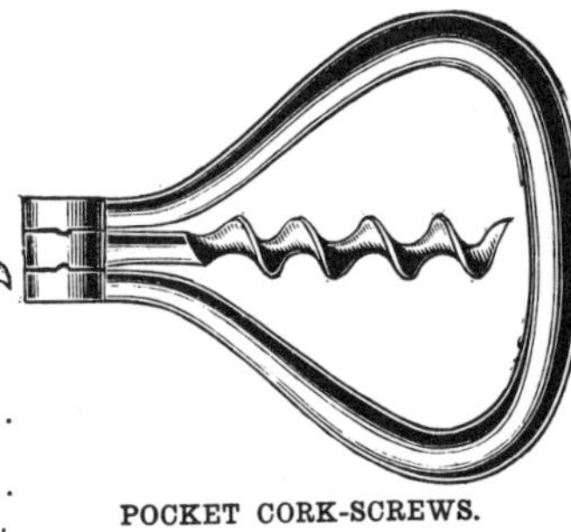

POCKET CORK-SCREWS.

No. 62. .. . .
No. 63. ....

No. 123, Bronzed Frame......

No. 13½, Closed.

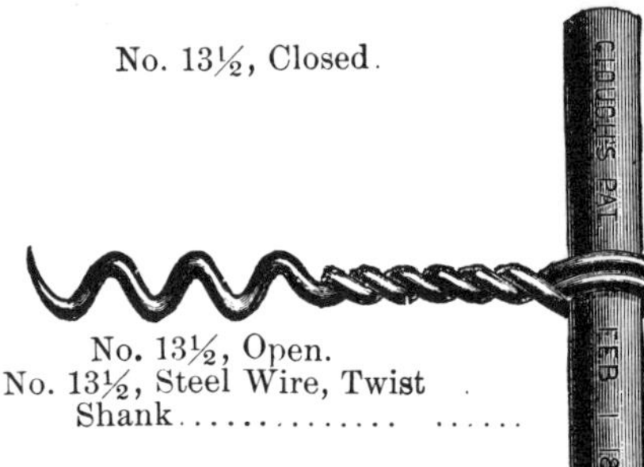

No. 13½, Open.
No. 13½, Steel Wire, Twist Shank............ ......

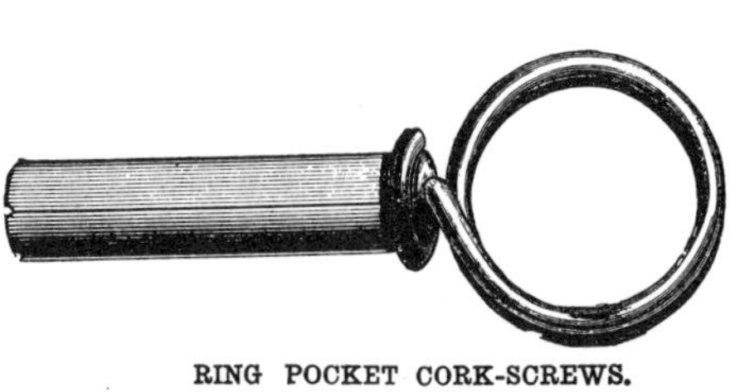

RING POCKET CORK-SCREWS.

Steel Wire, Nickel-Plated...... ....

A complete line of Cork-Screws, Champagne Taps, Shakers and Bar Supplies.

FISHING TACKLE.

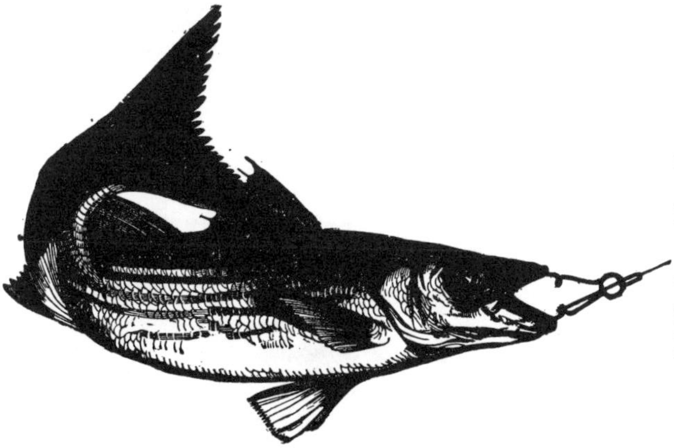

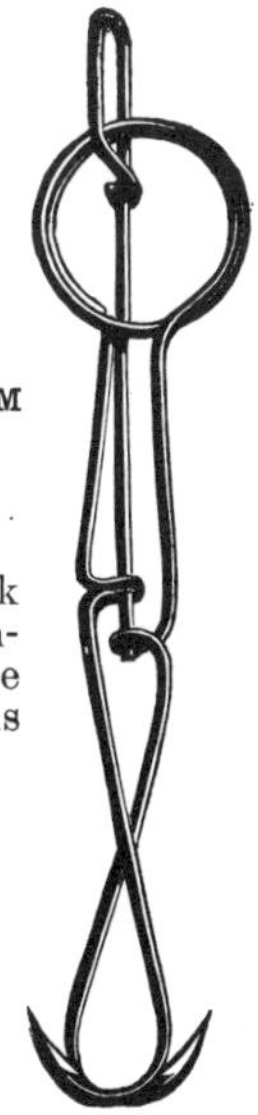

SNAP AND CATCH 'EM FISH HOOKS.

Price .. ..

This is the Hook that does the catching, as well as the holding after it is caught.

FISH HOOKS.—Plain and on Snells.

No. 13. **Kinsey.** No. 2–0. **Sproat.** No. 7. No. 2. **Carlisle.** No. 1. **Flatted Limerick.** No. 2–0. No. 1–0. **Ringed Limerick.**

Kinsey, Sproat and Carlisle Hooks on single or double gut.

Patent Fish Hooks, all Styles.

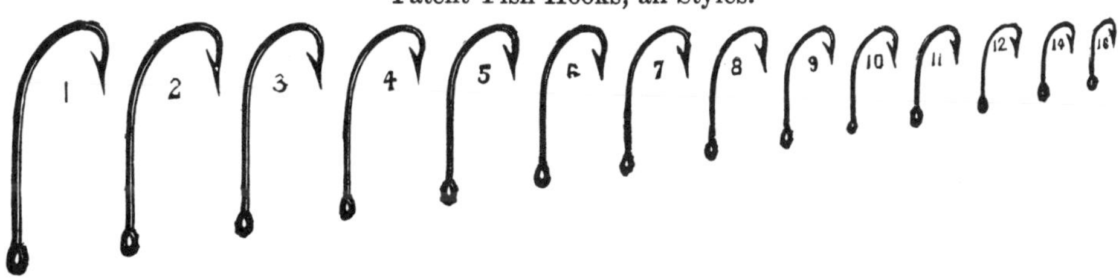

RINGED KIRBY FISH HOOKS.—Cast Steel.

Nos.....7–0	6–0	5–0	4–0	3–0	2–0	1–0	Nos.......1 to 14
......	......	......	......	......	......	......	......

FLATTED KIRBY FISH HOOKS.—Cast Steel.

Nos.....7–0	6–0	5–0	4–0	3–0	2–0	1–0	Nos.......1 to 14
......	......	......	......	......	......	......	......

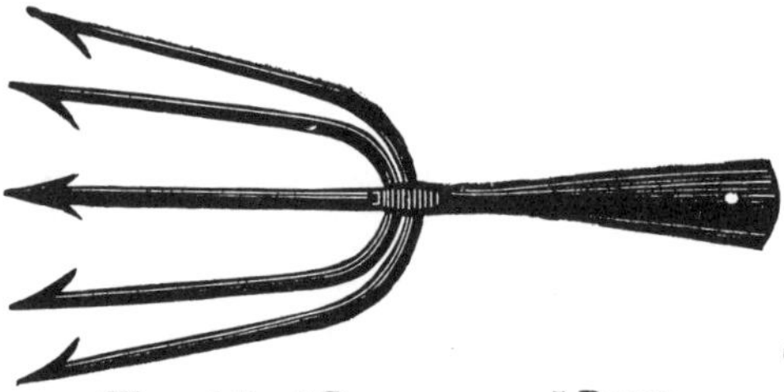

Spears (Wrought). 3 Prong...... 5 Prong......

ARTIFICIAL FLY HOOKS.

Trout and Bass Flies. Artificial Insects.

MANN'S KIDNEY SPOON HOOKS.

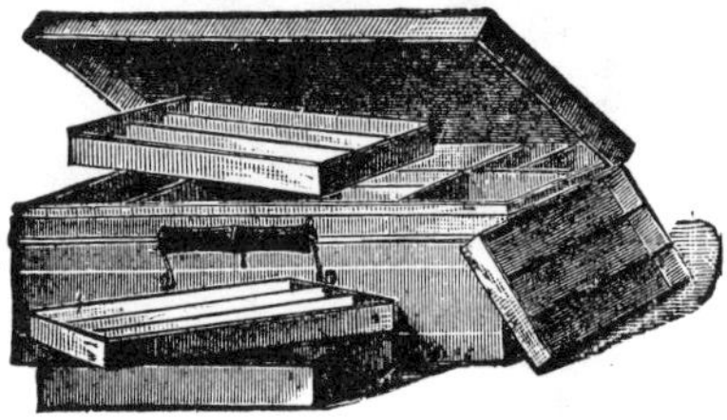

BAIT BOXES.

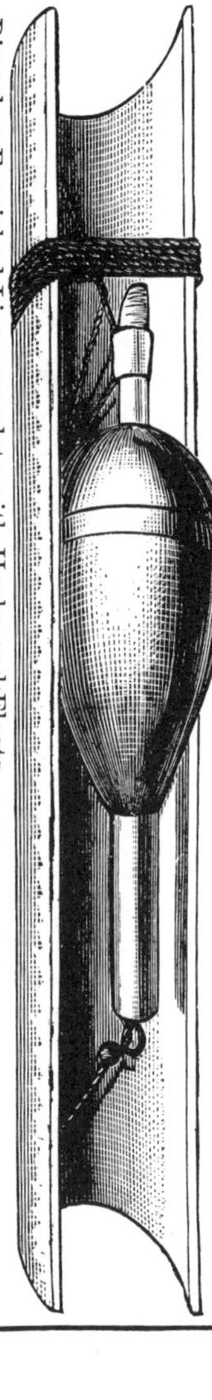

Rigged or Furnished Line, complete with Hooks and Floats...................... ......

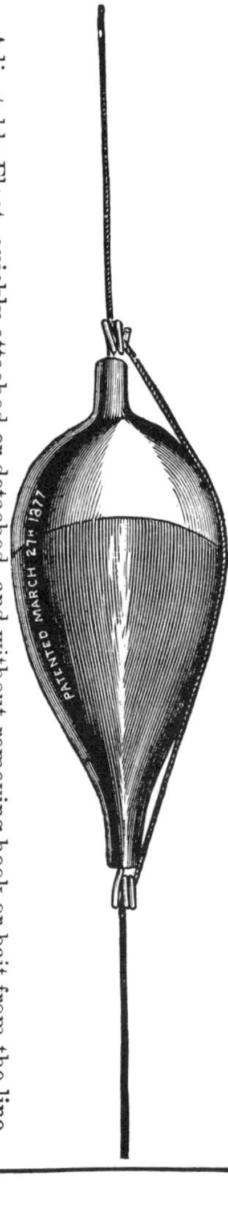

Adjustable Float, quickly attached or detached, and without removing hook or bait from the line.

Best Bound Cork Floats.

Barrel Shape.

PROTEAN MINNOWS —Cut No. 4.

Caledonian Minnows. Phantom Minnows

FLY BOOKS.—For Fly and Snell Hooks.

Ordinary .... Medium .... Fine ....

A good assortment in stock. Also Rubber and Britannia Drinking Cups, Fish Scales, Fly Nets, Landing Nets.

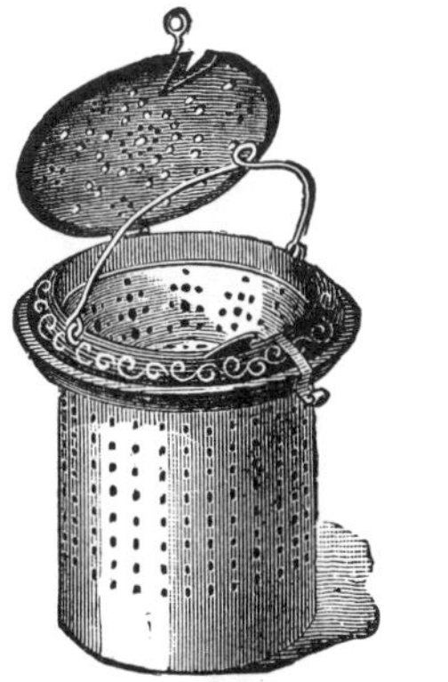

INSIDE PAIL REMOVED.

PAIL COMPLETE.

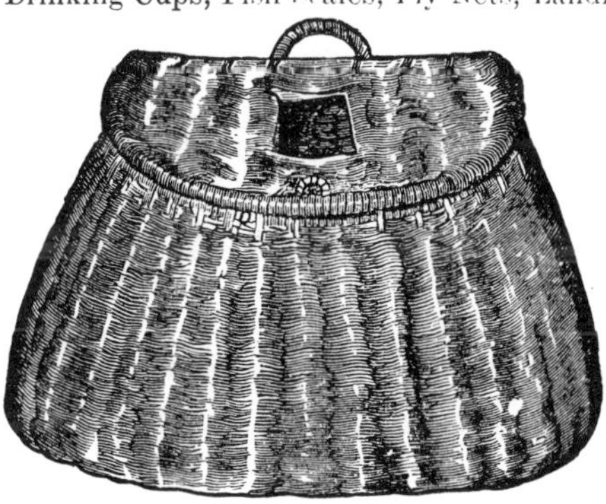

The inside pail can be removed and placed in the water the same as a "fish car," thus keeping the bait alive for an indefinite time. The pan which fits in the inside pail can be raised and lowered, thus affording an easy selection of bait without wetting the hand. The bait is kept alive during transportation (the critical time) by the continuous flowing of the water through the perforations, thus causing a never-failing supply of fresh air. Price ....

FISHING BASKETS.

Best French Trout Baskets.............................Nos. 1...... 2...... 3......

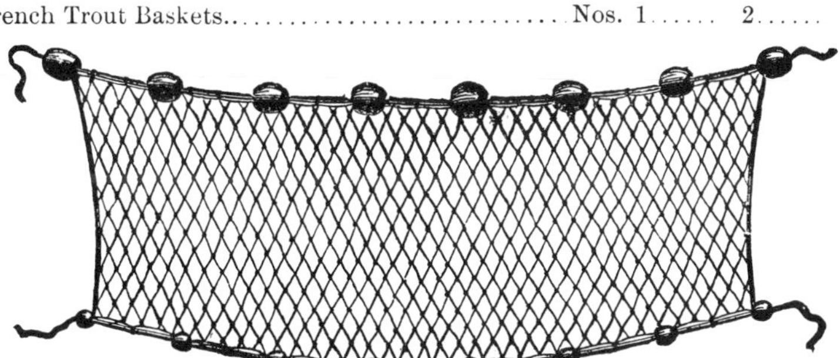

Minnow Seines, Mounted, Ready for Use, with Floats and Leads.

Length, 15 ft.; Width, 4 ft ....

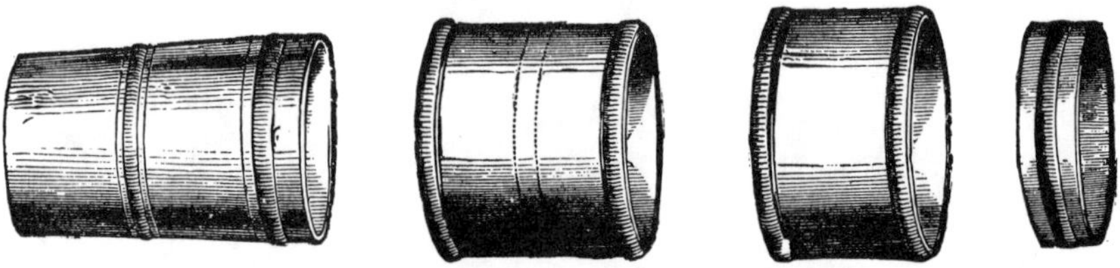

BUTT CAPS, REEL BANDS AND ROD FERRULES.

Nickel-Plated Mountings in Complete Sets, for Rod Making. Each Set consists of Improved Ferrules, Reel Bands, Butt Caps, Guides, Dowel Ferrules and 2 Metal Tips.

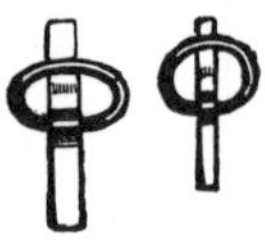

Plated Rings and Keepers.
Assorted Sizes.

8 9
Ring Standing Guides.
Brass and Nickel-Plated.
Assorted Sizes.

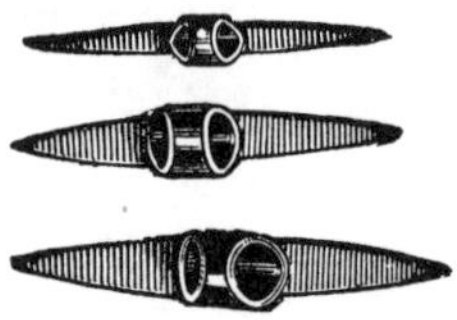

4, 5, 6.
Improved Tie Guides.
Brass and Nickel-Plated.
Assorted Sizes.

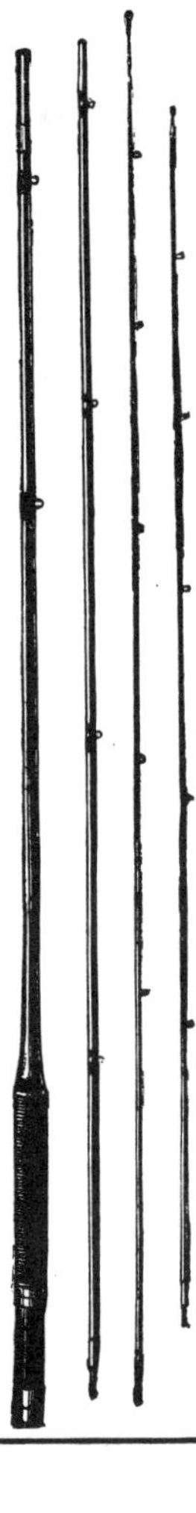

Brass Box Swivels.
Assorted Sizes.

5

Tube Tips.
Brass and Nickel-Plated.
Assorted Sizes.

LEAD SINKERS.
Common.

Nos. 4.... 5.... 6.... 7.... 8....

Patent Sinkers.

Nos. 6.... 7.... 8.... 9.... 10....

11.... 12 ...
Sizes differ from Common Sinkers.

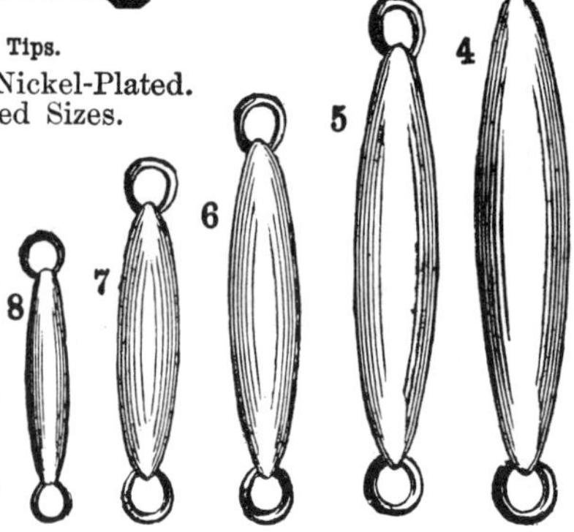

Full Size of Common Sinkers.

FISHING RODS.

It would be difficult for us to give the numbers and full description of our stock of Rods, as the styles are constantly changing, new Rods coming into the market every year. Suffice to say that our assortment in this line is complete.

Common Cane Poles...... ...... Japanese Cane Poles...... ......
Ash Jointed Rods.. ......
Japanese Cane, Bass.. ...... Fly.. ...... Trunk Rods.. ......
Calcutta Cane, Bass.. ...... Fly.. ...... Trunk Rods.. ......
Lancewood, Bass..... ...... Fly.. ...... Trunk Rods.. ......
Split Bamboo, Bass......... ...... Fly Rods................

We have ordered for the coming season a line of Fishing Rods which will be pleasing to look upon, we invite our friends to call and inspect them before making a purchase elsewhere.

FISHING LINES.

Our stock of Fishing Lines is quite complete.

Sizes of Common Lines, Cotton and Linen.

EUREKA FISH LINES.—Imitation Linen.

Nos. ...... 1 ...... 2 ..... 3 ...... 4 ...... 16 ft. Lines.

COTTON FISH LINES.

c.100 c.200 c.300 c.450

Nos. ...... 1 ...... 2 ...... 3 ...... 4 ...... 16 ft. Lines.

LINEN FISH LINES.

White Linen. . a.100 a.200 a.300 a.400 Drab Linen. . a.100 a.200 a.300 a.400

Nos .... 1 ..... 2 ..... 3 ...... 4 ..... Nos ....1 ..... 2 ..... 3 ... . 4 .....

Superior White Linen Line, 40 ft., in coils, 6 connected ....

Best Grass Lines, in coils, 6 connected .... Nos. 1 ...... 2 ...... 3 ......

Sizes of Braided Lines.

Braided Oil Silk Lines, 50 yards in coil, 2 coils connected .... Nos. 4 ..... 5 ......

This is the strongest and best selling Line; used mostly by our best fishermen.

Braided Silk Lines, 50 yds. on Block, 2 Blocks connected, assorted colors, Nos. 4... 5...

These Lines are very strong; the best we can buy.

BRAIDED LINEN LINES.

No. 5, Superior Variegated Linen Lines, on Blocks of 50 yds., 2 connected ....

BRAIDED TROT OR TROLLING LINES.

Drab Cotton, in 84 ft. Hanks, 2 connected .... Nos. 1 ...... 2 ...... 3 ......

We can supply you with any line desired.

FISHING REELS.

Unburnished, Plain Reels,

Plain Balance Handle Reels,

Multiplying Reels, with Drag,

Burnished Click Reels,

English Rubber Reels.

BALANCE HANDLE,

Multiplying Adjustable Click and Drag

REELS.

NICKEL-PLATED.

Kentucky Pattern Reels.

THE FOLLETT REEL.

Patented ....

This Reel surpasses all others in simplicity of construction and durability: can not get out of order, and will last a lifetime with proper care. The tension can be adjusted to run as easy as desired. The diameter of the Reel being larger, it will take in the line as fast as a multiplying reel. We think it the best low-priced Reel in the market.

Call and see our display of Reels.

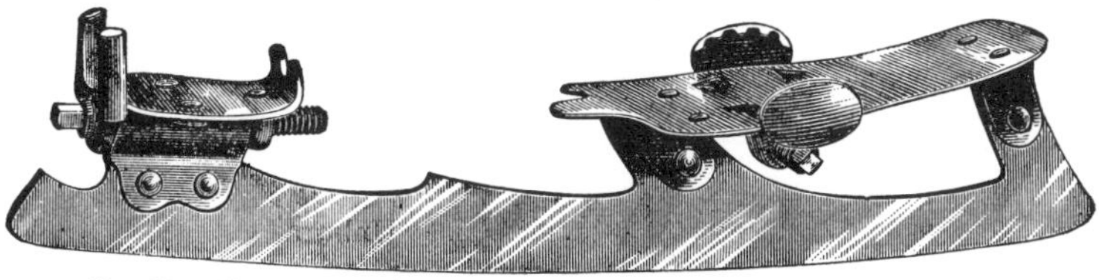

No. F. Sizes, 7, 7½, 8, 8½, 9, 9½, 10, 10½, 11, 11½, 12 in.
The heel plates, front plates and brackets are made from crucible steel; blades are fine finish.
Blued........................ ...... Nickeled...................... ......

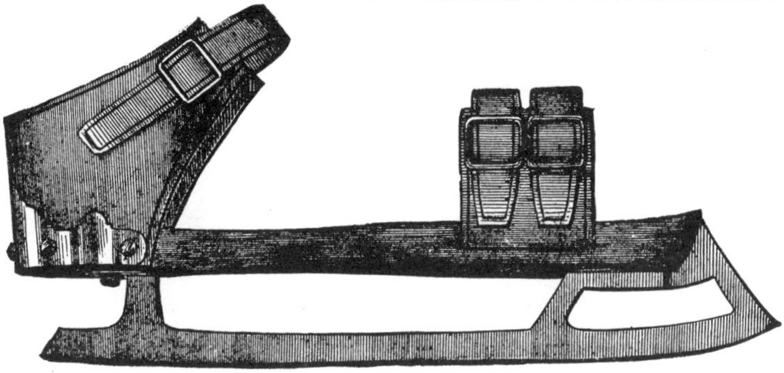

No. L W. Sizes, 7, 7½, 8, 8½, 9, 9½, 10 in.
Beech Wood Bottom, Russet Leather Straps, Nickel Heel Bands.............. ......

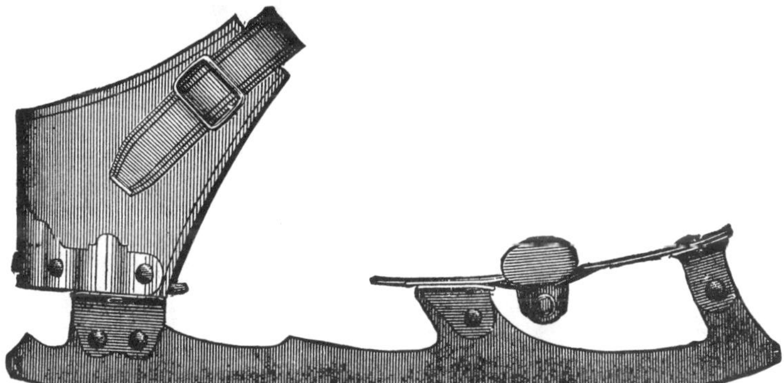

No. L E. Sizes, 7, 7½, 8, 8½, 9, 9½, 10 in.
Woods of seasoned Beech, polished, trimmed with best quality Russet Leather, Patent Lever Buckles, and Nickeled Heel Bands....... ....

ACME SKATES.

Can be instantly and firmly attached to any boot. No heel plates to clog up; no keys required to apply them.
Nickel Plated ....

SCIENTIFIC RINK ROLLER SKATES.

These Skates have been greatly improved in quality of material, style, finish and mechanical working of the parts. All the most intricate evolutions practiced on Ice Skates can be accomplished on these. Price.... ......
Youths' or Sidewalk Roller Skates.. ......

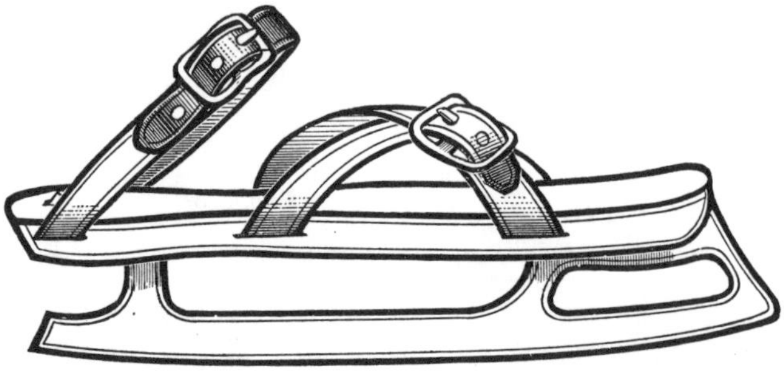

No. A. Sizes, 7, 7½, 8, 8½, 9, 9½, 10, 10½, 11 in.
Polished Beech Woods, Solid Heel Spur, Strapped with Short English Straps.... ......

No. B. Sizes, 7, 7½, 8, 8½, 9, 9½, 10, 10½, 11 in.
New Design, made from Superior Brand of Charcoal Iron. Japanned.......... ......

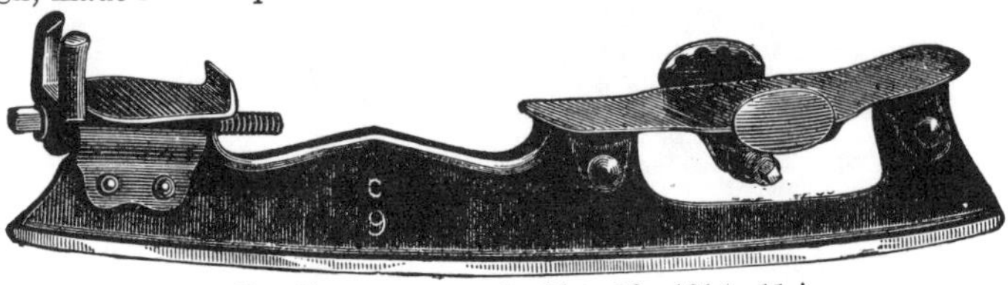

No. C. Sizes, 8, 8½, 9, 9½, 10, 10½, 11 in.
All clamp skate, no straps, no heel plates, self-adjusting; most durable cheap skate made....

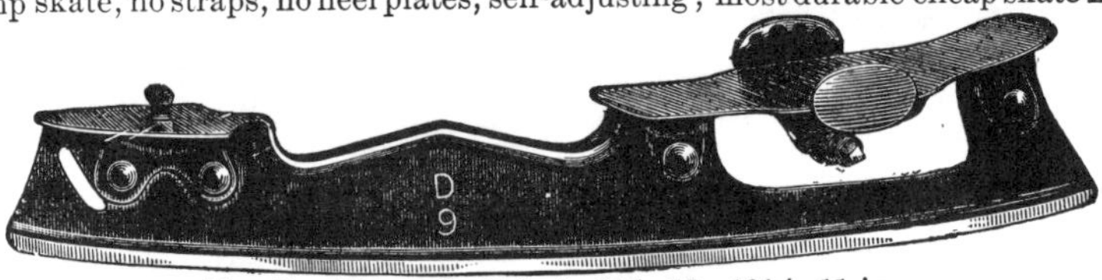

No. D. Sizes, 8, 8½, 9, 9½. 10, 10½, 11 in.
Same as above, but with Button, instead of Clamp, at Heel.................. ......

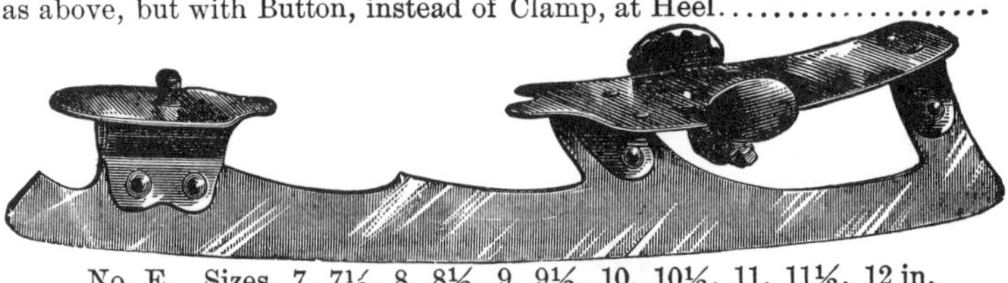

No. E. Sizes, 7, 7½, 8, 8½, 9, 9½, 10, 10½, 11, 11½, 12 in.
A fac-simile of the genuine Barney & Berry Skate, strong and well made. Curved Brackets made from steel and strongly riveted to Foot Plates. The Blades are fine finish.
Blued.......................... ...... Nickeled ....

Cut of Smith & Wesson Double Acting Revolver.

REVOLVERS.

Smith & Wesson, With Automatic Ejector, Nickel-Plated, Single Action,
32... ...... 38 Caliber.. ...... Double Action.. 32 ..... 38..Caliber ......
British Bull Dog, Double Action, Nickel-Plated ... 32.... ...... 44.. " ......
American Bull Dog, " " " .... 32.... ...... 38.. " ......
Forehand & Wadsworth, Double Action, " .... 32.... ...... 38.. " ......
Colts, Double Action, Nickel-Plated .... 38.. " ......
32 Long Revolvers, Nickel-Plated....Wood ...... Rubber...... Ivory Handles ......
22 " " " " ....Wood..... Rubber " ......
22 Short " " " Wood Handles, 7-Shot...................... ......

All the above kept in Pearl Handles.

SINGLE SHOT PISTOLS.

22 Caliber, Nickel-Plated ....
22 Blank, " " ....

Powder and Ball ....

Flobert Rifles and Target Pistols.

SHOT.

Drop Shot, Nos....000, 00, 0, BBB, BB, B, 1, 2, 3, 4, 5, 6, 7, 8, 9, 10, 11, 12 ......

Buck Shot, Nos.... 1, 2, 3, 4, 5, 6, 7, 8.. ......

LEROY TIN-COATED SHOT.--All Sizes.

This is a chilled shot. Does not lead the gun, and is used by all the best sportsmen. Sold at a slight advance on common shot.

CARTRIDGES AND SHOT SHELLS.

RIM FIRE CARTRIDGES.

No. 1, BB. Caps.
List Price, $4.00; case contains 10 M.

32 Blank.
List Price, $10.00; case contains 5 M.

22 Blank.
List Price, $5.00; case contains 10 M.

22 Short.
List Price, $5.00; case contains 10 M.

22 Long.
List Price, $6.00; case contains 10 M.

30 Short.
List Price, $9.00; case contains 5 M.

30 Long.
List Price, $10 50; case contains 5 M.

32 Short.
List Price, $10.00; case contains 5 M.

32 Long.
List Price, $11.50; case contains 2½ M.

38 Short.
List Price, $16.00; case contains 2½ M.

38 Long.
List Price, $18.00; case contains 2½ M.

41 Short.
List Price, $15.00; case contains 2½ M.

44 Short.
List Price, $23.00; case contains 2 M.

Discount ....

CENTRAL FIRE CARTRIDGES.

32 S. & W.
List Price, $11.00; case tains 5 M.

38 S. & W.
List Price, $13.50; case contains 2½ M.

44 Webley.
List Price, $16.50; case contains 2 M

Discount..........

Nos. 40, 45, 1⅞ Cartridges, for Remington's Hepburn Rifle. ......

GUN CAPS.

GD, SB, Am WP, Eley WP, Musket.
... ...

Powder Flasks, Shot Belts, Pouches; Gun Material, Tubes, Plugs, Nipples, Locks, Triggers, Hammers, Sears, Springs, Breeches, &c. Tube Wrenches, Bullet Moulds, Ramrod Tips, Gun Worms, Rifle Wipers, Cleaning Rods, and everything in the line.

POWDER.

RIFLE POWDER.

FG.

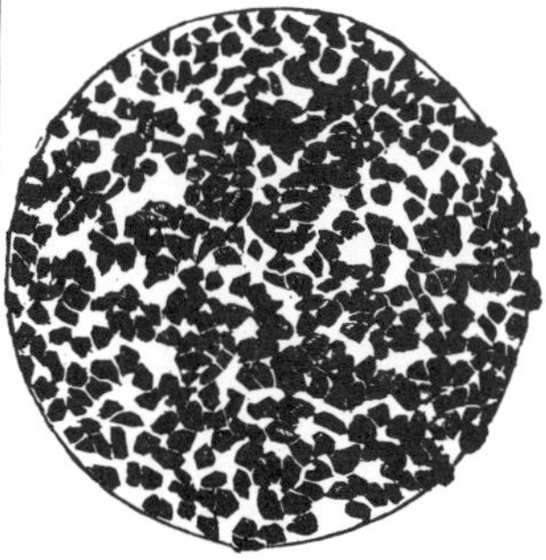

FFG.

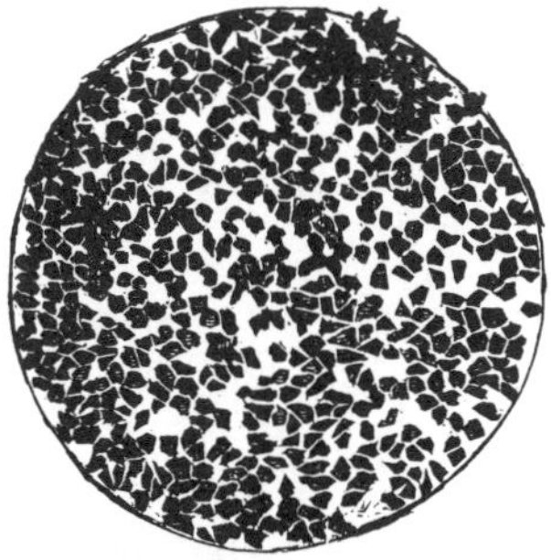

FFFG.

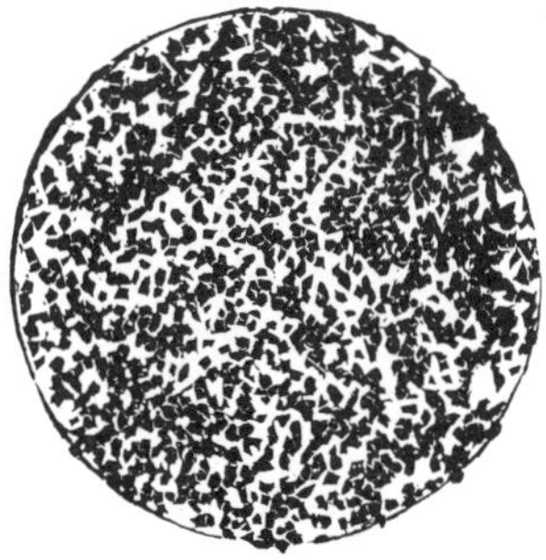

SPORTING POWDER.

FG.

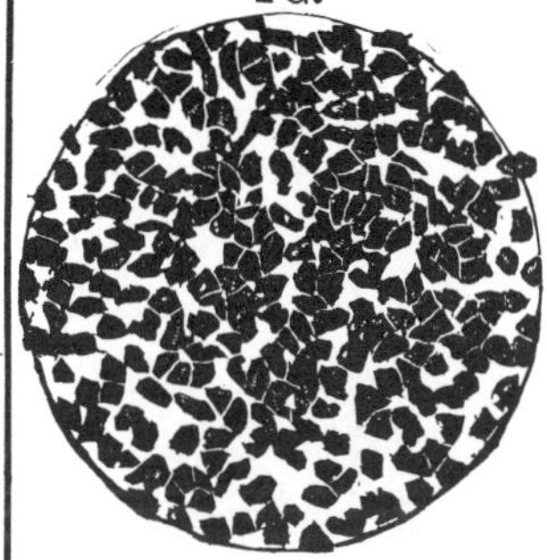

FFG.

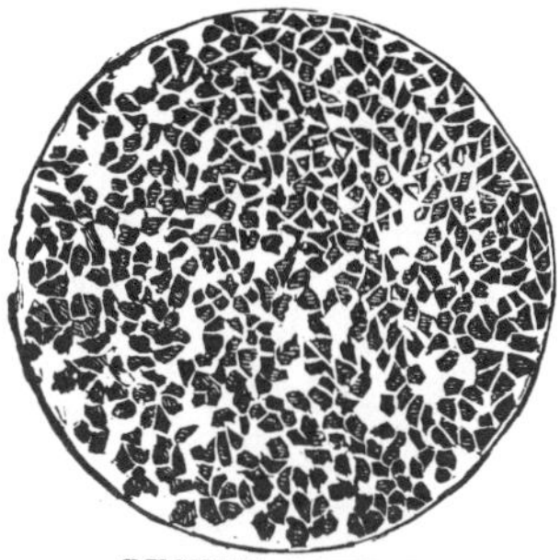

FFFG.

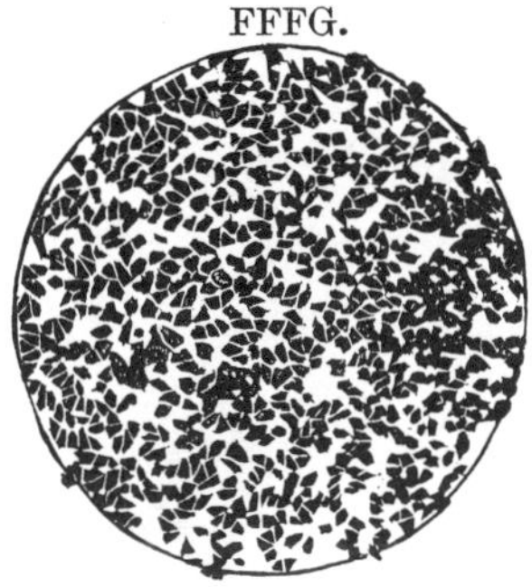

DUCKING POWDER.

1

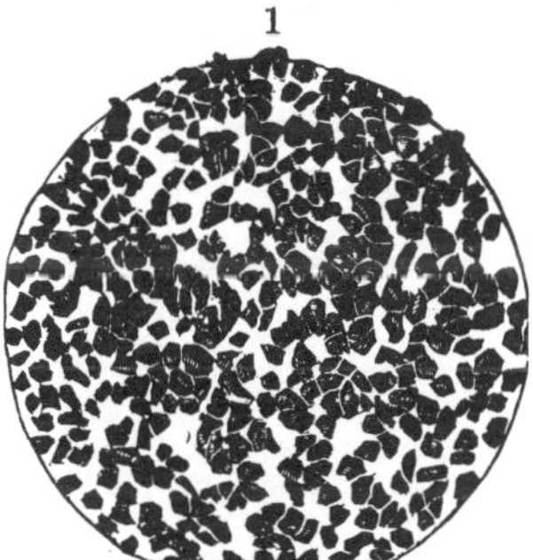

2

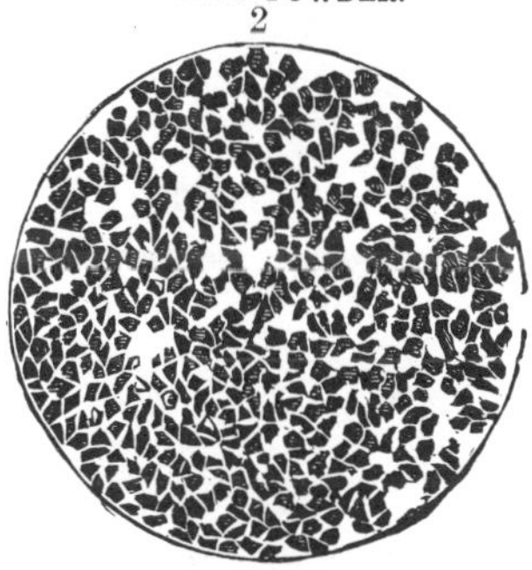

3

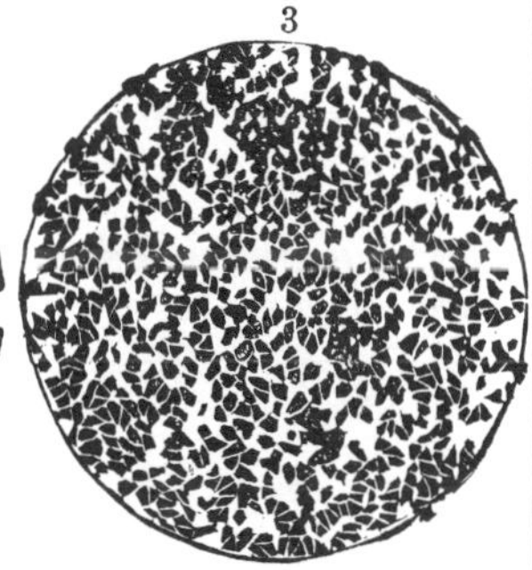

BLASTING OR MINING POWDER.

F.

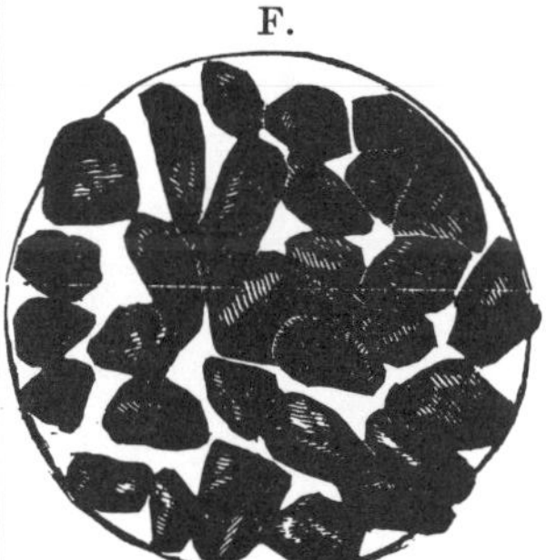

FF.

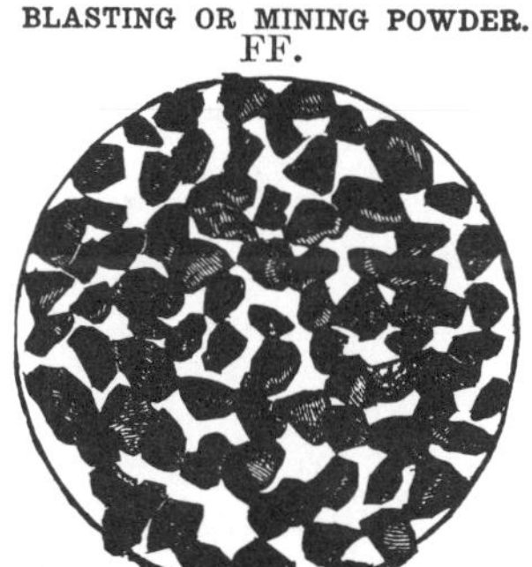

FFF.

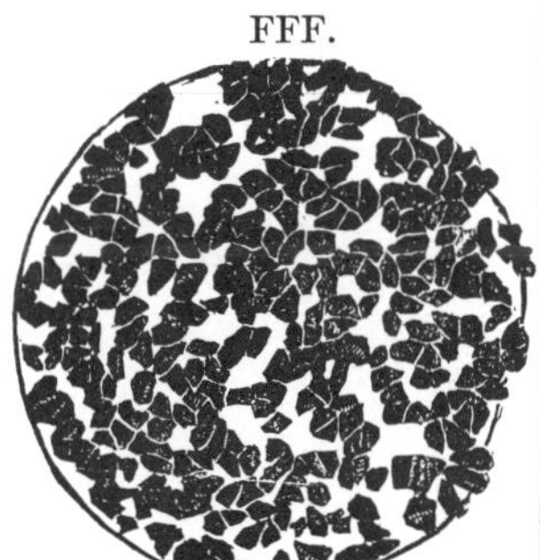

We furnish the above grains of Powder in the Austin, Hazard and Dupont makes.
Cuts kindly furnished by the Austin Powder Co.

VAJEN & NEW, INDIANAPOLIS, IND.

TOOL
DEPARTMENT.

This Catalogue contains a carefully selected list of fine Tools in nearly every branch. We are constantly adding to our stock New Tools. Should you not find what you want illustrated, ask or write for it.

Any Tool or Bill of Tools ordered from this department will be forwarded by return express, when possible, at the very Lowest Price. A reduction of 5% will be allowed on all mail orders from a distance for Tools, where the bill amounts to $100.00 or more. This is done to encourage mechanics to club together and order their Tools at one time.

In ordering give NUMBER, PAGE and a full DESCRIPTION of the article wanted, and give full instructions how to ship.

HATCHETS.

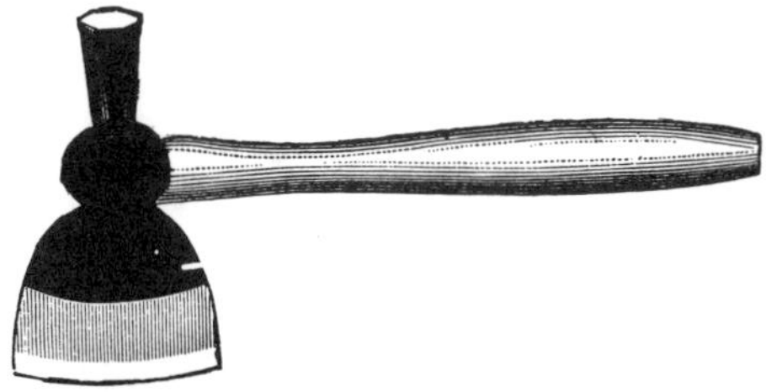

Shingling.

Nos.	1	2	3
Cast Iron	......	......	......
Cast Steel	......	......	......
Simmons'	......	......	......

Half.

Nos.	1	2	3
Simmons'	......	......	......

BARREL OR PACKERS' HATCHET.

Solid Steel, Octagon Pole. ....

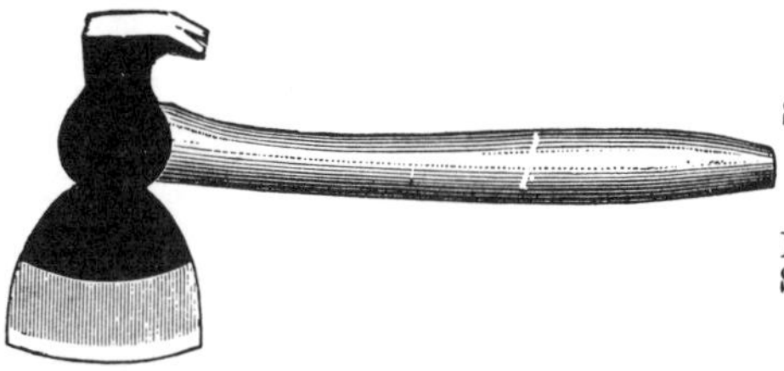

Claw.

Nos	1	2	3
Simmons'	......	......	......

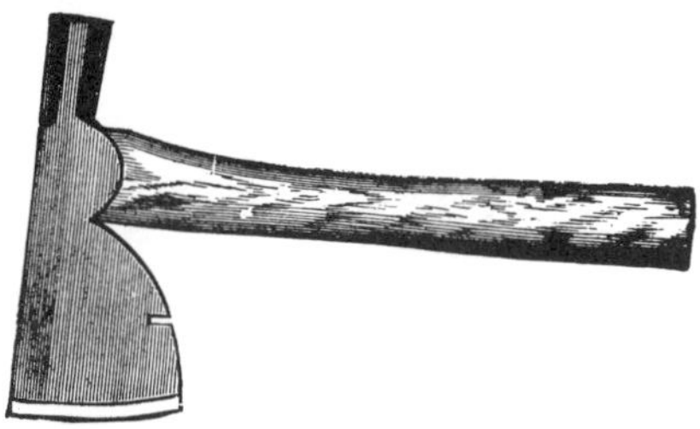

Solid Cast Steel Half.

Nos	1	2	3
Barton's	......	......	......

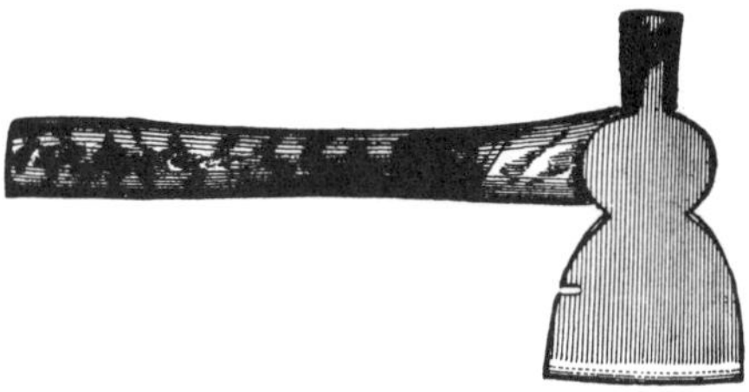

Solid Cast Steel Shingling.

Nos	1	2	3
Barton's	......	......	......

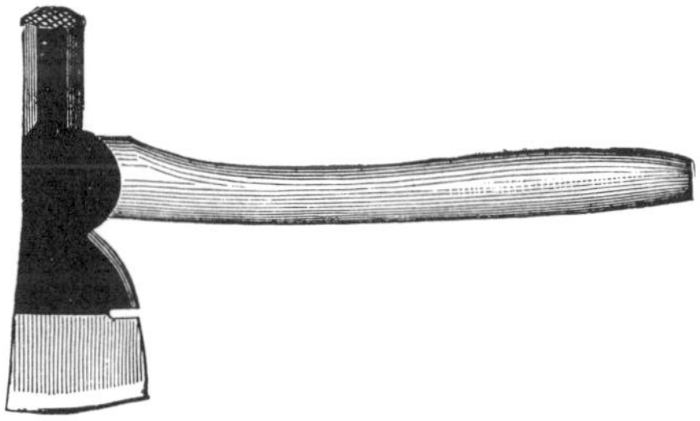

Lathing.

Nos	1	2	3
Simmons'	......	......	......

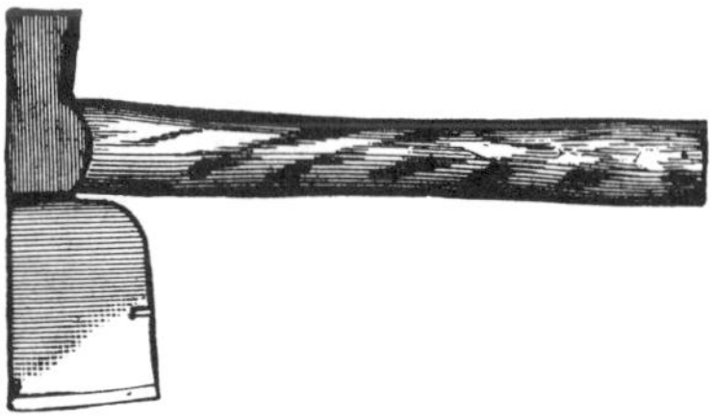

Solid Cast Steel Lathing.

Nos.	1	2	3
	......	......	......

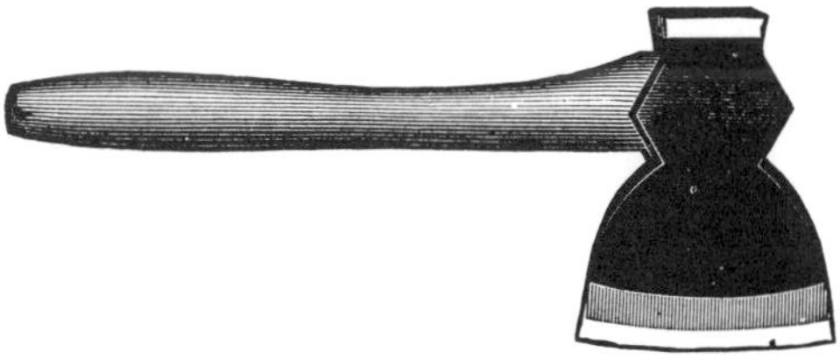

Broad or Bench.

Simmons'.......... Nos.... 1...... 2 ...... 3 ...... 4 ..... 5...... 6...... 7......

AXES, ADZES AND BUSH HOOKS.

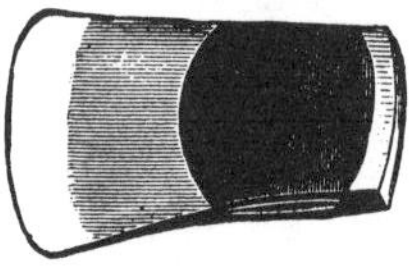

Plain.

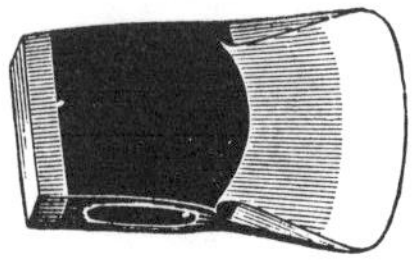

Beveled.

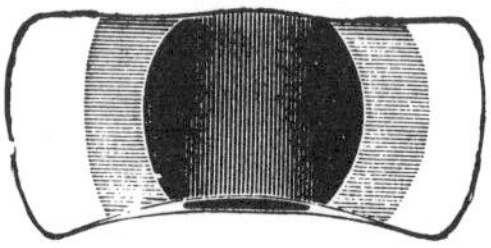

Double Bitted.

AXES.

Plain ....   Beveled ....

" Silver Steel ....   " Silver Steel ....

Double-Bitted Axes, 4½ to 5½ ℔ ....

Assorted, 3 to 4, 3¼ to 4¼, 3½ to 4½, 3¾ to 4¾, 4 to 5, 4¼ to 5¼, 4½ to 5½, 5 to 6 ℔.

Handled Axes......... ......   Second Grade Axes, Not Handled ....

Handled Boy's Axes, ...   Best........ ......   Common.......... ......

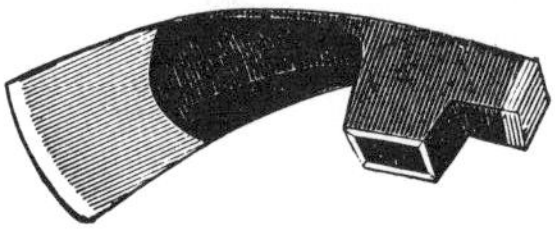

HOUSE CARPENTER'S ADZE.

Half Head ....   Flat Head.......... ......

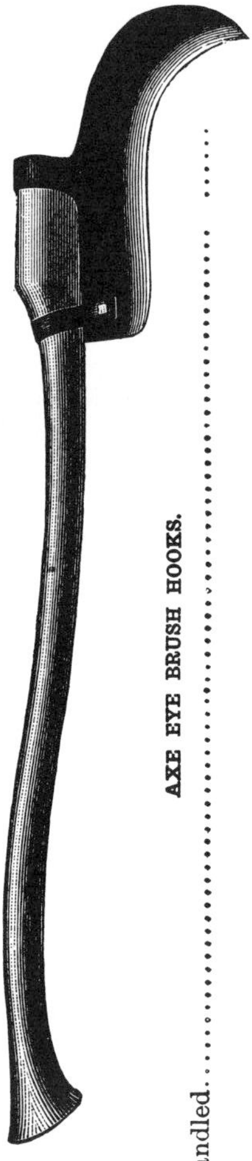

AXE EYE BRUSH HOOKS.

Handled...

HEAVY RAILROAD ADZE.

Price.. ......

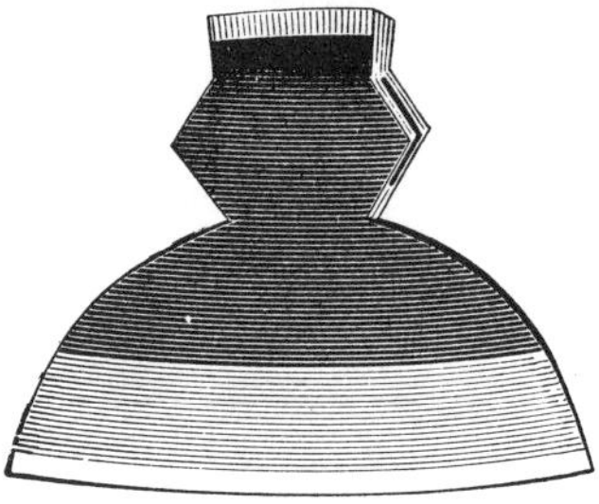

WESTERN BROAD AXE.

6 to 7 lbs.. ......

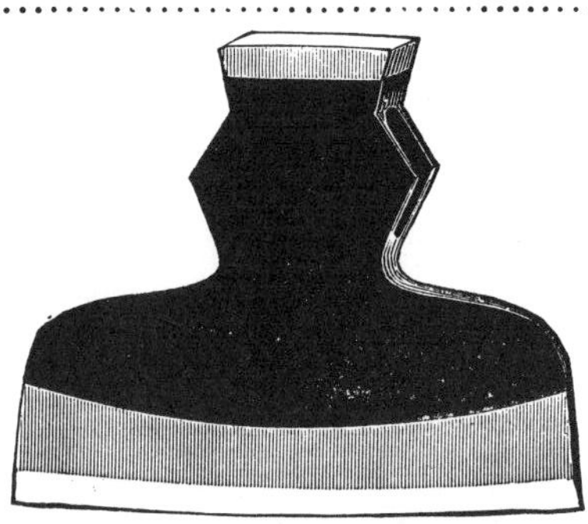

OHIO BROAD AXE.

7½ to 8 lbs...... ....

HAMMERS.

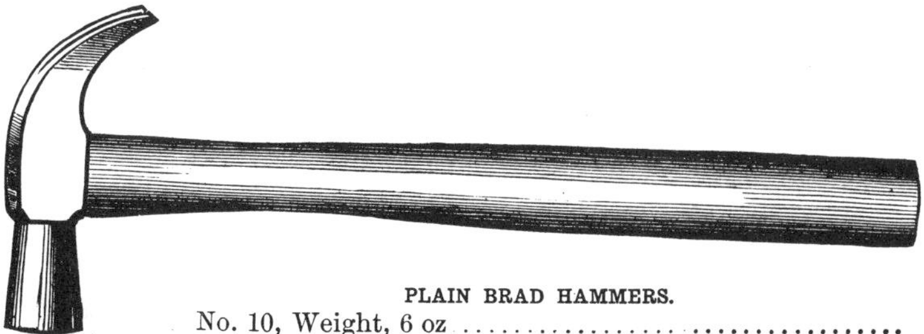

PLAIN BRAD HAMMERS.

No. 10, Weight, 6 oz ....

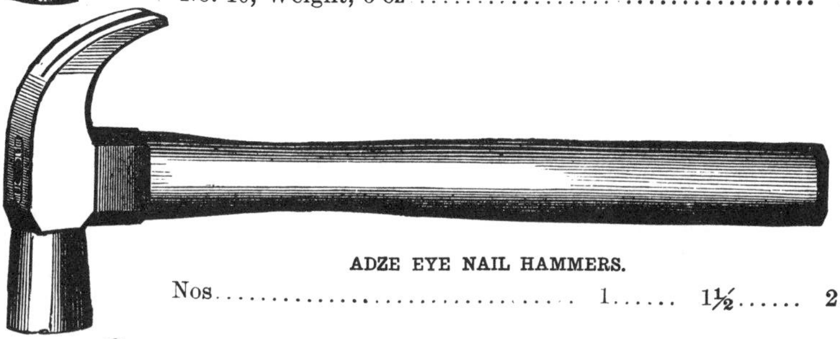

ADZE EYE NAIL HAMMERS.

Nos.................................. 1...... 1½...... 2......

CAST ADZE EYE NAIL HAMMERS.

No. 155.. ......

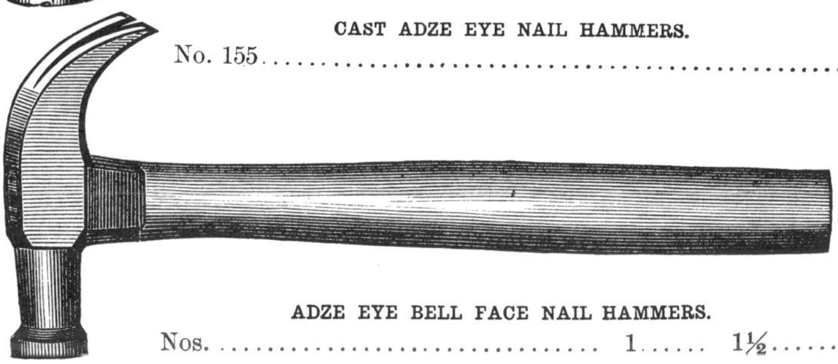

ADZE EYE BELL FACE NAIL HAMMERS.

Nos.................................. 1...... 1½...... 2......

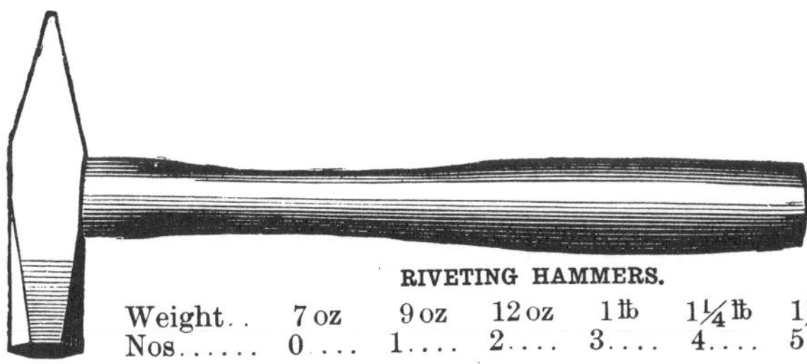

RIVETING HAMMERS.

Weight..	7 oz	9 oz	12 oz	1 ℔	1¼ ℔	1½ ℔	1¾ ℔	2 ℔
Nos......	0....	1....	2....	3....	4....	5....	6....	7....

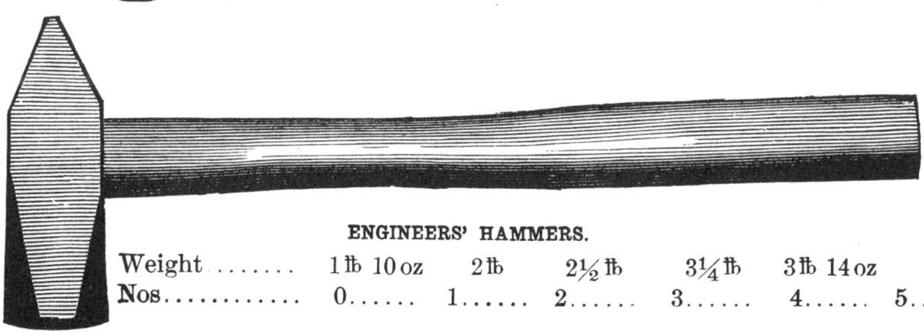

ENGINEERS' HAMMERS.

Weight	1 ℔ 10 oz	2 ℔	2½ ℔	3¼ ℔	3 ℔ 14 oz	5 ℔
Nos............	0......	1......	2......	3......	4......	5......

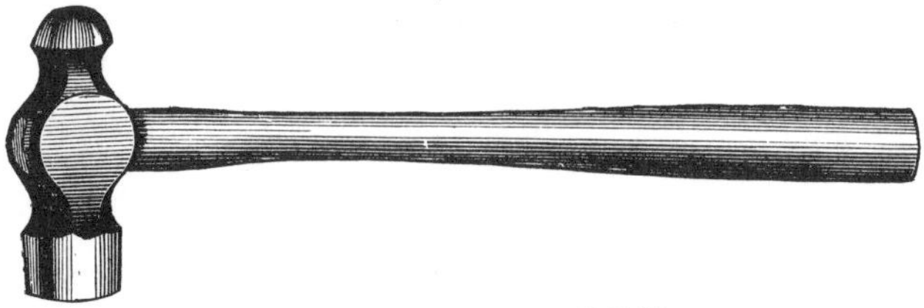

MACHINISTS' HAMMERS.—Ball Pien.

Weight	8 oz	12 oz	1 lb	1¼ lb	1½	1 lb 14 oz	2¼ lb	2½ lb	2¾ lb	3 lb	3¼ lb	3¾ lb
Nos....	0000....	000....	00....	0....	1	2...	3....	4....	5....	6....	7....	8....

Straight and Cross Pien, same size as above.

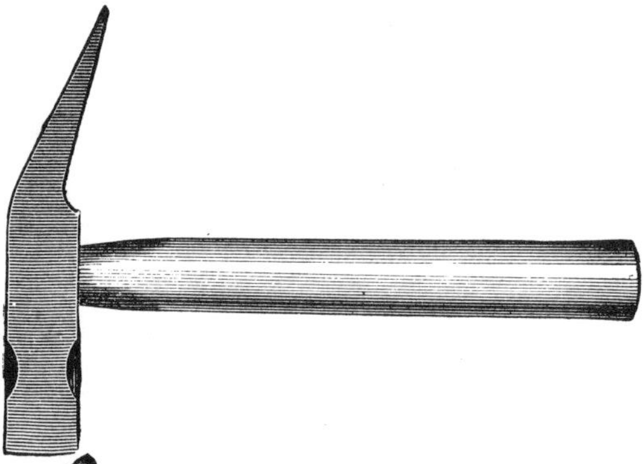

BRICK HAMMERS.

Weight............	1½ lb	2 lb
Nos..............	1......	2......

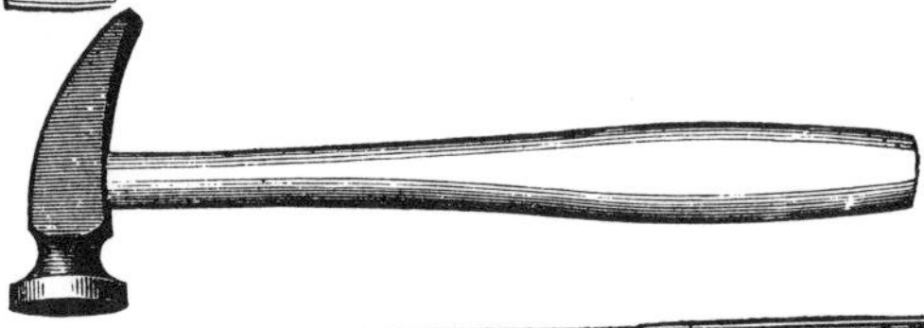

SHOE HAMMERS.

Nos.................	1	2
Steel................	......	......
Cast	......	......

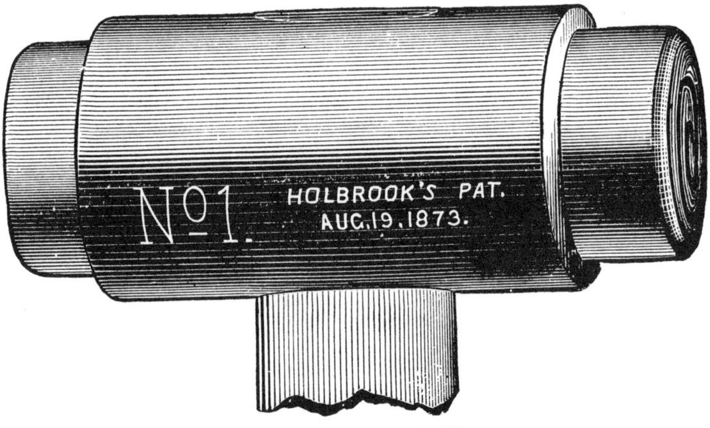

HIDE-FACED MALLETS.

Nos.. 1...... 2 .... 3 ..... 4 .....

One Pair of extra faces gratis with each mallet; when worn out they can be renewed at slight cost. These Mallets are invaluable for machinists, workers in brass, jewelers, etc.

RAW HIDE MALLETS.

Nos .... 0 ..... 1...... 2...... 3 ... 4......

Light Rawhide Mallets, made entirely of Rawhide, except handle; suited for many uses.

TACK HAMMERS AND CLAWS.

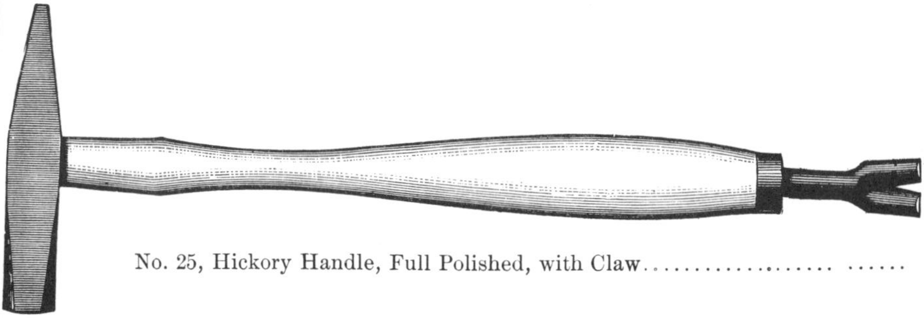

No. 25, Hickory Handle, Full Polished, with Claw.................. ......

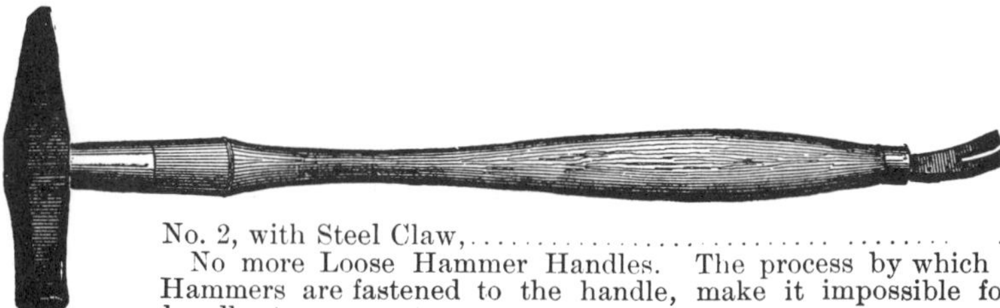

No. 2, with Steel Claw,.................................... ....

No more Loose Hammer Handles. The process by which these Hammers are fastened to the handle, make it impossible for the handles to come out.

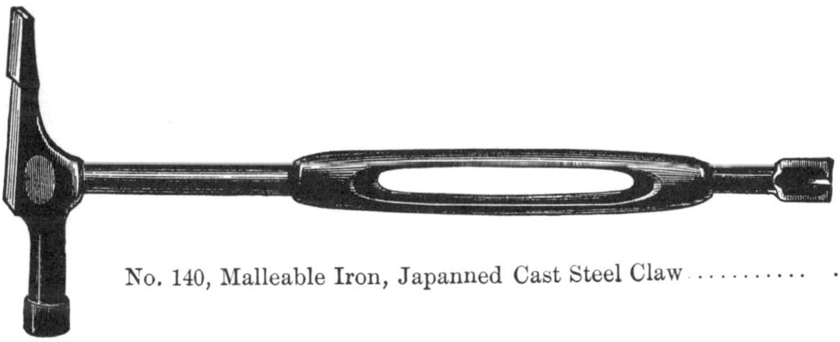

No. 140, Malleable Iron, Japanned Cast Steel Claw.......... ......

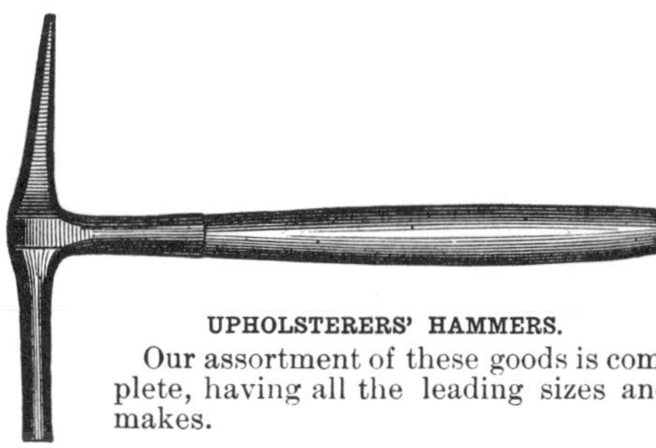

UPHOLSTERERS' HAMMERS.

Our assortment of these goods is complete, having all the leading sizes and makes.

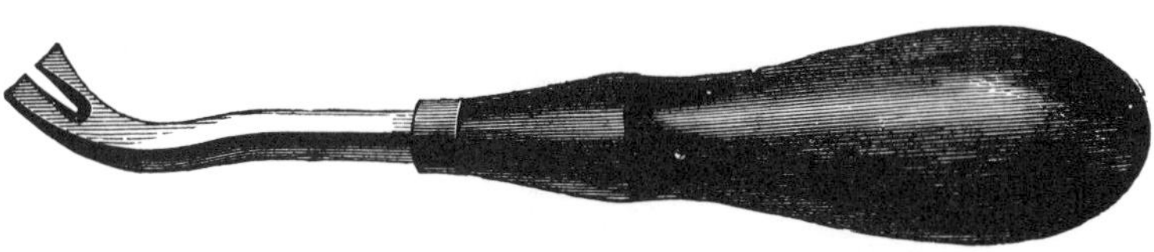

TACK CLAWS.

Polished Steel, Enameled Handles ....

Forged Cast Steel, Black Handles, Nickled Ferrule........................ ......

MASONS' TOOLS AND HAMMERS.

STONE CUTTERS' POINTS AND CHISELS.

STONE CUTTERS' MALLETS.
Assorted Sizes.

Mallet Headed Points and Chisels. Hammer Headed Points and Chisels. Marble and Carvers' Tools. Carvers Pitching Tools. A full and complete line of the above in stock.

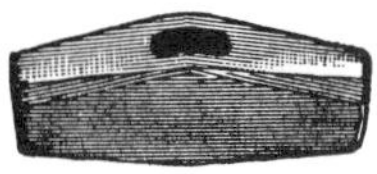

STONE MASH HAMMERS.

Solid Cast Steel, 6 to 30 lbs.......

BUSH HAMMERS.

Solid Cast Steel.......

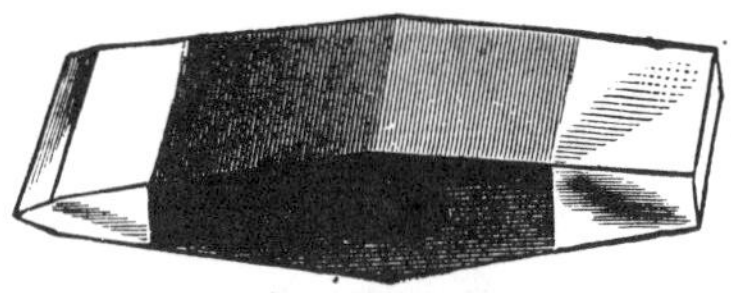

MASONS' HAMMERS.

Solid Cast Steel, 3 to 8 lbs.......

STONE SLEDGES.

Steel Face and Pien, 6 to 30 lbs.......

Solid Cast Steel, 6 to 30 lbs.......

BLACKSMITHS' SLEDGES.

Steel Face and Pien, 6 to 30 lbs.......

Solid Cast Steel, 6 to 30 lbs.......

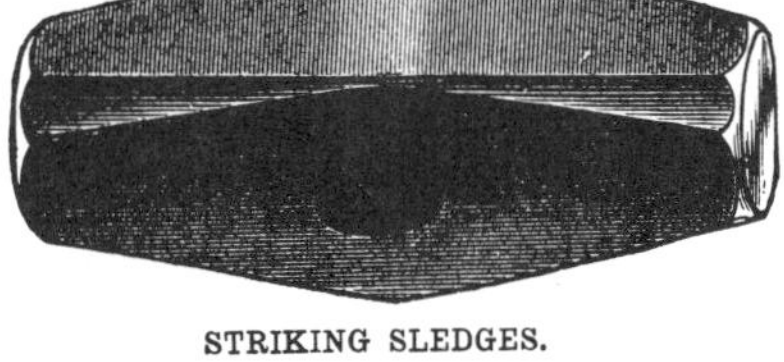

STRIKING SLEDGES.

Steel Face, 6 to 30 lbs.......

Solid Cast Steel, 6 to 30 lbs.......

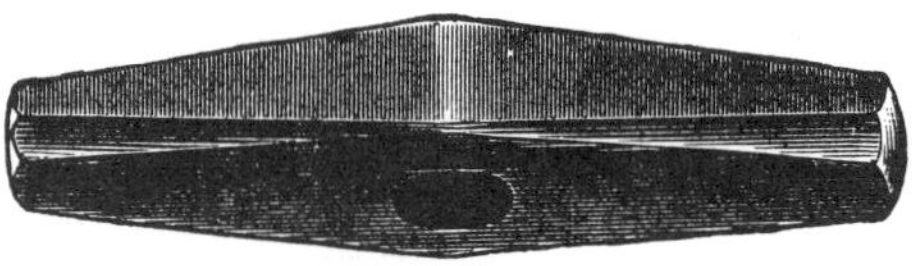

COAL SLEDGES.

Steel Face, 5 to 10 lbs.......

Solid Cast Steel, 5 to 10 lbs.......

SAW SETS.

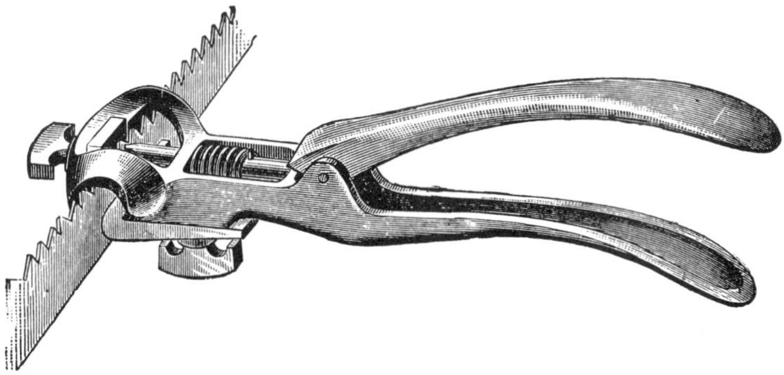

MORRELL'S SAW SET.

No. 1, For Hand and Rip Saws.. ......
No. 3, For Cross Cut Saws.. ......
No. 5, For Mill Saws ....

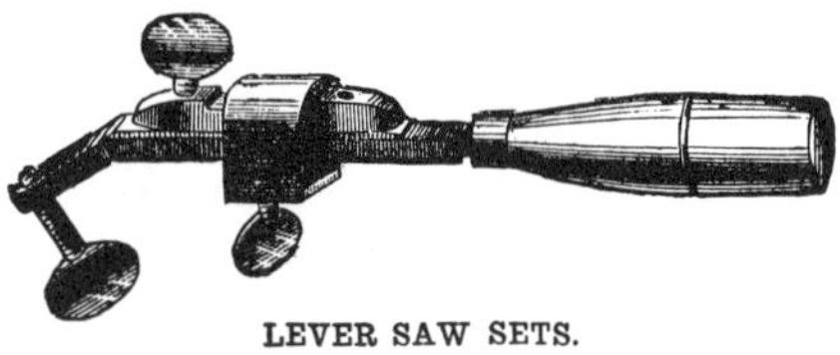

LEVER SAW SETS.

Cast Steel ....

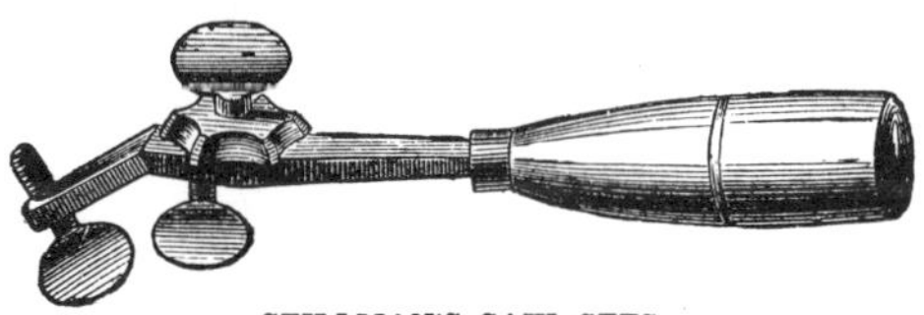

STILLMAN'S SAW SETS.

Small, for Hand and Rip Saws...... ......
Large for Mill Saws................ ......

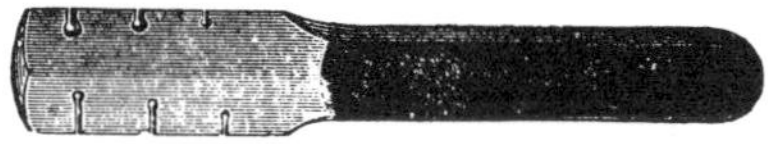

Bemis and Call's Plate Saw Sets.

Solid Cast Steel.................... ......

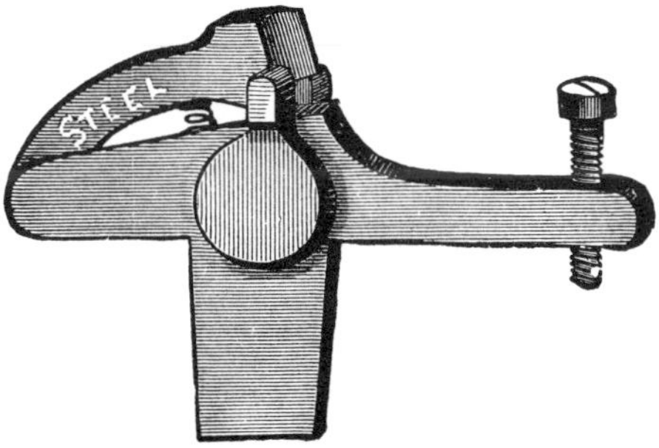

Aiken's Patent Hammer Saw Sets, Genuine....
" Pattern " " " " ....

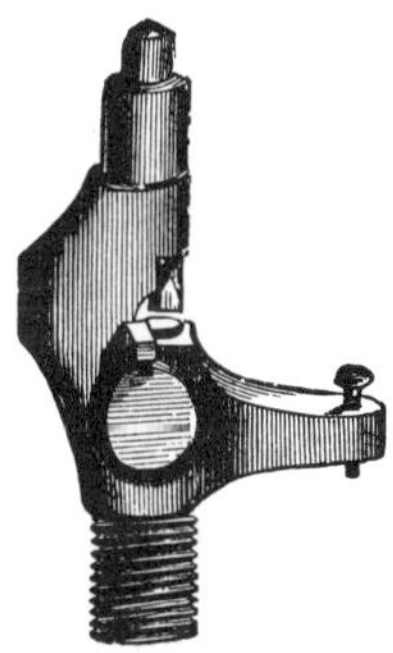

HAMMER SAW SETS.

Bemis and Call's "New Pattern." ......

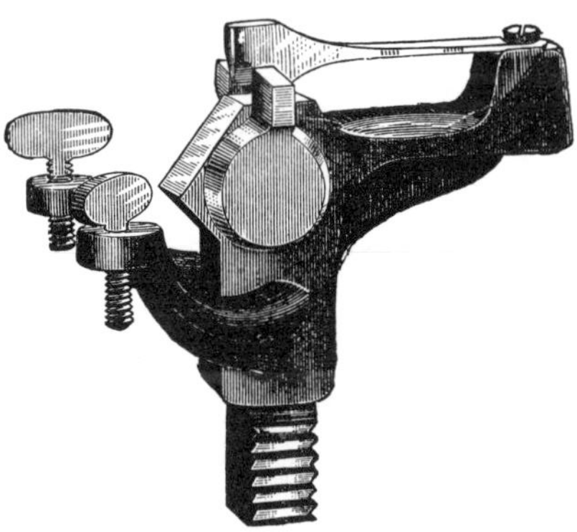

Bemis and Call's Spring Hammer Saw Set.................. ......

Bemis and Call's Cross-Cut Saw Sets...................... ....

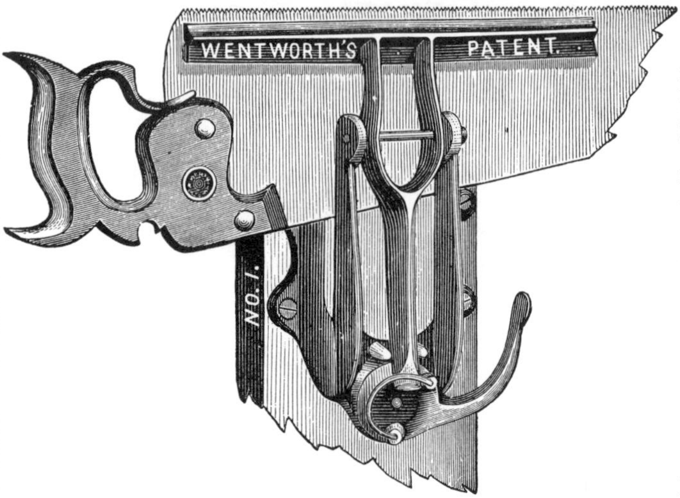

WENTWORTH'S PAT. SAW VISE.

It has a flexible rubber cushion or muffler between the jaws, which prevents any vibration, and renders saw filing noiseless. We guarantee it to make no more noise than filing on a solid piece of iron.

No. 1, Jaws, 10 in. long ....
No. 2, Jaws, 12 in. long ....

As harness clamp the No. 2 Vise is useful in stitching leather, repairing harness, etc.

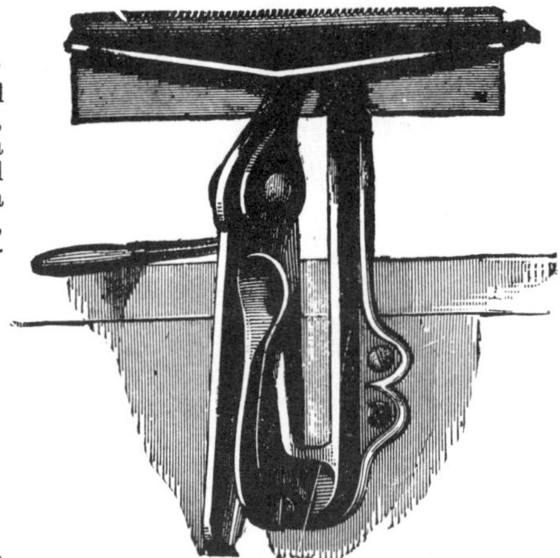

STEARNS' PAT. SAW VISE.

Nos ..... 0 ..... 1 ..... 2 ..... 3......

The jaws of these Vises are so constructed as to prevent vibration of the saw in filing, thereby lessening the noise, and causing a great saving of files. The jaws are planed to match perfectly. The No. 3 Vise has a screw clamp for attaching it to work bench, and a cam or lever for holding it in any position.

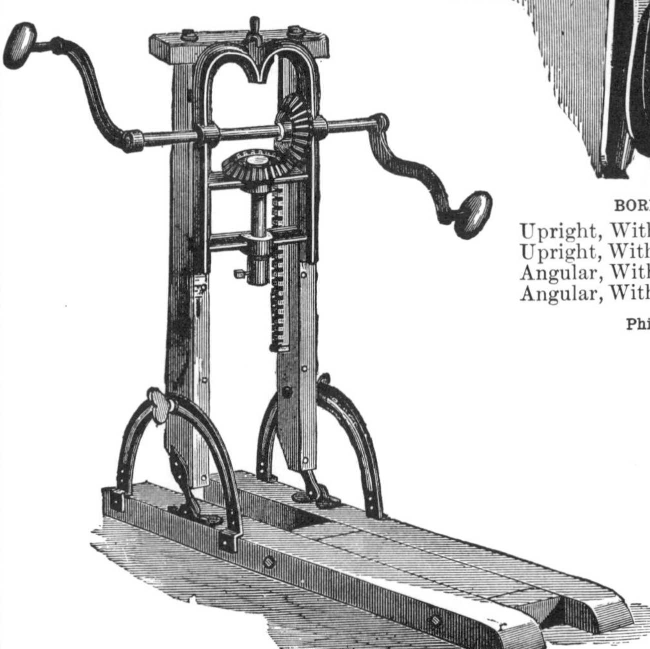

BORING MACHINES.

Upright, Without Augers ....
Upright, With " ....
Angular, Without " ....
Angular, With " ....

Phillips' Patent Boring Machine.

These machines are self-withdrawing. The depth of hole is set before boring by means of the movable collar, and without watching to see when the proper depth is reached, or stopping the boring movement, the auger returns of itself and is ready for another hole.

Angular, with Augers, ...

HAND SAWS.

In ordering, mention Length of Saw and Number of Teeth to the Inch Wanted.
Hand (or Cross-Cut) Saws are 6, 7, 8, 9, 10, 11, 12, 14 Teeth to the Inch.
Rip " " 4, 4½, 5, 5½ " " "

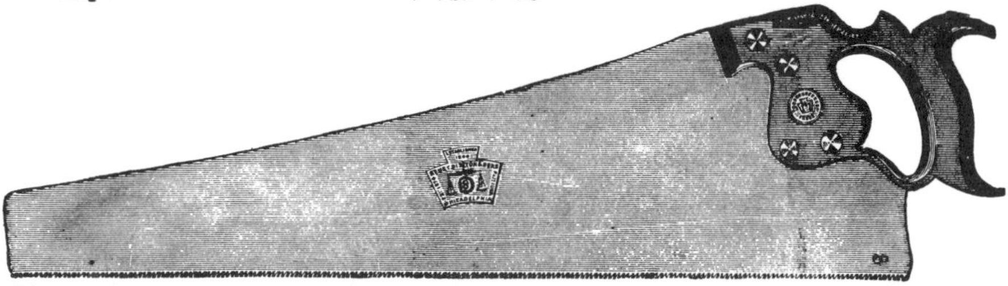

Disston's No. D 8, Spring Steel, Applewood Handle, Hand Saws, 26 in. long.... ......
" No. D 8, " " " " " " 28 in. " ....
" No. D 8, " " " " Rip " 28 in. " ....

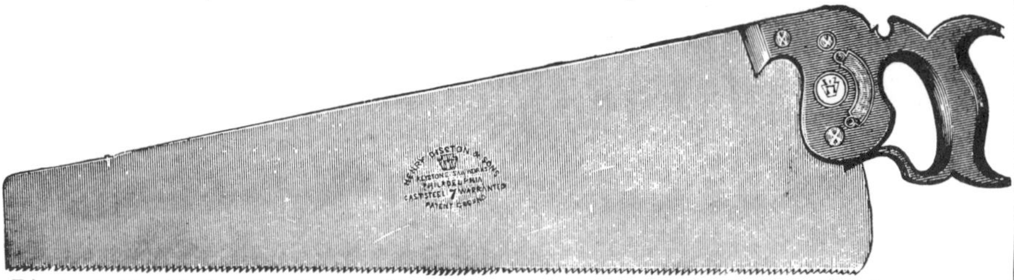

Disston's No. 12, London Spring, Hand Carved Handles, Highly Polished Blade, Etched, 26 and 28 in ....
Disston's No. 8, Spring Steel, Applewood Handles, Polished Edge, Grained Blade, Etched, 26 and 28 in.... ......
Disston's No. 7, Cast Steel, Beechwood Handles, Polished Edge, Grained Blade, Etched, 26 and 28 in. ....
"Vajen & New," Spring Steel, Applewood Handles, Polished Edge, Grained Blade, Etched, 26 in ....
"Charter Oak," Cast Steel, Beechwood Handles, otherwise same as V. & N. ... .
"Can't Be Beat," Same description as "Charter Oak,"...... ......

HAND RIP SAWS.

Disston's No. 12, London Spring, Hand Carved Handles, Highly Polished Blade, Etched, 28 and 30 in...... ......
Disston's No. 7, Spring Steel, Applewood Handles, Polished Edge, Grained Blade, Etched, 28 in...... ......
"Vajen & New," Same description, 28 in...... ......

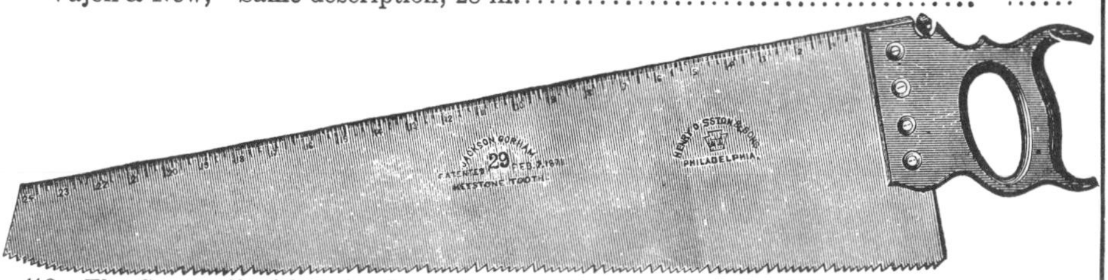

"On The Square," with 24 in. Rule Straight Edge and Square, 26 in...... ......

Disston's No. 7, Spring Steel, Applewood Handle, Polished Edge, Grained and Etched Blade, 20 in...... ......
"Vajen & New," Same description, 20 in...... ......

VAJEN & NEW, INDIANAPOLIS, IND.

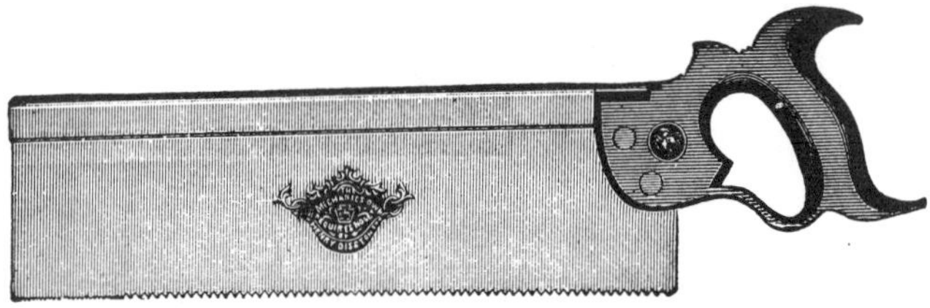

CAST STEEL BACK SAWS.

Disston's No. 4, Applewood Handle, Polished Edge, Blue Back,
Sizes, 8 .... 10 .... 12...... 14 ..... 16...... 18 in......

"Jackson," No. 1, Beechwood Handle, Polished Edge, Blue Back,
Sizes, 8...... 10...... 12...... 14...... 16......

CAST STEEL COMPASS SAWS.

Applewood Handle .... 10...... 12...... 14 in......

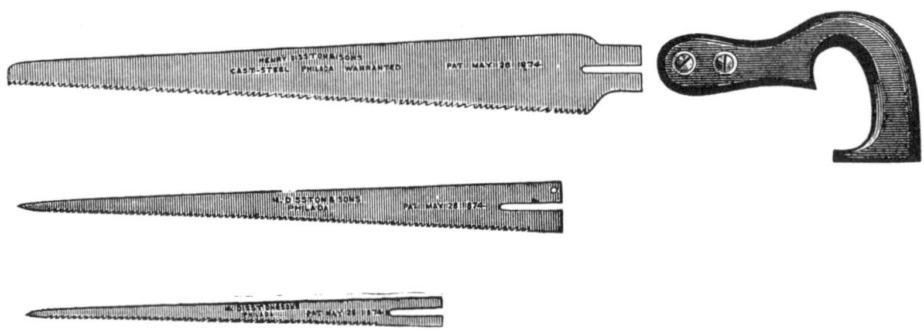

KEYHOLE SAWS.

Comprising One Blade each, Keyhole, Compass and Pruning Blade. Per Set ....

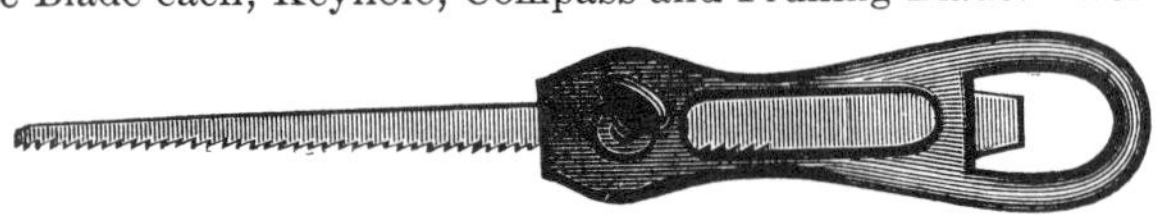

KEYHOLE SAW AND PAD.

Point can be Reversed and same carried in the pocket. Price .. ..

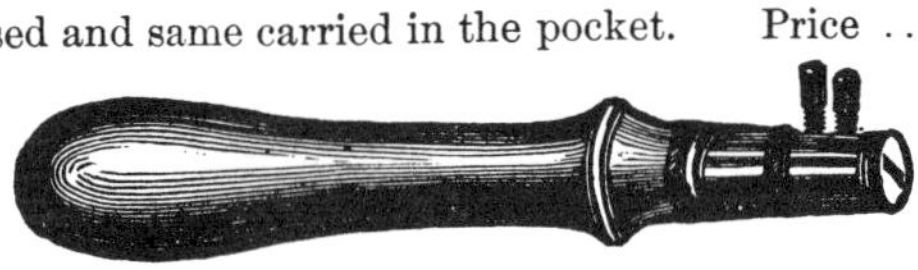

KEYHOLE SAW PAD.

Beech Handle, Brass Head, Iron Set Screws.................................... ......

No. 4.

No. 5.

SAW SCREWS.

No.2, Flush Brass ... No.3, Small Eagle.... No.4, Large Eagle.... No.5, Raised Brass....

See Hack Saws, Page 307. Meat Saws, Page 312.

CROSS-CUT SAWS AND HANDLES.

Cross-Cut Saws Furnished in any Regular Lengths Desired. All Saws Patent Tempered and Patent Ground.

Cast-Steel "Diamond" Cross-Cut Saws ....
Cast-Steel "Diamond," Thin Back, Cross-Cut Saws ....
Silver-Steel "Diamond," (With Handles and Gauge) ....

Cast-Steel "Champion" Cross-Cut Saws ....
Cast-Steel "Champion," Thin Back, Cross-Cut Saws ....

Concave Tooth "Dexter" Cross-Cut Saws, With Handles ....
Without Handles and Gauge ....

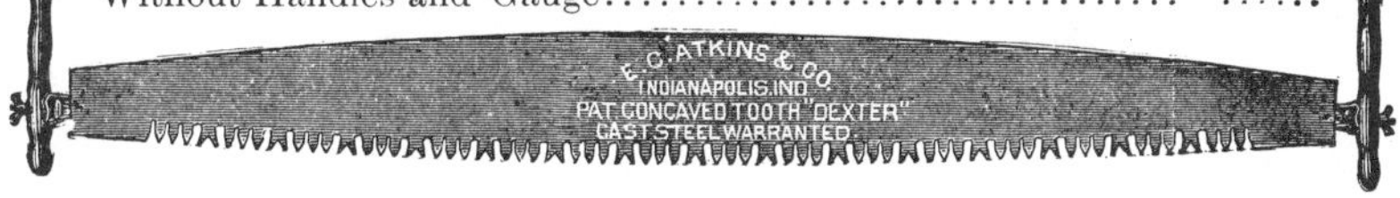

Hollow Back, Cast-Steel, "Diamond" Cross-Cut Saws ....
Hollow Back, Cast-Steel, "Champion" Cross-Cut Saws ....

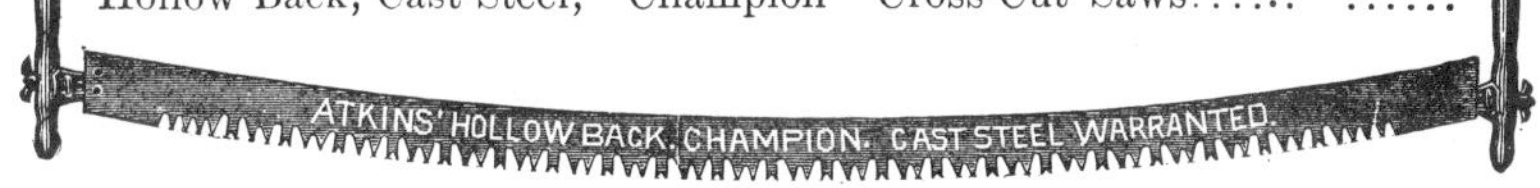

One-Man Cross-Cut, Champion Tooth ....
One-Man Cross-Cut, Cast-Steel, Diamond Tooth ....
One-Man Cross-Cut, Silver-Steel, Diamond Tooth ....

"V" Tooth Tenon Saws Furnished to Order.

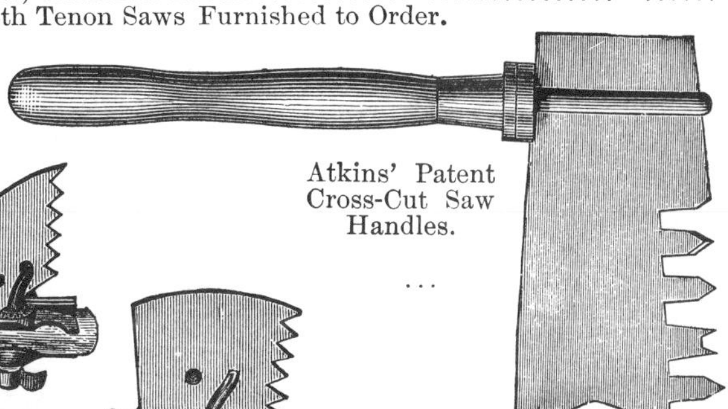

Atkins' Patent Cross-Cut Saw Handles. ...

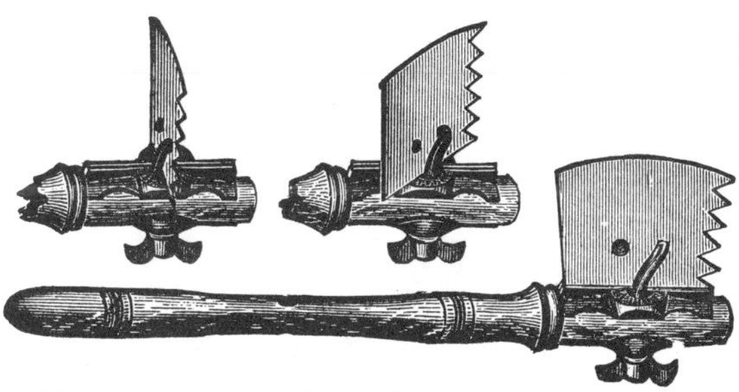

"Champion" Patent Cross-Cut Saw Handles ......
Atkins' Single Gauge Saw Tools ....
Atkins' Double Gauge Saw Tools ....
Atkins' Saw Tools, Complete ....

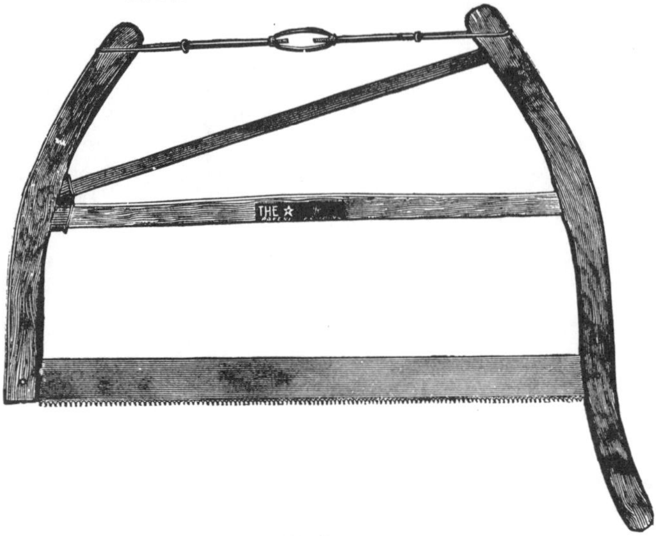

Common Frame, Complete, with No. 6 Blade...... ......
" " " " No. 1 " ....
" " " " No. 2 " ....
Extra " with Wood Brace, Complete, with No. 6 Blade...... ......
" " " " " " " No. 1 " ....
" " " " " " " No. 2 " ....
" " " " " Painted Red, with Superior Blade...... ......

Saw Rods, Regular Length, 22 in...... ......

No. 6, Disston's Cast Steel Wood Saw Blades, 30 in., Set and Sharpened...... ......
No. 1, Atkins' " " " " " 30 in., " " ....
No. 2, " " " " " " 30 in., " " ....

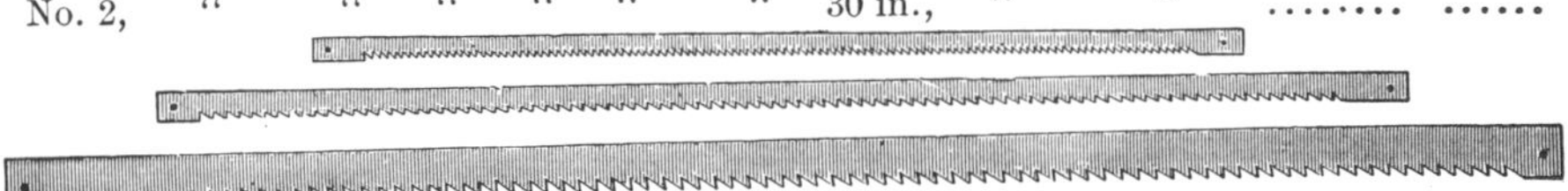

Felloe Webs, Turning or Chair Webs, Power Webs, Fay's Patent Scroll Saw Webs, Hack Saw Webs, Butcher Saw Webs. All in assorted Widths and Lengths.

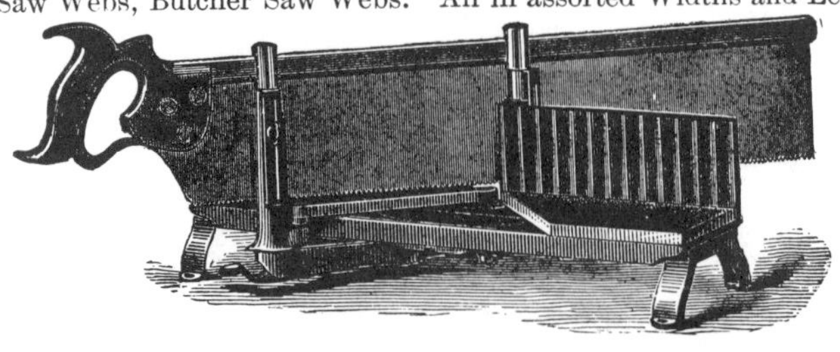

No. 1, "New Langdon" Mitre Box, with Saw, 20 in. long, 4 in. under the back.... ......
Larger Saws and Larger Boxes furnished to order.

LEVELS.

DAVIS' IRON LEVELS.

Adjustable Spirit Level, Plumb and Inclinometer.

No. 1, 6 in............
Simple, Durable and Accurate.

Cut of No. 2.
No. 2, 12 in .... No. 3, 18 in.....
No. 4, 24 in......

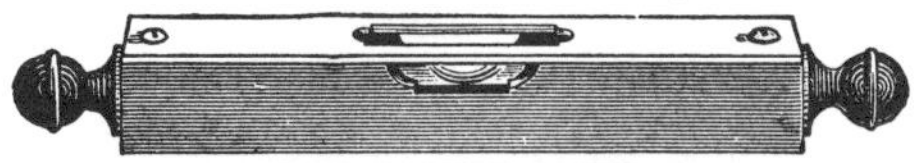

IRON POCKET LEVEL.

No. 14, 3 in........... ...... No. 15, 5 in. in length.... ......

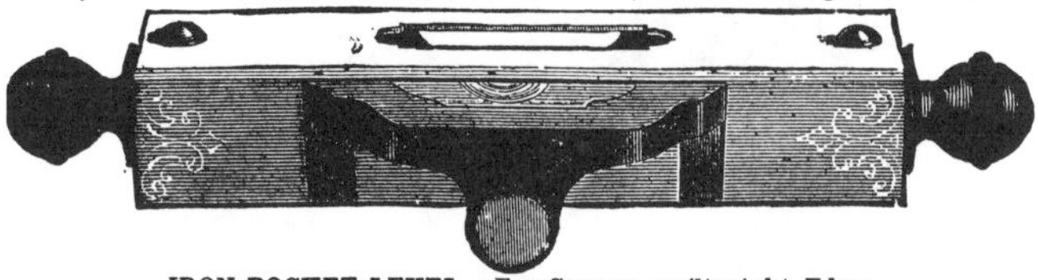

IRON POCKET LEVEL.—For Square or Straight Edge.

No. 17, 3½ inches in length.............................. ......

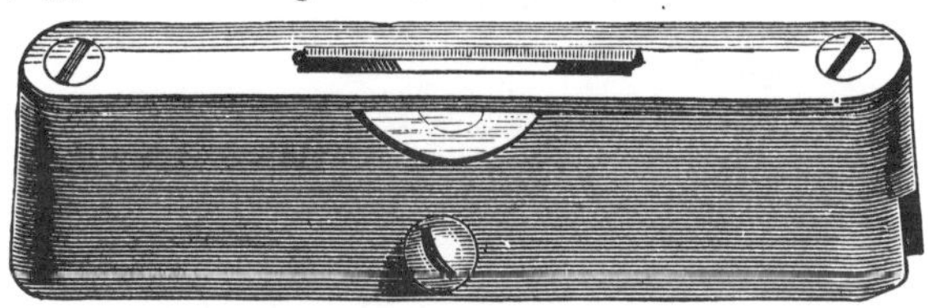

IRON POCKET LEVEL.

No. 46, Brass Top and Plate, a Superior Article............. ......

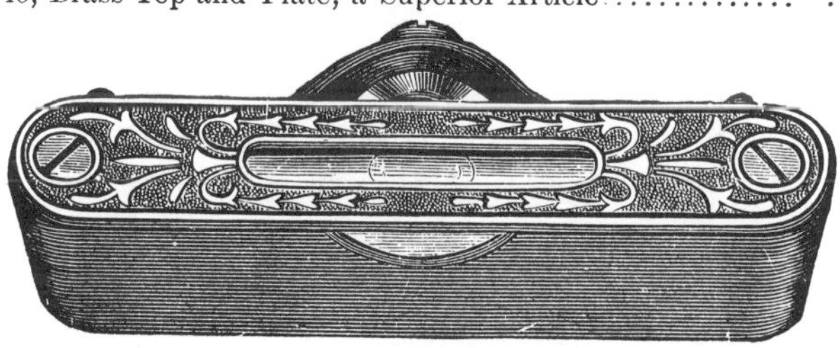

POCKET LEVEL.

No. 41, Iron, Brass Top Plate ....

PLUMBS AND LEVELS.

No. 102 Level, Arch Top Plate, 2 Side Views Polished, 10 to 16 in.....
No. 103 " " " " " " " 18 to 24 in......
No. 0 Plumb and Level, same as above, 24 to 30 in ....

PATENT ADJUSTABLE PLUMBS AND LEVELS.

No. 3, Arch Top Plate, 2 Side Views, Polished and Tipped, 26 to 30 in.................. ......
No. 4, Arch Top Plate, 2 Brass Lipped Side Views, Polished and Tipped, 26 to 30 in ....
No. 9, Mahogany, Arch Top Plate, 2 Ornamental Brass Lipped Side Views, Polished and Tipped, 26 to 30 in ....
No. 10, Mahogany, Triple Stock, 2 Ornamental Brass Lipped Side Views, Arch Top Plate, Polished and Tipped........ ......
No. 35, Patent Adjustable Masons' Plumb and Level for Plumb Bob and Line, 3¾ in wide, 42 in, long ....
Level Glasses. 1¾ in.... 2 in.... 2½ in.... 3 in.... 3½ in.... 4 in....

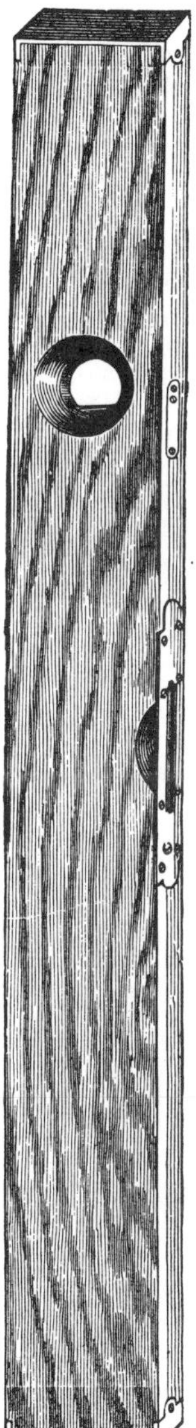

No. 3 Level.

No. 5.

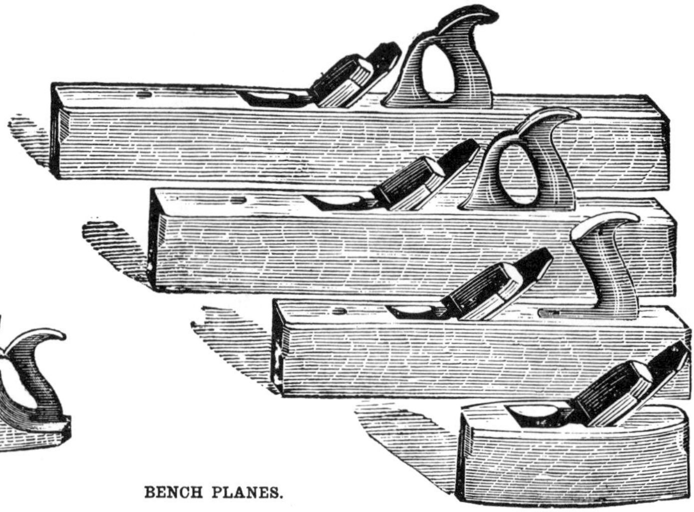

BENCH PLANES.

No. 1, Single Iron Smooth, Best Cast Steel, Polished Start, 2 to 2¼ in. Irons..... ....
No. 3, Double " " " " " " " 2 to 2¼ in. " ....
No. 5, " " " Solid Handle, Best Cast Steel, Pol'd Start, 2 to 2¼ in. Irons ....
No. 12, Single Iron Jack, " " " " " 2 to 2¼ in. " ....
No. 15, Double " " " " " " " 2 to 2¼ in. " ...
No. 18, Single " Fore, 22 in. " " " " " 2⅜ to 2⅝ in. " ....
No. 21, Double " " 22 in. " " " " " 2⅜ to 2⅝ in. " ....
No. 24, Single " Jointer, 26 and 28 in. " " " " " 2½ to 2¾ in. " ....
No. 27, Double " " 26 and 28 in. " " " " " 2½ to 2¾ in. " ....

RAZEE OR RECESS HANDLE PLANE.

No. 17, Double Iron Jack, Best Cast Steel, Polished Start, 2 to 2¼ in. Irons ....
No. 23, " " Fore, 22 in., Best Cast Steel, Polished Start, 2⅜ to 2⅝ in. Irons ...
No. 29, " " Jointer, 26 and 28 in., " " 2½ to 2¾ in. " ...

FANCY AND MOULDING PLANES.

No. 37, Beads, Single Box.. ⅛ to ½.... ⅝ to ¾ ... ⅞ to 1 .... 1¼.... 1½ in....
No. 41, Center Beads, Double Boxed.................... ⅛ to ½.... ⅝ to ¾ in ...
No. 47, Dadoes, Brass Side Stop.................................. ¼ to 1 in ...
No. 53, Fillister, with Cutter and Brass Side Stop ....
No. 72, Hollows and Rounds, Set of 9 Pairs.... Per Pair, 1 to 6.... Per Pair, 7 to 9 ...
No. 75, Match Planes, Twin or Separate .... ⅜ to 1 in....
No. 116, Rabbet Planes, Skew .... ½ to 1.... 1¼.... 1½.... 1¾.... 2 in....
No. 97, Panel Plows, Beech, with Screw Stop, with Handles, Boxed Fence ....
No. 100, " " " " Boxwood Arms, " " " ....
No. 106, " " Applewood, " " Screw Stop, " " ....

The Numbers above are the Saleable Numbers.

Ogees, Rev. Ogees, Ovolos, Nosing, Raising, Reeding, Sash and Moulding Planes.

PLANES.

FANCY WOOD AND IRON PLANES.

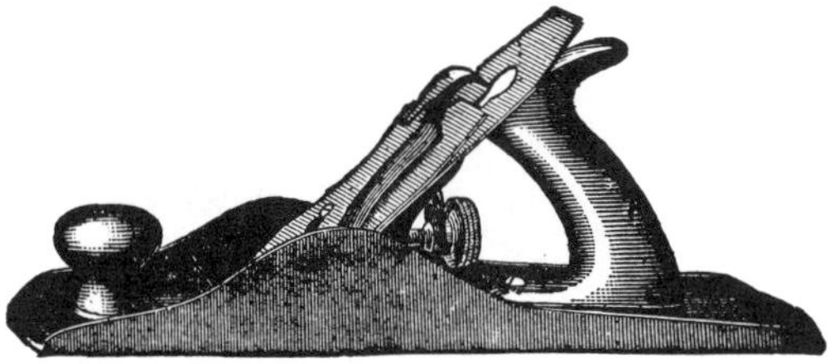

No. 5 Jack Plane, 14 in., 2 in. Cutter ... .
No. 6 Fore Plane, 18 in., 2⅜ in. Cutter .. ..
No. 8 Jointer Plane, 24 in., 2⅝ in. Cutter ......

No. 3 Smooth Plane, 8 in. long, 1¾ in. Cutter.... .... ..

Each Plane is Thoroughly Tested at the Factory and put in Perfect Working Order.

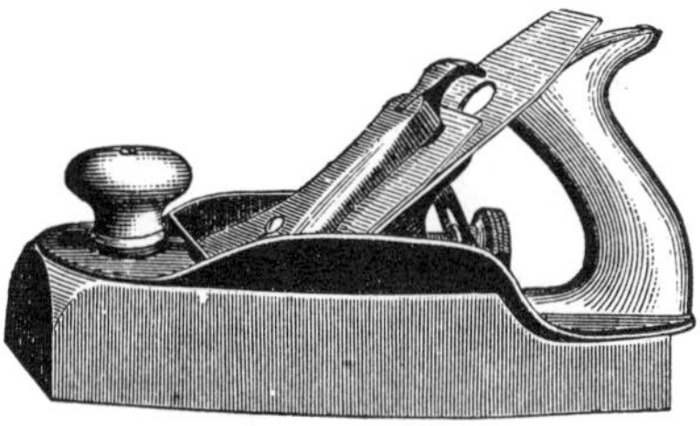

No. 35 Handled Smooth 9 in., 2 in Cutter....
No. 36 Handled Smooth 10 in., 2⅜ Cutter....

No. 22 Smooth Plane 8 in., 1¾ in. Cutter....
No. 23 Smooth Plane 9 in., 1¾ in. Cutter....
No. 24 Smooth Plane 8 in., 2 in Cutter....

For Beauty of Style and Finish, they are Unequaled, and the Superior Methods for Adjusting them readily in all their parts, render them Economical to the Owner.

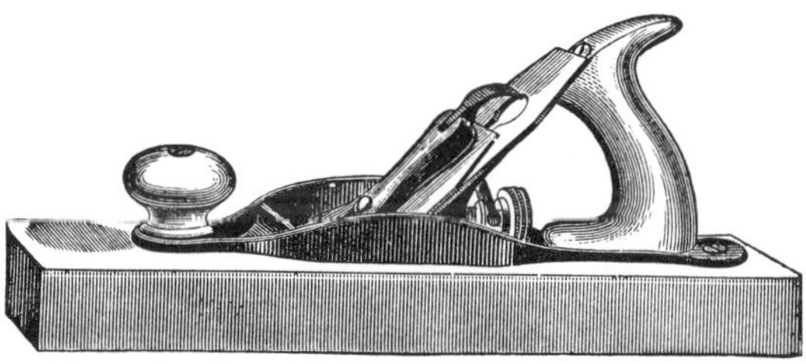

No. 26 Jack Plane 15 in., 2 in. Cutter.. ......
No. 27 Jack Plane 15 in., 2⅛ in. Cutter ....
No. 29 Fore Plane 20 in., 2⅜ in Cutter.. ......
No. 31 Jointer Plane, 24 in., 2⅜ in Cutter ....
No. 32 Jointer Plane, 26 in., 2⅝ in Cutter ....

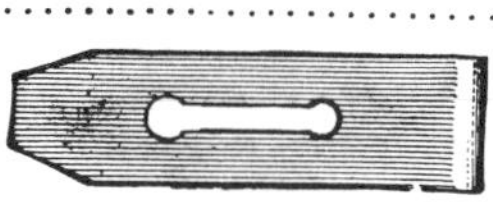

Bailey Plane Bits.

1¾ in .. 2 in ... 2⅛ in .. 2⅜ in... 2⅝ in ...

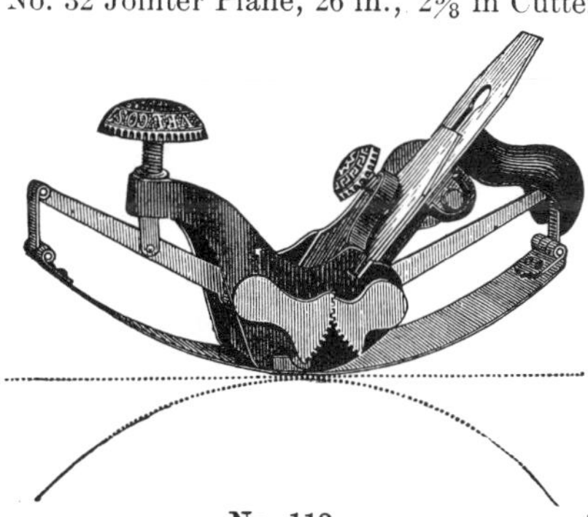

No. 113.

Improved Patent Adjustable Circular Plane.

No. 113, Adjustable Circular, 1¾ inch Cutter

This Plane has a Flexible Steel Face, which can be easily shaped to any required arc, either concave or convex, by turning the Knob on the front of the plane. By the peculiar construction of the plane, a smaller arc, either concave or convex, can be obtained than by any other similar tool.

BLOCK PLANERS.

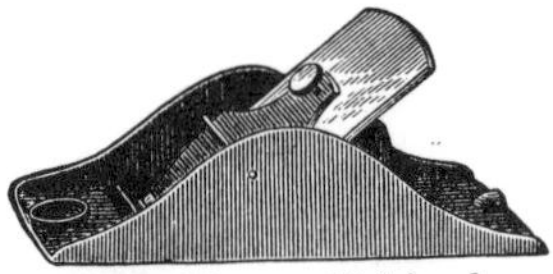

No. 101 Block Plane, 3½ in long, 1 in. Cutter.................... ......

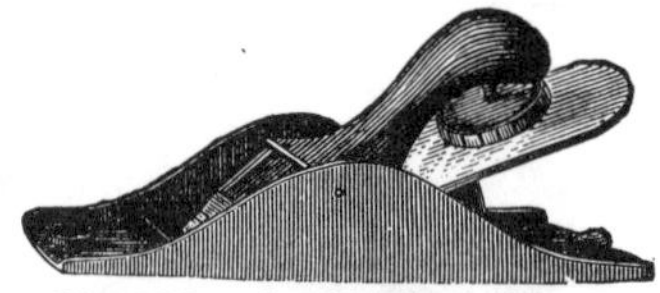

No. 102 and 103 Block Plane.
102 Plain........ 103 Adjustable........
5½ in. long, 1½ in. Cutter.

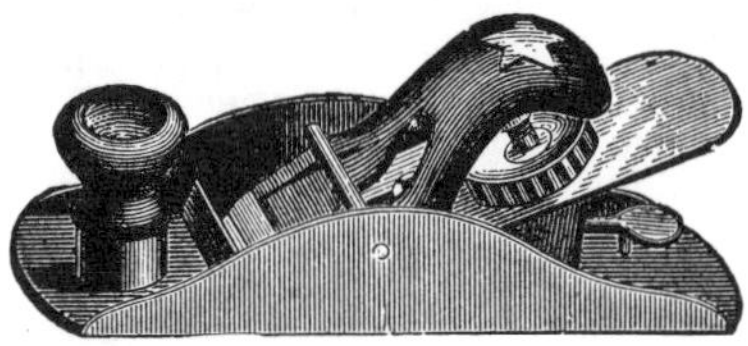

No. 110 Block Plane ....
No. 120 Block Plane, Adjustable... ......
7½ in. Long, 1¾ in. Cutter.

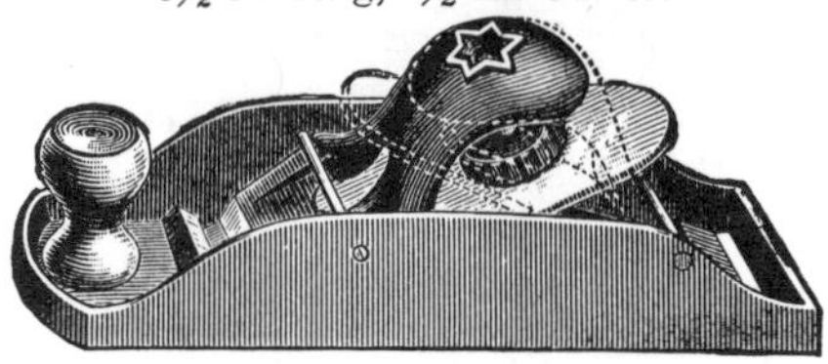

No. 130 Block Plane (Double Ender)......
8 in. long, 1¾ in. Cutter
Will plane close up into corners.

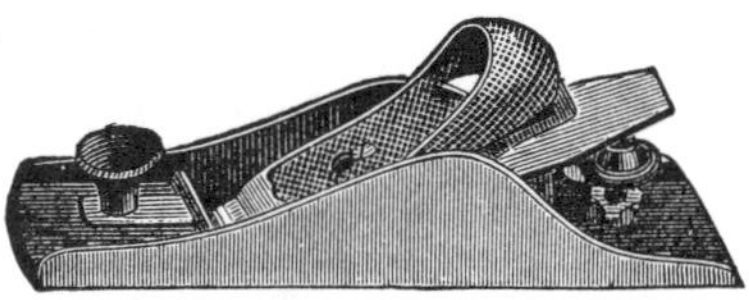

No. 9½ Excelsior Block Plane, 6 in. long, 1¾ in. Cutter............. ......

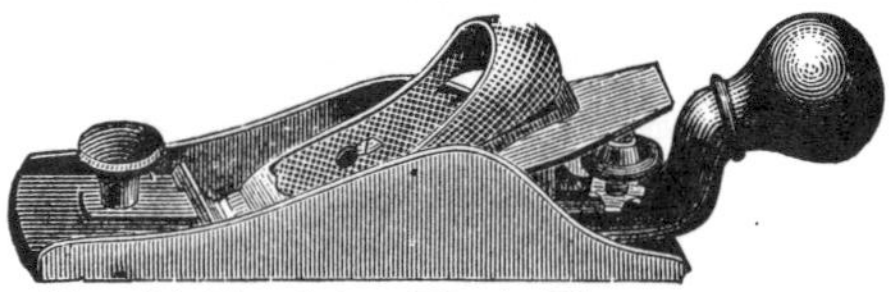

No. 9¾ Excelsior Block Plane, 6 in. long, 1¾ in Cutter....... ......
With Rosewood Handle.

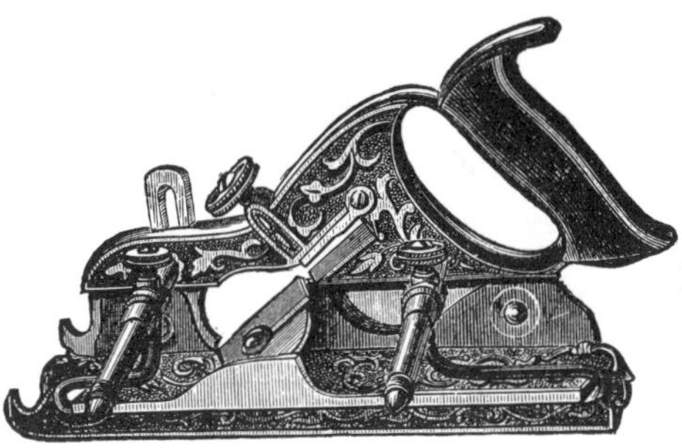

Cut of No. 41.

Bull Nose Rabbet Plane, 4 in. long, 1 in. Cutter.......... ......
To work close up into the corner.

No. 41 Miller's Patent Combined Plow, Fillister and Match Plane,... ....
Iron Stock and Fence.
No. 43 Plow and Match Plane combined ......
No. 45 Beading, Rabbet & Slitting Plane ......
No. 46 Taut's Pat. Dado Fillister & Plow ......
No. 50 Adjustable Beading Plane...... .....
The above Planes complete with Tools.

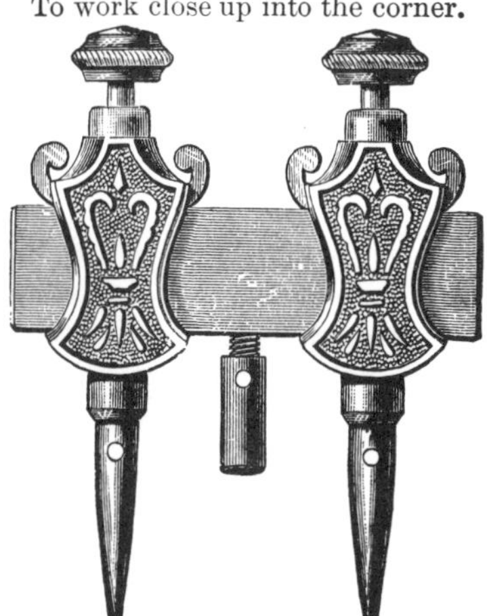

Improved Trammel Points, (Bronze Metal, Steel Points.)

No................. 1...... 2...... 3......

Points can be removed and replaced by the Pencil Socket which accompany each pair.

AWLS AND HANDLES.

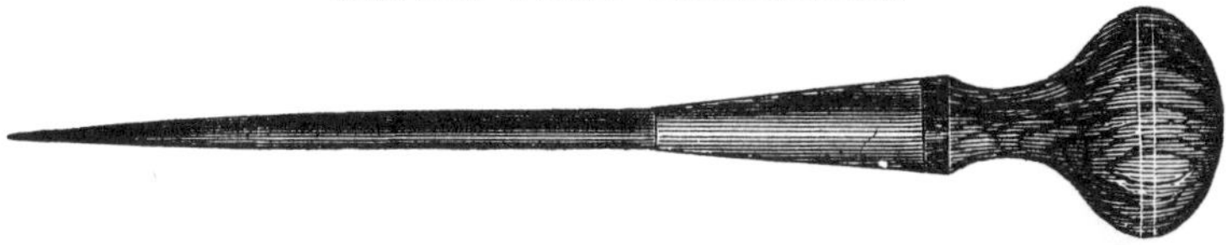

SOCKET SCRATCH AWLS.

Blades of Forged Cast Steel, All Polished.... ....

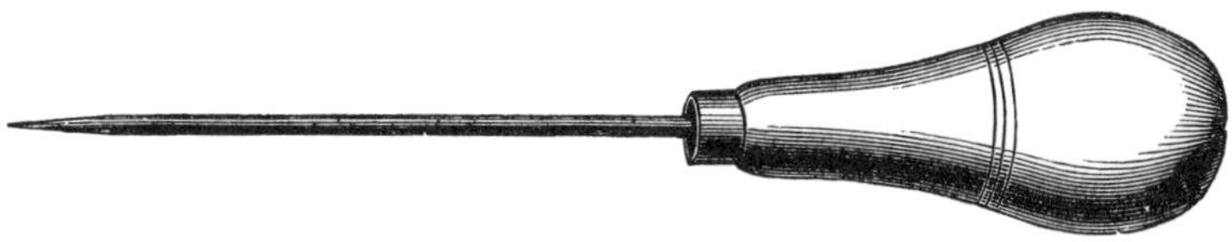

HANDLED SCRATCH AWLS.

Cast Steel, Polished Blades, Finished Handle, Brass Ferrule................. ......

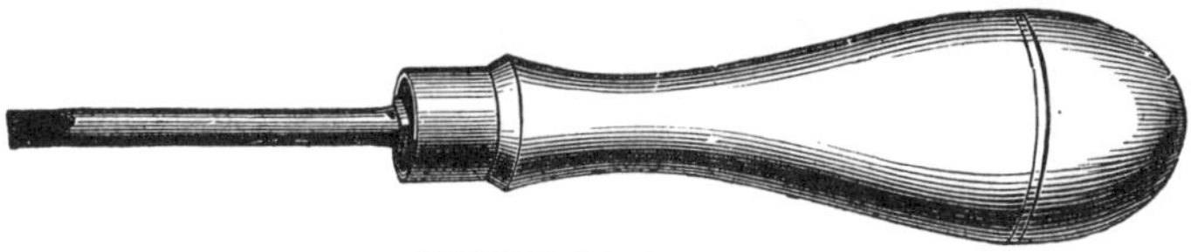

HANDLED BRAD AWLS.

Plain Handled Brad Awls, Brass Ferrules, Assorted, Small.................... ......
" " " " " " " Large..................... ......

HAND SAW HANDLES.

No. 3 Hand Saw Handles, Plain Edges ....
No. 2 " " " Varnished Edges...... ......
No. 1 " " " Cherry Varnished Edges ......

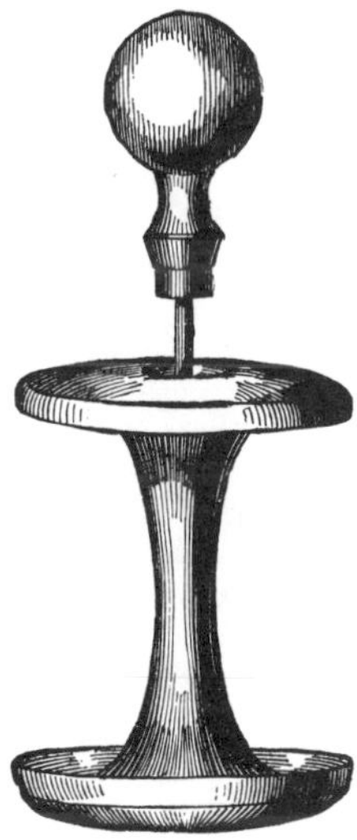

Chalk Line Reels.

Chalk Line Reels with Awl, ...

Chalk Line Reels, without Awls............

Fore Plane Handles.

Beech-wood, Plain.. ......

Jack Plane Handles.

Beech-wood, Plain.. ......

VAJEN & NEW, INDIANAPOLIS, IND.

MALLETS.

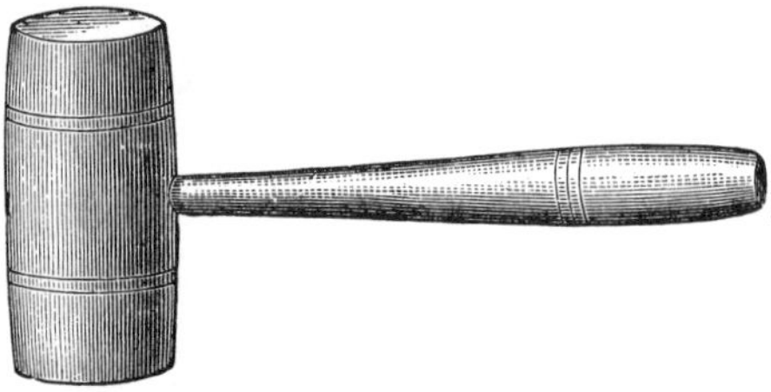

Tinner's Mallet.

No. 4 Round Hickory, 5½ in. long, Ass'd 2¼ and 2½ in. diameter, ...

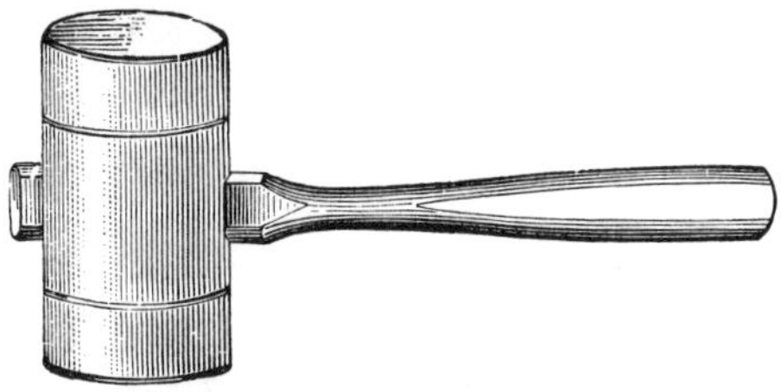

Round Hickory and Lignumvitæ Mallets.

No.		Length.	Diam.	
1,	Round Hickory Mortised,	5 in.	3 in.	....
2,	" " "	5½	3½	....
3,	" " "	6	4	....
5,	" Lignumvitæ "	5	3	....
6,	" " "	5½	3½	....
7,	" " "	6	4	....

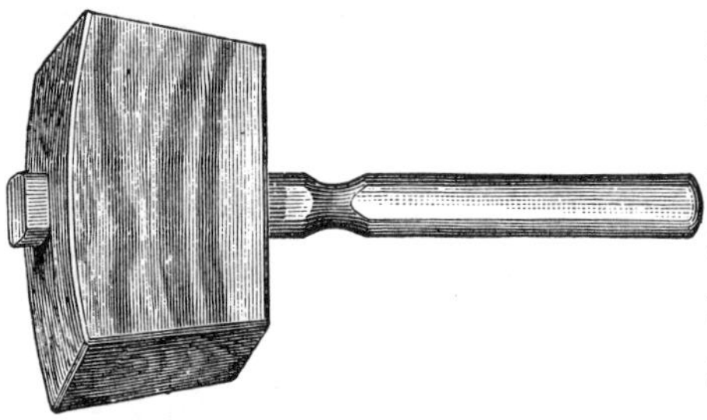

Square Hickory and Lignumvitæ Mallets.

No. 8 Square Hickory, Mortised, 6 in. long, 2½ x 3½ in. ......

No. 9 Square Hickory, Mortised, 6½ in. long, 2¾ x 3¾ in ......

No. 10 Square Hickory, Mortised, 7 in. long, 3 x 4 in ......

No. 11 Square Lignumvitæ, Mortised, 6 in. long, 2½ x 3½ in ......

No. 12 Square Lignumvitæ, Mortised, 6½ in long, 2¾ x 3¾ ......

No. 13 Square Lignumvitæ, Mortised, 7 in. long, 3 x 4 ......

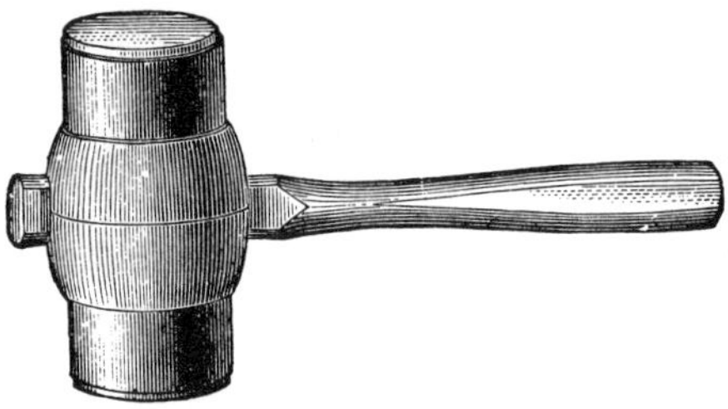

Hickory Iron-Bound Mallets.

No. 14 Round Mallets, Mortised, Iron Rings, 6 in. 4 in. diam. ......

No. 14½ Round Mallets, Mortised, Iron Rings, 5½ in. 3½ in. diam. .....

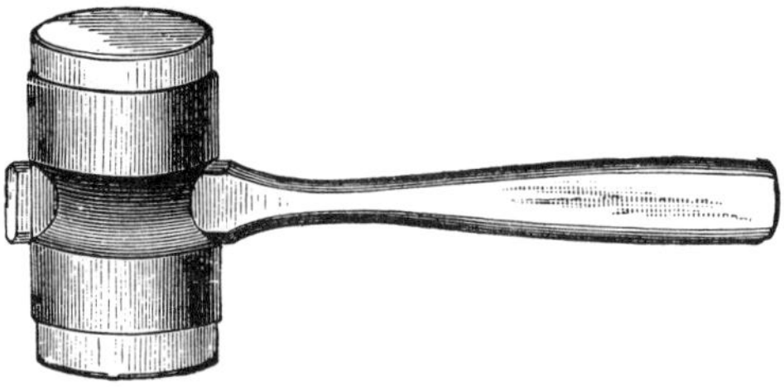

Iron Socket Mallets.

No. 16 Round Mallets Heavy Malleable Iron Socket, Mortised, Hickory Ends, 3 in. diam. .....

Also Engravers' and Ice Mallets, assorted sizes. See Raw Hide Mallets, page 237.

PATENT EXCELSIOR TOOL HANDLES.

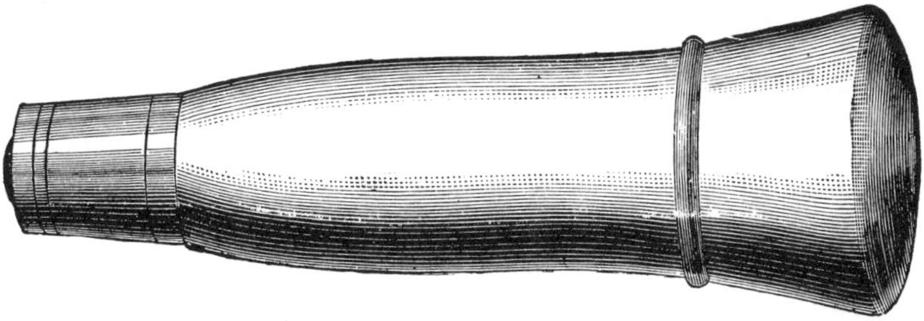

No. 1, Turkey Boxwood Handle, with 20 Tools ....

Buy this, if you would have the Best.

Cut of Tool Handle Nos. 2 and 3.

No. 2, Iron Handle, with 12 Tools.. ......

No. 3, Iron Handle, with 20 Tools.. ......

"Giant Tool Holders," Hollow Rosewood Handle, 6 in. long, with patent Swing Top and Cam Fastening. Tools are 2½ in. long and 3-16 shank, consisting of 1 Screw Driver, 1 Chisel, 1 Scratch Awl, 1 Gimlet, 1 Gauge, 4 Brad Awls, ...

Also, Other Wood Handle Tool Holders, 10 and 20 Tools; Cheaper Quality.

MARKING GAUGES.

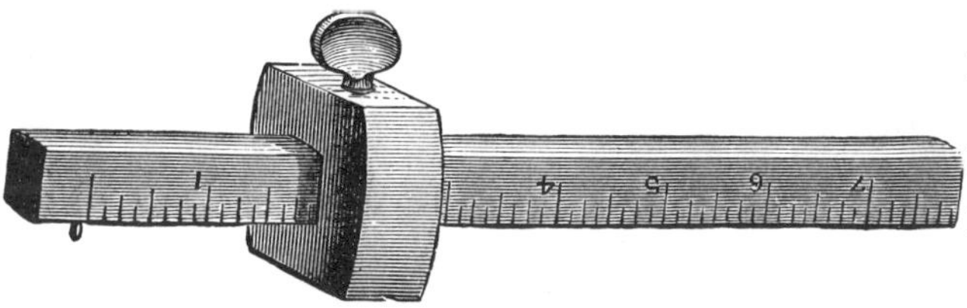

Cut of No. 0 Gauge.

No. 0, Beechwood, Boxwood Thumb Screw, Marked Steel Point ...

No. 61, Same, but with Oval Bar ....

No. 65, Oval Bar, Boxwood, Brass Plates, Brass Screw ....

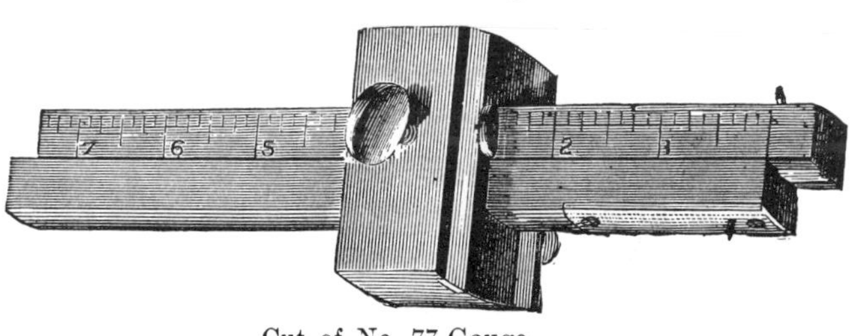

Cut of No. 77 Gauge.

No. 72, Beechwood, Dbl. Gauge, Marking and Mortise Combined, Boxwood Thumb Screw Oval Bar, Marked Steel Points.... ....

No. 77, Rosewood, Same as No. 72, but with Brass Thumb Screw and Shoe, ...

No. 84, Handled Slitting Gauge, with roller, 17 in. Bar Marked with Inches ....

No. 85, Panel Gauge, Beechwood, Boxwood Thumb Screw, Oval Bar, Steel Points ......

CHISEL AND AWL HANDLES.

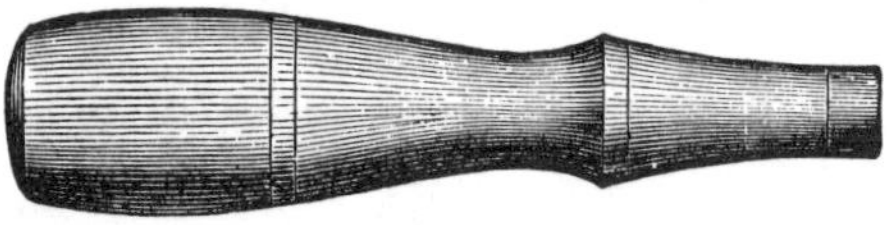

Tanged Firmer Chisel Handles.

Polished Hickory, Assorted Sizes.. .....

" Apple-tree, " " .....

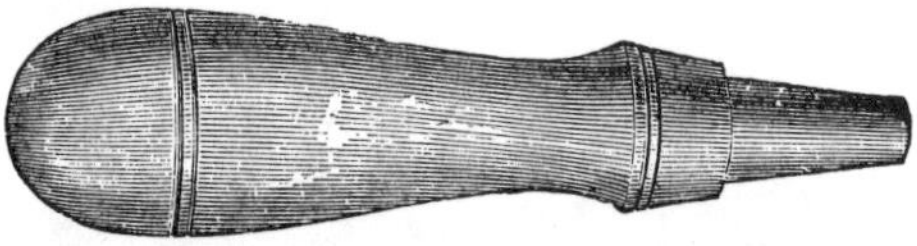

Socket Firmer Chisel Handles.

Polished Hickory, Assorted Sizes, ...

" Apple-tree " " .....

Socket Framing Chisel Handles.

Polished Hickory, Assorted Sizes,. ......

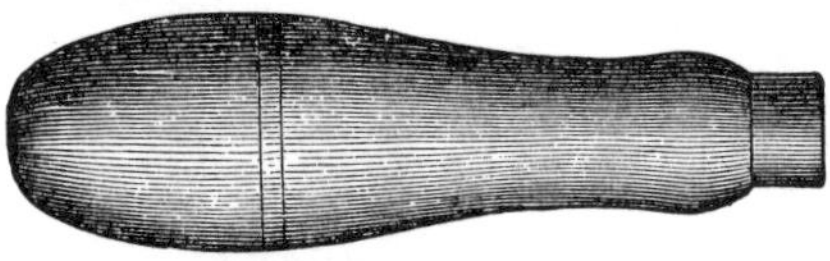

File Handles.

Bass-wood, Brass Ferrule, Ass'd Sizes, ...

Brad-Awl Handles.

Brass Ferrule, Ebony Finish.... ......

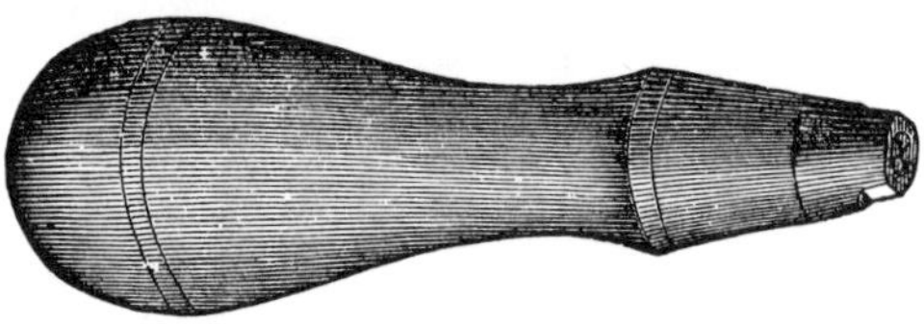

Carpenter's Tool Handles.

No. 8 Tool Handle, Steel Screw and Nut with Wrench..... ......

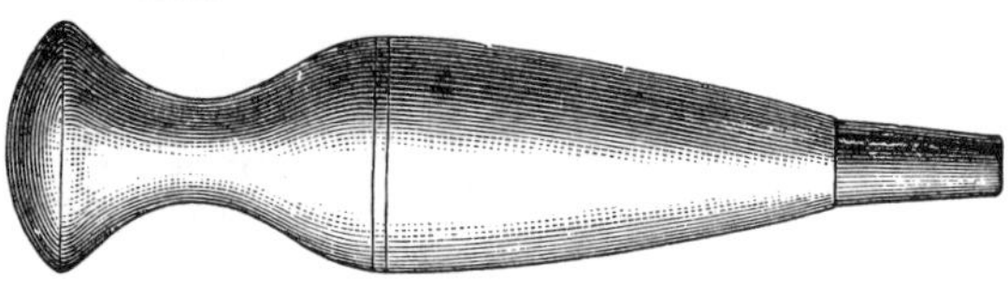

Common Sewing Awl Handles.

No. 10 Brass Ferrule ... .

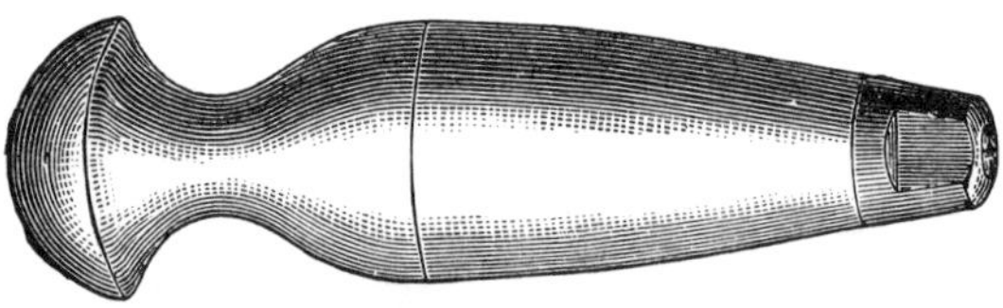

Patent Sewing Awl Handles.

No. 6½ Apple-tree, Steel Screw and Nut with Wrench ....

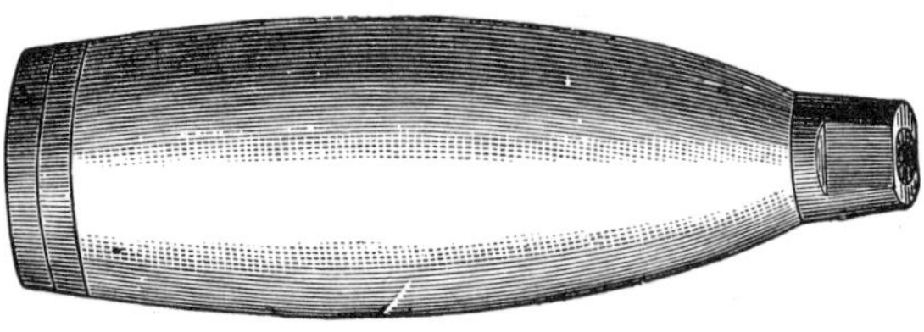

Patent Peg Awl Haft.

No. 7 Hickory, Leather Top Extra Large, Riveted, Steel Screw and Nut, with Wrench .. ..

No. 11 Common Peg Awl Haft, Hickory, Brass Ferrule............. ......

Walking Cane Board Measure, 8 lines, 9 to 16 feet graduation ......

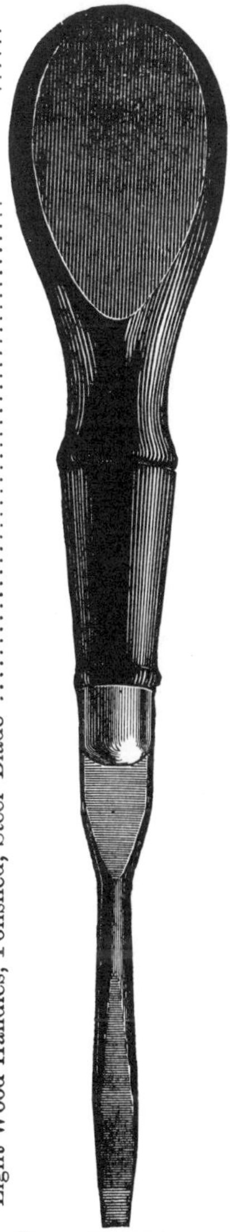

FLAT BLADE SCREW DRIVERS.

Black Ebony Handle, Best Quality, Inch Blade, 2 .... 3 .... 4 .... 5 .... 6 .... 7 .... 8 .... 10 .... 12 ....
Light Wood Handles, Polished, Steel Blade ......

ROUND BLADE SCREW DRIVERS.

Black Ebony Handle, Best Quality Only, Inch 2 ... 3 ... 4 ... 5 ... 6 ... 7 ... 8 ... 10 ... 12 ...

ELRICH SCREW DRIVERS.

Best Screw Driver for Small Machine Work, Inch ...... 2 ...... 3 ...... 4 ...... 5 ...... 6 ......
Champion Machinists', Inch ...... 12 ...... 15 ...... 18 ......

Cut of Double Acting Ratchet Screw Driver.

Double Acting, Inch ...... 4 .... 5 .... 6 .... 8 .... 10 .... 12 ....

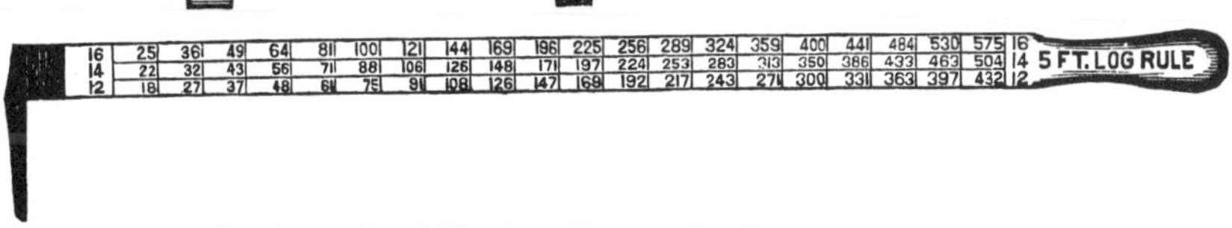

No. 14 Log Rule, 5 feet long, Steel Hook or Square Head ....

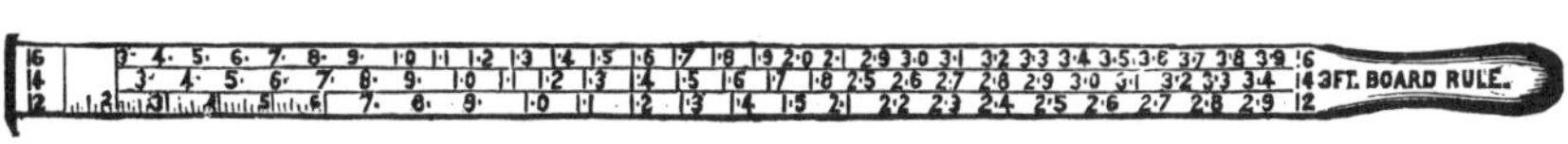

No. 3 3-Tier Board Rules ....
No. 5 " " " ....
No. 6 " " " ....

No. 8 4-Tier Board Rules ....
No. 10 " " " ....
Right or Left Hand with Steel Heads ......

VAJEN & NEW, INDIANAPOLIS, IND.

RULES.

STANLEY RULE AND LEVEL CO.

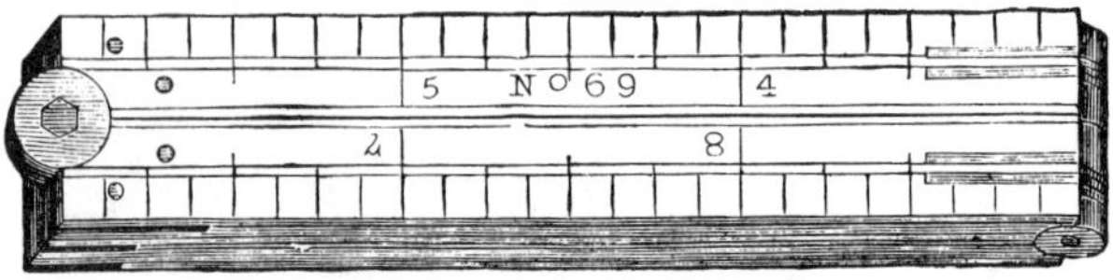

Boxwood, One Foot, Four Fold.

No. 69, Round Joint, Middle Plates, 5/8 in. wide, 8th, 16ths.....
No. 65, Square " " " 5/8 in. " " " .....
No. 65½, " " Bound, 5/8 in. " " " .....
No. 56, Arch " Edge Plates, 5/8 in. " " " .....
No. 57, " " Bound, 5/8 in. " " " .....

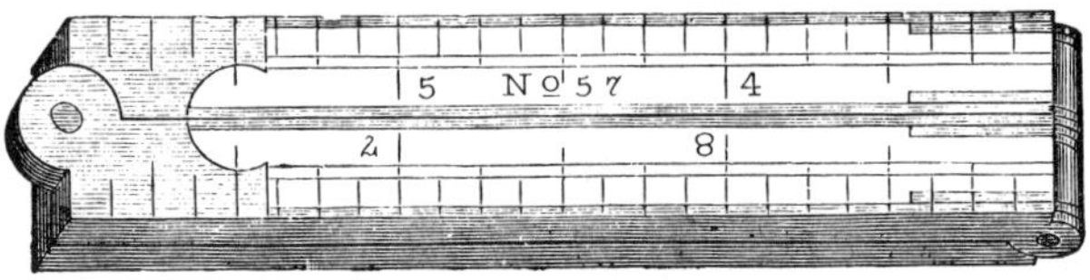

Ivory, One Foot, Four Fold.—8ths and 16ths.

No. 90, Round Joint, Brass Middle Plates, 5/8 in. wide, ...
No. 92, Square Joint, German Silver, Edge Plates, 5/8 in. ....
No. 92½, Same as No. 92, but with Middle Plates.......
No. 88, Arch Joint, German Silver, Bound, 5/8 in. wide,

IVORY, TWO FEET, FOUR FOLD.--8ths, 10ths, 12ths, 16ths, Drafting Scales.

No. 87, Arch Joint, German Silver Bound, 1 in. wide.. ....
No. 95, " " " " " 1⅜ in. " .. ....

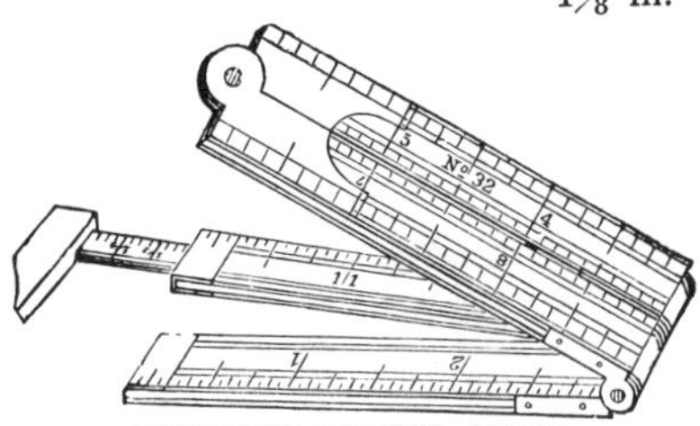

BOXWOOD CALIPER RULES.

No. 36, Square Joint, 2 fold, 7/8 in. wide, 6 in., 8ths, 10ths, 12ths, 16ths.......
No. 32, Arch Joint, Edge Plates, 4 fold, 1 in. wide, 12 in., 8ths, 10ths, 12ths, 16ths.......
No. 32½, Same as No. 32, Arch Joint, Bound.......

IVORY CALIPER RULES.

No. 38, Square Joint, German Silver, 2 fold, 6 in., 7/8 in. wide, 8ths, 10ths, 12ths, 16ths.......
No. 39, Square Joint, Edge Plates, German Silver, 4 fold, 12 in., 7/8 in wide, 8ths, 10ths, 12ths, 16ths.......
No. 40, Square Joint, German Silver Bound, 4 fold, 12 in., 5/8 in. wide, 8ths, 16ths.......

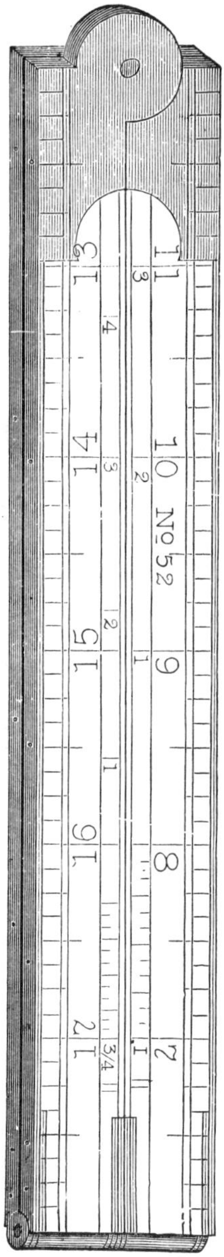

BOXWOOD, TWO FEET, FOUR FOLD.

No. 68, Round Joint, Middle Plates, 1 in. wide, 8ths, 16ths ...
No. 61, Same, Square Joint.......
No. 63, Square Joint, Edge Plates, Drafting Scales, 1 in., 8ths, 10ths, 12ths, 16ths ......
No. 84, " " Half Bound, " " 1 in., " " " " ......
No. 51, Arch " Middle Plates, " " 1 in., " " " " ......
No. 53, " " Edge Plates, " " 1 in., " " " " ......
No. 52, " " Half Bound, " " 1 in., " " " " .....
No. 54, " " Bound, " " 1 in., " " " " ......
No. 60, Double Arch Joint, " " " 1 in., " " " " ......
No. 53½, Arch Joint, Edge Plates, Inside Beveled Edges, Architect Scales.......
No. 77, Double Arch Joint, Drafting Scales, Bitted, 1⅜ in., 8ths, 10ths, 16ths... ......
No. 81, Same as No. 53, but Board Measure, 1⅜ in., 12ths and 16ths.......

CHISELS AND GOUGES.

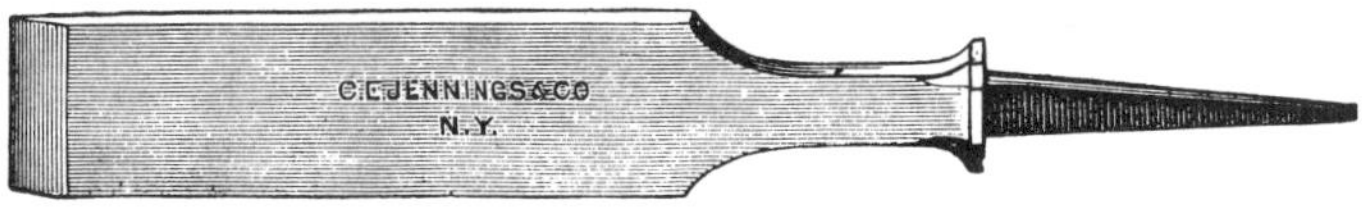

TANGED FIRMER CHISELS.—Solid Cast Steel.

Sizes	1/8	3-16	1/4	5-16	3/8	1/2	5/8	3/4	7/8	1	1 1/4	1 1/2	1 3/4	2 in.
Butcher's Firmer														
" Long Thin Paring														

Sizes	1/8	1/4	3/8	1/2	5/8	3/4	7/8	1	1 1/4	1 1/2	1 3/4	2 in.
No. 107 Barton's Firmer, Blade 6 in.												
No. 110 " Long Thin Paring, 9 in.												

Either of the above in Sets of 12 Chisels 1/8 to 2 inch

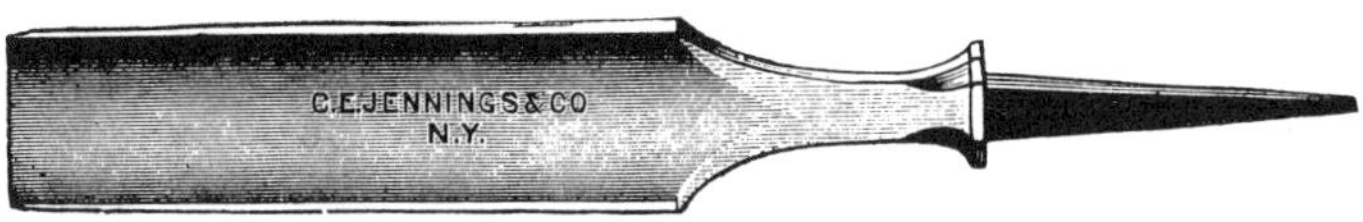

TANGED FIRMER GOUGES.—Solid Cast Steel.

Sizes	1/8	3-16	1/4	5-16	3/8	1/2	5/8	3/4	7/8	1	1 1/4	1 1/2	1 3/4	2 in.
Butcher's Firmer														

Sizes	1/8	1/4	3/8	1/2	5/8	3/4	7/8	1	1 1/4	1 1/2	1 3/4	2 in.
No. 113 Barton's Firmer (Inside)												
No. 116 " Long Paring (Bevel.)												

No. 116 in Flat, Medium, or Full Sweep. (All in Sets as above.)

TURNING CHISELS.—Solid Cast Steel.

Sizes	1/8	1/4	3/8	1/2	5/8	3/4	7/8	1	1 1/4	1 1/2	1 3/4	2 in.
Butcher's												

TURNING GOUGES.—Solid Cast Steel.

Sizes	1/8	1/4	3/8	1/2	5/8	3/4	7/8	1	1 1/4	1 1/2	1 3/4	2 in.
Butcher's												

MILLWRIGHTS' FIRMER CHISELS AND GOUGES.

Sizes	1/8	1/4	3/8	1/2	5/8	3/4	7/8	1	1 1/4	1 1/2	1 3/4	2 in.
No. 109 Barton's Chisel 9 in. Blade												
No. 115 Barton's Gouge												

(No. 115 in Flat or Full Sweep.)

Either of the above in Sets of 12 Chisels, 1/8 to 2 in.

CHISELS.

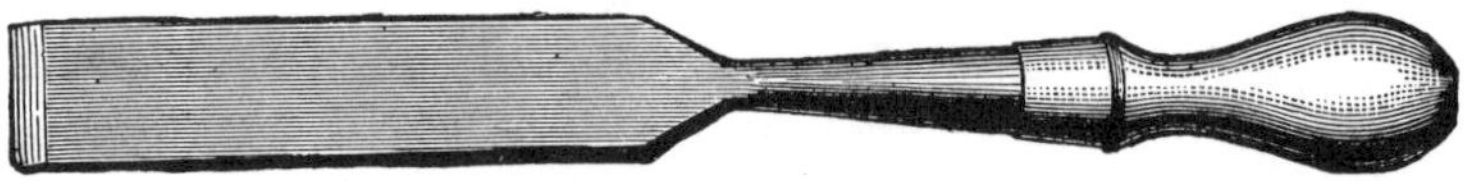

SOCKET FIRMER CHISELS.

Sizes	⅛	¼	⅜	½	⅝	¾	⅞	1	1¼	1½	1¾	2 in.
First Quality, Regular	....	....	....	....	....	....	....	....	....	....	....	....

BARTON'S SOLID STEEL SOCKET FIRMER CHISELS AND GOUGES.

Sizes	⅛	¼	⅜	½	⅝	¾	⅞	1	1¼	1½	1¾	2 in.
No. 97, Firmer Chisel, 6½ in. Blade	....	....	....	....	....	....	....	....	....	....	....	....
No. 100, Long Paring Chisel, 8 in. Blade	....	....	....	....	....	....	....	....	....	....	....	....
No. 101, Firmer Gouge, 6½ in. Blade	....	....	....	....	....	....	....	....	....	....	....	....
No. 104, Long Paring Chisel, 8 in. Blade	....	....	....	....	....	....	....	....	....	....	....	....

All of the above Handled. Either kind in sets, ⅛ to 2 in. (12 Chisels, 1 each of above sizes).

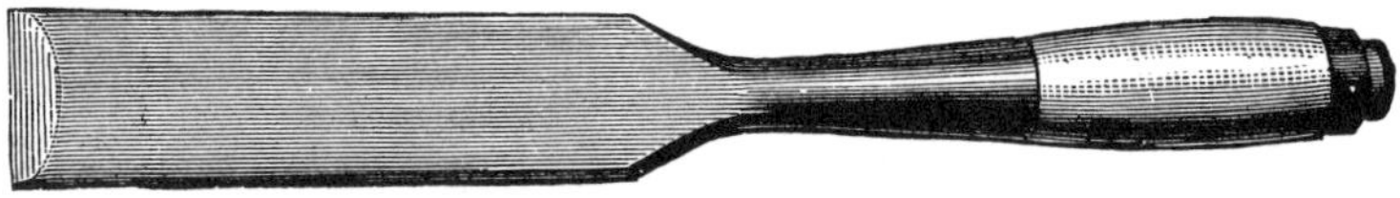

SOCKET FRAMING CHISELS.

Sizes	¼	⅜	½	⅝	¾	⅞	1	1¼	1½	1¾	2 in.
With Handles	....	....	....	....	....	....	....	....	....	....	....

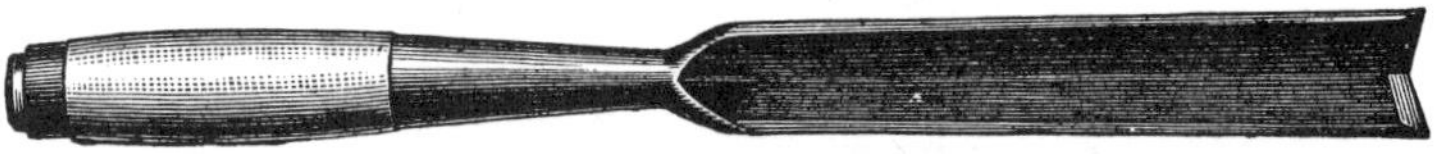

SOCKET CORNER CHISELS.

Sizes	½	¾	⅞	1	1⅛	1¼ in.
With Handles	....	....	....	....	....	....

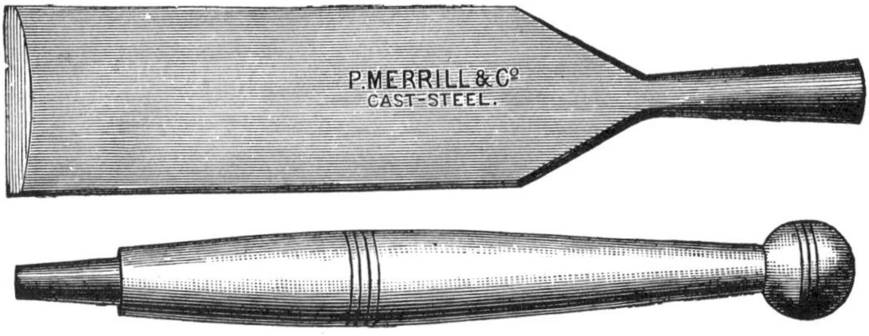

CARPENTERS' SLICKS.

Sizes	2½	3	3½	4 in.
With or without Handles	....	....	....	....

GERMAN STEEL SOCKET CHISELS.

Sizes	½	⅝	¾	⅞	1	1¼	1½	1¾	2 in.
Without Handles	....	....	....	....	....	....	....	....	....

TANGED MORTISING CHISELS.

Sizes	⅛	3-16	¼	5-16	⅜	7-16	½ in.
	....	....	....	....	....	....	....

S. J. ADDIS' CARVING TOOLS.

STRAIGHT.

SHORT BENT.

LONG BENT.

SWEEPS.

No. 1, No. 2

From	1-16 to ⅝	¾	⅞	1 in.
Per Doz	$3.60	$4.20	$4.80	$5.10

No. 3 to No. 9

Discount on Carving Chisels and Gouges......... ......

From	1-16 to ⅝	¾	⅞	1	1¼ in.
Straight	$4.20	$4.95	$5.55	$5.85	$ 8.10 Doz.
Long Bent	5.10	5.70	7.80	9.00	12.00 "
Short Bent	5.10	5.70	7.80	9.00	12.00 "

No. 10

From	1-16 to ½	⅝	¾ in.
Straight	$4.80	$4.80	$5.40 Doz.
Long Bent	5.10	6.30	7.80 "
Short Bent	5.10	6.30	7.80 "

No. 11

From	1-16 to ½	⅝	¾ in.
Straight	$5.40	$5.40	$7.20 Doz.
Long Bent	5.10	6.30	7.80 "
Short Bent	5.10	6.30	7.80 "

No. 41, No. 39, No. 45

From	1-16 to ½	⅝ in.
Straight Bent	$7.80	$7.80 Doz.
Long Bent	6.90	8.40 "
Short Bent	6.90	8.40 "

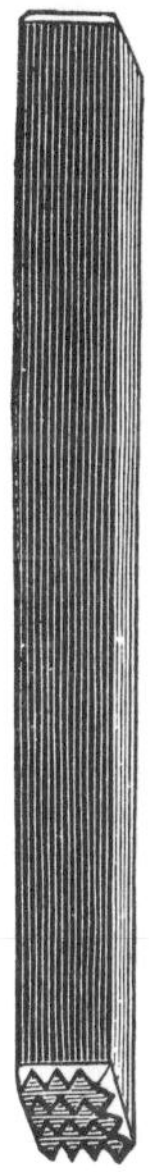

CARVERS' PUNCHES.

For producing a matted surface on carvings.

Per Doz. ....

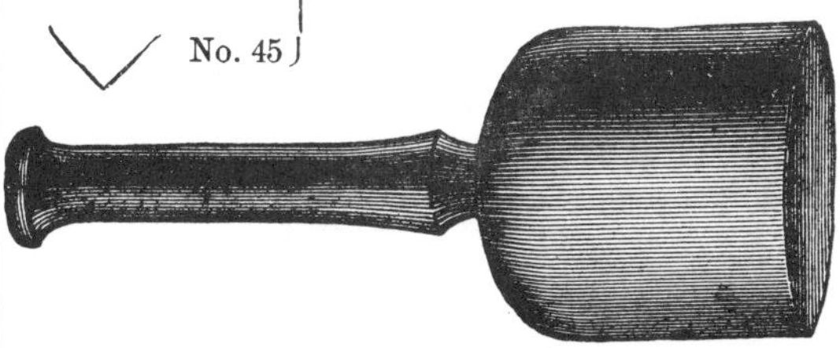

CARVERS' MALLET.

Lignumvitæ............... ......

DRAWING KNIVES AND SPOKE SHAVES.

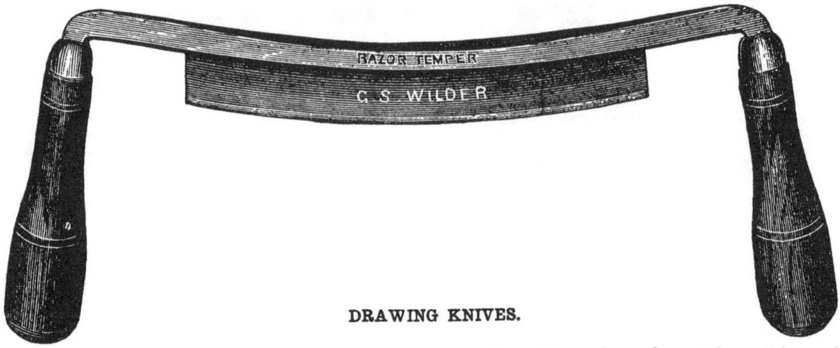

DRAWING KNIVES.

Inch	6	7	8	9	10	11	12
Common Razor Blade	....	....	....	....	....	....	....
Common Farmers	....	....	....	....	....	....	....
Barton's Razor Blade	....	....	....	....	....	....	....
Barton's Wagon, (Heavy)	....	....	....	....	....	....	....

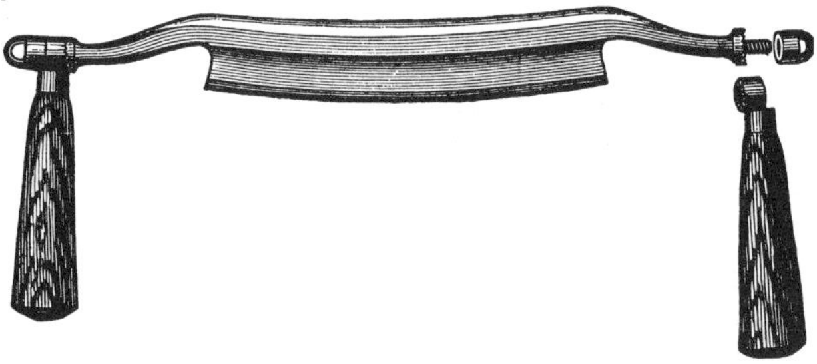

Adjustable Handle, Inch.. .... 7..... 8..... 9..... 10.....

SPOKE SHAVES.

Iron, No. 1 Plain............... ...... Iron, No. 7 Adjustable Cap......... ......

Iron, No. 2 Double........... ...... Iron, No. 9 Single Concave........... ......
Iron, No. 10, For Cutting inside Large or Small Circles........................ ......

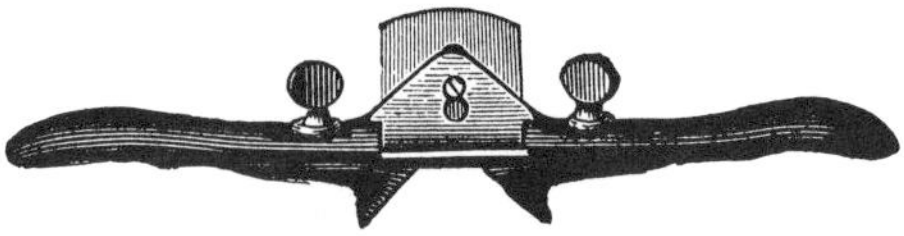

Patent Chamfer Spoke Shave ....

This Tool can be easily adjusted by means of the thumb-screws attached to the guides and will chamfer an edge any desired width up to 1½ inch.

Wood, Plain, Inch ... 2½..... 3..... With Plate, Inch ... 2½..... 3.....
Wood, with Plate and Adjustable Screw........................ 2½..... 3.....

AUGERS AND AUGER BITS.

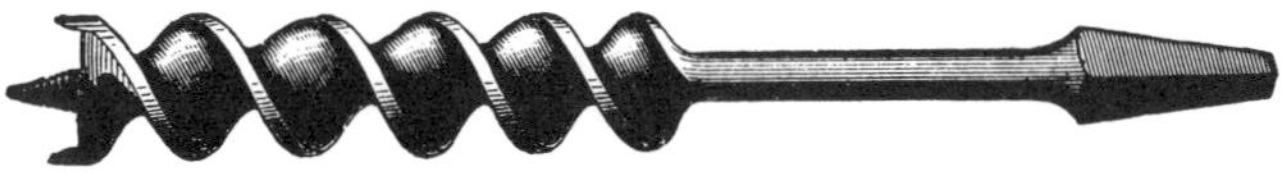

SOLID CAST STEEL AUGER BITS.—Extra.

3...... 4...... 5 ...., 6 .. .. 7...... 8 .... 9...... 10..... 11...... 12-16 in....
13..... 14...... 15...... 16 ..... 17...... 18...... 20 ..... 22...... 24-16 in....
In Sets, 24........ 32½ qrs. .... Discount........

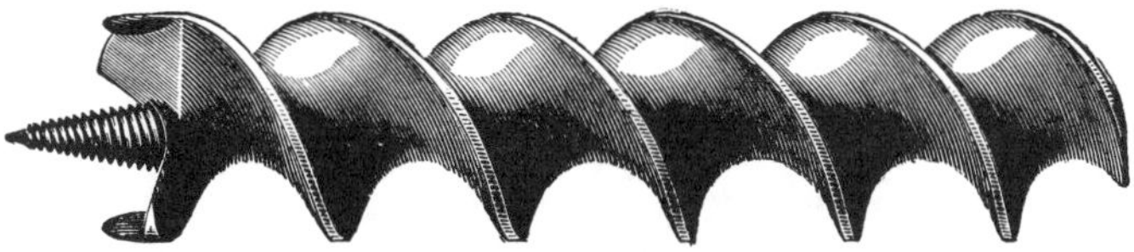

EXTENSION LIP AUGER BITS.

	3	4	5	6	7	8	9	10	11	12	13	14	15	16	18	20	24-16 in.
C. E. Jennings ...																	
Russell Jennings ..																	

In Sets, C. E. Jennings, 24 ... 32½ qrs.... Russell Jennings, 24.... 32½ qrs....
Discount........

LEWIS AUGER BITS.

3..... 4..... 5..... 6..... 7...... 8...... 9..... 10 ... 11. ... 12-16 in.....
13..... 14..... 15 ..... 16...... 17...... 18...... 20..... 22 .... 24-16 in.....
Discount........

COOK'S AUGER BITS.

3...... 4..... 5..... 6 ..... 7...... 8 .... 9..... 10 ..... 11...... 12-16 in....
13...... 14 .... 15 .... 16 ..... 17...... 18..... 20..... 22 .... 24-16 in .....
In Sets, 24 ..... 32½ qrs....... Discount ....

CAR BITS.—12 Inch Twist.

3 .... 4 .. 5 .... 6 ..... 7...... 8...... 9...... 10...... 11...... 12-16 in......
13 .... 14 ..... 15 ..... 16 ..... 17 .. 18..... 20 ..... 22 ... 24-16 in .....
Discount........

BORING MACHINE AUGERS.

½ to ⅞ ..... 1 .... 1⅛ ..... 1¼..... 1½..... 1¾..... 2 in .....
In Sets, 18...... 23 ..... 41 qrs. ..... Discount.......

CAST STEEL AUGERS.—With Nut.

½.... ⅝ .. ¾ ... ⅞.... 1.... 1¼ ... 1½ ... 1¾ ... 2 2¼ .. 2½ in.....
Discount........

SHIP AUGERS.—With or Without Screw.

½.. 9.. 10.. 11.. 12.. 13.. 14.. 15.. 16.. 17. 18.. 19.. 20.. 21.. 22 23 24-16 in...
Discount........

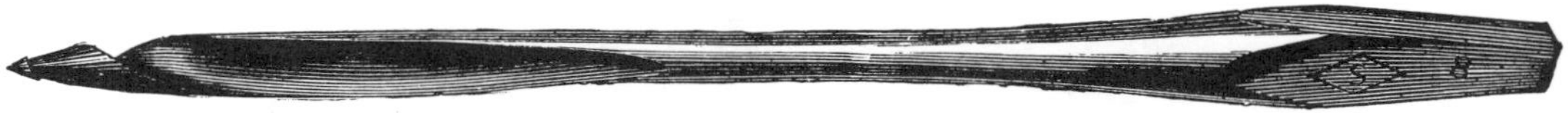

GERMAN PATTERN DIAMOND BITS.

Made from best quality Cast Steel, hardened and drawn to a very fine spring temper the entire length of the Bit.

Sizes.... 1.... 2.... 3.... 4.... 5.... 6.... 7.... 8.... 9.... 10.... 11.... 12-32....

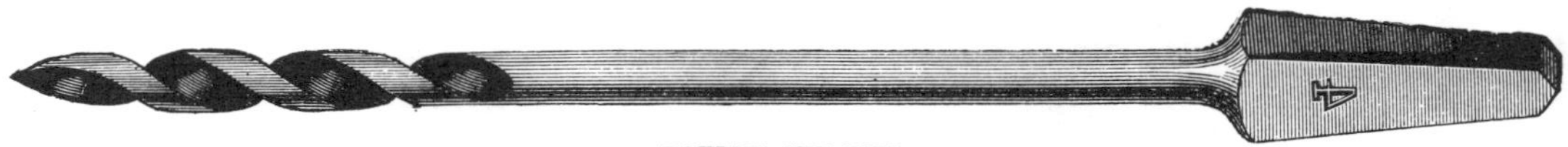

DOUBLE CUT BITS.

Nos............................ 0...... 1...... 2...... 3...... 4...... 5...... 6......

POD BITS.

Sizes .... 4...... 5 .... 6 .... 7...... 8 ..... 9...... 10-32 .....

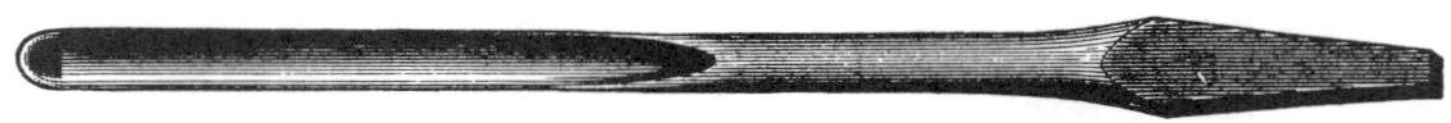

SPOON BITS.

Sizes................. 2.... 3.... 4 ... 5 ... 6.... 7.... 8.... 9.... 10... 12-32 ....

GOUGE BITS.

Sizes .... 2.... 3.... 4 ... 5.... 6.... 7.... 8.... 9 .. 10.... 12-32....

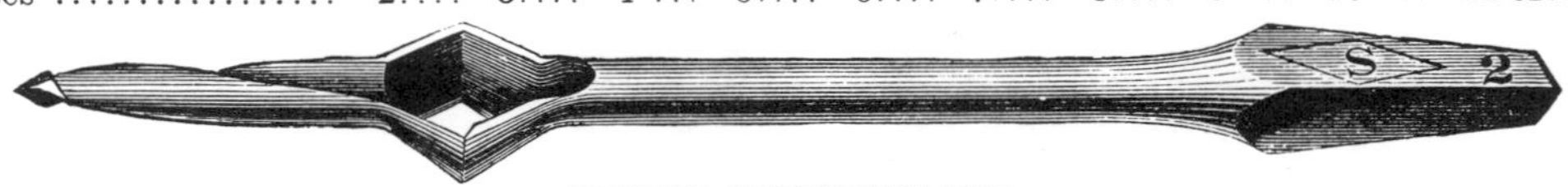

DIAMOND COUNTERSINK BITS.

Nos.. 0...... 1...... 2...... 3...... 4......

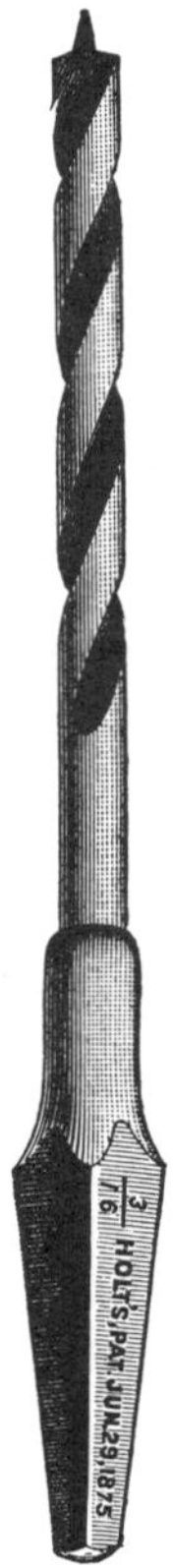

HOLT'S PATENT GIMLET BITS.

Sizes.......................... 3...... 4...... 5...... 6...... 7...... 8-32......

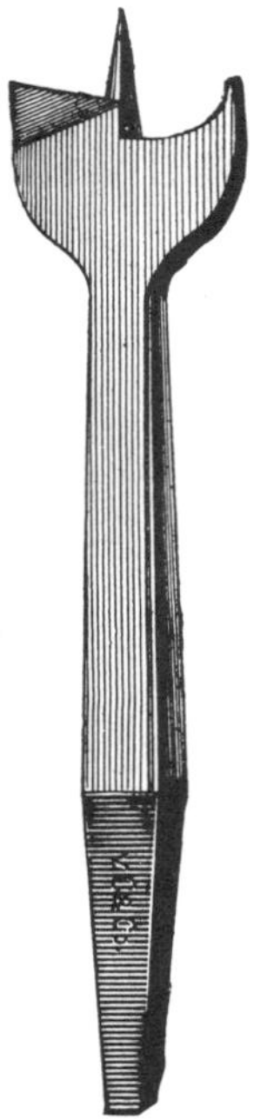

CENTER BITS.

Size...... ¼ to 1.... 1⅛.... 1¼.... 1⅜.... 1½.... 1⅝.... 1¾.... 2 in....

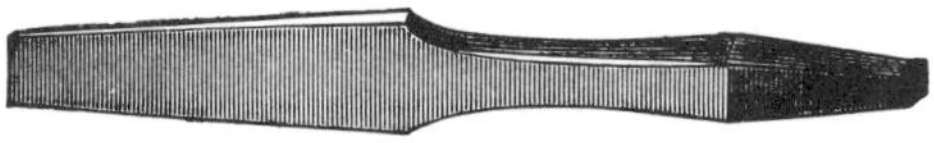

SCREW DRIVER BITS.

Nos. .... 0...... 1...... 2...... 3...... Assorted, 0 to 3

REAMERS.

Square........................ ...... Half Round........................ ......

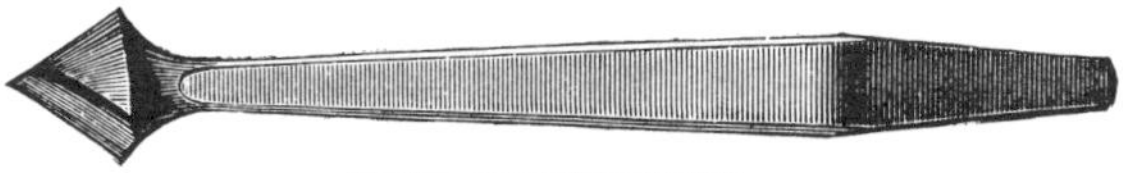

SNAIL COUNTERSINKS.

For Wood.. ......

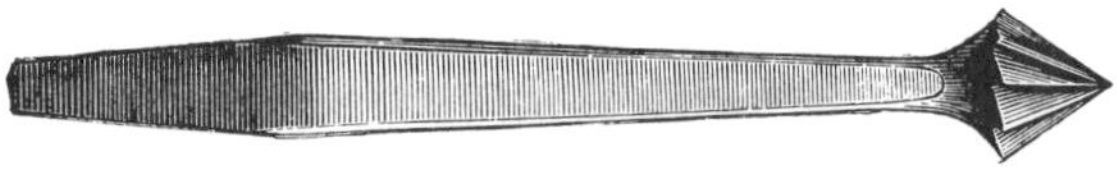

ROSE COUNTERSINKS.

For Iron or Brass.................................... ......

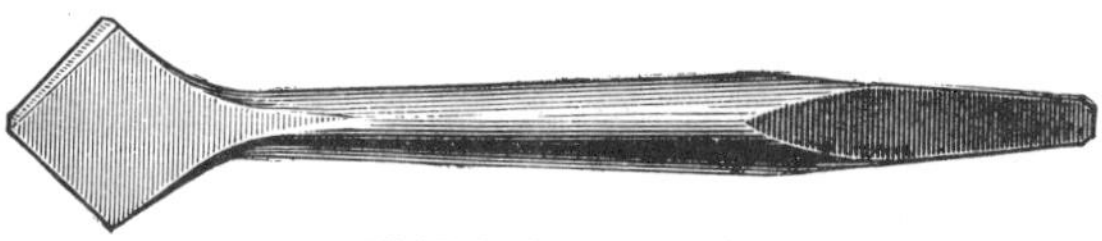

FLAT COUNTERSINKS.

For Iron ....

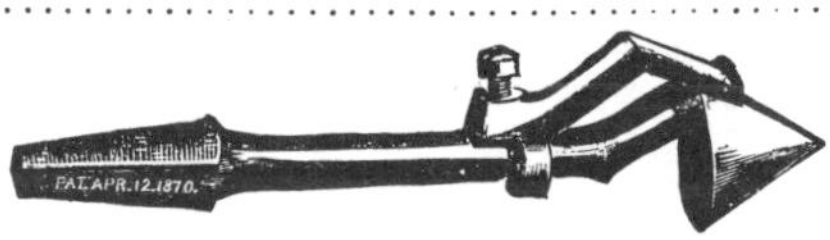

WHEELER'S PATENT COUNTERSINKS.

With Guage............ ...... Without Guage........ ......

BARBER'S PATENT COUNTERSINKS.

It can be used on any bit or drill not over one-quarter inch, and will not turn on the bit. It regulates the depth to be bored.

Price.......... ......

EXPANSIVE BITS.

Clark's, Small, Bores from ½ to 1½ in ....
" Large, " " ⅞ to 3 in...... ......
Derby, No. 1, " " ¾ to 2 in...... ......
" No. 2, " " ⅞ to 3 in...... ......

Clark's.

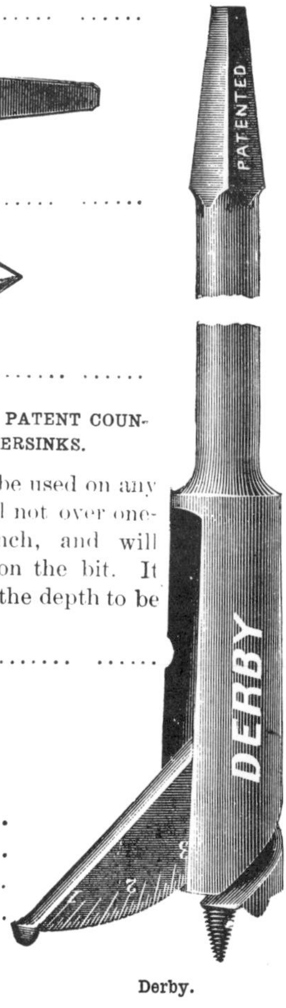

Derby.

GIMLETS AND WASHER CUTTERS.

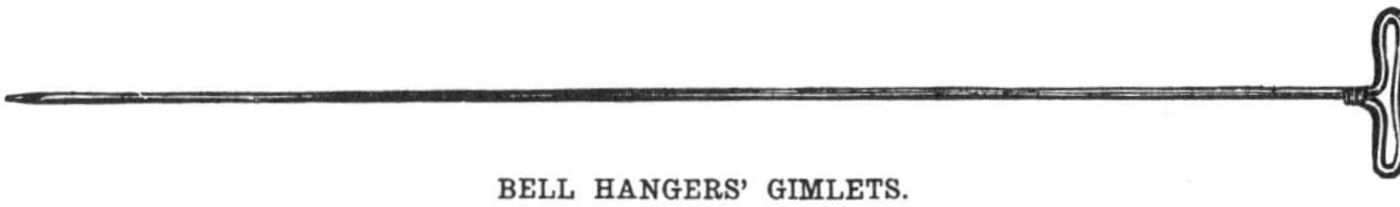

BELL HANGERS' GIMLETS.

¼ and 5-16 Inch, With Wood or Metal Handle ....

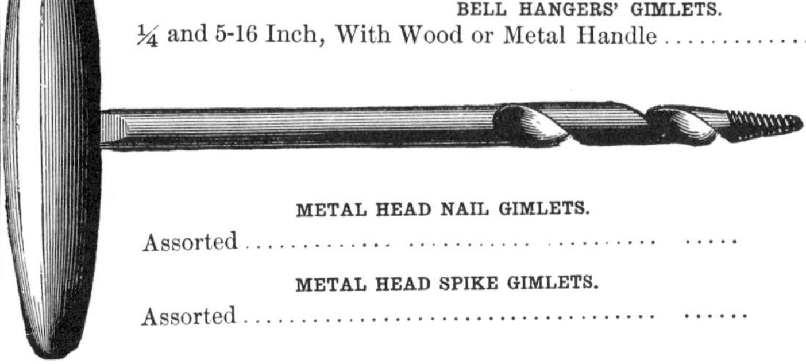

METAL HEAD NAIL GIMLETS.

Assorted ....

METAL HEAD SPIKE GIMLETS.

Assorted ....

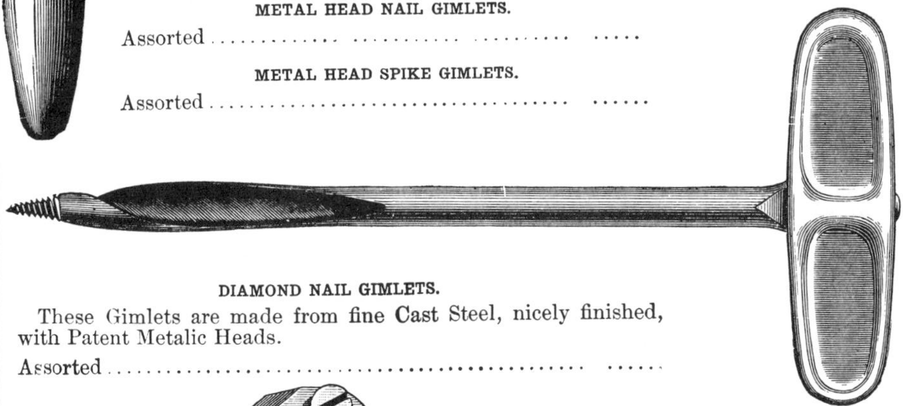

DIAMOND NAIL GIMLETS.

These Gimlets are made from fine Cast Steel, nicely finished, with Patent Metalic Heads.

Assorted ....

THE BEST COUNTERSINK.--For Metal or Wood.

Fits all Drills and Bits, from 1-16 to 3-16 inch. Can be sharpened quickly and easily. Costs very little money. Per doz.. ......

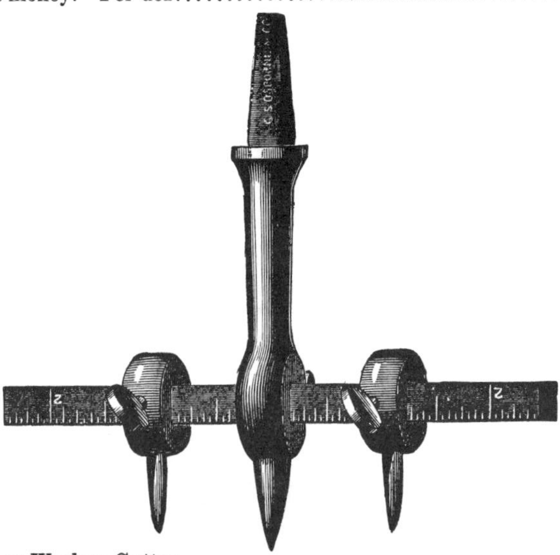

No. 45, Rosette or Washer Cutter ....

This is the Osborn Cutter; buy it in preference to all others.

BRACES.

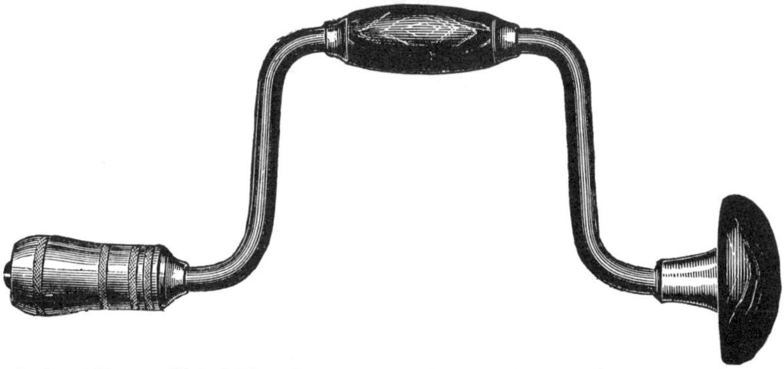

Barber's Steel Brace, Nickel Plated .. 6.... 8.... 10.... 12 .. 14 in. Sweep ...
Barker's Wrought Iron Brace, Plain. .... 8.... 10.... 12.... "

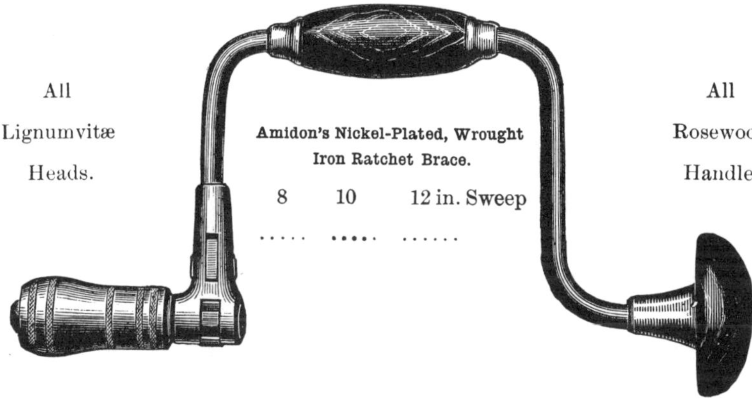

All Lignumvitæ Heads.

Amidon's Nickel-Plated, Wrought Iron Ratchet Brace.

8 10 12 in. Sweep

....

All Rosewood Handles.

Barber's Nickle-Plated, Steel Ratchet Brace.......... 8.... 10.... 12 in. Sweep....

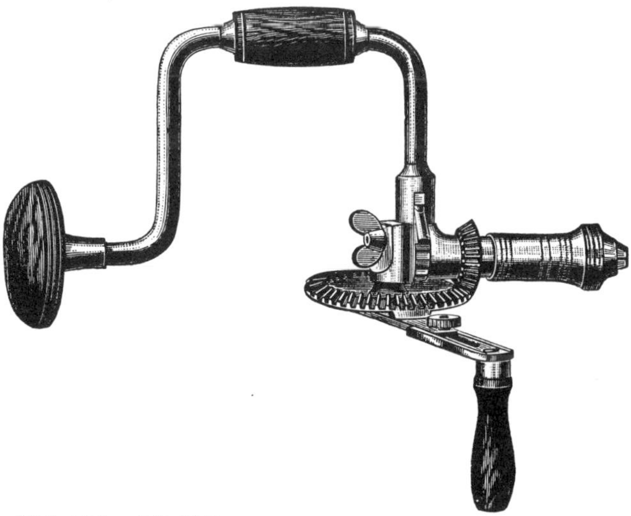

Millers Falls Nickel-Plated Drill Brace ....

The Gear Wheel can be removed on this, leaving a Ratchet Brace.

Robinson's Crank Wrench and Bit Brace ....

BRACES AND BIT HOLDERS.

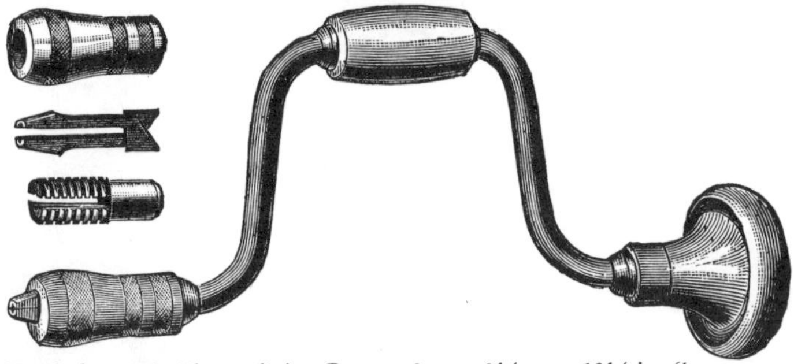

Bartholomew's Cheap Gripe Brace, 8.... 9½.... 10½ in. Sweep....

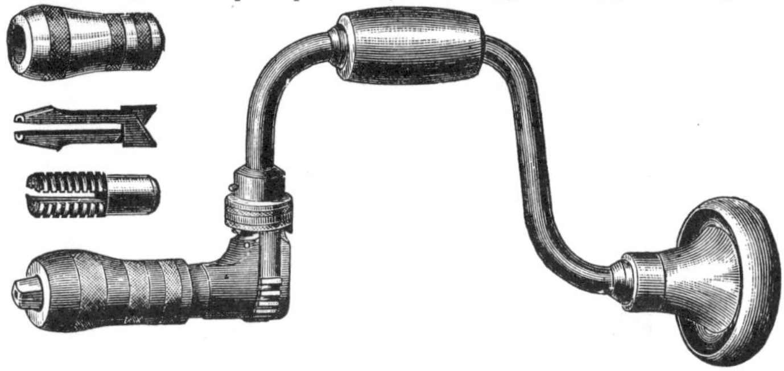

Bartholomew's Cheap Ratchet Brace...............10 in. Sweep.... .

Extension Bit Holder, Nickel Plated ....

Angular Bit Stock, Nickel-Plated...........................

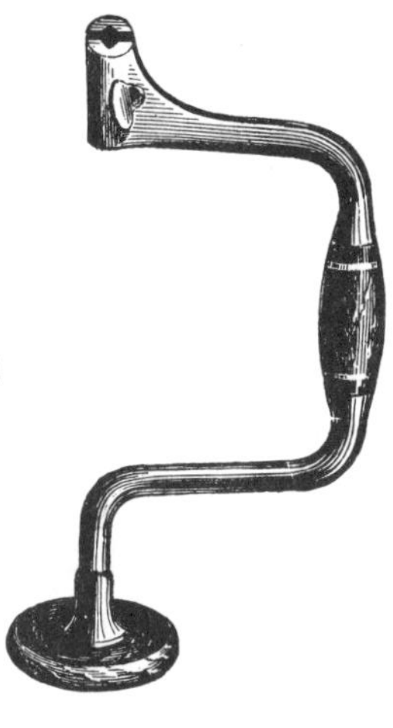

Spafford's Brace, Nickel Plated, Cocobolo Wood Head and Handle, ...

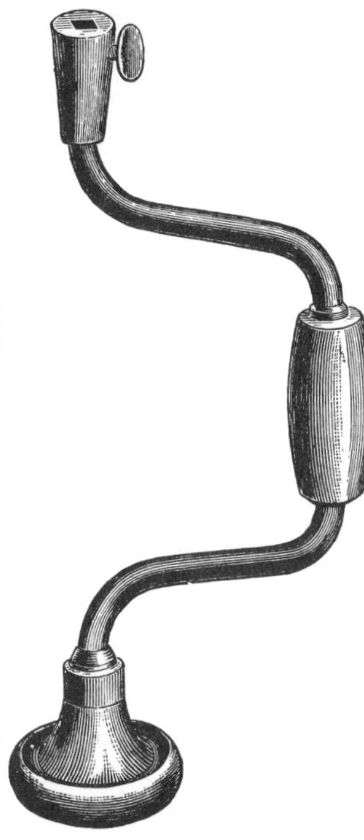

Ball Braces, No. 25, 8½ in. Sweep........ No. 30, 10 in. Sweep. ......
Made of Bright Malleable Iron, Nice Finished Handles.

HOLLOW AUGERS AND POINTERS.

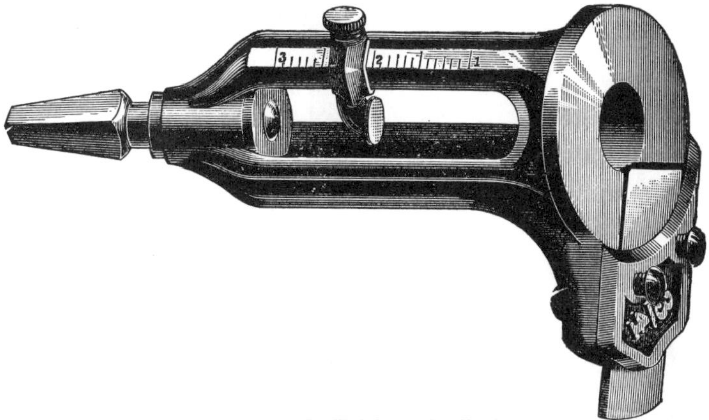

STEARN'S PATENT HOLLOW AUGERS.

The best single size Hollow Auger in the market, and the only one in which a stop, cperated upon a graduated scale, regulates the length of tenon.

Size	5-16	3/8	7-16	1/2	9-16	5/8	3/4	7/8	1 in.
No. 6 Without Bits	....	....	....	....	....	....	....	....	....

STEARN'S PATENT ADJUSTABLE HOLLOW AUGERS.

This justly popular Auger is made of steel, wrought and malleable iron, leaving no chance for breaking. The pivoted jaws, which move uniformly and center perfectly, are provided with a graduated scale or rule, by which the size of the tenon is regulated. To secure required length of tenon, a movable stop is operated upon a graduated scale, with rulings to sixteenths, adjustable from 1/4 to 1 1/4 inches.

No. 3 ....

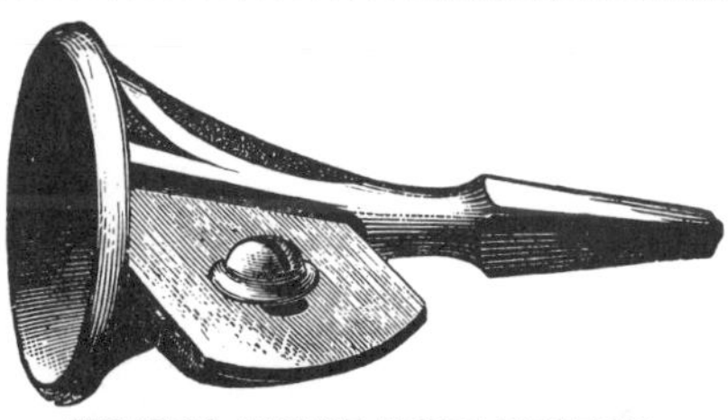

STEARN'S PATENT SPOKE POINTERS.

Have the knife held with two screws, and cut a much longer taper than the old style pointer. Will leave the spoke the exact size required for Hollow Auger.

No. 1 .... No. 2 ....

Dowel Pointers, pointing from 0 to 3/4. (See Cut) ....

VAJEN & NEW, INDIANAPOLIS, IND.

COOPERS' TOOLS.

BARTON'S TOOLS.

Adzes, No. 1...... 2......

Hollowing Shaves........ 7...... 8 in......

Froes, 8.... 9.... 10.... 12.... 14 in....

Hickory Drivers.

....

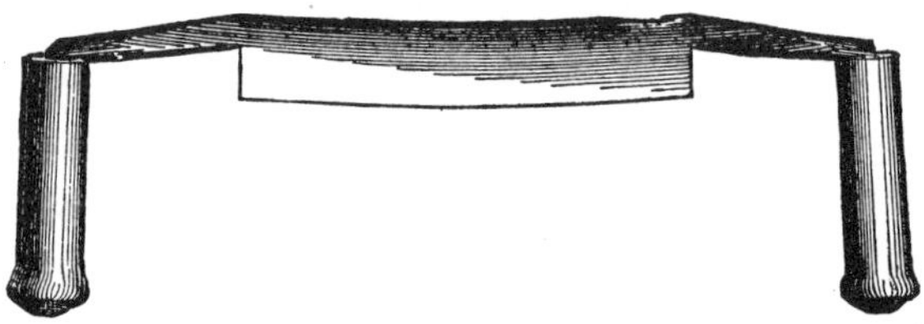

Heading Shaves.................................. 10...... 11 in... ..

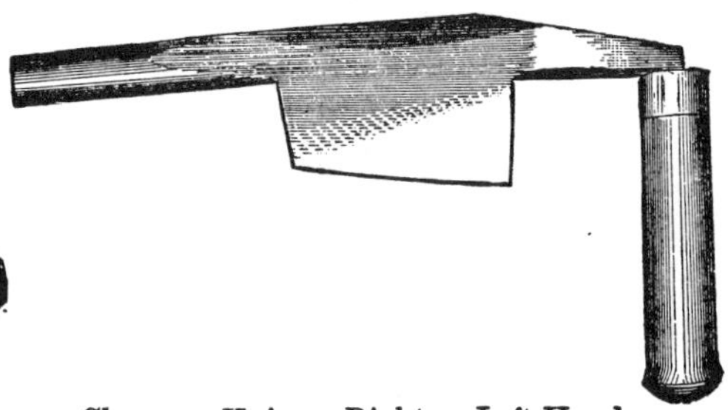

Champer Knives, Right or Left Hand.
5 5½...... 6 in......

Oval Driver.

......

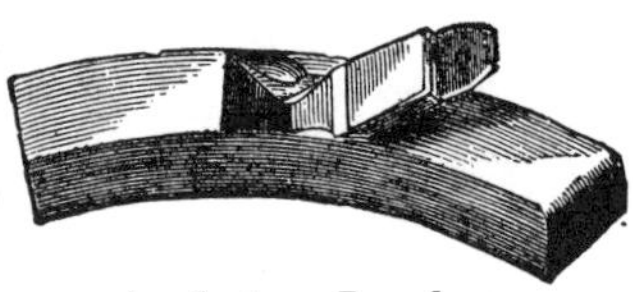

Apple-tree Levelers.

....

Hammers, Steel Face.
3½ to 4½ lbs... ..

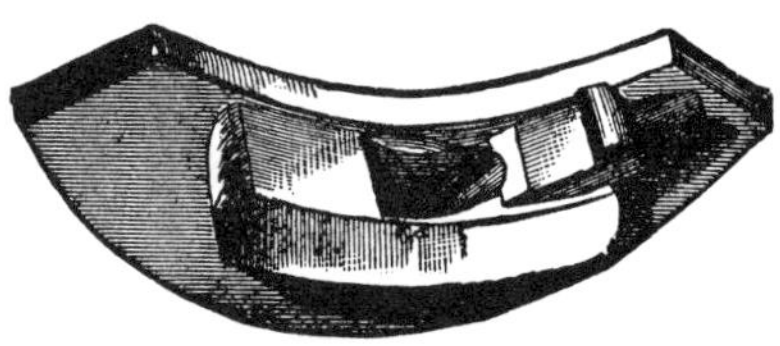

Tight Barrel Howels.

....

Spoke Shaves............

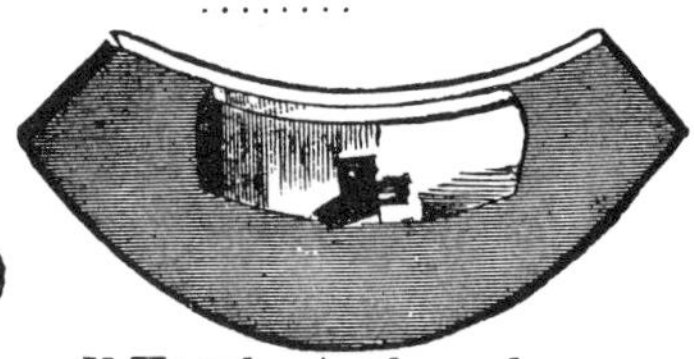

V Howels, Applewood.......

Coopers' Axes, Stave Shaves, Backing Shaves, Hoop Shaves, Paring Shaves, Scrapers, V Irons, Dowel Bits, Compasses, Tight and Oil Barrel Croze, Head Floats and Jointers, a full line in stock. Tress Hoops to order.

IRON BENCH SCREWS AND CLAMP HEADS.

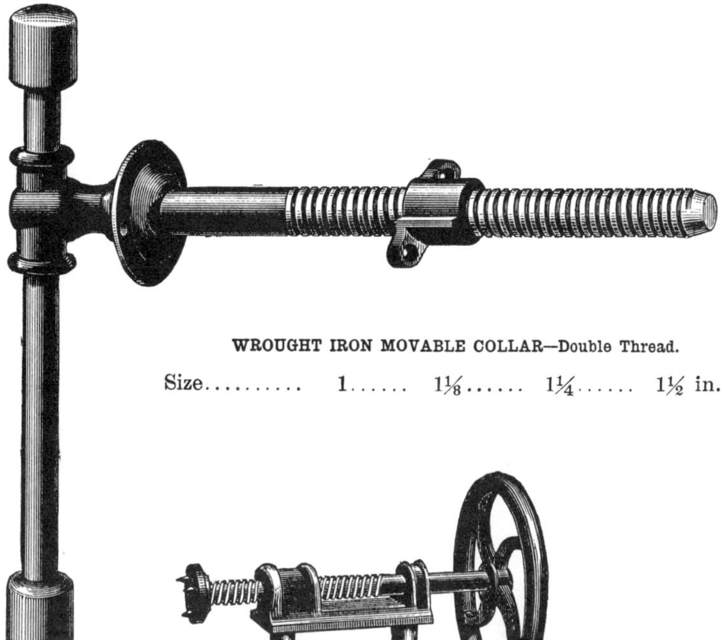

WROUGHT IRON MOVABLE COLLAR—Double Thread.

Size.......... 1...... 1⅛...... 1¼...... 1½ in.......

CARPENTERS' CLAMP SCREWS.

Wrought Screws, Double Thread.

No. 1............................ ...... No. 2.......................... ......

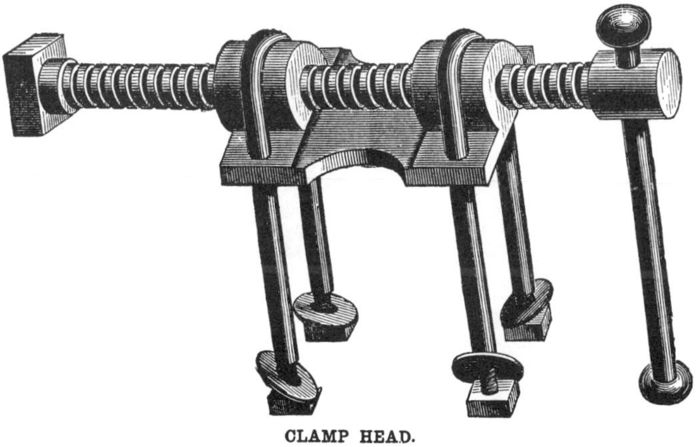

CLAMP HEAD.

No. 12, Wrought Screw, Double Thread.

Size... 1 .... 1⅛...... 1¼ in.......

BENCH SCREWS AND HAND SCREWS.

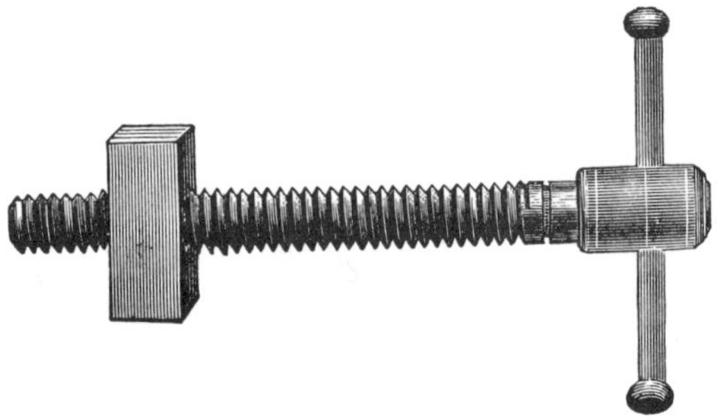

WOOD BENCH SCREWS.

V Thread, No. 185

Inch........ 2¼..... 2½ .....

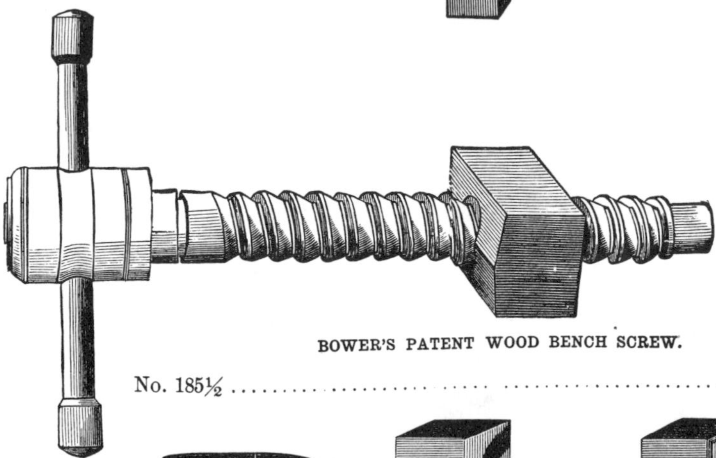

BOWER'S PATENT WOOD BENCH SCREW.

No. 185½ .... 2½......

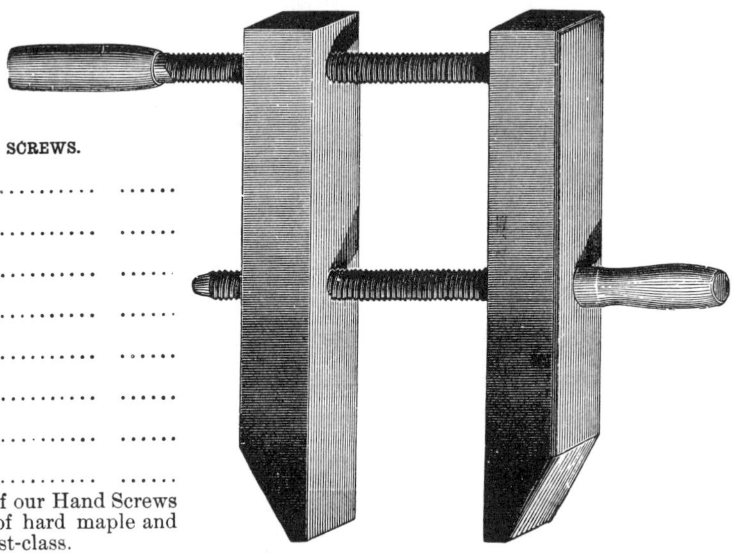

HAND SCREWS.

6 in.................. ......

8 in.................. ......

10 in.................. ......

12 in.................. ......

14 in.................. ......

16 in.................. ......

18 in.................. ......

20 in.................. ......

The jaws of our Hand Screws are all made of hard maple and are strictly first-class.

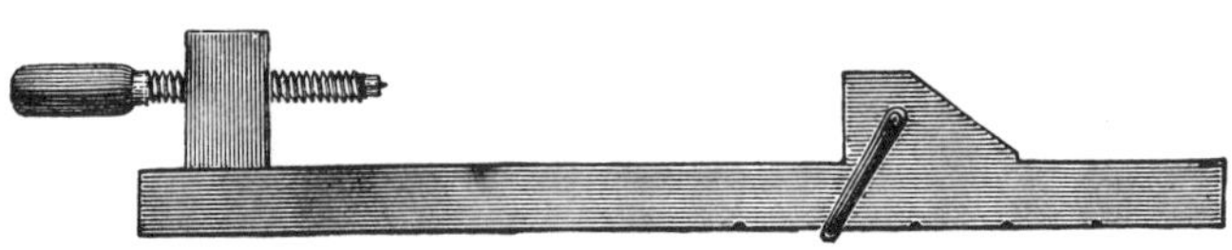

CABINET CLAMPS.

To Open.. 3..... 4..... 5 feet......

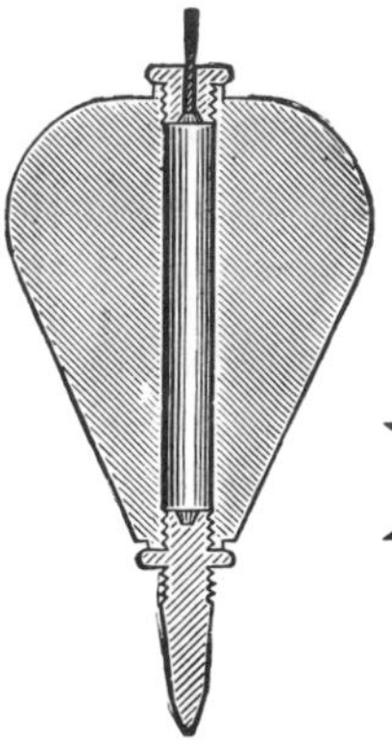

VAJEN'S PATENT REVERSIBLE PLUMB BOB.

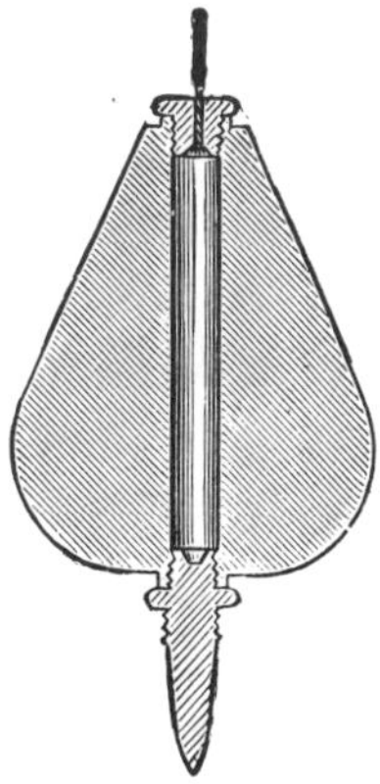

Patented November 14, 1882.

This new and perfect Plumb Bob, designed to overcome all the disadvantages of other Plumb Bobs, is capable of being adjusted to any and all the forms required by the Millwright, Mechanic and Civil Engineer, has no equal. It has the only proper shape for a Bob, having a hole extending entirely through it, with a reversible, well-tempered Steel Point and Screw Cap, which, being interchangeable, enables the Bob to be suspended in the several positions as shown in cuts. The hole in the center of the Bob affording protection for the point when not in use. By filing the shoulder the Bob can always be adjusted and made true. The Plumb Bob is made of brass and nickel-plated, furnishing as pretty and as valuable a tool as there is in the market. We recommend it in preference to all other combination bobs, and guarantee it to give perfect satisfaction. In four sizes.
1 Pound....... $2; 2 Pound ....$2.50; 3 Pound........$3; 4 Pound....... $4.
Discount to the trade..........

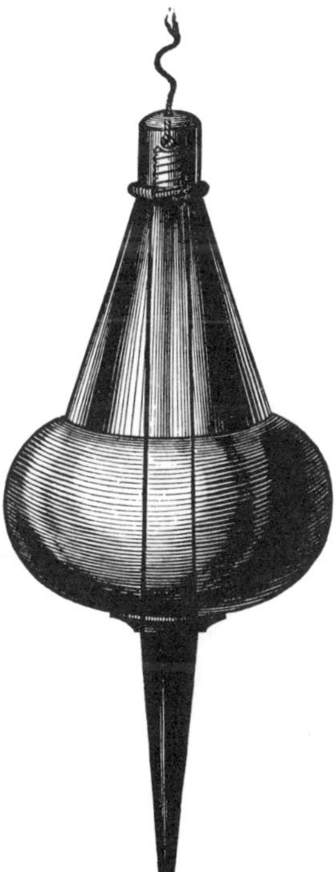

Sam Smith Bob.
Brass with Steel Point.
2 lb.... 2¾ lb.... 3½ lb....

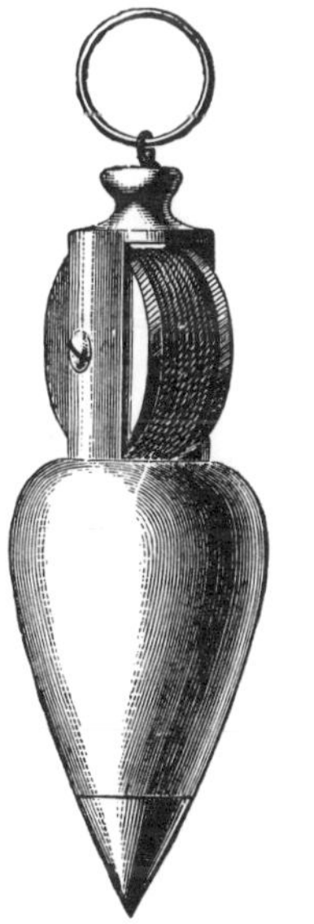

Stanley Bob.
With Reel and Line.
Iron ....
Bronze Metal.. ......

Bergen Bob.—Cut ½ Size.
Forged Steel, Weight 12 ounces, Furnished with Wooden Shell and Line. Nickel-Plated.... ......

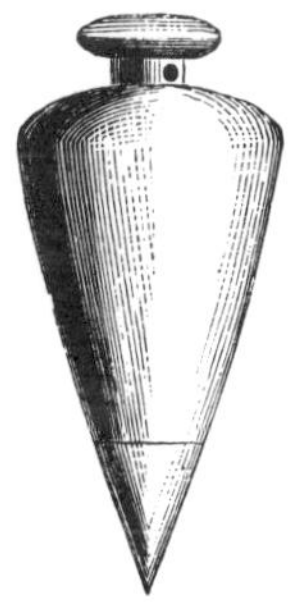

Brass Bob.—Steel Point.
5, 6½ oz.... 6, 12 oz....

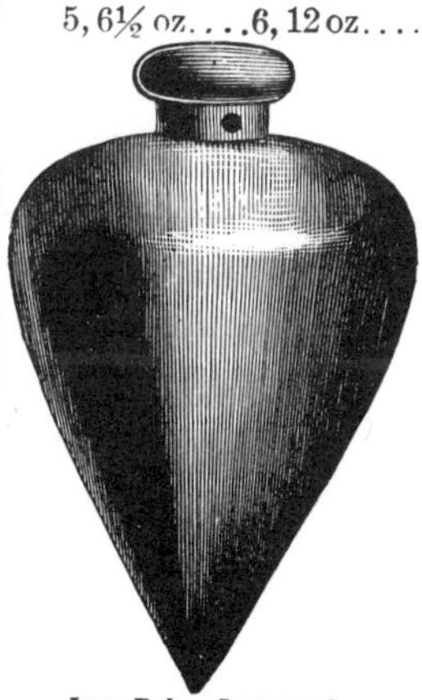

Iron Bob.—Japanned.
No.00, 18 oz.... 0, 42 oz....

Masons' Lead Bob.
Nos. 1 2 3
¾ lb...... 1¼ lb...... 2 lb......

MISCELLANEOUS TOOLS.

HAM TRYERS.

Best Cast Steel.. ......

NAIL SETS.

Round........................ ...... Octagon.................................. ......

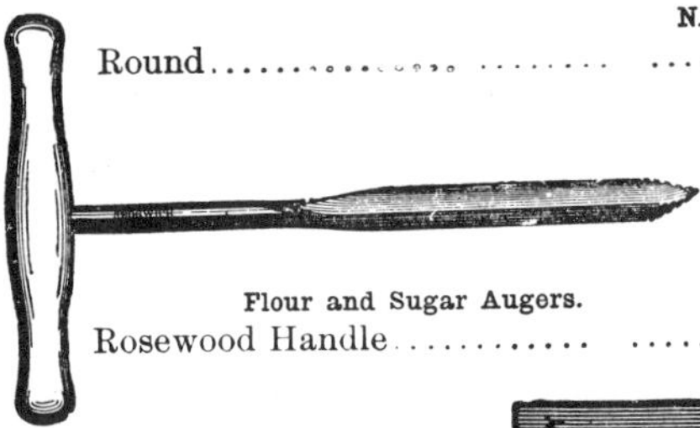

Flour and Sugar Augers.

Rosewood Handle............ ......

Saddlers' or Drive Punches.

Nos. 1 to 5.... 6 to 10.... 11 to 15....

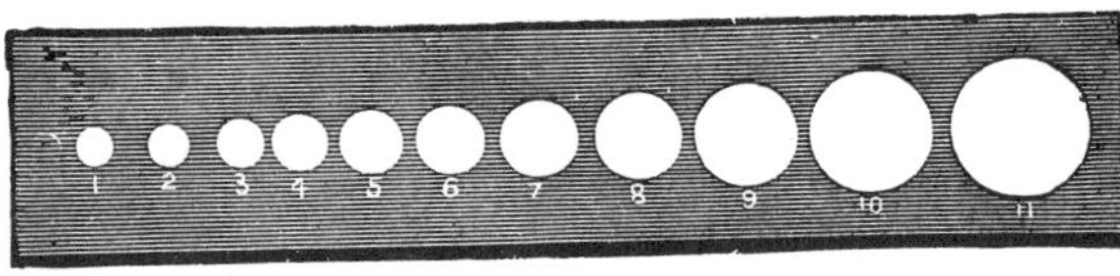

Belt Awls.

Cast Steel.......... ......

Plate Showing Sizes of Punches, Nos. 1 to 11.

Box Scrapers.

Double Handle........... ......

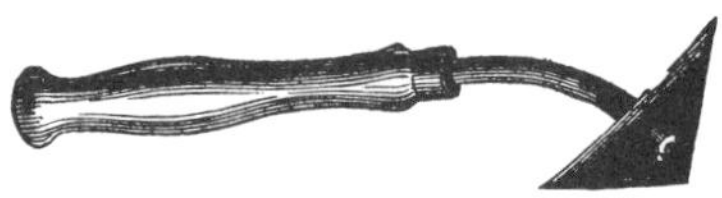

Triangular Box Scraper.

Solid Cast Steel Blade................. ......

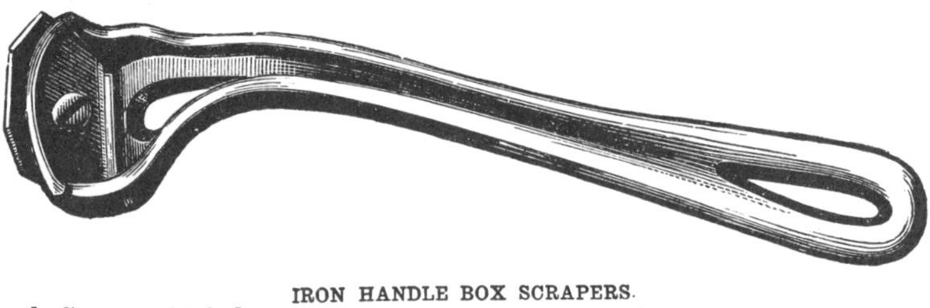

IRON HANDLE BOX SCRAPERS.

Japanned, Cast Steel Blade.. ......

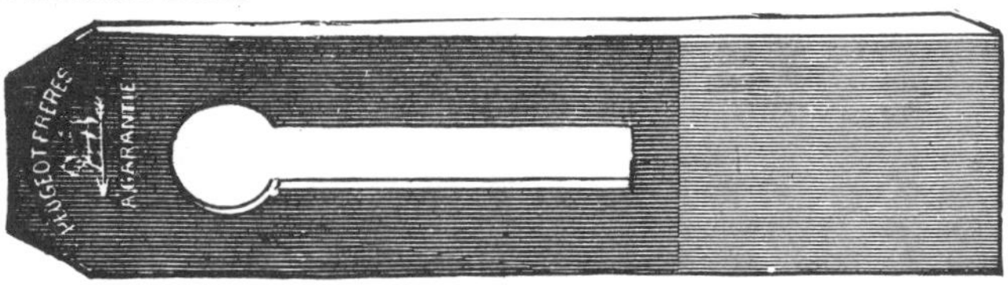

PLANE IRONS.

Inch	1¾	1⅞	2	2⅛	2¼	2⅜	2½	2⅝	2¾	3
Cut Single	....	...	....	....	....	....	....	....	....	....
Double	....	...	....	....	....	....	....	....	....	....

TRY SQUARES AND BEVELS.

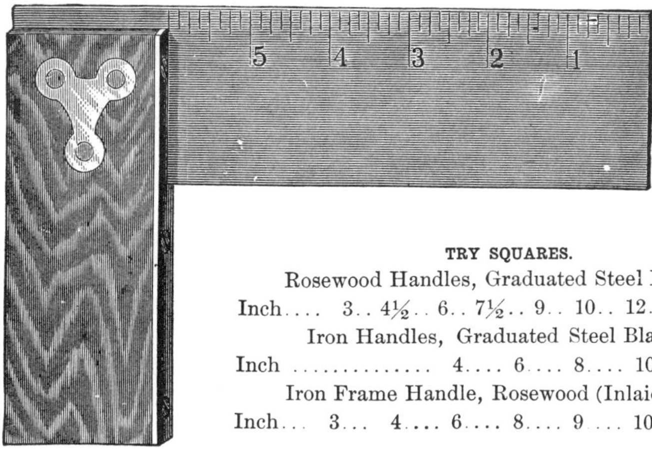

TRY SQUARES.

Rosewood Handles, Graduated Steel Blades.

Inch.... 3.. 4½.. 6.. 7½.. 9.. 10.. 12.. 15.. 18.

Iron Handles, Graduated Steel Blades.

Inch .... 4.... 6.... 8.... 10 . . 12....

Iron Frame Handle, Rosewood (Inlaid) Sides.

Inch... 3... 4.... 6.... 8.... 9.... 10.... 12....

Try Square and Bevel Combined,..............................Inch 6...... 8......

Plumb and Level Try Square,....................................Inch 7½.... ......

Improved Mitre Try Square, Cast Brass Handles,................Inch 7½.... ......

Patent Adjustable Try Squares.

Iron Handle, Graduated Steel Blade.

Inch........... 4.... 6....

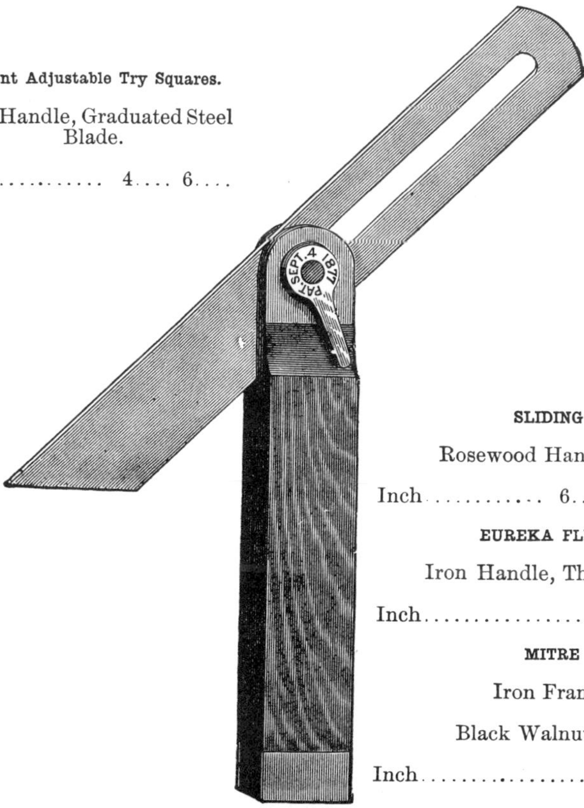

SLIDING T BEVELS.

Rosewood Handle, Brass Lever.

Inch........... 6.... 8.... 10.... 12....

EUREKA FLUSH T BEVELS.

Iron Handle, Thumb Screw at End.

Inch.................. 6.... 8.... 10....

MITRE SQUARES.

Iron Frame Handles.

Black Walnut (Inlaid) Sides.

Inch.................. 8.... 10.... 12....

STEEL AND COMBINATION SQUARES.

PLAIN STEEL SQUARES.

No.	Length.	Width.	Marked.	Polished.	Nickeled.
100,	2 ft.,	2 in.,	1-32, 1-16, 1-12, 1-10, 1-8, Brace and Board Meas......	......	......
2,	2 ft.,	2 in.,	1-16, 1-12, 1-8, 1-4, " " "	......	......
3,	2 ft.,	2 in.,	1-16, 1-12, 1-4, " " "	......	......
7,	2 ft.,	2 in.,	1-8, 1-4, 1 in., Board Measure	......	......
10,	1 ft.,	1½ in.,	1-12, 1-8, 1-4	......	......
12,	1 ft.,	1½ in.,	1-16, 1-12, 1-8	......	......

EAGLE SQUARES.

No.	Length.	Width.	Marked.	Polished.	Nickeled.
13,	2 ft.,	2 in.,	1-8, 1-4, 1 in., Brace and Board Measure......	......	......
14,	2 ft.,	2 in.,	1-8, 1-4, 1 in., " "	......	......

IRON SQUARES.

No.	Length.	Width.	Marked.	Polished.	Nickeled.
21,	2 ft.,	1½ in.,	1-8, one side	......	......
22,	2 ft.,	1½ in.,	1-8, two sides	......	......
24,	2 ft.,	2 in.,	1-8 " "	......	......

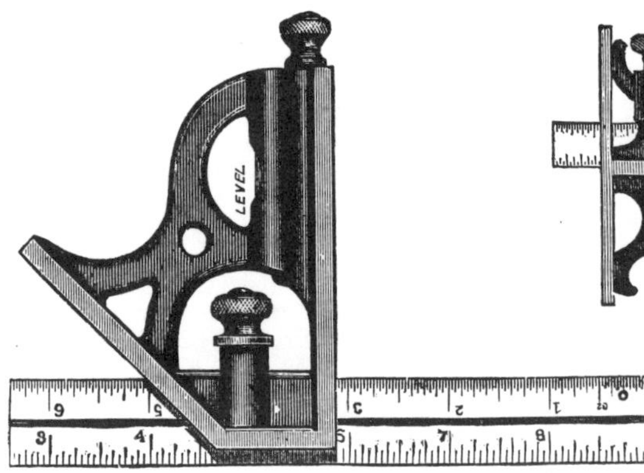

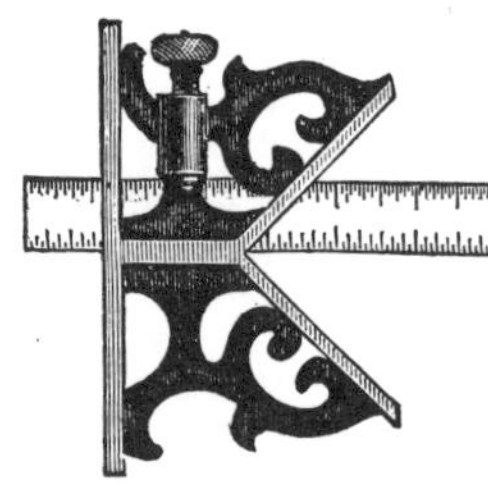

Chaplin's Patent Square and Mitre, Spirit Level and Plumb, Center Square, Draughtsman's T Square, Scribe and Marking Gauge.... ......

CENTER OR UNIVERSAL SQUARE.

A Mitre Head, Center Head and Adjustable Blade constitute a Set Complete.

Inch............ .... 6...... 9......

COMPASSES AND CALLIPERS.

COMPASSES.

Cast-Steel.

4 . . . 5 . . . 6 . .. 7 . . 8 . . 9 . . . 10 in . . .

COMPASS DIVIDERS.

Spring and Set Screw, Cast-Steel.

6 . . . 7 . . . 8. . . 9. . . 10. . . 12 . . 15 in . .

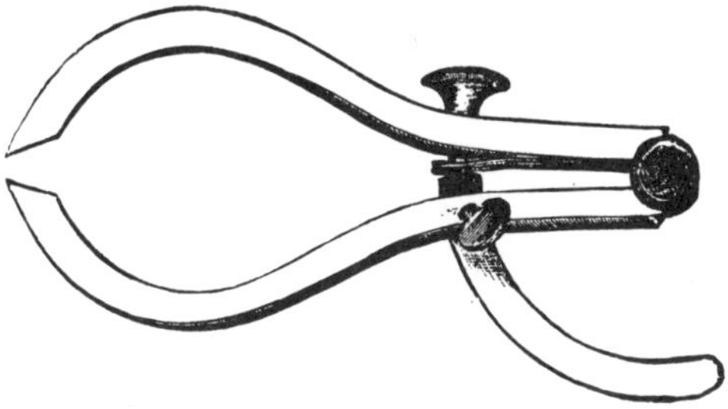

WING CALLIPERS.

Spring and Set Screw, Cast Steel.

5. 6. . . 7. . . 8. . . 10. . . 12. . . 15 in. . .

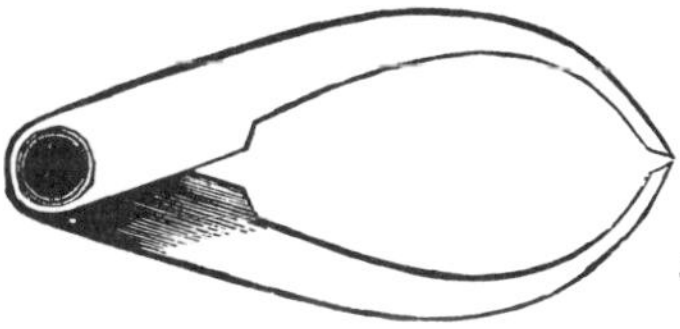

OUTSIDE CALLIPERS.

Cast-Steel.

3 . . . 4 . . . . 5 . . . . 6 . . 7 . . . 8 . . . 9 . . . 10 . . . 12 in . . .

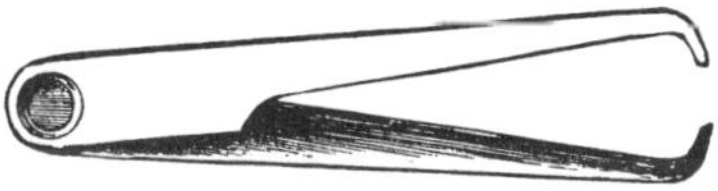

INSIDE CALLIPERS.

Cast Steel.

3 . . . . 4 . . . . 5 . . . . 6 . . . 7 . . . 8 . 9 . . 10 . . . 12 in . . .

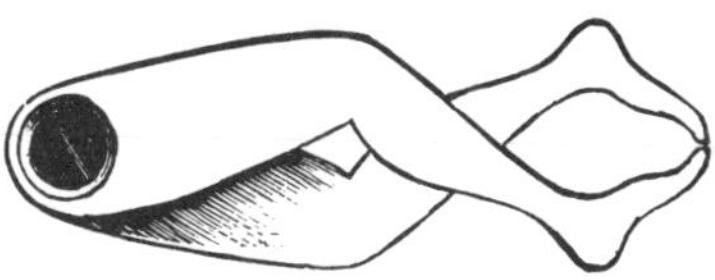

FANCY CALLIPERS.

Cast-Steel.

2½ in. . . . .

DOUBLE CALLIPERS.

Cast-Steel. For Measuring Inside or Outside.

3 . . . . 4 . . . 5 . . . . 6 in . . .

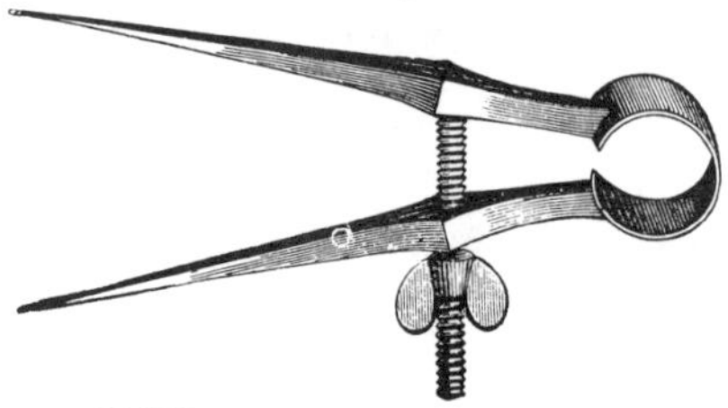

SPRING DIVIDERS.

Polished Cast-Steel.

Inch 2 to 6...... 7...... 8...... 10......

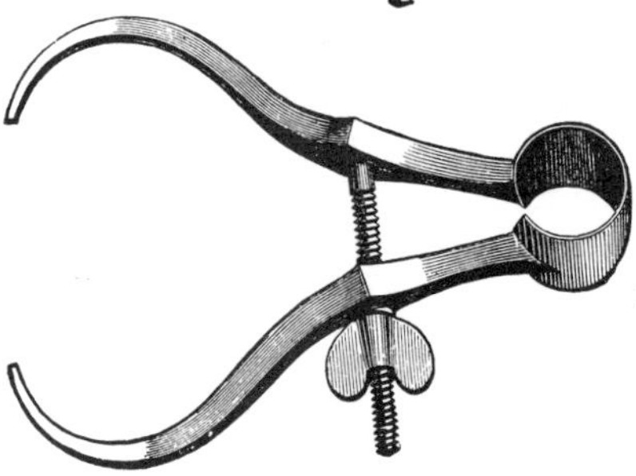

SPRING CALLIPERS.

Polished Cast-Steel.

Inch, 2 to 6...... 7...... 8...... 10......

This cut represents Cooke's Dividers with Calliper Points, which can be substituted for Steel Points, and will answer for Wood Turners and Machinists.

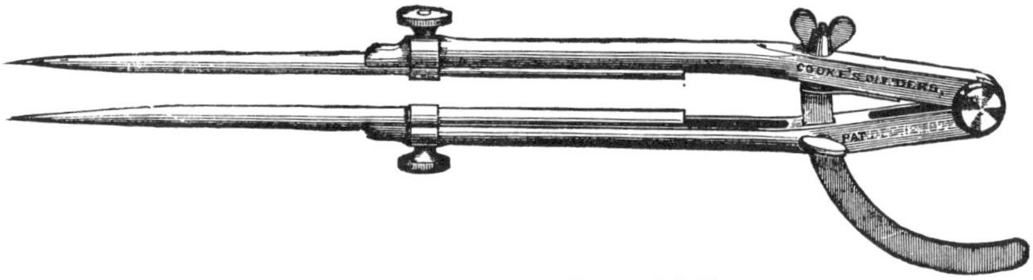

Cooke's Patent Extension Dividers and Callipers.

These Dividers answer every purpose of the Common Dividers, and give the advantage of an extension point, use of a pen or pencil, and use of Calliper Points. Adapted to the requirements of Architects, Machinists, Pattern Makers, Wheelwrights, Stair-Builders, Carpenters, in fact there is hardly a trade where they will not be in demand as soon as the goods are known.

2 Extension Points, 6...... 7...... 8...... 10 in ...... Calliper Points..........
1 Extension Point, 6...... 7...... 8...... 10 in ......

TIMBER SCRIBE.

Small.... .... Large............................ ......

HANDLES.

AUGER HANDLES.

Common, Assorted Regular .... Assorted Large ....
Adjustable, in Sets of Two, holding any size auger ....

CROSS CUT SAW HANDLES.

Common ....

AXE HANDLES.

Shaved, Oval .... Octagon ....
Turned, Extra .... No. 1 ....

Broad Axe Handles.

Reversible ....

ADZE HANDLES.

Carpenters', 32 in ....

HATCHET HANDLES.

No. 1, 13 in. .... No. 2, 14 in. .... No. 3, 15 in. ....

Broad Hatchet Handles.

Inch .... 16 .... 17 .... 18 ....

HAMMER HANDLES.

Round Eye, Inch		14	15	16 ....
Adze " "		13	14	15 ....
Riveting, "	10	11	12	13 ....
Machinists, "	18	20	22	24 ....

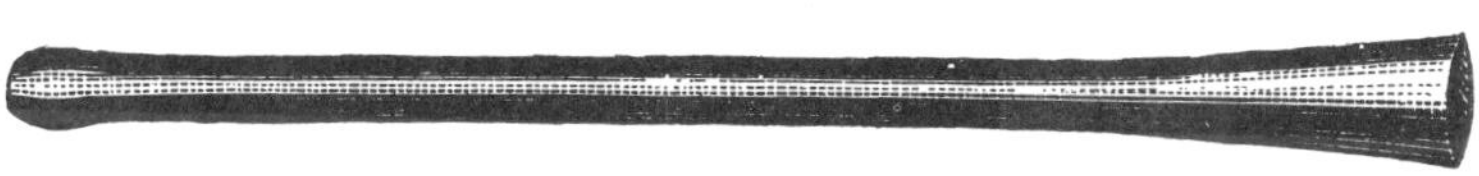

PICK HANDLES.

Railroad, No. 1 .... No. 2 ....
Drifting, Flat Eye, No. 1 ....
Coal .... Poll ....

SLEDGE OR MAUL HANDLES.

Inch .... 26 ...... 28 ...... 30 ...... 32 ...... 34 ...... 36 ......

Revised or American Price List of

FILES AND RASPS.

Inch. ☞ To	3	3½	4	4½	5	5½	6	7	8	9	10	11	12	13	14
Saw Files, Taper...	1 05	1 05	1 20	1 35	1 60	1 85	2 15	2 75	3 45	4 30	5 35	6 60	8 00	9 55	11 30
" " Slim	1 15	1 15	1 25	1 40	1 55	1 75	2 05	2 45	3 00	3 65	4 50	5 55	6 85	8 40	10 35
Pit Saw, blunt, s'gle cut	1 50	1 50	1 60	1 70	1 85	2 10	2 45	3 15	3 95	4 80	5 80	6 85	8 00		
Hook Tooth, " "	1 95	1 95	1 95	2 25	2 25	2 65	6 65	3 15	3 80	4 50	5 25	6 15	7 10		
Band Saw, Taper.....	1 70	1 70	1 85	2 05	2 35	2 65	3 00	3 70	4 50	5 50	5 50	7 50	8 75	10 00	
Double End, "	....	....	....	....	....	....	....	2 10	2 40	2 70	3 20				

Inch ☞ To	4	5	6	7	8	9	10	11	12	13	14	15	16
Bastard, Flat ..	1 50	1 70	2 00	2 40	2 90	3 50	4 15	4 80	5 80	6 85	8 15	9 75	11 55
" Half Round...	1 60	1 85	2 20	2 65	3 15	3 80	4 50	5 25	6 25	7 35	8 75	10 35	12 25
" Hand.........	1 60	1 85	2 20	2 65	3 15	3 80	4 50	5 25	6 25	7 35	8 75	10 35	12 25
" Round........	1 40	1 60	1 85	2 20	2 65	3 15	3 80	4 50	5 35	6 40	7 65	9 10	10 80
" Square........	1 40	1 60	1 85	2 20	2 65	3 15	3 80	4 50	5 35	6 40	7 65	9 10	10 80
" Knife.........	1 85	2 20	2 65	3 15	3 80	4 50	5 25	6 25	7 35				
" Mill..........	1 40	1 60	1 85	2 20	2 65	3 15	3 80	4 50	5 35	6 40	7 65	9 10	10 80
" " 1 round edge	1 50	1 70	2 00	2 40	2 90	3 50	4 15	4 80	5 80	6 85	8 15	9 75	11 55
Second Cut, Flat ..	1 75	2 00	2 35	2 80	3 35	4 00	4 75	5 60	6 65	7 90	9 40	11 20	13 30
" Half Round	1 85	2 10	2 55	3 05	3 65	4 35	5 20	6 05	7 20	8 50	10 10	11 90	14 10
" Hand......	1 85	2 10	2 55	3 05	3 65	4 35	5 20	6 05	7 20	8 50	10 10	11 90	14 10
" Round.....	1 65	1 85	2 10	2 55	3 05	3 65	4 35	5 20	6 15	7 35	8 75	10 50	12 40
" Square.....	1 65	1 85	2 10	2 55	3 05	3 65	4 35	5 20	6 15	7 35	8 75	10 50	12 40
" Knife......	2 10	2 55	3 05	3 65	4 35	5 20	6 05	7 20	8 50				
" Shafting...	....	....	....	...	....	....	....	....	6 65	.....	9 40		
" Surfacing ..	....	....	....	....	....	...	....	...	7 20				
Smooth, Flat.......	1 90	2 15	2 55	3 05	3 65	4 35	5 20	6 05	7 25	8 55	10 20	12 20	14 45
" Half Round	2 00	2 35	2 80	3 30	3 95	4 75	5 60	6 60	7 80	9 20	10 95	12 95	15 35
" Hand.....	2 00	2 35	2 80	3 30	3 95	4 75	5 60	6 60	7 80	9 20	10 95	12 95	15 35
" Round	1 75	2 00	2 35	2 80	3 30	3 95	4 75	5 60	6 70	8 00	9 55	11 40	13 50
" Square	1 75	2 00	2 35	2 80	3 30	3 95	4 75	5 60	6 70	8 00	9 55	11 40	13 50
Wood Files, Flat.....	1 50	1 70	2 00	2 40	2 90	3 50	4 15	4 80	5 80	6 85	8 15	9 75	11 55
" " Half Round	1 60	1 85	2 20	2 65	3 15	3 80	4 50	5 25	6 25	7 35	8 75	10 35	15 25
Cabinet Files	....	....	2 90	3 50	4 20	5 00	6 00	7 00	8 25	9 65	11 30	13 15	13 20
" **Rasps**.......	....	....	2 90	3 50	4 20	5 00	6 00	7 00	8 25	9 65	11 30	13 15	15 40
Wood " Flat.....	....	....	2 35	2 80	3 35	4 00	4 75	5 60	6 65	7 90	9 40	11 20	13 40
" " Half Round	....	....	2 55	3 05	3 65	4 35	5 20	6 05	7 20	8 50	10 10	11 90	14 10
Shoe " " "	....	....	2 45	2 65	3 10	3 75	4 60	5 70	7 00				
Horse " Plain.....	....	....	....	....	....	....	4 65	5 35	6 30	7 55	9 00	10 80	12 80

Discount..................

The above list applies to American Files only.

Our American Files are the best in the market, and each one fully guaranteed to do its work well. The above assortment includes the Files and Rasps in general use. For Special Work, we can furnish any other kind or size required.

REMARKS ON USING FILES.

A new file should be used with a light pressure on the work till the needle-like points of the teeth are worn away; after this, a much heavier pressure may be used with less danger of breaking off the teeth at their base. Many new files are violently diminished half their efficiency by a few careless strokes when first applied to the work.

FILES AND RASPS.

FLOAT CUT.

Float Cut.

Bastard.

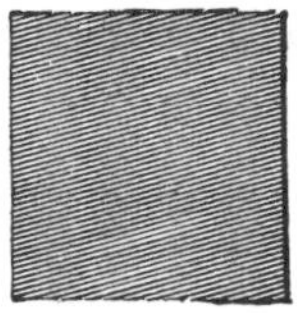
Second Cut.

Smooth.

Dead Smooth.

DOUBLE CUT.

Middle Cut.

Bastard.

Second Cut.

Smooth.

Dead Smooth.

RASP CUT.

Rasp Rough.

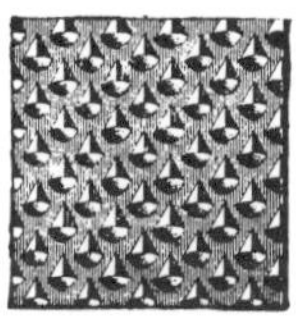
Middle Cut.

Bastard.

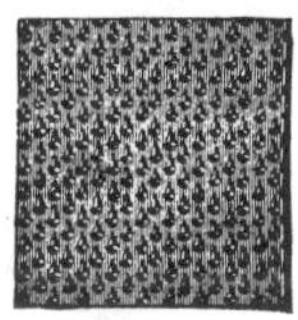
Smooth.

Dead Smooth.

FILES.

Flat Bastard.

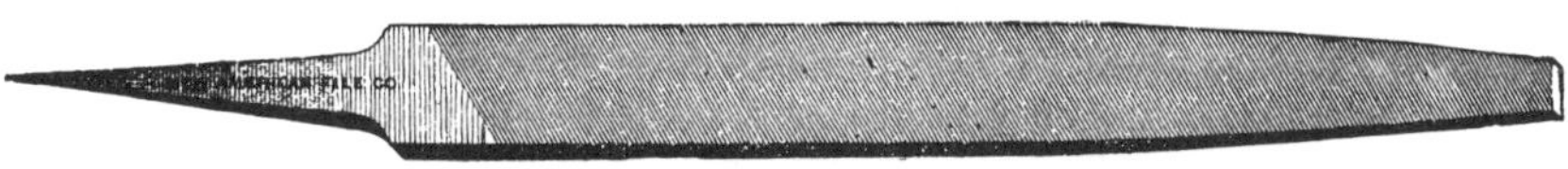
Mill Saw.

Flat Smooth.

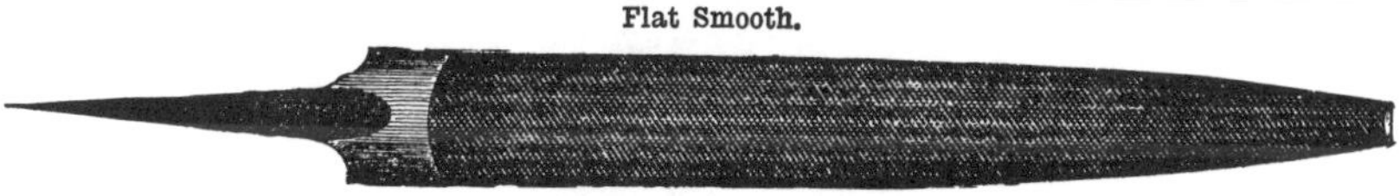
Half Round Bastard.

Half Round Smooth.

See List on Page 277.

FILES AND RASPS.

FILES.

Round Smooth.

Square Smooth.

Hand Bastard.

Pit Saw File.

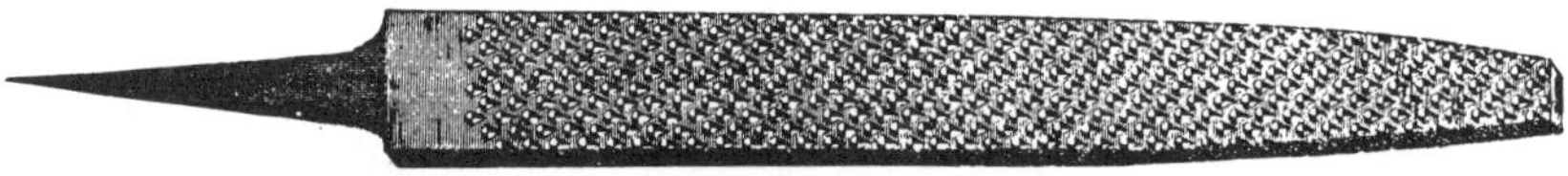

Flat Wood Rasp.

Three Square Taper Saw File.

Three Square Slim Taper Saw File.

Reversible Three Square Taper Saw File.

RASPS.

Horse Rasp.

Flat Shoe Rasp.

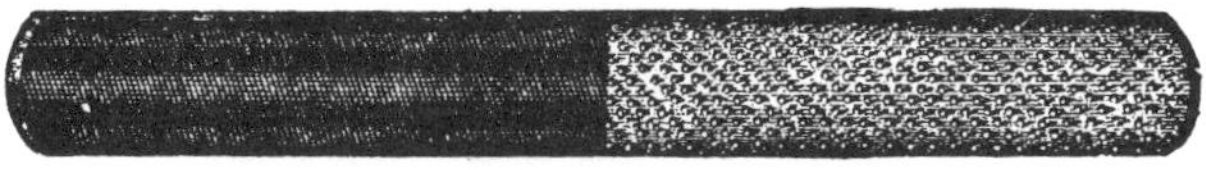

Half Round Shoe Rasp.

See List on Page 277.

STUBS FILES.

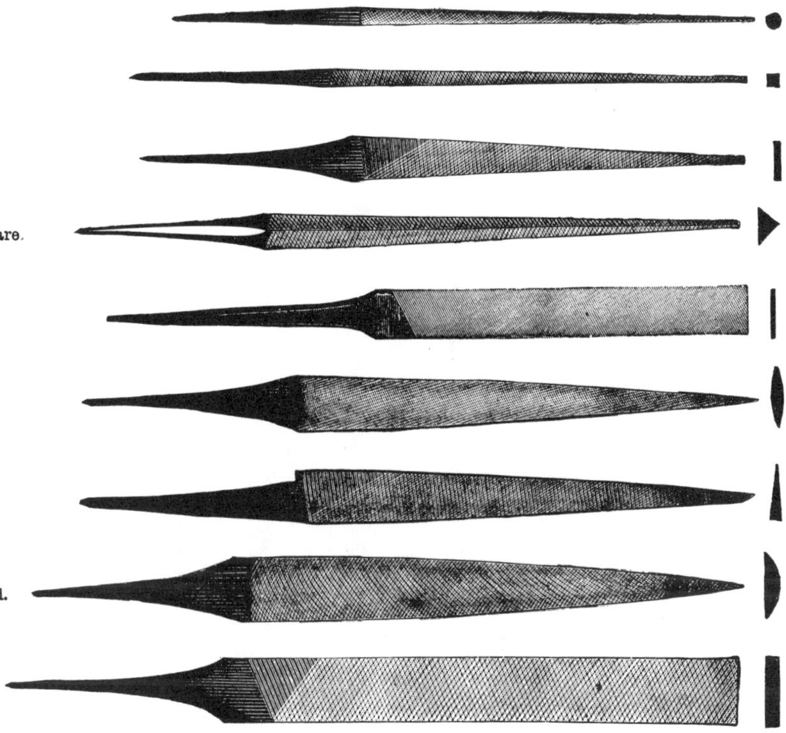

Round.

Square.

Warding.

Three-Square.

Equalling.

Crossing.

Knife.

Half Round.

Hand.

NEEDLE FILES.

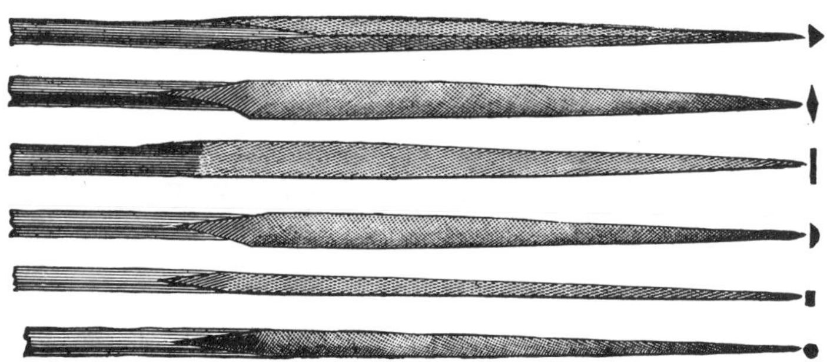

Three Squares.

Crossing.

Flat.

Half Round.

Square.

Round.

The above Files in Smooth and Bastard Cut. Sizes, 3, 3½, 4, 4½, 5 and 6 in.

Slotting Files, Die Sinkers' Files in Sets of 12, Jewelers' and Pattern Makers' Files. The best assortment of Files of the best makes at New York prices. Orders filled promptly.

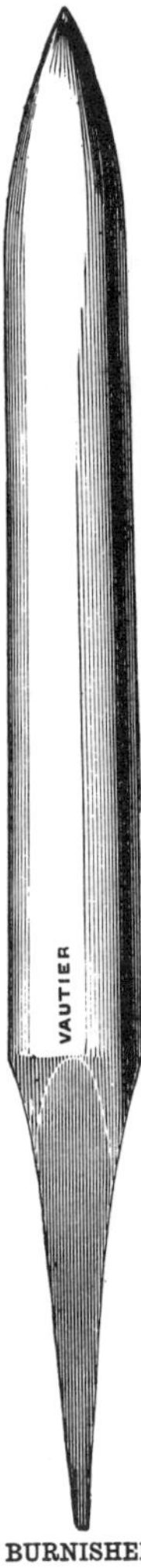

BURNISHER.

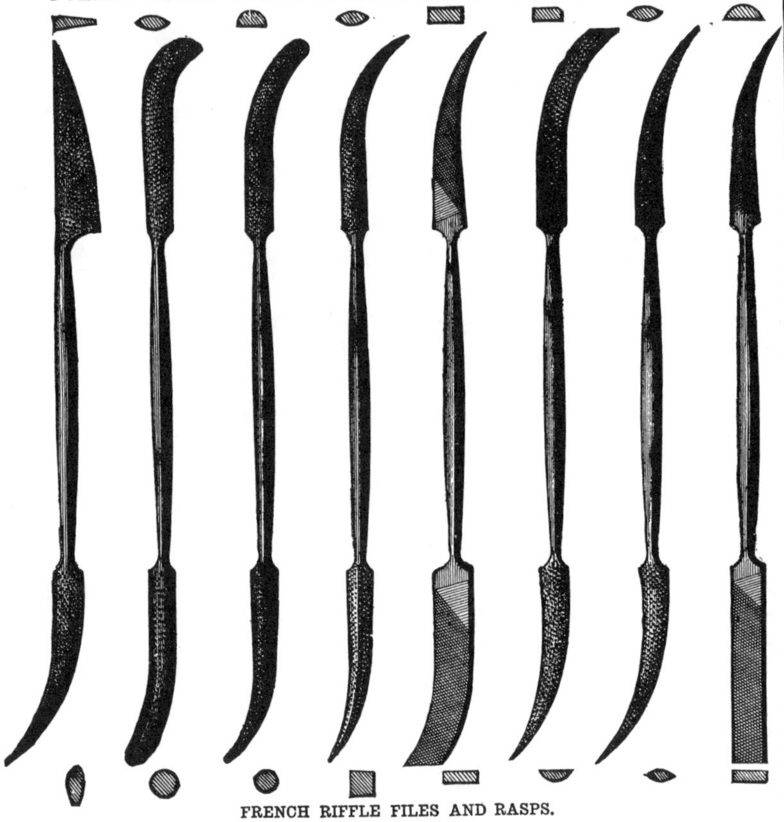

FRENCH RIFFLE FILES AND RASPS.

Known as the Best in the Market.

Sizes.......... .... 6 .... 7..... 8..... 9..... 10 in.....

Steel and Blood-Stone Burnishers in Assorted Shapes.

TRACING WHEELS.

Common.................. ...... Patent.................. ......

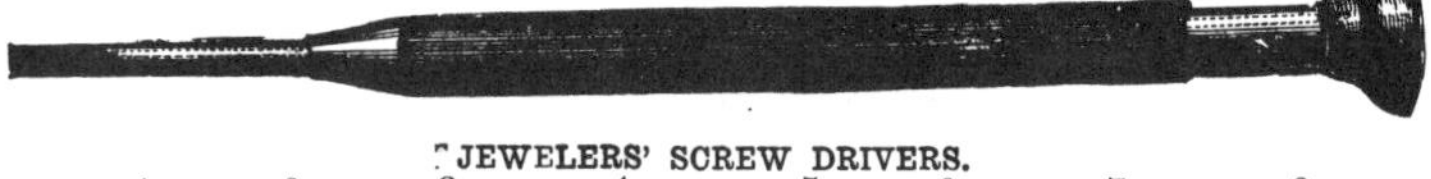

JEWELERS' SCREW DRIVERS.

1 2 3 4 5 6 7 8

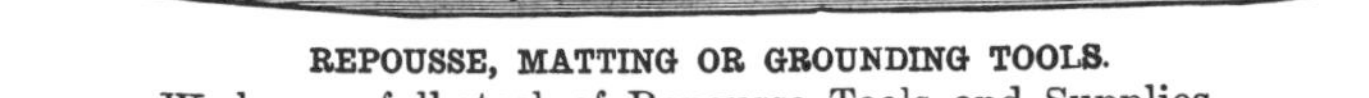

REPOUSSE, MATTING OR GROUNDING TOOLS.

We keep a full stock of Repousse Tools and Supplies.

CHASING TOOLS.

DRILL CHUCKS.

THE INVINCIBLE CHUCK.

Will take any Size Drill to ½ inch.

By the peculiar movement of the jaws, they will grip a drill stronger, and when desired release the drill more easily than any other chuck in the market. This is a new chuck, a $5.00 chuck. Should be seen by every mechanic. ....

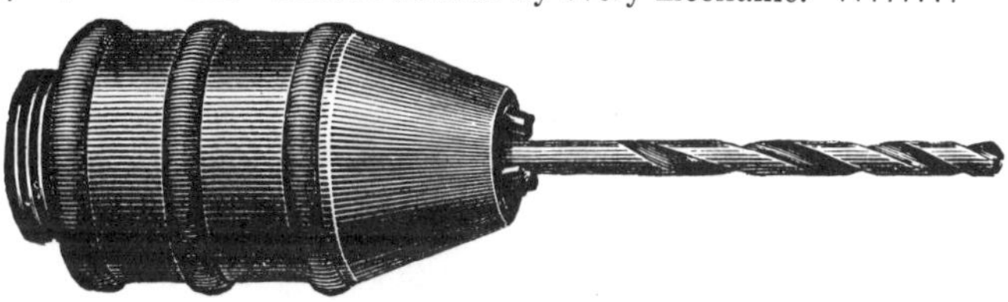

BEACH PATENT DRILL CHUCK.

The Best Known Chuck.

No. 0, holds to ⅛....No. 1, to ¼....No. 2, to ⅜....No. 3, 1-16 to ½....No. 4, 3-16 to ⅝..

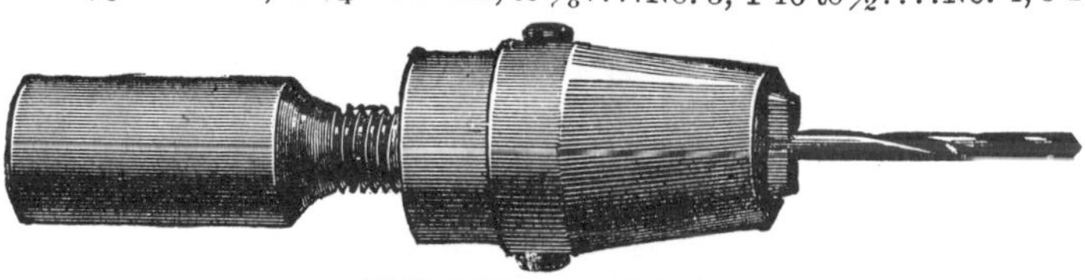

STAR CHUCK—Low Priced.

No. 1 Shank, ½ in. and 2 in. long, holds drills from 1-64 to ⅛ in................ ......
No. 2 Shank, ⅝ in. and 3½ in. long, holds drills from 1-32 to ¼ in.............. ......

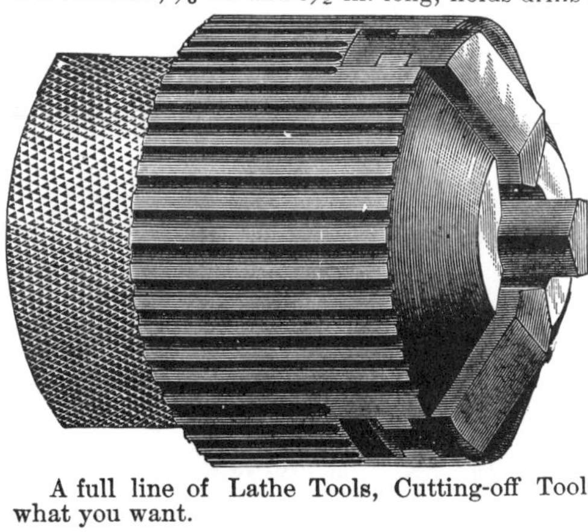

THE FOUR DOLLAR CHUCK.

Is made of steel, holds drills from 0 to 9-16 inch, perfectly true and firm and is guaranteed to give more satisfaction for the money than any other.

A full line of **Lathe Tools, Cutting-off** Tools. Chasers for Screws, etc. Write for what you want.

DRILL CHUCKS.

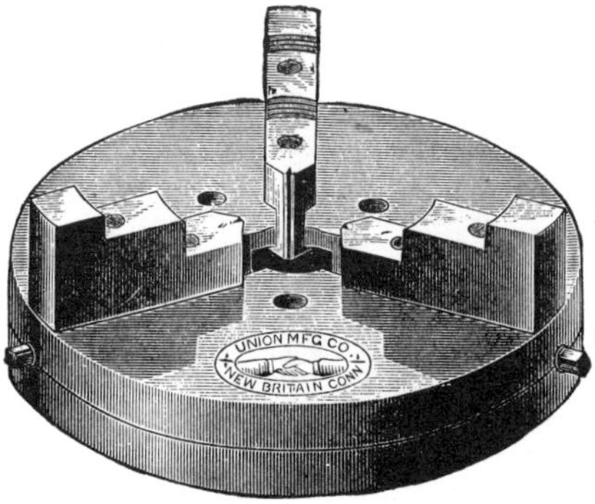

SKINNER'S COMBINATION CHUCK.

Including Bolts and Wrenches.

THREE JAWS.

4. . 6... 9... 12... 15... 18... 21... 24 in...

FOUR JAWS.

6.... 9.... 12.... 15.... 18... 21... 24 in...

Discount........

In ordering please state if common, reverse or inside jaws are wanted.

Can be made universal or independent.

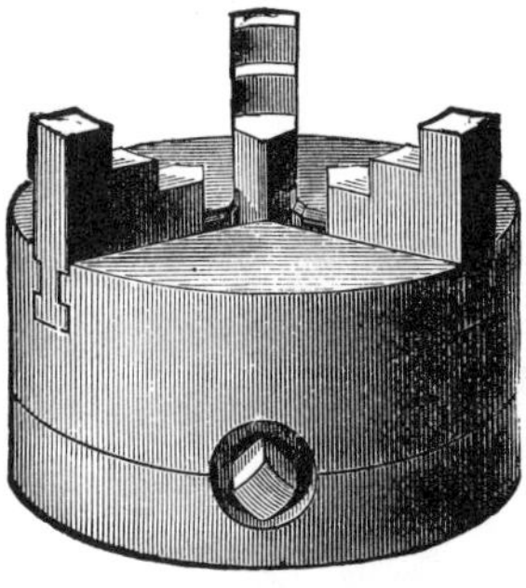

CUSHMAN'S CHUCK.

Geared Scroll Chuck.

3 inch............. ...... 4 inch............... ......

CUSHMAN'S AMATEUR CHUCK.

Especially adapted to Foot Lathes.

2 inch ... 2½ inch ....

Furnished with inside or outside jaws, or with both, as desired.

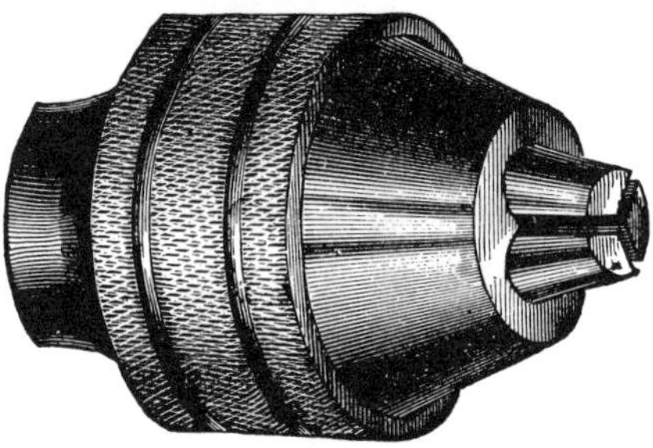

THE ALMOND DRILL CHUCK.

This Chuck will center and hold drills with a firm grip and is one of the best Chucks in the market. Three sizes.

No. 0, To hold from 0 to 3-16 inch.... ......

No. 1, " " " 0 to 5-16 inch.... ......

No. 2, " " " 0 to ½ inch.. ....

Discount........

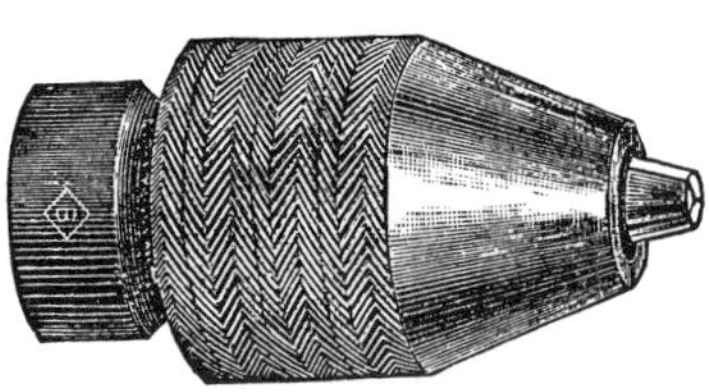

ARLINGTON CHUCK.

A thoroughly well made and finished Chuck, jaws are of hardened steel, self-centering, and of the simplest construction.

For Drills 0 to 3-16 in full................. ... ..

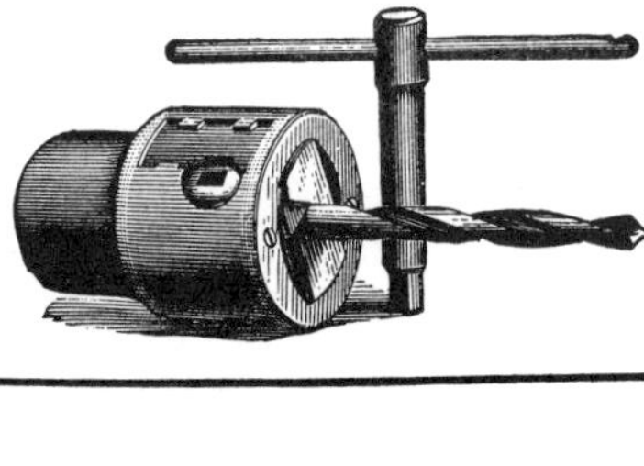

LITTLE GIANT IMPROVED DRILL CHUCK.

Self-Centering.

No. 00, Holds from 0 to ¼inch............. ......
No. 0, " " 0 to 7-16 inch.......... ......
No. 1, " " 0 to ⅝ inch ....
No. 2, " " 0 to 1 inch............. ......

Discount........

DRILLS, TAPS AND SCREW PLATES.

STRAIGHT SHANK DRILLS.

1/16, 5/64, 3/32, 7/64, 1/8, 9/64, 5/32, 11/64, 3/16, 13/64, 7/32, 15/64, 1/4, 17/64, 9/32, 19/64, 5/16, 21/64, 11/32, 23/64, 3/8, 25/64, 13/32, 27/64, 7/16, 29/64, 15/32, 31/64, 1/2

Also, Sizes Stubs Steel Wire Gauge from No. 1 to No. 65.

TAPER SHANK DRILLS.

1/4, 9/32, 5/16, 11/32, 3/8, 13/32, 7/16, 15/32, 1/2, 17/32, 9/16, 19/32, 5/8, 21/32, 11/16, 23/32, 3/4, 25/32, 13/16, 27/32, 7/8, 29/32, 15/16, 31/32, 1, 1 1/32, 1 1/16, 1 3/32, 1 1/8, 1 5/32

1 3/16, 1 7/32, 1 1/4, 1 9/32, 1 5/16, 1 11/32, 1 3/8, 1 13/32, 1 7/16, 1 15/32, 1 1/2, 1 17/32, 1 9/16, 1 19/32, 1 5/8, 1 21/32, 1 11/16, 1 23/32, 1 3/4, 1 25/32, 1 13/16, 1 27/32, 1 7/8, 1 29/32, 1 15/16, 1 31/32, 2

Discount ....

BIT STOCK DRILLS FOR METAL OR WOOD.

2/32, 3/32, 4/32, 5/32, 6/32, 7/32, 8/32, 9/32, 10/32, 11/32, 12/32, 13/32, 14/32, 15/32, 16/32, 17/32, 9/16, 5/8, 11/16, 3/4

Discount... ....

Steel Sockets for Taper Shank Drills and Straight Shank Machine Bits.

Taper. Plug. Bottoming.
MACHINE HAND TAPS.

MACHINISTS' HAND TAPS.

1/4	16, 18, 20 Threads....	11-16	...11, 12 Threads....
5-16	16, 18 "	3/4	....10, 12 " ....
3/8	14, 16, 18 "	13-16	.... 10 " ....
7-16	14, 16 "	7/8	.... 9, 10 " ....
1/2	12, 13, 14 "	15-16	... 9 " ....
9-16	12, 14 "	1 in	.. 8 " ....
5-8	10, 11, 12 "	Discount	....

Taps for Machine Screws, Nos. 4 to 24, 18 to 40 Threads.

SCREW PLATES.

4 Sets Dies, 4 Taps.

No. 00, 6 in., 1-16, 64; 3-32, 56; 7-64, 48; 1/8, 40.. .. ....
No. 0, 7½ in., 7-64, 48; 1/8, 40; 3-16, 32; 1/4, 24.... ....
No. 1½, 8 in., No. 6, 32; No. 8, 30; No. 10, 24; No. 14, 20..

No. 2½ B, 11½ in. long, 3 Sets Dies, 3 Taps, 5-16, 18, 3/8, 16; 7-16, 14.................... ....
No. 2½ C, 11½ in. long, 5 Sets Dies, 5 Taps, 1/4, 20; 5-16, 18; 3/8, 16; 7-16, 14; 1/2, 12 ....
No. 4 A, 19 in., 3 sets dies, 3 taps, 1/2, 12; 5/8, 11; 3/4, 10,....
No. 7 A, 22 in., 3 " 3 " 3/4, 10; 7/8, 9; 1 in.. 8,....

Extra Taps in Stock. Discount......

LIGHTNING SCREW PLATES.

Plate A, 10 in., 3-16, 1/4, 5-16, 3/8, 7-16.... ....
" AA, 18 in., 3-16, 1/4, 5-16, 3/8, 7-16, 1/2. ....
" B, 23 in., 1/4, 5-16, 3/8, 7-16, 1/2, 5/8, 3/4.. ....
" C, 26 in., 3/8, 7-16, 1/2, 5/8, 3/4, 7/8, 1 in. ....

Discount ....

Jewelers' Screw Plates, Taper Reamers, Tap Wrenches, King's Stocks and Dies.

The best assortment of mechanics' small tools in the State.

VAJEN & NEW. INDIANAPOLIS, IND.

DRILLING TOOLS, LATHE DOGS, ETC.

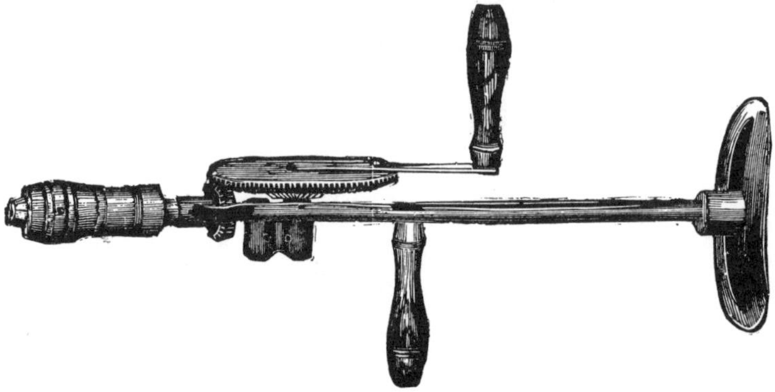

BREAST DRILLS.

Nos......................... 11..... 12..... 13.....

Cut is No. 13.

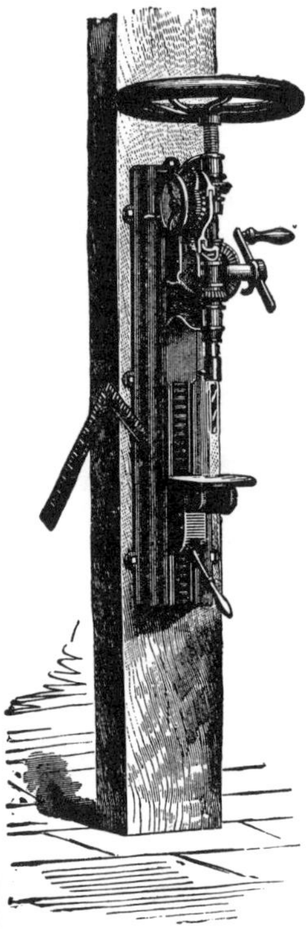

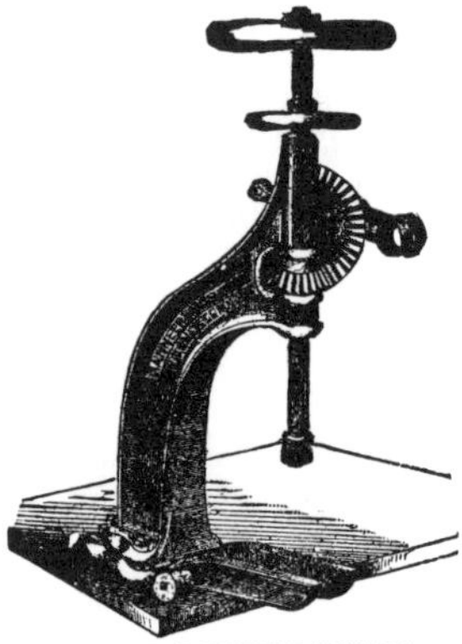

MANNER'S BENCH DRILLS.

Total Height, about 24 in.

Each................ ......

COMMON LATHE DOGS.

3/8	1/2	3/4	1 in.
....	....	....	....Each.

Also a full assortment of patent Lathe Dogs.

GREEN RIVER SELF-FEEDING DRILLING MACHINES.

No. 2, Drills to 3/4 in. Drill Bits should have 1/2 in. Shank, Diameter of Balance Wheel, 16 1/2 in. Drills to Center of 15 in. Circle. Weight, 130 lb. Complete........ ......

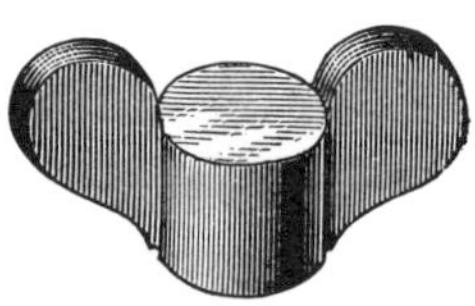

THUMB NUT BLANK.

Nos. 1.... 2.... 3.... 4... 5...

Forged or Cast. Cut is No. 1.

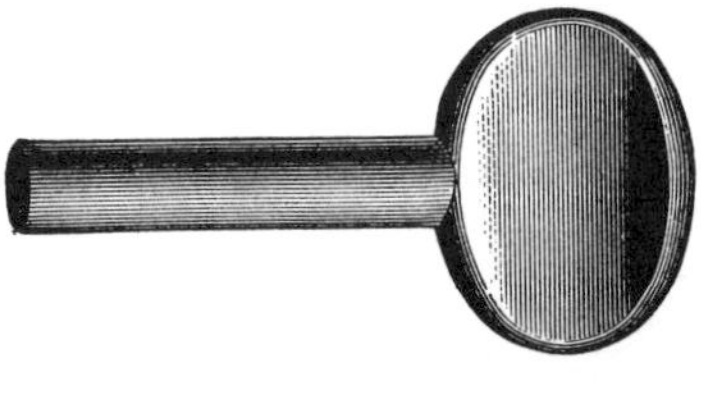

THUMB SCREW BLANKS.

From 3-16 to 3/8 Diameter, in Different Lengths.

Forged or Cast.

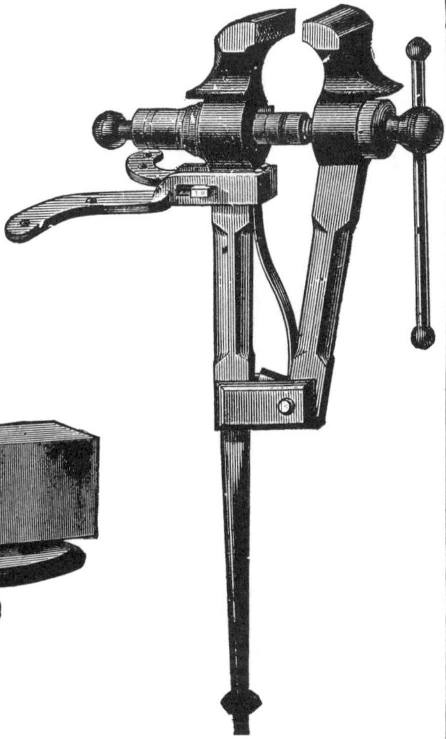

SOLID BOX VISES.

Nos.......... 40 ..... 55 ..... 70.....

Other Sizes furnished to order.

PARKER'S PARALLEL VISES.

Nos	1	2	3	4	5
Length of Jaws ...	$3\frac{5}{8}$	$4\frac{1}{4}$	$4\frac{3}{4}$	$5\frac{3}{8}$	$6\frac{1}{8}$ in.
Weight	23	34	$42\frac{1}{2}$	61	83 lb.
Price..............	......	......	......	......	......

Discount...........

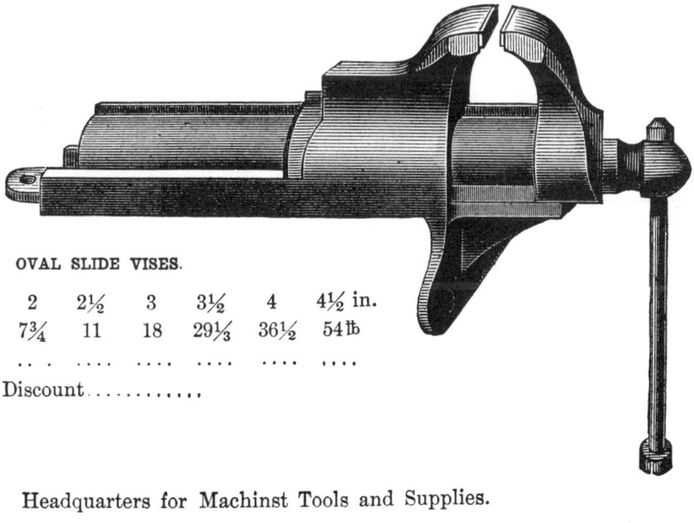

OVAL SLIDE VISES.

Length of Jaws,	2	$2\frac{1}{2}$	3	$3\frac{1}{2}$	4	$4\frac{1}{2}$ in.
Weight........	$7\frac{3}{4}$	11	18	$29\frac{1}{3}$	$36\frac{1}{2}$	54 lb
Price..........	.. .	....	....	....	....	....

Discount...........

COMBINATION VISES.

CHENEY'S COMBINED ANVIL AND VISE.

Size of Jaws	2½	3⅓	4	4½
No.	10	20	30	40....

This is a combination of three tools, namely: 1st, An Anvil having a chill-hardened and polished face. 2d, A Parallel Vice with a square thread wrought iron screw and jaws that are steel faced. 3d, It becomes an adjustable vise that will hold odd shaped articles, as shown in cut, by removing the steel pin.

Anvil and Vise with Drill Attached.

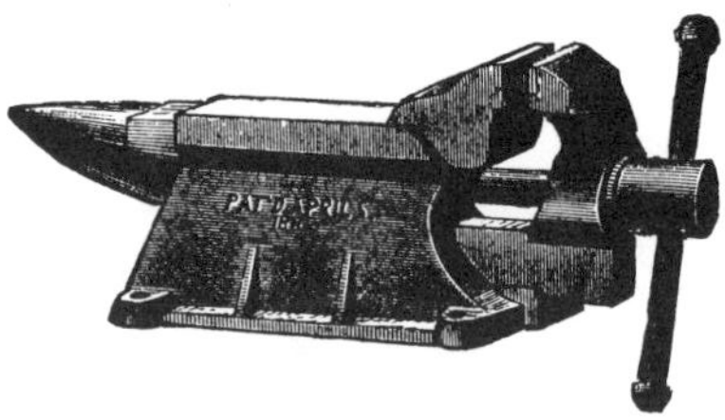

Anvil with Vice Attached.

COMBINED VISE ANVIL AND DRILL.

A valuable tool for Carpenters, Harness-Makers, Tinners, Locksmiths, Blacksmiths, Brewers, Millers, Farmers, etc. Three machines at the price of one.

Weight, 50 lb.; Total length, 19 in.; Widths of jaws, 4 in.; 1 in. deep. Face of Anvil 8½ x 3¼ inches.

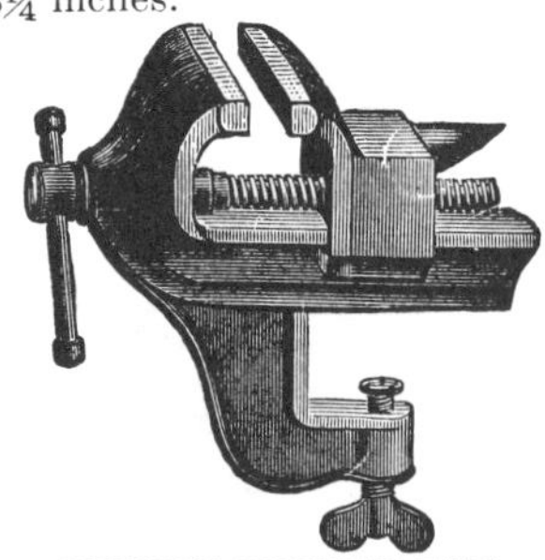

BONNEY'S DOMESTIC VISES.

With Clamp Attachment.

Size	1⅜	1½	2	2	2	2¾
Nos.	0....	1½....	2....	2½....	3....	4....
Size	2¾	2¾	2¾	2¾	2¾	
Nos.	5....	6....	7....	8....	9....	

Nos. 2½, 6, 7, 8 and 9 have steel jaws.

Stephen's Toggle Joint Vise.

Size of Jaw	2	2¾	3½	4½
Flat....	.....	.....	.....	.....
Swivel..	.....	.....	.....	.....

2 in. Nickel-Plated Flat.... Swivel....

WRENCHES.

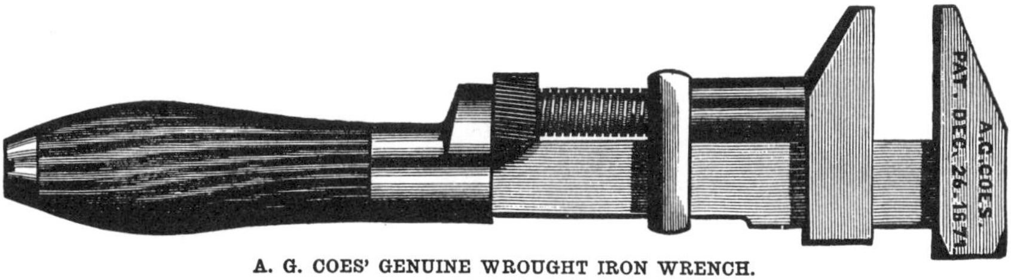

A. G. COES' GENUINE WROUGHT IRON WRENCH.

Black.............. 6...... 8 ..... 10...... 12...... 15...... 18...... 21 in......
Bright............. 6...... 8 ..... 10..... 12 ..... 15...... 18...... 21 in......

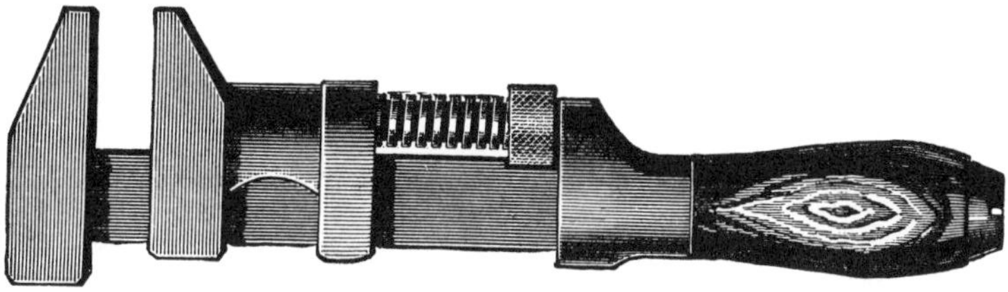

COES' PATTERN WROUGHT IRON WRENCH.

Black...................... 6...... 8...... 10...... 12...... 15...... 18 in......

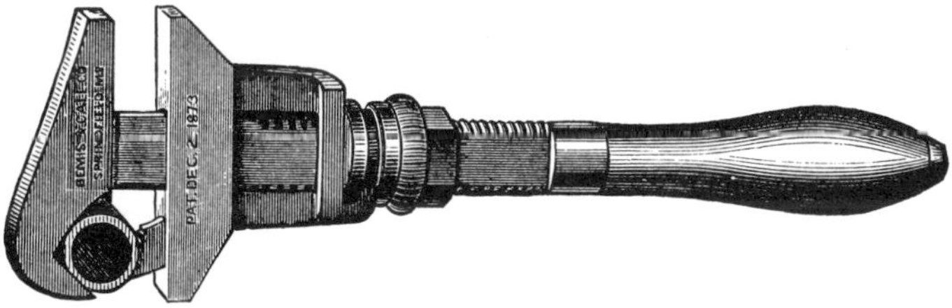

BEMIS & CALLS COMBINATION SHORT NUT WRENCH.

Bright.. 10...... 12...... 15 in......

ROUSE S PATENT PIPE WRENCH.

Drop Forged from Best Tool Steel. It is the latest and best Pipe Wrench in the market.

Length	6	8	10	12	14	18	24	36	48	60
Size Pipe	⅛ to ½,	⅛ to ¾,	⅛ to 1,	¼ to 1¼,	¼ to 1½,	¼ to 2,	¼ to 3,	½ to 4½,	½ to 5½,	½ to 8.
Price,	.....	......	......	......	......	......	......	......	......	......

BAXTER'S "S" WRENCHES.

Bright............................ 4...... 6.... . 8...... 10...... 12......

WRENCHES.

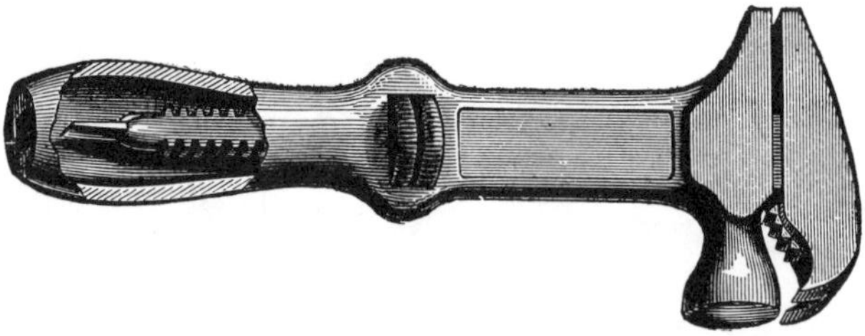

BOARDMAN'S COMBINATION WRENCH.

This combination comprises six useful tools, neatly and compactly arranged in a convenient form for practical use. These tools are: Screw Wrench, Pipe Wrench, Hammer, Nail Claw, Screw Driver, Bit Handle or Socket Wrench.

Nickel-Plated. Length .... 4½...... 6 in......

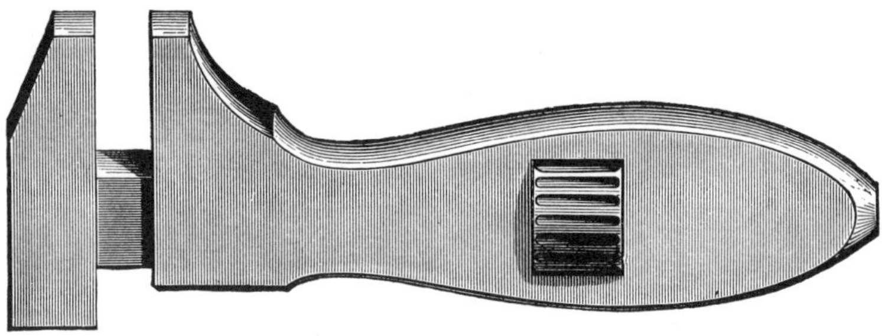

POCKET WRENCH.

Nickel-Plated. Length.......... .... 4...... 6 in......

MALLEABLE CARRIAGE WRENCH, JAPANNED.

Adjustable to all Sizes of Nuts.. ......

Green River Cross Wrench.

Price........

For Nuts 3-16, ¼, 5-16 & ⅜ in

This tool will be found very handy for nuts inside felloes of carriage wheels.

MALLEABLE CARRIAGE WRENCH.

Inch ⅞.... 1.... 1⅛.... 1¼.... 1½... 1¾... 2...

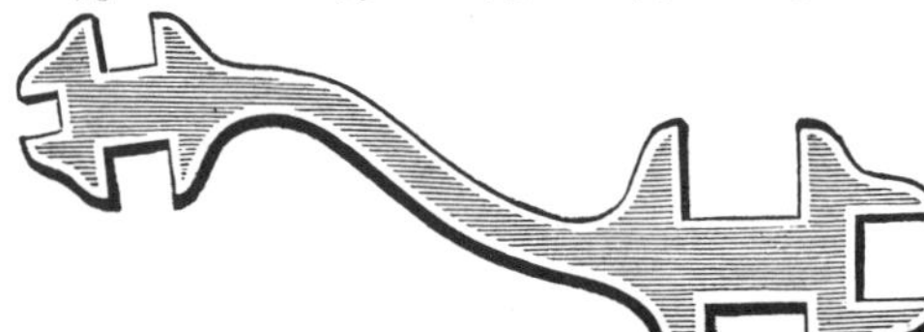

MALLEABLE "S" WRENCH.

9. ... 11..... 12 in....... ...

PUNCHES AND CLAMPS.

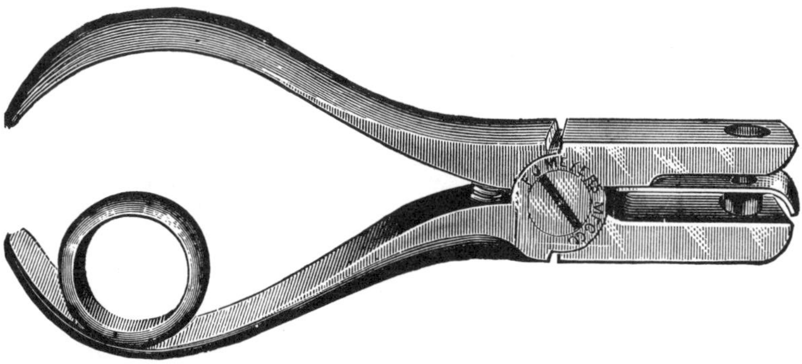

5 6 7 9 12 17 18 21 22 23 29 32 40 43 54 68 80 81 106

NEW IMPROVED CONDUCTORS PUNCH.

This new Ticket Punch is the best low priced Punch now in the market. It is made entirely of steel; it punches easy, and is neat, strong and very serviceable.

No. 3. . . . .

We have also other Fancy Punches, lower in price.

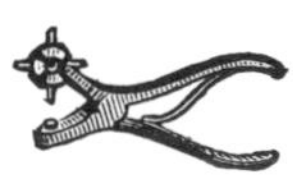

Revolving Spring Punch.

4 Tubes. . . . .
Assorted Sizes.

Spring Punches.

. . . .

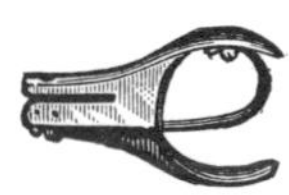

No 1. . . . .
Best Punch in use for any Ticket, including Thousand Mile, Commutation, Duplex or Similar Forms. Every Punch warranted.

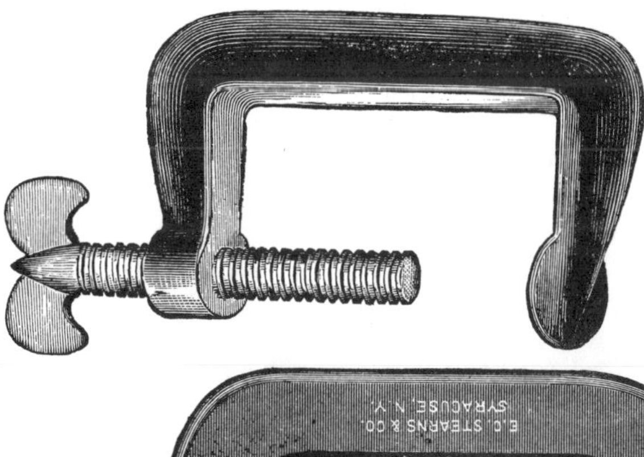

QUILT FRAME CLAMPS.

No. 1, Japanned. . . . .

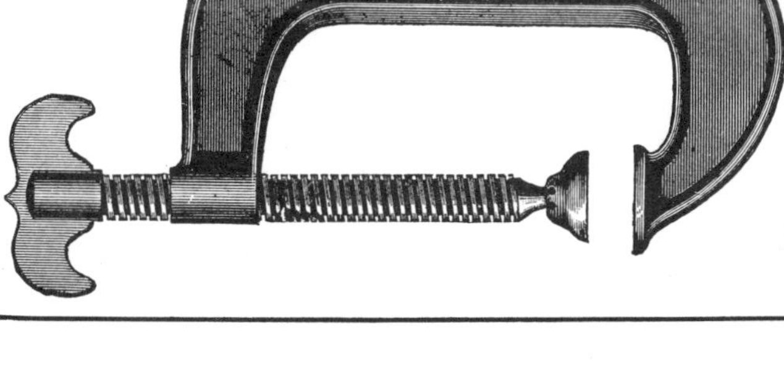

IMPROVED PATTERN SCREW CLAMP.

Wrought Iron Screws.

Inch, 3. . .4. . . .5. . . . 6. . .
" 7. . 8 . . 9 . 10 . .

The heaviest clamp made. It has the ball and socket and adjustable washer.

MISCELLANEOUS TOOLS.

GIANT NAIL PULLERS.

Small .... Large ....

BOX CHISELS.

Round .... Flat ....

JACK SCREWS.

Size	8x1½	10x1¾	12x1¾	12x2	14x2	16x2½
Each	......	......	......	......	......	......

Cast Frame, Wrought Iron Screw.

CROW BARS.

Iron .... Steel ....

Pinch Points will be sent, unless Wedge Points are ordered.

THE REEVES PATENT CANT HOOKS.

This Hook being self-adjusting it will take hold of any size log from 10 inches in diameter up to the largest log that grows, enabling one man to handle more timber and with greater ease, and at a less expense than he can with any other hook. It will take hold of square timber, which no other hook will do. It is made of the very best material, the entire hook is best steel, the handle the best seasoned hickory and the attachments are wrought and malleable iron.

THE GIANT CAR PUSHER.

Weighs only twenty-four pounds. With it one man may move twenty tons with ease. Oil or grease on the rail does not hinder the operation. Can be used at either end or middle of car.

Each ....

Weston's Patent Safety Double Lift Hoists.

This Hoist can be furnished in the following sizes; Capacity, 500, 1000, 1500, and 2000 lbs. Prices and description upon application.

....

MISCELLANEOUS GOODS.

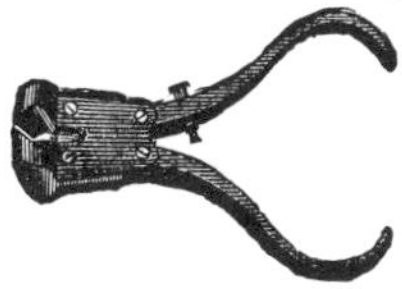

HALL'S CUTTING PLYERS.

Plain and Nickeled. See Page 307.

STEEL MARKING GAUGES.

6 Inch. ....

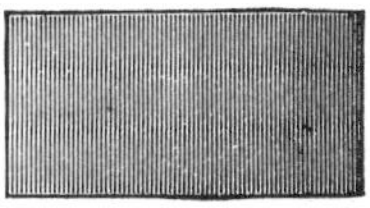

CABINET SCRAPERS.

Assorted Sizes, ...

ROUND PUNCHES.—Solid Cast Steel.

Inch,	½ to ⅞	1 to 1⅛	1⅛ to 1¼	1⅜ to 1⅝	1¾ to 2	2⅛ to 3
	......	......	......	......	......	......

MELTING LADLES.

Inch.... .... 2½...... 3...... 4...... 5...... 6 .....

HUNTINGTON'S PATENT EMERY WHEEL AGGRAVATOR.—Steel Cutter.

For Shaping, Sharpening and Removing Glaze from Emery Wheels.

The cut shows the form and construction of the tool. Its head contains a combination of a sharp-toothed cutter and discs set at right and left declination, thus producing a combination of cross-cutting and scraping effects, at the same time, that rapidly cuts the emery wheel, while the cutters are not perceptibly worn by contact with it.

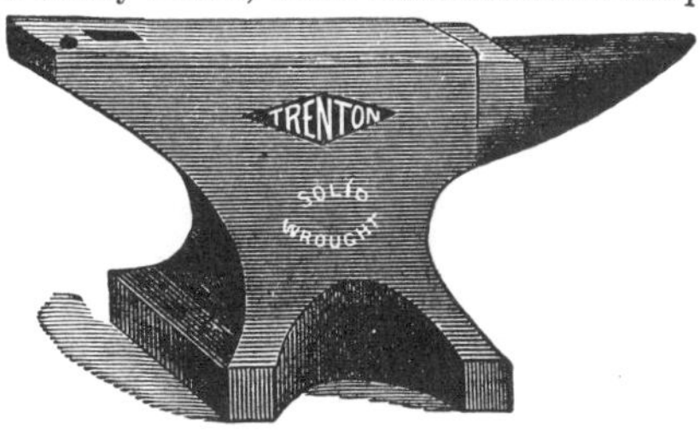

ANVILS. Jewelers', Mirror-Polished Face.

Size...........	1......	1½......	2℔......
Flat Jewelers...........		2......	3 in......

Eagle Anvils.

Nos...........	0	1	2	3	5
Weight, about..	10	15	20	30	40℔.
Price..........	....	....	....	....	....
Nos...........	5	6	7	8	9
Weight, about..	50	60	70	80	90℔
Price..........	....	....	....	....	....

From 100 to 800℔..................Per ℔......

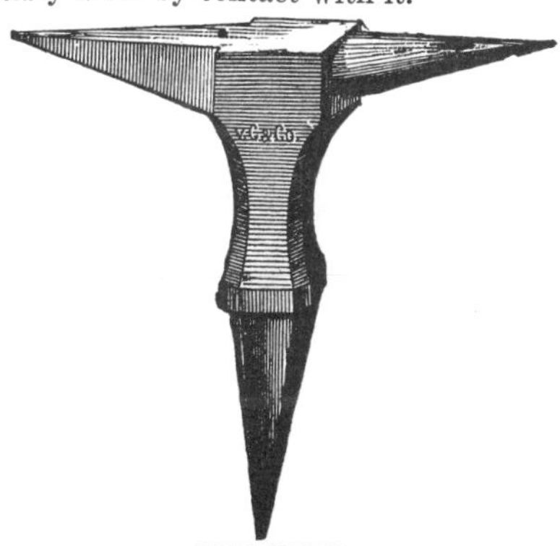

BICK IRONS.

For Jewelers. Mirror Polished Face.

Sizes, ¾.... 1.... 1½.... 2℔....

VAJEN & NEW, INDIANAPOLIS, IND.

HAND VISES AND BENCH STOPS.

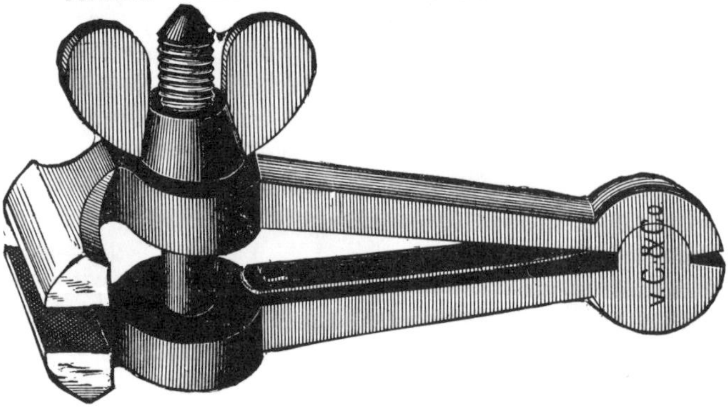

Hand Vises .... 2½..... 3..... 3½ .... 4 ..... 5 in .....
Hand Vises, Telegraph, 5½ in. with Hook.............................. ......

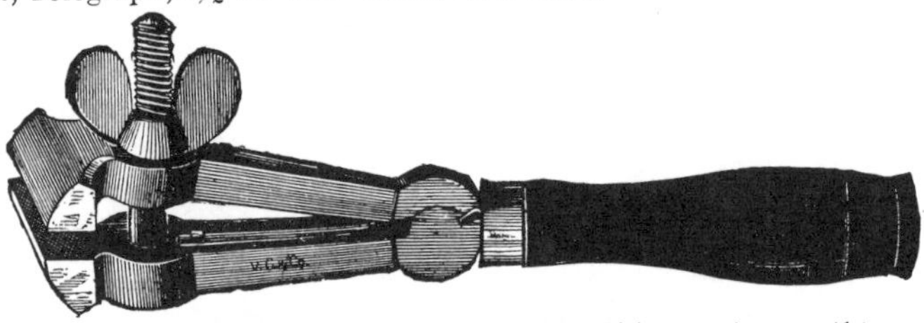

Hand Vises, Handled,..............2½.... 3.... 3½.... 4.... 4½.... 5 in....

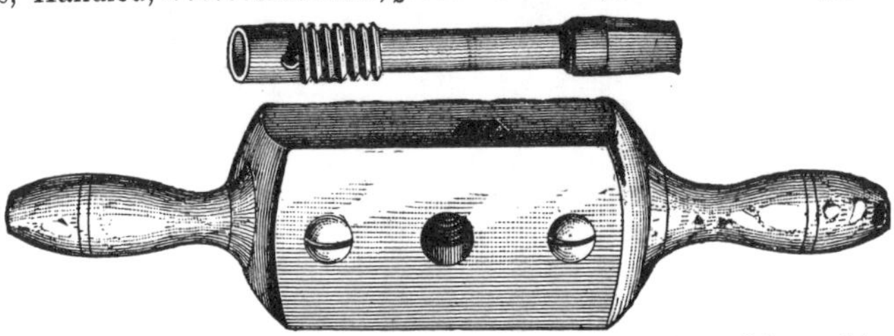

Screw Boxes.................... ¼.... ⅜ ... ½.... ⅝.... ¾.... ⅞.... 1 in....

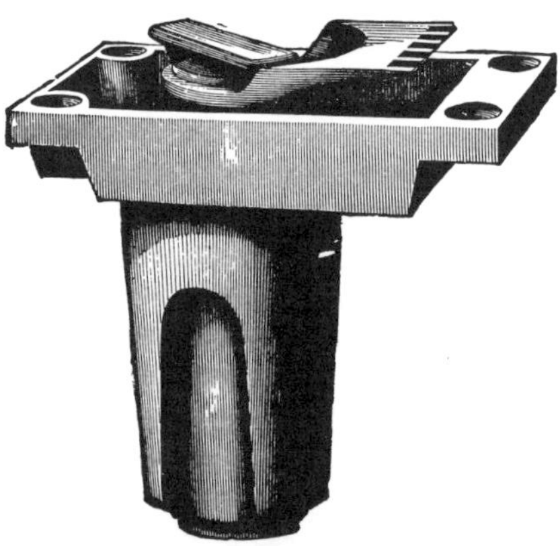

THE ECCENTRIC.

The Cheapest Good Bench Hook made .....

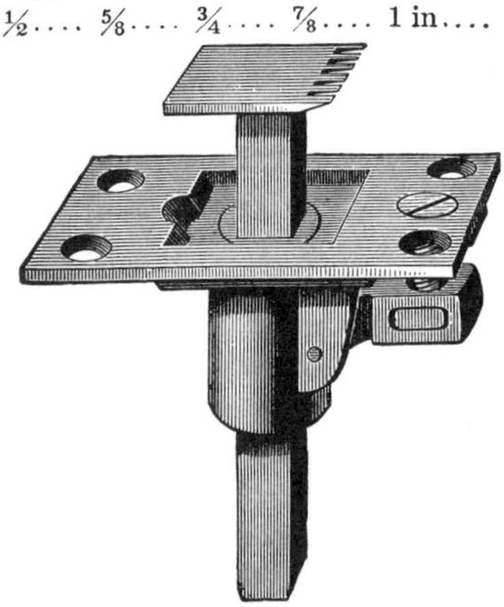

MERRILL'S BENCH STOPS.

Price.............................. ......

OIL STONES AND SLIPS.

No. 1, Washita, Size about 8x2x1 in., Not Mounted . . . .

No. 1, " Small, Size about 6x1½x¾ in., Not Mounted . . . .

Large " Assorted Sizes, Not Mounted . . . .

Washita Pocket Pieces . . . .

" Pen Knife Pieces . . . .

No. 1, Washita Round Edge Slips, Size 3½ to 5 x 1 to 1¾ in. . . . .

No. 1, Arkansas Oil Stone, in pieces from ½ to 1½ lb. . . . .

Arkansas Slips, Assorted Sizes . . . .

" Points, for Fine Work . . . .

No. 1, Hindostan " " Assorted Sizes . . . .

Hindostan Axe Stone, Assorted Small Sizes . . . .

" Round Edge Slips, Assorted Sizes . . . .

No. 1, Sand Stone, Assorted Sizes, for Shoemakers and Kitchen Use . . . .

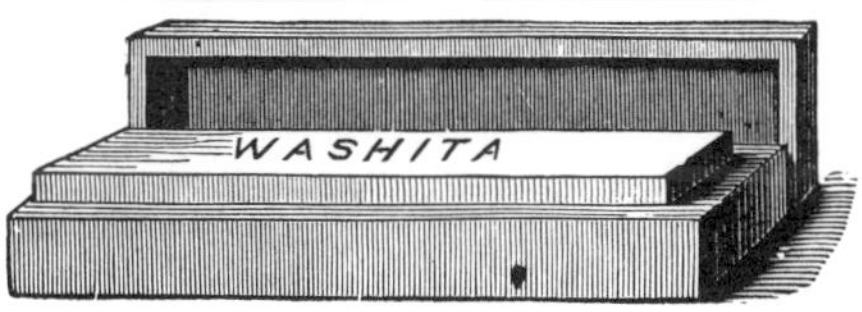

MOUNTED OIL STONES.

Washita and Arkansas, Assorted Sizes . . . .

Also, Small Oil Stone Wheels and Rubbers.

OILERS.

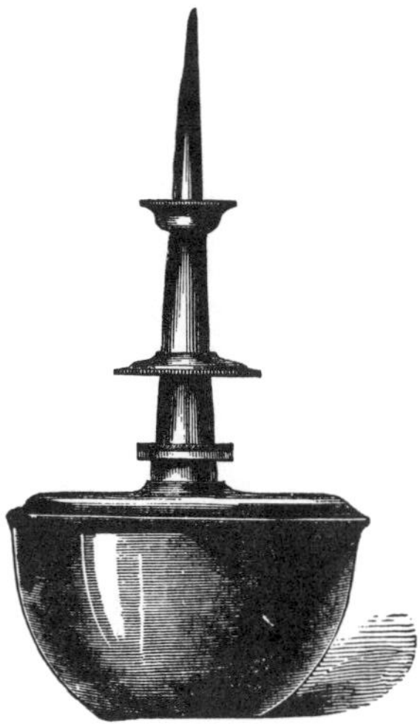

Olmstead's.

Nos.	0	1	2	3
Tin				
Zinc.				

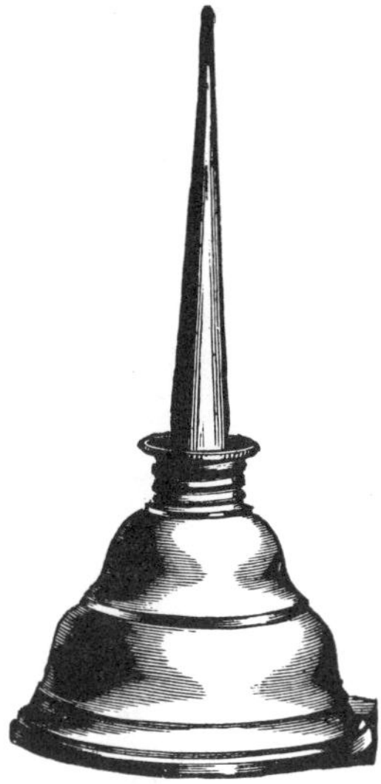

Chase's.

Nos.	0	1	2	3	4	5
Zinc.						
Copper.						
Brass						

Paragon.

Nos.	0	1	2	3	4	5
Zinc.						
Copper.						
Brass						

Polished Brass Engineers' Sets.

5 Pieces and Tray.................. ......

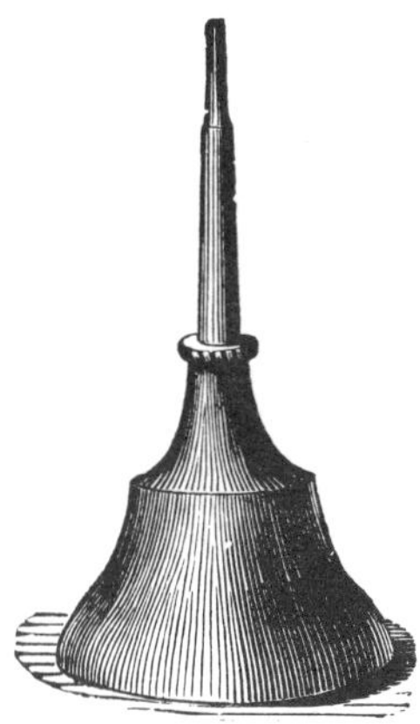

Malleable Iron.

Nos. 1 ... 2.... 3....

This is the most durable Oiler in the market.

Pocket and Bicycle Oilers.

Tin .. .. Nickel Plated... ......

Mowing Machine Oilers.

Straight or Bent Spout 1 Pint.... 1 Quart....

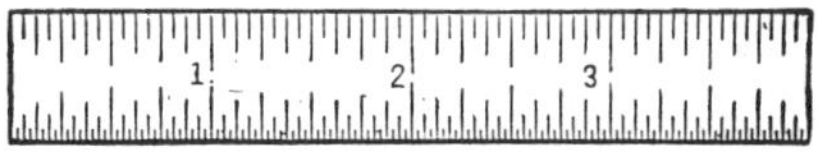

STANDARD STEEL RULES.

Sizes......... 1.... 2... 3.... 4.... 6 ... 9 ... 12... 18.... 24 in....

In several different makes and Graduations: Triangular Rules, Square Rules, Gear Rules and Shrink Rules.

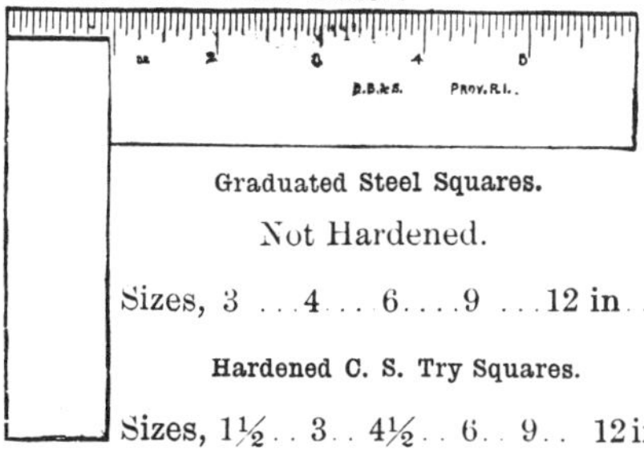

Graduated Steel Squares.

Not Hardened.

Sizes, 3 ...4 ... 6....9 ...12 in....

Hardened C. S. Try Squares.

Sizes, 1½.. 3.. 4½.. 6.. 9.. 12 in..

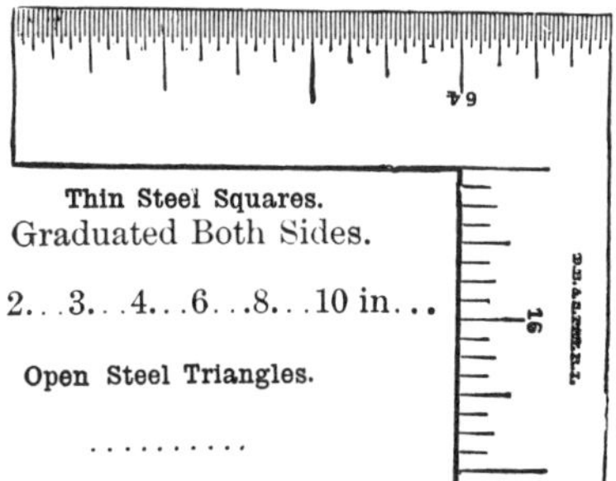

Thin Steel Squares.

Graduated Both Sides.

Sizes, 2...3...4...6...8...10 in...

Open Steel Triangles.

....

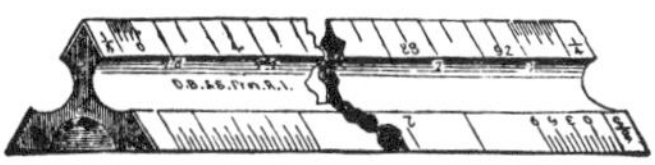

Metallic Triangular Scales.

12 in., Nickel-Plated, Very Light..... ......

Center Gauge.

Angles 60 degrees........ ......

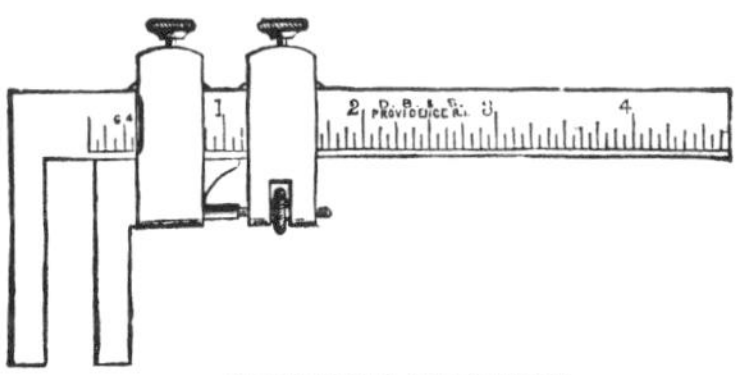

CALLIPER SQUARES.

Divided, one side to 64ths, other side to 100ths.

With or Without Adjustable Screws.

Sizes................ 2.... 4.... 9 in....

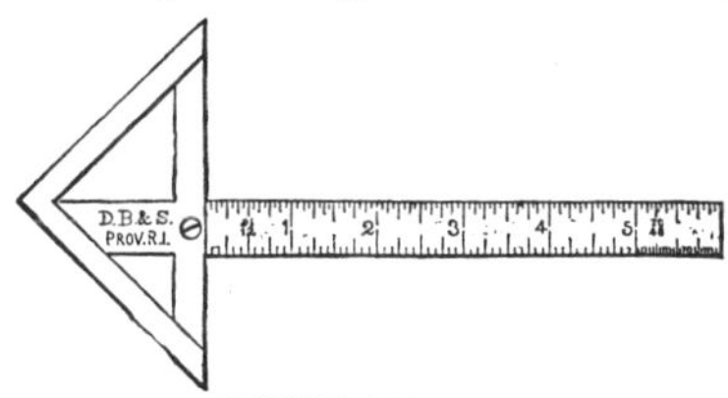

CENTRE SQUARES.

Sizes, 4.... 6.... 8 .. 10 .. 12 in....

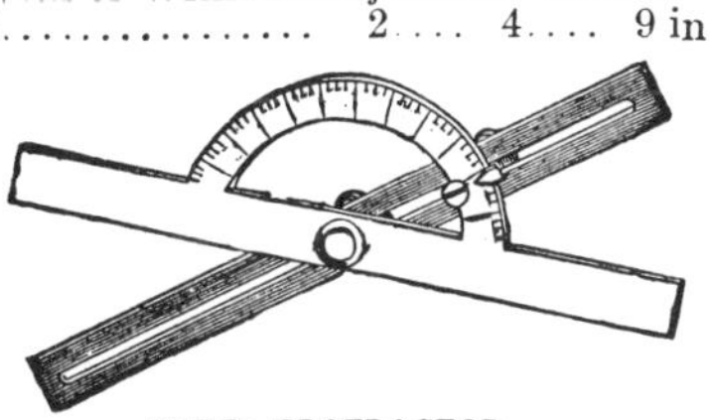

BEVEL PROTRACTOR.

6 in...... 10 in......Slide Arm.

SMALL UNIVERSAL BEVEL.

....

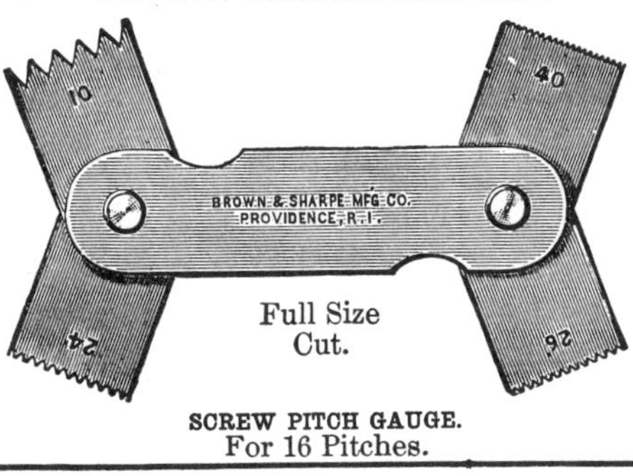

Full Size Cut.

SCREW PITCH GAUGE.

For 16 Pitches.

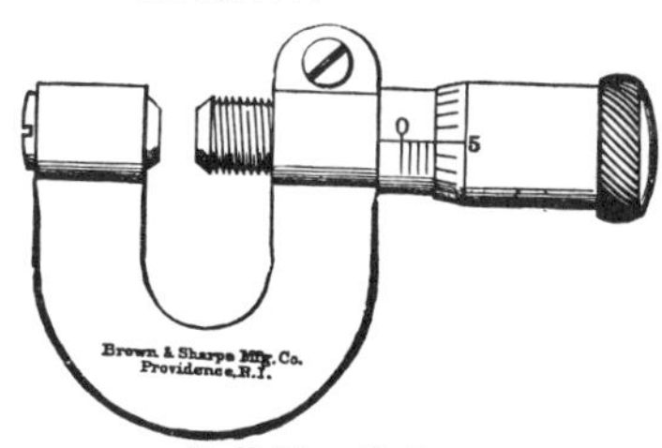

Full Size Cut.

POCKET SHEET METAL GAUGE.

Measure by thousands of an inch up to three-tenths of an inch.

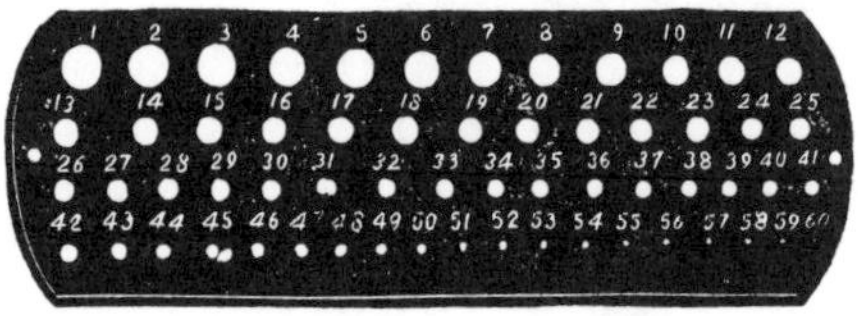

STUBS' STEEL WIRE GAUGES.

From Nos. 1 to 60 ... .

Used for Gauging Stubs' Bright Steel Wire and Twist Drills.

CAST STEEL WIRE GAUGES.

Small, No. 6 to 36.............. ......

Large, No. 0 to 36.............. ......

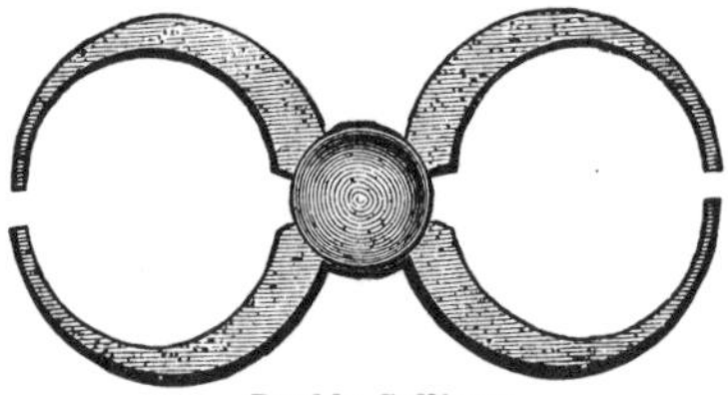

Double Callipers.

Brass, Plain..................... ......

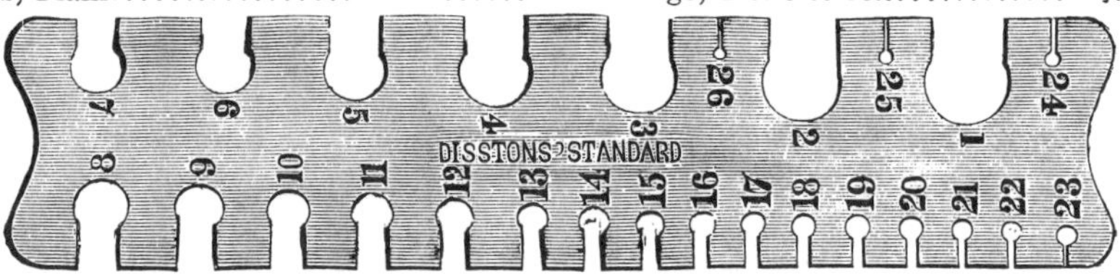

STANDARD WIRE GAUGE.—Accuracy Guaranteed.

Small, No. 1 to 26............. ...... Large, No. 0 to 36........... ....

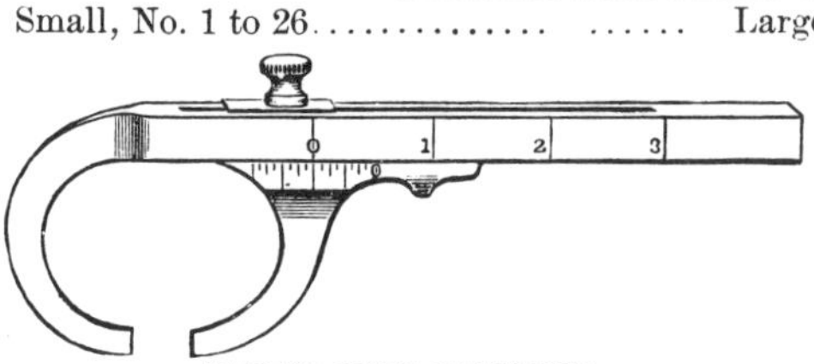

PATENT SLIDE CALLIPERS.

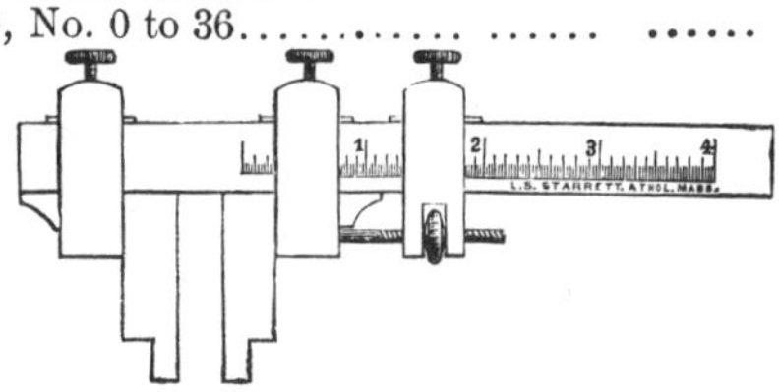

CALLIPER SQUARE.

4 in. with Adjusting Screw..... ......

NURLS OR MILLING WHEELS.

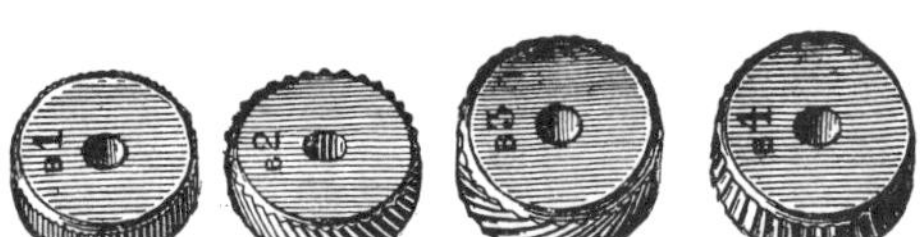

Nos. 1 and 2 are Flat, 3 and 4 Concave....

Lines straight across or diagonal are most used.

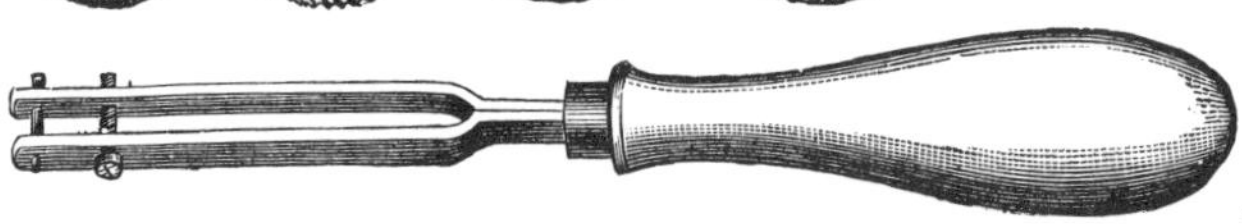

UNIVERSAL HANDLES.

For Milling Wheels.

Adjustable...... ......

CONCAVE SCRAPER.

STUBS' BROACHES.

No. 15 ..... 20 .... 25 ..... 30 ..... 35 ..... 40 ..... 45 ..... 50...... 55......

Broach Handles and Fancy Tool Handles.

EMERY WHEELS AND TOOLS.

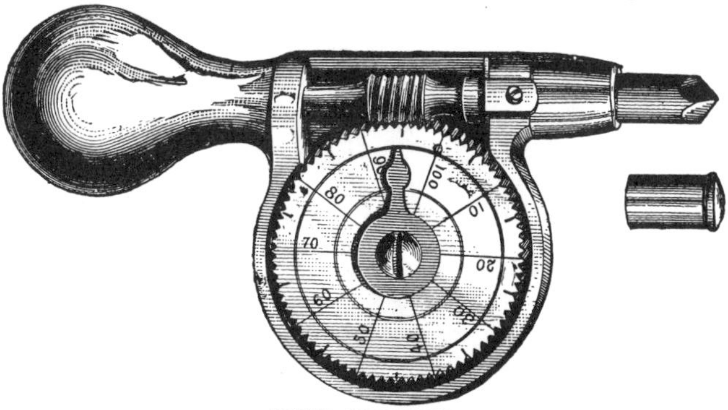

SPEED INDICATOR.

Single .... Double (either Right or Left)......... ......

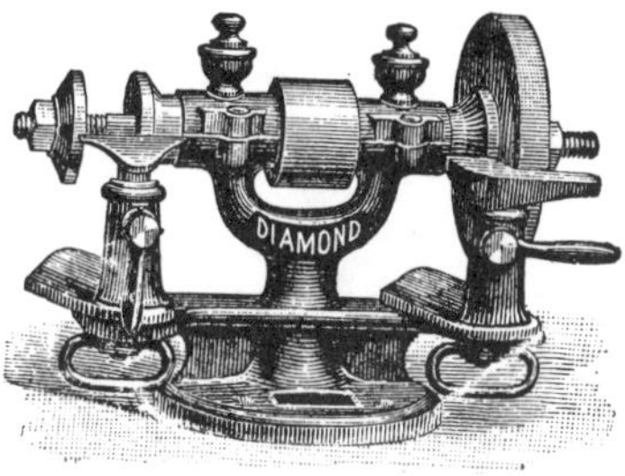

EMERY GRINDING MACHINE.

No. 2, To run 2 Wheels, up to 6 in....
No. 3, " 2 " " 9 in....

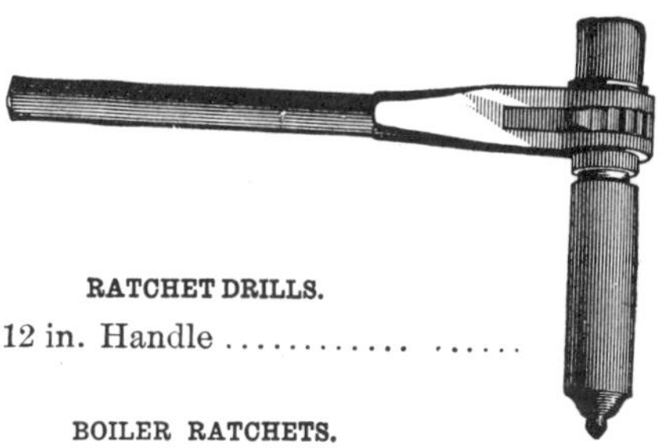

RATCHET DRILLS.

No. 2, 12 in. Handle ....

BOILER RATCHETS.

No. 2, 12 in. Handle ....

EMERY WHEELS.

Thickness	¼	½	¾	1	1¼	1½
Diameter, 6 in	......	......	......	......	......	......
" 8 in	......	......	......	......	......	......
" 10 in	......	......	......	......	......	......
" 12 in	......	......	......	......	......	......
" 14 in	......	......	......	......	......	......
" 16 in	......	......	......	......	......	......

Square, Round and Beveled Face, Same Price.

GROUND EMERY. In 10 lb. Cans.

Nos .... 8, 16, 18, 20, 24, 30, 36, 46, 54, 60, 70, 80, 90, 100, 120, 150...... Per Can.
Flour and Fine Flour...... ..... .Per Can.

MACHINISTS' TOOL CHESTS.

20x12x11............................ ......
22x13x12............................ ......

Chests made from selected Chestnut Wood, trimmed with heavy Bands and Bases, and nicely finished in hard oil finish.

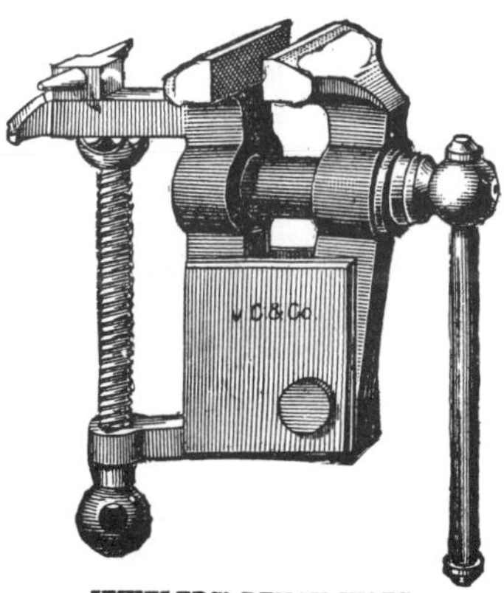

JEWELERS' BENCH VISES.
With Anvil, in the Different Sizes.

SURFACE GAUGES AND SAW SWAGES.

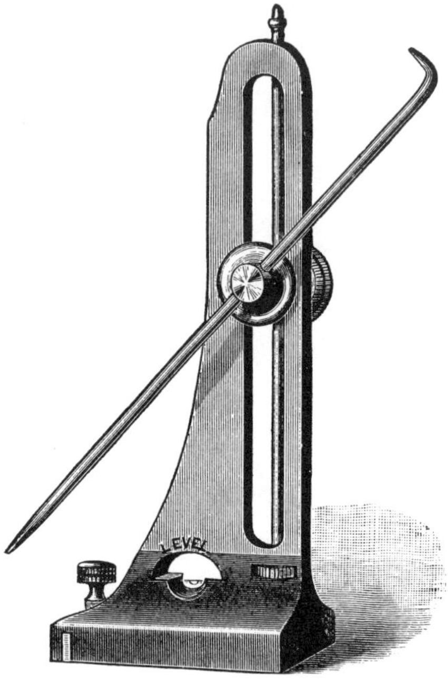

STANDARD SURFACE GAUGE.

8 in...

This Tool is provided with adjustable attachment for the quick and accurate adjustment of work on a line with the bed of a Planer, or parallel to its edge. It is also provided with a spirit level, making it a very convenient level and plumb as well as the best Surface Gauge made for machinists' use.

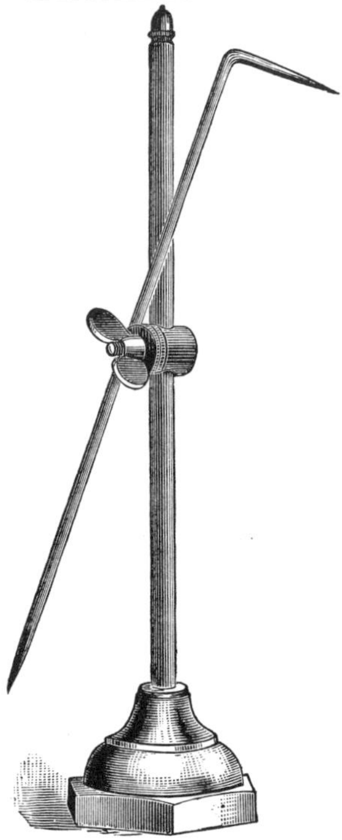

EXACT SURFACE GAUGE.

Small ...... Large ......

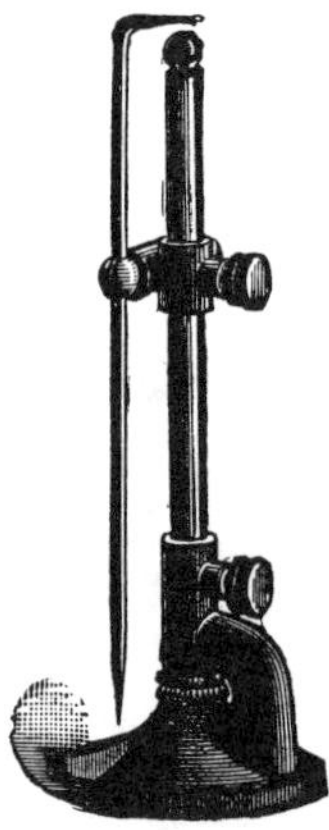

Starret's Pat. Surface Gauge....

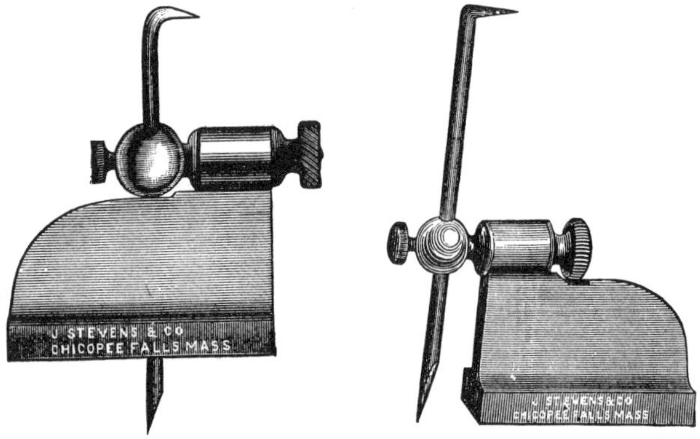

HATHAWAY'S COMBINATION GAUGE.

A new and useful instrument for machinists, tool makers, model makers, die sinkers, draughtsmen, etc. ......

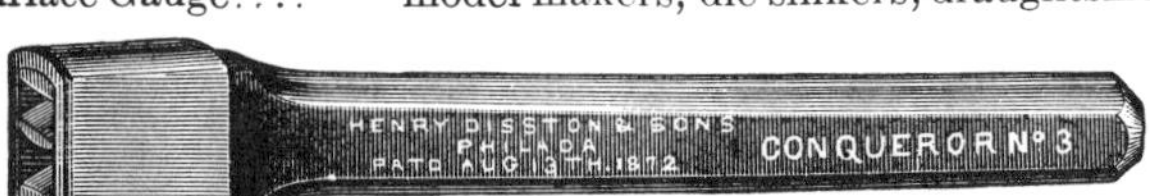

THE CONQUEROR SAW SWAGE OR UPSET.

Nos.. 0...... 1...... 2......

MISCELLANEOUS TOOLS.

For milling wire or castings for making screws, etc. Length, 1½ in.; diameter, ⅝ in.; size of hole, 3-32 in . . .
⅛ . . 5-32 . . 3-16 . . . . 7-32 . . . . ¼ . . . .
Larger Sizes, 5-16 . . . . 9-32 . . . . 11-32 . . .
⅜ . . .

NEW CENTRE REAMER.

This tool will be appreciated by every machinist. Accurately made of best cast steel. . . . .

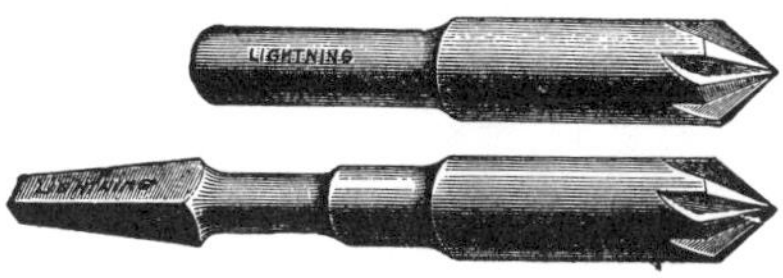

These Countersinks are of best material, so formed that they can be sharpened without losing shape. For use in drilling machines or bit braces. The round shanks for drilling machines and lathes are made ½ in. and 41-64th diam.

LIGHTNING TAPER REAMERS.

For Bit Brace. . . . .

Straight Shank. . . . .

These reamers are intended to make true, smooth holes when the punching or drilling is not quite perfect. Each reamer leaves a round, true cut hole. They will also be found useful for work on hard wood as well as on iron.

Size,	¼	5-16	⅜	7-16	½	⅝	¾ in.
Each	. . . .	. . . .	. . . .	. . . .	. . . .	. . . .	. . . .

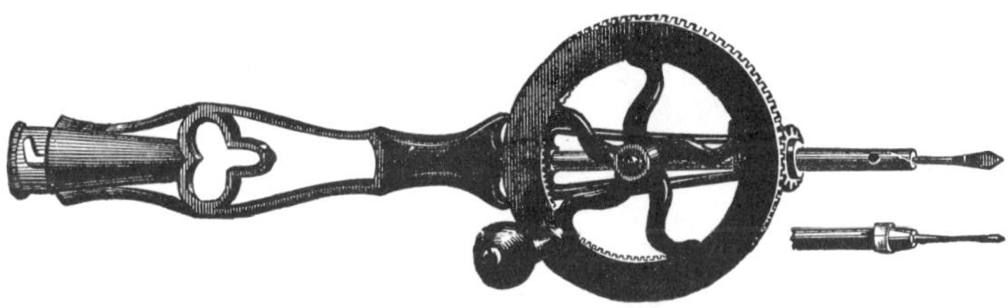

WHITNEY'S GEARED HAND DRILLS.

For Machinists, Metal Workers, Jewelers, Ornamental Wood Workers, etc. With six Tempered Drills, 1-32 to 3-16 inch, in a covered case which forms part of the handle.
With Adjustable Chuck and 6 Assorted Drills. . . . .

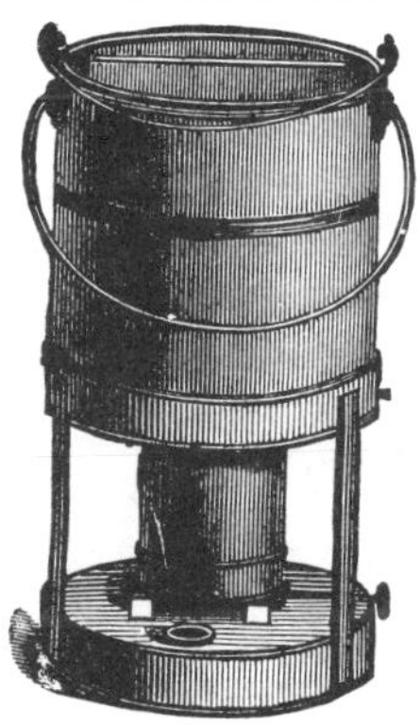

Kerosene Glue Pots.

No person using glue can afford to be without such an article. The cost of burning will not exceed from three to ten cents per day.

No. 3 . . . .

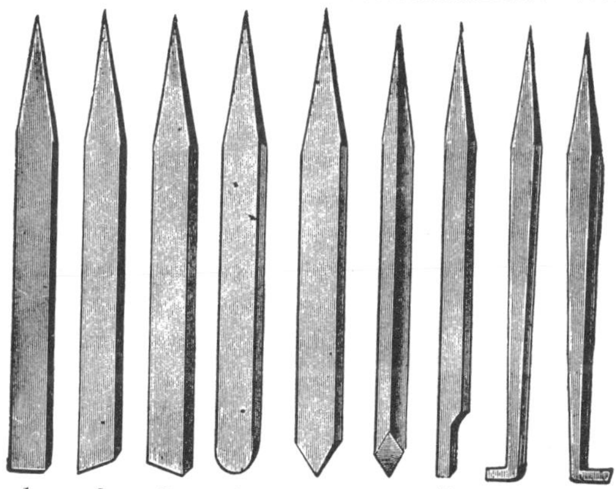

1 2 3 4 5 6 7 8 9

Hand Turning Tools for Metal, Hard Wood, Ivory or any hard material. The above cuts show the different shapes. They are all of one length, about 5 inches.

Price per set. . . . . Single. . . . .

ENGRAVERS' TOOLS AND SUPPLIES.

GRAVERS.

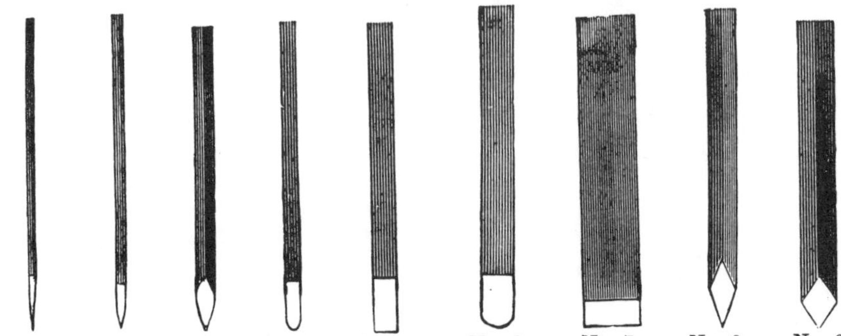

No. 1. Knife.	No. 2. Onglette.	No. 3. Oval.	No. 4. Round.	No. 5. Flat.	No. 6. ½ Round.	No. 7. Chisel.	No. 8 Lozenge.	No. 9. Square.

Stubs' and Vautier Gravers, Bent Gravers, Line Gravers,

Price of Gravers................ ...... Lining Tools........................ ......

Tint Tools, Assorted Shapes.. ......

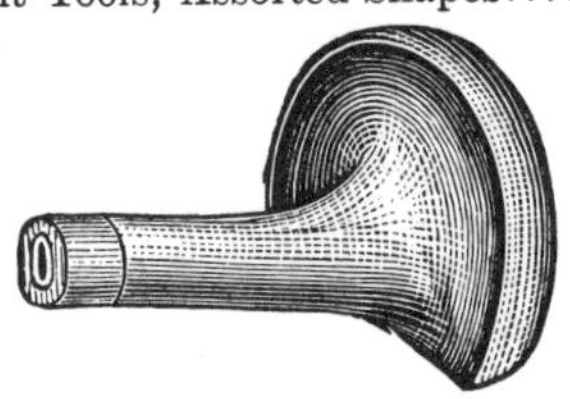

GRAVER HANDLES.

Assorted Shapes.. ......

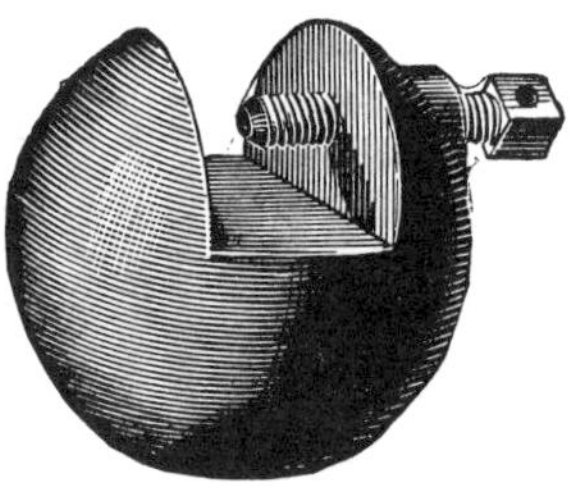

ENGRAVERS' BALLS.

Price............ ......

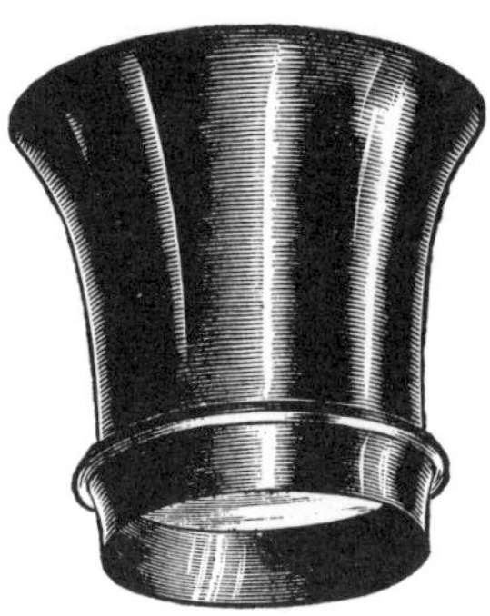

EYE GLASSES.

Price........... ......

EYE-GLASS STANDS.--Several Styles.

Price........... ......

LEATHER PADS.—Assorted Sizes.

For Engravers Ball............ ...... For Hand Engraving.............. ......

A Complete Line of Engravers' Tools.

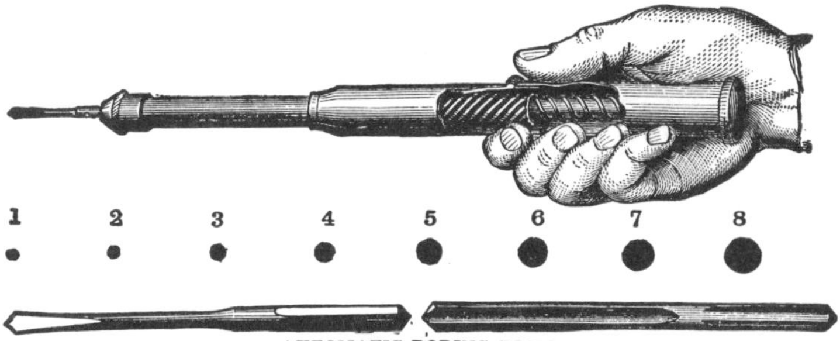

AUTOMATIC BORING DRILL.

Can be used in many places where the Bit-Brace, Gimlet or Brad Awl cannot... ......

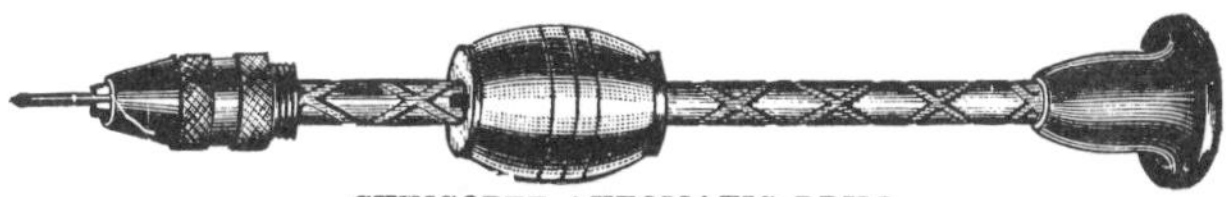

CHINCOPEE AUTOMATIC DRILL.

Continued motion in one direction with Chuck to hold Morse Twist Drills....... ......

GERMAN DRILL BRACES.

With Drills, Inch.................................... 9...... 10...... 12......

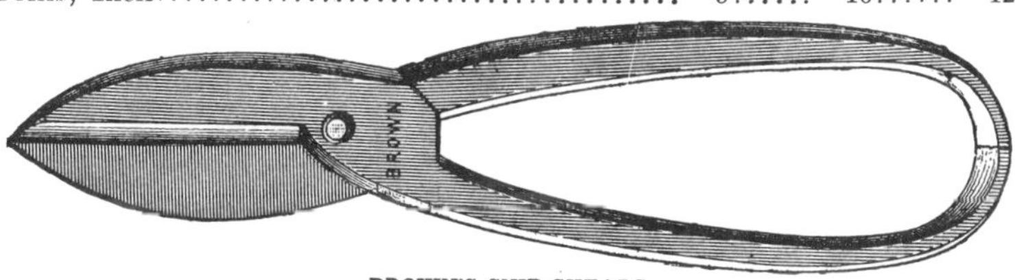

BROWN'S SNIP SHEARS.

Inch .... 5...... 6...... 7......

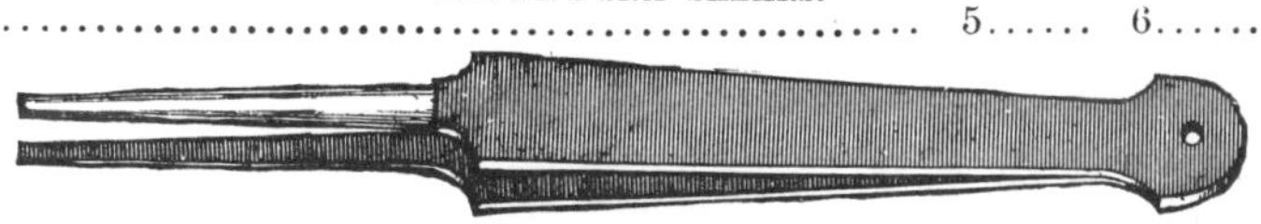

STEEL TWEEZERS.

Inch.. 3...... 4...... 5...... 6.....

BLOW PIPES.

Brass.

Plain, 8 .... 9.... 10 in ...

With Bowl 8.... 9.... 10...

Gas Blow Pipes.... ......

Glass Alcohol Lamps and Acid Bottles.

....

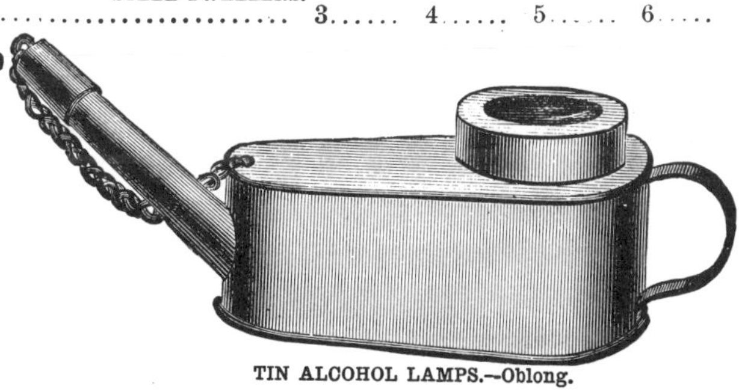

TIN ALCOHOL LAMPS.—Oblong.

....

Jewelers' Soft Solder.... ...... Silver Solder.... ...... Gas Heaters.... ......

JEWELERS' TOOLS AND SUPPLIES.

VAJEN & NEW, INDIANAPOLIS, IND.

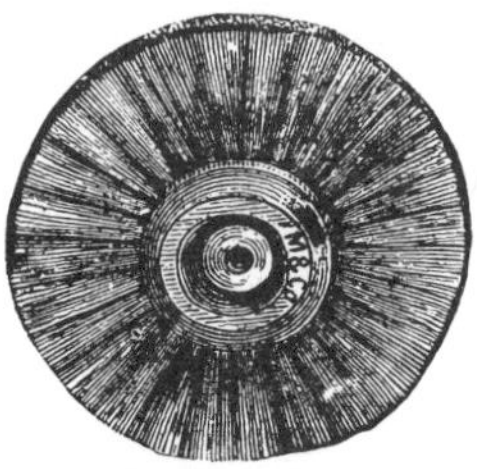

Bristle Wheel Brushes. ....

Wire Wheel Brushes. ....

Felt Polishing Wheels. ...

Cotton Buff Wheels. ....

Emery Wheels. ....

Oil Stone Wheels. ....

Jewelers' Brushes of all kinds.

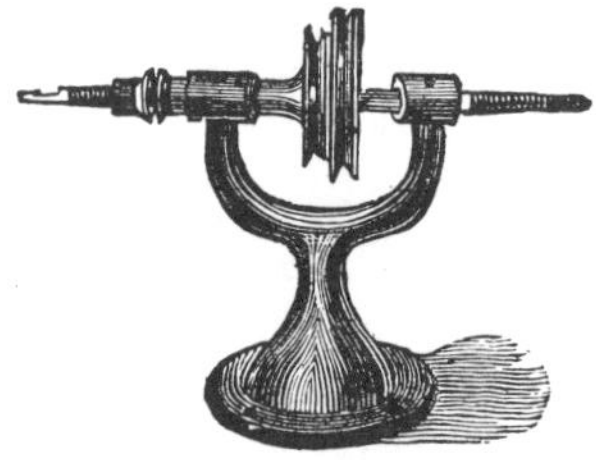

Polishing Head. ....

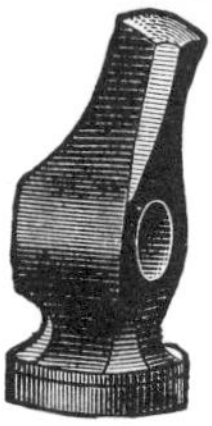

Single.

Double

STUBS' CHASING HAMMERS.

1....2 3....4 ...5....6 oz ...

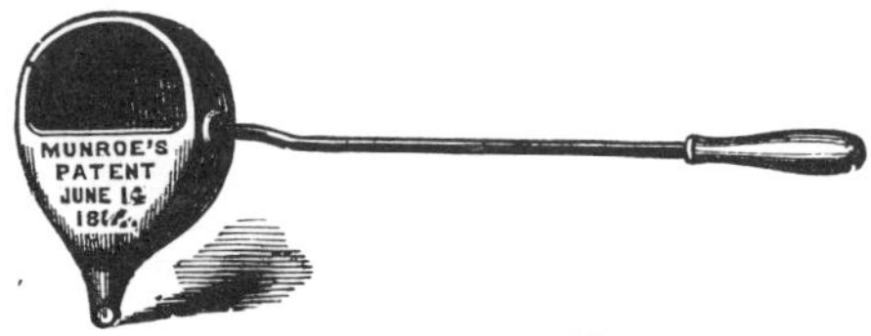

MELTING LADLES.

Self Skimming.................. ......

Spring Tongs for Crucibles. ....

Soldering Coppers.

Sand Crucibles.

No. 3's... 5's ...

3 in a nest.

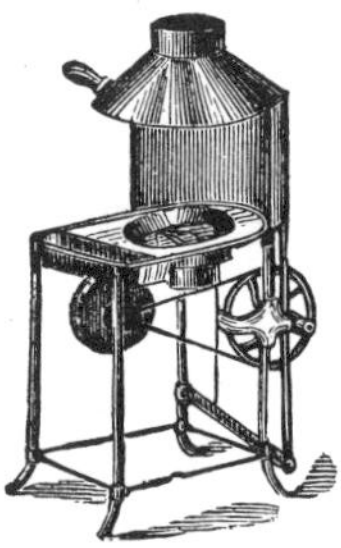

Jewelers' Forges.

With Hood.. ......

Without Hood......

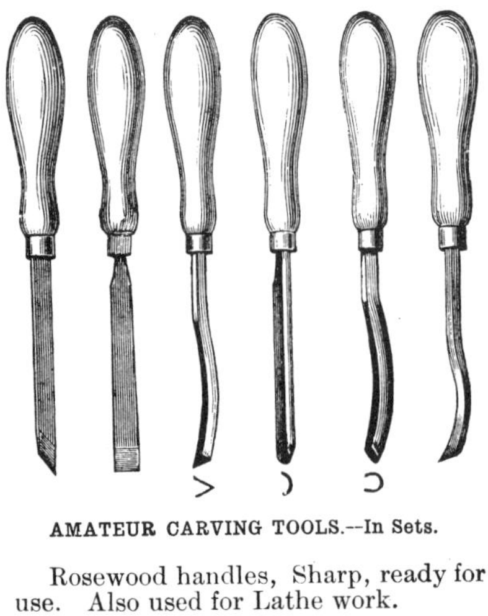

AMATEUR CARVING TOOLS.--In Sets.

Rosewood handles, Sharp, ready for use. Also used for Lathe work.

Prices furnished upon application.

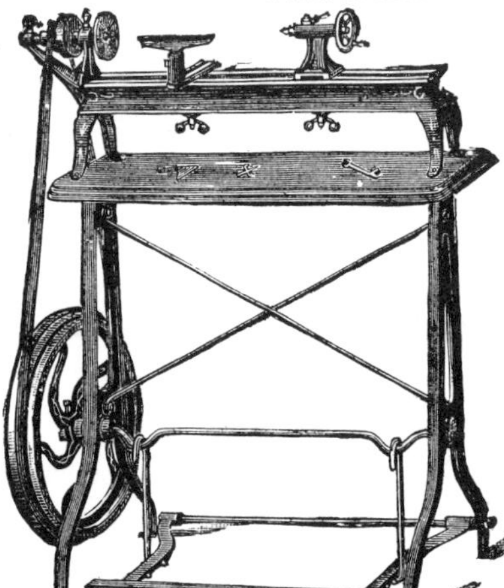

LATHE.

Swing 6 in., Between Centers 20 in., Balance Wheel 18 in., Weight 115 lbs.

This Lathe is very complete and perfect.

Lathe Attachment for Challenge Saw.

THE CHALLENGE SCROLL SAW.

We pronounce this the best finished, most complete and perfect scroll saw in the market. It has a patent tilting table, with hollow ball joint, upright drilling attachment, with improved drill chuck and improved dust blower. Just the machine for amateurs, model makers, jewelers, shell workers, printers, and all light scroll sawing in wood, bone, shell or metal. ......

THE CHALLENGE LATHE ATTACHMENT.

Made of iron and steel; length of bed, 18 in.; distance between centers, 11 in., and swings 4 in. Has a solid emery wheel for grinding and polishing. With this Lathe is furnished a set of best steel Turning Tools and a Screw Driver, packed in a nice box, ready for shipment. ......

Challenge Scroll Saw.

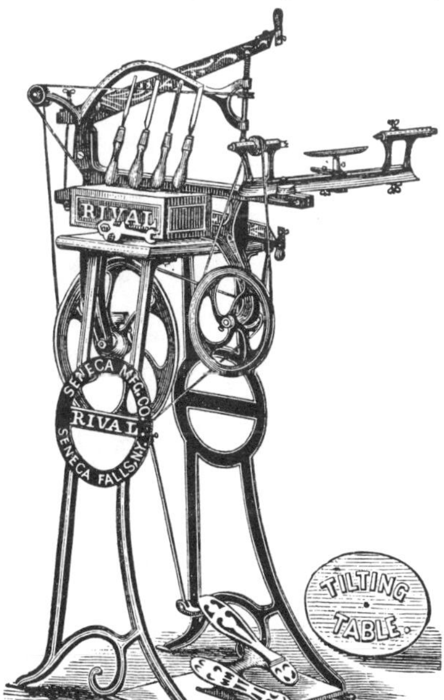

Rival Scroll Saw.

THE RIVAL SCROLL SAW.

This machine for beauty of design, simplicity of construction and practical use far excels any ever offered for the price. It has a patent tilting table, with hollow ball joint, an upright drilling attachment that cannot be found on any other saw for the price in the market. The table is polished and nickel-plated. This machine is designed for light work, sawing inch wood and under readily, but it will cut up to 1½ inch. ......

THE RIVAL LATHE ATTACHMENT.

This is a handy and useful attachment; will take work 9 in. long and 4 in. in diameter. It also has a solid emery wheel for grinding and polishing, also a set of three best steel Turning Tools and a Screw Driver; all packed in a nice box, ready for shipment. ......

Screw Driver.

Hand Drill.

Bracket Tools of All Kinds.

Bracket Wood, ⅛, 3-16 and ¼ in. thick, in Walnut, Cherry, White Holly, Rosewood, Cocoabolo, Ebony, Mahogany, Red Cedar.

Bracket Designs, all the Latest Patterns.

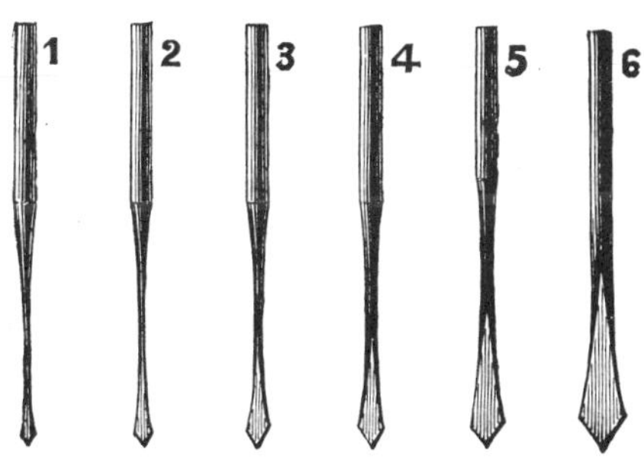

DRILL POINTS.

Cuts are Exact Size.

Set of Six.................... ......

SCROLL SAWS.

Hand Scroll Saw...... ......

This saw we keep in several grades, packed each saw in a paper box, with designs, saw blades, awl and impression paper, and full directions for using saw.

NEW LESTER IMPROVED.

This Saw is as near perfect as can be made for the money. Strong, durable and accurate. The iron work is nicely japanned, black with stripes of red and gilt, giving the machine a very handsome and rich appearance. The wood work is varnished, bringing out the beautiful grain of the ash; with emery wheel and drilling attachment, six drills, six saw blades, wrench, screw driver, two sheets of designs, and a nice box for small tools. Saw has nickel-plated tilting table.

With Lathe .... Without Lathe ...

No. 1. NEW ROGERS SAW.

Best Cheap Saw offered to the public; price....

The entire frame work is made from iron, painted and japanned black and ornamented with red and gilt stripes. With a dust blower and drill attachment, with tilting table. Six saw blades, wrench, sheet of designs and drill point.

BRACKET SAW BLADES.

10 ......
9 ......
8 ......
7 ......
6 ......
5 ......
4 ......
3 ......
2 ......
1 ......

A complete stock of Swiss, Griffin's and American Saw Blades.

PLIERS AND NIPPERS.

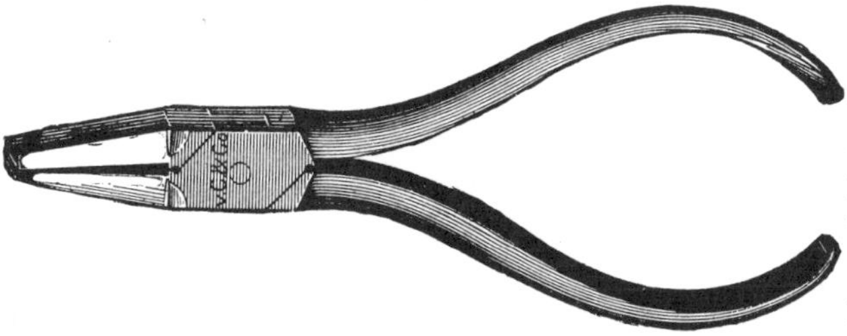

PLIERS.

Flat Nose.

Inch 3 3½ 4 4½ 5
Blk Steeled.. .. ..

Inch 5½ 6 7 8
Blk Steeled .. ..

Inch 3 3½ 4 4½ 5
Blk Stubs.. .. ..

Long Flat Nose.

Inch...... 4½.... 5....

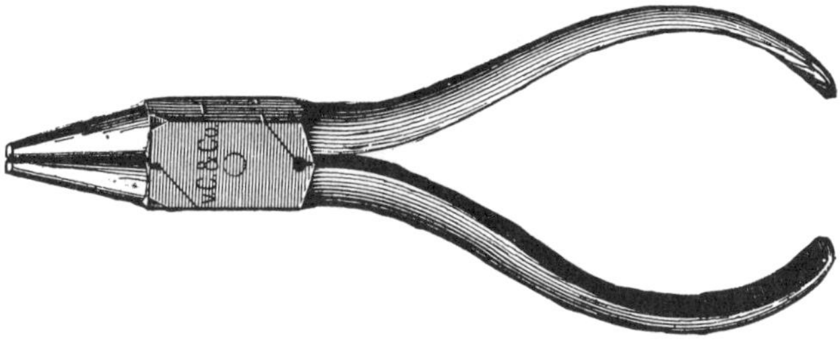

Round Nose.

Inch . . 3 3½ 4
Black Steeled ... ...

Inch........ 4½ 5 6
Black Steeled ... ...

Inch 3 3½ 4
Black Stubs . ...

Inch 4½ 5
Black Stubs.... ... ...

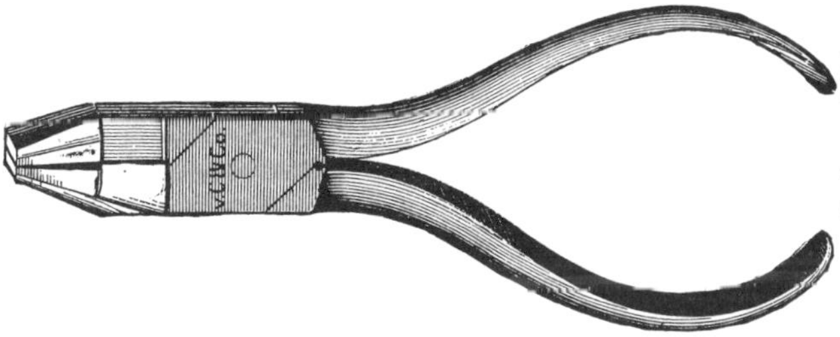

Side Cutting.

Inch...... 4 4½ 5 5½ 6
Blk C. S.. .. ..

Also, other styles of Side-Cutting Pliers.

Side-Cutting Telegraph Pliers, Stubs Pattern, extra heavy cast steel, best quality, 8 in. . ....

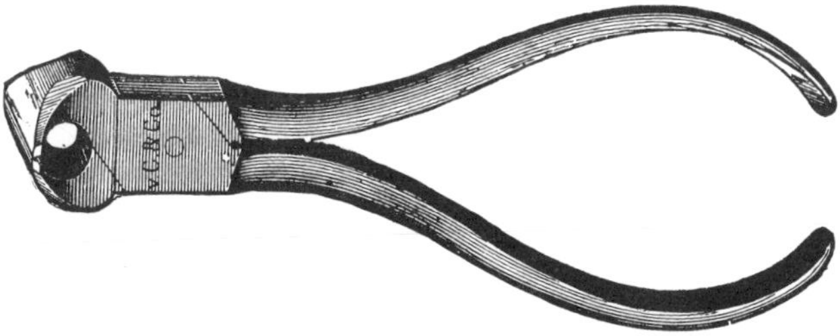

END CUTTING NIPPERS.

Inch 4½ 5 5½
Blk, ex.quality... ... ...

Inch........ 6 7 8
Blk, ex.quality... ... ...

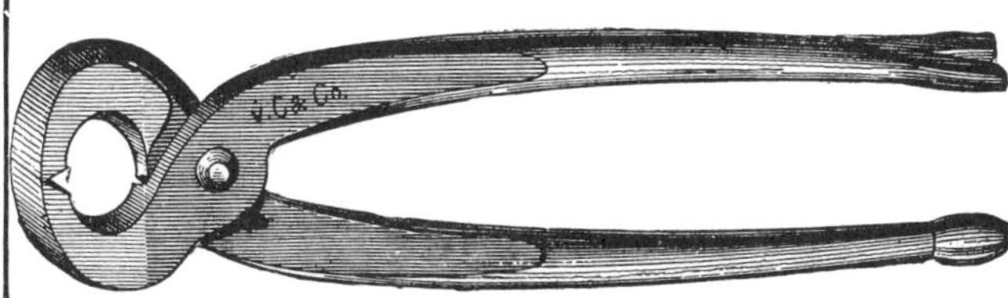

CARPENTERS' PINCERS.

Black. Polished Steel Jaws.

Inch.. 6... 7... 8... 9...

Button's Pat. Cast Steel Pliers and Wire Cutter Combined.

Inch 4½ 6 8 10
Polished.. ... ...

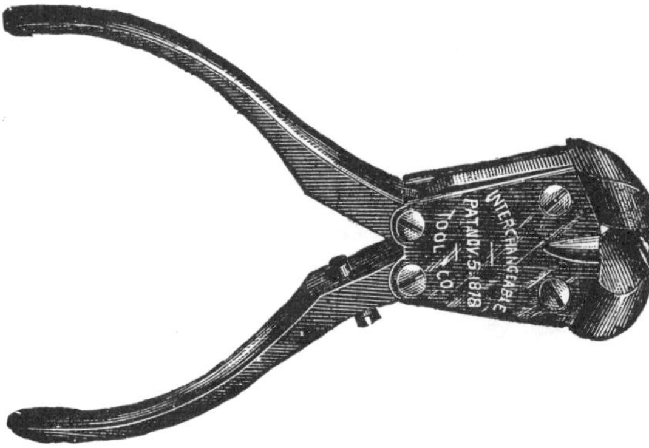

Hall's Patent Compound Lever Cutting Nippers.

With Interchangeable Jaws.

Nos.	1	2	4	6
Inch	4	5	7	8
Plain	....	....	....	....
Nickeled	....	....	....	....
Extra Jaws	....	....	....	....

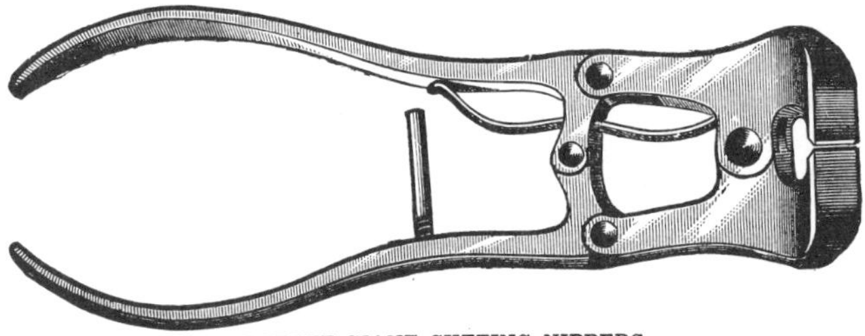

PATENT GIANT CUTTING NIPPERS.

5 Inch .... 7 Inch .... Extra Jaws.......... ......
Extra Springs .... 7 inches will cut wire up to 3-16 inch.

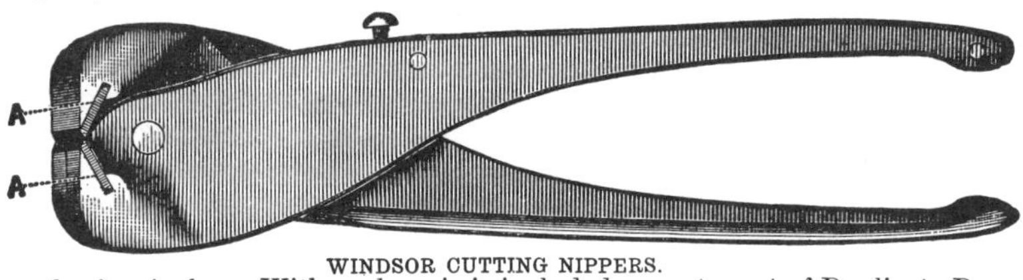

WINDSOR CUTTING NIPPERS.

Length nine inches. With each pair is included an extra set of Duplicate Reversible Double Edge Cutters. A A are reversible, which gives two sets of cutting edges with each set of cutters.

Price.................................. .... Extra Cutters..........per pair.

Extension Frame, Polished and Nickel-Plated.. ......
Blades, Inch.................................... 6...... 7...... 8...... 9......

HACK SAWS.

Inch.. 10...... 12......

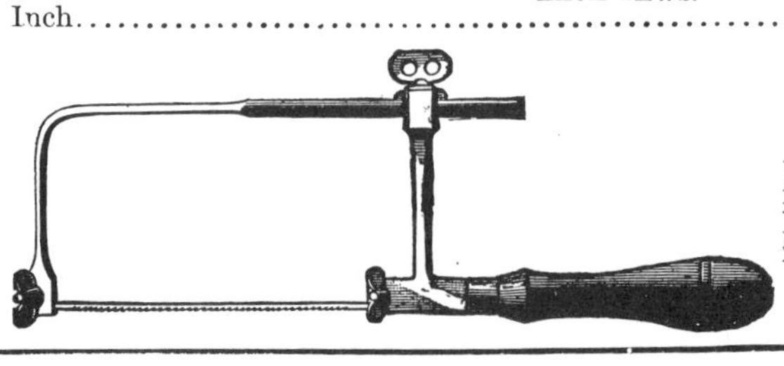

JEWELERS' SAW.

Made of Forged Spring Steel, with Rosewood Handle, Polished and Nickel-Plated. Will hold a saw from one to six inches in length.

Other Saws, pages 242 and 243.

DRAWING INSTRUMENTS.

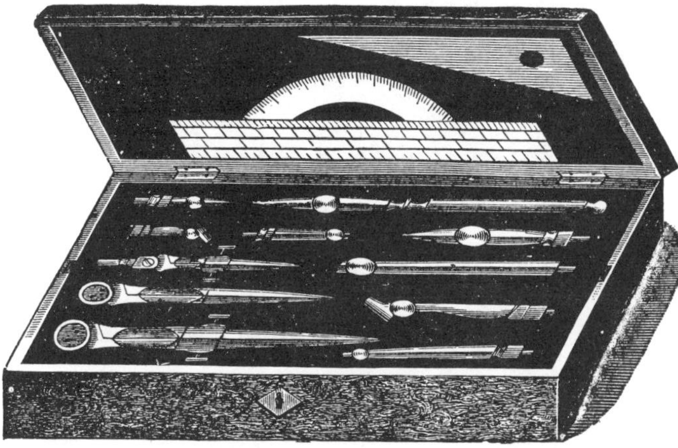

A full assortment of German and Swiss Drawing instruments in Cases and Separate. Drawing Papers, Tracing Cloth, Trammel Points, School Sets, Plotting Scales, Ruling Pens, Bow Pens and Pencils, Needle Points, etc.

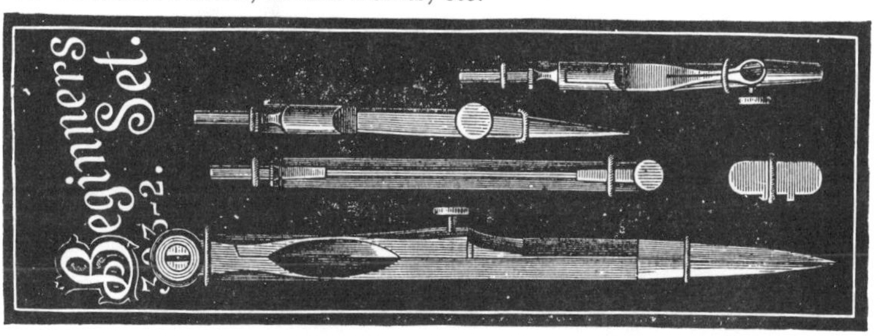

FRENCH INSTRUMENTS ON CARDS.

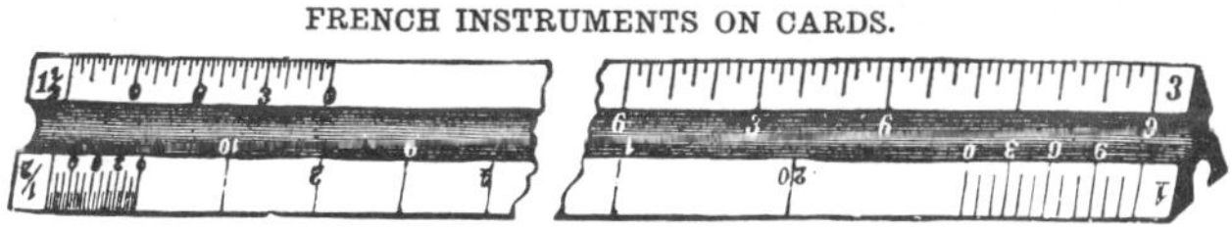

TRIANGULAR BOXWOOD SCALES.

Architects or Engineers.. 6...... 12 in......

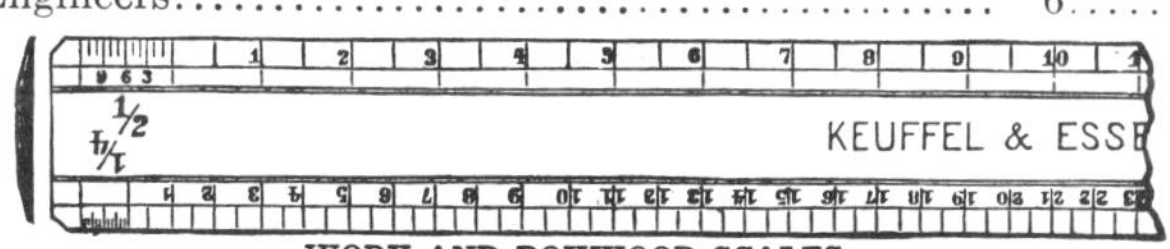

IVORY AND BOXWOOD SCALES.

Flat.. 6...... 12 in.....

DRAWING PINS OR THUMB TACKS.

German Silver Heads, Steel Points.. .....

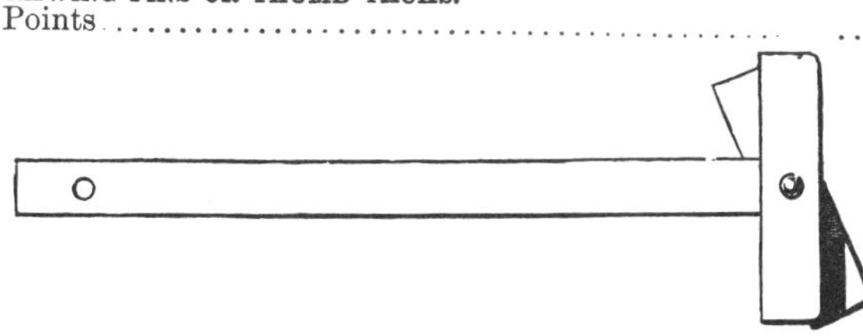

PEARWOOD TRIANGLES.

......

PEARWOOD T SQUARES.

Inch.................. 18........ 24........ 36........

Black Board Crane Compasses.

Land Chain, Iron, Brass Handles............................... 66...... 100 ft......

Ass Skin Case, ½ in. Cotton Tape .. 25 .. 30.... 40... 50.... 66.... 75.... 100 ft....
" " " ½ in. Holland " ... 25 ... 30.... 40.... 50.... 66.... 75.... 100 ft ...
Pat. Leather Case, ½ in. Holland Tape 25 ... 30 ... 40.... 50 ... 66 ... 75.... 100 ft ...
Bend " " ⅝ in. Heavy Corded Tapes .... 50 ... 66 ... 75.... 100 ft ...

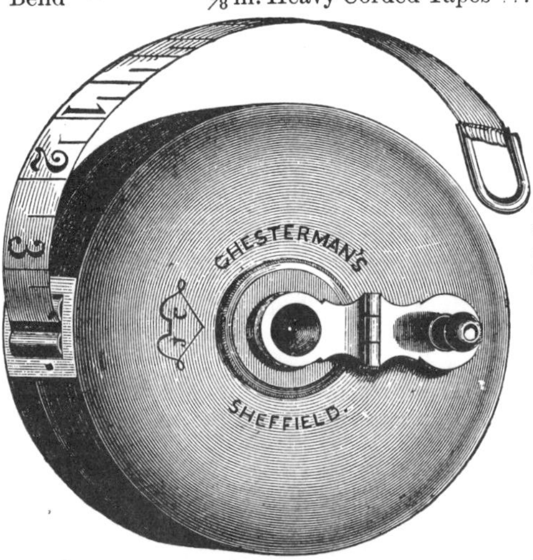

Chesterman's Tapes—Divided in either 10ths or 12ths.

Metallic ... 50 ... 66 ... 75.... 100 ft....
Steel .... 50.... 65.... 75.... 100 ft....

Spring Pocket Tapes.

Plated Case, Linen Tape, 3... 5.. 6 ft...
Plastic " " " 3.. 5 ft...
Nickeled " ⅜ in. " 3 5 6 8 12 ft.
.. ..

Steel Pocket Tapes--Spring.

3....4....5....6....8....12.... 15 ft....

MASONS' AND PLASTERERS' TOOLS.

VAJEN & NEW, INDIANAPOLIS, IND.

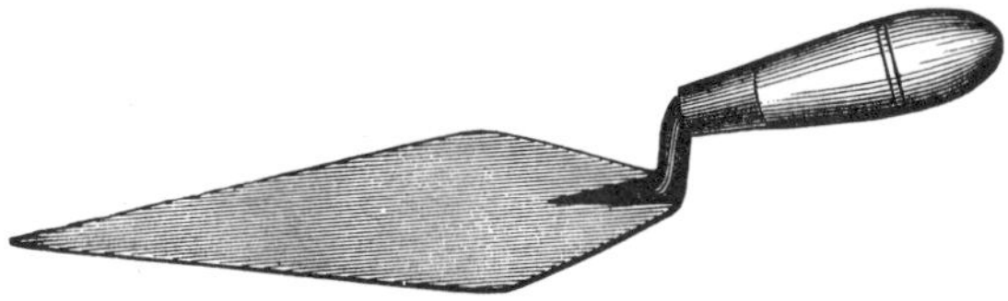

Brade's Brick Trowels--London Pattern.

Sizes........................ 10 ..... 10½...... 11...... 11½...... 12 in......

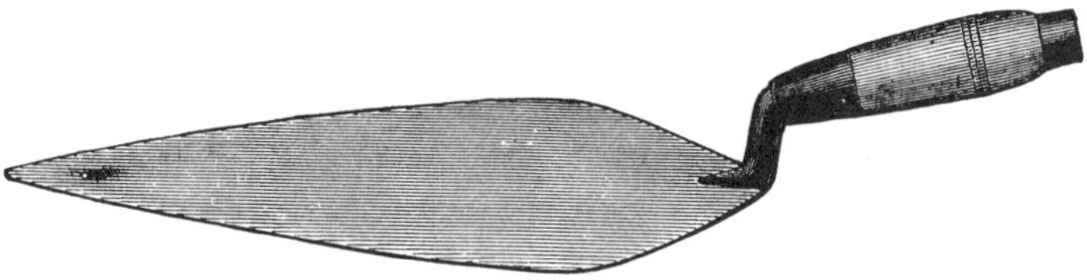

Common Brick Trowels.

Sizes................................ ...... 8...... 9...... 10...... 11 in......

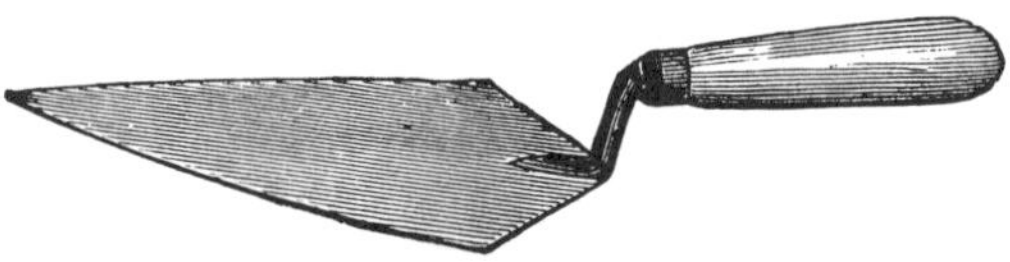

Pointing Trowels.

Sizes .... 4...... 4½...... 5 in......

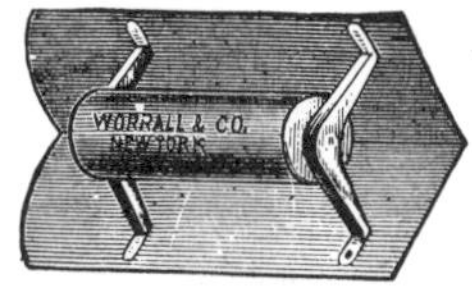

Corner Trowels.

Size .... 6 in .....

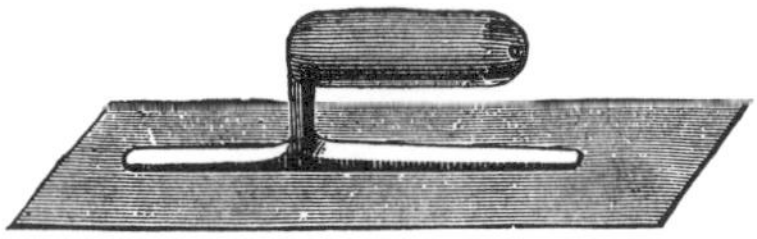

Plastering Trowels.

Sizes.. 10½...... 11...... 11½...... 12......

Improved Hock, with Patent Handles.

Derby Float, with Patent Handles.

We also have the Handles extra.

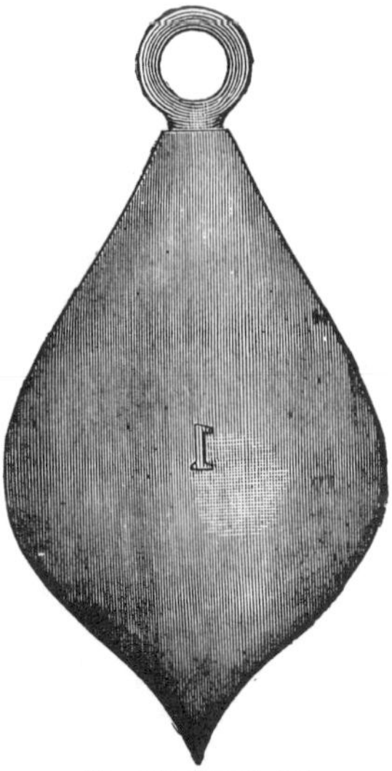

Mason's Plumb Bob.

Lead......... 2℔......

Mitre Rods, with Back.

Size.................................. 14 in......

TINNERS' TOOLS.

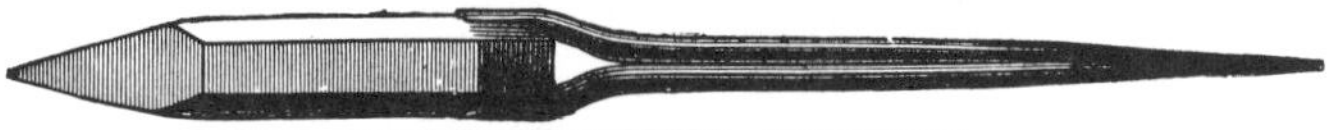

SOLDERING COPPERS.—Extra Finish.

Pounds to the Pair.. 2...... 3 ..... 4......

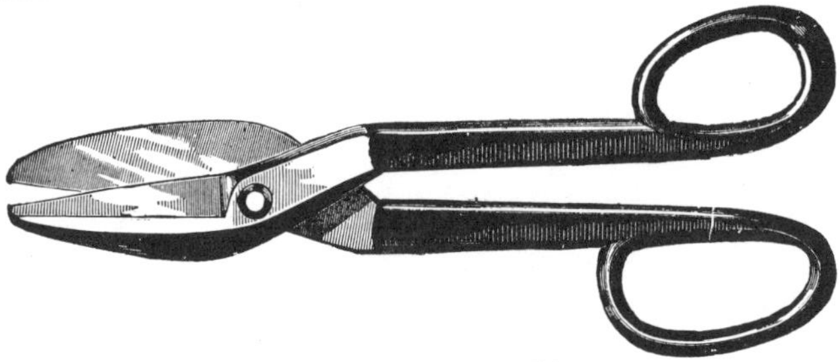

HAND SHEARS OR SNIPS.

Nos... 7 ..... 8 ..... 9......

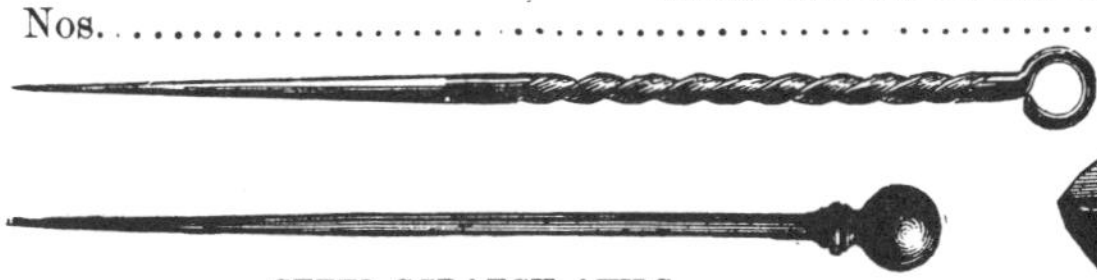

STEEL SCRATCH AWLS.

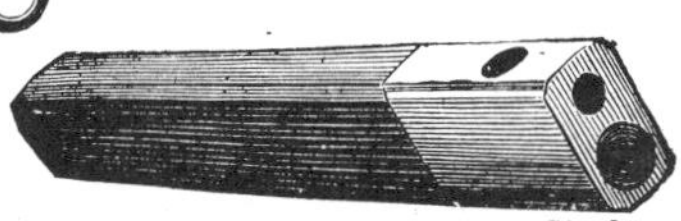

Rivet Sets and Headers.—Cast Steel.

Nos. 00 .. 0 .. 1 .. 2 .. 3 .. 4 .. 5 ..

6 .. 7 .. 8 ..

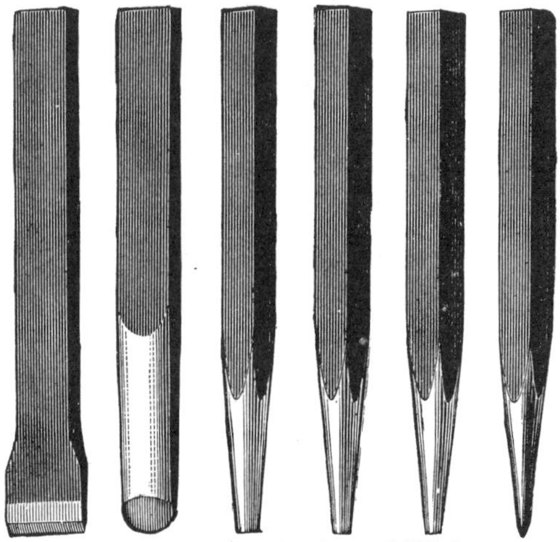

Solid Punches, Prick Punches and Chisels.

TINNERS' STOVES

Nicely Japanned, Double Damper, Base Burning, Reversible Flue, causing the fire to burn downward directly on the soldering coppers. This Stove or Fire Pot is provided with a grate and an ash pit. The top and bottom plate of the Stove, together with the spout piece, are of cast iron, and the body or jacket of sheet iron. A Tinner can not afford to make his own stove when he can buy this one, having all the new improvements, considering the low price at which it is sold.

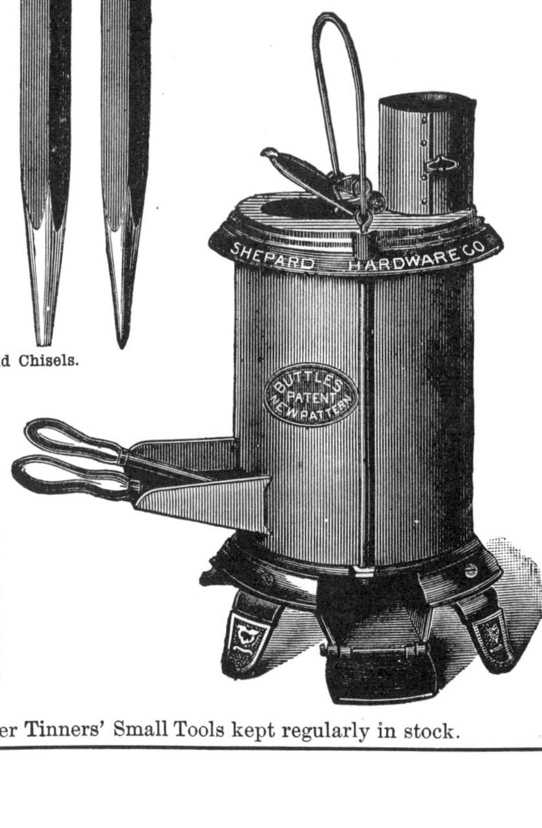

Tinners' Mallets and other Tinners' Small Tools kept regularly in stock.

BUTCHERS' TOOLS.

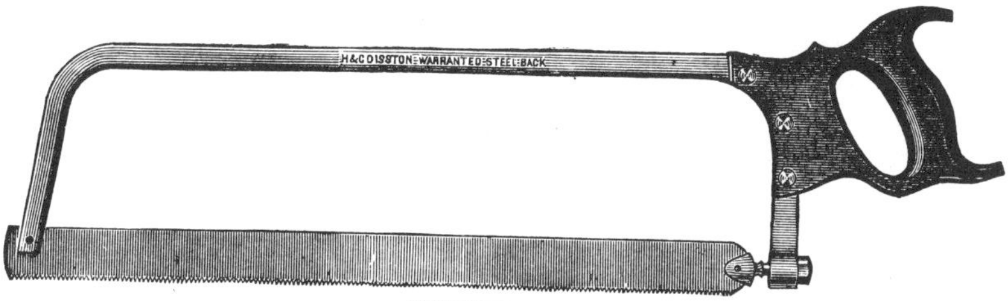

BUTCHER SAWS.

Flat Steel Back, Inch .... 18 ... 20.... 22 ... 24 ... 26....

FAMILY MEAT SAWS.

Inch,... 12 ..... 14...... 16......

Other Saws, pages 242 and 243.

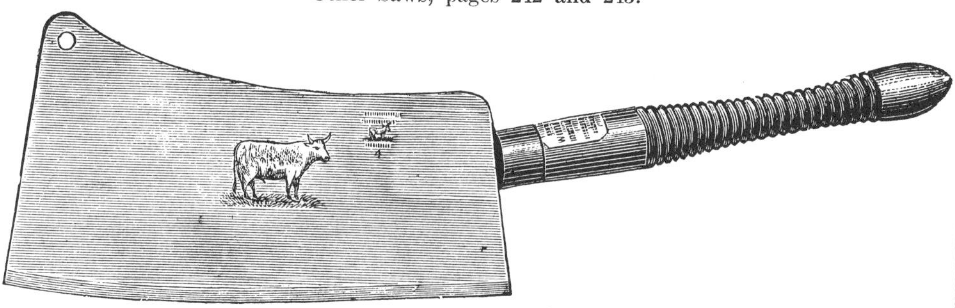

BUTCHERS' CLEAVERS.

Nos.	0	1	2	3	4	5
Inch	7......	8	9......	10......	11......	12......

BUTCHERS' BLOCK PINS.

No 1, 18 in. long, Polished .... No. 2, 18 in. long, Tinned........ ......

No. 3, 17 in. long, Tinned.......... ...... No. 4, 16 in. long, Milled ....

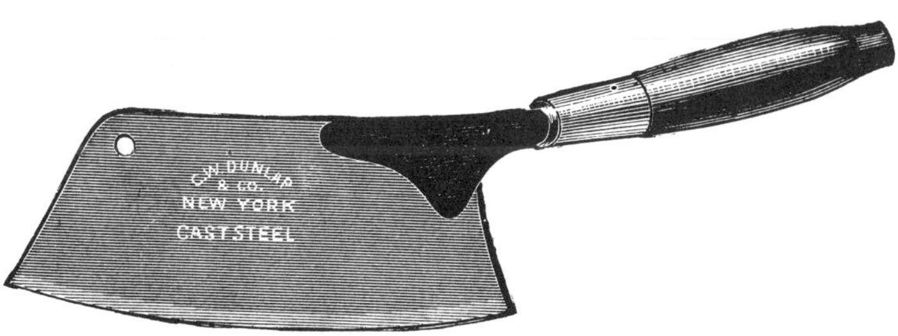

FAMILY CLEAVERS.

6 in. Blades, Cast Steel Forged Blades, Malleable Iron Shanks................. ......

Skewers, Inch.. 5...... 6......

VAJEN & NEW, INDIANAPOLIS, IND.

MEAT HOOKS AND BLOCK SCRAPERS.

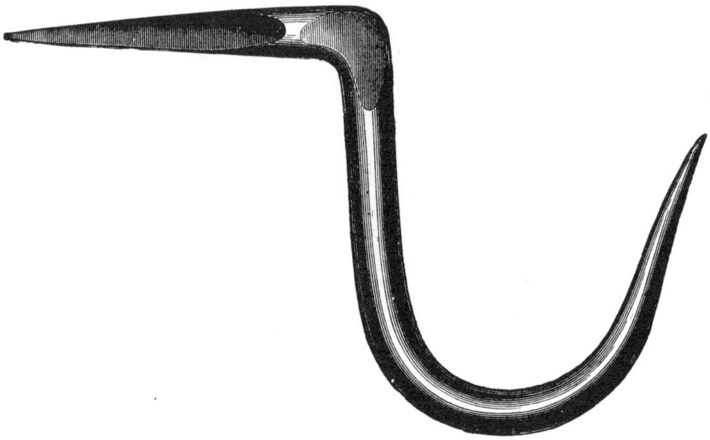

TINNED WROUGHT IRON MEAT HOOKS.

To Drive, Nos.	11......	12......	13	14......
To Screw, Nos.	21......	22	23	24......
To Screw on, Nos.	31......	32......	33......	34......
Bar Meat Hooks, Nos.	90, 5-16 in		92, ½ in.......	
S Meat Hooks, Nos.			65......	66......

TINNED WIRE MEAT HOOKS.

To Screw in, Nos.	43......	44......	45......

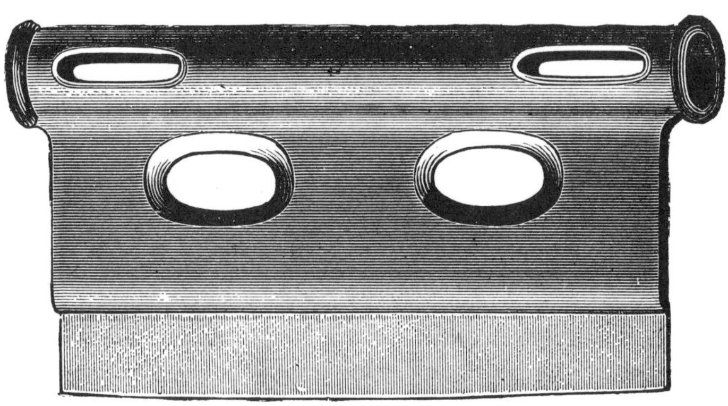

BUTCHERS' BLOCK SCRAPERS.

No. 26, Best Cast Steel Blades, Oil Tempered.................................. ......

HOG SCRAPERS.

Made of No. 18 Sheet Steel, Round ....

These are considered the best Instruments in use for the purpose.

MOULDERS' TOOLS.

Moulders' Dusting Brushes... ....
Steel Casting Brushes . Square, 3½ ... 4 ... 4½ in ... With Handle .. Round ......
Foundry Riddles, Steel, 2 .. 3 ... 4 ... 5 ... 6 ... 8 ... 10 ... 12 ... 14 ... 16 in. ......
Sand Screens. ....
Moulders' Bellows ...... 12 .... 14 ..... 16 in. ......
Moulders' Shovels ....

A complete line of Moulders' Tools; also Pattern Letters and Figures.

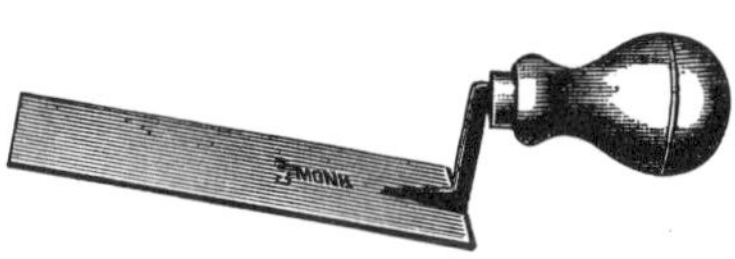

SQUARE TROWELS.

Length.	4	4½	5	5½	6 in.
1 in .	$6.00	$6.60	$7.20	$7.80	$8.40
1¼ in ..	7.20	7.80	8.40	9.00	9.60
1½ in...	8.40	9.00	9.60	10.20	10.80
1¾ in ..	9.60	10.20	10.80	11.40	12.00
2 in...	10.80	11.40	12.00	12.60	13.20

HEART TROWELS.

Width.	2	2¼	2½	2¾	3 in.
Doz....	$6.00	$7.50	$9.00	$10.50	$12.00

FINISHING TROWELS.

No. 2, $1.20 per doz. less than square.

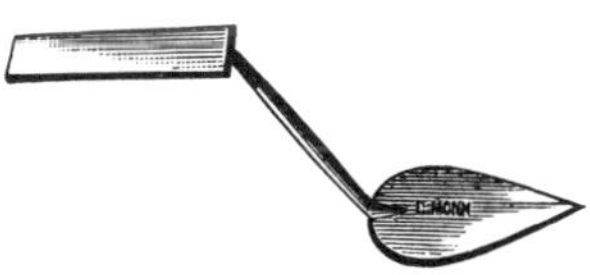

HEART AND SQUARE.

Width.	1	1¼	1½	1¾	2 in.
Doz....	$6.00	$7.50	$9.00	$10.50	$12.00

No. 1, 60c. per doz. less than square.

Bench Lifter ...	⅜	½	⅝	¾ in.
Doz	$5.40	$6.00	$6.60	$7.20

Stove Tool ...	⅜	½	⅝	¾ in.
Doz	$4.80	$5.40	6.00	$6.60

LIFTERS.--Per Dozen.

Lentgth,	10	12	14	16	18	20 in.
⅛ in.	$4.50	$5.25	$6.00	$	$	$
¼ in.	4.50	5.25	6.00			
⅜ in.	5.25	6.00	6.75			
½ in.	6.00	6.75	7.50	8.25		

Length,	12	14	16	18	20 in.
⅝ in.	$7.50	$8.25	$9.00	$	$
¾ in.	8.25	9.00	9.75	10.50	11.25
⅞ in.	9.00	9.75	10.50	11.25	12.00
1 in.	9.75	10,50	11.25	12.00	12.75

FLANGE LIFTERS.

½x14	½x16	⅝x14	⅝x16	¾x14	¾x16	¾x18	⅞x16	⅞x18	⅞x20	1x16	1x18	1x20
$12.75	$13.50	$13.50	$14.25	$14.25	$15.00	$15.75	$15.75	$16.50	$17.25	$16.50	$17.25	$18.00

Per Dozen.

SPOON.

Width	1	$1\frac{1}{4}$	$1\frac{1}{2}$ in.
Dozen	$6.00	$7.50	$9.00

FLUTE.

Width	$\frac{3}{8}$	$\frac{5}{8}$	$\frac{7}{8}$ in.
Dozen	$7.50	$8.25	$9.00

TAPER ROUND.

Width	$\frac{3}{4}$	1	$1\frac{1}{4}$	$1\frac{1}{2}$ in.
Dozen	$5.40	$6.00	$7.50	$9.00

BEAD.

Width	$\frac{1}{2}$	$\frac{7}{8}$	$\frac{3}{4}$ in.
Dozen	$6.00	$6.75	$7.50

SQUARE STRAIGHT.

Width	$\frac{1}{2}$	$\frac{5}{8}$	$\frac{3}{4}$	$\frac{7}{8}$	1 in.
Dozen	$5.25	$6.00	$6.75	$7.50	$8.25

CIRCULAR FLANGE.

Width	$\frac{1}{2}$	$\frac{5}{8}$	$\frac{3}{4}$	$\frac{7}{8}$	1 in.
Dozen	$10.50	$12.00	$13.50	$15.00	$16.50

DOUBLE SQUARE.

Width	$\frac{1}{2}$	$\frac{5}{8}$	$\frac{3}{4}$	$\frac{7}{8}$	1 in.
Dozen	$4.80	$5.40	$6.00	$6.75	$7.50

YANKEE.

Width	$\frac{1}{2}$	$\frac{5}{8}$	$\frac{3}{4}$	$\frac{7}{8}$	1 in.
Dozen	$5.25	$6.00	$6.75	$7.50	$8.40

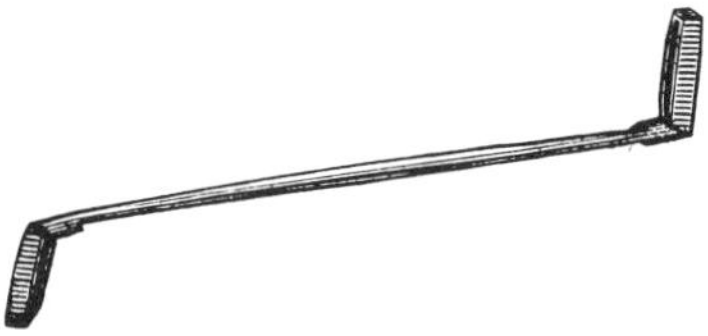

FLAT FLANGE.

Width	$\frac{1}{2}$	$\frac{5}{8}$	$\frac{3}{4}$	$\frac{7}{8}$	1 in.
Dozen	$9.75	$10.50	$12.00	$13.50	$15.00

FLAT AND CIRCULAR FLANGE.

Width	$\frac{1}{2}$	$\frac{5}{8}$	$\frac{3}{4}$	$\frac{7}{8}$	1 in.
Dozen	$12.00	$13.50	$15.00	$16.50	$18.00

FLANGE AND BEAD.

Width	$\frac{1}{2}$	$\frac{5}{8}$	$\frac{3}{4}$	$\frac{7}{8}$	1 in.
Dozen	$9.00	$9.75	$10.50	$11.25	$12.00

HALF ROUND CORNER.

Width	1	$1\frac{1}{4}$	$1\frac{1}{2}$	$1\frac{3}{4}$	2 in.
Dozen	$5.25	$6.00	$6.75	$7.50	$8.25

OVAL DOG TAIL.

Width	$\frac{3}{4}$	1	$1\frac{1}{4}$ in.
Dozen	$6.00	$6.75	$8.25

SQUARE CORNER.

Width	$\frac{3}{4}$	1	$1\frac{1}{4}$ in.
Dozen	$6.00	$6.75	$8.25

PIPE.

Dozen.............................. $5.40

PLUMBERS' TOOLS.

Chambers' Calking Chisels.............................. ....

Plumbers' Bending Pins.. ......

PLUMBERS' LADLES.

Inch........................... $2\frac{1}{2}$...... 3...... $3\frac{1}{2}$...... 4...... 5...... 6......

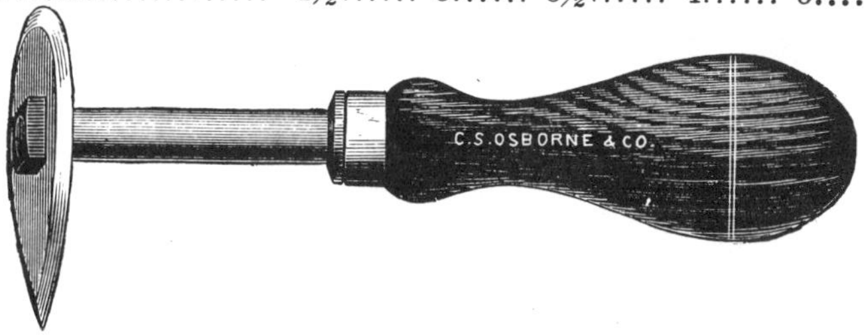

Plumbers' Shave Hooks, Oval, Half-Oval and Triangle ....

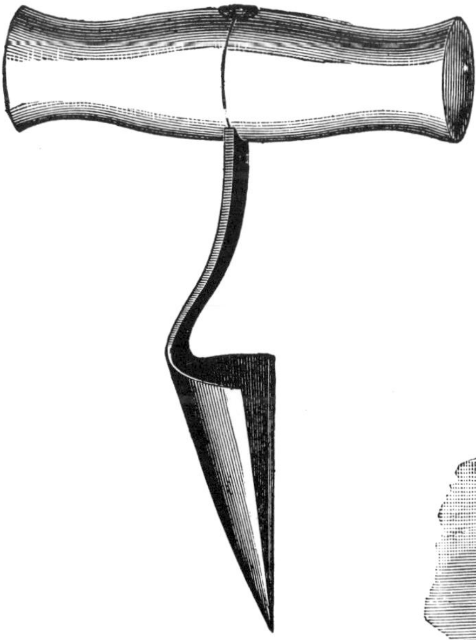

Plumbers' Tap Borers........ ......

Plumbers' Torches, Tin .... Brass.... ......

PLUMBERS' TOOLS.

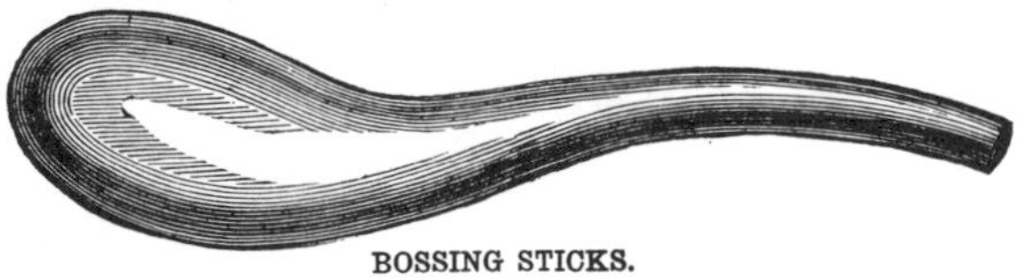

BOSSING STICKS.

Boxwood.. ......

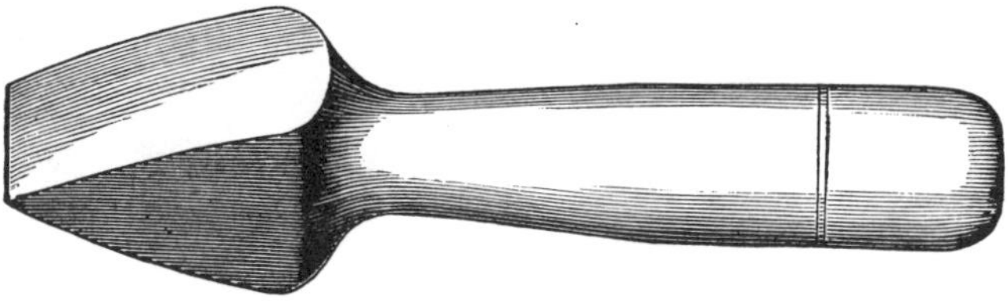

PLUMBERS' SIDE EDGES.

Boxwood.. ......

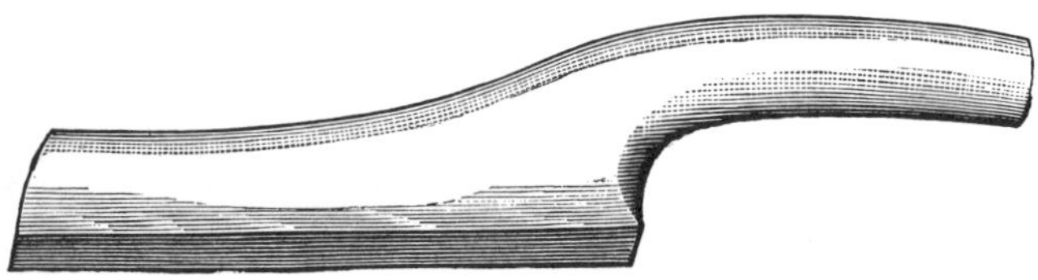

PLUMBERS' DRESSERS.

Boxwood.. ......

Plumbers' Soldering Irons ....

Copper Pointed Bolts.............................. ....

Copper Hatchet Bolts.............................. ......

Cape Chisels.............................. ......

Cold Chisels, from ¼ in. to 1 in. Bit.............................. ......

See Index for Miscellaneous Tools.

PLUMBERS' TOOLS.

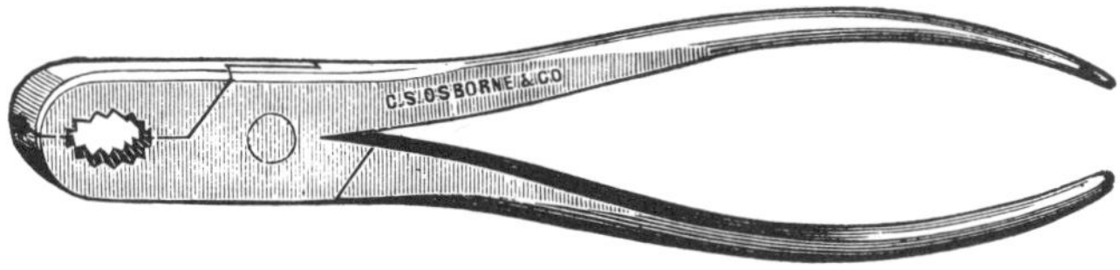

GAS PLIERS.—Best Cast Steel Polished.

Inch.................. 5...... 6 ..... Double Grip, ... 7 inch......

GAS PLIERS.--Cast Steel.

Inch.............................. 8 ..... 9..... 10 ..... 11...... 12.....

HALF-ROUND FILES.

All Sizes from 3 in. to 14 in.. ... .

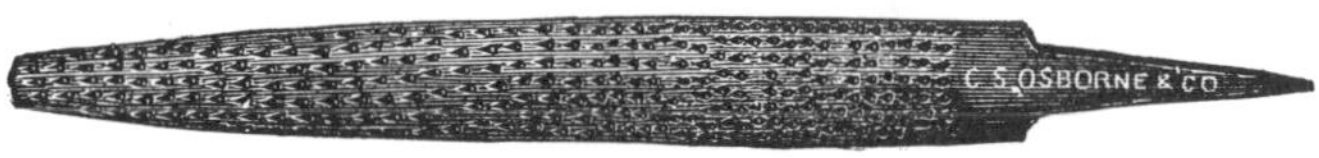

WOOD RASPS.

All Sizes from 8 in. to 16 in.. ......

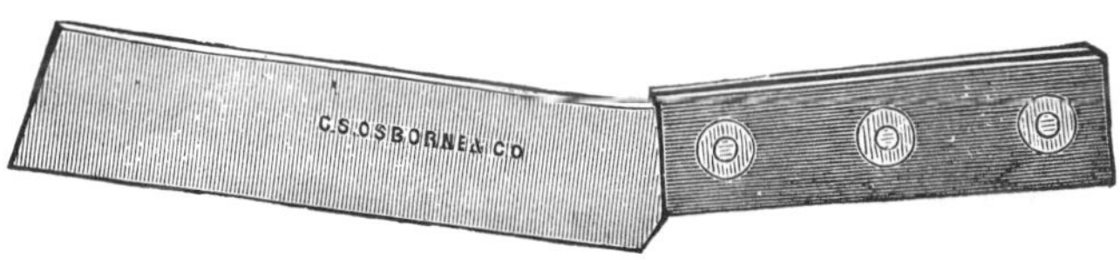

Plumbers' Clipping Knife ....

Plumbers' Double Edge Saws................ ......

Soil Brushes................................ ......

Plumbers' Boxwood Turn Pins................ ......

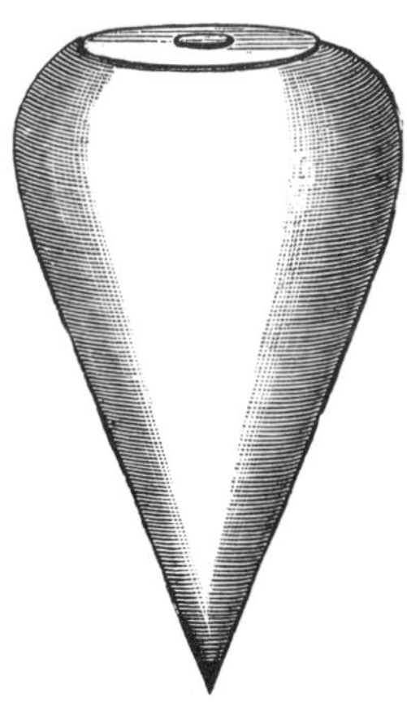

See Index for other Tools wanted.

PLUMBERS' TOOLS.

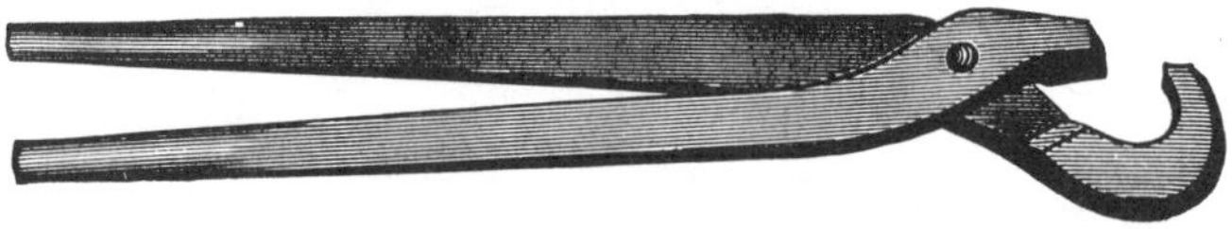

PIPE TONGS.—Steel Faced.

Sizes........ .. ¼ ... ⅜.... ½.... ⅝.... ¾ ... 1 ... 1¼ ... 1½ in.....

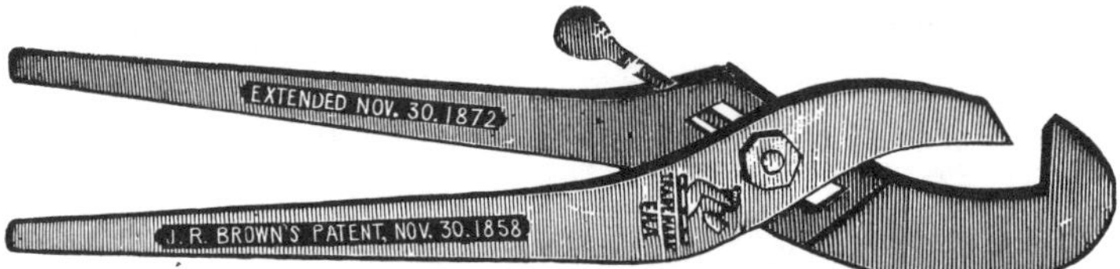

BROWN'S ADJUSTABLE PIPE TONGS.

No. 1, ⅛ to ¾ in.... ...... No. 2, ¼ to 1¼ in.... ..... No. 3, 1 to 2 in.... ......

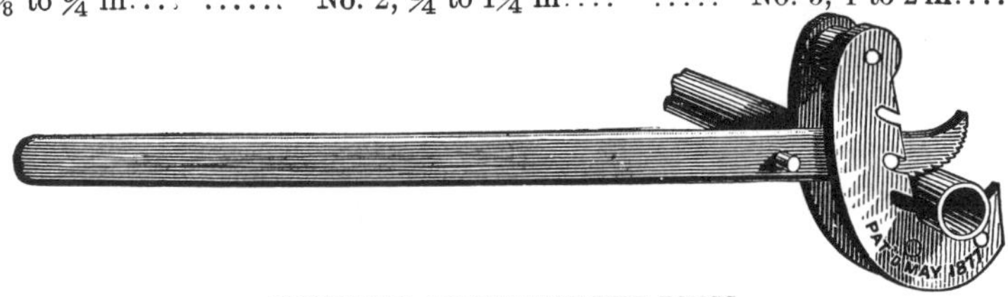

UNIVERSAL ADJUSTABLE PIPE TONGS.

Taking Ten Sizes of Pipe from ⅛ in. to 2½ in., Length 22 in. with Steel Jaws... ......

See Wrenches, pages 288 and 289.

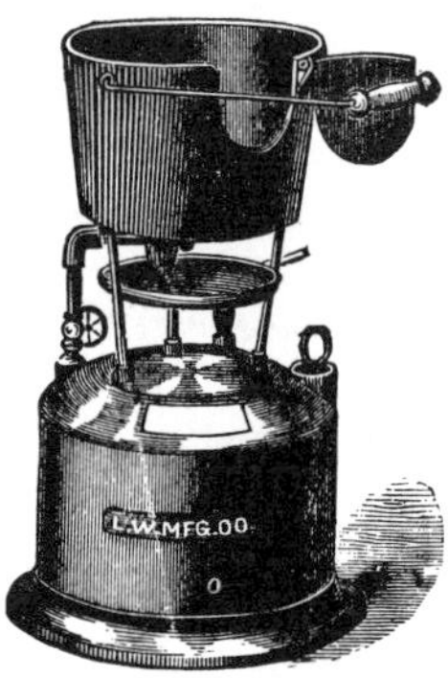

SOLDER POTS.

Inch	5	6	6½
Nos............	1........	2......	3........

PLUMBERS' BLAST FURNACE.

This Furnace is safe, simple in construction, and its effectivness will at once commend it to every one. Will melt 10 lbs. of solder in six minutes. We furnish the syringe for charging the furnace, with the furnace, without extra charge.

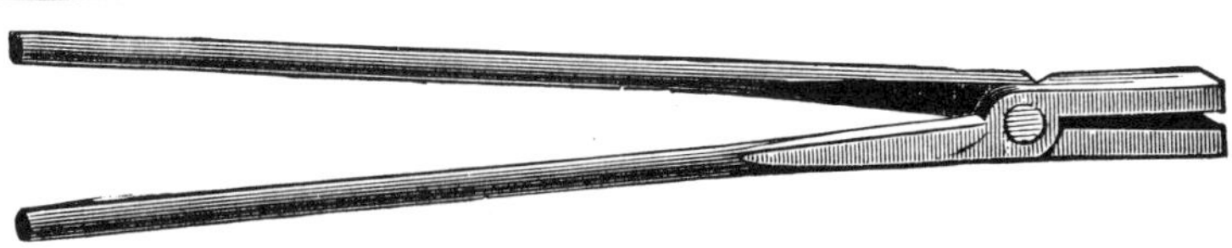

Blacksmiths' Tongs .... 22 in .....

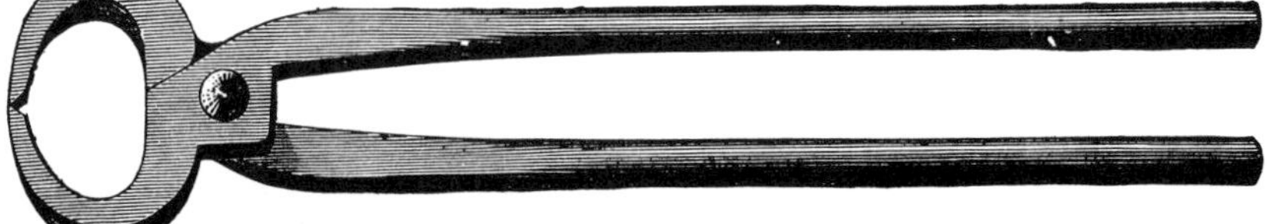

Blacksmiths' and Farmers' Pincers.................................... ......

Also, Farriers' Knives and Hammers.

VAJEN & NEW, INDIANAPOLIS, IND.

PICKS AND MATTOCKS.

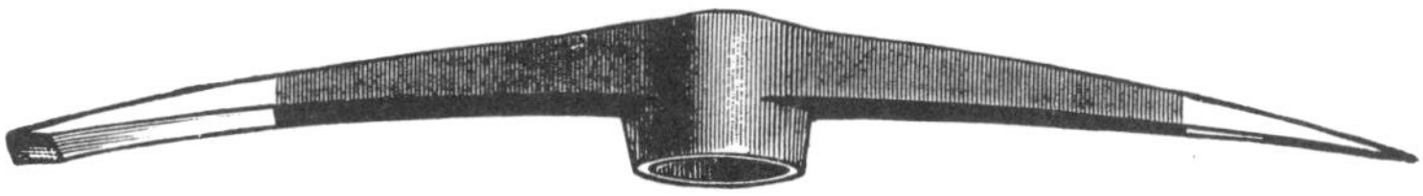

ADZE EYE RAIL ROAD OR CLAY PICKS.

Weights Assorted .... 5 to 6 lbs ..... 6 to 7 lbs...... 7 to 8 lbs......

RAIL ROAD TAMPING PICKS.

Weights Assorted .... 6 to 7 lbs ..... 7 to 8 lbs......

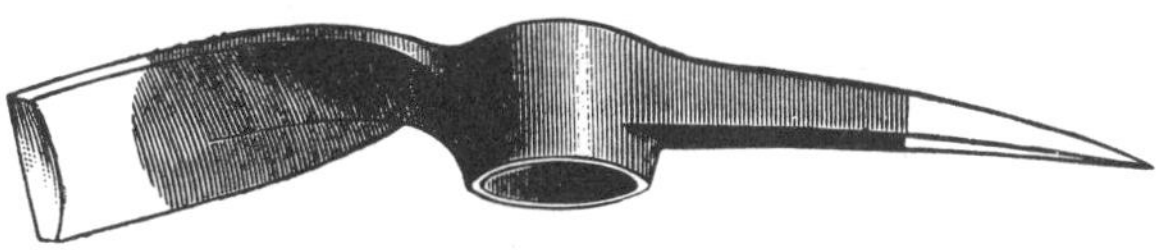

PICK MATTOCKS.

Average Weight .... 5 lbs......

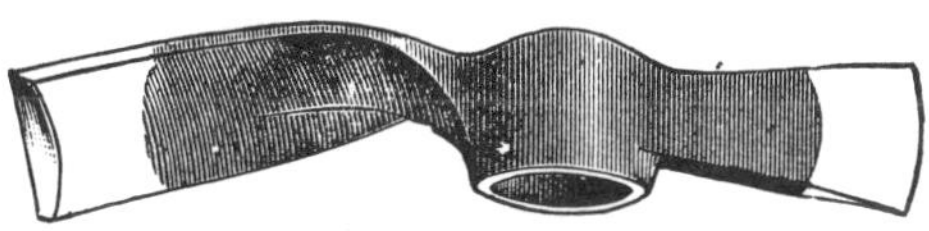

ADZE EYE MATTOCKS.

Short Cutter .... Long Cutter ....

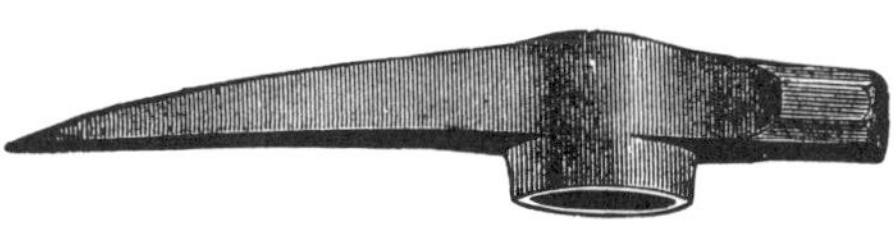

POLL PICKS.

No. 2, Weight 4 lbs................ .....

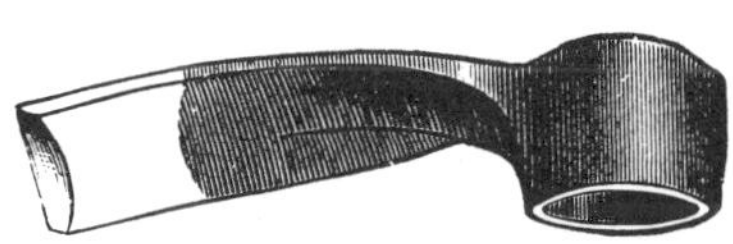

ADZE EYE GRUB HOES.

Nos............... 1...... 2......

COAL PICKS.

No. 2, Weight 2½ lbs.. ....

MILL PICKS.

Solid Cast Steel.............. ......

STONE PICKS.

Weights Assorted, 6 to 7 lbs.......... ......

ICE TOOLS.

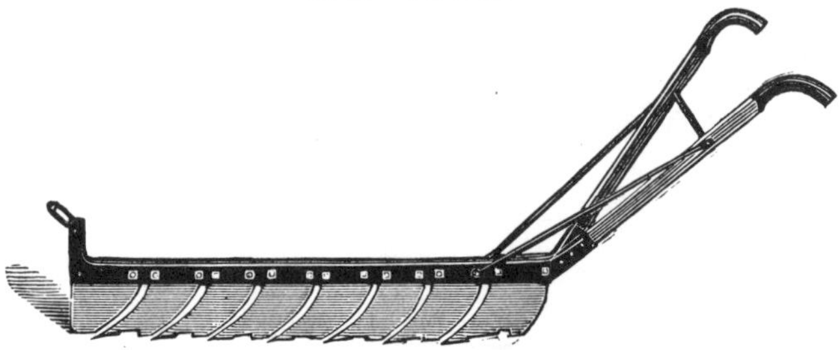

ICE PLOWS—With Patent Clearing Tooth.

Inch.......................... 6.... 7.... 8.... 9.... 10.... 11.... 12...

Markers, Nos.. 1...... 2......

Plows and Markers can be furnished with or without Stationary or Swing Guides.

The teeth of Plows and Markers are solid Cast Steel of the best quality that can be obtained.

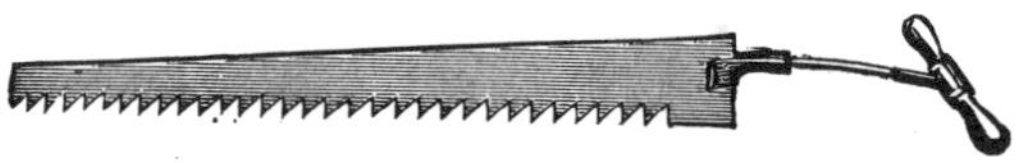

POND ICE SAWS.

Tiller Handle ....

ICE TONGS.

Hand Tongs.

Hand Tongs (Boston Pattern)...... Wagon Pattern........... ......

Hoisting Tongs .... Stowing Tongs........... ......

Family Ice Tongs.. ......

Family Ice Tongs.

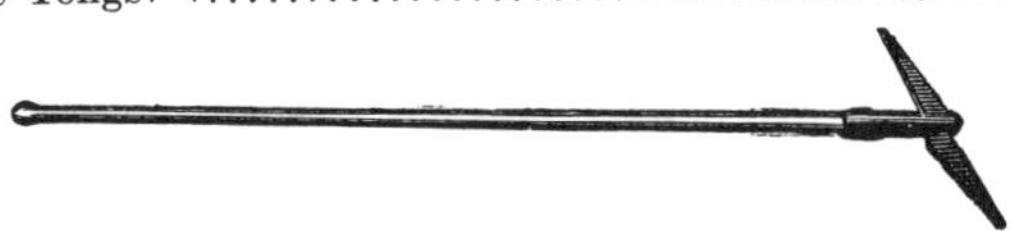

PATENT ICE HOOKS.

Turned Ash Handles................. 5...... 6...... 7..... 8...... 10ft......

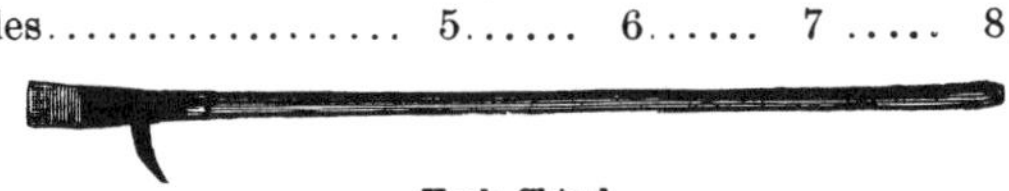

Hook Chisel.

ICE BALANCES.

To Weigh 300 lb by 5 lb.. ......

WAGON ICE SAWS.

Iron Handles ....

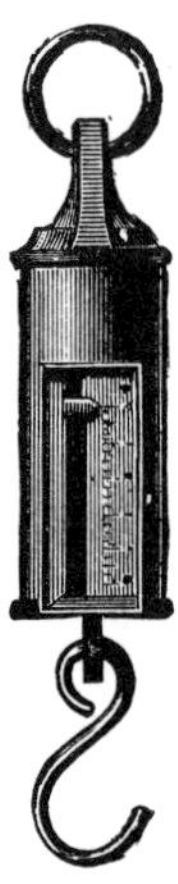

Ice Balance.

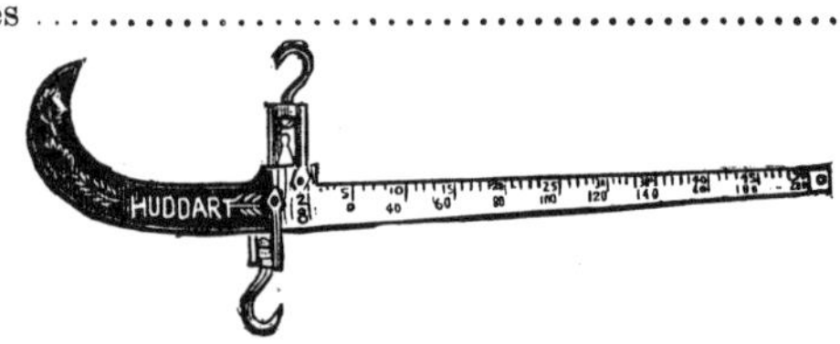

ICE BEAMS.

250 ...... 300........ 400 lb ....

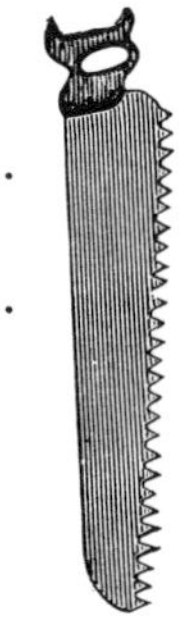

Wagon Saw.

We have a complete list of Ice Tools during the Ice season.

AWLS AND NEEDLES.

Patent Sewing Awls .... Patent Peg Awls.......... ......

Shouldered Peg Awls........... ...... Shouldered Brad Awls.......... ......

Saddlers' Awls ....

Bent Sewing Awls ....

SAIL NEEDLES.

Flat Seam .... Store...... .... Middle Bolt Rope. ......

LARDING NEEDLES.

Inch.. 6...... 8......

UPHOLSTERERS' NEEDLES.

Inch.............. 6...... 8...... 10...... 12...... 14...... 16...... ......

BENT PACKING NEEDLES.

Inch.................................. 3...... 4...... 5...... 6...... 8......

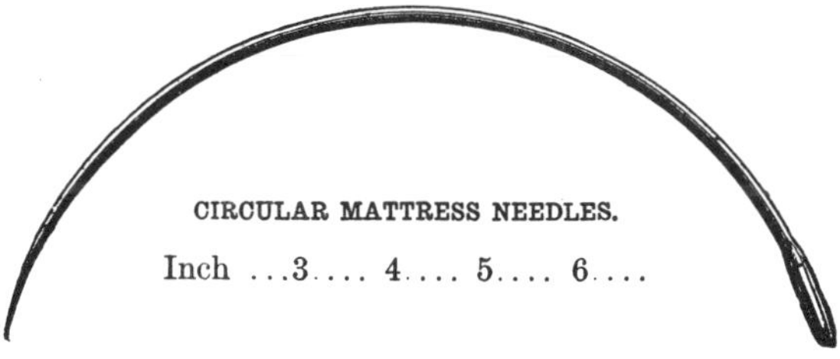

CIRCULAR MATTRESS NEEDLES.

Inch ...3.... 4.... 5.... 6....

Knitting Needles,	Nos	12	13	14	15 .....
Speying "	Inch...............................			2½	3 .....
Ham "	"				4 .....
Darning "	Nos....................	16	17	18	19 .....

2004 Price Guide Collectors Encycl. of 19th Century Hardware

The current values in this book should be used only as a guide. They are not intended to set prices, which vary from one section of the country to another. The publisher assumes no responsibility for any losses or gains incurred as a result of consulting this guide.

Page 2 - Common

Page 3 – Common

Page 4

2 x 2, $3^{1/2}$ x 4	$8-10
4 x 4, $4^{1/2}$ x 5	$15-20
5 x 5, $5^{1/2}$ x $5^{1/2}$, 6 x 6	$25-35

Page 5

Small to 3 x 3	$5
Larger sizes	$10

Page 6 – All on page $10-25

Page 7 – All on page $10-15

Page 8 – Common

Page 9 – Common

Page 10 – All on page $5-10

Page 11 – All on Page $5-10

Page 12 – Common

Page 13 – Top two Door Bolts $8-10
Bottom two Door Bolts $15-25

Page 14

Mortise	$15-20
Barrel	$20-25
Chain	$20-30

Page 15 – All on page $25-35

Page 16 – Bolts $30-50

Page 17

$1^{1/2}$ x 8, $1^{1/2}$ x 24	$20-40
$1^{1/2}$ x 30 & up	$50

Page 18

Cupboard Catches	$5-10
Window Catches	$5-10
Larger Window Catches	$10-15
Show Case	$5
Cupboard Bolts	$5-10

Page 19 – Cupboard Turns $15-25

Page 20 – All on page $2-5

Page 21 – All on page $2-5
Window Lock $5-10

Page 22

Top two Pulls	$3-5
Bottom two Pulls	$10-15

Page 23 – All on page $10-15
Second handle $2-4

Page 24 – All on page $2-4

Page 25 – All on Page $2-5

Page 26 – All on page $2-4
Top Hook $10-15

Page 27

Top two hooks	$10-15
Bottom hook	$4-6

Page 28 – All on page $15-20

Page 29 – All on page $15-20

Page 30 – All on page $10-15

Page 31 – Top Handle $15-20
All on page $4-5

Page 32 – All on page $5-15

Page 33 – Top three $5-10
All of Bottom row $1-2

Page 34 – Reference Only

Page 35 – Reference Only

Page 36 – Sliding Door Hangers $30-35

Page 37 – Top two $10-15
Springs-Rail $4-5

Page 38 – All on page $15-20

Page 39 – All on page $5-10

Page 40 – Top two rollers $4-5
Bottom two $10-20

Page 41 – All on page $10-15

Page 42 – Reference Only

Page 43 – Top two $25-35
Bottom $5-10

Page 44 – Door Bells $40-50

Page 45 – Door Bell Levers $30-40

Page 46 – Top Left $20-30
All others on page $5-10

Page 47 – All on page $10-15

Page 48 – All on page $10-15

Page 49 – Store door handle $40-50

Page 50 – All are
Store door handle w/latch $50-60

Page 51 – All are
Store door handle w/lock $50-75

Page 52 – Dead Locks & Latches $25 ea.

Page 53 – Locks $15 ea.

Page 54 – Lock $30-40

Page 55 – (notice pat. date) $50-75

Page 56 – Latches $15-25

Page 57 – Lock $40-60

Page 58 – Lock $10-20
Page 58 A – Reference Only

Page 59 – Lock $40-50
Page 59A – Reference Only

Page 60 – Sliding Door Locks $50-60

Page 61 – Reference Only

Page 62 – Lock $30-40

Page 63 $40-50

Page 64 – Top three $20-30
Bottom Sash $10-20

Page 65 – All on page $30-40 ea.

Page 66 $30-40

Page 67 – All on page $10-20 ea.

Page 68 – Door Knobs $15-20 ea.

Page 69 – Door Knobs $30-40 ea.

Page 70 – Door Knobs $40-50 ea.

Page 71 – Plate Escutcheons $2-5 ea.

Pages 72 thru 74 – Reference Only

Pages 75 thru 91
have been omitted because they only showed: screws, bolts, tacks, and rivets.

Page 92 – Till Locks $4-6 ea.

Page 93 – Chest & Till Locks $6-8 ea.

Page 94 – Chest & Till Locks $4-6 ea.

Page 95 – (2 Top) Trunk locks $8-10 ea.
(2 Bottom) Cupboard locks $4-6 ea.

Page 96 – All on page $4-6 ea.

Page 97 – All on page $3-5 ea.

Page 98 – Casters $3-5 ea.

Page 99 – Reference Only

Page 100 – All on page $1-3

Page 101 – Reference only

Page 102 thru 105 – Reference Only

Page 106 – Keys $10-15 ea.

Page 107 – Mail Boxes $40-50 ea.
Letter Plates $10-20 ea.

Page 108 thru 113 – Reference Only

Page 114 – Padlocks (Brass) $40-50
Padlocks (Nickle) $30-40
Padlocks (Scandinavian) $30-40

Page 115 – Padlocks $30-40 ea.

Page 116-117 – Reference Only

Page 118 – All on Page $4-6 ea.

Page 119 – Well Wheel $30-40
Hay Fork $15-25
All others on Page are $30-40 ea.

Page 120 – All on page $25-35 ea.

Page 121 – Rakes $15-25 ea.
Grass Hooks $5-10 ea.

Page 122 – Hay Forks $10-20 ea.

Page 123 – All on page $10-20 ea.

Page 124 – All on page $10-20 ea.
Bottom two Scoop Shovels $35-45 ea.

Page 125 – Top four Spades $25-35 ea.
Left Side Spade $30-40
Drain Cleaner $40-50 ea.

Page 126 – Shovels $10-20
Lawn Roller $

Page 127
Junior Mower $50-75
Senior Mower $100+
(they must be in mint condition)

Page 128-129 – Reference Only

Page 130 – Garden Hand Tools $4-8 ea.

Page 131 – Top two $30-40
Shears $15-25 ea.

Page 132
Hay Knives (top 2) $40-50 ea.
Rest on page $30-40 ea.

Page 133 – No. 20 Peg Break $25-35
Rest on page – Reference Only

Page 134 – Weather Vanes $500+
Cutting Box $50-60

Page 135 – Shovels $40-50 ea.
Rest on page – Reference Only

Page 136
Wagon $300+
Sleighs $150+ ea.
Store Trucks $40+ ea.
Warehouse Trucks $100+ ea.

Page 137 – Wood Barrows $75+
Steel $30-40
Scraper $50-60

Page 138 – Grind Stones Kitchen $40-60
Mounted $100+

Page 139 – Top Row $25-35 ea.
Spouts $10
Pokes $30-40
Halters $10-20

Page 140 – Reference Only

Page 141 – Reference Only

Page 142 – Hand Bells $30-40 ea.
Trip Bells $40-60 ea.
Hand Bells (Bottom) $40-60

Page 143 – Top $1000
Middle $60-75
Bottom $10-20

Page 144 – Body Strap $300+
Neck Strap $125
Chimes $150

Page 145 – Single Bells $5-25
Others $40+

Page 146 – Fire Place Sets $500
Stand on right $100
miscellaneous tools $10

Page 147 – All on page $3-10

Page 148 – Buckets (top) $10 ea.
Buckets (middle) $250 ea.
Coal Vases $200 ea.
Dog Irons $35 ea.

Page 149 – Fire Irons $40-50 ea.
Sets $200+
Bellows $60

Page 150 – All on page $40-50
Mrs. Potts Sad Irons $75+
Charcoal Irons $80-100

Page 151 – Top two $200+
Middle Fluting Machine $300+
Bottom Left Knox Machine $500+
Bottom Right Shephard $300+

Page 152 – No. 2 Coffee Mill $600+
Brighton Box Mill $150-200 ea.
Webbs Mill $150+ ea.

Page 153 – Brighton Side Mill $100+ ea.
Brighton Cracker Mill $175+

Page 154 – Peerless Wringer $75
Middle Wringer $50
Excelsior w/Bench $400+

Page 155 – Cherry Stoner $125
Tincture Press $150-175
Sausage Stuffer $175-225
Apple Parer $75
Vegetable Graters $100

Page 156 – Ice Cream Freezer
Top & Middle illustrations $50 ea.
Ice Cutting Machine $100+

Page 157 – Coolers
Top illustration $75
Middle illustration $75-100
Climax Filter (bottom) $125+

Page 158 – All on page $20-50 ea.

Page 159 – Bellows $60
Rest on page $10-20 ea.

Page 160 – Baskets $50+
Hods $20
Chain Pumps $175+

Page 161 – Reference Only

Page 162 – Scales $75-100
Steelyards $60+
Scale Beams $75

Page 163 – Scales $50
Pan $10-20

Page 164 – All on page $5-10

Page 165 – Top Left $100
Top Right $75+
Alarm Money Drawer $100+
Borers $15-20
Cutters $200

Page 166 & 167 – Reference Only

Page 168 – All on page $10-25 ea.

Page 169 – Reference Only

Page 170 – All on page $5-25 ea.

Page 171 – All on page $10-25 ea.

Page 172 – Top $50
Middle $75
Bottom $75

Page 173 – Top $100
Middle $50
Bottom $75

Page 174 – Reference Only

Page 175 – Wash Boards $10-20 ea.
Churns 1-4 $75-200
Unions 1-3 $75-200
Sieves $10-20

Page 176 – Top Two $100 ea.
Squirrel Cage $125
Wood Bird Cage $350
Hooks $10-20 ea.

Page 177 – Towel Rollers $20
Slaw Cutters $30-40
Kraut Cutters $75
Rolling Pins $35 ea.
Potato Mashers $20

Page 178 – All on page $10-25 ea.

Page 179 – Glue Pots $30-65 ea.
Maslin Kettles $35-100
Iron Mortars $40-100
Sugar Kettles $65-125

Page 180 – All on page $10-40

Page 181 – Toliet Set $150
Spitoons $40-100
Tea Pots $20-30

Page 182 – All on page $10-20

Page 183 – Boot Jack $40-50
Twine Box $50-60
Hooks $10

Page 184 – Top $40-75 ea.
Middle Factory $100+
Boss $25-30
Little Boss $30-40

Page 185 – Reference Only

Page 186 – Reference Only

Page 187 – Jack $50-75
Wedge $5-10
Mauls $15-25 ea.

Page 188 – Reference Only

Page 189 – Reference Only

Page 190 – Top $40-60
Middle $20-30
Bottom $60-70

Page 191 – All on page $5-10

Page 192 – Round Wire trap $5-10
Revolving Trap $40-50
Bottom Mole Trap $10-20

Page 193 – Top Fly Traps $30-40 ea.
Middle illus. $20-30 ea.
Bottom Poppers $10-20

Page 194 – Branding Iron $100
Rest on page for Reference Only

Page 195 – Reference Only

Page 196 – Reference Only

Page 197 – Reference Only

Page 198 – Reference Only

Page 199 – All on page $15-20 ea.

Page 200 – All on page $10-20

Page 201 – Collars $5-7.50
Locks $10-20
Safes $15-25

Page 202 – All on page $10-60

Page 203 – All on page $5-10

Page 204 – Razors (ea.) $5.00 up

Page 205 – All on page $5-25 ea.

Page 206 – Top $40
Bottom $35

Page 207 – Reference Only

Page 208 – All on page $5-10 ea.

Page 209 – Sets $20-30
Knives $5-10 ea.

Page 210 – All on page $10-20

Page 211 – All Knives $10-20
Cigar Cutter $40-60

Page 212 & 213 – All on page $5-10 ea.

Page 214 & 215 & 216 – All $10-20 ea.

Page 217 – Scissors $5-10 ea.
Reading Glasses $5-10
Rest on Page $2-5 ea.

Page 218 – All on page $5-10 ea.

Page 219 – All on page $20-25

Page 220 – Handcuffs $30-50
Nippers $10-20 ea.
Whistles $10-30 ea.

Page 221 – All on page $5-15 ea.

Page 222 – Reference Only

Page 223 – Bobbers $5-10
Spear $2-5
Minnows $35-50

Page 224 – All on page $15-35

Page 225 & 226 – Reference Only

Page 227 – All on page $40-75 ea.

Page 228 – All on page $40-60 ea.

Page 229 – All on page $40-60 ea.

Page 230 & 231 & 232 – Reference Only

Page 234 – All on page $25-40

Page 235 – Top $10-20
All others $40-60 ea.

Page 236 – All on page $5-10 ea.

Page 237 – All on page $5-10 ea.

Page 238 – All on page $5-10 ea.

Page 239 – Top Row $10-20 ea.
All others $20-40 ea.

Page 240 – All on page $10-25

Page 241 – Vise $30-40 ea.
Boring Machine $100-150

Page 242 – Saws $5-20 ea.

Page 243 – All on page $5-15 ea.

Page 244 – All on page $50-100 ea.

Page 245 – All on page $30-50 ea.

Page 246 – All on page $20-50 ea.

Page 247 – All on page $25-75 ea.

Page 248 – All on page $30-50

Page 249 – Top 6 Planes $30-40 ea.
#41 Plane $75-100
Bull Nose Rabbet Plane $15-25
Trammel Points $20-30

Page 250 – All on page $5-10 ea.

Page 251 – All on page $10-20 ea.

Page 252 – Handles for Reference Only
Gauges $15-25 ea.

Page 253 – Reference Only

Page 254 – Drivers $5-10 ea.
Rules $30-40 ea.

Page 255 – Rules $25-40 ea.

Page 256 – All on page $5-10 ea.

Page 257 – All on page $5-10 ea.

Page 258 – Reference Only

Page 259 – Top Two $30-50 ea.
Rest on page $25-60 ea.

Page 260 & 261 & 262 – Reference Only

Page 263 – All on page $5-20 ea.

Page 264 – Top Two Braces $20-30 ea.
Bottom $40-60

Page 265 – All on page $20-30 ea.

Page 266 – All on page $40-65 ea.

Page 267 – All on page $25-40 ea.

Page 268 – Reference Only

Page 269 – All on page $10-20 ea.

Page 270 – All on page $5-10 ea.

Page 271 – All on page $5-15 ea.

Page 272 – All on page $15-25 ea.

Page 273 – Plain Squares $10-20 ea.
Rest on page $30-40 ea.

Page 274 – All on page $5-15 ea.

Page 275 – All on page $5-30 ea.

Page 276 thru 281 – Reference Only

Page 282 & 283 – All on page $10-75 ea.

Page 284 – Reference Only

Page 285 – Drills $35-100 ea.

Page 286 – Vises $20-40 ea.

Page 287 – Vises $40-75 ea.

Page 288 – wrenches $15-25 ea.

Page 289 – wrenches $10-25 ea.

Page 290 – Reference Only

Page 291 – Top Nail Puller $20-30
Pusher $35-50
Hoist $30-40
Rest $10-20

Page 292 – All on page $10-30 ea.

Page 293 – All on page $15-30 ea.

Page 294 – Reference Only

Page 295 – Cans $5-10
Sets $50-75

Page 296 – All on page $5-40

Page 297 – All on page $10-50

Page 298 – All on page $20-100

Page 299 – All on page $30-50

Page 300 – Drill $20-40
Glue Pot $25-35
the rest – Reference Only

Page 301 – All on page $10-20

Page 302 – All on page $20-40

Page 303 – All on page $20-40
Forge $100+
Lathe $150+

Page 304 – Saws $250 ea.

Page 305 – Saws $175-225

Page 306 – All on page	$5-10 ea.	**Page**
Page 307 – All on page	$10-20 ea.	
Page 308 – Sets	$30-40	
Others	$10-20 ea.	
Page 309 – All on page	$10-50 ea.	
Page 310 – All on page	$5-15 ea.	
Page 311 – Tinners Tools	$5-15	
Stove	$300+	
Page 312 – All on page	$20-40	
Page 313 – Reference Only		
Page 314 – Moulders Tools	$10-100	
Page 315 – All on page	$5-10 ea.	
Page 316 – Tools	$10-20 ea.	
Torch	$30-40	
Page 317 – All on page	$10-20 ea.	
Page 318 – All on page	$10-20 ea.	
Page 319 – All on page	$15-25	
Blast Furnace	$175-225	
Page 320 – All on page	$20-40	
Page 321 – Ice Plow	$100	
Rest on page	$10-30	
Page 322 – Reference Only		